Acquisitions Editor: Daniel F. Pipp
Developmental Editor: Marisa L'Heureux
Project Coordination, Text and Cover Design: Proof Positive/Farrowlyne Associates, Inc.
Cover Illustration: James Watling
Photo Researcher: Karen Koblik
Production Manager: Willie Lane
Compositor: Better Graphics, Inc.
Printer and Binder: R. R. Donnelley & Sons Company
Cover Printer: The Lehigh Press, Inc.

Principles and Types of Speech Communication, **Twelfth Edition**

Library of Congress Cataloging-in-Publication Data

Principles and types of speech communication/Bruce E. Gronbeck . . .
    [et al.].—12th ed.
        p.   cm.
    Includes bibliographical references and index.
    ISBN 0-673-46804-6
    1. Public speaking.   I. Gronbeck, Bruce E.
PN4121.P72   1993   93-36231
808.5'1—dc20   CIP

94 95 96 9 8 7 6 5 4 3 2

Principles and Types of Speech Communication

Twelfth Edition

Bruce E. Gronbeck
The University of Iowa

Raymie E. McKerrow
University of Maine

Douglas Ehninger

Alan H. Monroe

HarperCollins*College*Publishers

CONTENTS

PART *1*
PROCESS

CHAPTER 1
THE PROCESS OF PUBLIC SPEAKING

CHAPTER 2
PUBLIC SPEAKING AND CRITICAL LISTENING

CHAPTER 3
GETTING STARTED: PLANNING AND PREPARING SPEECHES

PART *2*
PREPARATION

CHAPTER 4
CHOOSING SPEECH SUBJECTS AND PURPOSES   76

Chapter 7
Developing Ideas: Finding and Using Supporting Materials

Chapter 8
Adapting the Speech Structure to Audiences: The Motivated Sequence

Chapter 9
The Motivated Sequence and Patterns of Internal Organization

PART *3*
CHANNELS

PART *4*
TYPES

CHAPTER 17
ARGUMENT AND CRITICAL THINKING

CHAPTER 18
SPEECHES ON SPECIAL OCCASIONS

SAMPLE SPEECHES
FOR STUDY AND ANALYSIS

PREFACE

P rinciples and Types of Speech Communication has been a mainstay in the basic speech course, a celebrated leader in communication studies, for over half a century. Such longevity comes to textbooks that look both backward and forward: backward to the timeless principles of speech that are part of the EuroAmerican cultural experience and yet forward to the new ideas and challenges of today and tomorrow.

Signs of today's challenges are everywhere: the racial overtones in the Los Angeles beating of Rodney King; Native Americans suing their communities for land and fishing rights; the boat people of Southeast Asia and of Haiti testing America to see if it is still the Land of the Free and the Home of the Brave; the helplessness felt by onlookers to the not-so-civil wars of the Yugoslavian regions; the concern for the economic, political, and military implications of a disassembled Soviet Union. Even more locally, the challenge to effective communication is witnessed daily in communities that often seem seriously divided by race, religion, gender, age, sexual orientation, and socioeconomic status.

Ours has been called the Age of Diversity, the Era of Fragmentation—a post-modern epoch. Perhaps we just lost our innocence or our narrow-mindedness. Perhaps the electronic revolution did not wire us together, after all, but instead drove us into ourselves, out of our social bonds with others. Perhaps this, perhaps that. But, whatever the reason, it is more important than ever for people to communicate with people, to "get along," as Rodney King hoped we could, with the aid of solid oral communication skills.

That's what *Principles and Types of Speech Communication* always has been about: providing students across the decades with the skills they need to make a difference. The present authors of *Principles and Types of Speech Communication, Twelfth Edition*, have built upon the solid foundation laid by Alan H. Monroe (1903–75), former Professor of Communication at Purdue University, and Douglas Ehninger (1913–79), former Professor of Speech at the University of Florida and then at the University of Iowa. Professor Monroe made his mark in communication studies largely through the 1935 publication of this pedagogically innovative book, with its justly famous "Monroe's Motivated Sequence" and exploration of the factors of attention and types of imagery. Professor Ehninger complemented Monroe's social-scientific emphasis with his strong commitment to the philosophy and history of rhetoric. Both men took the measure of their times (Douglas Ehninger joined the book in the 1960s) and adapted *Principles and Types of Speech Communication* to their eras. And so have we. We aspire to keep this book what it's always been: the flagship of communication studies, the most respected introduction to the field.

New to This Edition

In this edition we have continued to offer the best advice the past has generated for speakers, but we have also looked forward. New elements and perspectives stand out:

1. ***Recognition that diversity in listeners' backgrounds is a fact of rhetorical life.*** "Tellin' 'em what they want to hear" is really very difficult these days, because most audiences are composed of many "they's": of people from groups with varying beliefs, attitudes, values, and ways of doing things. Speakers must not only watch their use of "he or she" but also be sensitive to ethnic, religious, and other cultural differences. Learning to analyze and then making your way through social differences in a time when they count for much calls upon your greatest human relations skills. *Principles and Types of Speech Communication,* Twelfth Edition, tries at every corner to help you refine those skills.

2. ***Greater sensitivity to the ethical issues facing speakers.*** In the eleventh edition, we extended the discussion of such ethical issues as plagiarism, sexism, and the bases of speaker credibility. We now have added a boxed feature, "Ethical Moments," that describes situations and poses questions about the moral decisions you must make in your speech preparation and delivery.

3. ***Occasional stops to think about particular aspects of communicating publicly in this era.*** Another feature, "What Others Are Saying," draws upon statements from public figures, reports of salaries that top-notch speakers make on the after-dinner circuit, and meditations on dimensions of communication today. Quotations and brief discussions of them are offered to give you a break in your reading—and to encourage reflection.

4. ***Expanded pedagogical support.*** In today's educational world there is much, much more to teacher preparation and materials than just the textbook. *Principles and Types of Speech Communication,* Twelfth Edition, continues to be a leader in pedagogical support services. Available with this edition are multiple videotapes, with a guide on how to use them; a booklet providing an orientation to the history of rhetoric and to rhetorical vocabulary; an Instructor's Manual that includes not only banks of questions but also tips for teaching, bibliographies, chapter-by-chapter reviews for lecturing, and additional, tested exercises prepared by the expert hand of Professor Kathleen German, Miami University of Ohio.

Accompanying these changes are revisions throughout all the chapters. You'll find important material on such topics as diversity, market-tested modes of audience study (with VALS, or Values and Life Styles, analysis, new to this edition), computer searches for information, audience segmentation and targeting, information processing, and motivational appeals and their organization. We also have augmented the discussion of gender-neutral language and refined the discussion of instructional speeches and oral briefings. In addressing the issue of cultural diversity, we have included in this edition excerpts and complete sample speeches from, among others, Native American speakers. We have reorganized the *Speaker's Resource Book* to make its individual sections more accessible and easier to use.

Strengths That Continue from Edition to Edition

Principles and Types of Speech Communication is such a highly respected text because of its particular strengths, and we have been sure to retain those characteristics in this revision.

1. ***Focus on both speechmaking in society and student presentations in classrooms.*** This book has an obligation to compel the students of communication studies to reflect seriously upon the Communications Revolution and its implications for responsible citizens. Throughout, we ask you to think about political, economic, religious, and social messages in your environment—to analyze them, to understand their strategic bases, and to learn to construct them. Yet, we realize that you are a student seeking to survive and grow in your own environment, the college or university campus; thus, you'll find many of our examples and illustrations drawn from campus life both in and out of class. This book asks you to assess your skills where you are, but also to look ahead to a complete life of involvement in your social, work, and political communities.

2. ***Emphasis on critical thinking and critical listening skills.*** This textbook always has been grounded in analysis: analysis of audiences, of the self, of one's purposes, of the occasions on which one speaks. Our surveys clarify, however, that today's student needs more than that. Speech classrooms are expected increasingly to teach the principles of critical thinking and critical listening—consumer-oriented techniques for examining messages, for assessing their characteristics, and for evaluating their claims in terms of logical and psychological criteria. Such defensive studies of critical thinking are central to *Principles and Types of Speech Communication,* Twelfth Edition, especially the chapters on listening (2) and argumentation/critical thinking (17) and various segments of the *Speaker's Resource Book.*

3. ***Up-to-date research in "Communication Research Dateline" segments.*** This textbook has prided itself on the firmness of its intellectual base: traditional rhetorical principles and contemporary communication research. The "Communication Research Dateline" boxes that appear in almost every chapter recognize the importance and usefulness of current research, reviewing studies and then pointing out their practical implications for communicators. Among the research traditions examined are those of advertising, survey research, nonverbal communication, psychology, intercultural communication, argumentation, and television studies. Not only will you find ideas you can use as a speaker, but "Communication Research Dateline" items will introduce you to the work of academic communication professionals.

4. ***Four-color presentation.*** Four-color presentations help you understand emphases, spot special features, translate diagrams and figures into meaningful concepts, and come to grips with the "real world" of communication as presented in four-color photographs. Your world is in color and so is this book.

5. ***Chapter-end summaries and critical thinking exercises.*** As the leading full-sized textbook in the field of communication studies, *Principles and Types of Speech Communication,* Twelfth Edition, uses a full communication vocabulary; it teaches you how to talk precisely about public speaking. Because of that stress on vocabulary, we have added to the end of each chapter both a summary and a list of terms for easy review. New exercises stressing analysis and critical thinking are included in the chapter-end materials as well.

Overall, we know this edition of the most popular public speaking textbook of the twentieth century has merged traditional and innovative features to keep it at the forefront of communication studies. Both instructors and students can use this book. Its *Speaker's Resource Book*—the shorter segments at the end—make *Principles and Types of Speech Communication* marvelously flexible as a teaching and a learning instrument.

Acknowledgments

We owe a great debt to those instructors who took the time to review the previous edition and the manuscript for the current edition:

David E. Bradbury, Wilkes University
Kent R. Colberet, University of the Pacific
Stanley Richard Coleman, Louisiana State University at Eunice
Ray Dahlin, Palomar College
Charles Fuller, Texas Southern University
Mark A. Gring, Ohio State University
Dayle C. Hardy-Short, Idaho State University
Lawrence A. Hosman, University of Southern Mississippi
Rita C. Hubbard, Christopher Newport University
C. W. Mangrum, Southeastern Oklahoma State University
Janet K. McKenney, Macomb County College
Aileen R. Sundstrom, Henry Ford Community College
Meleia Utley, Dyersburg State Community College
Beth M. Waggenspack, Virginia Polytechnic Institute and State University

Special thanks, again, to Kathleen German, who transformed the Instructor's Manual into the most innovative manual in the field. As well, Christopher, Jakob, and Ingrid Gronbeck continue to contribute their talents for library research and their attempts to keep their father current. Gratitude is owed, too, to the University of Iowa Center for Advanced Studies, especially its director Jay Semel and its administrative secretary Lorna Olson; the facilities and warm conversation provided by the Center during the year of revision made it all go most smoothly.

We also thank HarperCollins College Publishers for the resources and talents it invested in this project. The master plan for the edition took shape under Communication Editor Dan Pipp and then was executed under the careful watch of Developmental Editor Marisa L. L'Heureux, who untangled and worked to blend our prose. The word-by-word manuscript preparation was handled by Gail Savage, with Senior Picture Editor Karen Koblik capturing the tenor of the book in its illustrations and with Allison Ellis of the Permissions Department keeping us legal. And finally, we were pleased with the marketing work done by Peter Glovin and the army of enthusiastic sales representatives who carried this book into the field—and to you.

You, of course, are the bottom line. We thank you for examining it. We thank you not only for using this book, but for your singular commitment to excellence in public speaking, in order to both improve your own fortunes and to make this world a better place for human beings. Your commitments make our work worthwhile, and we thank you for them.

Bruce E. Gronbeck
Raymie E. McKerrow

PART ONE

PROCESS

"*What other power [than eloquence] could have been strong enough either to gather scattered humanity into one place, or to lead it out of its brutish existence in the wilderness up to our present condition of civilization as [people] and as citizens, or, after the establishment of social communities, to give shape to laws, tribunals, and civic rights?*"

Cicero
De oratore *I.33*

1

The Process of Public Speaking

I n 1989 Henri Mann Morton, a member of the Cheyenne nation, addressed a multicultural conference. She both welcomed and yet feared the effects of cultural diversity in the United States in these words:

> I am the granddaughter of those who welcomed many of our grandmothers and grandfathers—your grandparents—to this country. It is now our country.
>
> We were multi-tribal; heterogeneous as the indigenous people of America, and following Anglo contact exchanged the term "multi-tribal" for "multi-cultural," so we could embrace those who came to live with us.
>
> Prior to non-Indian contact, we as American Indians were culturally diverse. We were familiar with the concept of "cultural diversity," and recognized that those cultural differences made us strong. Cultural diversity made for strength—there was/is strength in cultural diversity. Cultural diversity makes our country strong. It has made us a great nation and we all have an opportunity to achieve the American dream.
>
> American Indians are the minority of minorities. They number 1.5 million; less than one percent of our population. Though small in numbers we are the fastest growing ethnic group, with a young population. Unfortunately, they are American society's "miners' canaries."
>
> The treatment of American Indians indicates the political-economic-social-humanistic climate of this country. It signals a shift from a healthy environment to one that is dangerous, if not lethal.[1]

On the opening night of the 1992 Democratic National Convention in New York City, the third keynote speech was given by Barbara Jordan, the former congresswoman from Texas who was, in 1976, the first female African-American to keynote a national party convention. Dealing forthrightly with the issue of race relations in this country, she argued as follows:

> We need to change the decaying inner cities to places where hope lives. As we undergo that change we must be prepared to answer Rodney King's haunting question, "Can we all get along?" Can we all get along? I say, I say we answer that question with a resounding yes! Yes! Yes! Yes.
>
> We must, we must, we must change, we must change that deleterious environment of the eighties, that environment which was characterized by greed and hatred and selfishness and mega-mergers and debt overhang. Change it to what? Change that environment of the eighties to an environment which is characterized by a devotion to the public interest, public service, tolerance, and love. Love. Love. Love. Love.
>
> We are one, we Americans, and we reject any intruder who seeks to divide us on the bases of race and color. We honor cultural identity. We always have, we always will. But separateness is not allowed. Separateness is not the American way. We must not allow ideas like political correctness to divide us and cause us to reverse hard-won achievements in human rights and civil rights. Xenophobia has no place in the Democratic party. We seek to unite people, not divide them.
>
> As we seek to unite people, we reject both white racism and black racism. This party, this party, this party will not tolerate bigotry under any guise. Our strength, our strength in this country is rooted in our diversity. Our history bears witness to that fact. *E pluribus unum.* "From many, one." It was a good idea when our country was founded, and it's a good idea today.[2]

That two recent speeches by female members of minority groups would deal with matters of cultural diversity, racial divisions, and yet social unity was no accident. By mid-1992, the United States had been rocked by a series of incidents that suggested the country was in danger of splitting apart along racial lines. The so-called "Rodney King incident"—a videotaped, physically forceful beating of an African-American man by white police and the officers' subsequent acquittal—precipitated spring riots in Los Angeles. That summer, the lyrics of rapper Ice-T's song "Cop Killer" were considered incendiary. The previous fall, in the confirmation hearings of Supreme Court nominee Clarence Thomas, both racial and sexist slurs appeared in public print. As Christmas 1992 approached, Spike Lee's film *Malcolm X* renewed concerns over the development of separated African-American and white communities in America. Untotaled clashes between and among African-Americans, Latinos, other ethnic enclaves, and skinheads unsettled the neighborhoods of most American cities on most days. The early nineties were tense times in the Land of the Free.

Social division along racial lines is but one of the cleavages that shows itself nightly on television. Men battle women for elected office, for managerial and entry level jobs, and over custody rights of children at the time of divorce and charges of sexual discrimination and harassment. College and university campuses are alive with debate over "political correctness": concern about giving members of the political left or right access to student audiences, about racial and gender quotas in faculty hiring, about what constitutes sexual or racial harassment, about what authors should be read in basic literature and history classes.

Young adults demand that older ones quit discriminating against them when it is time to hire new employees, while older Americans complain that they're too often fired to make room for cheaper, younger workers. Yankees and Southerners accuse each other of not understanding their respective cultures. There still are cities in the U.S. where the Italians and the Irish talk little to each other, where church steeples signal not only religious preferences but also sociocultural groupings, and where the people living in a "gentrified" neighborhood don't associate with the single parents on welfare living across the street.

Some days it seems amazing that anyone can talk to anyone else. Some days it seems like *E pluribus unum* was a cruel joke perpetuated on the rest of us by a group of old, eighteenth-century men who had no idea, really, of what they were talking about. "Out of many, one"?

Public Speaking in an Age of Diversity

The remarks of Morton and Jordan are signs that even mainline public spokespersons have become frustrated by the divisions that threaten to crack open this country. The difficulty was clearly articulated by Jordan: we believe in and regularly affirm *cultural diversity*, even while we know it is essential that we maintain *social unity* to achieve common goals both locally and globally. How can a people recognize and honor its "manyness," its **diversity**, while working together as a "oneness," as a nation? How can we achieve *E pluribus unum*?

Two answers are usually given to that question, and this book is about the second. First is the matter of common activity. People who work together, play together, fight a common enemy, or seek a common goal usually find out that people are people. When men and women teach together, they better appreciate each other's strengths; when Latinos and whites serve on community boards together, they generally discover shared hopes for their neighborhoods. Sharing work and play can lead to shared views.

But, mere association is not enough. Most people need more than proximity to get to know and understand someone else, and this fact gives rise to the second answer. They need to talk. They need to chat about their teenage years, children, disgust with local government, favorite basketball teams, commitments. They need to argue over abortion or statehood for the District of Columbia or tax credits for kids in college. They need to verbally construct bridges between female and male, brown and white, immigrants and Native Americans. In their diversity, they must speak to become one.

Public speaking is a primary vehicle for recognizing individual identity even as a group of people seeks to share common ideas, values, action plans, and identities. If we had no need to share information and ideas, attitudes and values, plans and projects, or images of what we hold in common, we wouldn't have to talk. But we have those needs, we talk publicly, and we must become better at such talk.

The Functions of Speechmaking in Society

Both speaking and listening skills are important because *public communication* for centuries has been the glue that holds societies together. A sense of sharing, the "with-ness" part of the Latin root *cum-munis* (to work publicly with) of the English word *communication*, bonds people together. Without public communication, societies could not organize into working and living groups, mark the passage of individuals from childhood to adulthood to retirement, debate and make decisions about difficult issues, and change society in necessary ways. Because oral communication flows directly between individuals, it is the preferred form of communication in times of joy and crisis. When there is an occasion to celebrate or a crisis to face, leaders inevitably give speeches, because speech unites diverse peoples.

More specifically, public speeches perform four important functions for a society:

1. *Speeches are used for self-definition.* Especially on such occasions as Memorial Day, the Fourth of July, dedications of community centers, and political conventions, communities (societies and their sub-units) define themselves, indicating what they stand for, what it means to be a member of the community. Just as churchgoers recite creeds and credos aloud, so societies regularly review their defining tenets through speech. That's why national political conventions have keynote addresses. "Speak that I may know you" is an old adage grounded in the shared experiences of many generations.

2. *Speeches are used to spread information through a community.* The president announces the latest plans for a European economic summit through public talk; the Surgeon General holds a press conference to

*In the Age of Communication, it is impor-
tant that you learn to speak publicly and to
analyze the messages of public speakers
from around the world [Emperor Akihito of
Japan (top), United States President Bill
Clinton (center), Russia's President and
Prime Minister Boris Yeltsin (bottom)].*

update AIDS research findings; the mayor uses a radio interview to spread the word on next week's downtown jazz festival. Most information, of course, is distributed via print or electronic display, but spoken information is so much more personalized that important ideas are very often spoken directly to you. Even when offering ideas across national boundaries, world leaders still speak through translators, because of the personal nature of talk.

3. *Speeches are used to debate questions of fact, value, and policy in communities.* Human beings always have fought through their differences with each other. As civilizations advanced, verbal controversy replaced much of physical combat, and the art of public debate was born. From government to the workplace, arguing one's way through to a decision is an important function of talk.

4. *Speeches are used to bring about individual and group change.* For centuries persuasion has been the heart of public talk. The earliest books about public speaking dealt exclusively with persuasion as the most important kind of talk. Societies must adapt to changes in their environments, values, and practices; if change is to occur, most people must be persuaded to accept it.

Speechmaking, therefore, performs four broad social functions in communities. Whether one is talking about community broadly (as in a community of nations) or narrowly (as in a community of friends), collectivities simply could not exist and work without multiple forms of public communication.

The Need for Speech Training in the Age of Diversity

It is clear you need public speaking skills to live productively in the Age of Diversity. Unless you have the speaking talents necessary to engage in committee discussions, presentations to clients, and interactions with your managers, you may be in trouble on the job.[3] Your speechmaking skills also affect your ability to change people's minds at neighborhood or coffee room meetings, city or student councils, political conventions and public hearings, and the innumerable associations, clubs, and pressure groups that lobby the government. The power of public talk is as important in government as it is in the world of work.

You will become a fully developed, thinking, and forceful human being to the degree that you've learned and practiced speechmaking and other oral communication skills. Ultimately, you speak not only to serve others but also to achieve your own goals on the job and in the public forum. You might even have fun doing it; human beings talk with others both to survive and to play a little.

Before you plunge into the activities that will improve your speaking skills, however, it is helpful to visualize the whole process, to think about the various elements that comprise communication in general and public speaking in particular. The rest of this chapter will examine those elements, the competencies they require of you, and matters of fear and ethics that you face as a speaker.

Basic Elements in the Speechmaking Process

It's time you started thinking seriously and more technically about the speechmaking you are about to study and practice. Speechmaking is comprised of a number of elements: a *speaker*, the primary communicator, gives a speech, a continuous, purposive oral *message*, to the *listeners*, who provide *feedback* to the speaker. Their exchange occurs through various *channels* in a particular communication *situation* and *cultural context*. Consider each of these elements individually.

The Speaker

A speaker must consider four key elements in every speech exchange or transaction:[4] his or her (a) purpose; (b) knowledge of subject and communication skills; (c) attitudes toward self, listeners, and subject; and (d) degree of credibility.

The Speaker's Purpose.   Every speaker has a purpose. You speak to achieve a goal. That goal can be as simple as a desire for social exchange or as complex as the desire to alter someone's ideas and actions. As you think about your purposes, you may wish to entertain, call attention to a problem, refute an assertion, ward off a threat, or establish or maintain your status or power.

The Speaker's Knowledge.   Your knowledge of the subject and mastery of communication skills affect the character of your message and your effectiveness. If you have only surface knowledge of a topic, listeners feel cheated; they want you to say something important, new, relevant, interesting. To succeed you also need to acquire and refine a series of fundamental speaking skills. This book focuses on especially important skills: setting communication goals, finding and assembling relevant information, organizing messages in coherent and powerful ways, illustrating them visually, and delivering them with clarity and punch.

The Speaker's Attitudes.   Your attitudes toward your self, your listeners, and your subject significantly affect what you say and how you say it. We all have mental pictures of ourselves—self-concepts or **self-images** of the kinds of individuals we are and of how others perceive us.[5]

THE SPEECH COMMUNICATION TRANSACTION

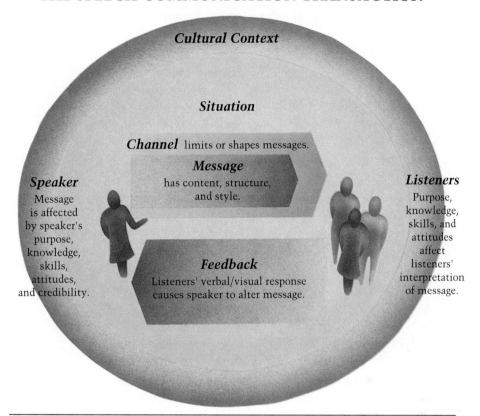

Cultural Context

Situation

Channel limits or shapes messages.

Message
has content, structure,
and style.

Speaker
Message
is affected
by speaker's
purpose,
knowledge,
skills,
attitudes,
and credibility.

Listeners
Purpose,
knowledge,
skills, and
attitudes
affect
listeners'
interpretation
of message.

Feedback
Listeners' verbal/visual response
causes speaker to alter message.

Your self-image influences the way you speak in particular situations. Suppose you're giving a speech in class about chlorofluorocarbons and the possibility of replacing them in aerosol spray devices. If you have little confidence in your abilities and if you haven't done research, you'll tend to speak hesitantly; your voice will become weak, your body stiff, and you'll watch the walls rather than your audience. If you're convinced of your vast superiority over your listeners, you might move to the other extreme, becoming overbearing and overly familiar, disregarding listeners' needs, and riding roughshod over their feelings. Ideally, you'll find a middle way when discussing alternatives to chlorofluorocarbons, with enough self-confidence to believe in your usefulness to your listeners and enough sensitivity to treat them with respect.

Part of your treatment of audiences comes from your *power relations* with them and the ways you perceive them—as instructors or fellow students, supervisors or employees, subordinates or equals. Giving a speech

A speaker brings four key elements to every speech transaction: a communicative purpose; knowledge of the subject and communication skills; attitudes toward self, the listeners, and the subject; and a certain degree of credibility.

about chlorofluorocarbons in front of a teacher who's grading you involves an unequal power relationship; giving the same speech to a student research committee of which you're a member involves a equal relationship. Your attitudes differ from audience to audience, and you adjust your speaking style accordingly. You have other attitudes that may affect your talk:

1. *Are you comfortable in the speaking situation, or does it make you feel strange?* For example, a speech classroom will make you feel awkward at first, and that feeling will affect your speeches, but as you grow more at home your attitudes will improve—and so will your skills. Most people usually take a while to get used to speaking in church, clubs, or civic groups.

2. *Are you comfortable with your subject and your mastery of it?* Is it interesting to you, or did you pick it because an article in *Time* set it up

for you? Does anyone else care about it? Can you make them care? Do you really know enough to speak about hiring quotas in front of a mixed-racial group? Your answers to these questions will be reflected in the ways you use your voice and body, in the intensity of your language and demeanor, and even in your selection of materials.

The Speaker's Credibility.   The listeners' estimation of a speaker's credibility will affect the speaker's success. Speaker **credibility** is the degree to which an audience judges a communicator trustworthy, competent, sincere, attractive, and dynamic. The idea of credibility is rooted in the classical Greek concept of **ethos**, a word that means *character*. Research has repeatedly demonstrated that a speaker who can raise an audience's estimation of his or her own trustworthiness, competency, sincerity, attractiveness, and dynamism will heighten the impact of the speech. Research has verified the following generalizations, among others:

1. References to yourself and your experience—provided you're not boasting or excessive—tend to increase your perceived trustworthiness and competence. References to others (authorities) tends to increase your perceived trustworthiness and dynamism.

2. Using highly credible authorities to substantiate your claims increases your perceived fairness.

3. If you can demonstrate that you and your audience share common beliefs, attitudes, and values, your overall credibility will increase.

4. Well-organized speeches are more credible than poorly organized speeches.

5. The more sincere you are, the better chance you have of changing your listeners' attitudes.[6]

As these generalizations suggest, you and your message are inseparable in people's minds. Your audience's perception of you is the key—Aristotle called it the most important aspect of persuasion—to your effectiveness.

The Message

Your messages often are referred to as your *ideas* or *information*. In public speaking, three aspects of the message—content, structure, and style—are especially important.

The Content of the Message.   The message of a speech does not consist merely of facts and descriptions. A speech's **content** is the substantive and valuative materials that form the speaker's view of this topic, of the world. So, the content of a speech on so-called notebook computers is more than a recitation of brands, model numbers, and features; the content is the way that the speaker shapes that information for an audience's use. Such shaping often shows up in the central idea guiding the speech, such as "Three factors—price, preference in diskette operating systems, and uses—should guide your decision on which notebook computer to purchase." In speeches, content is comprised of information plus the ways it is packaged for others.

The Structure of the Message.   Any message you transmit necessarily is structured in some way, simply because you say some things first, others second, and so on. Even if you ramble, listeners look for patterns. It's important, therefore, to provide a pattern in order to guide their search for coherence. That structure may be as simple as numbered points ("First I'll discuss . . . , next I will . . . and finally I'll . . .") or as complex as a full outline with points and subpoints.

The Style of the Message.   Just as you must select and arrange the ideas you wish to convey to listeners, so too must you select words, arranging them in sentences and using them to reveal your self-image to others. Selecting and arranging words and revealing yourself to be a certain kind of person are matters of style.

Given the innumerable words from which to choose, the great varieties of sentence structures, and even the many possible self-images available to speakers, many styles are possible. Styles can be personal or impersonal, literal or ironic, plain or elevated, philosophical or poetic. Such labels refer to particular combinations of vocabulary, syntax (sentence structure), and images of the speaker. What we call style, therefore, really has little to do with the elegance (stylishness) of language. Rather, it refers to those aspects of language that convey impressions of you, of details of the world, and of emotional overtones.

The Listener

Like speakers, listeners have purposes in mind; they are partners in transactions. The way they think about what's said is affected by their (a) purposes; (b) knowledge of and interest in the subject; (c) level of listening skills; and (d) attitudes toward self, speaker, and the ideas presented.

The Listener's Purposes.   Listeners always have one or more purposes when they come to your speeches. No less than speakers, they're looking for rewards. For example, you may attend an on-campus presentation by actor-activist Ted Danson in part to be entertained, in part to learn something about the environmental causes he champions, in part just to see what a star looks and sounds like in person. Such purposes might form your expectations; you'd be disappointed if he didn't refer to any of his movies or his long run in the TV show *Cheers*, and if he only talked about Hollywood without discussing the dangers to our oceans. Speakers must take listeners' purposes into account or risk rejection.

The Listener's Knowledge and Interest Levels.   In speaking situations, listeners' knowledge of and interest in the subject significantly affect how they respond to the message. When speaking, one of your jobs is to figure out how much listeners know about your topic and whether they have any personal stake in it. You can give only the most elementary speech on prestressed concrete to an audience that knows nothing about cement; if you talk to a structural engineering class, it's quite another matter. You must assess the levels of knowledge and interest in your audience. Such assessment must include an analysis of your cultural differences and how they will affect the audience's reception of your speech. What shared experiences can you call upon when talking with this audience?

The Listener's Command of Listening Skills.   Listeners vary in their abilities to process oral messages. Some people were raised in homes in which complex oral exchanges occurred, and others weren't. Some people have acquired the ability to follow long chains of reasoning, while others struggle to get the point. Most younger children cannot concentrate on difficult speeches, while most college students already have been taught to do so. What you must do is constantly scan your audience, looking for signs of comprehension and confusion.

The Listener's Attitudes.   Listeners' attitudes toward themselves, the speaker, and the subject affect how they interpret and respond to speeches. Listeners with low self-esteem, for example, tend to be swayed more easily than those with stronger self-images. Listeners who feel their opinions are confirmed by the views of the speaker are also more easily influenced than those holding contrary ideas. Moreover, as a rule, people seek out speakers whose positions they already agree with and retain longer and more vividly those ideas of which they strongly approve.[7] **Audience analysis** is one of the keys to speaking success, because you need to know much about people's attitudes before you can reach them.

Feedback

You may think of public speaking as communication flowing in one direction, from speaker to listener. But information, feelings, and ideas flow the other way as well. **Feedback** is information that listeners return to speakers about the clarity and acceptability of ideas.

Two kinds of information are provided by feedback. By looking for frowns or other signs of puzzlement, or, in a classroom, seeing how well students do on tests, speakers can learn whether their ideas have been comprehended clearly. Speakers also look for cues to the acceptability of their ideas; audiences can boo, look disgusted or antsy, or even leave the room. Being able to read feedback for signs of *comprehension* and *acceptability* is important, for this skill allows you to make mid-course adjustments in the speech.

Suppose you're giving a speech on child abuse. You might distinguish between punishment and abuse by referring to various modes of spanking. If you see wrinkled brows of puzzlement, you might elaborate by comparing withholding dessert and withholding all food or between just raising your voice and shouting at children about how bad and rotten they are. Each time, you'd try to show a difference between nonabusive and abusive discipline. Or, if you quote an expert on the subject and some listeners still look skeptical, you might add another authority as well as descriptions of such incidents of abuse. Throughout all this, you might not be able to convince everyone that your distinction between punishment and abuse is workable, but at least you might convert a few doubters. Feedback thus is a return message from audience members that tells you how much progress you've made and how far you've yet to go to reach your goals.

The Channels

The public communication transaction occurs across multiple channels. The **verbal channel** carries words, society's agreed-upon symbols for ideas. The **visual channel** transmits the gestures, facial expressions, bodily movements, and postures of the speakers and listeners; these tend to clarify, reinforce, or emotionalize the words or to transmit needed information about the audience's state of mind to the speaker. The visual channel sometimes is supplemented with a **pictorial channel**—visual aids such as diagrams, charts, graphs, sketches, and objects. The **aural channel**—also called the **paralinguistic channel**—carries the tone of voice, variations in pitch, loudness, and other vocal modulations; the aural channel carries cues to the emotional state of the speaker and the tone (ironic, playful, serious) of the speech.

Because these four channels are seen and heard simultaneously, the overall message is really a combination of several messages flowing through all of the pathways. Communication via multiple channels is what makes public speaking such a rich and subtle transactive experience. You must learn to shape and control the messages moving through all four channels.

The Situation

What you say and how you say it are affected significantly by the situations in which you're speaking. You don't talk the same way at work as you do at a party. Your speech is affected by the physical setting and the social context in which it occurs.

Physical Setting.   The physical setting influences listeners' expectations as well as their readiness to respond to your speech. People waiting in the quiet solemnity of a cathedral for a service to begin have very different expectations from theatergoers who've spent $75 to see a revival of *Cats* on Broadway. Listeners who gathered in 1992 at an open-air political rally to hear H. Ross Perot diagnose the problems in Washington, D.C., anticipated very different sorts of talk than those gathered in a political science class on minority politics.

Even furniture and decor make a difference. Soft chairs and muted drapes help to put discussants at ease and to promote productive exchange. The executive who talks to an employee from behind a massive walnut desk in the middle of an opulently decorated room with large windows looking down from the twenty-fifth floor gains a communication advantage from that setting; it connotes power, authority, and command over others.

Social Context. Even more important to message reception than physical setting is the social context in which speeches are presented. A **social context** is a particular combination of people, purposes, and places interacting communicatively. In a social context, *people* are distinguished from each other by such factors as gender, age, occupation, power, degree of intimacy, ethnicity, and knowledge. These factors in part determine how you "properly" communicate with others. For example, you're expected to speak deferentially to your elders, your boss, a high status person in politics or the church, or a judge. Women on the assembly line relate to each other informally; women in the military talk to each other in accordance with the rules of rank.

Certain *purposes* or goals are more or less appropriately communicated in different social contexts. Thus a memorial service is not the context for attacking a political opponent; a "meet the candidates" night is. Some *places* are more conducive to certain kinds of exchanges than others. Public officials are often more easily influenced in their offices than in public forums, where they tend to be more defensive; sensitive parents scold their children in private, never in front of their friends.

Societies are governed by customs, norms, and traditions that become the bases for communication rules. **Communication rules** are guides to communication behavior, specifying what ought to be said, how, to whom, and in what circumstances. Some communication rules tell you what to do: "An audience will better remember what you have to say if you break it into three or five main points." Others tell you what to avoid: "Don't wander aimlessly across the stage while talking because it will distract your audience." Such rules, of course, can be broken; some wandering speakers are nevertheless listened to, probably because they have so many other virtues. Occasionally, rule breaking is inconsequential; sometimes, however, it determines success or failure, and it always involves a certain amount of risk.[8]

The Cultural Context

Finally, elements of communication may have different meanings depending upon the **culture**, or society within which the communication is taking place. Each culture has its own rules for interpreting communication signals. Some societies frown on taking second helpings of food, while in others, it's a supreme compliment to the host or hostess. Negotiating the price of a T-shirt is unheard of at Sears in Atlanta, yet it's a sign of active interest in an Istanbul bazaar or at a Cleveland garage sale. Communication systems operate within the confines of cultural rules and the expectations of members of any given society.

Cultural rules and expectations become important in two situations: during *intercultural contact* and *cross-cultural presentations.* When talking to members of other societies on your home turf, you might offend them by violating some rule that they bring with them to your speech. A common violation that occurs during intercultural contact is too much familiarity or informality with a new acquaintance. To call people by their first names in public, for example, is simply not acceptable in many countries.

Your problem may be even greater, of course, if you attempt to speak in public in another country. During such cross-cultural presentations you risk violating not only personal standards of interaction but the rules of the situation operating at that time and place. Americans soon learn that they cannot joke publicly about royalty in England in the same way that they can joke about the president's family in the United States. If you are going to speak in various countries, you have to learn the communication rules governing the ways to introduce a person to an audience, to quote appropriate authorities, and to refer to yourself and audience members correctly. Rules for such communication situations tend to vary from country to country.

To tap into the cultural context for public speaking is to grapple with the most fundamental questions of diversity and sociality—how people in various countries interact with each other and transact public business. The cultural context for public speaking is the ultimate source of the communication rules you've been taught.

Because speeches almost always represent transactions whose appropriateness is determined by cultural rules or expectations, throughout this book you'll find explicit pieces of advice—do's and don'ts. It's not really "wrong," for example, to skip a summary at the end of your speech, but most audiences expect one. If you omit it, the audience might question your **communication competence**—your ability to construct a speech in accordance with their expectations. These sorts of expectations do not have to be followed slavishly, because conditions and even speaker talents vary from situation to situation; however, you should follow the rules of communication most of the time because you want listeners to evaluate your ideas, not your communication skills.

Speakers and listeners, messages and feedback, channels, context, and culture—these are the primary elements of the public speaking process. Sooner or later you need to become expert at managing all of them in ways that make you a more effective communicator for the following reasons:

1. *A change in one element usually produces changes in others.* During a
   speech on learning to use the campus computer system, for example,

your attitude will affect your language and delivery, your listeners' attitudes toward you, and even the feedback that you receive from them.

2. *No single element controls the entire process.* You may think the speaker controls the entire process, but, of course, the speaker doesn't, because listeners can tune in or tune out, and because cultural expectations often affect the listeners' perceptions of the speaker's talents.

Overall, therefore, public speaking is a *transaction*. Inherent in this idea of transaction is the notion of exchange: you prepare a speech to give your listeners, and, in turn, they give you their attention and reactions or feedback. From among all of the things you could say, you actually select only a few and tailor them to the listeners' interests, wants, and desires, so that they can absorb and accept them. And, just as you assert your right to speak, they assert their right to listen or not. *Public speaking is a communication transaction, a face-to-face process of mutual give-and-take.*

Skills and Competencies Needed for Successful Speechmaking

Because public speaking is an interactive process through which people transact various kinds of business, you must acquire certain skills (psycho-motor abilities) and competencies (mental abilities to identify, assess, and plan responses to communication problems). From the beginning of your coursework, four basic qualities merit your attention: (a) integrity, (b) knowledge, (c) sensitivity to listener needs and to speaking situations, and (d) oral skills.

Integrity

Your reputation for reliability, truthfulness, and concern for others is your single most powerful means of exerting rhetorical influence over others. Integrity is important, especially in an age of diversity, when various groups in a fragmented culture are wary of each other and each other's purposes. Listeners who haven't had personal experience with a particular subject or representatives of particular social groups must be convinced of your trust and concern for them. You must earn their trust while speaking if you are to succeed.

Knowledge

Expertise is also essential. No one wants to listen to an empty-headed windbag; speakers simply must know what they're talking about. So, even though you have a lot of personal experience with criterium bike-racing, take time to do some extra reading, talk with other bikers and shop owners, and find out what aspects of the topic interest your potential listeners before giving a speech about it.

Rhetorical Sensitivity

Sometimes we talk publicly for purely *expressive* reasons—simply to give voice to ourselves. Usually, however, we speak for *instrumental* reasons, to pass on ideas or to influence the way others think or act. The most successful speakers are "other directed," concerned with meeting their listeners' needs and solving their problems through public talk. These speakers are rhetorically sensitive to others.

Rhetorical sensitivity refers to speakers' attitudes toward the process of speech composition.[9] More particularly, rhetorical sensitivity is the degree to which speakers (a) recognize that all people are different and complex, and hence must be considered individually; (b) avoid rigid communication practices by adapting their messages and themselves to particular audiences; (c) consciously seek and react to audience feedback; (d) understand the limitations of talk, sometimes even remaining silent rather than trying to express the inexpressible; and (e) work at finding the right set of arguments and linguistic expressions to make particular ideas clear and attractive to particular audiences.

Being rhetorically sensitive doesn't mean saying only what you think an audience wants to hear. Rather, it's a matter of careful self-assessment, audience analysis, and decision making. What are your purposes? To what degree will they be understandable and acceptable to others? To what degree can you adapt your purposes to audience preferences while maintaining your own integrity and self-respect? These questions demand that you be sensitive to listener needs, the demands of speaking situations, and the requirements for self-respect. Rhetorical sensitivity, then, is not so much a skill as a competency—a way of thinking and acting in the world of communication.

Oral Skills

Fluency, poise, voice control, and coordinated body movements mark you as a skilled speaker. These skills don't come naturally; they're developed through practice. Such practice is not a matter of acquiring and rehearsing with a bag of tricks. Rather, your practice inside and outside your classroom should aim at making you an animated, natural, and conversational speaker. Many successful public speakers—discounting those speaking in the high ceremonial situations of politics and religion—seem to be merely *conversing* with their audiences. That should be your goal: to practice being yourself, to practice conversing with others in public.

Overcoming Speech Anxiety

As you think about speaking publicly, you're likely to feel some anxiety because you don't want to fail. This fear of failure or embarrassment may be even stronger than your desire to speak, leading to speech anxiety.

Research distinguishes between two kinds of speech anxiety: state apprehension and trait apprehension.[10] **State apprehension** refers to the anxiety you feel in particular settings or situations. For example, perhaps you can talk easily with friends but are uncomfortable when being interviewed for a job. This sort of apprehension is also known as *stage fright* because it's the fear of performing that leads to your worries or embarrassment. Extreme stage fright has physiological manifestations: clammy hands, weak knees, dry mouth, and a trembling or even cracking voice. Its psychological manifestations include mental blocks (forgetting what you're going to say), vocal hesitation and nonfluency, and an internal voice that keeps telling you that you're messing up your speech. The knowledge that you're being evaluated by others intensifies these anxious moments.

While some aspects of nervousness are characteristic of the situation, others are a part of your own personality. This kind of apprehension, called **trait apprehension**, refers to your level of anxiety as you face any communication situation. A high level of such anxiety may lead people to withdraw from any situation that requires interpersonal or public communication with others. By attacking your trait fears of speaking in public, you'll be in a better position to reduce your overall level of social anxiety. Although there's no foolproof program for developing self-confidence, there are some ways to achieve the confidence necessary to complete the speaking task:

1. *Realize that tension and nervousness are normal and, in part, even beneficial to speakers.* Fear is a normal part of living; learn how to control it and make it work for you. Remember that the tension you feel can provide you with energy and alertness. As adrenaline pours into your bloodstream, you experience a physical charge that increases bodily movement and psychological acuity. A baseball pitcher who isn't pumped up before a game may find his fastball has no zip. A speaker who isn't pumped up may come across as dull and lifeless.

2. *Take comfort that tension is physiologically reduced by the act of speaking.* As you talk and discover that your audience accepts you and understands what you're saying, your nervousness will tend to dissipate. Physiologically, your body is using up the excess adrenaline it generated; psychologically, your ego is getting positive reinforcement. Shortly after you've begun, you realize that your prior preparation is working in your favor and that you've got the situation under control. The very act of talking aloud reduces fear.

3. *Talk about topics that interest you.* Speech anxiety arises in part because of self-centeredness; sometimes you're more concerned with your personal appearance and performance than with your topic. One means of reducing that anxiety is to select topics that thoroughly interest you—topics that take your mind off yourself. By doing this, you make the situation topic-centered rather than self-centered.

Shyness and Public Speaking

Do you think of yourself as shy? If so, does shyness affect your willingness and ability to speak in public? Many people think of themselves as shy, but some people suffer from heavy-duty speech fright to the point of paralysis.

A leading psychologist, Stanford's Philip G. Zimbardo, defines shyness as "an apprehensiveness about certain social situations due to excessive preoccupation with being critically evaluated, resulting in a variety of behavioral, physical, cognitive, and emotional reactions." Shyness comes in many forms. It's a matter of bashfulness at one extreme and social paralysis at the other, with the middle ground being a state in which you lack self-confidence and are easily embarrassed. About 40 percent of American college students describe themselves as shy, another 40 percent say that they used to be shy, and about 15 percent see themselves as shy in certain situations. To get at the roots of shyness, Zimbardo and his colleagues developed *The*

4. *Talk about subjects with which you're familiar.* Confidence born of knowledge increases your perceived credibility and helps you control your nervousness. Have you ever wondered why you could talk at length with friends about a hobby, sport, or political interests without feeling anxious, only to find yourself in a nervous state when standing in front of an audience to talk about something you just read in *Newsweek*? Knowing something about the subject may be part of the answer: subject mastery is closely related to self-mastery.

5. *Analyze both the situation and the audience.* The more you know about the audience and what is expected of you, the less there is to fear. In the speech classroom, students are usually less nervous during their third speech than during their first. They're more comfortable with the audience and are more aware of the demands of the situation. The same is true of other settings as well: careful analysis of the audience and its expectations goes a long way toward reducing a natural fear of the unknown.

Stanford Shyness Survey, a tool used to diagnose shyness and its sources in specific individuals.

Using such instruments as the Shyness Survey, therapists can tailor treatment programs to individual needs: (a) They can help individuals build new social skills, teaching them *how* to act in situations that are new or strange. (b) They can suggest exercises to boost self-esteem if it appears that a person consistently thinks of him or herself in negative terms. (c) If a shy person's physiological reactions are dominant, therapists can teach the individual anxiety management—breathing exercises, relaxation techniques, muscle-flexing, and so on. (d) Occasionally, therapists organize group and individual sessions devoted to "cognitive reorganization"; here, individuals learn the bases of their shyness, come to understand that it need not destroy social relations, and attribute different sorts of significance to it than they had before. (e) Group sessions can also be used as practice arenas, just as your speech classroom is, where shy people can be guided through their interactions with others step by step.

Shyness is probably at the base of what we usually call "speech fright" or "communication apprehension." If you are shy, one of the goals you ought to set for yourself in this classroom is the control and redirection of those feelings. Talk with your instructor, and perhaps other professionals on campus, if you want help.

FOR FURTHER READING
Zimbardo, Philip, Paul Piklonis, and Robert Norwood. "The Silent Prison of Shyness." Office of Naval Research Technical Report Z-17. Stanford, CA: Stanford University (November, 1974); Zimbardo, Philip. *Shyness: What It Is, What to Do About It.* Rev. ed. Reading, MA: Addison-Wesley, 1990.

6. *Speak in public as often as you can.* Sheer repetition of the public speaking experience will not eliminate your fears, but will make them more controllable. Speaking a number of times in front of the same group can help reduce your fright. Repeated experiences with different audiences and situations also will help you increase your self-assurance and poise, which, in turn, will lessen your apprehension. Force yourself to speak up in class discussions, join in conversations with friends and others, and contribute in meetings of organizations to which you belong. Find time to talk with people of all ages. Attend public meetings and make a few comments.

There are no shortcuts to developing self-confidence about speaking in public. For most of us, gaining self-confidence is partly a matter of psyching ourselves up and partly a matter of experience. The sick feelings in your stomach may well always be there, at least momentarily, but they needn't paralyze you. As you gain experience with each of the essential steps—from

Communication and Your Career

I n many chapters of this text, you will find a *Communication Research Dateline* highlighting a particular aspect of research on the public-speaking process. This first one centers on research dealing with communication and your career.

Since the early 1970s, members of the Speech Communication Association, the national professional organization for speech communication teachers and scholars, have been interested in the relationship of speech training to postcollege employment. In 1972, the SCA published its first book on the subject, *Career Com-* *munication: Directions for the Seventies.* That book discussed the applications of speech training for students interested in particular careers—counseling, the ministry, police work, telephone company positions, retail sales, direct sales, teaching, and management (focusing on the Sears, Roebuck program). Fifteen years later, following several other general and specific books on job hunting, a broader and more useful book appeared: Al Weitzel's *Careers for Speech Communication Graduates* (1987). In it, Professor Weitzel brings research findings to bear on the great variety of tracks in speech

selecting a subject to practicing the speech—your self-confidence as a speaker will grow.

The Ethics of Public Speaking

No introductory chapter to a public speaking textbook is complete without a reference to the ethics of public speaking. In helping people define who they are, in assembling and packaging information for others, in seeking to persuade them to think or act in a certain way, you run into many ethical questions. Is it ethical to make explicitly racial references when defining a people? Should you tell both sides of the story when you are giving people

communication education; on the image that communication majors and the outside world have of speech students; on some career options (in particular, the skills needed for careers in training and development, public relations, law, teaching, sales or marketing, and other positions); on some techniques for maximizing employability (including working at internships, joining professional organizations, improving your communication skills, and the like); and on simple steps to find appropriate employment.

A point worth underscoring that comes from this career-related research is that, after completing your communication training, you can profitably pursue either (1) "communication" careers (the ministry, education, politics, advertising, sales, broadcasting, filmmaking, writing, editing, and so on) or (2) "noncommunication" careers (careers that emphasize other special skills, such as accounting, scientific research, insurance, computer science, engineering, nursing, and the like). That is, oral (and written) communication skills, as indicated by some of

the sources cited in reference note 2 in this chapter, are useful to virtually *any* entry-level position in American education, business, government work, service industries, or other occupations. No matter what you will do after graduation, think of communication skills training as training for your life's work.

FOR FURTHER READING

Bolles, Richard Nelson. *What Color Is Your Parachute? A Practical Manual for Job-Hunters & Career Changers.* Berkeley, CA: Ten Speed Press (published annually); Kennicott, Patrick Curtis, and L. David Schuelke, eds. *Career Communication: Directions for the Seventies.* New York: Speech Communication Association, 1972; Weitzel, Al R. *Careers for Speech Communication Graduates.* Salem, WI: Sheffield Publishing Co., 1987; Weitzel, Al R., and Paul Gaske. "An Appraisal of Communication Career-Related Research." *Communication Education* 33 (April 1984): 181–94.

information on a new wonder drug? Can you in good conscience suppress certain kinds of information when you're trying to change people's minds? These and hundreds of other ethical questions face you as you prepare and deliver speeches. Whether you want to or not, you make decisions with moral implications many, many times—even when you're building a comparatively simple speech.

No one can presume to tell you precisely what ethical codes you ought to adhere to when giving a speech. Given a textbook's educational mission, however, we'll regularly raise ethical questions and urge you to deal with them. Throughout the book, you'll encounter "Ethical Moments," features that will confront you with a problem and ask you to think through it. Confronting and working through ethical dilemmas will make you a more thoughtful speaker.

Chapter Summary

We live in an Age of Diversity, characterized by a fragmented population and subgroups within society separated from each other even while needing a sense of the whole to live together. Speaking skills are important to society because we collectively use speeches for *self-definition; information giving; debate about questions of fact, value, and policy;* and *individual and social change.* A useful model of public speaking incorporates six elements and their variable aspects: *the message* (content, structure, style); *the speaker* (speaker's purpose, knowledge, attitudes, and credibility); *the listeners* (listeners' purposes, knowledge of subject, command of listening skills, attitudes); *the channels* (verbal, visual, pictorial, and aural); *the situation* (physical setting, social context); and *culture* (social and communication rules). Because public speaking is a complex *transaction,* you need certain skills and competencies to be successful: *integrity, knowledge, rhetorical sensitivity, oral skills,* and *self-confidence* and *self-control.*

References

1. Henri Mann Morton, "Strength Through Cultural Diversity," in J. Blanche, ed., *Native American Reader* (Juneau, AL: Denali Press, 1990), 196–97.

2. Barbara Jordan, keynote speech to the 1992 National Democratic Party Convention, July 13, 1992, New York City, telecast on the C-SPAN television network; personal transcription.

3. Carol H. Pazandak, "Followup Survey of 1973 Graduates, College of Liberal Arts" (Minneapolis: University of Minnesota, 1977) (multilith); Jack Landgrebe and Howard Baumgartel, "Results of the Graduate Requirement Questionnaire for College of Liberal Arts and Science Alumni" (Lawrence: College of Liberal Arts, University of Kansas, n.d.) (typescript); "Instruction in Communication at Colorado State University" (Ft. Collins: Colleges of Engineering, Colorado State University, July 1979) (multilith); and Edward Foster et al., "A Market Study for the College of Business Administration, University of Minnesota, Twin Cities" (Minneapolis: University of Minnesota, November, 1978) (multilith). These studies all indicate that graduates in the working world find communication skills to be essential for both hiring and promotion. See also this chapter's *Communication Research Dateline.*

4. The word *transaction* is being used to indicate that public speaking is not a one-way mode of communication. Just as the speaker offers a message, so the listeners in return offer messages in the form of feedback. Speakers and audiences have mutual obligations to be forthright and honest in their appraisal and treatment of each other. Each thus plays complementary roles during public speeches, and hence the word *transaction* clearly applies to this sort of communication exchange. For a more complete discussion of this concept, read the classic essay on it: Dean C. Barnlund, "A Transactional Model of Communication," in *Language Behavior: A Book of Readings,* ed. Johnny Akins et al. (The Hague: Mouton, 1970), 53–71.

5. On the interrelationships between self-concept and communication, see Gail E. Myers and Michelle Tolela Myers, *The Dynamics of Human Communication: A Laboratory Approach,* 3rd ed. (New York: McGraw-Hill, 1980), Ch. 3, "Self-Concept: Who Am I?" 47–72.

6. Still the most complete summary of research on credibility is Stephen W. Littlejohn, "A Bibliography of Studies Related to Variables of Source Credibility," *Bibliographic Annual in Speech Communication: 1971,* ed. Ned A. Shearer (Annandale, VA: Speech Communication Association, 1971), 1–40. For supplements, see Erwin P. Bettinghaus and Michael J. Cody, *Persuasive Communication,* 4th ed. (New York: Holt, Rinehart & Winston, 1987), Ch. 5, "The Influence of the Communicator," 83–104.

7. For more information on such matters, see Stephen W. Littlejohn and David M. Jabusch, *Persuasive Transactions* (Glenview, IL: Scott, Foresman, 1987), Ch. 3, "Persuasion and the Individual," 44–75.

8. For a fuller discussion of physical and social context, see Loretta A. Malandro and Larry Barker, *Nonverbal Communication* (Reading, MA: Addison-Wesley, 1983), Ch. 6, "Environment," and Ch. 11, "Culture and Time," 179–210, 344–370. The best review of research on communication rules is found in Susan B. Shimanoff, *Communication Rules: Theory and Research,* Sage Library of Social Research (Beverly Hills, CA: Sage, 1980).

9. See Roderick P. Hart and Don M. Burks, "Rhetorical Sensitivity and Social Interaction," *Speech [Communication] Monographs,* 47 (1980): 1–22. Some similar points are made in Wayne Brockriede, "Arguers as Lovers," *Philosophy and Rhetoric,* 5 (1972): 1–11.

10. James McCroskey, "Oral Communication Apprehension: A Summary of Current Theory and Research," *Human Communication Research,* 4 (1977): 78–96.

Key Terms

audience analysis (p. 13)

aural channel (p. 14)

communication competence (p. 16)

communication rules (p. 15)

content (p. 11)

credibility (p. 11)

culture (p. 15)

diversity (p. 4)

ethos (p. 11)

feedback (p. 13)

paralinguistic channel (p. 14)

pictorial channel (p. 14)

rhetorical sensitivity (p. 18)

self-image (p. 8)

social context (p. 15)

state apprehension (p. 19)

trait apprehension (p. 19)

verbal channel (p. 14)

visual channel (p. 14)

Problems and Probes

1. In a notebook set aside for the purpose, start a Personal Speech Journal. The contents will be seen by only you and your instructor, who may call for the journal at intervals during the term. In your first entry, write about yourself in relation to the six basic qualities needed for successful speechmaking. (If you

have not engaged in an exercise like this before, it should be a fascinating source of enlightenment for you.) Consider your integrity. In what areas do you feel you have the most knowledge? In what areas would you wish to research to gain more knowledge? Look around your classroom at your classmates who will be your listeners this term. What do you know about their needs? What do you know about the speaking situation you are about to face? What do you still need to learn? What oral skills do you already possess and what others do you wish to gain? Finally, consider your own self-confidence and control in light of the task before you.

2. Identify and describe three speech transactions in which you participated during the past week. In at least two of these encounters, you should have been the speaker initiating the interaction. Formulate answers to the following questions:

    a. In which of the three situations—person-to-person, small group, or public communication—did each of these three transactions take place?

    b. What channel or channels did you use?

    c. What was your communicative purpose in each case?

    d. To what extent do you feel you accomplished your communicative purpose in each transaction? Why?

    e. What was the extent of your message-preparation in each of the three instances? If preparation was more mandatory and/or more extensive for one situation than for others, explain why this was so.

    f. Show how, in one of these transactions, the physical setting probably influenced what happened. In another, explain how the social context tended to affect the outcome.

Communication Activities

1. To the extent that the physical facilities of the classroom permit, your instructor will arrange for members of the class to seat themselves in a large circle or in smaller groups around two or three separate tables. Informality should be the keynote in this particular activity. After the instructor has completed a brief self-introduction, each class member will provide a self-introduction based generally on the following pattern:

My name is _____.

My major (or my major interest) is _____.

I am enrolled in this college/university because _____.

In addition to a grade credit, what I hope to get from this course in speech communication is _____.

2. Working in pairs, present pertinent biographical information about yourself to the class member who is your partner. Your partner, in turn, will prepare a short speech introducing you to the group. You will do the same for your partner. When these speeches have been completed, draw up a composite picture of the audience to whom you will be speaking during the remainder of the term.

3. Interview the leader of a local group that schedules public lectures, the director of the campus speakers' bureau, or another person in a position to

discuss the speech skills that are characteristic of professional speakers. Bring a list of those skills to class and be prepared to compare your notes with those of others.

4. Prepare a two-to-three-minute presentation on the topic "a speech I shall always remember." In specifying why you consider a particular address notable, focus on one or more of the factors in the speech communication process discussed in this chapter.

2

PUBLIC SPEAKING AND CRITICAL LISTENING

L istening is an activity that we all too often take for granted. After all, we say, we have been listening to others since birth—with this amount of practice, why should we bother to study it formally? Since listening takes up much of our daily lives—estimates run as high as 45 percent of our communication time spent in attending to what others say— we must be fairly proficient at it by now.[1] While these statements may make sense, your past experience with your own listening behavior, as well as that of others, strongly suggests that habitual practice does not always result in proficiency. As a character in one of the late science fiction writer Theodore Sturgeon's novels lamented, "Did you ever talk to someone who simply and totally listens? Do you know how rare that is?"[2]

The importance of "simply and totally" listening cannot be overestimated. In general, listening to others is the means by which we understand ourselves better, learn what others expect of us, and obtain the information and ideas necessary to make informed decisions. Corporations have long recognized that poor listening, which occurs often in meetings and in communication between superiors and subordinates, harms productivity and morale within the company. In response, corporations have instituted workshops and other training sessions to improve skills at all levels. As one study reports, almost half of the Fortune 500 companies provide training in listening skills.[3] The Sperry Corporation, for example, has used listening as its advertising theme—"We understand how important it is to listen"—and has a comprehensive program for training its employees.[4] In your own experience as a student, you may have faced the consequences of *not* listening to someone's instructions on how to perform a chemistry experiment, to the oral presentation of the next day's assignment, or to the orally presented schedule for the next exam.

Chapter 1 focused briefly on the listener as audience member. In this chapter we will discuss listening behavior in general, as it functions within the classroom and in other contexts. Barriers to effective listening behavior, and ways to counteract them, will be presented. Finally, your responsibilities as a speaker in improving the chances of being *listened to* will be discussed.

Types of Effective Listener Behavior

At the most general level, there are two discrete types of listening behavior: empathic and critical. Both share three attributes. First, *all listening aims at comprehension.* If you don't understand what you're hearing, you can do very little with the information presented. If your ultimate goal is to act or to give advice on the basis of the spoken word, comprehending is the initial prerequisite—whether you are sitting in your living room conversing with friends, attending a corporate board meeting, listening to a friend explain a problem, or receiving the next assignment in class. People often are poor listeners because the human mind can comprehend many more words per minute than speakers can produce clearly. A listener can mentally handle more than 400 spoken words per minute, yet the average speaker produces between 125–175 words per minute. Thus, the listener needs only about 20 to 25 seconds of every minute to comprehend what the speaker is saying. The resulting time lag—the spare moments when close attention is not needed—provides a tempting route to non-listening. "Dropping out" to think about other things may be fine, but only if you can remember to "drop in" again on the message. Therein lies the difficulty in effective listening.

The second attribute of all listening activity is that it is a *transactional process.* The audience in face-to-face situations sends a message back to speakers. Listeners can provide three types of feedback: (1) **direct feedback** in the form of verbal or written comments; (2) **indirect feedback**, as in nods, laughs, frowns, and other nonverbal signs that indicate whether a person understands the message and is or is not accepting it; and (3) **delayed feedback**, such as when classroom speakers are graded by their peers and/or the instructor on their performance.

Thus, listening is not a one-way street—"I talk; you listen"—but rather is a dynamic, transactional process in which both speakers and listeners participate to create meaning. This leads us to the third common feature: *listening is an interpretive act.* Both speakers and listeners modify each other's thoughts and actions, one by making a speech and the other by reacting to it. The "meaning of the message" is not something unique to the

Listening Behavior

There are several approaches to the study of listening behavior. Some of these focus on theoretical *models* of the processes involved. Goss, for example, takes an "information processing" approach to listening. There are three stages to the model:

(1) *signal processing*—transmitting the message to the listener. This stage causes problems only if the speech is unclear, poorly spoken, or the language being used is unfamiliar to listeners;

(2) *literal processing*—taking the words spoken at face value in assessing their probable meaning. This is the first stage of meaning assessment, and it focuses on the denotation of the words used;

(3) *reflective processing*—listening to evaluate. This goes beyond the literal stage to determine what else may be contained in the message (for instance, inferences, motives, and speaker credibility).

In a recent study, Beatty and Payne connected the Goss model of listening to the concept of cognitive complexity, which refers to the levels of complex thinking or variety of different thoughts a stimulus produces in the mind. They found that as complexity increases, one is better able to recall information presented. In terms of listening, this suggests that as you bring more ideas to bear on what you're hearing, your own ability to listen effectively, as measured by comprehension and recall, will increase.

Another approach to listening research has focused on "the relationship between listening skills and individual performance." In their study, Michael Papa and Ethel C. Glenn hypothesized that a listening training program would improve employees' ability to adapt to a new computer system. They concluded that there was "strong evidence that listening ability impacts on employee productivity levels with new technology" and that "the provision of listening train-

speaker, nor is it wholly "inside" the receiver. Rather, meanings are created by the interaction of both parties involved in the exchange.

An analogy to drama may clarify what is meant by the interpretive act.[5] When a writer creates a play, he or she may intend to convey certain meanings. When a director stages the play, some of those meanings will be altered. An actor will further alter the meaning of the play through the interaction of his or her experience and personality with the script. Finally, what each audience member takes away as the play's meaning is a complex integration of that person's own knowledge and experience, the author's

ing programs improves employee's ability to perform with new technology."

Beverly Sypher, Robert Bostrom, and Joy Hart Seibert examined the relationship between listening and factors associated with one's communication ability, job level, and upward mobility. As in the case of Papa and Glenn, they used the Kentucky Comprehensive Listening Test to evaluate the relationships. They also distinguished between several types of listening behavior. Their conclusions regarding "short term listening" (STL) and "lecture listening" (LL) included the following observations: (1) Persons with persuasive ability and sensitive to social contexts have higher levels of skill in both STL and LL. (2) There is some evidence that a person's listening skill has a positive impact on job level; the better the skill, the higher the job. (3) There also is some evidence to support the notion that better listeners are more upwardly mobile within an organization.

M. H. Lewis and N. L. Reinsch, Jr., examined behaviors contributing to effective and ineffective listening. In a study of listening behavior in a bank and a hospital, they found that the work setting did not influence the kinds of behaviors that people appreciated or disliked. Effective behaviors included maintaining eye contact when listening to others, generally appearing attentive to the person talking, and following directions to demonstrate that you did listen. Ineffective behaviors included not following directions, not reacting verbally or nonverbally to the message, talking to others while someone is speaking, and not recalling prior messages (perhaps indicating a pattern of not listening).

FOR FURTHER READING

Goss, Blaine. "Listening as Information Processing." *Communication Quarterly,* 30 (1982): 304–07. Goss, Blaine. *Processing Communication.* Belmont, CA: Wadsworth Publishing Co., 1982. Beatty, Michael J., and Steven K. Payne. "Listening Comprehension as a Function of Cognitive Complexity: A Research Note." *Communication Monographs,* 51 (1984): 85–89. Papa, Michael J., and Ethel C. Glenn. "Listening Ability and Performance with New Technology: A Case Study." *Journal of Business Communication,* 25 (Fall, 1988): 6–15. Sypher, Beverly Davenport, Robert N. Bostrom, and Joy Hart Seibert. "Listening, Communication Abilities, and Success at Work." *Journal of Business Communication,* 26 (Fall, 1989): 293–303. Bostrom, Robert N. *Listening Behavior: Measurement and Application.* New York: Guilford Press, 1990. Lewis, Marilyn, and N. L. Reinsch, Jr. "Listening in Organizational Environments." *Journal of Business Communication,* 25 (1988): 49–67.

intent, and the performance as fashioned by the director and actors. The words of Shakespeare's *Macbeth* may remain the same, but different directors, performers, and audiences will create divergent views of the significance and meaning of the play. While audience members may disagree about "what the play means," it also isn't uncommon for them to agree on the quality of the performance. Thus, different audience members may take away the same essential interpretation from the event.

The same process of interpretation is taking place in organizations when superiors talk to subordinates, and in the classroom when students present

THE TYPES OF FEEDBACK

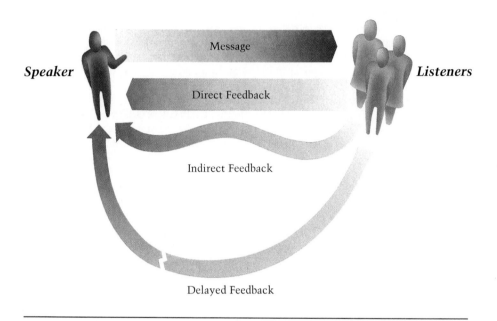

Speaker ... *Listeners*

Message

Direct Feedback

Indirect Feedback

Delayed Feedback

speeches to their peers. Given the manifold possibilities in any interpretation of oral talk, the refrain "I told them—they just didn't listen" may not be as true as its speaker believes.

Empathic Listening

Empathy involves putting yourself in the place of another—seeing an event from his or her perspective and coming as close as possible to understanding his or her feelings or attitudes.[6] The most common context for empathic listening is in therapeutic settings. In **therapeutic listening**, the auditor (as single listener) acts as a sounding board as the speaker talks through a problem, works out a difficult situation, or expresses deep emotional stress or confusion. Empathic listening is not confined to professional people, such as teachers, lawyers, or therapists. In your own life, you undoubtedly have found yourself playing the role of a "sympathetic ear." Although empathic listening most often occurs in interpersonal situations, and generally in more private settings, it may also be required of audiences in a public speaking situation. For example, empathic listening would be required when a sports star apologizes for unprofessional behavior, a televangelist confesses on nationwide television to moral failure, or a classmate reviews a personal problem and asks friends for help in solving it.

Equally important occasions for listening with empathy occur in times of joy, as when someone wants to tell others about a new love, a new baby, a promotion at work, or an award at school. People seek others both in times of triumph and in times of turmoil. In empathic listening, special social bonding between the speaker and listener occurs; the speaker-audience relationship itself can become the focus of attention and a cause for celebration.

Critical Listening

Whereas empathic listening attends to the person as a result of what is said, **critical listening** attends directly to the message, to what is being communicated. It may be easier to understand the dimensions of critical listening by considering what it is *not*. First, the opposite of critical listening is **passive listening**. In preparing to study, you may turn the stereo on; you may require one kind of sound to drown out all others so you can concentrate. Occasionally, you "tune in" to the music, but not for long. Your focus of attention remains on the text. While this example suggests a positive role for passive listening, not all instances of passivity are helpful. As you listen to a lecture, you're passively listening to the primary message if you don't think about or analyze the ideas being offered. If the message has important implications for your beliefs or actions (such as taking a test on the material in the near future), your passivity could have negative consequences.

Second, critical listening is *not* negative listening; the goal isn't necessarily to criticize what is being said. Rather, it's listening in order to retain the *option* of critique—that is, by knowing what is said you can decide how you wish to respond. Thus, critical listening demands that listeners become fully engaged with the message, not just so they understand it, but so they can interpret it, judge its strengths and weaknesses, and determine its worth. You practice listening critically when you evaluate commercials for their sexist or ethnical content, political campaign speeches for their inane or false claims, theatrical performances for their artistic merit, or oral arguments for or against some plan of action in the community or at work. When listening critically, you decide to accept or reject a claim, to act or delay action on a project, to decide whether to offer praise or blame.

Appreciative Listening.   There are two predominant types of critical listening: appreciative and discriminative listening. The primary purpose of **appreciative listening** is to judge the aesthetic value of what you hear, whether a speech, a dramatic play, a musical, or a jazz ensemble performance. One might, for example, listen to Martin Luther King, Jr.'s "I Have a Dream" speech or John F. Kennedy's Inaugural Address with the principal goal of appreciating their illustration of the art of public speaking—hearing King's resonant voice or recognizing the force of metaphor as an argument for change, or listening to Kennedy's superb verbal style. Recognizing these

Martin Luther King, Jr., presented his "I Have a Dream" speech at the 1963 March on Washington.

elements can explain why both presentations have become exemplars of public oratory.

Regardless of the reason, appreciative listening requires active rather than passive participation. In order to appraise an event's actual significance to you and your community, you need to employ certain evaluative criteria, and that can only be done if you engaged yourself fully and attentively in the proceedings (see Chapter 18). Thus, appreciative listening aims at making *value judgments* about the speaker, the presentation, and the event itself.

Discriminative Listening. In **discriminative listening**, the goal is to evaluate the *reasons* being offered through the message—to either believe an idea or to act on the basis of a proposal. The discriminative process involves drawing inferences about both stated and unstated matters—about what speakers are really saying, about whether the claims being made are cogent or well-founded. By listening carefully to what the speaker is claiming, and to the reasons that support the claim, you will have a basis for determining whether the claim is reasonable or not. To assess what is "really meant," you may need to evaluate tone of voice or recognize that the "unsaid" is more important than the "said" in a given situation. For example, you may conclude how angry your friends are with you based not so much on *what* they say as on *how* they say it. Likewise, a president's attitudes toward a foreign policy controversy such as Iraq's reluctance to allow United Nations' inspection teams access to certain areas is determined as much by what is left unsaid as by the public pronouncements. Do the public statements reflect a sincere attitude or are they merely *pro forma* comments designed to deflect criticism? Do they clearly imply a firm commitment to find the truth or are they simply the "right words" for the occasion, regardless of personal intent? The crucial question in such situations is this: Can you place your trust in what the speaker is saying, and by accepting the belief or acting on the claim, find that you have not misplaced your trust?

Discriminative listening involves making choices about the worth of claims; it is the basis for making informed decisions about how you live your life. Whether such decisions concern "Should I study for the exam?" or "Should I present the proposal to my employer?" or "Should I disagree with the professor?" the accuracy of your decisions depends on your prior listening behavior. If you have been only half-there during class lectures, you will not know what to study. If you have not been paying attention to your employer's solicitations for new ideas, your speculation about her response to your proposal will produce more anxiety than necessary. If you have not noticed the tone of your professor's statement that criticism is welcomed, you cannot be sure whether it is.

When you are a member of an audience, you need to decide on a specific listening approach. When listening in a critical mode, appreciative listeners are highly selective. They watch for metaphors, listen to speaking tones, and search out memorable phrases. Discriminative listeners, on the other hand, work hard to catch every piece of information relevant to some proposal, judge the soundness of competing arguments, and consciously select criteria which would justify accepting or rejecting a proposal. Empathic listeners must decide when to reinforce speakers positively through applause or other signs of approval, thereby serving a therapeutic purpose.

As your skill in listening increases, and as you think explicitly about your own purposes *before* attending a speech, you'll find your experiences with public presentations becoming more pleasurable and complete. Listening effectively, regardless of purpose, provides a firm foundation for conclusions about what is going on around you.

Barriers to Effective Listening

To be effective, both speaker and listener must accept the fact that listening is a joint responsibility. Both must make reasonable efforts to insure that intended messages are taken in, comprehended, interpreted, and responded to in an appropriate manner. Even when people make the required effort, problems can still arise. Few of us are good listeners, since we tend to drop out more often than we drop in. Although estimates of the average listening comprehension rate vary, researchers agree that we do not utilize our full listening potential.[7] Some studies indicate that we may understand only one-fourth of the information we receive aurally.

As a speaker, you need to know the barriers to effective listening in order to adjust your message and to diminish their potential negative effects. Four of the barriers are most responsible for poor listening habits: (1) weak extrinsic motivation; (2) personal constraints; (3) environmental constraints; and (4) poor timing of message.

Weak Extrinsic Motivation

Studies indicate that being told to listen is an ineffective strategy. Being told *why* one should listen, and providing relevant rewards or punishments as incentives, increases the extrinsic motivation to listen.[8] **Extrinsic motives** stand outside the specific act being performed; they function as reasons to pay attention to the act. For example, if your class lecturer doesn't offer any guides as to what to listen for and why, one of two possibilities will occur. Either you will listen closely to everything and take copious notes in the hope that later you will be able to sift out essential material, or you will despair of ever knowing what to listen for and tune out. What will make you expend extra energy on your task is the extrinsic motive: a decent grade. If the extrinsic motive is not very strong, you will simply become a passive listener and hope that studying outside of class will make up the difference.

Personal Constraints

The presence or absence of an *internal desire* to listen will affect how well you pay attention to a message. Listening is not an automatic response to most stimuli that reach us. Although the wailing of a siren as a fire truck roars past will generally command our attention, the sonorous tones of a tired, unenthusiastic speaker will not. Your *past experiences* also may affect how well you listen. Sometimes a speaker's words will trigger a memory of the past or remind you of some present engagement—on these occasions your mind wanders to personal thoughts, plans, or needs.

Your *attitudes, values,* and *beliefs* also can cause you to interpret spoken messages personally. When you don't agree with the message, you spend mental time debating with the speaker, planning what to say if you have the opportunity. In the meantime, the speaker goes on, unaware that you're missing the full development of her or his ideas. Listeners' mental debates can trip them up, as the speaker blithely must respond to uninformed questions with the remark: "As I said in my presentation. . . ." Much faulty listening can be attributed to the fact that auditors haven't given the speaker the benefit of a complete presentation before drawing conclusions about the accuracy and justifiability of the claim.

PERSONAL AND ENVIRONMENTAL CONSTRAINTS ON LISTENING

Competing demands on your attention usually allow you to hear and symbolically process only part of a spoken message. Listening with full discrimination rarely occurs.

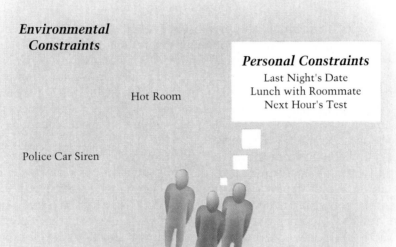

Environmental Constraints

Hot Room

Police Car Siren

Uncomfortable Chair

Personal Constraints
Last Night's Date
Lunch with Roommate
Next Hour's Test

Attitudes toward the speaker also color a person's internal desire to listen effectively. For example, if you've heard that an instructor lectures poorly, you'll enter the classroom with a negative mind-set. Chances are that your preset notions will be confirmed, not necessarily because the instructor is boring everyone, but because you allowed the person's reputation to interfere with the reality of the communicative situation.

That personal constraints matter to others is clear. As one study suggests, being lazy, closed minded, opinionated, insincere, bored, or otherwise inattentive are some of the traits that college students see as barriers to effective listening.[9]

Environmental Constraints

The physical communication setting also can work against effective listening. Distractions draw attention away from the speech. Seats can be too hard or otherwise uncomfortable; the person next to you might be whispering to someone in the next row; the room may be too drafty or too hot and stuffy; a police car with its siren blasting may pass by an open window. Paying attention to your own physical well-being and comfort or to other external distractions can inhibit your concentration on the message as the primary stimulus.

Poor Timing

The Greeks understood the importance of the "fitting moment" for speech—the right time to present an idea or argue for an action. Their term for it was *kairos*; ours is **rhetorical timing**.[10] This concept is as relevant for listeners as it is for speakers. There are good and bad times for attempting to attend to a message, as explained in the preceding discussion of personal and environmental constraints. If you have just taken out a loan for a new car, you may not be in the best mood to hear an urgent appeal for money for a social cause, no matter how justified the need.

You probably have an intuitive understanding of what it means to speak or to listen at an opportune moment. Your life is full of both good and bad episodes in which appropriate timing was a key ingredient in your success or failure. You've learned from experience that listening to an instructor on a "review day" has positive consequences; you've learned that listening to instructions when you're unsure how to perform a task saves you from later embarrassment.

Strategies for Effective Listening

Let us now examine your responsibilities as a listener, and the ways in which you can improve your listening behavior as a member of an audience, either in a classroom, social, or work setting. This section also will suggest ways to improve listening skills through an analysis of *self*, *speaker*, and *message*.

Listener Analysis of Self

To become a better listener in public settings, you first must identify your listening habits and preferences—your internal desire to listen—and think about them in terms of their productivity. How useful have these habits and preferences been in the past? Have they enabled you to listen as well as you should? If not, should you change your approach? Think about the times when you felt you were a good listener, when listening well was easy, and when you understood and recalled the most important parts of the message.

What types of settings were these? What kinds of things did you do to keep your attention focused on the speaker and his or her message? Think also about the negative experiences, those times when listening was difficult. Why was it difficult to listen? Was your internal desire to listen insufficient to the task? Were you, for example, uninterested in the topic, bored, or too tired to stay with the speaker for the time required?

Another way to analyze your listening habits is to consider what you are looking for when you listen. Do you focus your attention on what the speaker is asking or requesting—her or his "bottom line"? Or do you first want to know the context, the historical background for the request and why it is being presented at this time? Or, are you more interested in examining the reasons being offered in support of the request or proposed action?

Wood and Bennett have labeled these orientations as **results, process,** and **reasons**.[11]

- If you become impatient when listening to someone because he or she is not clear about what they want, the chances are you are a results oriented listener. You want to get on with the task at hand, and not waste time with unimportant details.
- If you are more concerned about how the request or action affects others and about how the decision to implement the request is reached, you are a process oriented listener.
- If you want to know why something is being proposed or argued, you are a reasons oriented listener.

Some listeners will focus most of their behavior on one listening style while others may vary styles according to the situation. Factors such as the degree of sensitivity attached to the message, who is talking, how you feel about the person speaking, and how much risk there is in accepting or rejecting the message will affect the style adopted.[12]

After assessing your listening behavior, you can begin to correct habits that have proven ineffective by preparing to listen. Before you enter the communication event ask yourself the following questions.

What is my purpose in listening? Do I expect to gain information and understanding, to offer advice, or to make a critical decision based on the speaker's presentation? What is the extrinsic motive—the incentive—for listening? Think, for example, about your reaction to the professor's announcement that "This material will be on the next test." You'll probably pay particular attention, making sure that you understand and can recall it as needed. In this instance, there is sufficient extrinsic motivation to focus on the message. In another case, listening may be influenced by your personal interest in the subject matter or by your commitment to assist a friend, based on the information you receive. Whatever your motive for listening, recognizing why you are listening can better prepare you to analyze the important features of the message.

To prepare for a communication transaction, you must determine your purpose in listening. In receiving advice, for instance, consider the personal importance of the message and attend to it accordingly.

Am I impartial about the message being presented? If you're not willing to allow the speaker to complete his or her presentation before you draw conclusions, you may be wasting the speaker's time and your own. Try setting aside your personal feelings or attitudes about the topic, and give the speaker a chance to develop the message to its fullest extent. If you are critical of the message, your criticism will be stronger if you exercise the patience to hear the speaker out. Suspending initial judgment will enable you to listen more carefully to the arguments presented and to offer an appropriate refutation; you will be less vulnerable to the charge "If you had only listened to what I said. . . ."

How much do I know about the topic? If you are unfamiliar with the topic but at least curious about it, the chances are greater that you will listen effectively. If you know a good deal about the topic, you can listen to compare your information with that provided by the speaker. How complete are her or his ideas? Are they accurate, up-to-date, and fairly presented? As long as you control the process of comparative analysis, resisting the temptation to drop out and mentally check off items, before returning to the presentation, you have a basis for evaluating the worth of the idea.

What trigger words cause me to stray from the central message? As you hear words that bring up thoughts that are irrelevant to the occasion, resist the temptation to let your attention stray. For example, a classmate mentions *test* while describing a psychology experiment, and the word reminds you that you have an exam in the afternoon, and you haven't studied all of the material. As difficult as it is to put that issue aside, now is not the time to worry, since you can't study effectively while the speaker is talking. Or you may find your attention wandering because the speaker uses unfamiliar words.

What do I expect from this speech? Be realistic in setting your personal expectations. If the speaker is a classmate, the chances are that she or he is not an authority on the topic but has done sufficient research to offer a fairly complete summary of what experts are saying. If, for example, your classmate is giving a speech about the stock market, you'll be disappointed if you hope for hot tips on how to invest your money, or for the secret to successful investing. If you expect only to increase your understanding about how the stock market operates, your reason for listening will more closely match what the speaker can provide.

What do I know about the situation? If you can anticipate the length of the speech, you will do a better job of controlling your listening behavior. Assigned speeches in your class usually have a time limit; hence you can prepare to concentrate for a preset time in listening. If you are attending a lecture, you should be prepared for a presentation that will last at least an hour. By practicing your concentration skills in listening to the shorter classroom speeches, you will gradually improve your ability to focus attention on key ideas during longer presentations. Ask yourself if the situation calls for an evaluation of the performance's worth, as in appreciative listening, or if you'll be expected to make decisions on the basis of the presentation, as in discriminative listening. Knowing in advance what is expected of you will prepare you to adopt the appropriate listening strategies.

How favorable is the listening environment? Become aware of the physical constraints that may impede effective listening in particular environments. If you are engaged in therapeutic listening, a loud gathering may be the wrong setting. If your goal is to critically appraise a performance or to make decisions on the basis of reasons offered by a speaker, recognize that the physical environment may not be conducive to these ends. Noise from the air conditioning fan, a hot and stuffy room, or large columns that block your view of the speaker all impact listening effectiveness. Sitting nearer the speaker, if possible, will improve your chances of concentrating on the message. If it's possible to listen in relative isolation, your ability to concentrate on a message will increase. You also may ask the speaker for permission to tape the presentation so that you can listen to it later. Listening alone will improve your comprehension and retention of the message.[13] If you cannot alter the physical environment, recognizing the potential problems will help you guard against their intrusion into your concentration.

How appropriate is the timing of the message? As with the physical environment, the timing of the message is something else you may not be able to affect. But, if you are aware that the timing is not to your liking and that you cannot change it (many students dislike 8:00 A.M. classes, for example), you will be better able to make the best of the situation. To the extent possible, control the timing.

Listener Analysis of the Speaker

Speaking does not occur in a vacuum. Both speaker and listener bring personal experiences to the communication environment. In doing so, the listener attends not only to the message the speaker transmits but also considers the speaker's credibility. The following questions may assist your evaluation of a speaker and of his or her effect on the way you receive the message.

What do I know or think about this speaker? If you've heard the speaker before and enjoyed the speaker's presentation, you'll probably respond positively to a new encounter. If you agree with the speaker's position on political issues, you are more highly motivated to listen than if you disagree. If you dislike or disagree with the speaker, your views will probably color your perception of the person *and* of the message. If you take the position that the best defense is a sound knowledge of the opposition, you can increase your desire to listen carefully while building the strongest case for your position.

How believable is the speaker? People tend to answer this question based on previous experiences with the speaker or on advance information. If you know that the speaker has misled an audience on a previous occasion, you may expect similar treatment. If you suspect false information, you need to confront the speaker and show how it weakens the claim.

Is the speaker responsive to your needs? If the speaker has done her or his job well, there will be elements in the speech that meet your expectations, provide the information you seek, or satisfy your general desire to listen. For example, if the President of the United States were to visit your campus, would you expect him to discuss current national issues? If he spent his entire speech extolling the achievements of his administration, would your personal needs be met? Would you expect him to be aware of local issues and comment on them? If he did not, would your personal expectations have been satisfied? In a more informal setting, in which people have a chance to interrupt each other, a speaker who monopolizes talk lessens listening behavior. A speaker in such a situation who does not ask you probing questions about your interests will not invite close attention to what is being said.[14] Your interest in listening is tied closely to whether the speaker is meeting your personal needs.

What is the speaker's attitude toward this presentation? Listeners determine whether a message is worthy of attention in part by the attitudes that the speaker projects through both nonverbal and verbal cues. A speaker who appears flippant or insincere creates an obstacle to productive listening.

Listeners' interest in a communication transaction is tied closely to whether the speaker meets their personal needs. An effective communicator fulfills listeners' expectations, provides information they seek, or satisfies their general desire to listen.

Even a speaker who is genuinely interested in the audience may have distracting habits or mannerisms. Have you experienced a speaker who paced back and forth while speaking, with no real purpose associated with the physical movement, or who played with a pencil or paper clip while talking, or who spoke so slowly and in such measured tones that you couldn't follow the train of thought?

When such distractions occur, as they inevitably will, try to focus on the ideas being presented. Repeat the central points to yourself to help you ignore the distractions, or try taking notes on main points, to help you focus more precisely on the ideas as they are developed. If the problem is random movements of the speaker, listen with your ears rather than watch with your eyes. If the problem is a distracting mannerism, ignore it and concentrate on the message.

Are cultural differences relevant? Cultural differences may influence how a speaker organizes and addresses listeners. They also may affect the listeners' expectations. For example, Asian speakers talking about management techniques may be more focused on the development of personal relationships than on the bottom line. If you are a results oriented listener, you need to embrace the speaker's natural proclivity to address issues in a manner suited to that person's culture. If you interpret variations in style and approach as *different* rather than *wrong*, the attitude will help you focus on what is being said.

Listener Analysis of the Message

The message is the speaker's product, the reason for being for the speech occasion. The message provides information, gives advice, or urges decision making or action. As such, the message is the principal focus of your attention. As a receiver, you can focus your energy on the message by structuring your listening behavior in terms of the following questions.

What are the main ideas of the speech? Try to discover the speaker's purpose for speaking and list the ideas that the speaker presents to fulfill that purpose. Usually these can be found by determining the *central idea* or *claim* and identifying the main ideas used as explanation or support. Listen for specifics in light of the overall structure of the speech.

How are the main ideas arranged? The answer to this question will assist you in identifying and later recalling the main ideas. If you become aware early on that the main ideas are arranged in a chronological or spatial pattern, or that the assessment of cause is followed by a listing of effects, you can track the speech's progress from one point to the next. This takes the guesswork out of determining where the speaker will go next in the development of the speech, and makes it easier to structure or outline in your own notes.

Are the main ideas adequate and related to one another? Once you have identified the main ideas, you can attend more critically to their validity. You will be more likely to accept messages you see as carefully planned and fully researched. When the speaker offers inadequate justification, your motivation to listen can lessen. By noting the relationships between and among ideas, between and among claims and supporting evidence, you will be able to evaluate the adequacy of the message.

What types of supporting materials are used to develop the main ideas? In evaluating the worth of the message, consider such things as the timeliness of the data, the quality of the sources, and the specific content of the speech as it unfolds. Supporting materials should clarify, amplify, and strengthen the main ideas of a speech. Listening carefully to the support material provides the basis for evaluating the significance or worth of the speaker's central idea or claim.

Notetaking in the Classroom: Practicing Critical Listening Skills

The strategies discussed in this chapter relate to your current situation as a student in a speech class, as well as to other listening contexts. A useful initial approach to improving your critical listening skills in the classroom is to concentrate on notetaking. Studies indicate that taking notes enhances comprehension and recall following a presentation.[15] Taking notes over many years of classroom listening may have helped you perfect a method that works for you. On the other hand, when you are faced with unfamiliar material, you may be tempted to write everything down, or at least as much detail as possible. When you review your notes later, you hope that they will make sense.

If you concentrate too hard on taking notes, you may discover they are relatively meaningless because you did not *listen* to the message. You heard what was said, but you did not take the time to think about the content. Studies indicate that *interchanging* notetaking with listening is better than either attempting to listen and take notes concurrently, or taking no notes at all.[16] By alternating between listening and writing notes, you can control when you write, as well as when you listen. You also have a better chance to put down in abbreviated form what you understand about the presentation, and will find the notes are more useful in later review for an exam.

Second, as you take notes or simply listen to a speaker, whether in the classroom or elsewhere, follow this pattern: review, relate, and anticipate. *Review* what a speaker has said, both during and immediately after the presentation. Take the time to summarize the main points of the message and any factual material that appears essential. The task of reviewing will be easier if you also *relate* the message to what you already know. Consider how consistent the message is with your own knowledge, and how you might use this additional information at a future time. Finally, *anticipate* what the speaker might say next. Once you are aware of the pattern of development, what is the logical direction of the speech? Whether the speaker obliges you and does the "logical" thing is less important than the fact that you are interacting with the logic of the speech as you perceive it and are in a position to follow the ideas to their completion. Reviewing, relating, and anticipating are useful activities given the difference between your rate of comprehension and the speaker's rate of speaking.

There are several other ways you can enhance your classroom experience by actively seeking to improve listening habits. For example, use the speech course as a place to sharpen your listening skills through critiquing the speeches of other students. Take part in post-speech discussions as a means of checking your own understanding of main points and support material. Constructive criticism accomplishes two goals: it provides a beginning speaker with much-needed reaction from peers, and it forces you, as a listener, to attend closely to the message. In this way, both you and the speaker benefit. You also can listen critically to discussions, lectures, oral presentations, and student-teacher exchanges in other classes, identifying effective and ineffective communicative techniques in a variety of different settings. By listening carefully to speakers outside of class, and noting how well their audiences listen, you can develop your own understanding of what works and why.

Speaker Responsibilities

As we have already seen, effective listening depends on the speaker fulfilling certain responsibilities. The following material highlights strategies that you, as a speaker, can use to facilitate listener comprehension. These can be discussed in terms of speaker related strategies and message related strategies.

Speaker Related Strategies

Several of the primary variables which affect listening are related to speaker characteristics:[17]

Rate of delivery.   Speaking between 125 and 250 words per minute is an acceptable average rate for listener comprehension. While listeners can comprehend much faster rates of speech, this speed allows them to process the message, to engage in reviewing, relating, and anticipating activity while the message is being presented, and to take notes.

General fluency of speech.   The easier a speech is to hear, the more effective listening behavior becomes. If listeners must strain to hear the speaker or to comprehend words spoken in a thick accent, their listening focus will be on these factors instead of the message. Speak clearly (and more slowly if you have a strong accent) and avoid frequent pauses or false starts.

Visibility.   Position yourself so that you can be seen by all listeners. This will enable them to focus more easily on the message. If there are columns or other obstructions that the seating arrangement has not taken into account, suggest that people move to unobstructed viewing areas.

Credibility.   As noted, your credibility will influence an audience's perception of you and your message. If you have had an earlier negative experience with the audience, you should realize that while your credibility may be low, it is not necessarily fixed at that level. By presenting a well-prepared, cogently argued speech, delivered with sincerity and conviction, you can go a long way toward improving the audience's estimate of your competence.

Speaker likability.   If the audience is already positively disposed toward you, your message has a better chance of being received favorably. If the audience is negatively disposed, the advice concerning credibility applies here as well. Even if audience members don't like you as a person, you can strive to present your ideas in a manner that garners their respect for you as a competent, well-meaning individual with an idea to offer. Direct listener attention to your message rather than to your personal relationship with them.

Similarity in values.   Critical listening depends in part on the audience's perception of the degree of similarity between its values and your own. If the values are generally in accord, you can expect listener activity to be fairly high. If the values are in discord, you can expect some listeners to tune you out. You will learn more about strategies for dealing with discrepant values in Chapter 16.

Adaptation to cultural differences.   Being aware of the listening styles of your audience and the ways they prefer to have issues addressed will go a long way toward insuring their active listening behavior. If you remove idiomatic expressions that would be unfamiliar to foreign members of your audience, you'll make it easier for them to track the meaning of your message. You also won't be as likely to give unintended offense if you suit your language to the culture of the audience.

Message Related Strategies

As suggested earlier, controlling the message enhances your chances of being listened to in a critical manner. The following attributes of message design will improve your chances of being heard.

Clear, unambiguous language.   The clearer your message, the less confused your listeners will be. In turn, they will have less reason to drop out and neglect to return. When presenting concepts that are difficult to comprehend, restate them in different ways so your listeners can understand the material.

Active voice.   In stylistic terms, use the active rather than the passive voice to give greater emphasis to ideas. Active voice emphasizes the "doer of the deed"; passive voice emphasizes the recipient of the action. Instead of saying "It was decided by the board of directors to postpone action," say "The board of directors decided to postpone action." Using passive voice consistently may create equally passive listeners, because it makes the speaker appear less involved in the actions he or she is describing.

Organized message.   In preparing your speech, adopt a pattern of organization and use it consistently in the development of the main ideas. Anticipate points where your listeners may have difficulty following the speech, and build in internal summaries or transitions to guide them to the next idea.

Capturing and holding attention.   Although some listeners will come to the presentation highly motivated to listen actively, others may not. Speakers must constantly be on the lookout for lapses of attention and continuously take steps to secure it.[18] James Albert Winans, a twentieth-century communication scholar, put the matter succinctly when he observed "attention determines response." Attention and strategies for gaining it are discussed in Chapter 3.

In addition to these strategies, any action you can take as a speaker to crack the barriers to effective listening will enhance the impact of your message. If possible, control factors in the physical environment, such as noise and temperature, to reduce distractions. Time your presentation to meet the needs and expectations of the audience. If your listeners perceive that you are making a sincere effort to communicate, they will tend to make the effort necessary to be more effective listeners.

Your response to feedback is one sign of your desire to communicate effectively. Watch for nonverbal cues from the audience, and if you notice signs of confusion, quickly reassess the way you are presenting the information. You can exert more control over audience comprehension and listening behavior by rephrasing unclear points, by summarizing to clarify and reemphasize your main points, and by presenting a cogent overall summary of the speech's significance—its value to the audience in terms of their own interests. If time permits, ask for questions, and use the answers as opportunities to clear up any confusion or misunderstanding.

Chapter Summary

A common feature of all listening behavior is the desire to *comprehend* a message. In addition, listening is a *transactional* enterprise—a two-way street, a joint responsibility of speaker and listener to maximize the transmission of ideas. Third, listening is *interpretive;* meaning is not the sole property of either speaker or listener, but is created by both participants in the act of communication. Listening is *empathic* when the objective is to put yourself in another person's place, to assume that person's feelings as your own. *Critical* listening is neither *passive* nor *negative*. Rather, it is active attendance to what is said, with a view to evaluating the worth of a performance or an idea. *Appreciative* listening attaches value to a speech or event; *discriminative* listening evaluates a speaker's *reasons* to determine whether they are worthy of adoption. In any type of listening, both parties must be sensitive to its points of breakdown; *extrinsic motives, personal* and *environmental constraints,* and *poor timing* can impede effective listening behavior. Through the analysis of *self* as listener, the *speaker,* and the *message,* you as a listener can exert greater control over your own behavior and improve your comprehension and recall of the message. Through conscious attention to your responsibilities as a speaker, you can help diminish the potential causes of poor listening, enhance your credibility, and increase the chances your message will be received favorably.

References

1. See studies reviewed by Andrew Wolvin and Carolyn Coakley, *Listening* (Dubuque, IA: William C. Brown Co., 1982), ch 1.; and Kittie W. Watson and Larry L. Barker, "Listening Behavior: Definition and Measurement," in Robert N. Bostrom, ed., *Communication Year-*

book 8 (Beverly Hills, CA: Sage Publication, 1984), 178–94. Hereafter cited as Watson and Barker.

2. Theodore Sturgeon, *Godbody* (New York: Donald I. Fine, Inc., 1986), 88.

3. A. D. Wolvin and C. G. Coakley, "A Survey of the Status of Listening Training in Some Fortune 500 Companies," *Communication Education*, 40 (1991): 152–64.

4. Gary T. Hunt and Louis P. Cusella, "A Field Study of Listening Needs In Organizations," *Communication Education*, 32 (1983): 393–401.

5. John R. Stewart, "Interpretive Listening: An Alternative to Empathy," *Communication Education*, 32 (1983): 379–92.

6. See Ronald C. Arnett and Gordon Nakagawa, "The Assumptive Roots of Empathic Listening: A Critique," *Communication Education*, 32 (1983): 368–78; Karen B. McComb and Fredric M. Jablin, "Verbal Correlates of Empathic Listening and Employment Interview Outcomes," *Communication Monographs*, 51 (1984): 353–71.

7. For a discussion of these issues, see Carl Weaver, *Human Listening* (Indianapolis, IN: Bobbs-Merrill Publishers, 1972), ch. 1; Lyman K. Steil, Larry L. Barker, and Kittie W. Watson, *Effective Listening: Key To Your Success* (Reading, MA: Addison-Wesley, 1983).

8. Michael J. Beatty, R. R. Behnke, and D. L. Froelich, "Effects of Achievement Incentive and Presentation Rate on Listening Comprehension," *Quarterly Journal of Speech*, 66 (1980): 193–200; Larry R. Smeltzer and Kittie W. Watson, "Listening: An Empirical Comparison of Discussion Length and Level of Incentive," *Central States Speech Journal*, 35 (1984): 166–70; Charles R. Petrie, Jr., and Susan D. Carrell, "The Relationship of Motivation, Listening Capability, Initial Information, and Verbal Organizational Ability to Lecture Comprehension and Retention," *Communication Monographs*, 43 (1976): 187–94.

9. S. Golen, "A Factor Analysis of Barriers to Effective Listening," *Journal of Business Communication*, 27 (1990): 32.

10. See Bruce E. Gronbeck, "Rhetorical Timing in Public Communication," *Central States Speech Journal*, 25 (1974): 84–94.

11. This discussion is based on Rosemary V. Wood and Ruth T. Bennett, "Secrets of Successful Communicators—How They Get What They Want," *Business Quarterly*, 52 (Summer, 1987): 24–27; Bennett and Wood, "Effective Communication Via Listening Styles," *Business*, 39 (April–June, 1989): 45–48.

12. John S. Fielden and Ronald E. Dulek, "Matching Messages to Listening Style," *Business*, 40 (October–December, 1990): 55–57.

13. Michael J. Beatty and Steven K. Payne, "Effects of Social Facilitation on Listening Comprehension," *Communication Quarterly*, 32 (1984): 37–40.

14. See McComb and Jablin; John A. Daly, James C. McCroskey, and Virginia P. Richmond, "Judgments of Quality, Listening, and Understanding Based Upon Vocal Activity," *Southern Speech Communication Journal*, 41 (1976): 189–97.

15. Robert N. Bostrom and D. Bruce Searle, "Encoding, Media, Effect and Gender," in Bostrom, *Listening Behavior: Measurement and Application* (New York: Guilford Press, 1990), 25–41; Mary Helen Brown, Enid Waldhart, and Robert N. Bostrom, "Differences in Motivational Levels and Performance on Various Listening Tasks," in Bostrom, *Listening Behavior*, 144–54.

16. See Watson and Barker.

17. See Watson and Barker.

18. See Watson and Barker.

19. Blaine Goss, "Listening as Information Processing," *Communication Quarterly*, 30 (1982): 304–07; Blaine Goss, *Processing Communication* (Belmont, CA: Wadsworth, 1982); James J. Floyd, *Listening: A Practical Approach* (Glenview, IL: Scott, Foresman, 1985).

20. Michael J. Beatty and Steven K. Payne, "Listening Comprehension as a Function of Cognitive Complexity: A Research Note," *Communication Monographs*, 51 (1984): 85–89.

Key Terms

appreciative listening (p. 33)

critical listening (p. 33)

delayed feedback (p. 29)

direct feedback (p. 29)

discriminative listening (p. 34)

empathy (p. 32)

extrinsic motives (p. 38)

indirect feedback (p. 29)

passive listening (p. 33)

results/reasons/process listening (p. 39)

rhetorical timing (p. 38)

therapeutic listening (p. 32)

Problems and Probes

1. How effectively do you listen to others? In this exercise, you are asked to assess your attentiveness as a listener in a variety of situations. On a scale of 1–10 (with 10 being high), rate your listening behavior in the following situations:

_____ a. In a class in which you're interested in the subject.

_____ b. In a class in which you're not interested in the subject.

_____ c. In a social conversation setting, such as having coffee with friends or relaxing with co-workers.

_____ d. In a work-related situation, where a supervisor or boss is giving instructions.

_____ e. In a conversation with a close friend.

_____ f. At a lecture you are attending out of personal interest.

_____ g. At a lecture your professor assigned; you expect to be tested on the material.

First, think about your responses. If there are differences in listening "quality" across these settings (and it would be surprising if there weren't), what accounts for them? Second, ask five close friends—people who have observed you in situations similar to those above—to rate your behavior in each situation. Are there significant variances between your assessment and the perceptions of others? What might account for them? (See Steil, Barker, and Watson, *Effective Listening*, for an alternative "self-report" of listening skills.)

2. The Greek concept of *kairos* was introduced in a discussion of *rhetorical timing*. As you go through a typical day interacting with friends and listening to peers or professors present material in your classes, keep an informal diary of the relationship between appropriate timing and your own listening behavior. Which times were most appropriate for listening, and why? Which were not, and why? What can you do as a listener to control the appropriateness of timing when listening to others? Use the notes in your informal diary in a small group discussion of timing as it relates to listening.

3. Listening is rarely taught as an entire college course yet is acknowledged as an essential skill in the workplace. Should listening be focused on more than it is? Outline your response and be prepared to discuss this issue in class.

Communication Activities

1. You have been asked to give a brief speech to a group of prospective high school teachers. Your topic is "Ways of Faking Attention as a Listener in a Classroom." Develop a three-to-four minute speech in which you describe specific mannerisms that students use to appear attentive when they aren't.

2. You are to present a brief oral statement to a philosophy class on the significance of this quotation from the philosopher Epictetus: "Nature has given to man one tongue, but two ears that we may hear from others twice as much as we speak" (circa 300 B.C.E.). Using information from this chapter and other sources on listening (see the References for this chapter), develop a four-to-five minute speech explaining why this statement is still true about communication relationships.

3. Working in small groups in the classroom, test listening and comprehension skills. Each person in turn will explain a technical term to the others in the group (you might select one from another subject you are studying, such as "existentialism," "black hole," or "oxymoron"). As one group member presents his or her term, the others will listen without taking notes, then write on a notecard what they think they heard. After all explanations have been heard, each speaker should collect the cards on his or her presentation and compare the written understanding with the original explanation. If there are discrepancies, discuss with group members what might have helped them listen more effectively, including the possibility that the explanation was unclear or otherwise deficient.

4. For any round of speeches in your class, your instructor can ask that each student listen to the speech being presented and write down the speaker's main points and purpose as the listener understands them. Following each speech, the class members can compare their lists with what the speaker thought he or she was presenting. For this exercise, focus on what the speaker might have done to enable class members to listen more effectively, in order to reduce any discrepancies that arose between presentation and reception of the message.

3

GETTING STARTED:
PLANNING AND
PREPARING SPEECHES

T he first two chapters have provided a foundation for understanding the *process* of public speaking. Now we'll turn our attention to the *practice* of speech, beginning with planning. All speech teachers have heard students say, "Well, yeah, I knew what I wanted to do. It just didn't come out right and I made a fool of myself." When their teachers probe a little—did you know the precise point you wanted to make? had you found and carefully arranged supporting arguments? had you phrased your key ideas ahead of time?—the answer is usually "No, I didn't have time for that stuff."

Now, you can't learn everything there is to know at once about the intricacies and shortcuts of speech preparation and speechmaking, but you can learn enough about the basics now to get yourself thinking and acting in more rhetorically sound ways. Having a **rhetorical frame of mind** means thinking your way strategically through the decisions you have to make as you prepare for any speech: (1) selecting and narrowing the subject; (2) determining your purposes; (3) determining a central idea or claim; (4) analyzing the audience and occasion; (5) gathering the speech material; (6) making an outline; and (7) practicing aloud in preparation for actually delivering the speech. These may seem like a lot of decisions. True enough, they are. But systematic planning and purposeful decision making are two essentials for platform success. They save you time and keep you from wandering aimlessly through the library or waiting endlessly at your desk for inspiration. In this chapter, we'll briefly examine each of the seven steps.

THE ESSENTIAL STEPS IN SPEECH PREPARATION

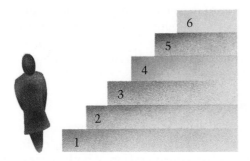

6 Practicing Aloud

5 Arranging Materials into an Outline

4 Gathering the Speech Material

3 Analyzing the Audience and Occasion

2 Determining the Central Idea or Claim

1 Selecting and Narrowing the Subject

The Essential Steps in Speech Preparation

There's no magical formula for getting ready to speak. However, if you generally follow the series of seven steps—either in the order presented here or in another that works for you—you'll be ahead of the game and ready for an audience. At the end of the chapter, we'll explore three other subjects you ought to think about before talking publicly: finding an appropriate method of preparation, gaining and holding listeners' attention, and projecting self-confidence.

Selecting and Narrowing the Subject

Oddly, one of the most difficult jobs many speakers in classrooms face is choosing a subject. Three important considerations should guide your selection process:

- What do you know something about?
- What are you interested in talking about?
- What topics can you relate to the audience's situation and interests?

You might begin by listing those topics that you know about, circling the ones you're willing to talk about in front of others, and thinking about ways you can relate them to your listeners. Before committing yourself to a firm choice, however, check your possible subjects in the next two steps: Be sure that your choice fits the purposes your instructor intends and that you can phrase your choice as a strong central idea or claim.

Once you've selected a workable topic, narrow it so that you can cover it in the time allowed. How much can you say about a particular subject in five minutes? You can't relate everything you know about professional baseball, but you could discuss such topics as the classification system (rookie clubs, single A, double A, triple A, and major leagues), the importance of the reappearance of the Northern Lights League in 1992, the divisional system in the National and American leagues, or the joys of contemporary baseball fiction. The narrower your subject, the more fully (and clearly) you can explain or support essential points. *Narrower subjects covered with more examples and materials usually are more interesting than once-over-lightly talks.* Include a variety of illustrations, data, authoritative quotations, and other supporting materials.

Determining the General and Specific Purposes

Once you have completed the first step, you can focus more precisely on why you want to talk about this subject. What do you want this speech to accomplish? Answering this question involves consideration of both general and specific purposes.

General Purpose.   What is the state you wish your listeners to be in when you complete the speech? For example, are you trying to tell them something they do not—but should—know? Are you seeking to alter the way they feel about a social, economic, or political issue? Are you interested in having them do something as a result of your speech? Answering "yes" to one of these questions will help focus your **general purpose**.

Specific Purpose.   Given your topic, specifically what do you want the audience to know, value, or do? Within the context of a general purpose, a **specific purpose** focuses attention on the particular, *substantive* goal of your presentation. Once this is determined, you'll be in a position to describe the exact response you want from your listeners: "I want my audience to understand the classification scheme for levels of professional baseball." In this instance, you want to inform your audience (general purpose), but, more specifically, you want to teach them about the different levels of expertise they're likely to encounter at the different levels of professional baseball.

Determining the Central Idea or Claim

For most speakers, this step flows directly from the preceding one. Can you state your message in a single sentence? If you are seeking to explain an idea or inform an audience about a process or event, that sentence is the **central idea**. It is a declarative statement that summarizes your speech: "The reemergence of the Northern Lights League in 1992 reshaped the structure of professional baseball." In speeches that aim at persuading an audience to adopt a specific attitude or take a particular action, the **claim** summarizes the intent of your argument: "The reappearance of the Northern Lights League in 1992 improved professional baseball in three important ways."

By this point in the planning process, your speech should be focused precisely on what you wish to convey to your audience. The central idea, in

Ethics and Public Speaking

O ccasionally, we'll include a boxed area devoted to "ethical moments"—ethical decisions public speakers must make in preparing and delivering their talks. Some of these moments will fit you and your circumstances, and some won't. In either case, we hope that you'll take an ethical moment and think about the problems presented and their solutions in your life. Some of these problems might be discussed in class. Here are some typical ethical questions that you might face in the speeches you'll give this term:

1. When is it fair to borrow other people's ideas and words, and when is it not? Need you acknowledge everything you learned from others? Must you cite sources for everything?

2. You recognize that a major portion of a speaker's informative speech came from an article that you read last week. The speaker does not cite the source. During the critique session, should you blow the whistle on the speaker? Should you instead talk with the person later? Or tell your teacher? Or let it go?

3. An article says exactly what you intended to say about the use of pesticides on garden vegetables. Then you find a more recent article claiming that new research contradicts the first article. Should you ignore the new evidence?

4. An authority whom you wish to cite uses the words *perhaps, probably, likely,* and *often.* Should you simply strike those words from a quotation that you wish to use to make the statement sound more positive? After all, you're not tinkering with the ideas, only the strength of assertion.

5. There are four minutes left in your class period. If you keep talking, there'll be no time left for a critique of your position. Should you extend your speech by four minutes?

6. A student in your class disagrees strongly with your analysis of the crack problem in the United States. You know that he was in a substance abuse program a year ago. You expect that if you bring this student's past up in response to his challenge, it will deflect focus from his point of view. Should you go for the deflection?

Ethical moments such as these will face you regularly, both in your speech classroom and throughout the rest of your life. Taking a few moments to consider such situations, and even articulate your position in discussion, can save you many, many embarrassing times later. Know what your moral stands are and know why you take them *before* you face ethical dilemmas on the platform.

the context of your general and specific purposes, serves as a constant guide as you move into the heavier sections of preparation. By thinking of each speech as an instrument for winning particular responses from audiences, you're able to simplify your research and direct your organization of materials. The tasks you complete in your head before you go to the library will save you incredible amounts of time and energy once you're there.

Analyzing the Audience and Occasion

While it's tempting to focus speech preparation on yourself—your goals, fears, and interests—listeners, not you, are the targets of your speeches. A good speech, therefore, not only reflects you but also is responsive to the interests, preferences, and values of the audience to whom it's presented. You must regularly ask yourself: "How would I feel about this topic if I were in their place?" "How can I adapt this material to their interests and habits, especially at points where their experiences and understanding differ from mine?" To answer such questions, you need to analyze the people that compose the group—their age range, gender, social-political-economic status, origin, backgrounds, prejudices, and fears. While you cannot interview everyone, of course, you need to get some sense of how they'll react to your central idea or claim.

In other words, you need to probe the listeners, finding out how much they know, how interested they are in hearing more, what they believe and value, and what their probable attitudes are toward you and your position. In a public speaking class, you can estimate these factors by listening to comments made during class discussions and by asking some class members what they think. In other circumstances, gathering this information is more difficult, requiring you to become more creative in assessing the audience. Regardless of how it's done, **audience analysis** is a primary determinant of success.

You also need to consider the setting and circumstances in which you're speaking:

- Are there specific rules or customs that you need to know and follow?
- How long will you have to speak?
- Will you precede or follow other speakers who could influence your reception?
- What impact will events before or after your speech have on topic selection, phrasing of your central idea or claim, or supporting materials?
- Will the physical circumstances be amenable to your speaking style? If not, can you alter them?

The answers to these questions can affect your speech. You might have to shorten it because your time has been shortened, for example, or maybe you'll need to ask for a microphone you hadn't planned on using. Perhaps you'll want to change your speech to answer a point the person speaking before you made. Analyzing the occasion involves both serious, substantive issues and such mundane matters as physical comforts. Examining such issues in advance is the key here. You want to be as forewarned and as comfortable as you can be in the circumstances you face when it's your time to speak.

Gathering the Speech Material

Now you're ready to assemble some ideas and information to fill out your speech. You need (1) to comb your mind to see what you already know and to figure out how much of it is relevant to your central idea or claim and then (2) to find the additional information elsewhere. You almost inevitably have to gather additional information to develop, expand, or reinforce what you already know and believe.

You may wish to talk to others, such as friends or local experts, to check out your perceptions. Critical listening is important here. You undoubtedly will want to gather other materials from newspapers, magazines, books, government documents, or radio and television programs. You'll soon learn some traditionally solid sources: the "News of the Week in Review" section of *The New York Times*; the news weeklies (*Time, Newsweek, U.S. News and World Report*); the breadth of magazines surveyed in *Readers' Guide to Periodical Literature* and more specialized indexes; and all of the annuals, yearbooks, almanacs, and so on that fill the reference area of your library. You'll even learn to consult more sophisticated sources of the type we'll review in Chapter 5.

Arranging Materials into an Outline

Once you've compiled your materials, you have to sort them. Developing a preliminary outline of main ideas will help. An outline lets you see how your various materials relate to your central idea or claim, shows you where you have plenty of (or too little) material, and makes the structure of your speech clear to you. You'll probably jockey back and forth between your materials and your outline, looking for just the right fit between what you *know* and what you can *justify* publicly to a critical audience.

We will examine outlining in more detail later. For now, follow two rules: (1) arrange your ideas in a clear and systematic order and (2) preserve the unity of your speech by making sure that each point is directly related to your specific purpose and central idea or claim.

Practicing Aloud

With your outline completed, you're ready for the most terrifying task of preparation: practicing your speech. This is not easy! You can feel like a fool talking aloud in your room; the sound of your voice rings hollow and you find that some of the materials you wrote out come off as simplistic, clichéd, stiff, or silly. Nevertheless, you've got to practice aloud to (1) improve some of the decisions you've already made and (2) work on your delivery skills.

Speech preparation involves gathering the materials you need to build the speech, arranging them into an outline, and practicing your delivery. Preparation and practice lead to effective performance.

Give practice a chance. It can save your communicative life. Talk through your outline aloud, in a full (not a mumbling) voice; that will help you to get used to the sound. Repeatedly read through the outline until you've made all the changes that seem useful and until you can express each idea clearly and smoothly. Then, putting the outline aside, think through the speech silently, point by point, to make sure that it's fixed in your head. Now, try to talk through the outline without looking at it, but by looking at a card with only a one-word cue for each idea. On your first trials, you may inadvertently leave out some points. That's okay. Practice until all of the ideas come out in their proper order and the words flow easily, all the time talking in full voice. Finally, if you dare, get a friend to listen to your speech, give you direct feedback, and help you practice making eye contact with a real person.

These seven steps, from selecting and narrowing a subject through practicing aloud, take you to the brink of public speaking with real audiences. Good work on preparation pays off in effective performance.

Delivering Your First Speeches

For most beginners, delivering their first speeches is very difficult. Many feel anxious and nervous. You may say to yourself, "I'm too nervous to stand up there." "What do I do with my hands?" "Will people think I'm a jerk?" Self-doubts, from actual fright to a more general lack of self-confidence, creep into every speaker's mind; the trick is to learn to control them. In the remaining part of this chapter, we'll examine three strategies for self-control: (1) selecting the right method of presentation, (2) focusing not on yourself but on capturing and holding the attention of your listeners, and (3) communicating self-confidence.

Selecting the Method of Presentation

Which method should you use to present your speech? Your choice should be based on several criteria, including the type of speaking occasion, the seriousness and purpose of your speech, your audience analysis, and your own strengths and weaknesses as a speaker. Attention to these considerations will help you decide whether your method of presentation should be (1) impromptu, (2) memorized, (3) read from a manuscript, or (4) extemporaneous.

The Impromptu Speech.   An **impromptu speech** is delivered on the spur of the moment with little preparation. The speaker relies entirely on previous knowledge and skill. When an instructor in a meteorology class calls on you for an explanation of the jet stream's course through the atmosphere, you don't have time to prepare more than a quick list of three or four words to remind you of points you want to make. Impromptu speeches are given in rhetorical emergencies—at public meetings, in classes, in conventions. When using this method, try to focus on a single idea, carefully relating all significant details to it. Avoid the rambling, incoherent "remarks" that the method too often produces.

The Memorized Speech. As its name implies, the **memorized speech** is written out word for word and then committed to memory. Although a few speakers are able to do this well, it presents problems for most of us. Usually memorization results in a stilted, inflexible presentation; speakers tend to be either excessively formal and oratorical or hurried, pouring out words with no thought as to their meaning. Using a memorized speech makes it difficult to adjust to feedback while speaking. If you do memorize your speech, remember that you tend to use more formal language when writing than when speaking. Be sure that your speech doesn't sound like a written essay.

The Read Speech. Like the memorized speech, the **read speech** is written out, but in this method the speaker reads from a manuscript. If extremely careful wording is required—as in the president's annual message to Congress, in which a slip could undermine domestic or foreign policies—the read speech is appropriate. It also is used in the presentations of scholarly papers, where exact, concise, often technical exposition is required.

The ability to read a speech effectively is valuable in certain situations, but it shouldn't be done unnecessarily. No matter how experienced you are, when you read your message, you'll inevitably sacrifice some of the freshness and spontaneity necessary for effective speechmaking. You'll also have trouble reacting to feedback and may be tempted to use more formal, written language. If you do use this method, talk through the speech over and over to ensure an effective oral style.

The Extemporaneous Speech. Representing a middle course between the memorized or read speech and the impromptu speech, the **extemporaneous speech** requires careful planning and a good outline. This whole chapter has been aiming at preparing you to present an extemporaneous speech. Working from your outline, practice the speech aloud, expressing the ideas somewhat differently each time through it. Use the outline to fix the order of ideas in your mind, and try out various wordings to develop accuracy, conciseness, and flexibility of expression. Through such preparation, you'll be able to deliver the actual speech from a few notes.

If the extemporaneous method is used carelessly, the result will resemble a bad impromptu speech, a fact that sometimes leads to a confusion of these two terms. When well-used, however, the method will produce a speech that is nearly as polished as a memorized one but more vigorous, flexible, and spontaneous. The best lecturers at your college or university undoubtedly are extemporaneous speakers. Most of the advice in this textbook assumes the use of the extemporaneous method.

THE FACTORS OF ATTENTION

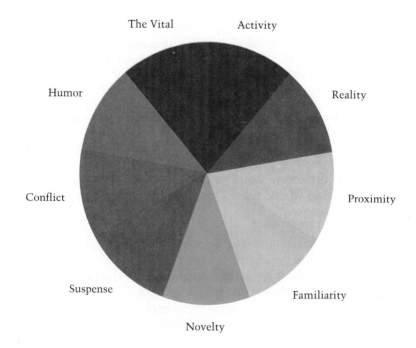

Capturing and Holding Attention: Nine Factors

Listeners' behaviors vary considerably, thanks to the thoughts and sensations in their internal and external environments. Essentially, your listeners need reasons for *wanting* to listen. Even when you have their attention, it tends to ebb and flow. So, you must constantly watch for lapses. James Albert Winans, a twentieth-century pioneer in public speaking instruction, expressed the problem succinctly: *Attention determines response.* If you cannot gain and hold it, you're in deep trouble. If you can, you have a chance to drive home your points.

What is **attention**? For our purposes, it can be thought of as *focus* on one element in a given environment, with the result that other elements fade from the perceptual field.[1] For example, in April of 1968, Martin Luther King, Jr., went to Memphis, Tennessee, to support striking African-American sanitation workers in their demands for improved wages. The evening of April 3 he spoke in a hot, crowded church about the history of civil rights, about his joy to be living "just a few years in the second half of the twentieth century,"[2] about the tense times in his life, about his upcoming Poor People's Campaign that was planning a March on Washington, and about Christian injunctions to social action. Videotapes of the speech show an audience interacting with King, moving and jostling, laughing and talking. But the audience became quiet and transfixed as he moved through the conclusion of the speech:[3]

> We've got some difficult days ahead. But it really doesn't matter with me now because I've been to the mountaintop. And I don't mind. Like anybody I would like to live a long life. Longevity has its place, but I'm not concerned about that now. I just want to do God's will, and He's allowed me to go up to the mountain, and I've looked over and I've seen the Promised Land. I may not get there with you, but I want you to know tonight that we as a people will get to the Promised Land. So I'm happy tonight, I'm not worried about anything. I'm not fearing any man. Mine eyes have seen the glory of the coming of the Lord.

As King finished, the crowd then erupted in long, sustained applause and even cheers. That crowd had talked and shouted through the speech, then was quieted as it focused intently on King's prophetic concluding words, and finally exploded in joy and appreciation as King's concluding religious image broke through their focus and returned them to the church, Memphis, the strike, and the problems of 1968 America.

Few of us will ever absolutely rivet onto ourselves the undivided focus of an audience in the way King did just before his assassination. Yet, we all can work to gain and hold attention. A *vigorous and varied delivery* will help. Likewise, your reputation and trustworthiness (positive *ethos*) can command respect—and attention. *Lively and picturesque language* gives audiences word-pictures and makes it easier for them to stay with you. Fundamentally, however, you'll capture and hold attention through the types of ideas you present. Some types of ideas or images have greater attention value than others.

Ideas can be presented in a variety of ways that have high attention value. Often called the **factors of attention**, these include the following:

- Activity
- Proximity
- Novelty
- Conflict
- The Vital
- Reality
- Familiarity
- Suspense
- Humor

Activity.   Suppose you have two TV sets side by side. One shows Natalie Cole performing motionless behind a microphone; the other carries one of her music videos—a complete production number with motorcycles, dry-ice clouds, and three back-up singers fully choreographed. Which one will you look at? In the same way, ideas that "move" tend to attract attention. Stories with suspense, uncertainty, fast action, and excitement usually have attention value.

Like ideas, the speech as a whole should move; it should march or press forward. Nothing is so boring as talk that seems to stand still, providing far too much detail on a minor point. Instructions and demonstrations, in particular, demand orderly, systematic progress. Keep it moving!

Reality.   The earliest words you learned were names for tangible objects—"Mama," "milk," "dog." While the ability to abstract or generalize is one of the marks of human intelligence, there still persists in all of us an interest in concrete reality, the here-and-now of sense data. When you speak, refer to specific events, persons, places, and happenings. A few paragraphs ago, we might have written: "Consider, for example, a preacher who is reviewing his church history and present circumstances." Such a depersonalized anecdote about "a preacher" doesn't carry the punch, human interest, and memorableness of one about a specific person. Audiences can hang ideas on specific details.

Proximity.   A direct reference to something nearby in time and space often orients an audience that is wondering what you're talking about. Consider the following: "Do you realize how much fast food is consumed on this campus? Within four blocks of this classroom are nine restaurants, including a McDonald's, a Wendy's, and a Pizza Hut. Two are local submarine houses. Even the student union runs a fast-food bar. A key question you patrons face is this: What are your lunch habits doing to your nutrition—to your body and mind?" Such an introduction brings the topic home.

Familiarity.   Especially in the face of new or strange ideas, references to the familiar are attention-sustaining. A common device here is the *analogy*. If a speaker explains that the London postal or zip codes are arranged like directions on a compass, with the initial letters indicating directions and the next set of numbers representing degrees or positions, then the speaker is using something familiar to explain something unfamiliar. The familiar is comfortable, reassuring. Thus, many a speaker opens with allusions to Washington, Lincoln, and Kennedy; cites a piece of conventional wisdom; or refers to an experience that most everyone has had. If not too clichéd, the familiar is attention-gaining.

Novelty.   As the old adage has it, when a dog bites a man, it's an accident; when a man bites a dog, it's news. Novel happenings or unusual developments attract wide notice. Two special types of novelty are *size* and *contrast*. In a speech on the high cost of national defense, a speaker caught the attention of his audience with this sentence: "Considering that it costs more than $5000 to equip an average soldier for combat, it is disquieting to learn that in a year his equipment will be 60 percent obsolete."[4] The attention-getting power of numbers is even greater when thrown into contrast. Former vice presidential candidate Geraldine Ferraro, in comparing the earnings of men and women, made this observation:[5]

I wanted to find out how many women in America earn more than $60,000 a year. I picked that number, frankly, because that is what I, as a member of Congress, earn. I learned that there are only 18,000 women in the entire United States, working full-time, who earn more than $60,000. We represent just one-tenth of one percent of all the women who work full-time in America. By contrast, 885,000 men, 2.1 percent of full-time male workers, are in the $60,000 plus bracket.

In using novel materials, be careful not to inject elements that are so different or unusual as to be unfamiliar. Listeners must at least know what you're talking about. They ought to be able to relate what you're saying to things they know and, if possible, have experience with.

Suspense.   Much of the interest in mystery and detective stories arises from uncertainty about their outcome. Films such as *The Hunt for Red October* or *The Russia House* have so many twists that they leave viewers spellbound. When giving a speech, you can create uncertainty by pointing to puzzling relationships or unpredictable forces.

Introduce suspense into the stories you use to illustrate your ideas, building up to a surprising climax. For example, you might begin a speech on retardation with the scenario of a developmentally disabled child; then, after describing the causes of retardation and care for the retarded, reveal that you've been talking about your brother.

Conflict.   Controversy compels attention; consider the ratings of prime-time TV soap operas that emphasize extremely strong interpersonal conflicts in their plots. Conflict, like suspense, suggests uncertainty; conflict, like activity, is dynamic. When President Jimmy Carter wanted to convince the American people of the seriousness of the energy crisis, he talked about it as "the moral equivalent of war"; when President George Bush wanted to get Americans involved in the fight against drug abuse, he talked about "the war on drugs" and promised an "assault on every front."[6] The idea of war, of conflict, gave their speeches a sense of urgency.

Humor.   Listeners usually pay attention to a speech when they're enjoying themselves. Humor provides a change of pace and a chance for listeners to participate more actively in the transaction by sharing their laughter; humor is a great link between speaker and audience, and between listeners. It also tends to relax both speaker and audience. And, too, humor is a great way to revive an audience when it's sagging. When using humor to capture or hold attention, follow two guidelines:

1. *Be relevant.* Beware of wandering from the point, and of telling a joke just for the sake of telling a joke. If the humor doesn't reinforce an important idea, leave it out.

2. *Use good taste.* Consider the occasion. You don't want to tell a knee-slapper during a funeral, and off-color stories most of the time will offend some audience members.

The Vital. Finally, people nearly always pay attention to matters that affect their health, reputation, property, or employment. When you hear "Students who take an internship while in college find jobs after graduation three times as fast as those who don't," you're likely to pay attention. Appealing to the vital, therefore, is a matter of *personalizing* your speech, making it unavoidably relevant, not just to the group, but to specific individuals in your audience.

In 1938, while Angelina Grimke addressed a general meeting of the abolitionist societies, a mob raged outside, preparing to destroy the meeting hall. She referred to the tumult in her speech, saying "What if the mob should now burst in upon us, break up our meeting and commit violence upon our persons—would this be anything compared with what the slaves endure?"[7] At that moment, every individual in her audience most likely felt the horror of slavery.

Each of these nine attention getters and holders should be in your arsenal of rhetorical weapons. They give your speech sparkle and spunk and keep you and your words squarely in the listeners' external and internal perceptual fields. The nine factors of attention are designed to keep audiences curious, alert, and tuned in.

Communicating Confidence

The third matter you need to think about when speaking in front of a real audience is yourself. In Chapter 1 we discussed speech anxiety and some ways to overcome it. Now you need to consider how you can convey an air of dynamism and self-assuredness to your listeners.

Many students ready to give their first speech ask, "How should I deliver my speech? How can I communicate a sense of self-confidence to an audience?" The following guidelines are a start to answering those questions.

1. *Be yourself.* Act as you would if you were having an animated conversation with a friend. Avoid an excessively rigid, oratorical, or aggressive posture. At the same time, don't become so comfortable in front of the group that you sprawl all over the lectern. When you speak, you want your listeners to engage you in a kind of conversation and to focus on your ideas, not the way you're presenting them.

2. *Look at your listeners.* Watch their faces for reactions. Without this feedback, you can't gauge the effectiveness of your speech or make adjustments as you speak. Also, people tend to mistrust anyone who doesn't look directly at them. They also may get the impression you

Kemp on Listening and Judging for Yourself

We live in a democracy that allows us to select or reject those who govern us. An important ingredient in the selection process is the candidate forum or debate. These events are held at almost every level of government: city council, state assemblies, U.S. senators, etc.

Too often the people viewing these contests have relied on the media to make a decision as to who did the better job in the debates. But if we are to cast the vote, then the citizen should be equipped to make judgments about the political candidates.*

And that citizen, of course, is you. Television commentators, expert reporters, celebrity judges, spin doctors, candidates, and others knock around the networks and television stations, telling you how to think about the politics you view on the news and special electoral events. No matter how many experts you hear, however, your vote counts the same as each of theirs. You must listen, you must evaluate. You are responsible for your own actions.

* Robert L. Kemp, *A Voter's Guide to Political Debate* (Clayton, MO: The Alan Co., 1992), p. 21.

don't care about them and aren't interested in their reactions. *In speaking, the eyes have it!*

3. *Communicate with your body as well as your voice.* Realize that as a speaker you're being seen as well as heard. Bodily movements and changes in facial expression can help clarify and reinforce your ideas. Keep your hands at your sides so that when you feel an impulse to gesture, you can do so easily. If there is no lectern, don't be afraid to let your notes show. If you're working from an outline, use a hard backing to hold the papers firm. (This also makes your nervousness less visible!) If you have notecards, hold them up so you can see them clearly. Don't hide them; then referring to them becomes obvious. Avoid the impulse to curl your papers or fold your cards. Let your body move as it responds to your feelings and message. If you hear a tremor in your voice or see

one in your hand, remember that neither is as noticeable to listeners as to you. Overall, if you're being yourself, appropriate bodily responses will flow from the act of communicating.

Learning to Evaluate Speeches

Now that you and your class are ready to give your first speeches, your classroom can function as a laboratory for studying and evaluating speech materials and delivery. The evaluation form on page 68 is designed to help sharpen your critical listening skills as well as your sensitivity to the fundamentals of the speechmaking process. You can use it in classrooms and in real-life settings around your campus or community. It is easily adapted, too, for use while listening to televised public addresses.

Use the form as a checklist to focus your listening. Depending on the assignment, the audience, and the demands of the occasion, some checkpoints on the form will be more significant and applicable than others. For now, use the form as a general guide; later, concentrate upon those parts of it that are relevant to specific assignments.

As you participate regularly in postspeech evaluations, even of early classroom assignments, do not hesitate to provide direct feedback to your classmates. Constructive criticism is both positive and negative—but it is always personally supportive. Telling someone both what worked and what you would suggest be changed provides beginning speakers with much-needed feedback, and it forces you, the listener, to formulate your thoughts and come to grips with your own standards and expectations. In this way, both you and the speaker gain. As another strategy in this class, you also can read the sample speeches in this text, analyzing them systematically to isolate the communication cues that facilitate listener comprehension and acceptance.

Sample Speech

The following speech by Alicia Croshal of Troy State University (Alabama) is well adapted to a student audience and an informative speech assignment. It's simply put together, with an orienting introduction (Paragraph 1), and then a body broken into four parts (history, Paragraphs 2–4; psychological functions, Paragraph 6; anthropological uses, Paragraphs 7–12; and newsworthiness, Paragraphs 13–15), and finally a two-paragraph (16–17) conclusion. Ms. Croshal was very good at documenting her information and providing details that could engage an audience's interests; she used humor well. While she might have better set off each main point and dealt with its implications, overall this speech is a competent effort.[8]

SPEECH EVALUATION FORM

The Speaker

- ☐ poised?
- ☐ positive self-image?
- ☐ apparently sincere?
- ☐ apparently concerned about the topic?
- ☐ apparently concerned about the audience?
- ☐ apparently well prepared?

The Message

- ☐ suitable topic?
- ☐ clear general purpose?
- ☐ sharply focused specific purpose?
- ☐ well-phrased central idea or claim?
- ☐ adequately supported (enough, varied, trustworthy sources)?
- ☐ supporting materials tailored to the audience?
- ☐ introduced adequately?
- ☐ concluded effectively?
- ☐ major subdivisions clear, balanced?
- ☐ use of notes and lectern unobtrusive?

Transmission

- ☐ voice varied for emphasis?
- ☐ voice conversational?
- ☐ delivery speed controlled?
- ☐ body alert and nondistracting?
- ☐ gestures used effectively?
- ☐ face expressive?
- ☐ language clear (unambiguous, concrete)?
- ☐ language forcible (vivid, intense)?

The Audience

- ☐ all listeners addressed?
- ☐ their presence recognized and complimented?
- ☐ their attitudes toward subject and speaker taken into account?

The Speech As a Whole

audience's expectations met?

_____

_____

_____

_____

short-range effects of the speech?

_____

_____

_____

_____

long-range effects?

_____

_____

_____

_____

possible improvements?

_____

_____

_____

_____

Gossip: It's Worth Talking About
Alicia Croshal

Gossip has a bad reputation. It hasn't always had, and it doesn't always deserve it. Allow me to give you the real scoop. It's so juicy that I'm going to develop four main points instead of three! First, I will give you a brief overview of the history of gossip. Then, I'll explain how it fulfills psychological needs, how it functions anthropologically; and finally, how gossip is real news. /1

R. B. Sterling, in his article "Some Psychological Mechanisms Operative in Gossip," published in *Social Forces* in 1956, tells us that the West African Ashanti Indians, upon learning a tribe member gossiped about a leader, cut off the perpetrator's lips. In American culture, Ann Landers voices mores for society in an August, 1985, column which appeared in the Philadelphia *Enquirer*. It was entitled "Gossip is the Faceless Demon that Breaks Hearts and Ruins Careers." She quotes a poem, "My name is gossip, I maim without killing and my victims are helpless. They cannot protect themselves against me because I have no name and no face." /2

The word "gossip" hasn't always had a bad connotation. It comes from an Old English word "godsibb," referring to men's drinking companions and their camaraderie. In 1730, Benjamin Franklin wrote a gossip column for the Philadelphia *Gazette* and was rather proud of it. By the beginning of the Nineteenth Century, gossip started to mean idle talk and tattling. Even the dictionary definition changed. The Oxford English dictionary stated: "Gossip is trifling, or groundless rumor; tittle-tattle." /3

By the turn of the Twentieth Century gossip had a totally bad connotation and denotation. It became a code word for malicious slander and insults. It no longer had anything to do with good relationships. Gossip became synonymous with fear. /4

Despite its bad reputation, I'm going to talk some more about gossip. I will discuss not only the negative aspects of gossip, but also enlighten you about some of its positive aspects. /5

Gossip is psychologically useful. Ralph Rosnow and Gary Fine, in their book *Rumor and Gossip*, published in 1976, reveal their findings that people with fewer friends or less popularity gossip because they have a strong need for contact. They feel that they gain esteem by having the "inside scoop." Lewis H. Lapham, in "Gossiping About Gossip," *Harper's*, 1986, says that people with a strong need for attention, or people who need to be the center of attention to feel important, thrive on celebrity gossip. Gossip reinforces group cohesiveness—it gives us a sense of belonging. /6

Psychologists help us understand how gossip fulfills individual needs. Anthropologists study life in other cultures and in their own cultures. Gossip reporters do the same. Anthropologists are considered objective scientists who gather knowledge for the sake of knowledge. Gossip reporters are considered to gather knowledge to further their own fame and wealth. And they do. Louella Parsons, in Hollywood in 1925, had the power to make or break celebrities. She made people flock to movies on her word alone. In 1938, Hedda Hopper gave Louella some competition. They both had authority. In 1940, Walter Winchell wrote newspaper articles and had radio audiences that exceeded 50 million people. He also had the power to make or break. He made Sinatra. He broke the editor of *New Yorker* magazine, Harold Ross. Now, I'm not just spreading gossip about Winchell. I learned this straight from the pen of Herman Klurfeld who, in 1961, wrote *Winchell—His Life and Times.* /7

Gossip reporters and anthropologists have a firm code of ethics. For example, Louella Parsons in her 1961 book *Tell It to Louella* wouldn't reveal some juicy scandals or print unverified information. She said, "I've kept secrets and watched others profit from my keeping them. I've covered up infidelities and scandals and then seen them publicly proclaimed, frequently by the protagonists themselves." /8

For 40 or 50 years, gossip reporters focused on eccentricities rather than evils. The payoff for readers is that they learn to function in their own culture. They get the straight dope, learn about overcoming addictions and feel closer to celebrities or other people by knowing tidbits of information. /9

Anthropologists seek out other cultures and live and learn with them. Gossip reporters get information without requesting it and usually just check out the facts for accuracy. Both pass on the knowledge and help us (the public) understand our own culture and other cultures better. /10

Gossip is helpful in understanding our world. Authors Levin and Arluke published a book in 1987 entitled *Gossip: The Inside Scoop.* They tell us that the difference between news and gossip is that gossip serves to remind people of their community norms and values. Sociologist James West in his 1945 novel *Plainville USA* notes that ". . . people report, suspect, laugh at and condemn the peccadilloes of others; and walk and behave carefully to avoid being caught in any trifling missteps of their own." /11

On the other hand, in 1986 an article appeared in *Harper's* entitled "Gossiping About Gossip," Author Mark C. Miller of Johns Hopkins University reported his discovery that very few powerful people get smeared by the press. At least not with everyday-type gossip. That is . . . not until Watergate. But reporters still refused to print gossip when preserving the image of a government official if it served the greater good. The Kennedy brothers are a good example. They were treated with kid gloves by the mass media. No one knew about Jack's affair with Marilyn Monroe or his infamous list of lovers. In the case of Ted Kennedy, no one knew about his drinking or philandering or that he cheated on his college exams. Well, not until Chappaquidick. But at Chappaquidick someone got more than hurt or embarrassed. Someone got killed and the police and the press were not willing to cover it up. /12

Gossip is sometimes the only source of accurate news. Survivors of catastrophes such as floods, fires and earthquakes "gossip" about their experiences and actually give us first-hand, eyewitness accounts of the events. /13

News is front-page gossip. Gossip is news in the "living" section. News is verifiable, substantiated by many sources. Gossip comes from several sources, usually unnamed. /14

It is common knowledge that the government leaks gossip in the guise of news to ensure "national security." /15

Our notion of gossip as small talk is bad press. Gossip is more positive than negative. Unethical revelation and distortion is more the exception than the rule. Gossip has a long, healthy history, it serves psychological needs and anthropological functions, and is a means of getting and reporting accurate news. Gossip is anything but trivial. It is big business and a major part of how we function within ourselves and in society. /16

Gossip is worth talking about. /17

Chapter Summary

In preparing a speech, you face seven main tasks: *selecting and narrowing the subject; determining the general and specific purposes; determining the central idea or claim; analyzing the audience and occasion; gathering the speech material; making an outline;* and *practicing aloud.* Going through these seven steps prepares you to deliver speeches to audiences. As you prepare your first speeches, you'll need to *select an appropriate method of presentation* (impromptu, memorized, read, extemporaneous); to *capture and hold attention* by using one or more of the nine *factors of attention* (activity, reality, proximity, familiarity, novelty, suspense, conflict, humor, the vital); and to *communicate confidence.*

References

1. Psychologist Philip G. Zimbardo has likened attention to "a spotlight that illuminates certain portions of our surroundings. When we focus our attention on something and thus become conscious of it, we can begin to process it cognitively—converting sensory information into perceptions and memories or developing ideas through analysis, judgment, reasoning, and imagination. When the spotlight shifts to something else, conscious processing of the earlier material ceases and processing of the new content begins." In *Psychology and Life*, 12th ed. (Glenview, IL: Scott, Foresman and Co., 1988), p. 225.

2. Martin Luther King, Jr., "I've Been to the Mountaintop," in *Contemporary American Voices: Significant Speeches in American History, 1945–Present*, ed. James R. Andrews and David Zarefsky (New York: Longman, 1992), p. 115.

3. King, p. 120.

4. Neal Luker, "Our Defense Policy," a speech presented in a course in advanced public speaking at the University of Iowa.

5. Geraldine Ferraro, "Women in Leadership Can Make a Difference," in *Representative American Speeches, 1982–1983*, ed. Owen Peterson (New York: H. W. Wilson Company, 1983).

6. Jimmy Carter, "The Energy Problem," April 18, 1977, in *Presidential Rhetoric (1961 to the Present)*, ed. Theodore Windt, 4th ed. (Dubuque, IA: Kendall/Hunt, 1987), 238; "Text of President's Speech on National Drug Control Strategy," *The New York Times*, 6 September 1989, A–10.

7. Angelina Grimke [Weld], "Address at Pennsylvania Hall, 1838," reprinted in *Man Cannot Speak for Her*, ed. Karlyn Kohrs Campbell (New York: Praeger, 1989), 2:27.

8. Alicia Croshal, "Gossip: It's Worth Talking About," *Winning Orations; 1991*, ed. Larry G. Schnoor (Mankato, MN: The Interstate Oratorical Association, 1991), pp. 1–3.

Key Terms

attention (p. 61)

audience analysis (p. 56)

central idea (p. 54)

claim (p. 54)

extemporaneous speech (p. 60)

factors of attention (p. 63)

general purpose (p. 54)

impromptu speech (p. 59)

memorized speech (p. 60)

read speech (p. 60)

rhetorical frame of mind (p. 52)

specific purpose (p. 54)

Problems and Probes

1. Listed below are two groups of three statements about a single topic. Read all three statements in each group and write what you believe to be the claim of the group's message. Compare your phrasing of the claims with those of members of your class.
   a. Many prison facilities are inadequate.
   b. Low rates of pay result in frequent job turnovers in prisons.
   c. Prison employees need on-the-job training.

   a. There is a serious maldistribution of medical personnel and service.
   b. The present system of delivering medical service is excellent.
   c. Rural areas have a shortage of doctors.
2. Rewrite each of the following statements, making it into a clear and concise central idea for a speech:
   a. "Today I would like to try to get you to see the way in which the body can communicate a whole lot of information."

b. "The topic for my speech has to do with the high amount of taxes people have to pay."

c. "A college education might be a really important thing for some people, so my talk is on a college education."

Now rewrite the last two statements (b, c) as claims. Be ready to present your versions in a class discussion.

3. Select a general subject area for an in-class speech of three to four minutes. Write a brief essay indicating the process involved in narrowing the subject, determining the general and specific purposes, and determining the central idea or claim. In addition, briefly analyze the audience and the occasion. What major concerns need to be considered in developing a speech for this audience and occasion?

4. Attend a lecture on campus or in your community. As you listen to the speaker, concentrate on the method of presentation. Has the speaker thought through the essential steps outlined in this chapter and responded adequately to each? Write a brief report focusing on what the speaker does well and/or poorly in meeting each of the steps.

Communication Activities

1. Following the principles and guidelines presented in this chapter, prepare a three-to-four minute speech to inform. Narrow the subject carefully so that you can do justice to it in the allotted time. Concentrate on developing ways to gain and hold the audience's attention. Hand in an outline along with a brief analysis of the audience and the occasion when you present the speech. In your analysis, indicate why you think your approach to attention will work in this situation.

2. Listen to the first speeches delivered in class. What strategies are used to gain and hold attention during the speeches? Are these effective strategies? What would be more effective uses of the devices discussed in this chapter? Be prepared to discuss your reactions in class.

PART TWO

PREPARATION

" *L*et no one however demand
from me a rigid code of rules such as most authors of
textbooks have laid down. . . . If the whole of rhetoric could
be thus embodied in one compact code, it would be an easy
task of little compass: but most rules are liable to be altered
by the nature of the case, circumstances of time and place,
and by hard necessity itself. Consequently, the all-important
gift for an orator is a wise adaptability since he is called
upon to meet the most varied emergencies. "

Quintilian
Institutio Oratoria *I.xiii.1–2*

4

CHOOSING SPEECH SUBJECTS AND PURPOSES

C hapter 3 surveyed the steps involved in preparing a speech. This chapter will discuss in more detail the first two of these steps—selecting a suitable subject and determining the central purposes of the speech. Several factors affect your decision about what to speak on and why you want to speak. Whether the occasion is an in-class assignment or a presentation to an outside group, your own knowledge, the audience's needs, and the special demands of the occasion play a part in the rhetorical choices you make. Although you may need to alter your choices as you develop a speech, you will begin with these two concerns.

Selecting the Subject

Several factors may limit your degree of freedom in selecting a subject. On some occasions, your choice will be determined, at least in part, by the group to whom you will speak. Usually, you are invited to speak because you have specific expertise or knowledge to share with the group. As part of the invitation, you'll be asked to address a particular issue, policy, or question that relates to your work, community involvement, or special skills. The occasion also may limit your choice of subject. For instance, you may be speaking at a public hearing on a proposed rezoning of your neighborhood so your remarks need to focus on issues relevant to the local officials and community members present. While you may have other concerns about recent community actions, this is neither the time nor the place to present them, unless you can demonstrate their clear connection to the rezoning issue.

On other occasions your freedom to choose a subject and your approach will be virtually unlimited. An in-class speech assignment often asks that you seek to inform or persuade but allows you freedom in selecting a subject. If an invitation to speak at a breakfast meeting of a local service organization is generally phrased, you may have greater latitude in selecting a subject. If, for example, you were asked to address current environmental issues, you could focus on local concerns about closing town dumps or hazardous waste disposal or choose more general concerns about depletion of the ozone layer or the devastation of the rain forests. Similarly, if you were invited to address your hometown school board on your general concerns as a former student, you could focus on the balance between college-oriented course work and vocational training, on the issue of sports versus academics, or on the issue of adding mathematics and science training in the high school. In each instance, your choice would be affected as much by your personal interests as by the needs of the audience.

When you are confronted with a speech assignment, the following guidelines will help you select a subject that's appropriate to the rhetorical situation.

Select a subject about which you already know something and can find out more. Begin with an inventory of what you already know. This will help you focus your ideas and distinguish between strong and weak choices (less familiar topics are weaker choices). If you need to update statistical data or locate additional examples to flesh out your basic knowledge, consider whether the needed information is readily accessible. Additional research is easier if you know something about the subject because you will have a better idea about potential sources of information. Selecting a topic familiar to you also increases your self-confidence as you rise to speak.

Select a subject that interests you. Resist the temptation to speak on an issue that is more interesting to the audience than it is to you. This is an invitation to disaster. When you select such a topic, gathering information will be unexciting, and your presentation will reflect your lack of enthusiasm. If you have a personal interest in an issue, your commitment to the topic will come across to the audience. You'll find that researching the issue is of greater interest and that the speech "comes together" much more easily.

Select a subject that will interest your audience. This may sound as though it contradicts the advice above, about following your own interests. Talking without regard to the audience, however, may leave you with a subject that interests an audience of one—you. You need to balance your interest with the needs and interests of the audience. Resist the temptation to force a topic on listeners because you think "it's good for them to hear this." It may be, but will they listen? A topic may interest listeners for one or more of the following reasons:

- *It concerns their health, happiness, or security.* For instance, you might talk to senior citizens about changes in Medicare regulations or to college students about recent employment trends.
- *It offers a solution to a recognized problem.* You may suggest ways your group could raise funds in order to participate in a national conference, or you may suggest ways college students might protest cuts in financial aid.
- *It is surrounded by controversy or conflict of opinion.* You might speak on the proposed relocation of a town dump to a site near your campus or on proposed strategies to implement recycling in the community.
- *It provides information on a misunderstood or little understood issue.* You might speak to a local business group about the community service contributions of college students or to the class about the services provided by the campus writing and math centers.

Select a topic appropriate to the occasion. A demonstration speech on body-building might go over very well in your speech classroom, but bringing a dog to class to demonstrate training commands may not work equally well. Consider whether the occasion is the right setting for what you want to do. The same speech on body-building may not be appropriate at the dedication of a new senior citizens' center, but a speech describing the need for exercise at all ages and the new center's exercise room would be fitting.

In sum, whether the topic is assigned or is a free choice, it's advantageous to approach it in ways that play off your strengths. Any speech must reflect interests that you and your audience share and must be appropriate to the speaking occasion. If you have difficulty thinking of such a topic—and selecting the topic area is often the most taxing and time consuming part of the process—study the list of subject categories on the endsheets of this textbook. The topics listed there are very general and don't exhaust the possibilities, but they may trigger ideas, especially more narrowly focused ones.

Narrowing the Subject

A general subject is of little value until it's narrowed down to a manageable size. Narrowing a subject to a more precise speech topic involves three primary considerations:

Narrow your subject so that you can discuss it adequately in the time allotted for the speech. If you are responding to an in-class speech assignment that will last 5 to 7 or 8 to 10 minutes, you cannot begin to do justice to "The Growth of the Winter and Summer Olympics Since Early Times." Instead, you might give an overview of the newest sports recognized for Winter or Summer Olympic competition, or you might discuss the impact of pro players on the Olympic amateurism ideal, using the "Dream Team" as your prime example. Put simply: fit the topic's breadth to the time you have to speak.

Narrow your subject to meet the specific expectations of your audience. Listeners expecting to hear an informative presentation on clear-cutting rain forests may be upset if you request their financial support for an environmental group formed to counter the devastation. The announced purpose of the meeting, the demands of the particular context, and group traditions can influence an audience's expectations of what it is to hear. Violate audience expectations only when you feel it's absolutely essential; be prepared for and willing to accept the consequences if you break with those expectations.

Gauge your subject so that it's neither above nor below the comprehension level of the audience. If, for example, you want to talk about laser technology or the existence of "black holes" to students in your speech class, focus your attention on basic, elemental principles. If the audience were a group of senior physics majors, the nature and complexity of the material you present would necessarily change.

Narrowing a subject amounts to finding one, two, or three points that you can establish, clarify, or support in the time limit allotted to you. For example, suppose you decide to talk informatively about science fiction. Within that general subject area there are numerous subtopics, including:

- The beginnings of science fiction—Shelley's *Frankenstein*
- The differences between science fiction and fantasy
- The nature of "hard science" in science fiction novels
- Major writers of science fiction—such as Heinlein, Clarke, LeGuin, Asimov
- Asimov's Three Laws of Robotics
- The nature of "space opera" as science fiction
- The major periodicals publishing science fiction
- The history of the Hugo Award for science fiction writing
- Recent literary trends in science fiction
- Major science fiction films
- The use of science fiction to present a political message
- Images of women in science fiction
- Art and science fiction

Even with this list of subtopics, you will need to narrow further to select one that meets both your knowledge and interest and that of your listeners, is appropriate to the occasion, and fits the time available. Consider the following possibilities as you sift through the above subtopics to select a speech that would meet a 5 to 7 minute time limit:

1. *Subjects I know something about:*

    - The differences between science fiction and fantasy
    - Major writers of science fiction

- Asimov's Three Laws of Robotics
- "Space Opera"
- Political messages in science fiction
- Major periodicals in science fiction
- Images of women

2. *Subjects interesting to me:*

- All except art and science fiction

3. *Subjects potentially interesting to audience* (speech class):

- Science fiction versus fantasy
- "Hard science" in science fiction
- Major writers of science fiction
- Asimov's Three Laws of Robotics
- "Space Opera"
- Political messages in science fiction
- Images of women
- Science fiction films

4. *Subjects appropriate to the occasion* (informative speech situation in speech class):

- All are appropriate

5. *Topics I can talk about in the time available* (note: this may require further narrowing of the above):

- *Two* or *three* major differences between science fiction and fantasy
- An introduction to the works of one major writer or to a writer's major series (e.g., Asimov's *Foundation* series)
- The image of women in Anne McCaffrey's *Crystal Singer*
- Political message in LeGuin's *Always Coming Home*

6. *Topics I can fit to the audience's comprehension level:*

- Most difficult: "hard science" issues, depending on the audience's background in science
- All other topics: within the general knowledge level of the audience, even if they haven't read science fiction novels

7. *Topics that will meet their expectations in this rhetorical situation:*

- Any of the above topics: meets the general expectations of the audience for an informative speech

The process of narrowing may lead to a subject that is "best" for a particular occasion, or as the previous sample process indicates, it may leave you with several possibilities. If that is the case, you need to decide which subject, given your time limit, will best fit your interests as well as those of the audience. Which topic can you make the most interesting—which can you involve the audience in as you talk?

In sum, selecting and narrowing involves the following considerations:

1. Analyzing your own experiences and background for subjects about which you are knowledgeable and interested,
2. Thinking about your audience's interests and abilities,
3. Considering the demands of the rhetorical situation, and
4. Narrowing the subject area by using the above criteria to develop a subtopic that you can cover adequately in the time allotted and that is in accordance with the expectations of the audience and the requirements of the situation.

Determining the Purposes

Once you know what you want to talk about, the next task is to consider a series of "whys" already implicit in much that's been discussed: Why do *you* wish to discuss this subject? Why might an *audience* want to listen to *you*? Why is this topic appropriate to *this occasion*? These *whys* can be easily answered by considering the following three points in sequence: think about the general purposes that people have in mind when they speak in public, consider your own specific purposes, and then focus on the central idea or claim that expresses the principal message you wish to communicate. In addition, if you phrase a working title for your speech it may help you keep your principal aim in speaking firmly in mind as you engage in the remaining tasks of preparation.

General Purposes

The **general purposes** for speaking reflect the "end states" you wish to create in your audience. Do you wish your listeners to *be informed* as a result of your message, to *be persuaded* that your proposals are worth acceptance, to *be moved to action* on the basis of your appeals, or to *be entertained* by the way you phrase your message? While these "end states" are not mutually exclusive (you may make a moral point through humor, for example), they are sufficiently discrete to discuss.

Usually, you talk to others publicly because you possess some knowledge of potential relevance and benefit to them or because you hope to alter their fundamental beliefs about events in their world, their attitudes toward life, or the actions they have been or ought to be taking. Unless you're a comedian, you'll use entertainment as a general purpose to convey information or persuade the audience to accept or act on your ideas. Therefore, we'll focus on speeches designed to inform, to persuade, or to actuate. We'll consider the types of speeches that accompany each of these general purposes later in

THE GENERAL PURPOSES OF SPEECH

To Inform	Clear Understanding
To Persuade	Acceptance of Ideas
To Actuate	Action
To Entertain	Enjoyment and Comprehension

the text, with a major emphasis on the processes of informing and persuading. In this section we will consider the major *goals* of informative, persuasive, and actuative speeches.

To Inform.   When your object is to help listeners understand an idea, concept, or process, or when you seek to widen their range of knowledge, the general purpose of your **speech** is **to inform.** This is a primary goal of elected officials when they seek to explain their actions to their constituents, of college professors when they teach chemistry, speech, philosophy, art, or any other subject, and of supervisors when they explain how to use new equipment to plant workers.

To evoke understanding, you must change the level or quality of information your listeners possess. By providing examples, statistics, illustrations, and other materials containing data and ideas, you seek to expand or to alter their concrete knowledge about an idea, policy, process, concept, or event. Just "telling them the facts" may not be enough. Not only must an informative speech provide raw data not previously known or not perceived in a particular way, but its message and supporting materials must be structured and integrated in such a way that listeners perceive the whole. For example, an informative speech on how to build a stereo set or how to conduct a successful science experiment must include the necessary information and must present it in an orderly sequence of steps. Understanding in these instances depends not only on learning *what* to do, but also on *when* and *why*.

In some cases, your listeners may be familiar with the information you wish to present, but still lack understanding. They may, for example, know what a set is in mathematics, but not be able to work within the rules of set theory. This means they have not yet integrated their knowledge into a usable whole, so your job as an informative speaker is to help the audience structure their own knowledge into a new, more meaningful body of information that they can use.

Speakers who attempt to alter listeners' behavior must go beyond the mere presentation of facts to appeal to listeners' psychological needs and desires.

When your purpose is to clarify a concept or process, to introduce your listeners to new material, terms, and previously unknown relationships, your objective is to inform. The response you seek from an informative speech is primarily conceptual or cognitive—some adjustment in the audience members' body of knowledge. Several types of speeches are considered informative: speeches of definition or denotation, demonstrations, oral instructions, reports from committees or task forces, lectures, and so forth. In each instance, *information transmission and sharing* are the primary thrusts of the presentation.

To Persuade or to Actuate.   The purpose of a **speech to persuade** or **to actuate** is to influence listeners' minds or actions. Because both have similar goals, we'll consider them together. While it may be argued that all speeches are persuasive to some degree, there are many situations in which speakers have outright persuasion or action as their primary purpose.[1] For example, promoters and publicists try to make you believe in the superiority of certain products, persons, or institutions. Lawyers seek to convince juries of the guilt or innocence of the accused. Social action group leaders exhort tenants to believe in the need for city codes to protect their rights. Politicians debate campaign issues and strive to influence voters as to who should represent their interests in state legislatures, Congress, or the White House.

Beyond speaking to influence your listeners' beliefs and attitudes, you also may go a step further and try to move them to action. Speakers may urge specific action: buy the product, vote for innocence, join in the protest, vote for the preferred candidate. Or, you may want listeners to contribute money, sign a petition, carry an organ donor card, or participate in a demonstration. The distinguishing feature of an actuative speech is that, instead of stopping with an appeal to beliefs or attitudes, you ask your listeners to alter their behavior in a specified way.

To influence or alter your listeners' beliefs and actions, you need to present well-ordered arguments that are supported by facts, figures, examples, and the opinions of experts. You'll also find it necessary to do more than simply state the facts. Persuasion involves psychological as well as logical processes; you need to use motivational appeals relevant to listeners' desires and wants as part of the overall rationale for changes in behavior. To change minds and move people to action you must be sensitive to the rational and motivational aspects of audience psychology, topics that will be discussed at length in later chapters. For the present, keep in mind the principle that facts alone, even if "air-tight" as far as the case for change is concerned, are often insufficient to move people to change their behavior. Consider all of the information connecting cigarette, cigar, and pipe smoking to various forms of cancer, as well as to the issue of passive smoking. If facts alone were sufficient, wouldn't people stop smoking? What motivational appeal will lead a listener to take action in such an instance? Thus, persuasion and actuation involve far more complex tasks than simply telling people what you think.

To Entertain.   To entertain, amuse, or provide other enjoyment for the listener is frequently the general purpose of an after-dinner speech, but talks of other kinds also may have enjoyment as their principal aim. A travel lecture, for example, contains information but also may entertain an audience through exciting, amusing tales of adventure or misadventure. Club meetings, class reunions, and similar gatherings of friends may provide the opportunity for a "roast" of one or more of the people present. In these situations, the effective use of humor is a key ingredient in being judged funny as opposed to tasteless by the audience.

A **speech to entertain** is *not* just a comic monologue. The humor in speeches to entertain is purposive. Even the humor at a roast is intended to convey affection and genuine appreciation for the talents of the person being honored by friends and colleagues. Think of some of the great humorists: Mark Twain used humor to inform Eastern audiences about life in the Midwest; Will Rogers used his radio talks and commentaries on political realities during the Depression to help create a sense of American unity and common effort; more recently, Art Buchwald never tires of showing us our foibles and moral dilemmas; and columnist Dave Barry uses humor to make us aware of social needs. In short, a speech to entertain is humorous yet serious. Forms of public-speaking humor, such as evening entertainments, parodies, and satires, are subtle and often difficult to master; we will discuss them later in this book.

If you are contemplating a humorous speech or planning to use humor in a speech that is primarily meant to inform or persuade, consider whether you're accustomed to using humor in your everyday encounters with others. Attempting to be funny when it isn't natural to your personality or attempting to tell a humorous story that falls flat with your audience leaves you in an uncomfortable position. The pause that should be filled with laughter may be filled with silence—an awkward moment to say the least, especially if the attempt at humor is the beginning of your speech.

As you have learned, to inform, persuade or actuate, and entertain are the general end-states that guide your reason for speaking. Just as subjects are narrowed to subtopics, and often further, your general purpose needs to be narrowed to more specific ones in order to focus audience attention on the content of your presentation.

Specific Purposes

In addition to your general purpose, your speech will have one or more **specific purposes** representing your actual goals. The choices available to you will depend on your interests as well as the needs of the audience and demands of the occasion. You will undoubtedly make some of your purposes explicit as you present your ideas. For example, you tell your listeners precisely what you want them to understand or do as a consequence of listening to your presentation. Some specific purposes may remain private, known only to you; for example, you hope to make a good impression on the audience or receive a high grade on the presentation but you are not likely to make these purposes explicit.

Specific purposes can be short-term or long-term. If you are speaking to members of a local food cooperative on the virtues of baking their own bread, your short-term purpose may be to get people to try your recipe; your long-term objective might be to induce them to change their food-buying and food-consuming habits.

Theoretically, you may have any number of public and private, short-term and long-term specific purposes when you speak. Practically, however, you will want to reduce your list of goals to a *dominant* one—with all others enhancing the likelihood of success of your primary objective. Given this reduction, we can define *the* specific purpose as *the response you wish to elicit from the audience.* Formulated into a clear, concise statement, this specific purpose delineates exactly what you want the audience to understand, enjoy, feel, believe, or do.

Suppose, for example, that as part of a student teaching assignment, you are asked to explain to a high school civics class how the Democratic and Republican party caucuses work. If the objective is to prepare them to

THE PRIVATE AND PUBLIC PURPOSES OF SPEECH

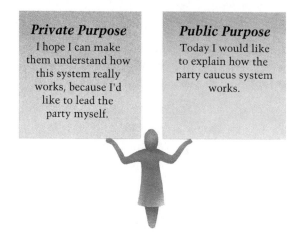

> **Private Purpose**
> I hope I can make them understand how this system really works, because I'd like to lead the party myself.

> **Public Purpose**
> Today I would like to explain how the party caucus system works.

analyze citizen participation in the upcoming state elections, your purposes would include the following: (1) in terms of the subject, you want to demonstrate that caucusing allows for grassroots participation in the electoral process, to review step-by-step the actual caucus procedures that each party uses, to explain what the caucus rules on voting for a candidate allow and do not allow; (2) in terms of the classroom task, you want to define the goals of the assignment and clarify their role in analyzing participation; and (3) in terms of yourself, you want to show the students that you are knowledgeable and competent to speak on the issue, as well as to show an observing teacher or supervisor that you are well-organized and can present ideas clearly. The first specific purpose addresses a long-term goal of creating understanding of a process. The second is short-term—unique to this assignment. The personal goals are private rather than public. All of these specific goals can be summarized, however, in a statement of *the* dominant specific purpose: "to show members of the class how they can participate in the party caucus of their choice."

Central Ideas or Claims

Once you have settled on the dominant response that you wish from the audience, you are ready to compose the central idea or claim that will form the controlling thought of your speech. The **central idea** is a statement that captures the essence of the information or concept you are attempting to communicate to an audience; a **claim** is a statement that phrases the belief, attitude, or action you wish the audience to adopt. *Central ideas are charac-*

teristic of informative speeches, while claims form the core of persuasive and actuative speeches. Speeches to entertain also have a controlling thought—either as a central idea aiming to convey information or as a claim aiming to make a moral point or exhort to action through the use of humor or other devices.

Both central ideas and claims share the same function: they identify the primary thrust of your message. Thus, precise phrasing of your central idea or claim is crucial because it focuses the audience's attention on *your* reasons for speaking, rather than on *their* reasons for listening. Assume, for example, that you're giving an informative speech on the use of science fiction to present political messages. Each of the following central ideas suggests a different emphasis for the speech:

1. Science fiction novels are as much about the present as they are the future.
2. Ursula LeGuin's novel *Always Coming Home* carries an implicit political message about how we should live our lives in the present.
3. The political worlds created in science fiction must remain believable. Hence the genre cannot escape making choices that reflect the writer's preferences; we learn their politics by reading the fictional works.

A speech on central idea 1 would be developed differently than one on either idea 2 or 3 and would utilize different kinds of material for support or illustration. The first version stresses the idea that science fiction, although ostensibly set in the future, actually tells us something about our everyday lives. The second version focuses on the same theme but develops it through a close analysis of one work by a major writer. The third version states that authors' political views are reflected in their writing and would cite examples from novels that enable one to discern those views.

Phrasing a claim is an even more crucial preparatory step than casting the central idea, because the wording colors the emotional tone of the message and its line of development; it also suggests the relationship between you and your audience. Note the effect of the following examples:

Varying the audience's perception of your intensity:

1. "Clear-cutting in the world's rain forests is *unwise.*"
2. "Clear-cutting in the world's rain forests is *a despicable act.*"
3. "Clear-cutting in the world's rain forests is *a moral outrage.*"

As you move from version one to three, feelings are phrased with greater intensity; each successive version expresses your attitude in harsher, more graphic language.

Varying the reasons for taking some course of action:

1. "Make use of the Writing Lab because it will help you in your English courses."

2. "Make use of the Writing Lab because you will get higher grades in all courses in which writing is expected."
3. "Make use of the Writing Lab because better writing will lead to better jobs on graduation."

These three examples vary the rationale for the action you wish listeners to take. Presumably, one can act for a variety of rationales; phrase your claim in a way that captures what you think will be the most compelling reasons for *this particular audience.* In this instance, each reason may be further developed as part of an overall speech on using the Writing Lab. Each reason may tap interests or needs of different listeners; overall, the hope is that you touch each listener with a reason persuasive enough to motivate him or her to act on your advice.

Varying the evaluative criteria for judging something:

1. "The city's landfill is an *eyesore.*" (aesthetic judgment)
2. "The city's landfill is a *health hazard.*"(personal-safety judgment)
3. "While the city's landfill is cheaper than other solid-waste removal options, we should still explore other means of handling garbage." (political value judgment)

Each of these claims condemns a community facility. The first version judges the landfill's lack of beauty, the second considers its safety and health costs, while the third acknowledges it is a cheaper alternative but implies the community should value safety above economic cost. Were you to advocate the first version, you would need to demonstrate that (a) aesthetic values are important criteria for judging community resources such as landfills and (b) that the physical appearance of the landfill harms the image the city wishes to maintain. For the second version, you would need to argue that significant health hazards are in fact present, and that they should be a matter of grave community concern. In defending the third version, you would need to document the relative expense of various solutions, while noting that cost alone should not be the sole criterion—health and safety issues should be paramount. In each case, selecting particular criteria will control the main features of the speech's ultimate development.

When you've decided the general and specific purposes of your speech and considered ways to phrase central ideas and claims, you have the elements for initiating your speech outline. These points will focus your research efforts, because they will indicate the type and quantity of information needed to accomplish your goals. As examples of the process, consider the following illustrations:

Informative Speech

Subject: Science Fiction

General Purpose: To Inform

Specific Purposes: (* indicates dominant purpose, recast as central idea)

To show how science fiction conveys a political message

CENTRAL IDEAS AND CLAIMS

The relationship between central ideas and claims can be summarized as follows:

General Purpose	Inform	Persuade/Actuate	Entertain
Specific Purpose	Central Idea	Claim	Central Idea or Claim

---

* To explain LeGuin's use of political themes
  To convey confidence in handling the subject
Central Idea: LeGuin's novel *Always Coming Home* contains a political message.
Actuative Speech
Subject: Accident insurance for youth sports groups
General Purpose: To Actuate
Specific Purposes: (* indicates dominant purpose, recast as claim)
* To have city officials purchase insurance for their recreational programs
  To show how such protection can be provided at a reasonable cost
  To be perceived favorably by the audience.
  To overcome opposition to spending money on this type of protection
Claim: The City Council should authorize the purchase of the accident insurance plan I am offering for its youth sport programs
Supporting Reasons
a. because such protection is essential in the event of a lawsuit
b. because the policy I am offering is less costly than others available
c. because the city cannot rely solely on the accident insurance purchased by the families of youth participants[2]
  As the above illustrations indicate, central ideas and claims make different demands on the audience. Where central ideas focus on explanation and

Precise phrasing of your central idea or claim is important, because your wording captures the essence of your subject matter and purpose and focuses audience attention on your reasons for speaking.

clarification to disseminate information, claims focus on giving audiences reasons to believe or act in a certain way. The speech to entertain encompasses both possibilities, since its goal may include either informing or persuading an audience. Focusing attention on a set of specific purposes enables you to decide which one will govern the presentation's content. Determining general and specific purposes clarifies your primary goal and helps ensure that your audience will understand *why* you are speaking, even if they disagree with your ideas.

Wording the Working Title

To complete your initial thinking about purposes, you often will want to write down a **working title**. Although it may seem odd or even unnecessary to consider a title during the preliminary stages of speech preparation, there are several concrete advantages of doing so. First, a working title highlights the key concept or idea that the speech content will reflect. The working title assists in determining what will be relevant or irrelevant, central or peripheral, or significant and insignificant in the development of the speech. Second, speakers often are required to announce titles ahead of time, in order to allow for publicizing the event. Just as a title helps the speaker focus on content, it assists those who might attend in deciding whether the speaker's subject is of interest. Local business meetings also may ask for a title to use for advance publicity in the local paper or in the organization's newsletter or meeting announcement. The following guidelines will assist you in selecting and phrasing a working title.

A title should be relevant to you, the audience, and the occasion. If you were to give a speech on business and political ethics, you might consider a title such as "The Eleventh Commandment," as did the speaker who claimed that the commandment "Thou shalt not steal" has been supplanted in some business and political circles by another: "Thou shalt not get caught." The title created some curiosity about the speech, as audience members wondered what would be added to the Ten Commandments they already knew. Just as important, the title reflected the significance of the subject by connecting it to a set of commandments whose importance already was accepted.

A title should be provocative and productive. Linda G. Stuntz, Acting Deputy Secretary of Energy for the Bush Administration, delivered a speech at MIT's Center for Energy and Environmental Policy Research (April 30, 1992). The title of her speech, "The Environmentally Ugly American," reflected the image of the inconsiderate American and was meant to focus attention on her primary claim "that while the United States, of course, has challenges . . . we are hardly the evil empire of environmental deregulation that some would have you believe."[3] The title was worded in such a way that audience members would not know for certain which side of the issue she would defend—that we were in fact ugly Americans or that we were not. By capturing the essence of the dispute in this way, she engaged the attention of her audience and helped listeners retain the central point of her message.

As you contemplate the provocative nature of possible titles, also *seek to make the title productive.* If an audience is initially hostile to you or your message, a provocative title may distance them further. Had Stuntz titled her address "As Protectors of the Environment, We Are Not Ugly Americans," she would have alerted her audience more clearly to the central point of her message, but she would also have turned off those who might disagree. Such a provocative title would have lessened her chances for a fair hearing. Do not create irritation or raise questions of your sensitivity to audiences through your title.

The title should be brief. Imagine the effect of announcing your title as "The Effects upon High-Track, Mean-Track, and Low-Track High School Juniors of Pretesting for Senior Year Competency Testings." Besides not being terribly clear, the title is far too long and doesn't do much to engender curiosity or arouse interest in your audience. A better choice might be "Tracking Juniors: A Means to Successful Testing as Seniors?" or "A Pretest in Time Saves Nine—or More." These two may lack some precision, but they are decidedly more engaging and provocative than the first choice.

When committing to a title for advance publicity, select a general phrase. If you have to commit to a title well in advance, you want to preserve flexibility in how you develop the speech itself. The title "Science Fiction as Political Statement" is sufficiently precise to give the audience an idea of your general topic area while allowing you to alter the development of the subject as you plan the speech. When college professors are asked to present a paper months in advance of actually writing it, they'll develop a working title that's broad enough to cover a variety of specific issues and concerns. By the time they arrive at the convention, they're ready to indicate the more precise area to be covered.

Remember that your working title is just that—something to start with. As you gather your supporting materials, you may become excited about some aspect of your subject matter that you hadn't planned on covering. Simply change your title to reflect your new direction or emphasis. If you've already committed to a title, you may find that your new direction doesn't coincide with the expectations you've set up. When you present the speech, explain your reasons for altering the announced focus of the presentation; if you convey your reasons with enthusiasm and sincerity, the audience will, in all likelihood, accept your new direction and purpose.

Selecting Subjects and Purposes: Strategic Choices

The preceding discussion has focused on the general and specific purposes in terms of the *desired response* you wish to obtain from your audience. What remains is to examine some of the reasons you may elect to (or have been asked to) inform, persuade, or entertain your audience. Some of the factors that will determine your actual decisions include an assessment of private and ultimate aims, the listeners' authority to act, their pre-existing attitudes, the nature of the speech occasion, and the time available to speak.

Private and Ultimate Aims

You must take into account your own interests and abilities as you select subjects and purposes. Few of us can talk convincingly or even sincerely about something in which we have little or no interest; few of us dare move into specialized areas in which audience members have more expertise than we do. Furthermore, at times we must think through carefully how much we are willing to risk personally in front of others. For example, suppose you work for a firm that you're convinced is patently sexist in its promotion policies. The past record clearly suggests that it seldom promotes women to upper-level managerial positions. You find that you are given a chance to talk about promotions at an open meeting of the firm. How far do you go? What do you say?

Your **private aim** may be one of getting your frustrations heard, regardless of the consequences. Your **ultimate aim** is to get some women, including yourself, into higher managerial positions. A harangue on the evils of sexism, replete with threats to report the firm to an equal opportunity agency, might satisfy your private aim, but would harden others' resistance to change.[4] After thinking through the situation, you might decide on a less risky course, such as an informative speech with the specific purpose (cast as a central idea) of presenting a review of the numbers of men and women promoted within the firm to upper levels of management over the last ten years. You also could point out the number of females ready for promotion within the company and discuss the "head-hunting" agencies that keep records of women interested in and qualified for managerial positions.

Casting your speech as an *informative* speech, rather than as an *actuative* one, would allow you to unite your private and ultimate aims in a message that satisfies your private convictions and enhances your future upward mobility within the firm. If this option seems to be one of "wimping out," you'll need to confront your own conscience, make a deliberate choice, and say what you feel has to be said by casting your ideas as an assertive claim, regardless of the consequences.

Listeners' Authority or Capacity to Act

For a speaker to demand of students that they should "abolish all required courses" is futile; any decision concerning course requirements is in the hands of the faculty. In this case, the listener's **authority to act** is non-existent. They would be better advised to act within their power to affect change, such as conducting a collegewide survey of student attitudes about required courses to present to the faculty or print in the campus newspaper. Or, students from different majors could talk at a general meeting of the faculty about the impact of the requirements on their own programs of study. As a speaker, limit your specific purposes and claims to behaviors that are clearly within the domain of the audience's authority or power.

Listeners' Pre-existing Attitudes

A group of striking workers who believe they are badly underpaid and unfairly treated by their employer probably would be hostile to suggestions that they return to work under existing conditions. They might, however, approve plans to submit the issues to arbitration by a disinterested person whose fairness and judgment they respect. If the listeners' **pre-existing attitude** is hostile to your message, you might, in a single speech, be able to convince them that there's merit in your side of the issue. You'll be hoping for too much if you expect the audience to disavow their current beliefs and embrace yours, or to take positive action on the basis of your request. In this instance, you must adjust your specific purpose to what you can reasonably obtain from the audience, given its past history, experiences, and present attitudes. Don't ask for a response you cannot reasonably expect from people holding their particular feelings or beliefs.

The Nature of the Speech Occasion

Normally, you should strive to meet the normal or traditionally accepted expectations at any event. Violating audience expectations can have negative consequences; hence, you should willingly go "against the grain" only

Public speaking elicits certain mental and behavioral responses from listeners. Their attitudes, the nature of the speech occasion, and the time limits imposed on the situation all affect the speaker's task of preparing a message.

when your principles dictate a response that's divergent from the listeners'. When that isn't the case, consider the appropriateness of your remarks in terms of what's expected by the **nature of the speech occasion**. To ask for contributions to a political campaign fund might be appropriate at a pre-election rally, but to pursue this specific purpose at a memorial service for a public official would be decidedly out of place. An athletic awards ceremony is hardly the occasion for a presentation denigrating the administration's support for athletic programs. Be sure your specific purpose is adapted to the mood and spirit of the occasion on which you are to speak.

Time Limits

Time limits may be imposed by those who invited you to speak or may be dictated by the nature of the occasion. The amount of time available will have a major impact on what you can accomplish. For example, you may be able to induce a hostile audience to postpone a decision without talking very long; however, if your goal is to change their feelings and convictions so they endorse your proposal, you'll need more than a few minutes. Similarly, if your subject is complex, you may be able to achieve listener comprehension in a 15-minute speech. You may, however, need to give one or more additional speeches to convince the audience that action on the basis of the information you offer is in its best interests. Don't attempt to secure a response that an audience cannot give in the time available.

Chapter Summary

When you have *selected* a subject that meets your needs and those of the audience and occasion and *narrowed* it to fit the occasion and time available, your speech preparation will be off to a sound start. You will have decided on an *informative, persuasive,* or *actuative* purpose, or you will have elected to *entertain* the audience through humor. With this in mind, you also will have determined how many *specific purposes* that you can handle in this situation. From among this number, you will have determined which specific purpose will be the dominant one and recast it as your *central idea* or *claim* being advanced in the speech. Selecting a *working title* highlights the general thrust of your speech. Finally, you will have considered five strategic issues—*private* and *ultimate aims, listener authority or capacity to act, listeners' pre-existing attitudes,* the *nature of the speech occasion,* and *time limits.* You will have begun to use these strategies in choosing appropriate material to accomplish your objectives in speaking.

References

1. It can be argued that all speeches are persuasive. *Any* change in a person's stock of knowledge, beliefs, attitudes, or ways of acting represents the kind of adjustment in one's mental and emotional state that can be attributed to persuasion, as long as symbols were employed to induce the change. From a psychological perspective, it may be argued that it's impossible to separate "informative" and "persuasive" messages. We're taking a *rhetorical* perspective, in which the symbols used to evoke a certain kind of response, as well as the strategies employed in that process, provide an *orientation* that's overtly one of informing, persuading, actuating, or entertaining an audience, Hence, you'll find separate discussions of these later in the textbook. See Gary C. Woodward and Robert E. Denton, Jr., *Persuasion & Influence in American Life* (Prospect Heights, IL: Waveland, 1988), ch. one.

2. You may be better able to specify the relevant reasons once you've gone on to the next step, analyzing the audience.

3. Linda G. Stuntz, "The Environmentally Ugly American," *Vital Speeches,* 58 (June 15, 1992): 527.

4. From a research perspective, there are several theories or psychological models that can be used to explain this "hardening" process. Within *consistency theory,* any message that is inconsistent or "discrepant" with a person's other beliefs will cause that person to react negatively to it. *Dissonance theory* explains the same process by arguing that when two perceptions clash explicitly, a person experiences dissonance or disharmony; because we prefer consonance or harmony between or among our beliefs, we take actions to remove the forces of disharmony. These actions can take the form of discrediting the source of the message or discrediting the "facts" that are presented. Another theory stresses an individual's *latitudes of acceptance* and *rejection.* This approach argues that each of us can tolerate discrepant information or attitudes counter to our own position, but that there are limits to how far we will go. Because they fall within our range of acceptance, appeals to beliefs or attitudes that call for relatively small adjustments in our current position on an issue are likely to be successful. Appeals that fall outside, or belong to our latitude of rejection, are likely to make us stronger than ever in our original position. On topics where we have very little information or little

direct involvement, our latitude of acceptance is very wide, but on topics where we think we know a lot or have a very strong opinion, our latitude is likely to be very narrow. Part of a speaker's job in analyzing an audience is in determining the range of acceptance and rejection as it relates to the particular speech being prepared. For reviews of these and other theories, see R. P. Abelson, et al. (eds.) *Theories of Cognitive Consistency* (Chicago: McNally, 1968). For practical applications see Woodward and Denton; and Stephen W. Littlejohn and David M. Jabusch, *Persuasive Transactions* (Glenview, IL: Scott-Foresman, 1987).

Key Terms

authority to act (p.93)

central idea (p.86)

claim (p.86)

general purposes (p.81)

nature of the speech occasion (p.94)

pre-existing attitude (p.93)

private aim (p.92)

specific purposes (p.85)

speech to actuate (p.82)

speech to entertain (p.84)

speech to inform (p.82)

speech to persuade (p.83)

time limits (p.94)

ultimate aim (p.92)

working title (p.90)

Problems and Probes

1. The speaker must take the *occasion* into account every time he or she plans to give a speech. Consider your classroom as the occasion—the room, classmates, and instructor. How does each of these affect your choice of a subject? Does the room's location, size, or configuration permit certain types of demonstration speeches but not others? What are the students interested in hearing about, either as informative or persuasive speeches? Has your instructor indicated that certain topics aren't suitable for presentation in class? Develop short answers to each of these questions, and be prepared to discuss them in small groups during a class session. The class might use this discussion as the basis for preparing an "Issues Survey" that provides more precise data on interests and attitudes on a wide variety of topics.

2. Attend a speech or lecture on campus with a small group of classmates. As you listen to the presentation, each student should take notes on the following: *general purpose, specific purpose,* and statement of *central idea* or *claim.* When you compare your notes after the presentation, how much agreement is there about these factors? What accounts for any discrepancies in agreement? In addition, how well does the speaker meet your needs as an audience member? How is this done, or not done? Discuss your reactions with the group during a class session.

3. Attend an event on campus or in the community where you expect to hear a humorous presentation. If the expectation is realized, how does the speaker

accomplish this objective? Does the speaker use humor successfully or unsuccessfully? Take notes on your perceptions of the event, and be prepared to discuss why this event did or did not work as an entertaining occasion.

4. As a class or small group, study a recent controversial presentation on campus or in the community, or one that stirred national feelings (e.g., Dan Quayle's criticism of Murphy Brown's decision to have a child without benefit of marriage, delivered prior to the 1992 presidential campaign). Consider the situation the speaker faced, the possible general and specific purposes that might have been operative, and the announced and hidden aims that might have influenced the choice of material. Discuss your interpretation of the event. How did the purposes and aims identified affect the choice of material in the presentation? Was the choice appropriate for the audience and occasion? Was it an ethical decision on the part of the speaker?

Communication Activities

1. Deliver a brief impromptu speech on a topic that interests you. Your instructor will allow a question and comment period so that listeners can indicate whether the topic interests them or the degree to which you were able to arouse interest.

2. List five topics that would be inappropriate for speech presentations in class. During class, present a brief speech in which you indicate why each would be inappropriate. Note what might happen if such presentations were made (for example, cutting the head off a live chicken as part of a demonstration speech [it has happened!]).

3. Working in small groups, prepare an "Issues Survey": each group member will come to class prepared with five suitably narrowed subjects for an informative speech and five for a persuasive speech (there may be some overlap). Discuss your list within your group, sorting out overlapping ideas in order to develop one list. Have one person collate the list in readable form and bring it to the next class, with copies for everyone in the class. Using a simple three-point scale (1 – very interesting; 2 – interesting; 3 – very uninteresting), have class members respond to the subject lists of the various groups. The instructor and one or two students will collate responses and prepare a master copy for everyone in class. Select one informative or persuasive topic that scores among the lowest (most uninteresting) on this final list, and develop a speech that has arousing audience interest as a specific purpose.

4. Rewrite each of the following statements, making each into a clear and concise *central idea* for a speech:

   a. "Today I would like to try and get you to see the way in which the body can communicate a whole lot of information."

   b. "The topic for my speech has to do with the high amount of taxes people have to pay."

   c. "A college education might be a really important thing for some people, so my talk is on a college education."

Now rewrite statements b and c as *claims;* be ready to present your versions during a class discussion.

5

ANALYZING THE AUDIENCE AND OCCASION

Public speaking is **audience** and **occasion centered.** As earlier chapters have stressed, it's crucial that your remarks meet the needs and interests of the people you address and are deemed appropriate to the speaking occasion. Both of these objectives depend on your listeners' perceptions of their needs and their expectations regarding the occasion. Thus, selecting and narrowing a subject and framing a central idea or a claim all require that you consider your audience, as do the remaining steps in speech preparation. It's time to look more closely at the audience and the occasion. In the words of Donald C. Bryant, since ancient Greece the essence of the rhetorical process has been that of "adjusting ideas to people and people to ideas."[1]

Analyzing listeners individually would be a time-consuming task, so the most efficient way to adopt messages to audiences is to analyze them as members of a group. Look for common situational and psychological factors to help you target your messages to the people you're addressing. Identifying the roles and physical characteristics of your listeners (demographic analysis) will help you account for their psychological attributes (psychological profiling). One theme will be stressed throughout this chapter: *The goal of audience analysis is to discover which facets of listeners' demographic and psychological characteristics are relevant to your speech purposes and ideas.*

The examination of the situation or occasion is closely related to that of the audience's characteristics. As noted in Chapter 3, members of society tend to have rather strong expectations of what will (and will not) be said on certain occasions. For example, a preacher at the funeral of a man who had serious shortcomings as a generous and giving person won't dwell on these qualities. The preacher probably will say only that this man, like us all, was not a perfect human and go on to praise the man's virtues. To violate the tradition of funerals as times to celebrate a person's life by giving a speech that condemns the person's vices probably would cause the family and friends of the deceased to rise up in anger. You must be sensitive to the demands that the occasion places on your choice of themes and language.

Relating the demands of the audience to the demands of the occasion is a difficult task because both are so varied. If you're to secure your goals, however, you must learn to analyze both, and to adjust your speech accordingly. As you work through this procedure, it helps to consider the second theme running through this chapter: *An "occasion" includes a time and place set aside for particular events and activities; speakers must learn what people expect on those occasions and meet those expectations as completely as possible.* After discussing the audience and occasion, this chapter concludes with advice on how to use the results of your analyses to construct arguments and ideas for your speeches.

Analyzing the Audience Demographically

A **demographic analysis** is a study of the social and physical traits people hold in common. Many of these analyses are available to the public or are accessible with some research. Drawing inferences about psychological characteristics is based in large part on the information gleaned from this kind of analysis. When you begin to look for demographic characteristics, you will want to ask the following questions:

- *Age:* Will the expected listeners be primarily young, middle-aged, elderly, or will the group more likely be of mixed ages? Is there a special relationship between age groups, such as parent/child or teacher/student?
- *Gender:* Will the listeners be predominately female or male, or will the group be split?
- *Education and Experience:* How much will be listeners already know about the subject? Does their educational or experiential background allow them to grasp easily the essential ideas I want to convey?
- *Group Membership:* Do these people belong to groups that represent specific experiences, attitudes, or identifiable values?
- *Cultural and Ethnic Background:* Do audience members predominately belong to specific cultural or ethnic groups? Are my listeners likely to share a common heritage?

The importance of demographic analysis for you as a speaker doesn't lie in simply finding answers to such questions. Rather, *the key is to decide if any of these demographic factors will affect your listeners' ability or will-ingness to understand and accept what you want to say.* That is, does a particular group affiliation, age, or gender factor have any *relevance* in the situation you face? Does it influence the rhetorical choices you make in selecting a subject and developing its central idea or claim?

For example, if you're addressing a group of citizens gathered to hear proposals for new low-income housing, you should consider all of the above questions. For example, your adaptation to this group of citizens might well assume that most of them will be young to middle-aged, many will be family members, and some will bring children to the meeting. Others in the audience will be elderly living on fixed incomes who are unable to afford more expensive housing. You also may assume, if you know something about the neighborhood, that they belong to one or more specific ethnic groups and that you'll have to relate to them in terms of their cultural backgrounds. You might also assume that some will be on Aid to Families with Dependent Children, others will be employed in low-paying jobs, others unemployed, and others will be in job training programs. With these demographic characteristics in mind, you will probably adapt to your lis-teners by using these strategies: (1) avoid technical jargon; (2) consider-ing that children may be present, limit your remarks to the essential items; (3) give examples demonstrating that you understand that the audience members are looking for low-income housing by necessity, not choice; and (4) convey an attitude that shows you're genuinely interested in moving the project forward in order to improve their living conditions.

Demographic analysis can help you select and phrase your key ideas. It sensitizes you to crucial factors that may influence your choice of themes, examples, and other supporting material. If your analysis is cursory or incomplete, you decrease your chances of being understood and agreed with. Even when you're aware of the demographic characteristics, you may still create problems with your choice of language. Speaking to a group of African Americans, for example, and referring to them as "you people" and "your people" will demonstrate your lack of sensitivity or judgment (as Ross Perot discovered to his dismay when he addressed such an audience during the opening weeks of his 1992 presidential campaign). Appropriate use of demo-graphic information can help you avoid such problems and convey a sensi-tive and caring attitude toward your listeners.

Analyzing the Audience Psychologically

Dividing audience members into **psychological profiles** on the basis of their beliefs, attitudes, and values also helps you adapt to their needs and inter-ests. This is especially important if you intend to influence your listeners' thinking on issues. You need to know what ideas they already accept before you can help to alter their thoughts and actions. Sometimes careful demo-graphic analysis will create such groupings naturally and provide clues

THE VARIETIES OF BELIEF

	Beliefs of Fact	*Beliefs of Opinion*
Fixed Beliefs	Americans who exercise live longer, healthier lives.	Exercise is boring.
Variable Beliefs	I might live longer and be healthier if I exercised.	It might be fun to jog with Ed and Nancy.

about what your audience members will be thinking. For example, members of a salmon fishing club generally will be in favor of rules and regulations that facilitate their goal of enjoying their sport. They will be against damming rivers and streams if they feel such action will hinder fish migration. Members of a quilting society are proud of their heritage as quilters and can be expected to oppose attempts to sell famous quilts collected by national museums (such as in the current controversy over actions by the Smithsonian to sell historic quilts to private collectors). At other times, when data are limited, you'll have to take a chance and draw inferences about audience positions on issues. This section will examine some of the ways you can use beliefs, attitudes, and values to inform and persuade audiences.

Beliefs

Beliefs are ideas about what is true or false in the "real world." They arise from firsthand experience, evidence read or heard, authorities who have told us what is true, or even blind faith. For example, you might believe that "Apples come in different sizes and colors" (firsthand experience), that "The Lupini Business College has a 90 percent success rate in getting their graduates jobs" (college promotional literature), that "Learning is life-long" (a belief your parents and instructors have told you), or that "Getting an education increases your chances of landing a good job" (something you hope is true).

Beliefs, like colors, come in many different shades; they vary in the degree of *certitude* with which we hold them and in the degree of *intensity* with which we are committed to them. We hold some beliefs to be externally verifiable—*facts*—while others are personal *opinions*. Some beliefs are *variable*, or open to change, while others are *fixed*. Both facts and opinions can be either fixed or variable. The following examination of these qualities will assist you in speaking before audiences.

Facts and Opinions.   **Facts** are strong beliefs that you think are open to independent investigation and verification. When you say, "It's a fact that apples are nutritious," "Research has proven that infant blue whales gain an average of 10 pounds per day," or "It's a fact that university tuition has risen more than the cost of living," you're claiming relative certainty about these beliefs. You believe you have hard evidence to support these statements and that others can verify their accuracy. In sum, a fact is a belief you hold with relative firmness and think is supported with strong evidence.

Opinions are another matter. When you identify a belief as an opinion, such as "It's my opinion that our current administration is neglecting jobs" or "In my opinion, he's right," you're signaling that your statements are personal; they express your own judgment. Indirectly, you also are suggesting that your views may not be as well supported by hard evidence as are other beliefs you refer to as "facts" and that your commitment may be less strong as a result.[2]

Since both facts and opinions are matters of belief, however, their "truth" can be relative. Some statements are easily verifiable as true: "This is SPC 101"; "My name is (fill in . . .)"; "Refusal to use protective skin creams when sunbathing will increase the chance of developing skin cancer." Others are not as easily verifiable, even though supported by hard evidence: "SST overflights will significantly reduce the ozone layer"; "Depletion of the rain forests will have a devastating effect on the earth's environment." In yet other instances, the line between fact and opinion is blurred. In colonial America, for instance, many people knew "for a fact" that regular bathing caused illness, just as their ancestors knew that the earth was flat and located at the center of the universe. If an opinion is widely held, it may be construed as a fact by those who accept it, if for no other reason than it's common knowledge. In preparing to speak, remember that opinions and facts are psychological concepts that can be held both individually and collectively.

Before you speak, it's important to assess how committed your audience may be to particular beliefs, for three basic reasons:

1. *You can reinforce or alter people's beliefs by using the same strategies people use when acquiring beliefs in the first place.* For example, knowing that audiences often establish beliefs based on statements by authorities will encourage you to use authoritative testimony to influence your listeners' views.

2. *Such assessments should help you outline some of the appeals you can make within your speech.* If audience analysis shows that your audience considers sensitivity to their culture important, you can develop appeals that demonstrate an awareness of and appreciation for their cultural habits. If your listeners are business people, you'll go further using hard, empirical data rather than loose generalizations to support your proposals.

3. *These assessments allow you to set realistic expectations as you plan your talk.* Not all audience beliefs are equally amenable to change through speeches. You shouldn't try to accomplish impossible goals in a single speech. You probably will encounter psychological resistance if you try to destroy too many facts and fixed beliefs.

Making appropriate choices in adapting beliefs to audiences will be discussed in more detail later in the chapter.

Attitudes

Attitudes, the second facet of psychological profiling in selecting arguments and appeals, may be defined as tendencies to respond positively or negatively to people, objects, or ideas. Attitudes express individual preferences or feelings, such as "Democracy is the best form of government," "Discrimination is wrong," "The Vietnam War Memorial is a fitting tribute," and "My public speaking class is awesome."

In expressing our preferences, predispositions, reactions, and basic judgments, attitudes predispose us toward certain behaviors. We tend to do the things we like and to avoid doing those we dislike. As a speaker, you should consider the dominant attitudes of your audience. Expecially relevant are the audience's attitudes toward you, your subject and purpose, and the occasion. One dramatic example of the strength of attitudes can be seen in Ross Perot's foray into presidential campaigning. At one point, well before he declared his official "non-candidacy" (only to later reenter the race in time to participate in the presidential debates), Perot actually led both President Bush and Bill Clinton, the Democratic nominee. Public disgruntlement with the economy was such that Perot's potential candidacy had great appeal. Coca-Cola's experience in introducing a "new Coke" also demonstrates the strength of attitudes; the public's loyalty to the original formula was such that Coke was forced to reintroduce its long-standing Coke as Coca-Cola Classic™.

The Audience's Attitudes Toward the Speaker.   Your audience's initial attitude toward you as a speaker will be based on what they know about you before you speak. As you speak, they will assess how you present yourself and reevaluate their impression. Two factors are especially important regarding your reputation: (1) the amount of respect listeners hold for you and your subject, and (2) the listeners' feelings of friendliness toward you.

You can enhance your listeners' respect for you and your subject in several ways. Doing adequate research and presenting clear evidence during your speech provide evidence of your sincerity and expertise. Acknowledging that the audience's own beliefs and judgments are worthy of respect demonstrates your sense of fairness. Using language that's appropriate to the occasion and sensitive to the audience's background and experience shows that you're interested in talking to them, not lecturing them. You can strengthen your listeners' friendliness toward you by (1) speaking energetically to support how important the topic is to you and should be to them, (2) appearing alert but comfortable in your role as a speaker, (3) showing a sense of humor appropriate to the situation, and (4) expressing your interest in your audience as individuals.

The Audience's Attitudes Toward the Subject.   Whether your listeners are highly interested, downright apathetic, or neutral toward the subject will influence how they respond. Some researchers place *prior audience attitudes* among the most critical audience variables that determine speaking success.[3] If listeners feel unfavorable toward the message, they may distort its substance, refuse to listen, or even heckle you, leave the room, or seek to discredit you following the speech. Listeners who feel threatened by the message will use these and other defense mechanisms to maintain their own beliefs and to avoid an accurate perception of your intent as a speaker.

As you prepare your speech, there are several ways to minimize potentially negative consequences. If your audience analysis indicates a large portion of your audience will be apathetic, you can stress ways in which the problem you're discussing directly affects them. You can seek to involve them in the subject by beginning the speech with a series of questions designed to increase their interest and awareness. Above all, you need to neutralize the audience's apathy by drawing connections between your subject and their own lives.

Interest (or lack of it) is only one aspect of an audience's attitude toward your subject. *Expectancy* is another. For example, as soon as listeners hear that a speech will be about the Los Angeles riots, some will instantly form favorable or unfavorable attitudes (even before they know what position you will take). For example, listeners may be looking for a concrete solution to a problem, not simply an exposition on how serious the problem is. Your goal, on the other hand, is to get them to think more carefully about what kinds of solutions are acceptable, rather than jump ahead to embrace any solution. The introduction of your speech can deal with these potential problems: (1) acknowledge that some in the audience may have other expectations and that, if time permits, you would be happy to consider these expectations as part of a question-answer period; (2) indicate what you're prepared to do and why; and (3) demonstrate your willingness to be open-minded on the issues. From that point on, you will need to bear in mind the potential problems that listener expectations can cause and adapt accordingly.

The Audience's Attitudes Toward Your Speech Purpose.   Many of your listeners will come to hear your speech with preset attitudes toward your purpose. For example, some may resent having to listen to you rather than someone else who should have been selected; others may be eager to learn new ideas; still others may be looking for an opportunity to argue with you (sometimes seriously, at other times just for the fun of it). Since audience disposition is seldom uniform, you are best served by considering which attitudes are major obstacles to achieving your goal. Listeners will have one of the following attitudes toward the belief or action you propose:

1. favorable but apathetic;
2. apathetic to the situation;
3. interested in the situation but not sure what to think or do about it;
4. interested in the situation but hostile to the *proposed* attitude they are to accept or the action they're asked to take; or
5. hostile to any change from the present state of affairs.

Determining the predominant attitude of your audience toward your subject and purpose should guide you in selecting your arguments and developing the structure and content of your message. As suggested earlier, if your listeners are apathetic, begin your speech with a point of compelling interest that connects directly to their own lives. If they're hostile to the proposal, you may wish to introduce it more cautiously, emphasize a basic principle with which you know they agree, then relate your proposal to it. If you're speaking on a highly controversial topic, with strong arguments on both sides, a cautious or timid beginning won't be in your best interest, especially if the audience already suspects or knows the position you'll advocate. Neither will a hard line stance that treats the opposing view as totally lacking in merit be in your best interest.

In a situation like this, recognize that gaining a fair hearing is more likely than converting your audience to your views. Make clear your respect for them, even though you disagree with their stance, and openly acknowledge the differences that divide you. In this way, you can advance your position while recognizing that their views also have merit. They may still disagree, but if your presentation is open and candid, they will be that much more likely to hear you out. If the audience is interested but undecided, provide concrete evidence in the form of factual illustrations, testimony, and statistics to support your proposal. If they're favorable but not aroused, try to motivate them by using appeals based on the desire for pleasure, independence, power, creativity, ego satisfaction, and the like.

Values

The third important facet of the psychological profile is values. **Values** are the basic components that organize one's view of life. They're habitual ways of looking at the world or responding to problems. Values are more basic than either attitudes or beliefs; they represent broad categories that in turn motivate many of your specific beliefs and attitudes. Thus, you may hold a certain value, such as "Life is precious." That value can be expressed in an attitude toward a specific action, such as "I am in favor of a helmet law for motorcyclists." Values are normally grounded in specific beliefs. In this example, the reasoning might be as follows: "I believe helmets save lives; hence I favor the proposal to require them; after all, life is precious and everything we can do to protect it should be done."

In this way, values form the foundation for beliefs and attitudes that cluster around them. Because of interrelationships among values, they tend to form consistent clusters that reinforce and repeat one another. Not only are values clustered, but the clusters will mean different things to different people. Dan Quayle discovered the multiple meanings a value may convey—the beliefs and attitudes it engenders—when he briefly mentioned the Murphy Brown show's depiction of its lead character's pregnancy. He spoke in terms similar to those represented by the value cluster profiled in the graphic display (see p. 107), and his remarks were quite acceptable to many in his immediate audience but caused widespread controversy when his remarks were published. Quayle also discovered that there is no telling what an audience or the media will find of interest; this was only one example he used in a longer speech that dealt with many other issues, yet it *became the speech* in the eyes of many. If you choose to speak to a particular audience on a particular topic, you also must be cognizant of the impact that your remarks may have should they be communicated to the general public.

When values exist in broad mixtures of compatible values and their attendant attitudes and beliefs they comprise **value orientations** or **ideologies.** These orientations are often shared by groups of people. Over the last three decades, for example, Americans have read about the establishment, the silent majority, the counterculture, the Puritan ethic, yippies and yuppies, new politics, the new world order, skinheads, neo-liberals, and Perot-Conservatives. Social and political value orientations come and go. During their active life, however, they have a tremendous influence on how people view ideas and actions associated with these ideological orientations. Value orientations also can serve as the identity of a nation, as in the United States' commitment to democracy. As the Yugoslavian clashes over the right to "homeland" demonstrate, differences in value orientations may lead to bloodshed.[4]

Discovering the values that your listeners are most likely to bring to bear on issues is a critical part of audience analysis. When you present information, your audience is likely to value sound preparation and accurate sharing of factual data. If they sense you're misleading them or neglecting some data that might help them comprehend the material, they will be less likely to grant you the respect you seek. In a persuasive setting, if your audience suspects that your ideas are premised on weak or unsound values, they will

VALUES AND RELATED BELIEFS/ATTITUDES

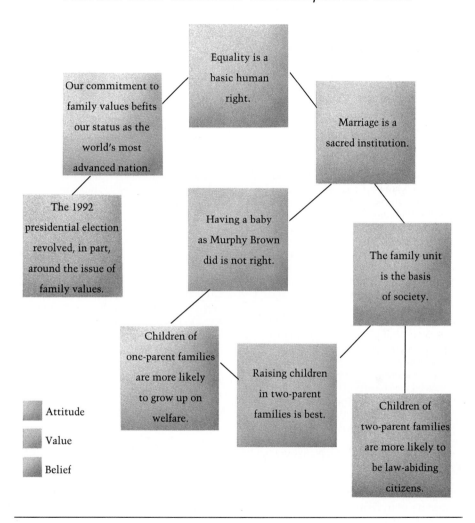

be more likely to reject your views, regardless of the quality of your argument.

Locating *common ground* with your audience with respect to values is of paramount importance if your goal is to persuade them to adopt a belief or a course of action. For example, persuading members of a local business group to lend financial support to a collegewide job fair will be easier if you know the listeners see themselves as a service group that contributes both money and time to community projects. You can appeal to this value by showing how the job fair will give students a chance to meet and visit with those

A Costly Misperception

Assume the following has occurred:

Andrew carefully prepared, then delivered a persuasive speech to his public speaking class, warning them of the wickedness of drinking and the pitfalls of dating. At first he did not notice the smiles that suddenly froze on faces or the stony gazes of his audience. Even his instructor stared for a few minutes before she began to make notes on Andrew's critique sheet. Andrew went on to explain how they could find help in his religion. Mouths became hard lines and eyes turned toward desktops and the ceiling as he proceeded with his speech, oblivious to the reactions. Eventually Andrew noticed the changes in his listeners and thought to himself, "They probably feel guilty—I'm really getting through to them—finally!" Following the speech, his classmates were silent when asked for responses and avoided him for weeks after the speech. At the next class, the instructor handed back his critique with the suggestion that Andrew more carefully analyze his audience's attitudes toward drinking and dating and think about more effective ways to introduce his religious stance as a response to the problems cited.

Drinking and dating are common concerns for Andrew's audience. The ethical issue in this instance is central to an effort to remain true to our values and beliefs and at the same time gain a fair hearing from those who oppose our views. Assuming these are realistic statements, how might Andrew have won his audience over without compromising his religious beliefs?

who may be prospective employers. In this way, you can describe the job fair in terms benefiting the larger community while introducing students to the demands they will meet upon graduation. Unless you can locate and develop this sense of common ground, you may well be in communication trouble. The search for common ground is the critical last step in audience analysis.

Analyzing the Speech Occasion

Sometimes analyzing the occasion is simple: you know you're attending a Public Relations Student Society of America meeting, you have been there often, and you know what is expected from you when called on to present a 5- to 10-minute report on internship opportunities in the local area. At other

An "occasion" is a set of activities that occurs in a predetermined time and place to fulfill collective purposes for and by people who have been taught the special meanings of those activities.

times, the occasions are complex, with many rules governing what can be said, who can talk, how and when people can talk, and in what manner you must treat other people. In deciphering the needs of occasions like these, you need to understand why occasion has such an influence on the act of speaking, then explore how best to analyze those influences profitably.

The Idea of an Occasion

To formalize the definition suggested earlier, an *occasion* is a set of activities that occurs in a time and place set aside expressly to fulfill collective goals of people who have been taught the special meanings of those activities. Unpacking this definition will be helpful in understanding its importance to public speaking.

. . . in a time and place. Regular occasions, such as religious services, usually occur at special times (often Fridays, Saturdays, or Sundays) in special places (often in buildings identified as churches, mosques, or synagogues). Special events, such as political conventions, happen at specific times in halls designed to accommodate the large number of people present. Those times and places take on special meanings of their own. Sunday morning in the United States is a special time for some religious groups; few other special occasions besides church are allowed to occur then. The places

where justice is handed down—courtrooms—are specially designed to emphasize permanence (made of marble), spaciousness (high ceilings in oversized rooms), elevation (the bench raised above all other chairs so the judge looks down on everyone else), and impartiality (a black robe to hide the individualized features of the judge). As such, courtrooms have come to be known as quiet, decorous places where respect is shown to all parties.

. . . *fulfilling collective goals.* Most important, perhaps, people design occasions to meet the particular needs of particular groups. For example, worship (church), justice (courts), passage to adulthood (bar mitzvahs, confirmations, debutante balls, and commencement ceremonies), remembrance of basic values or heroes (monument dedications and holidays such as Memorial Day), and recognition of leadership and power (inaugurals and coronations). These are all activities in which individuals tend to participate as part of a group; a one-person ceremony or dedication doesn't mean much. A group ceremony does because it recognizes the importance of those belonging to the group, its claims upon its membership, and the group's power to confirm status upon people.

. . . *special meanings.* You do not enter the world knowing how to pray, to cheer, to dedicate, to mourn with others, or to inaugurate. Those are all *social* activities you must learn, either through instruction or through imitation.[5] Knowing and understanding what is expected of you and others is a sign of belonging to a particular group. Outsiders do not possess this knowledge; insiders do.

The purposes, complexity, and even formality of occasions vary widely. A presentation to your public relations club may be an informal yet important occasion; other occasions, such as funerals and political conventions, are much more formal. No matter what their formality, however, all occasions are governed by *rules* (do's and don'ts), by *roles* (duties or functions that different people perform), and judgments of *competency* (assessments about how well people play their parts). Occasions normally carry with them rather precise expectations of what will happen, to whom it will happen, who will participate, and how they will take part.[6]

Audience Expectations on Speech Occasions

As noted earlier, occasions can be relatively informal (presenting your ideas to classmates during a class discussion) or formal (accepting an award for your theatrical accomplishments). Whether informal or not, however, a speech occasion shares characteristics with most other occasions:

- The *set of activities* that constitute a speech (standing or sitting in front of an audience, talking in a sustained fashion for [usually] an agreed upon period of time, for a particular purpose) is known to both speaker and audience members. For example, unless someone is an outsider, he or she will know what to expect when you rise to speak to the local Rotary Club about your experiences as a Rotary International Scholarship student in Germany last year.

- The *time and place* of speeches usually are determined in advance. You often are told how long to speak and when, and the room in which you're speaking may be designed to accommodate speeches—a raised platform, a lectern, audience members seated in front of you and facing you, audiovisual equipment you may require, and perhaps a microphone to facilitate speaking in a large room. The whole setting says, "This is a place for public speaking and not interpersonal chitchat." Not all settings are so accommodating; you may need to take time to allow your audience to move their chairs in order to face you, and you may need to alter the place from which you speak. In these situations, the audience often is used to the limitations of the setting, so they aren't bothered by the extra effort needed to facilitate communicating with them.
- The *collective goals* that a task is to fulfill are likewise known ahead of time when a speech is announced. Both you and your audience usually know the general purpose of your talk—to inform, persuade, actuate, or entertain. Some occasions are so formal that listeners also understand your specific purposes, as when you nominate someone for office during the election portion of a business meeting, when you pay tribute to a valued employee upon her retirement, or when you describe the latest trends in the stock market to your investment club. The knowledge of purposiveness that speaker and audience share is vitally important in bonding them together and in ensuring that communication actually will occur; shared knowledge comes from mutual understanding of the occasion.
- Both you and your listeners have been taught *how to speak (and to listen) on particular occasions.* No one came into the world knowing how to give a speech in general, much less construct a particular type of speech suited for a precisely defined audience—such as after-dinner talks, quarterly sales reports, or speeches supporting a proposed energy conservation policy. That is one of the reasons you're in this class: to learn more about speaking on particular occasions.

A speech occasion is every bit as demanding as any other social or political event. This means that speech occasions, like other occasions, are characterized by rules, roles, and judgments of competency—in other words, by audience expectations. The common lore about public speaking is filled with communication rules: Don't mumble. Trusted speakers are more effective than mistrusted ones. Extemporizing speeches, other things being equal, is preferable to reading them. In an introduction, orient audience members by giving them reasons for listening, forecasting the development of your speech, and gaining their attention. The larger the audience, the larger your gestures must be.

As you can tell, these communication rules come from several sources—social scientific study, experience, and things your grandmother or your textbook told you. As noted in Chapter 1, you can sometimes can get away with violating such rules in a speech. You might, however, pay a price. For

Speech occasions, like other occasions, are characterized by rules, roles, and judgments of competency.

example, a speech that never seems to end can be a problem if the audience expects you to talk only 15 to 20 minutes. You may be able to circumvent the time by suggesting that the complexity of the topic requires a fuller, hence longer, explanation or by speaking in an enthusiastic, engaging, and at times, humorous manner. If you simply ignore these strategies and forge ahead, your audience may believe you're deliberately flaunting the communication rules, and write off your message. Ignoring rules can be risky.

The matter of roles is a bit more complicated. There is no good scheme for classifying all of the possible roles speakers play. So far, we have discussed general roles—informer, persuader, entertainer—and suggested other, more specific ones. Thus, on one occasion, your role might be that of an instructor (listeners expect to learn something), an arguer (listeners are looking for a rational, well-supported, well-reasoned presentation), a nominator (listeners want to know why they should cast their vote for a candidate), or a eulogist (listeners expect to hear someone praised for his or her accomplishments and/or personal qualities). Whatever your role, your performance should conform to audience expectations. If you violate a role expectation, perhaps by preaching when people are expecting dispassionate analysis, you could get into trouble. A president of a corporation who prepares a comic monologue in place of her or his serious "state of the firm" to stockholders would be in grave difficulties because of playing an inappropriate role.

If you cannot offer clear information, rational arguments, or compelling motivational appeals, your listeners might judge you to be incompetent. A positive judgment of competency is a sign you have learned well your society's or group's way of talking publicly; a negative assessment means you still have important things to learn about speaking before an audience in a particular situation (the judgment may have little bearing on how you handle other occasions). The negative assessment also may mean that you were aware of the constraints and chose to ignore them for reasons of your own, in which case you accept the consequences, but believe the price is worth paying because you didn't sacrifice your principles or ideas. Some standards for judgment are general, such as the standards for delivery and appropriate language choice (see Chapters 12 and 14). Many, however, are attached to specific occasions. By tradition, a presidential inaugural address must begin with, among other things, the phrase "fellow citizens," in recognition that the president, unlike a king, is "one of us." Also by tradition, first-year members of the United States Senate do not speak but are expected to listen and learn their role. Then, in their second year, they can deliver their "maiden speech," awaited by others interested in the oratorical power of the yearling politician. A senator who speaks too soon is considered brash, unthinking, and in violation of tradition—in a word, incompetent.[7]

Audiences expect speakers to follow tradition and other demands posed by the occasion. Thus you'll need to know what is required to be ready to speak effectively.

Factors to Consider When Analyzing Occasions

You'll have to learn the specific demands of particular occasions each time you speak. However, there are some general issues common to most speaking situations that can be generalized, including queries about the nature of the occasion, the prevailing rules, the physical conditions, and the events preceding or following your speech.

The Nature and Purpose of the Occasion.   Listeners may attend because they want to, or because they have to. A **voluntary audience** attends a speech primarily because of interest in the speaker or subject. A **captive audience** is required or expected to attend, perhaps at the explicit invitation of a manager or under threat of a failing grade on an assignment. In general, the more captive your audience, the less initial interest members will show and the greater will be their resistance to accepting your information or your point of view.

In either situation, your considerations are the same. Are your subject and purpose in line with the reason for the meeting, or are you merely seizing the occasion to present some ideas you believe are important to convey at this time? Are you one in a series of speakers whom the audience has heard over a period of weeks or months? If so, how does your speech relate to those previously presented? These are important questions to consider when you're analyzing the nature and purpose of the occasion. In other words, nature, purpose, and interest level often dictate the general decisions you make in your approach to the speech.

For example, if you're the last speaker in a special series on ethics in business, you should obtain a list of the prior speakers and their announced titles. This will give you a general sense of the kinds of speakers (presumably some will be known to you) and their orientation to issues. You can then fill gaps in the subjects or themes addressed, insofar as your expertise allows, or you can take a different approach to common themes.

If the audience is captive, you'll have to work harder to show how the subject relates to their personal lives. You might go so far as to acknowledge that many would rather be elsewhere and contrast that with the significance of what you're to cover.

The Prevailing Rules or Customs.   Will there be a regular order of business or a fixed program into which your speech must fit? Is it the custom of the group to ask questions of the speaker after the address? Do the listeners expect a formal speaking manner? Will you, as the speaker, be expected to extend complimentary remarks or to express respect for a tradition or concept? Knowing the answers to these questions will help you avoid feeling out of place and will prevent you from offending your audience with an inappropriate word or action.

In addition to probing these general customs, you may need to go a step further by discovering any occasion-governed specific rules for formulating your message. If you're delivering a report on some research you've undertaken, you'll be expected to review other's research before you discuss your own study, or at minimum, show that you're familiar with the general conclusions drawn from prior research. A member of the U.S. Senate must always refer to an opponent as "The Honorable Senator from _____," even if he or she thinks the person dishonorable or is about to disagree violently with the person. The speaker at the Friars Club in New York is expected to mercilessly but good-naturedly verbally abuse the person who is the object of that evening's "roast." By knowing the prevailing rules and customs in advance of presenting your speech, you'll be in a position to determine whether your remarks fit the occasion or whether you need to violate certain rules to get your ideas across.

The Physical Conditions.   Will your speech be given outdoors or in an small conference room, with members seated at a round table? If outdoors, is the weather likely to be hot or cold, dry or wet? Will the audience be sitting or standing? If sitting, will the members be crowded together or scattered about? If you are in a conference room, will you be able to work from your notes or prepared text in a relaxed and casual atmosphere? When the setting impinges on your ability to effectively address your audience, consider ways you can involve the audience in moving closer together, in changing locations to avoid excessive heat or moisture, or in giving them time to stretch and get comfortable. In how large a room will the speech be presented? Will you be using an electronic public address system? Will the audiovisual equipment you need be provided, or must you bring your own?

Again, you will need to be prepared for the unexpected in making certain your visuals can be seen in the speech setting, and in ensuring your ability to set up and use efficiently their equipment or your own. Will you be seen and heard easily? Are there likely to be disturbances in the form of noise or interruptions? For example, if you're one of several people speaking concurrently at a convention, you may find your room is part of a subdivided ballroom and that the speakers on each side are rather more loud than necessary. If nothing else can be done to alter the situation, you can move the audience as close to you as possible and speak more loudly and distinctly than you usually would.

Events Preceding or Following Your Speech.   At what time of day or night will you give your speech? If it immediately follows a heavy meal or a long program, you can deal with the potential drowsiness and reduced listener interest by acknowledging their mental and physical state, and giving them time to stretch and otherwise get comfortable. If you're the "warm-up" act before the principal address or event, be especially careful to follow the requisite customs and rules so you don't give offense. If you know who will introduce you and how, you can consider whether that approach affects how you begin and develop your speech. If there are other items on the program, considering what are they and their individual tone and character will give you a sense of how the group functions, and perhaps a clue as to its basic values.

Using Audience Analysis in Speech Preparation

Neither demographic analysis nor psychological profiling is an end in itself, nor will merely thinking about the speech occasion produce foolproof speech preparation strategies. Rather, you carry out these twin analyses to discover what might affect the reception of you and your message. You're searching for relevant factors that can affect the audience's attitudes toward you, your subject, and your purpose. These factors, in turn, should guide your rhetorical choices with respect to subject matter, themes covered, language used, and the appropriateness of visual aids in the speech setting. What you learn about your listeners and their expectations through systematic investigation has the potential to affect every aspect of your speech—right down to the way you deliver your thoughts.

Audience Targeting: Setting Realistic Purposes

There are few occasions in which the choice of general speech purpose—to inform, to persuade or actuate, to entertain—is problematic. Once you have passed beyond this step, you need to determine what you can hope to accomplish with a particular audience in the time available. As you think about **targeting your audience,** five considerations are relevant: your specific purpose, the areas of audience interest, the audience's capacity to act, their willingness to act, and the degree of change you can expect. While what appears to be a reasonable or realistic aim may fall short of your actual goal, working within these parameters will make it far easier for you to obtain audience support for your ideas. Moving too far beyond what is realistic will, in general terms, increase the risk that your listeners won't follow you, even if they're in sympathy with the thrust of your remarks.

Your Specific Purpose.   Suppose you have a part-time job with your college's Cooperative Education Office. You're familiar with its general goals and the programs, and you have sufficient personal interest to speak about these to other campus groups. What you have discovered about different audiences should help you determine appropriate specific purposes for each. If you were to talk to a group of incoming first-year students at new student orientation, for example, you would know these things beforehand:

- They probably know little or nothing about the functions of a cooperative education office (they have few, if any, fixed beliefs about the office).
- They probably are predisposed to look favorably on cooperative education once they know how it functions (given their own career aspirations).
- They probably are, at their stage of life and educational level, more concerned with practical issues such as selecting their courses, seeing an advisor, registering, and learning about basic degree requirements (whether a foreign language is required for English majors; whether a calculus course is required for business majors). While they want to be well-positioned to make the most of their junior or senior year, learning specifics about what they can do "if and when" is not a high priority at this time. Hence, they may require external motivation (provided by your arguments and illustrations) to develop interest in the subject.

Speakers must determine what they can expect to accomplish with a particular audience in the time they have available.

- They are likely to see you as an authoritative speaker, especially if you're introduced (or introduce yourself) as a staff member from Cooperative Education, and are willing to listen to what you have to say.

Given these audience considerations, you probably should keep your presentation fairly general; explain the principal functions of Cooperative Education, review the prerequisites that must be met in order to be qualified (for example, having selected a major and completed a set number of courses). Stress the ways that a cooperative education experience can give them an early start on a possible career or serve to introduce them to new career possibilities, all while earning academic credit. You might phrase your specific purpose as follows: "To brief incoming first-year students on the range of service offered by the Cooperative Education Office." That orientation would include a basic description of each service and a general appeal to use the services to make some curricular decisions.

Were you, instead, to talk about this subject to a group of college juniors, you would address the audience differently. You would know these things beforehand:

- They are more likely to be aware of the general goals and programs of the Cooperative Education Office, but they may be misinformed or uninformed about details.

- They have generally positive feelings about the advantages of cooperative education, but some may be unsure of whether it's well suited to their major or career interest, or aren't sure they meet the prerequisite conditions for enrollment.
- They tend to value education pragmatically—that is, for how it's prepared them to earn a "decent living."
- They may view your qualifications with somewhat more scepticism since you're one of their peers.

Given these factors, you should be much more specific in some areas. You should describe your own recent experience as a "Co-op" student or, if you have yet to enroll in one, those of students who have completed the experience. First-person stories will help convince the audience that a wide variety of students can avail themselves of this opportunity and that all they need do is check with the office to see if they can qualify. In addition to fleshing out particulars about the "what" of cooperative education (for example, can you enroll if the placement site is two hours away in your hometown, and you plan to enroll during summer session?), you will need to spend time on the "how": What steps should students take if they're interested in enrolling? Should they pursue employers on their own? If they know an employer, can he or she be involved? By presenting a variety of narratives demonstrating the breadth of the experience, you also erase any doubts about your expertise. You might phrase your dominant specific purpose in this way: "To inform juniors about the benefits gained by enrolling in Midstate University's Cooperative Education Program." Your subordinate purposes might include "Demonstrating the ease with which students can enroll in the program" and "Illustrating that almost every student may be served."

Areas of Audience Interest.   You can use both demographic analysis and psychological profiling to help you decide what ideas will interest your listeners. This is critical in narrowing your topic choice and choosing specific ideas to develop. Suppose you know something about communicating with diverse cultures. An audience of new management trainees for an international firm would be very interested in hearing about how communication may differ as one moves from a Japanese to a Latin American market; an audience of mid-level managers for the same company could want to know more, if only to assess for themselves whether a new training program should be put on-line; an audience of vice-presidents and regional managers would want to know how insensitivity to communication across cultures may affect employee morale and company productivity and profits. The characteristics of the occasion also will be helpful to consider. Who will attend is often a function of the kind of situation you're entering; a national holiday will bring those people who normally venerate the ideals represented by the holiday such as Memorial Day or the Fourth of July.

Sometimes, however, you will want to create a new set of interests in an audience. For example, you might want to inform a group of eastern college students about the exciting new directions taken by southwestern artists. Some audience members may already have more than a passing interest in art, while others are relatively uninformed and uninterested. For those already interested, you can draw connections to the kinds of painting and sculpture that is invigorating art in southwestern states. For those without interest, you may work from the general value they place on broadening their horizons. You also might underscore your interest by being energetic in presenting the ideas and by using two or three prints that will enable the audience to see what you're talking about. For this speech, you might phrase your central idea as "Knowing more about southwestern art will expand your interests in positive ways." Phrasing the central idea in this way ties the subject to a more general interest in expanding one's experiences and knowledge.

The Audience's Capacity to Act. As noted in the section on narrowing speech subjects, limit your request to an action that lies within your listeners' range of authority. Don't ask them to accomplish the impossible. To demand of a group of college students that they take direct action to stop the killing of innocent dolphins is unrealistic, especially if you're in the corn belt of the United States. However, you can ask them to boycott tuna and other products associated with tuna harvesting that are not marked "dolphin safe." You can also urge them to write their local congressional representative to implore their support for more stringent fishing regulations protecting dolphins.

Sometimes your audience analysis will reveal that different segments of your audience have varying capacities to execute actions. In that case, you will want to address those segments separately in the action step of your speech. In talking with a local school's PTA about instituting an after-school program of foreign language and culture instruction, you will want to target each subgroup with a different call to action:

- *Parents*: "Prepare a petition for the school board, enroll your child or children in the program, and help us find community volunteers to work in it."
- *Administrators*: "Seek funding from the school board for the after-school program."
- *Teachers*: "Volunteer at least one after-school period a week to help with instruction."

By using this method, each call for action is suited to the range of authority and talent possessed by each subgroup among their listeners. (This will be discussed further in the section on audience segmentation later in this chapter.)

The Audience's Willingness to Act.   Not only must you be concerned with audience authority, but also with audience will. You'll need to assess the degree to which listeners are willing to put themselves on the line on behalf of your ideas or proposals. For example, a speech soliciting blood donors has a better chance of success when given at a fraternity or sorority meeting about service projects than it does in your speech classroom. People attending the meeting are committed to the idea of public service or they wouldn't have come to listen. On the other hand, people in your classroom are strongly aware that you're "practicing" public address; hence, they're usually more distanced from you, more attuned to the quality of your appeals and style of speaking and less caught up in the spirit of advice-following. They are difficult listeners to reach because they hear so many appeals from fellow students during the term.

Your assessment of an audience's will or desire may influence the wording of your claim. Addressing a fraternity or sorority or a panhellenic council comprising both groups, you might phrase a claim in this fashion: "Running a campuswide blood drive is the best service project our organization can undertake this semester." Dealing with the same subject in your speech classroom would suggest a different claim: "You should give blood as a matter of personal commitment to human beings in need." The first version acknowledges the purpose of the meeting (identifying a service project) and acknowledges the willingness of the listeners to act on some project. The second version plays down or ignores the occasion (classroom speech), because that occasion doesn't encourage listeners to take your advice. Instead, the wording personalizes the subject, allowing the speaker to tug on at least a few heart strings. Thus, willingness to act is usually related to listeners' expectations in a situation and should be taken into account when you phrase your goals or purposes.

Degrees of Change.   Finally, as suggested earlier, you must be realistic in targeting the degree of change you can reasonably hope for. In an informative context, there is a natural limit on how much information you can present about the topic, due to the time limits and the complexity of the subject. For instance, it would take more than a 5-minute speech to do justice to the controversy surrounding the changes in saltwater fishing stock. Demographic factors such as age, work experience, and educational development will influence how much change you can affect. Also, deciding whether the information is new or is already known will influence how much material you can cover in a single speech. Talking to lobster fishermen off the coast of Maine is one thing; addressing a group of Iowa farmers is quite another when you're deciding what is known and understood about saltwater fishing.

How intensely can you motivate your listeners to react positively to your ideas or proposals for action? If your listeners are strongly opposed to downtown renovation, a single speech, no matter how eloquent, probably won't reverse their opinions. One attempt may only neutralize some of their objections; to aim at some rather than all objections is a more realistic goal. If your prespeech analysis indicates that your listeners vehemently oppose locating a work-release prison facility in your community, you can probably persuade many of them to contribute funds to the defeat of the proposal, to work long hours as volunteers at a variety of activities, such as picketing, lobbying, and telephone marathons; however, if they're only moderately opposed to the facility, you might ask for a small monetary donation and no actual time commitment.

In other words, audience analysis should help you determine how to phrase your specific purpose, central ideas, and claims for maximum effectiveness. The understanding you gain about your audience in this manner also gives you a more realistic expectation of the degree of change possible in behavior, beliefs, attitudes, values, and commitments to action.

Audience Segmentation: Selecting Dominant Ideas and Appeals

The preceding demographic analysis and psychological profiling of relevant beliefs, attitudes, and values focus on targeting your audience as a group. Keep in mind, however, that no matter how people are crowded together, arranged in rows, or reached electronically, they're still individuals. Although influenced by culture and society, each person holds unique beliefs, attitudes, and values. Each is a unique product of experience and thought. You also function as a unique individual when approaching the audience as a speaker.

Ideally, it would be most effective if you could approach each listener one-on-one. Sometimes you can, but such communication is time consuming and inefficient in matters of broad public concern. Imagine for a minute the president of this country talking to each one of us individually. If you assume 160 million adults and 5 minutes per person, it would take 300 million minutes or over 570 years of nonstop talking! Rather than take that approach, it's no wonder politicians have resorted to television to broadcast their messages simultaneously to millions of viewers. Candidates have found that they can simulate the atmosphere of personal conversation through their delivery and choice of language. In so doing, they can begin to think of listeners as individuals hearing the message in the privacy of their homes.

They and their advisors have adopted a technique long familiar to advertisers: audience segmentation. **Audience segmentation** is a matter of dividing a mass audience into subgroups, or "target populations," that hold common attitudes, beliefs, values, or demographic characteristics. The earlier illustration of addressing parents, school administrators, and teachers in terms of their different capacities to act is an instance of such segmentation. A typical college-student audience might be segmented by academic standing (freshmen through seniors), academic majors (art through zoology), classroom performance (A through F), and even extracurricular activities (officer training programs, varsity sports, recreational clubs, political groups).

Accurately Identifying Subgroups/Segments.   Identifying subgroups must be accurate and relevant to the speech purpose and occasion. This will not only allow you to better phrase your appeals, but it will help you avoid irritating your listeners unnecessarily. A speaker who began, "Because all you girls are interested in efficient cooking, today I want to talk about four ways a food processor will save you time in the kitchen," would probably alienate two subgroups in the audience. The females probably would be irritated by being called "girls," and by the assertion that all females are interested in cooking; the males who cook also would be offended by having been excluded. The appeal would be better phrased "Because everyone who cooks is interested in efficiency. . . ." This appeal aims at the proper audience segment—those who like to cook.

In finding ways to talk about controversial issues, be sure to avoid stereotyped references to people and to groups and avoid blanket condemnation of groups of people. When possible, work around controversial issues; when that is not possible, know the risks ahead of time and decide to what extent you wish to or must confront specific subgroups that will be present in your audience. When you do challenge these subgroups' beliefs, attitudes, and sacred values, cite ample and unbiased evidence in support of your position. Analyzing the occasion will be useful because particular occasions may bring one or more subgroups to the speech setting. An invitation to speak before a community senior citizen's group would imply a subgroup that is older than the average community member. Speaking at a community rally in an ethnic neighborhood also implies that your audience will be predominantly associated with the area's particular ethnic heritage.

Selecting Relevant Psychological Statements.   Audience segmentation should also help you identify statements of belief, attitudes, and values to include in your speech. If you can accurately identify the relevant subgroups, you can include psychological appeals for each in your speech, thereby greatly increasing the personal appeal and potential effectiveness or your message. Suppose you were to give a speech to a longstanding private men's club about the importance of including women in its membership. Your initial segmenting of the audience tells you that the club is composed of businessmen, medical professionals, and lawyers. By thinking of the club as segmented into such subgroups, you should be in a position to offer each some reasons to support your proposal. You might outline the appeals in this way:

Claim: "The membership of this private men's club should be extended to include women."

1. For doctors and other medical professionals: A large percentage of the hospital staff is composed of women in all roles, including physicians,

nurses, physical therapists, and administrators. Their expertise and commitment to helping others is compatible with the club's founding philosophy.

2. For those from community businesses: Women control a large proportion of the financial resources of the community as investors, property owners, and heads of households. They could offer a significant contribution to the success of the organization.

3. For legal professionals: As in the other instances, women are represented and valued in their respective roles; hence it makes no sense to exclude their representation in the club. In fact, to do so implicitly devalues them.

This is just a sketch of several basic appeals. In an actual speech, each would be expanded, with specific examples indicating how women can make a difference in the life of the organization. From these brief beginnings, however, you can see how each is based on beliefs and attitudes you assume are important to segments of the audience. There is an implicit reference to medical ethics based on serving humankind, to business commitments, to financial responsibility and success, and to the legal profession's commitment to justice. Thus, audience analyses, in combination with audience segmentation, are valuable tools for selecting your main lines of appeal and argument.

Choosing Among Valuative Appeals.   Finally, as you might guess, audience segmentation will help you select a valuative vocabulary for your speeches. Even informative speeches, as we will discuss more fully later, need to contain appeals to audience interests. You can use a **valuative vocabulary** to motivate different segments of the audience to listen to and accept your information. For a class demonstration speech, you might introduce your speech in this way:

> Today I want to teach you three basic techniques of Oriental cooking—cutting meats and vegetables, using spices, and quick-cooking your food in a wok. If you learn these techniques, you'll expand your range of expertise in the kitchen [*personal value*], you'll save money on your food and energy bills [*economic value*], you'll prepare more-than-satisfying meals for your friends [*social value*], and you'll prepare more nutritious, healthful meals for everyone [*pragmatic value*].

With that statement, you give your audience four different reasons for listening and will have a good chance of appealing to every listener. If you want, you also can tell them that the meals will be beautiful, thereby adding an *aesthetic value* to your set of appeals.

Valuative appeals are even more important to persuasive and actuative speeches. These speeches are attempts to alter people's values, in concert with their supportive beliefs and attitudes, and their behaviors. You do so only insofar as your appeals address these value clusters in concrete terms and, especially to those subgroups who disagree, appear reasonable and worthy of consideration. For example:

> **Claim:** "The United States should adopt immediate, severe economic sanctions against those nations, such as China and South Africa, who routinely violate basic human rights."

1. *Politically,* getting tough with nations that consistently violate citizens' rights will increase international respect for the United States' commitment to support human rights. If successful, such action may also gain a voice for previously disenfranchised peoples or groups.

2. *Pragmatically,* economic sanctions are effective and avoid violence. Nations violating human rights are more likely to respond to economic sanctions than to verbal threats.

3. *Psychologically,* we will increase the importance of basic human rights throughout the world if we take them seriously enough to enforce them.

4. *Culturally,* treatment of groups or people as equals may enhance their opportunity to contribute to the development of their nation. Everyone will be richer because the nation is recognizing and valuing the heritage of all of its citizens.

5. *Economically,* individuals who have been denied access will have the opportunity to participate more fully in the resources of their nation.

While this segmentation of appeals has not used every conceivable value term, the procedure should be clear: (1) Think through possible reasons people might accept your claim in valuative terms. (2) Then use a valuative vocabulary to phrase your actual appeals for acceptance.

In conclusion, understanding your audience is certainly the most crucial step of speech preparation. The competent speaker makes many decisions about topic, specific purposes, phrasing for central ideas and claims, dominant appeals, and phraseology based on demographic and psychological profiles of audience members. To assist in completing these tasks, you need to do these things: (1) think through your personal experiences with identifiable groups in the audience; (2) talk with program chairpersons and others who can tell you who will likely be in the audience and something about their interests or positions on issues; (3) ask speakers who have addressed this or similar audiences what to expect; and (4) interview some people who will be there to find out more about their beliefs, attitudes, and values—their range of concerns.

These are not especially easy tasks, for most of us don't possess the resources of public opinion polls and extensive social-psychological target group profiles. You probably won't be able to identify precisely all possible facets of listeners' minds and habits; however, if you learn all you can about them and use that knowledge to make key prespeech decisions according to those factors that are relevant and potentially influential, you will significantly improve your chances for success.

Sample Analysis of an Audience

This chapter has surveyed an array of choices you must make as you analyze your audience and occasion. If you work systematically, one step at a time, these choices will become clearer. Observe how one student analyzed her audience as she prepared a speech to promote an increased understanding of acquired immune deficiency syndrome (AIDS).

Audience Analysis: Understanding AIDS

I. Basic Speaking Situation
   A. Title: "The Great American Plague: AIDS"
   B. Subject: What we should know about the crisis in American health—acquired immune deficiency syndrome
   C. General Purpose: To persuade
   D. Special Purpose: To prove to members of a local political action caucus that AIDS poses a national health threat
   E. Specific Audience: The political action caucus is a community group whose function is to promote political consciousness and action in the community. It consists of varied membership, including local housewives, business proprietors, the town mayor, the Chair of the State Republican Committee, and approximately a dozen interested listeners. A synopsis of the monthly meeting is broadcast over local radio stations and is included on the editorial page of the local newspaper (reaching a secondary audience).
   F. Claim: "The caucus should be alerted to the crisis in national health."

II. Audience Analysis
   A. Demographic Analysis
      1. Age: Of the individuals attending the meeting, most are between thirty and sixty-five. The spectators are approximately twenty to thirty. Except for appeals to future events, age is probably not an important factor. The speaker is significantly younger than members of her audience (twenty-one). She will need to enhance her credibility as a speaker to compensate for her relative youth and inexperience.
      2. Gender: The caucus is a mixed group with slightly more women than men. Given the topic and claim, there may be an initial attitude that AIDS is not a threat to either women or heterosexual males.

3.   Education: Approximately one-third of the listeners have completed a B.A. degree in varied fields, including political science, pharmacy, nursing, home economics, and accounting. All but four of the remainder have finished high school, several have taken college courses. While several health professionals in the audience are familiar with disease history and control, most listeners are acquainted with the topic only through media coverage.

4.   Group Membership: All listeners are politically active registered voters. Although they do not necessarily share party affiliation, they all agree that participation in the democratic process is vital.

5.   Cultural and Ethnic Background: Ethnic background is primarily European but should not be a factor on this topic. The community was shocked by the news of the recent AIDS death of a former resident. All members of the caucus were born and/or raised in this small Midwestern community with a mixed rural–small business economy.

B.   Psychological Analysis

1.   Beliefs

a.   Accepted Facts and Beliefs: Anyone who contracts AIDS will die of it. There is nothing that can currently be done to stop the disease. The incidence of AIDS is concentrated in homosexual populations primarily on the East and West Coasts. The resident who died had just moved to San Francisco, where it is thought that he may have contracted the disease.

b.   Fixed Beliefs (beliefs reinforced throughout one's life and central to thinking): Homosexual behavior is morally wrong and should not be condoned. Only one or two members of the caucus would even consider hiring, renting to, or politically endorsing a person known to be homosexual. The medical profession has accounted for most breakthroughs in disease control and treatment.

c.   Variable Beliefs (beliefs that one holds less firmly and can change in the face of opposing evidence): Most probably believe that a degree of tolerance should be shown to members of unusual religious or political factions. Several would agree that the sexual revolution of the 1960s brought some advantages, such as greater openness, more individual responsibility, and better understanding of human sexuality.

2.   Attitudes

a.   Audience Attitude Toward Speaker: The members of the caucus probably consider the speaker to be naive and idealistic on the topic. Her youthfulness severely undermines her credibility.

b.   Audience Attitude Toward Subject: The listeners are certainly hostile toward those they feel are guilty of spreading AIDS—the "promiscuous gay population." While they are curious about AIDS because of recent media attention, they are probably not very concerned. They do not consider themselves likely targets of the disease.

c.   Audience Attitude Toward Purpose: Most are basically apathetic. While they are curious about the disease, they do not really care about it since they think it will not touch their lives. Several members are hostile, given their strong personal religious attitudes toward homosexuality.

3. Values

   a. Predominating Values: The political value of "majority rule" is strongly held by every listener. There is a positive commitment to democratic process and a pride in community political involvement at the state and national levels. They see themselves as "common people—the heart of America," fulfilling the American dream. Caucus members often point to community progress in civil rights issues, general educational reforms, and high voter turnout during elections.

   b. Relevant Value Orientation: Ideologically, while caucus members are voicing democratic principles, they are practicing those ideals in a limited sphere. They are promoting fair treatment for some minority issues, such as equal rights, but are unaware of or are denying others. It would be counterproductive to point out this hypocrisy to the group, since they take a great deal of pride in themselves and their local accomplishments.

III. Adaptive Strategies

  A. Audience Targeting

    1. Specificity of Purpose: To defuse one set of suspicions, to make it clear that this is not simply "a gay cause." While the speaker should recognize the importance of a good moral climate in this country, she also must stress the practical importance of treating disease regardless of moral issues. The speaker should emphasize that everyone's health may be affected if the disease is allowed to spread unchecked through ignorance or neglect.

    2. Areas of Audience Interests: Make sure to use the caucus members' fixed and anchored beliefs and values to advance the speaker's own goals. Stress their commitments to the welfare of the community and nation, their beliefs in the democratic process, and the rights of citizens in minority factions. Encourage their feelings of pride in previous civic accomplishments and challenge them to face the coming AIDS crisis. In other words, show them that it is in their self-interest to confront and discuss unpopular issues for the well-being of the entire community.

    3. Audience's Capacity to Act: The immediate goal is to increase their awareness of the AIDS crisis and encourage them to discuss it in future meetings. Point out that other Midwestern communities have debated the issues involved as they were faced with enrolling infected children in local schools. Stress predictions of future infections affecting broader populations. Overcome audience apathy and hostility by encouraging members to discuss the disease in other groups, such as the local PTA, religious organizations, and community service groups.

    4. Degrees of Change: Do not demand immediate commitments or political action. Push instead for an open forum for future debate on the issues.

  B. Audience Segmentation

    1. Accurate Identification of Subgroups: Emphasize the nature of the

caucus' political rather than moral or personal involvement in community issues. Avoid stereotyping or judging religious or dogmatic individuals or groups. Deemphasize the sexual aspects of the issue. While these aspects might gratify the curious, they would strengthen the resistance of listeners who associate the disease only with those they consider to be undesirable members of the community.

2. Relevant Psychological Statements: Recognize the group's excellent efforts at political reform in local projects. Remember that listeners have taken the time to attend, and their commitments should be recognized. Stress the farsightedness of the group on difficult issues, such as this one. Point out that, in a democracy, fair play requires that each side be given equal time and consideration before anyone reaches a final decision. Aim the bulk of the speech at gaining assent to openminded discussions.

3. Relevant Valuative Appeals: Underscore the virtues of democratic process, freedom of expression, and the rights of all American citizens. Encourage pride in previous caucus accomplishments and channel motivation toward achieving new goals. Highlight, too, the fundamental importance of both medical and political progress in achieving success.

With this prespeech audience analysis completed, the next steps in preparing the speech are clearer. The audience analysis points to the kinds of supporting materials needed. The speaker has these options:

1. Look up the history of AIDS in the United States.
2. Find out projected levels of AIDS infection in the future. This material should be available through the Centers for Disease Control and Prevention in Atlanta, Georgia.
3. Identify the populations that are currently infected by AIDS—men, women, children, homosexual, heterosexual.
4. Read local newspaper articles concerning former community residents who died of AIDS.
5. If possible, interview community residents who knew an AIDS victim.
6. Search out examples of people who have contracted the disease, including schoolchildren in Midwestern towns and medical personnel.
7. Develop a "typical" disease profile—what occurs in the body and how it copes with the disease.
8. Interview local medical authorities to discover the kinds of treatment currently used and the chances of AIDS occurring in local residents.
9. Read expert opinions and discussions of the disease, especially concerning the rates of infection. Identify potential supporting material, such as authoritative statements, statistics, explanations, or illustrations.
10. Prepare a list of other Midwestern communities that have held community discussions or adopted measures regarding AIDS.

11. Anticipate and list potential questions and objections to the topic itself.
12. Check local and state medical codes and guidelines regarding infectious disease.

Chapter Summary

Public speaking is *audience* and *occasion* centered. The primary goal of audience analysis is to discover the aspects of listeners' *demographic* and *psychological* backgrounds that are relevant to your speech purposes. Once you can profile your listeners, you can adapt your speech purposes and ideas to them. Demographic analysis concentrates on describing such audience characteristics as *age, gender, education, group membership,* and *cultural and ethnic background.* Psychological profiling seeks to identify the relevant *beliefs, attitudes, and values* of your listeners.

Analysis of the *occasion* complements that of the audience. An occasion is a set of activities that occurs in a time and place set aside for the express purpose of fulfilling collective goals for and by people who have been taught the special meanings of those activities. You should attempt to analyze your speech occasion's *rules for speaking, habitual roles played by both speaker and audience,* and *standards for competency* that will be applied to your speech. All of this should help with *audience targeting*—that is, determining realistic specific purposes, the areas of audience interest, the audience's capacity and willingness to act, and the degree of change you can expect. The analysis of audience and occasion also will assist you in *audience segmenting*—creating basic appeals that accurately identify subgroups, applying psychological statements that are relevant to their life, and using appropriate valuative appeals.

References

1. Donald C. Bryant, *Rhetorical Dimensions in Criticism* (Baton Rouge: Louisiana State University Press, 1973), 19.

2. For more discussion, see Milton M. Rokeach, *Beliefs, Attitudes, and Values: A Theory of Organization and Change* (San Francisco: Jossey-Bass, 1968); and his *The Nature of Human Values* (New York: Collier-Macmillan, Free Press, 1973).

3. For recent studies of how attitudes affect the persuasive process, see Daniel O'Keefe, *Persuasion: Theory and Practice* (Newbury Park, CA: Sage Publishers, 1990) and Kathleen Kelly Reardon, *Persuasion in Practice* 2nd ed. (Newbury Park, CA: Sage Publishers, 1991).

4. On values and their role in communicative decisions, see Douglas Ehninger and Gerard Hauser, "Communication of Values," in *Handbook of Rhetorical and Communication Theory,* ed. Carroll C. Arnold and John Waite Bowers (Boston: Allyn and Bacon, 1984), 720–48.

5. In his now classic examination of culture and language, Edward T. Hall argues that you learn about culture and social expectations in three ways: formally (when someone tells you what to do), informally (when you learn by imitating others), and, when you are older, technically (when you learn *why* members of a culture do certain things and not others). See Hall, *The Silent Language* (Greenwich, CT: Fawcett, 1959), Chapter 4, "The Major Triad," 63–91.

6. For a broader, cultural discussion of occasion, see Elihu Katz, "Media Events: The Sense of Occasion," *Studies in Visual Communication*, 6 (1980): 84–89.

7. For a discussion of competency as grounds for assessing speaker success, see Bruce E. Gronbeck, "Ronald Reagan's Enactment of the Presidency in His 1981 Inaugural Address," in *Form, Genre, and the Study of Political Discourse*, ed. Herbert W. Simons and Aram A. Aghazarian (Columbia, SC: South Carolina University Press, 1986), 226–45.

Key Terms

attitudes (p. 103)

audience centered (p. 98)

audience segmentation (p. 121)

audience targeting (p. 116)

captive audience (p. 114)

demographic analysis (p. 99)

facts (p. 102)

occasion centered (p. 98)

opinions (p. 102)

psychological profiles (p. 100)

valuative vocabulary (p. 123)

value orientations (p. 106)

values (p. 105)

voluntary audience (p. 113)

Problems and Probes

1. Working in small groups, study the speaking situation that faces you in your classroom. Begin with an audience analysis. What are the most common elements shared by your class members? In what areas are they the most different? Develop a questionnaire that will help you discern less readily observable aspects of their beliefs, attitudes, and values. These questionnaires will be collated and used in future class sessions.

2. Working in small groups, study the occasion of presenting a speech in your classroom. Note the nature and purposes of the occasion. What are the prevailing rules and customs you must follow? What physical conditions affect the way you speak? Try to predict the events that will precede and follow classroom speeches. Submit your group's list of findings; they will be collated and circulated as a general summary of the "protocol" for giving speeches.

3. Examine the conditions surrounding a speech that the press has reported to be stirring controversy, either locally, nationally, or internationally. Using the relevant themes developed in this chapter, write an analysis that answers these questions: What kinds of assumptions might the speaker have made in advance of the presentation? Would better audience and occasion analysis have pre-

vented the controversy or altered its nature? From an ethical perspective, should the speaker have changed her or his subject, themes, or language?
4. Read or listen to a speech in which the values, attitudes, and beliefs of the listeners are hostile to the speaker's purpose. Analyze the speech to ascertain how the speaker attempted to minimize or reduce hostility in seeking to influence the audience to accept the ideas.

Communication Activities

1. After your instructor has divided the class into four-person groups, meet with the other members of your group and, using the "sample analysis of an audience" as a guide, discuss the next round of speeches to be presented—the nature of the audience and occasion, the topic you intend to use, your general and specific purposes, the development of your central idea or claim, your speech plan or outline, and useful kinds of supporting materials. Criticize each other's plans and preparation, offering suggestions for changes and more specific adaptations to your particular classroom audience. Following the discussion, write up a more refined analysis for your next speech, using the "sample analysis" as a guide, and hand it in.
2. As a student of speech communication, you can learn something about the principles of audience analysis by observing how such public opinion pollsters as Dr. George Gallup, Jr., analyze "the great American audience" to derive the samples on which they base their predictions. Working in small groups, research these methods in books, magazine articles, and newspaper surveys, and report on them orally. The report could be handled as an informal class discussion, or each member of the group could individually report to the class his or her findings.
3. Present your findings for *Problems and Probes* questions 3 or 4 orally, instead of writing a formal report.

6

Determining the Basic Appeals

Chapter 5 emphasized the importance of audience analysis. Who people are, what experiences they've had, what they believe, and what they think is appropriate to say on various occasions all determine how they'll respond to your speeches. Equally important are their **motives**— their basic biological, physical, social, and emotional needs, wants, and desires.

If you've ever gone to a professional football game or one played at a large university, you may have noticed that you're surrounded by appeals for you to act: to *buy* a product advertised on billboards or the trailing signs pulled by airplanes overhead, to *cheer* loyally for the home or visiting team, to *join* the alumni or athletic support group, to *eat* a hot dog or *wear* a souvenir cap. To buy, cheer, join, eat, or wear—all these are appeals for you to act in a way desired by a communicator. Often, such appeals are expanded to include reasons for acting:

- "Buy a Mercury and save!"
- "Show your support for the defense!"
- "Join the alumni association in return for all the college has given you!"
- "What's a football game without a Red Hot?"
- "Let the world know where you're from!"

Determining and effectively using basic appeals is the focus of this chapter: what are some of the reasons you can suggest for people to think or act as you'd like them to? The first section will focus on motivational studies of individual behavior, including a discussion of the various clusters of motivational appeals. Then, we can get more practical, giving you advice on using your knowledge of motives and motivational appeals to increase the power of your messages.

Motivation and Motives: The Analysis of Human Behavior

To understand the workings of basic appeals in speeches, we need to investigate relationships between them and human behavior. For our purposes, human behavior can be divided into (1) activity that is the result of *biological* needs, drives, or stimuli, and (2) activity that is the result of *social* motives, desires, and deliberate intent.[1] The motive to eat when hungry or to sleep when tired is the result of biologically determined needs or drives. External stimuli such as a stuffy room can also affect your physiological state; attending classes between noon and 1:00 P.M. affects students' concentration because they're used to eating then. Satisfying a **biological need**, then, is a matter of giving in to or meeting a physiological urge.

Social motives are individual goals, desires, or behaviors that are the result of acting in accordance with your understanding of what others expect or value. A person's desires to achieve success on a speech, to feel wanted or needed by others, and to be the kind of person others admire are all examples of social motives. They come from your personal experiences within your family or with groups of friends, in work environments, and in your community. Some social motives are related to how you want to see yourself (as a nice or good person), and others to what you want from the world: higher pay, approval from teachers and friends, awards. Think of social motives as prods to thought or action arising from ways you see yourself in relationship to others.

Overall, while most biological and social motives are relatively enduring, some social motives are subject to change. People confronted by strong political or religious experiences operate from new motives. Or, social motives change from situation to situation; you may try to demand respect from your friends in informal conversation but show respect to the owner of the company you work for when talking about your job. Your social motives change over time—your drive for power and glory on the job probably will diminish as you near retirement. Motives to some degree or another are part of dynamic psychological processes, capable of being altered explosively or gradually—often through the power of speech.

The Classification of Motives: Clusters

We now are ready to talk about speechmaking. First, we'll discuss two classification systems that can help you group or cluster together individual motives. Then, we'll define "motivational appeal" and examine individual motives as they get cast into words in your speech.

McClelland's Motive Types.   Generally, we think of three primary cluster motives: affiliation, achievement, and power or social influence. **Affiliation motives** include those focused on the desire to belong to a group, to be well liked and accepted. **Achievement motives** are related to both intrinsic and extrinsic desire for success, adventure, creativity, and personal enjoyment. **Power motives** attach to activities in which influence over others is the primary objective.[2]

Shortly, we'll illustrate each of these types of motives. For now, think of this classification system as useful when you're trying to find a center or middle for your appeals to motive. The distinction between *affiliation* and *power* is critical: are you going to appeal to your listeners' sense of belongingness or to their sense of dominance? It's important as well to think of the relationships between *power* and *achievement* motives: do you approach audience members with a focus on their desires to control others or their hopes for personal development and self-satisfaction? McClelland's motive types help you think strategically about how to approach an audience.

Maslow's Hierarchy of Needs.   Another approach to the study of motives was proposed by Abraham Maslow. Maslow's hierarchy of needs has had a major impact on consumer-oriented studies of marketing and sales and in the field of communication studies. Maslow presents the following categories of needs and desires that drive people to think, act, and respond:

1. *Physiological needs:* for food, drink, air, sleep, and sex—the basic bodily "tissue" requirements

2. *Safety needs:* for security, stability, protection from harm or injury, structure, orderliness, predictability, freedom from fear and chaos

3. *Belongingness and love needs:* for devotion and warm affection with lovers, spouses, children, parents, and close friends; for feeling a part of social groups; for acceptance and approval

4. *Esteem needs:* for self-esteem based on achievements, mastery, competence, confidence, freedom, and independence; for recognition by others expressed in reputation, prestige, recognition, and status

5. *Self-actualization needs:* for self-fulfillment, to actually become what you potentially can be; to actualize your capabilities, being true to your essential self, what you *can* be you *must* be; to know and understand, to satisfy an aesthetic sensibility.[3]

These needs and desires interrelate biological and social motives. In Maslow's theory, the five levels or stages function as a **hierarchy of prepo-**

MASLOW'S HIERARCHY

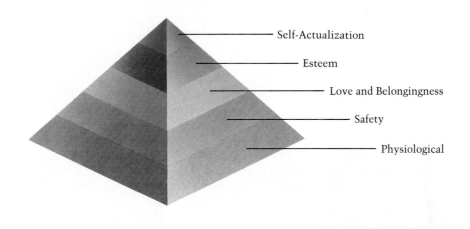

- Self-Actualization
- Esteem
- Love and Belongingness
- Safety
- Physiological

tency. That is, lower-level needs usually must be satisfied in whole or in part before higher-order desires become operative. Thus, the homeless have little time and energy to worry much about esteem or self-actualization, so appeals to such needs would fall on deaf ears in the soup kitchens of American cities. At the other end of the socioeconomic scale, it's often difficult to get the rich and famous to understand the importance of the welfare system as a safety net for the homeless because they have no physiological and few safety needs unmet in their own lives. To Maslow, needs or motivational appeals must be aimed at that level in the hierarchy where individuals' lives are centered.

Like McClelland's clusters of motive types, Maslow's hierarchy helps you map general strategy. Analyzing your audience in order to estimate which approaches to needs are best can help you frame your principal appeals—to physiological and safety appeals (which you might use in time of struggle or physical deprivation), to love and belongingness appeals (valuable on topics that feature our sense of being part of a group), or esteem and self-actualization (which are excellent when urging individuals to improve themselves). Centering your messages on the physical, the social, or the individual is the kind of speech strategy suggested by Maslow's hierarchy.

The Classification of Motives: Motivational Appeals

The idea of motive clusters helps you map general strategy, but how can you use the idea of motives to build specific lines of argument into your speeches? How can you translate psychological theory into rhetorical practice? The answer to both questions is, through the use of motivational

Motivational appeals are attempts to make salient and relevant a series of motives within an audience through visualization or attribution. Product advertisers use motivational appeals to influence the buying behavior of carefully segmented audiences.

appeals. A **motivational appeal** is an attempt to code or translate a social motive into language. So, "prestige" is a social motive. "If you're elected president of this organization, people will look up to you" is an attempt to work an appeal to prestige into the language of a speech.

You have two choices when attempting to encode motives into the language of speech: you can attempt to visualize a situation in which someone is acting upon because of some motive, or you can attribute a motive to someone acting in a particular way. Some examples of the process of **visualization** and the process of **attribution** should help.

Suppose you wanted your classmates to join in a demonstration against a proposed tuition hike when the Board of Regents is in town next month. While most, of course, would like to see the school hold the line on tuition, many would be reluctant to protest publicly. Your best bet to engage them might well be to visualize various motives:

Just think of what we can accomplish. If we all (*affiliation*) gather in front of the Administration Building, we can show the regents that this is a serious matter. We can show the regents that we're as much a part of the decision-making process as they are (*authority*) and that our voice (*independence*) deserves to be heard as much as theirs. When we present our petition to the President of the Board, even after he's tried to ignore us (*perseverance*), he'll see that we're serious and will have to admit we've got a right to be heard (*success/display*). There's no need to be afraid (*fear*) when you're among friends (*companionship*) in a cause that's right (*pride*). On that day, we'll demonstrate our solidarity (*loyalty*) and force the Board (*aggression*) to listen to our side of the story!

You also can couple motivational concepts directly with other concepts through what technically is called "a process of attribution."[4] Suppose you've shunned going to church because you've always thought of religions as conformist, authoritarian, dominating, repulsive, and destructive. One night, however, you go to a religious meeting where people seem to accept you for what you are and where the minister talks about the *adventure* of worship within a community where *companionship* and *loyalty* to others are valued. Upon reflection you decide you may have misconstrued the church's motivation and even misanalyzed yourself. What happened? You changed the former attributions of "churchness" in your mind, which caused your previous behavior, to new ones that will guide your personal behavior. You replaced the old association between "going to church" and the attributes of conformity, authority, and dominance with a new association between church and the attributes of adventure, companionship, and loyalty. This sort of realignment of some object/idea/person and attributed motives occurs often in persuasive speeches.

Motivational appeals, therefore, are verbal attempts to make a series of motives salient and relevant to an audience. Motivational appeals work through visualization (*verbal depiction*)[5] or attribution (*verbal association*) in order to produce a change in thought or deed in your audience. As we examine individual motivational appeals, always remember to consider your ethical responsibilities in various situations: motivational appeals ought to be appropriate to the moral standards of your community (see the "Ethical Moments," on pp. 153.

Motive Clusters: Examples of Motivational Appeals

Present in all of us is a near infinite number of needs and desires to which others might direct their appeals. Listing them could be an endless process. Nevertheless, we need some starting point, and so you'll find a prepared list of appeals in the table on page 139. These motivational appeals have been used by successful speakers, product advertisers, and political persuaders to tap the motives for action in their audiences. By understanding the general thrust of each **motive cluster** and its specific appeals, you'll be in a good position (1) to choose among appeals we've identified here when preparing your speeches, and (2) come up with others we don't deal with here. In selecting specific appeals, be guided by one principle: *motivational appeals work only when they are relevant to audience members and when they have features that listeners can visualize or can couple with attributes on which they want to act.*

The Affiliation Cluster

Affiliation motives are dominated by a desire for acceptance or approval. They're more focused on the social or interpersonal bonds between people than with personal success or power over others.[6] All motives falling into

MOTIVE CLUSTERS

Affiliation	*Achievement*	*Power*
Companionship	Acquisition/saving	Aggression
Conformity	Success/display	Authority/dominance
Deference/dependence	Pride	Defense
Sympathy/generosity	Prestige	Fear
Loyalty	Adventure/change	Autonomy/independence
Tradition	Perseverance	
Reverence/worship	Creativity	
Sexual attraction	Curiosity	
	Personal enjoyment	

this cluster, therefore, depend upon the importance of the group or collectivity to your listeners. Here are some examples of such motives and appeals to them.

Companionship. *"Birds of a feather flock together."* The human being is the one weakest of all animals, and ill equipped to survive alone. We all need others—their presence, recognition, touch, help. Maslow saw belongingness as the most important human need once basic physiological needs are satisfied. Thus, appeals to companionship fill sermons, political testaments, and ads for a majority of consumer products. Such appeals can be phrased explicitly, as in "We care about you," "Join our group and find the fellowship of kindred souls," or the ever-present TV appeal, "Thousands of people like you have found. . . ." The appeal also may be more indirect; whenever people recite a creed or credo in church, they affirm not only their common beliefs but also their membership in a group.

Conformity. *"You've got the right one, ba-by!"* For the last two decades, advertisements for soft drinks have worked to convince you that "your kind of person" drinks Coke, Mountain Dew, or Pepsi. "The Pepsi Generation"™ explicitly stressed conformity, and the "You've got the right one, ba-by!" campaign always shows groups of people approving of Ray Charles's endorsement of that cola. Commercials stressing where "the in-group dances," what "the serious jogger wears," and what "all true Americans believe" appeal to you to imitate others and conform to some norm. Extensive social scientific research on the power of *social comparison* and conformity pressures amply documents the power of this appeal.[7]

Deference/Dependence.   *"Nine out of ten doctors recommend. . . ."* When we perceive that others have wisdom, experience, or expertise superior to our own, we defer to their knowledge and even to their judgment. We live in an age of specialized knowledge and, hence, great expertise. This is why testimony is such an important kind of supporting material and why direct appeals to follow the lead of others appear in almost every successful speech.

Sympathy/Generosity.   *"You could be the parent this child has never known for a dollar a day."* Appeals such as this one appear in numerous magazine ads asking you to support efforts to save children around the world through financial foster-parenting. All appeals to giving, to support for others, and to self-sacrifice in the name of the common good are based on the assumption that your *social self* (the part of you that is bonded to others) will overcome your *private self* (the inward-directed part of you). Appeals to a giving motive remind you of your obligations, not to yourself, but to the society of which you're a part.

Loyalty.   *"The camaraderie becomes something that you carry the rest of your life with those individuals. Sometimes you never get a chance to see those individuals again, but in your heart you know you'd do anything for them because they did that for you in a situation which could have gotten them killed."*[8] In these words Vietnam vet Ron Mitscher tried to describe the loyalty he felt to his fellow soldiers. Periodically, these vets celebrate their membership in "the Brotherhood," as they call their group and renew their commitments to each other. Speakers often ask listeners to be loyal to friends, family, organizations, states, geographical regions, and country. Such appeals rarely appear in change-oriented speeches but tend to dominate appeals to those who already share the speaker's beliefs and values. They're typical of *reinforcement speeches.*

Tradition.   *"Let us go forward, determined to serve selflessly a vision of man with God, government for people, and humanity at peace. For it is now our task to tend and preserve, through the darkest and coldest nights, that 'sacred fire of liberty' that President Washington spoke of two centuries ago, a fire that tonight remains a beacon to all the oppressed of the world, shining forth from this kindly, pleasant, greening land we call America."*[9] This appeal, like the one to loyalty, works off the audience's sense of the past, off the listeners' desire to maintain close association with past values, actions, or events. It's little wonder that President Ronald Reagan spoke the words just quoted as part of a speech called "The Conservative Cause." They were conserving words, words that called upon a vision of the past to help form a vision of the present.

Visions of the past, of traditional values, are the foundations of present institutions, which is why politicians, the clergy, bank presidents, and other

Garry Wills Reads Lincoln's Gettysburg Address

[Lincoln] did not come to present a theory, but to impose a symbol, one tested in experience and appealing to national values, with an emotional urgency entirely expressed in calm abstractions (fire in ice). He came to change the world, to effect an intellectual revolution. No other words could have done it. The miracle is that these words did. In his brief time before the crowd at Gettysburg he wove a spell that has not, yet, been broken—he called up a new nation out of the blood and trauma.*

arry Wills also said that "Words were weapons, for him, even though he meant them to be weapons of peace in the midst of war." Much of our speech is flippant, uninspired, meant only to do the mundane work of daily life. But, some occasions— Lincoln at Gettysburg, Martin Luther King, Jr., at the March on Washington, Barbara Jordan at the 1976 Democratic convention—call for words that weave a spell. Such words turn basic appeals into weapons that smite both immediate audiences and those reliving the speech in the future.

* Garry Wills, *Lincoln at Gettysburg: The Words That Remade America* (New York: Simon & Schuster, 1992), 174–75.

institutional representatives never tire of calling it up. The past is stationary, stable; we use it to guide us into the unknown future—hence its great rhetorical strengths. Even those pushing for new ideas often try to ground them in past principles: "This new health insurance plan is simply a modernization and extension of our continuing tradition of concern for the welfare of our workers."

Reverence/Worship. "But in a larger sense we cannot dedicate, we cannot consecrate, we cannot hallow this ground. The brave men, living and dead, who struggled here, have consecrated it far above our power to add or detract."[10] In these words President Abraham Lincoln invoked a sense of reverence for the dead of both the North and South after the bloody battle at Gettysburg, Pennsylvania. In doing so, he recognized ordinary human beings' inferiority—to those who make the supreme sacrifice, to nature and the cosmos, to the deity that humbles us in its magnitude and timelessness. Going beyond deference, the appeal to reverence or worship leads to submission or dependence. Such reverent submission can take three forms: *hero worship, reverence for institutions,* and *divine worship.* As a speaker, you can't really create a sense of reverence in others; but, if you know ahead of time what range of objects, people, and institutions your listeners are likely to revere, you can refer to or describe those subjects. Some of the strongest appeals to reverence these days can be found in environmentalist literature and speeches.

Sexual Attraction.   *"Nothing gets between me and my Calvin's."* With that campaign, Calvin Klein used an appeal that has sold you deodorant, hair rinse and spray, beer and liquor, automobiles—and blue jeans. This particular campaign depended upon an American stock technique, *double entendre.* The "gets between me and my" suggests both brand loyalty and, of course, the sensual appeal of wearing jeans without wearing underwear— a nearly perfect combination of appeals, two for the price of one.

As you look closely at most appeals based on sexual attraction, you'll find their potency lies not so much in their allusion to particular actions as it is in a more general idea of personal physical attractiveness that connects with your desire to imitate or to belong to a select group. In most ads these days, the verbal appeal to sexual attraction is approached indirectly ("When you want to look your best . . ."). Generally, as a speaker you're advised to keep such appeals under firm control; it's too easy to be charged with bad taste or sexism. It is possible to make such appeals responsibly, but you'll have to work at it.

The Achievement Cluster

Achievement motives are focused on individual urges, desires, and goals—a concern for self, for excellence, prestige, success. The fourth and fifth levels of Maslow's hierarchy generally fit here; once your basic physiological and social needs are satisfied, you become centered on personal accomplishment. These motivational appeals are aimed at individual members of the audience.

Acquisition/Saving.   *"Earn good money now in our new Checking-Plus accounts!"* We live in an era of investment clubs, Supplemental Retirement Accounts (SRAs), and more investment counselors than bankers. The appeal to acquire possessions and money is a potent one in our society. *Reward* is the name of many a game, including appeals that are materialistic ("Be the first on your block to own a . . ."), social ("Become one of the select few who . . ."), and spiritual ("Lay up for yourselves treasures in heaven").

Motivational appeals to acquisition target the individual rather than the group; hence they fit into the achievement cluster and are used in speeches calling for personal action.

Success/Display. *"Successful executives carry the Connerton electronic organizer."* "To make maximum use of your talents, act today to . . ." "Be the envy of your neighborhood!" Such appeals depend upon your interest in making a mark, in reaping the reward you deserve because of your talents and abilities. The TV ads that encourage you to read the *Wall Street Journal,* for example, appeal to your desire to successfully control something very complicated and to move your way up the financial and even corporate ladder. Such motivational appeals often appear in speeches in which the speaker's goal is to get listeners to not only be successful but to display that success to others; thus, they are centered on your sense of individuality within specifically defined social contexts.

Pride. *"Be proud of America. Support the troops."* So far as appeals to pride are concerned, the Gulf War of 1991 certainly was a high point in most people's lives. Banners, newspaper and billboard ads, television appeals, and presidential speeches hammered on pride. Over 80 percent of America supported the president's conduct of that operation; the appeal was strong. Appeals to pride tighten our loyalties to others, and when coupled with an appeal to adventure ("Be all that you can be in the Army") or creativity, they can move people to great exertion. Hence, actuative speeches calling for extra effort often contain appeals to pride.

Prestige. *"L'ORÉAL—Because you're worth it!"* As with pride, this appeal is to an individual's sense of worth—to a person's place in a community or within a power structure. Ads for luxury cars, fine clothes, and expensive personal grooming products use the appeal to prestige, implying that owners of these products have reached the high point of their lives. An appeal to listeners' desires for prestige may be associated with affiliation: do listeners value driving a Lexus because they will be seen as members of an elite group, or would they be turned off by such a pitch? You often need to do some audience testing to see how to best couple appeals like that of prestige with others.

Adventure/Change. *"Taste the High Country!"* Beer commercials and recruiters for the armed services ("Join the Navy and see the world!") regularly appeal to adventure. The human soul yearns for escape and release; we seek risk as a way to validate our own worth. In release and risk, however, are potentials for danger, and not every listener is willing to be put into danger. Appeals to adventure are seldom used as a speaker's primary thrust; they tend to work only when individuals are ready for change but still need a nudge to move them to action.

Perseverance.   *"If at first you don't succeed, try, try again."* Pieces of conventional wisdom like this saying recognize that change does not come easily and that individuals must be taught to be patient as they seek a better life. Many motivational appeals tap into the way that people persist, even when change seems impossible. Especially potent are appeals to the future: "We shall overcome" (civil rights song), "Let the word go forth from this time and place . . . that a new generation . . ." (John Kennedy's inaugural address). Visualizing what the future will be like if listeners work hard can be an effective appeal in persuasive speeches, especially ones that promote new ideas.

Creativity.   *"Draw me."* You've seen the ads in magazines: a sketch of a girl or man, perhaps a line drawing of an animal, that you're asked to draw and have evaluated to see if you should enroll in the Famous Artists' School. As Maslow noted, the height of self-actualization is a sense of individualized abilities and talents, and such ads appeal to that need. The appeal is especially great to those for whom creativity is an extraordinarily strong goal. For most listeners, however, this appeal rarely can stand alone. Most ads that challenge your creativity cite not only personal enjoyment but also mention material rewards, suggesting that hidden talents as an illustrator can earn you big money.

Curiosity.   *"Have you ever wondered what a well-trained American student can do to make an African tribal village a better place to live?"* Children take apart alarm clocks to find out where the tick is, and adults crowd sidewalks on a cold day to watch a celebrity filming a movie. Curiosity is sometimes "idle"; more often it's a driving force behind such high achievers as explorers, inventors, scholars, and mountain climbers. Appeals to curiosity, as you might imagine, don't work well with people worried about more basic needs, but, especially with college-aged people or others looking for changes in their lives, it helps you gain and sustain attention.

Personal Enjoyment.   *"Let the good times roll!"* Perhaps the most totally self-centered appeal is the appeal to pleasure. Maximizing one's pleasure, as Freud told us at the beginning of this century, is one of the two (along with avoiding pain) driving forces of the individual. In most persuasive speeches there can be appeals to enjoyment, recreation, rest, relief from home and work pressures, aesthetic pleasure, or just plain fun. Advertisers, politicians, and preachers regularly use this motivational appeal to break through your skepticism.

The Power Cluster

All appeals in the power cluster focus on influence or control over others or the environment. All motives in this group feature appeals to one's place in the social hierarchy, a dominating place. Although people with power motives seek to manipulate or control others, not all uses of power are negative. With power comes social responsibility—the demand that power be used in socially approved ways to benefit the group, community, and society. Actually, it is the relationship between power and affiliation, in McClelland's terms, that determines how constructively power is wielded; one of your ethical challenges is to reconcile appeals to power and affiliation. You'll want to consider that relationship when framing motivational appeals to power.

Aggression.   *"We have not raised armies with ambitious designs of separating from Great Britain and establishing independent States. We fight not for glory or for conquest. We exhibit to mankind the remarkable spectacle of a people attacked by unprovoked enemies, without any imputation or even suspicion of offense."*[11] With these words, John Dickinson, the "Pennsylvania Farmer," as he called himself in pamphlets, urged the colonists to fight back against the British in the spring of 1775. Because human groups tend to be very hierarchical, our biological urge to fight for rights and territory is translated into appeals to personal and social competition. Ad after ad tells you how to "get ahead of the crowd" or "beat the competition to the punch." You must be careful with this appeal, especially when you identify an "enemy." Blatant negative appeals to aggressive action must always be examined for their fairness. If you're too aggressive, the appeal may *boomerang*—generating sympathy for rather than anger against the enemy.[12]

Authority/Dominance.   *"If the FDA [Food and Drug Administration] will not protect us, we must protect ourselves."*[13] When Samantha Hubbard built that argument in a speech attacking the irradiation of food, she was appealing to our natural desire to dominate our environment before it dominates us. The appeal depends on the listeners' willingness to see themselves as stronger or more important than they are now; it taps into a common desire to control our own lives. Thus it is used often in actuative speeches.

Defense.   *"If I were an American, as I am an Englishman, while a foreign troop was landed in my country, I never would lay down my arms— never—never—never!"*[14] In speaking these words when encouraging England to get out of America in 1777, former Prime Minister William Pitt recognized the power of an appeal to a defensive position. The line between attack and self-defense may seem a thin one at times, yet it's important to maintain it. It's seldom socially acceptable to attack someone else for no reason, which Pitt accused the British of doing; defending oneself against the attack of another, on the other hand, is perfectly acceptable in most instances. Thus, President Bush worked hard in 1991 to portray the U.S. role in the Persian Gulf as one of defense rather than offense.

It is usually acceptable to protect one's own interests or "to save the lives of our children and our children's children." Such appeals tap our basic safety needs. The appeal is linked to power in terms of listeners' ability to control their own environment, to exert authority over their collective needs through the defense of vital interests.

Fear. *"Friends don't let friends drive drunk."* This slogan of an extended MADD (Mothers Against Drunk Driving) campaign makes double use of the fear appeal: It appeals to your fear of not being a true friend as well as to your fear of accidents involving drunk drivers. The range of fear appeals is great. Fear can be productive, as when an individual is driven to achievement or acts of courage while under duress. Fear also can be negative, as when fear-based prejudice produces socially unacceptable behavior toward others. The power of fear makes its way into many advertising campaigns: "Speed kills," "Ring around the collar!" "American Express: don't leave home without it." In using fear appeals, stay within the range of acceptable taste; we know that hyper-strong appeals are much less effective than medium-range appeals.[15]

Autonomy/Independence. *"Free should the scholar be—free and brave. Free even to the definition of freedom, 'without any hindrance that does not arise out of his own constitution.'"*[16] When Ralph Waldo Emerson spoke these words a century and a half ago, he was working hard to convince American intellectuals to maximize their independence from European thought. You, too, hear such appeals often: "Be your own person; don't follow the crowd." Appeals to "know yourself" and "be yourself" are like appeals to adventure—both draw their force from our struggles for independent achievement. The expression of individuality is almost always a powerful motive. It works especially well in persuasive speeches in which the speaker asks listeners to commit to a belief or to vote for someone different from all the rest. H. Ross Perot's "independent" presidential campaign in 1992 was based on just such an appeal.

A Final Comment

You may have noticed that some appeals in the three clusters seem to contradict each other. Fear appeals may be to antithetical to adventure; generosity seems opposite to aggression. Of course human beings are bundles of contradictory impulses, balancing urges and making decisions between personal gratification and public good. McClelland's analysis of motive types is based on just such observations of human behavior. Your *ethos*—your ethical standing in a community—is related directly to your choice of motivational appeals. You cannot avoid that fact.

As a result, this discussion of individual motivational appeals is not designed to present the human psyche as if it were orderly and consistent. Rather, we're trying to give you a basic understanding of human motivation and of various kinds of appeals you can use to enhance your rhetorical effectiveness. Even in all of their confusing aspects, humans nonetheless usually act in a motivated way. Hence we turn next to questions concerning the use of these appeals in speech development.

Using Motivational Appeals in Speech Preparation

The material we've discussed thus far raises an extremely important question: *How do you decide which motivational appeals to use in your speech?* That's a difficult question to answer, of course, because so much depends on the specific group of listeners you face, the occasion, and even your own preferences and motives for speaking. In general, however, three factors in the speaking situation should guide your thinking about motivational appeals: (1) the type of speech you are to give, (2) the demographical characteristics of your audience, and (3) your personal predilections.

Throughout the discussion of motivational appeals we've suggested that thinking about the *type of speech* you're delivering helps you select appeals. For example, appeals to individuality often appear in persuasive and actuative speeches, the goals of which are to free people from previous modes of thinking. Suppose you're attempting to persuade your classmates to pursue a flexible Bachelor of General Studies degree instead of the usual B.A. or B.S. The topic is a perfect candidate for appeals to individuality:

Claim: For many students, the B.G.S. is the best available college degree.
1. *[appeal to creativity]* Without a major and with few requirements, the B.G.S. allows you to build a program suited to your individual desires.
2. *[appeal to adventure]* Break away from the crowd and do something unique in structuring your life here.
3. *[appeal to curiosity]* Explore subjects as deeply as you wish.
4. *[appeal to success]* Get a feeling of achievement from designing and completing your own program.

In contrast, speeches can tap into collective motives—tradition, companionship, defense, deference, conformity, and loyalty. When your speech topic depends upon collective action—e.g., asking people to help set up and run a dormitory-based recycling program—your best bets are appeals with an affiliative flavor.

Exploring the *demographic characteristics* of your audience members— their age, educational level, and so on—will also help you sort through possible motivational appeals. As noted, for example, people who have less need to be concerned about survival or safety needs are more likely to respond to appeals to creativity, independence, personal enjoyment, and

Targeting Motivational Appeals

To be successful, motivational appeals must be targeted to the appropriate audience. Advertising campaign experiences offer support for the twin benefits of audience analysis and appropriately devised appeals. For example, when Tostitos was launched as a new product, the target was female heads of households who watched daytime television. The commercials' spokesperson talked to mothers about the quality of Tostitos as a snack for their children. When later research indicated that the primary purchasers were 18-to-34-year-old adults, the ads were changed, and their timing was shifted to approximate the viewing habits of the new target audience. Instead of talking to mothers, the spokesperson talked to characters of popular television series the audience might have watched when they were younger ("Leave It to Beaver," "Mr. Ed"). The commercials aired on such evening television shows as "St. Elsewhere" and "Cheers." Sales doubled.

Over time, a company might wish to keep a particular identity relationship with a particular audience, as in the case of Betty Crocker. Rather than stay with the same "model" of a woman likely to symbolize a consumer of Betty Crocker products, the company has maintained its appeal to traditional values yet updated the image to stay in tune with the times. In a case of identity change, William Underwood altered its "devil"

generosity. As Maslow's hierarchy of prepotency suggests, a speech on urban renewal presented to inner city tenement dwellers should feature discussions of food, shelter, and safety rather than achievement and self-actualization. Younger people are notoriously vulnerable to appeals to sexual attraction and adventure. Appeals to endurance or perseverance are potent with older listeners. Appeals to ethnic traditions and a sense of belonging work well with homogeneous audiences gathered to celebrate such occasions as Hispanic Heritage Week (*Cinco de Mayo*) or Norwegian Independence Day (*Syttende Mai*).

Consider, too, McClelland's analysis of motive types, particularly the relationship between affiliation and power motives. Suppose you're trying to organize a labor union for the nonprofessional employees at your school. Examine the following sets of motive appeals:

Betty Crocker, 1936

Betty Crocker, 1986

trademark for deviled ham—in 1959, the then-ninety-two-year-old symbol was changed from one reflecting an evil image to a "smiling, impish Satan."

These and similar changes by other companies indicate a marked sensitivity to the effectiveness of particular consumer-oriented appeals. Additional examples, such as the changes in prod-uct images for Marlboro cigarettes and Budweiser beer, also suggest a continual search for motivational appeals that will enhance product identification and sales.

FOR FURTHER READING
Cohen, Dorothy. *Advertising.* Glenview, IL: Scott, Foresman and Company, 1988.

On joining the union for reasons of affiliation:
1. [conformity]: All your friends are joining.
2. [dependence]: The union has leaders with the strength to stand up for your rights.
3. [sympathy]: Unions better understand the way you live and what you need than university professors do.

On joining the union for reasons of power:
1. [aggression]: If you don't fight for your rights, who will?
2. [dominance]: With the union, you can take charge of your workplace and run it properly.
3. [fear]: Without a union, you can be dismissed from your job at any time and for any reason.

If you attempt an audience analysis that allows you to estimate the strength of your listeners' affiliative and power motives, you're in a position to structure either one of these speeches. *Never* will it be the case, of course, that the audience is all affiliation- or power-oriented; life's not that simple. But assessing tendencies will help you select the appeals you want to feature.

Finally, always look to your *personal predilections*—your own beliefs, attitudes, and values—when framing motivational appeals. Ask yourself questions like these: "Am I willing to ask people to act out of fear, or am I committed instead to higher motives such as sympathy and generosity?" "Do I actually believe in the importance of loyalty and reverence as they relate to this situation?" Use the appeals that *you* think are important and that *you* can defend to yourself and others.

The speech on pages 151–53 was written by a fourteen-year-old eighth-grade student and presented as part of a citywide oratorical contest in Boston, Massachusetts. While there are some technical problems with the speech (the language is unsophisticated and the level of thought development is well below that of college students), it nonetheless contains a powerful message. Note particularly how the girl uses motivational appeals: does she make a powerful indirect appeal to achievement by telling a story that illustrates its opposite? How does Maslow's hierarchy or prepotency relate to this speech? What does the narrative (story-telling) structure add to the strength and force of the appeals?

Combining Motivational Appeals

As we've suggested throughout this chapter, you can unify motivational appeals to aim them at homogeneous audiences or you can diversify them to target segments of your listeners. Targeting strategies can be seen in the following arguments for a speech by a travel agent urging students to take a summer trip to Europe:

[acquisition and savings]	I.	The tour is being offered for a low price of $2000 for three weeks.
[independence]	II.	There'll be a minimum of supervision and regimentation.
[companionship]	III.	You'll be traveling with friends and fellow students.

In this example, you have one motivational appeal each from the achievement, power, and affiliation clusters.

If you're appealing to self-centered interests—to private fears, monetary gain, acquisition, or pride—recognize that people may not wish to acknowledge that these motivations underlie their actions. For example, even though some people contribute to charitable causes to get tax deductions, this probably isn't the rationale they want to acknowledge publicly. As a

A Much More Meaningful Life
Shanita Horton

My name is Shanita Horton and I am a black, fourteen-year-old young lady living in the city of Boston. I have a lot to say about drugs and crime. Drugs are one of Boston's major problems and also has affected me personally. /1

I have firsthand experience on the devastating dangers of drugs because some-one real close to me has been addicted. She started drinking at the age of seventeen and stayed drunk most of the time, not really caring about herself or anyone else. /2

By the age of twenty, alcohol no longer gave her the feeling she needed so she began smoking marijuana and heroin. She had a little girl now to take care of which she really could not do that well because she was high most of the time. /3

So she let the little girl go live with her grandmother. Now she had no one to take care of but herself and things really started to go downhill. Being under-educated and having no job to support her habit, she had begun a life of crime. Her criminal activities resulted in her going to MCI-Framingham. /4

At the age of twenty-two she had given birth to another little girl. When that little girl was two months old she went to live with her godmother because her own mother was on her way back to Framingham prison. How can one's life continue on such a destructive merry-go-round, never getting better, always worse? /5

At the age of twenty-four not only was she in jail again but she had given birth to another little boy while she was in there. This little boy was born with webbed hands and feet but he is now six years old and has had surgery on his hands. But there's nothing they can do with his feet. Can you imagine how embarrassing that will be when he gets older and his friends start talking about where they were born? /6

Luckily for this little boy, he went to live with his grandmother and older sister. Because of the lady's continued destructive behavior, her oldest daugh-ter, at the age of twelve, decided to commit suicide and end it all. She took a lot of pain killers and passed out. Luckily for the little girl, she did not die and older people in the community gave her extra support. /7

This lady I'm talking about is now thirty-one years old and things aren't any better. She was released from Framingham prison for the umpteenth time about a year ago. It was on a Thursday that she came home. Saturday, two days later, she was rushed to Boston City Hospital on an overdose of heroin. /8

Drugs and crime broke this lady's family apart. The only reason I know the story so well is because this lady is my mother. /9

My mother's life will soon be ending because she is dying of AIDS. But because of the grace of God and because of some other people that believe in me and encourage me to realize my fullest potential, I will have a much more meaningful life than my mother. /10

So even though I cannot change what has happened in the past, I can always want a much more positive future because I do believe everyone has something positive to contribute to society. /11

I wrote this speech prior to my mother's recent passing. She died on March 31 and I would like to dedicate this to her memory. Thank you very much. /12

Shanita Horton, "A Much More Meaningful Life," *Boston Sunday Globe,* 22 May 1988.

speaker, therefore, you usually need to combine more selfish with more selfless appeals: "Your tax-deductible contribution to the Suicide Hotline will save countless lives next year" [*acquisition plus sympathy*].

The Appropriate Use of Motivational Appeals

Using motivational appeals with tact and judgment is important to your speechmaking success. The appropriateness of any motivational appeal generally depends upon (1) your speech purpose, (2) expectations arising in the audience on this particular occasion, and (3) your beliefs and values. Some additional communication rules can guide your selection and use of motivational appeals:

1. *Avoid blatant or overly aggressive appeals.* Don't say, "Mr. Henry Hawthorne, the successful banker, has just contributed handsomely to our cause. Come on, now. Imitate this generous and community-spirited man!" Better in most situations is something like, "Local banker Henry Hawthorne has started the ball rolling with his contribution—now it's your turn!" Don't insult your audience's intelligence; be tactful.

2. *Organize your appeals effectively.* When should you introduce a powerful appeal, at the beginning or the end of a speech? While this question can't be answered definitively, it's one you need to consider. If listeners need to be jolted out of a lethargic or indifferent state, you may need a strong opening appeal. On the other hand, if listeners are ready to do something about a problem, you're well advised to build toward a climax, saving your big appeal for the end so as to channel their enthusiasm in the preferred direction. (See Chapter 8 for more help here.)

3. *Use motivational appeals judiciously.* There's no rule about how many appeals a speech should contain. Two primary considerations are (a) the amount of time you have to develop your argument and your viewpoints and (b) the degree of audience approval or disapproval. If time is short,

Your Ethical Boundaries

What are your ethical limits? What are the appeals *you* wouldn't make? Consider the following examples:

1. In 1988 George Bush attacked Michael Dukakis for being governor of a state with a furlough program that let criminals out of jail on weekends. Some of those released were accused of rape and other crimes. Dukakis indeed was governor in Massachusetts when that program was functioning, though he later stopped it. Would you hold him accountable for the criminals' behavior?

2. In 1988 Michael Dukakis attacked George Bush for picking J. Danforth Quayle as his vice-presidential running mate, saying that five times in this century the vice president has had to take over as president and accusing Bush of showing bad judgment. Would you have attacked Bush in this manner, accusing (without saying so) his running mate of gross incompetence?

3. In 1992, the United States signed all of the environmental treaties put forth at the Rio de Janiero international conference save one—the treaty encouraging biodiversity. Instead, the president of the United States pledged $150 million to be spent on biodiversity projects and said the United States would con-

tinue to support such projects, but could not tie up all of its economic interests in a pledge. Would you have attacked President Bush?

4. Would you show third-graders pictures of mouth sores and completely decayed teeth as a way of getting them to brush and floss better?

5. Would you threaten grandmothers with loss of their life savings if they don't move their money out of savings and loans and into a "safe" bank?

6. Would tell your classmates that they can earn up to five thousand dollars a month selling encyclopedias, even though commissions average only three hundred dollars a month?

Sometimes, as we've suggested in this chapter, audiences will rise up in protest when your appeals become too sleazy, although it's sometimes amazing how much tolerance listeners and viewers seem to have. Even when audiences don't appear to complain, however, you must remember your reputation: your credibility, your *ethos,* is created largely by what you say and by what others think about what you say.

Know your own limits. In that way, you're not going to be surprised when listeners question your motives. Be ready to defend your choices. In the process, anything you do to promote the common good and the basic humanity of others will earn you many points in life.

you're probably better off fully developing two or three lines of motivation instead of shooting off half a dozen appeals. If listeners already are positively predisposed, you'll need fewer direct motivational appeals so you can concentrate principally on those designed to spur action. Conversely, if listeners are hostile, you'll probably want to segment the audience and offer various appeals to individual segments, as was suggested in Chapter 5.

You may even wish to make one appeal into a kind of theme or refrain, letting it hold others together. This technique was used recently by United Way: "Thanks to you, it works—for all of us" *[success plus generosity]*. They could then work into their ads various other appeals—to generosity, tradition, companionship, creativity, pride—as parts of the messages. The refrain, like an advertiser's slogan, held the whole series together, making the entire ad campaign present a single view of giving.

4. *Use appeals ethically.* Even in a free society, there are ethical boundaries that, when crossed by an overzealous speaker, produce public condemnation. So, while presidential political campaigns are filled with attacks on the opposition, anyone who goes too far is likely to be reprimanded. When Mary Matalin, the deputy manager of the Bush-Quayle campaign in 1992, attacked the Clinton-Gore campaign for its "unprecedented hypocrisy" and suggested that Clinton may have been guilty of marital infidelity, her innuendo got an apology even from President Bush for having gone too far.[17] The social penalties for overstepping moral boundaries can be severe, and you must decide the degree to which you're willing to risk social censure for the positions you take and the ways you advocate them.

Chapter Summary

One can think of motives as *springs*—needs or desires tightly coiled and waiting for the right appeal or verbal depiction to set them off. When worked by a skillful speaker, these motives can convert the individuals in an audience into a cohesive group ready to think and act in ways consistent with your purpose. Motives are either *biological needs* or *social motives*; all are *dynamic*. Motives also are interactively related to each other; they are *clustered* into *affiliation, achievement,* and *power* groups (McClelland) and organized into a *hierarchy of prepotency* (Maslow). Considering the *type of speech, audience demographics,* and *personal predilections* help a speaker select motivational appeals. When selecting motivational appeals for your speeches, avoid *blatant appeals, organize* appeals effectively, select an *appropriate number of appeals,* and use them in *ethically sound ways.*

References

1. Katherine Blick Hoyenga and Kermit T. Hoyenga, *Motivational Explanations of Behavior: Evolutionary, Physiological, and Cognitive Ideas* (Monterey, CA: Brooks/Cole, 1984), ch. 1. Psychologists are divided over several important issues. For example, some argue that all motives are innate (Maslow's theory assumes motives are instinctual), while others (e.g., McClelland) argue that at least some are learned. (See citations below.) Likewise, psychologists differ on the issue of conscious awareness of motives: are we aware of the drive, and if not, how do we control it? We won't get into such controversies but take the position that, whether innate or learned, conscious or not, motives are the *foundations for motivational appeals* and, hence, are reasons for action; it's that characteristic that makes them important to the student of public speaking.

2. Hoyenga and Hoyenga; Donald R. Brown and Joseph Verloff, eds. *Frontiers of Motivational Psychology: Essays in Honor of John W. Atkinson* (New York: Springer-Verlag, 1986); Abigail J. Stewart, ed., *Motivation and Society: A Volume in Honor of David C. McClelland* (San Francisco: Jossey-Bass, 1982); Janet T. Spence, ed., *Achievement and Achievement Motives* (San Francisco: W. H. Freeman, 1983).

3. Abraham Maslow, *Motivation and Personality*, 2nd ed. (New York: Harper & Row, 1970). In the 1970 revision, Maslow identifies two additional desires—to know and understand and an aesthetic desire—as higher states. These frequently operate as part of the satisfaction of self-actualization, and hence we've included them in that category.

4. For a discussion of motivation and attribution, see Hoyenga and Hoyenga. To review attribution theory and communication studies more generally, see Alan L. Sillars, "Attribution and Communication: Are People 'Naive Scientists' or Just Naive?" in Michael E. Roloff and Charles R. Berger, eds., *Social Cognition and Communication* (Beverly Hills: Sage Publishing, 1982), 73–106.

5. To understand the power of verbal depiction, read Michael Osborn, "Rhetorical Depiction," in *Form, Genre, and the Study of Political Discourse,* eds. Herbert W. Simons and Aram A. Aghazarian (Charleston: University of South Carolina Press, 1986), 79–107.

6. Hoyenga and Hoyenga, ch. 4. A classic work on affiliation is Stanley Schachter, *The Psychology of Affiliation: Experimental Studies of the Sources of Gregariousness* (Stanford, CA: Stanford University Press, 1959).

7. For discussions of conformity and social comparison theory, see Mary John Smith, *Persuasion and Human Action: A Review and Critique of Social Influence Theories* (Belmont, CA: Wadsworth, 1982), esp. chs. 7 and 11.

8. From an interview with Ron Mitscher, Vietnam vet, for *Parallels: The Soldiers' Knowledge and the Oral History of Contemporary Warfare,* ed. J. T. Hansen, A. Susan Owen, and Michael Patrick Madden (New York: Aldine de Gruyter, 1992), 137.

9. Ronald Reagan, "The Conservative Cause," speech delivered in 1982, in *Presidential Rhetoric (1961– to the Present),* ed. Theodore Windt, 4th ed. (Dubuque, IA: Kendall/Hunt, 1987), 316.

10. Abraham Lincoln, "Gettysburg Address," speech delivered in 1863, reprinted in Gary Wills, *Lincoln at Gettysburg: The Words That Remade America* (New York: Simon & Schuster, 1992), 261. This is what Wills calls the "spoken text" rather than the "final text." His book provides a fascinating account of the speech's development, delivery, and later course through history.

11. John Dickinson, "The Declaration on Taking Up Arms," speech delivered 6 July 1775, in *The World's Best Orations*, ed. David J. Brewer (St. Louis: Ferd. P. Kaiser, 1899), 5:1855.

12. For a description of the boomerang effect, see Stephen W. Littlejohn and David M. Jabusch, *Persuasive Transactions* (Glenview, IL: Scott, Foresman, 1987), 79, 92.

13. From Samantha L. Hubbard, "Irradiation of Food," speech reprinted in Bruce E. Gronbeck, et al., *Principles of Speech Communication*, 11th brief ed. (New York: HarperCollins Publishers, 1992), 354.

14. William Pitt [the Elder], "The Attempt to Subjugate America," speech delivered in 1777, reprinted in *The World's Best Orations*, ed. David J. Brewer (St. Louis: Ferd. P. Kaiser, 1899), 3:1070.

15. On fear appeals, see Erwin P. Bettinghaus and Michael J. Cody, *Persuasive Communication*, 4th ed. (New York: Holt, Rinehart & Winston, 1987), 158–61; See also Hoyenga and Hoyenga, 154–67.

16. Ralph Waldo Emerson, "The American Scholar," speech delivered in 1837, reprinted in Brewer, 10:2005.

17. "Bush Aide Apologizes for Mudslinging," *The Daily Iowan* August 4, 1992, 5.

Key Terms

achievement motives (p. 134)   motives (p. 132)
affiliation motives (p. 134)   motive cluster (p. 138)
attribution process (p. 136)   power motives (p. 134)
biological need (p. 133)   social motives (p. 133)
hierarchy of prepotency (p. 134)   visualization process (p. 136)
motivational appeal (p. 136)

Problems and Probes

1. Examine the series of advertisements included in this chapter. What are the major motivational appeals used to entice consumer approval and affect behavior? Are the appeals well suited to your interests as a potential consumer? Note that a motivational appeal may be used both in an illustration and in printed form to reinforce each other and the appeal of the ad as a whole. Be prepared to discuss your evaluations in a small group setting during class and to contribute to general class discussion on the effectiveness of the various appeals.
2. What relevant motivational appeals might you use in addressing each of the following audiences? Be ready to discuss your choices in class.
a. A group of farmers protesting federal agricultural policy
b. A meeting of prebusiness majors concerned about jobs
c. Women at a seminar on nontraditional employment opportunities

d.   A meeting of local elementary and secondary classroom teachers seeking smaller classes
e.   A group gathered for an old-fashioned Fourth of July picnic
3. Bring to class examples of at least five different motivational appeals excerpted from a speech or speeches. What are the appeals, and how are they used in the context of the entire speech? Do they add to or detract from the speaker's persuasive effort? What other appeals, given the situation, might the speaker have used? Combine your examples and analysis in a brief written report.

Communication Activities

1. Present a 3-to-4-minute speech in which, through the combined use of three related motivational appeals, you attempt to persuade your audience to accept a particular belief or engage in a specific action. (For example, combine appeals to adventure, companionship, and personal enjoyment to persuade listeners to go on a group tour of Europe, or combine sympathy and pride to elicit contributions to a charity drive being conducted by a campus group.) At the conclusion of your speech, ask a classmate to identify the motivational appeals you used. If other class members disagree with that identification, explore with the class the reasons your appeals did not come through as you intended and what you might have done to strengthen their impact.
2. In a small group class discussion, talk about some principles or guidelines that might differentiate ethical from unethical appeals. In the course of the discussion, answer the following questions: (a) Under what conditions would you consider a motivational appeal to listeners' needs or desires an entirely ethical and legitimate means of persuasion? (b) Under what conditions might the same appeal be considered unethical or inappropriate? (c) Where does the ethical responsibility rest: with the speaker, with the audience, or in adherence to a list of external criteria (any of these, all of these)?
3. Assume you have a friend who is considering dropping out of school. Which motivational appeal would you use to convince your friend to continue his or her education if you wanted to direct those appeals to your friend's desire for affiliation, achievement, or power? Do the same with Maslow's hierarchy of needs and desires. What factors are helpful in distinguishing among these general clusters or levels of motives? Illustrate your appeals with specific examples or statements. Discuss your results with classmates in a small group setting during class.

7

Developing Ideas:
Finding and Using
Supporting Materials

B eing an effective speaker depends on more than an analysis of audience and occasion. You also must have something to say. The collection of substantive materials to fill out and support your ideas is at the core of the speech preparation process. If your purpose is to explain how students can obtain summer internships, for example, you can't simply assert the central idea "Summer internship opportunities are all around you." You must make the idea concrete through the use of clear examples of internships easily available to the students. Similarly, if you wish to argue "Nuclear power is a safe means of providing cheap electricity," you need to be able to define what you mean by "safe" and "cheap" in the context of other alternatives for providing electricity. In this case, the claim calls for statistical evidence on the likelihood of another Three Mile Island disaster, and on how nuclear power compares cost-wise to other alternatives.

The forms of supporting materials identified in this chapter, therefore, are the medium of exchange between your ideas and your audience. While the motive appeals discussed in Chapter 6 assist you in tying ideas and proposals to motives for human action, clear and compelling supporting materials bring your ideas to life. In both cases, motivational appeals and supporting materials must be seen by the audience as relevant to their needs, whether the task is to understand, to be persuaded, or to act.

The forms of supporting material discussed in this chapter function to *amplify, clarify, or justify the beliefs, attitudes, and values you wish to convey to your audience.* This chapter will first define and illustrate commonly used forms of supporting materials, then consider where these may be found. Finally, we'll consider ways these may be recorded and used to further your central ideas and claims.

What to Look For: Forms of Supporting Materials

The most commonly used supporting materials fall into six general categories: (1) explanation, (2) comparison/contrast, (3) illustration (hypothetical/factual), (4) specific instance, (5) statistics, and (6) testimony.

Explanation

An **explanation** is a description or expository passage that makes a term, concept, process, or proposal clear or acceptable. Explanations tell what, how, or why; they are useful in showing the relationship between a whole and its parts. They may also make it easier to understand concepts that are difficult to envision or grasp. As with other forms of support, explanations have to be well reasoned and clearly presented in order to be understood.

Explanations of "What."   Explanation may assist you in telling an audience what something is by giving meaning to previously unknown events, situations, or concepts. Student speaker Mary Hoffman offered the following description of the fillings you get when you have a tooth cavity:[1]

> Silver-amalgam fillings, the dull silverish fillings that many of us have in our mouths, have been in use for more than one hundred and fifty years, according to the October 15, 1990, issue of *Newsweek*. Silver amalgam is really only 35 percent silver and 50 percent mercury. The compound also contains zinc, copper, and tin. This combination of metals is used because it is both strong and durable. Fillings must withstand the stress of constant chewing, and silver amalgam is well suited to handle that pressure.

Having explained what the compound contained, Hoffman went on to argue that the mercury in fillings is potentially dangerous to our health.

At the same time, a brief explanation can do more than tell "what" something is. By illustrating why silver amalgam contains the properties it does, Mary Hoffman also answers an implicit audience question—why should it be used?

An explanation can be more lengthy when the picture a speaker wants to develop is complex. Wendy Liebmann, President of WSL Marketing, develops the image of the future in her depiction of twenty-first–century America in a speech before the "Drug Store of the Future" Symposium:[2]

> Picture it. *Twenty-first century* America. It will begin as an age of immigration. People will flock to her shores from Haiti and Cuba, from Mexico and

China, from Hong Kong and Uzbekistan. Sometimes by choice. Often by necessity. Often through no free will of their own.

Arriving in their millions, they will land in Los Angeles, Seattle, Miami, and stay just where they land, in a ghetto-like community reminiscent of their homeland.

Like their 20th century counterparts, they will come looking for the American Dream. A chance to work for a living, to earn enough to feed their families, to practice their own religion, and hold their own political views—with no fear of persecution. They will come to be Americans. But different Americans, diverse Americans, maintaining a strong sense of their own heritage and the character of the land from which they came.

They will *not* assimilate as fast as they can learn the language. In fact, English will never be their primary language. They will be proud of their national tongue.

They will not cast off their foreign ways. They will not dress like Americans, eat like Americans, speak like Americans, live like Americans, as those in the 20th century. Instead they will retain the essence of their own distinctive culture.

By showing that the American culture of the next century will be an ethnic mosaic, Liebmann underscores the need for businesses to adapt to the needs of diverse cultures. In so doing, she offers a clear picture of "what" the American experience will be like in the early years of the next century and beyond.

Explanations of "How."   Explaining how something works or is done is another way to support ideas. If your central idea is to explain the process of chair caning, as was P. Dorothy Gilbert's, the task could be completed as she did:

The intricate patterns of cane or reed you see on chair seats make the process seem mysterious and all too artistic for most of us. On the contrary, as I will demonstrate to you today, anyone can learn to cane a chair in order to restore a valuable antique or to save a family heirloom. Chair-caning involves five easy-to-learn steps. First, soak the cane to make it pliable; then, clean out the holes through which the cane will be stretched. Next, weave the cane or reed through the holes in four to seven operations. Fourth, tie off the pieces of cane underneath the chair. Finally, lace a heavier piece of cane over the holes to cover them. Let me describe each step, one at a time.

Explanations of "Why."   Explanations that account for a thing's existence or for a certain state of affairs are common in persuasive and actuative speeches. Giving reasons for why something exists or what forces cause its occurrence lays the foundation for proposing solutions. If we understand why something happens, we're better prepared to deal with its effects and the appropriateness of potential remedies. For example, this argument was presented by LaDonna Harris, speaking as president of Americans for Indian Opportunity:[3]

Explanations of how things work, with demonstrations of portions of a total process, can help increase audience attention and interest.

Basically, the dominant society in the United States does not believe in the continued existence of tribal peoples, societies and governments. The assumption continues to be that Indians, belonging, as it were, to societies at a more primitive stage of evolution than Euro-American society, will eventually be absorbed in the Euro-American "melting pot." Somehow, it's anathema to the dominant U.S. psyche for a person to choose to maintain his or her group identity. Differentness, perhaps because of the fear of "mixed loyalties" generated by the country's immigrant history, is seen almost as unpatriotic, as un-American. Perhaps it is because many immigrant Americans gave up their group identities, they gave up who they were, that they have this messianic need for tribal people to give up who they are, to give up their group identity.

This explanation clarifies why, in Harris's view, forces are at work to assimilate Native Americans into mainstream society rather than respect their differentness. She offers a reason for society's failure to recognize the Native Americans' right to pursue their own culture. In addition, her discussion draws on independence versus conformity as specific motivational appeals.

You'll find an explanation of "how" in Brooke Anderson's discussion of Semtex's properties. Following her description, Anderson went on to explain why someone could pass through airport security so easily with a device containing the plastic explosive:[4]

> It [Semtex] is virtually invisible to an x-ray. The x-ray machines in airports do not show plastics clearly, and the explosives are so chemically stable, that until detonation they don't even give off a detectable vapor. Plastic explosives absorb more low energy x-rays which are less penetrating than high energy x-rays, which is why a plastic bomb can pass right through x-ray detection devices without the operator batting an eye of suspicion.

There are general guidelines for using explanations. Keep your explanations relatively brief and to the point. Complex, detailed explanations may be more accurate, but they may also confuse your audience. Second, keep your explanations concrete. Specific images and examples, references to size or color, and relating the unknown to the familiar are ways to help an audience "see" what you are explaining. Finally, combine explanations with other forms of supporting material. In the example cited above, Harris went on to define what it means to be tribal by citing specific instances: "one cannot be 'an Indian.' One is a Comanche, an Oneida, a Hopi. One can be self-determining, not as 'an Indian,' but as a Comanche, an Oneida, etc."[5]

Comparison/Contrast

Comparison or **analogy** points out similarities between something that listeners already know, understand, or believe and something that they don't. For instance, you might explain the game of cricket to an American audience by comparing it with baseball, or explain how you can mold Semtex by comparing it to modeling clay. Analogies may be either *figurative* or *literal*.

Figurative Analogies/Comparisons.   These forms of support involve phenomena that, though basically different, exhibit comparable properties or relationships. **Figurative analogies** function especially well in clarifying ideas or concepts. Dr. Louis Hadley Evans, minister-at-large for the Presbyterian Church, drew these figurative analogies to distinguish between the terms "deist" and "theist":[6]

> To you the world is what: a clock or a car? Is it a huge clock, that God once made, that He wound up at the beginning and left it to run of itself? Then you are a *deist*. Do you believe that it is rather a car that God once made, but that does not run without His hand on the wheel, without His ultimate and personal control? Then you are a *theist*.

In this example, the speaker clarified two terms and an abstract concept (God) by comparing two machines whose operation is familiar to the audience. The notion of independence (clock) vs. dependence (car) helped the audience discriminate between two terms whose meaning may be either unknown or unclear.

As another example of comparing unlike things, consider Lincoln's answer to critics of his administration's policies during the darkest days of the Civil War. Lincoln compared the government's plight with that of the legendary tightrope walker, Blondin, in crossing the Niagara River:

> Gentlemen, I want you to suppose a case for a moment. Suppose that all the property you were worth was in gold, and you had put it in the hands of Blondin, the famous rope-walker, to carry across the Niagara Falls on a tightrope. Would you shake the rope while he was passing over it, or keep shouting to him, "Blondin, stoop a little more! Go a little faster!" No, I am sure you would not. You would hold your breath as well as your tongue, and keep your hands off until he was safely over. Now the government is in the same situation. It is carrying an immense weight across a stormy ocean. Untold treasures are in its hands. It is doing the best it can. Don't badger it! Just keep still, and it will get you safely over.

Comparing things that are unlike one another is an excellent means of clarification. Lincoln's analogy functions well for those convinced of its accuracy; they would be more likely to leave his administration alone lest it fall. Such analogies may be vivid and memorable, but they have limited value in justifying a claim. Those who reject the similarity argued in Lincoln's comparison could simply respond that they wouldn't give Blondin their gold in the first place, thus rejecting Lincoln's argument.

Literal Analogies/Comparisons.   If your purpose is to show why a claim should be accepted or an action taken, it's more effective to compare phenomena that are *alike*, using **literal analogies**. Thus, you might argue that placement of a homeless shelter in the community will not be harmful to the local residents because similar shelters have been created in other communities without producing negative effects.

In another setting, John Jacob, president and CEO of the National Urban League, outlined the Marshall Plan for America that had been proposed by the League:[7]

> One of the vehicles to move toward parity can be the Urban League's Marshall Plan for America.
> It's an outgrowth of our history and our mission. Back in the 1960s the then head of the National Urban League, Whitney M. Young, Jr., called for a Domestic Marshall Plan of investments in social and economic programs to help black people overcome centuries of oppression and disadvantage.
> His model was the Marshall Plan of the late 1940s, when the U. S. sent billions to rebuild Europe after World War II. . . . That Marshall Plan worked—but America never implemented Whitney's domestic Marshall Plan. If it had, many of today's problems would not exist. But it's not too late to learn from the mistakes of the past.

By calling forth the benefits of the postwar Marshall Plan and by linking the League's proposal by name to that program, Jacob goes a long way toward establishing the intent of his literal analogy.

Because it attempts to base a conclusion on a parallel instance, an analogy used as proof must meet a rigorous test: *the instances compared must be closely similar in all essential respects.* In Jacob's case, the audience must see major similarities in the goals and potential outcomes before acting on a domestic Marshall Plan. If the audience sees large differences between the situations, the argument is weakened considerably. In essence, audiences are faced with the question of whether the similarities outweigh the inevitable differences. You must answer this question clearly when you construct an analogy as justification for a claim.

Contrast.   **Contrast**, on the other hand, focuses on differences between things. In this example, Harris extends her explanation by contrasting the dominant view with that of "tribalness":[8]

> The tribal concept as regards differences is quite contrastive to the Euro-American one. Differentness, rather than being seen as a problem to be eradicated, is seen as a contribution to the whole. In tribal society the group does not dominate the individual, it nurtures individuals so that strong, idiosyncratic individuals contribute to the strength of the group. Each person's understanding, each person's perception from his or her place in the universe enables the group to make better decisions. Difference does not equate good/bad, better/best, hierarchy, domination and conflict. Difference is coordinated in terms of contributions made toward the good of the whole.

In presenting twin explanations of what it means to be Euro-American and tribal, Harris is better able to move on to a fuller explanation of the dilemmas faced by tribal peoples.

Contrast effectively supports specific arguments aimed at demonstrating the presence or absence of progress or change. For example, Janet Martin, vice president of a Canadian bank, CIBC, used contrasting examples to show the progress women have made:[9]

> Even in traditionally male-dominated fields of study such as engineering, women have increased their numbers. The 1970 undergraduate class at the University of Toronto's faculty of engineering included 33 women—just slightly over one percent of the students. In the 1990 class, there were 465 women or almost 17 percent.

Martin went on to illustrate that other industries had analogous results in the employment opportunities for women. For instance, she indicates that where only 33 percent of middle managers in banking were women in 1986, by 1992 that number increased to 48 percent. In this way, Martin effectively integrates an achievement motive appeal and evidence to support the claim that things are better than they were (though she does go on to note that senior management positions still elude large numbers of women).

Comparison and Contrast Used in Combination. Comparison and contrast also work in concert to strengthen an argument. For example, former U.S. Secretary of Health, Education, and Welfare Joseph A. Califano, Jr., traveled the country, addressing audiences composed of both smokers and nonsmokers. By combining comparisons and contrasts, he warned the smokers and psychologically reinforced the nonsmokers in this fashion:[10]

> The tragic consequences of [smoking] are dramatically evident if we compare the later health consequences of smoking for two sixteen-year-olds: one who smokes a pack a day and one who does not. According to one estimate, the sixteen-year-old smoker has one chance in ten of developing a serious lung disease: lung cancer, emphysema, or chronic bronchitis, for example—providing he or she manages to avoid a crippling or killing heart attack. By contrast, the nonsmoker will have one chance in one hundred of contracting a serious lung disease, and will have only half the risk of the smoker of suffering a heart attack.

When analogy or comparison and contrast are used in a speech, they add vividness to the ideas that are represented.

Illustration

An **illustration** is a detailed example in narrative form. It may be used to describe in detail conditions as they now exist or to picture the results of adopting the proposal you advocate. An illustration has two principal characteristics: (1) it uses *narrative form*—recounting a happening or retelling a story; and (2) it contains vividly described *details*. There are two types of illustrations: hypothetical, describing an imaginary situation, and factual, describing an actual happening.

Hypothetical Illustration. An imagined narrative, a **hypothetical illustration** is believable if its details are consistent with known facts. An audience will judge the illustration on the presumed likelihood of its actually occurring. Wendy Liebmann used this technique successfully to describe the scene a twenty-first–century consumer would face: [11]

> Picture it. A 21st century retailer where *selection* of merchandise defines the image, credibility and essence of the store. No longer the same merchandise

replicated store after store after store as in the 20th century. Instead a tightly tailored mix defined by the nature of the store and the community in which it operates.

Picture it. An apparel store designed to attract value-conscious, style-conscious consumers. A narrow mix of quality fashion basics in multiple colors and fabrications. No sales. Just everyday great values.

A quick and easy store to shop. A mistake-proof selection. Mix anything with everything for faultless fashion. A constant change in mix of merchandise to pique the shopper's interest. Need help, just ask and it's there. A different size, a different color, a different fabric. Not in that store. Not in another store. "We'll special order it from our factory." And it will be delivered to your door, within days, free of charge.

In creating a hypothetical illustration, you can manipulate facts at will, as long as your construction remains plausible to your audience. In Liebmann's illustration, the value lies in believing that such a scenario of marketing and consumer tastes would in fact be possible, let alone desirable. She structures her speech with this scenario in mind. Her consistent and prolonged narrative provides a well-balanced, comprehensive picture of life in the next century. Given that her audience is attending a symposium on "The Drug Store of the Future," it's evident that such an approach is highly relevant; the audience is more predisposed to listen to such scenarios than a different audience might be. The illustration fits the occasion.

A hypothetical illustration also is useful in explaining how something is done; you can create a person, then picture that individual going through the steps of the process. If you want to engage the audience even more, select the name of an audience member for your imaginary situation. Although the hypothetical illustration may set up your premise, it falls short of justifying it. Because you can manipulate the details of your illustration, the audience may be understandably reluctant to accept your premise just on your say-so. In her presentation, Liebmann prefaced her construction of a 21st-century store with the argument that cultural diversity would be the norm, that the "melting pot" idea is fast becoming an obsolete and inaccurate description of the American culture. In so doing, she prepared her audience for highly stylized stores catering to the needs of specific communities, rather than simply merchandising fashions for "everyone."

Factual Illustration.   A **factual illustration** is a narrative that describes in detail a situation or incident that has occurred. Because details are brought into the story and because the incident actually happened, factual illustration frequently has high persuasive value. In a speech calling attention to the trend toward hospitalizing troubled youths, student speaker Todd LaSala tells the following story:[12]

"They put me on drugs right away," remembers then 13-year-old Cynthia Parker. "They told me I was depressed, and then they told me I was suicidal.

That really threw me. . ." Ms. Parker had just been admitted to a private psychiatric hospital in Minnesota. There she was immediately bombarded by strong medications, placed in a windowed observation room where therapists could peer in at any time, and disciplined by being rolled up in a blue gymnasium mat. Cynthia was institutionalized for neglecting her homework, failing to clean her room and picking fights with her sister. Now I don't know about you, but I would hardly call that a "conduct disorder," I would call it adolescence.

Implicit in this illustration is an appeal to sympathy—listeners could identify with the kind of actions Cynthia Parker committed, and sympathize with her plight. LaSala goes on to provide additional examples of the trend in support of his claim that this was not always the most appropriate response to the needs of troubled youth. His narrative stimulates interest and attention to the additional examples and lends strong support to his claim.

Keep three considerations in mind when selecting an illustration, whether hypothetical or factual:

1. *Is it clearly related to the idea it is intended to support?* If the connection is difficult to perceive, its impact on the audience will be far less than you desire and the illustration won't accomplish your purpose.

2. *Is it a fair example?* An audience can be quick to notice when the example seems farfetched or out of character with the kinds of situations or events they're familiar with. Believability is even more crucial when your illustration is hypothetical. If your illustration truly is the exception to the norm, you'll have to show how it's possible for that scenario to exist despite audience belief to the contrary.

3. *Is it vivid and impressive in detail?* If this quality is absent, you lose the advantage of using an illustration, so be sure your illustrations are expressed in concrete, compelling language.

When you and your audience can answer all three questions in the affirmative, you can rest assured that your illustrations will have a solid, positive impact; they'll support your central ideas or claims.

Specific Instances

A **specific instance** is an *undeveloped* illustration or example. Instead of describing a situation in detail, you simply refer to it in passing. The reference should be to an event, person, place, or process that your audience already is familiar with, or can readily comprehend if the information is new. For example, Cinda Schmechel opened her speech with the following reference: "A tall glass of ice water. Nothing can beat the clear and natural taste of it on a steamy August day."[13] The quick reference achieved her goal of gaining attention as well as orienting her audience to the topic: the potential shortage of clean water and its consequences.

Specific instances most often are used to make an idea clear and understandable, or to add punch to a particular claim. Listing specific instances helps you create the impression that the issue is significant, is widespread, or is worthy of consideration. Henri Mann Morton used specific instances to illustrate the central role played by Native Americans:[14]

> We must remember that—
> America's first cultures were Native American.
> America's first workforce was Native American.
> America's first men were Native American.
> And America's first women were Native American.

With these statements, she adds vivid force to the claim that Native Americans have an important cultural legacy in their own right. The listing needs to be supplemented with additional proof. When the examples are not as familiar to the audience or reader, the speaker remains vulnerable to the charge that the instances are nonrepresentative or nonsignificant.

Statistics

Not all numbers are **statistics**; some numbers are simply used for counting. Statistics, on the other hand, are numbers that *show relationships* among phenomena; they emphasize magnitude (large; small), describe subclasses or parts (segments), or established direction (trends). Because statistics reduce great masses of information into potentially meaningful categories, they're useful both in clarifying a situation and in substantiating a disputable claim.

Magnitudes.   Statistics can be used to describe a problem's significance or degree of seriousness. Student speaker Brad Hoeschen utilizes statistical information in demonstrating the potential for fraud in charity drives:[15]

> [I]f you or I were contacted by the National Children's Cancer Society and asked for information to be sent to us, we would receive a lovely colorful pamphlet, inside of which would be a pie chart telling us 95% of all money taken in goes to help the charity. Yet underneath the pie chart are the words net profit. Net profit is the amount of money remaining after fundraising fees have been taken out of the gross profit, thus completely misleading us. The 1989 edition of the United States Attorney General's Report on Fiscal Responsibility for non-Government Organizations reveals in that year the National Children's Cancer Society raised $2.5 million. After fundraising costs only $105,000 was left for the charity, not even enough for one bone marrow transplant, and barely 1½ cents on every dollar. Meanwhile the charity's fundraiser out of Houston, Texas, received a $700,000 stipend, nearly seven times that which went to the charity itself.

A speaker can use statistics to describe a situation or to sketch its scope or seriousness. By reducing large masses of information into generalized categories, statistics clarify the nature of a situation and substantiate a potentially disputable claim.

In this example, Mr. Hoeschen also adds comparative illustrations to show the significance of the numbers—by showing that the $105,000 was equivalent to only 1½ cents of every dollar actually raised and that the fundraiser earned seven times more than the actual amounts available to cancer patients. By translating statistical information into more understandable units, you add to the impact of the numbers themselves.

Segments.   Statistical information can also be *segmented*, in order to show relationships between and among parts. Segmenting allows you to advance a specific claim, showing how the parts compare, or how they illustrate the strength or weakness of an argument. Student speaker Eddie Hunter, for example, used poll results in this fashion to show that incumbent politicians are not always unwanted by their electors:[16]

> Nobody forces people to vote for incumbents. Last October the *New York Times* reported a New York Times-CBS Survey, which found 44% of those surveyed believed their representative deserves re-election, while 40% say they want someone new. However, these percentages swing dramatically when people are asked about Congress as a whole. Only 20% then say most lawmakers deserve re-election, while 67% would give new people a chance. Apparently people perceive everyone else's legislator as the bad guy.

As Hunter's example illustrates, the most important value of statistics does not lie in the numbers themselves but in how they're interpreted and used. In contemplating the use of statistical data, answer this question: "What do these numbers mean or demonstrate?" The argument takes on strength from the statistics, but only if you interpret their meaning very clearly. In Hunter's case, when the separate poll results are compared, there is support for the argument that "If they're in, vote them out" doesn't apply across the board.

Trends.   Statistics often are used to point out *trends,* or indicators that tell us where we were and are now and where we may be heading. The comparison of statistical data across time allows one to say that a particular phenomenon is increasing or decreasing, and speculate about the values implicit in that movement. Martin's comparison of the growth of women in engineering studies, cited earlier (pp. 164), illustrates the advantage of using concrete numbers to show trends. Student speaker Kelly McInerney used comparative data to point to the increasing problem with pit bulls: "The National Center for Health Statistics reported that the increase in pit bull attacks has been dramatic, from 20% in 1980 to 62% in 1988. . . . Today, the ever increasing list of attacks and fatalities from pit bulls forces the American public to take a stand."[17] Having established the magnitude of the increase over the eight-year period, McInerney has an easier time identifying the problem as serious and worthy of urgent attention. She also provides a context for interpreting the results by noting in advance the nature of the trend and its significance, providing supporting evidence, and indicating its implications.

When you use statistics to indicate magnitude, to divide phenomena into segments, or to describe trends, keep these guidelines in mind:

1. *Translate difficult-to-comprehend numbers into more immediately understandable terms.* As noted earlier, Brad Hoeschen increased the impact of his information by translating larger numbers into smaller, more manageable units—it's easier to conceive of 1½ cents of every dollar than to think in terms of $105,000 as a proportion of $2.5 million (p. 168).

2. *Do not be afraid to round off complicated numbers.* "Nearly 400,000" is easier for listeners to comprehend than "396,456"; "just over 33 percent" is preferable to "33.4 percent," and "approximately one-third" is even more preferable.

3. *Whenever possible, use visual materials to clarify complicated statistical trends or summaries.* Hand out a mimeographed or photocopied sheet of numbers; draw graphs on the chalkboard; prepare a chart in advance. Such aids will allow you to concentrate on explaining the significance of the numbers, rather than on making sure the audience hears and remembers them.

4. *Use statistics fairly*. Arguing that professional women's salaries increased 12.4 percent last year may sound impressive to listeners until they realize the women are still paid almost one-quarter less than men for equivalent work. In other words, provide fair contexts for your numerical data and comparisons.[18]

Testimony

Testimony, the opinions or conclusions of others, adds weight to your central idea or claim. It may simply make listeners aware of a problem or further heighten interest in it, or testimony may add to the impressiveness of an idea, as when you quote a famous person's witty saying. At other times, this sort of support lends credibility to an assertion. While you may have significant personal experience and knowledge about a specific problem, often you also need to support your ideas and claims with others' evidence. That information can come in two basic forms: (1) *paraphrased* restatement of the source's ideas or information, complete with source citation; and (2) *verbatim* or exact statement from the source, complete with source citation. With reference to *paraphrasing*, consider the following brief examples of how student speakers have utilized research or other information in support of claims:

Claim: Pit bulls are responsible for serious injury.
Support: "In a study conducted by Sacks and Sattin for the September 15, 1989, issue of the *Journal of the American Medical Association*, they found that pit bulls were responsible for 42 of 101 deaths. . .that is three times the rate at which German Shepherds, the next most likely dog to attack, kill."[19]

Claim: Your medical records may be shared with more people than you think.
Support: "In practice your records may not even go directly from the doctor or hospital to the company requesting the information. Many insurers use reporting agencies to collect such information. As *Newsweek* of June 12, 1990, points out, one databank that is especially questionable is the Medical Information Bureau (MIB), which represents nearly 800 North American insurance companies and stores medical data on some 13 million Americans. As *U. S. News and World Report* of October 13, 1989, tells us, if you have ever filled out an application for health or life insurance, you're probably on file with the MIB and your medical records are an open commodity."[20]

Claim: "Sustainable agriculture practices are possible without the use of chemicals."
Support: "Another example of good sustainable agriculture is Fred Kirshenman. According to an article in the May 21, 1990, issue of *Time* magazine, when this farmer from Medina, North Dakota, discovered that the soil on his 3,100 acre farm was getting harder to till and he was having to apply more expensive pesticides and fertilizers, just to achieve the same yield, he

became the first person in his township to stop using agrichemicals, and the results were worth it. By rotating crops and using special plowing techniques he was actually able to improve the quality of his soil and still maintains an average harvest of thirty-three bushels of wheat per acre, which is as good, if not better than any of his neighbors who use conventional farming."[21]

In paraphrasing, be sure that your restatement accurately reflects the information—that it doesn't distort or otherwise exclude important cautionary statements or qualifying claims regarding the information. Taking information out of context requires care in making certain that the data capture the essence of the original source's meaning or intent.

There are other times when you will want to depend on the actual words of another person or agency in presenting support for your claims. For example, in showing that lawyers are in support of "preventive law," student speaker Sarah Nagel provides verbatim evidence: "Former ATLA (Association of Trial Lawyers of America) President Russ Herman even went so far as to make the theatrical pitch, 'We plead with you, particularly the journalists, to put us out of business.'"[22] By citing the president of an organization, the speaker lends credibility to her generalization about support. To support the notion that the fillings dentists put in your mouth are dangerous, Hoffman uses the words of an actual dentist: "Atlanta dentist Ron Dressler states, 'I have over three hundred scientific references on mercury toxicity and I can no longer in good conscience put those things in people's mouths.'"[23] Such personal testimony illustrates that dentists themselves take the issue seriously.

All testimony, whether paraphrased or verbatim, should meet the twin tests of pertinence and audience acceptability. When used to strengthen a statement, rather than merely to amplify or illustrate, testimony also should satisfy four other criteria that are more specific:

1. *The person being quoted or paraphrased should be qualified, by training and experience, to speak on the subject being discussed.*

2. *Whenever possible, the authority's statement should be based upon firsthand knowledge.* An Iowa farmer is not an authority on a South Carolina drought unless he or she has personally observed the conditions. However, using a journalist's summary of the drought, as published in a national news weekly, would lend appropriate authoritative support.

3. *The judgment expressed shouldn't be unduly influenced by personal interest.* Asking a political opponent to comment on the current president's job performance will likely result in a biased opinion. But sometimes you may find individuals least likely to support a claim coming out in favor of your ideas; this form of "reluctant testimony" has a

THE FORMS OF SUPPORTING MATERIAL

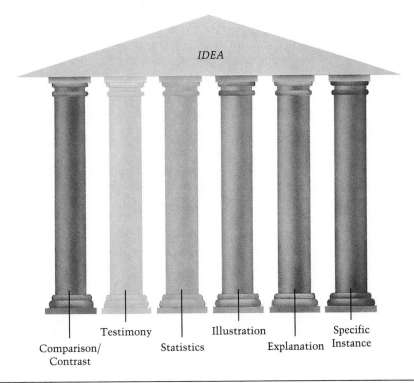

IDEA

Comparison/
Contrast

Testimony

Statistics

Illustration

Explanation

Specific
Instance

distinct advantage, since it's clear the person has little to gain from the position taken.

4. *The listeners should realize that the person quoted or paraphrased is an authority.* Using sources of information readily known to your audience will add support to your ideas. You may, as did Nagel and Hoffman in the above examples, have to tell the audience who the speaker is. When citing testimony, don't use big names for their own sake alone—make certain their expertise is relevant to the situation you're discussing. If your audience doesn't recognize the persons cited or their qualifications, add that information to the speech.

Finally, always acknowledge the source of an idea or particular phrasing of a point you're making. You want to avoid being guilty of *plagiarism*—claiming someone else's ideas, information, or phraseology as your own. This is the same as if you stole an item—hardly a way to bolster your credibility. Never underestimate the intelligence and experience of your audience to the point that you believe you will get away with citing infor-

Checklist for Supporting Materials

You should evaluate your supporting materials when you plan your speech. Answer the questions on this checklist as you consider supporting materials.

General Considerations:

_____ 1. Have I included sufficient supporting material?

_____ 2. Are my supporting materials distributed throughout my speech?

_____ 3. Do I provide extra support for confusing or controversial ideas?

_____ 4. Are my supporting materials interesting and clear?

_____ 5. Do I adequately credit the sources of my supporting materials?

Explanation:

_____ 1. Are my explanations short and direct?

_____ 2. Do I provide other forms of supporting materials in addition to explanations?

Comparison and Contrast:

_____ 1. Is at least one of the items in the comparison or contrast familiar to my listeners?

_____ 2. Is the basis of the comparison clear?

_____ 3. Is the contrast distinct enough?

Illustration:

_____ 1. Is the illustration clearly related to the idea it is intended to support?

_____ 2. Is the illustration typical?

_____ 3. Is the illustration vivid and adequately detailed?

Specific Instance:

_____ 1. Have I provided enough specific instances?

_____ 2. Can listeners easily recognize or understand the instances I mention?

Statistics:

_____ 1. Are my statistics easy to understand?

_____ 2. Have I rounded off complicated numbers?

_____ 3. Should I use visual materials to clarify complicated statistics?

_____ 4. Am I using statistics fairly?

Testimony:

_____ 1. Is the authority quoted qualified to speak on the topic being discussed?

_____ 2. Is the authority's statement based on firsthand knowledge?

_____ 3. Is the authority's opinion subject to personal influence or bias?

_____ 4. Do my listeners know the authority's qualifications?

mation without attributing it to appropriate sources. Trust in your credibility and integrity is easily broken if you pretend another's ideas or information is your own.

Where to Look for Information: Sources of Supporting Material

We are living in the Information Age—from television to fax machines, from print media to electronic mail, we are inundated with more data than we can hope to digest. As a speaker, therefore, you need never lack information; the key task is to locate that which is most relevant to your purpose. Any research requires a game plan. This section will review the major sources of information and suggest where to look for particular kinds of data.

Accessing Printed Materials

The most common source of supporting materials is the printed word—newspapers, magazines, pamphlets, and books. Through the careful use of a library—and with the help of reference librarians—you can discover an almost overwhelming amount of materials relevant to your speech subject and purpose.

Newspapers.   Newspapers are obviously a useful source of information about events of current interest. Moreover, their feature stories and accounts of unusual happenings provide a storehouse of interesting illustrations and examples. You must be careful, of course, not to accept as true everything printed in a newspaper, for the haste with which news sometimes must be gathered makes complete accuracy difficult. Your school or city library undoubtedly keeps on file copies of one or two highly reliable papers, such as *The New York Times*, the *Wall Street Journal*, and the *Christian Science Monitor*, and probably also a selection from among the leading newspapers of your state or region. If your library has *The New York Times*, it is likely to have the published index to that paper. By using this resource, you can locate accounts of people and events from 1913 to the present. Yet another useful and well-indexed source of information on current happenings is *Facts on File*, issued weekly since 1940. Also, *News-Bank* provides monthly listings on microfiche of news events from different areas.

Magazines.   An average-sized university library subscribes annually to hundreds of magazines and journals. Some—such as *Time*, *Newsweek*, and *U.S. News & World Report*—summarize weekly events. *The Atlantic* and *Harper's* are representative of a group of monthly publications that cover a wide range of subjects of both passing and permanent importance. Such magazines as *The Nation, Vital Speeches of the Day, Fortune, Washington Monthly,* and *The New Republic* contain comment on current political, social, and economic questions. For more specialized areas, there are such magazines as *Popular Science, Scientific American, Sports Illustrated, Field and Stream, Ms., Better Homes and Gardens, Today's Health, National Geographic,* and *Archaeology.*

This list is, of course, merely suggestive of the wide range of materials to be found in periodicals. When you are looking for a specific kind of information, use the *Reader's Guide to Periodical Literature,* which indexes most of the magazines you will want to refer to in preparing a speech. If you need more sophisticated material, consult the *Social Science Index* and the *Humanities Index.* Similar indexes also are available for technical journals, publications from professional societies, and the like. A reference librarian can show you how to use them.

Yearbooks and Encyclopedias.   The most reliable source of comprehensive data is *Statistical Abstracts of the United States,* which covers a wide variety of subjects ranging from weather records and birthrates to steel production and election results. Unusual data on Academy Award winners, world records in various areas, and the "bests" and "worsts" of almost anything can be found in the *World Almanac, The People's Almanac, The Guinness Book of World Records, The Book of Lists,* and *Information Please.* Encyclopedias, such as the *Encyclopaedia Britannica* and *Americana Encyclopedia,* which attempt to cover the entire field of human knowledge, are valuable chiefly as an initial reference source or for background reading. Refer to them for important scientific, geographical, literary, or historical facts; for bibliographies of authoritative books on a subject; and for ideas you won't develop completely in your speech.

Documents and Reports.   Various governmental agencies—state, national, and international—as well as many independent organizations publish reports on special subjects. Among governmental publications, those most frequently consulted are the hearings and recommendations of congressional committees or those of the United States Departments of Health and Human Services and of Commerce. Government documents can easily be explored through the *Congressional Information Service Index.* Reports on issues related to agriculture, business, government, engineering, and scientific experimentation are published by many state universities. Such endowed groups as the Carnegie, Rockefeller, and Ford Foundations and such special interest groups as the Foreign Policy Association, the Brookings Institution, the League of Women Voters, Common Cause, and the United States Chamber of Commerce also publish reports and pamphlets. Although by no means a complete list of all such pamphlets and reports, *The Vertical File Index* does offer you a guide to some of these materials.

Books.　There are few subjects suitable for a speech on which someone hasn't written a book. As a guide to these books, use the subject-matter headings in the card catalog of your libraries. Generally, you will find authoritative books in your school library and more popularized treatments in your city's public library.

Biographies.　*The Dictionary of National Biography* (deceased Britishers), the *Dictionary of American Biography* (deceased Americans), *Who's Who* (living Britishers), *Who's Who in America, Current Biography,* and more specialized works organized by field contain biographical sketches especially useful in locating facts about famous people and in documenting the qualifications of authorities whose testimony you may quote.

Accessing Nonprint Materials

Useful, up-to-date information also can be found in nonprint resources. The broadcast media and computer memory banks contain today's opinions and facts, not yesterday's set type. Learning to access nonprint resources keeps you abreast of late-breaking information.

Radio and Television Broadcasts.　Lectures, discussions, and the formal public addresses of leaders in government, business, education, and religion are frequently broadcast over radio or television. Many of these talks are later mimeographed or printed by the stations or by the organizations that sponsor them. Usually, as in the case of CBS's "Meet the Press" or National Public Radio's "All Things Considered," copies can be obtained for a small fee. If no manuscript is available, you may take careful notes or audiotape the program (as long as you make no public use of that tape). When taking notes, listen with particular care in order to get an exact record of the speaker's words and meanings. Just as you must quote items from printed sources accurately and honestly, so are you obligated to respect the remarks someone has made on a radio or television program and to give that person full credit.

Computerized Searches.　Your library may subscribe to one or more computerized data bases. These function much like a printed index. To access a data base, you need to work with a reference librarian in determining what *descriptors* (key words) to enter. An average-sized university library probably has access to upward of two hundred data files, such as ERIC, BIOSIS, Infotrac, PsychInfo, AGRICOLA, Datrex, and MEDLINE.

You also might be able to use one or more of the available public data bases. For example, BRS/After Dark is available by subscription to those with personal computers and a modem (a communication device that links computers through phone lines); CompuServe, Prodigy, The Source, and

Dow Jones News/Retrieval are other major consumer-oriented data base services that can be accessed through a modem and computer hookup.

These sources can be valuable time-savers, because they will search for and print lists of articles available in your specific research area. Data bases involve expense, however. Libraries often charge for computer time spent in searching and printing your information, and public data bases charge an initial fee plus per-hour charges for on-line time. Yet, in an age of information explosion, they can save you a tremendous amount of time and put you in contact with far more material than you could reasonably assemble using only a card catalog and a few reference works.

Generating New Information

At times you will find it necessary or useful to generate information on your own. Two common approaches are to conduct interviews with appropriate persons and to construct and distribute a questionnaire.

Conducting Informational Interviews.   The goal of an **informational interview** is clear: to obtain answers to specific questions. In conducting the interview, you hope to elicit answers that can be woven into your speech text. Further, the answers can increase your general understanding of a topic so that you avoid misinforming your audience or drawing incorrect inferences from information obtained through other sources. The interviewee may be a "content expert" or someone who has had personal experience with the issues you wish to discuss. If you are addressing the topic of black holes, who better to help you than a physicist? If you are explaining the construction of a concrete boat, you might contact a local civil engineer for assistance. If, on the other hand, you wish to discuss anorexia nervosa, it may be helpful to interview a person who's suffered through the disorder. Interviews can provide compelling illustrations of human experiences.

There are three general guidelines to observe in planning an informational interview:

1. *Decide on your specific purpose.* What precise information do you hope to obtain during the interview? One caution: if you are interviewing a controversial figure, you may not be best served by engaging in an argument or by assuming a belligerent or self-righteous manner. Even if you disagree with the answers being given, your role isn't that of Perry Mason, seeking to win a jury's vote by grilling the witness. This doesn't mean that your purpose cannot encompass tough questions or questions that seek further clarification of answers that seem "not right." You can raise such questions without provoking an argument.

2. *Structure the interview in advance.* The beginning of an interview clarifies the purpose and sets limits on what will be covered during the session. You also can use this time to establish rapport with the person being interviewed. The middle of the interview comprises the substan-

tive portion: information being sought is provided. Structure your questions in advance so that you have a rough idea of what will be asked when. The interview may not follow your list exactly, but you will have a convenient checkpoint to see whether all the information you need has been presented. Finally, you will find the list useful as you summarize your understanding of the major points. This will help you avoid misinterpreting the meaning given to specific points by the person interviewed. The following format is an example of one you might follow in an informational interview:

I. Opening
    A. Mutual greeting
    B. Discussion of purposes
        1. Reason information is needed
        2. Kind of information wanted
II. Informational Portion
    A. Question #1, with clarifying questions as needed
    B. Question #2, with clarifying questions as needed
    C. [and so on]
III. Closing
    A. Summary of main points
    B. Final courtesies

3. *Remember that interviews are interactive processes.* There is a definite pattern of "turn-taking" in interviews that allows both parties to concentrate on one issue at a time and assists in making the interview work for the benefit of both parties. The interactive pattern requires that both parties be careful listeners, for one person's comments will affect the next comment of the other. You'll need to remain flexible and free to deviate from your interview plan as you listen to the answers to your questions. You'll have to listen to what is said and almost simultaneously think ahead to the next item on your list of questions. Should you forge ahead or ask intervening questions to clarify or elaborate on a previous response?

Communicative Skills for Successful Interviewers.   From this discussion of interviewing and structures for communicating, it should be clear that adept interviewers must have certain communicative skills.

- *A good interviewer is a good listener.* Unless you take care to understand what someone is saying and to interpret the significance of those comments, you may misunderstand. Because questioning and answering are alternated in an interview, there is plenty of opportunity to clarify remarks and opinions. You can achieve clarification only if you are a good listener (see Chapter 2).

- *A good interviewer is open.* Many of us are extremely wary of interviewers. We are cynical enough to believe that they have *hidden agenda*—unstated motives or purposes—that they are trying to pursue.

One common way to generate new information is to conduct an informational interview. The interviewee may be an expert on the content of the speech or someone who has had personal experience with the issue under discussion.

Too often interviewers have said they "only want a little information" when actually they were selling magazine subscriptions or a religious ideal. If, as an interviewer, you're "caught" being less than honest, your chances for success are vastly diminished. Frankness and openness should govern all aspects of your interview communication.

- *A good interviewer builds a sense of mutual respect and trust.* Feelings of trust and respect are created by revealing your own motivation, by getting the person to talk, and by expressing sympathy and understanding. Sometimes, of course, your assumptions of integrity and goodwill can be proved wrong. To start with suspicion and distrust, however, is to condemn the relationship without giving it a fair chance.

Sending Letters and Questionnaires.   If you need more data than you can find in the library and don't have access to an expert, you can write away for information. This is always risky, as you may not receive the information in time for the presentation. Be sure to write as soon as you have decided on a topic. If you're requesting general information, be as specific about the purpose of the request as you can; this will assist your respondent in forwarding what you are looking for. A letter to the Department of Housing and Urban Development asking "Do you have any information on housing?" is unlikely to be answered satisfactorily, if at all. As you ask for information, explain why you have been unable to locate it on you own. Respondents who think they are being asked to do your work for you will probably be unwilling to help.

On other occasions, you may wish to discover what a group of people knows or thinks about a subject. If, for example, you wanted to give a speech on a proposed halfway house for the mentally ill, you might survey residents in the vicinity. You could send a questionnaire to people chosen randomly from the phone book or to all living within a three-block radius from the proposed home. If you're seeking information on a new college drinking policy, you could survey dormitory residents or members of several classes. With the results, you could construct your own statistical summaries for presentation as part of your speech.

When developing a questionnaire, keep these several guidelines in mind:

1. Be sure the form explains the exact purpose of the questionnaire and the procedures to follow in responding to the questions.
2. Keep the form short and to the specific points you wish to have responses on.
3. For ease of summarizing, use closed questions (for example, ask for "yes/no" responses where appropriate and use such categories as "strongly agree/agree/disagree/strongly disagree" if you want ranges of opinion).
4. Phrase questions in clear, neutral language. Do not use loaded terms (for example, "Do you wish to see mentally unbalanced, unpredictable people living next to your children?").
5. Pilot-test the form with a few people to see whether the instructions are clear and to determine if any questions need to be rephrased.
6. If mailing the questionnaire, include a stamped, self-addressed envelope to encourage returns.

Recording Information in Usable Forms

When you find the information you have been looking for, either photocopy it or take notes. Whether you keep your notes on 4-by-6-inch cards or in a notebook, it is helpful to have an accurate, legible record of the materials

A SAMPLE NOTECARD

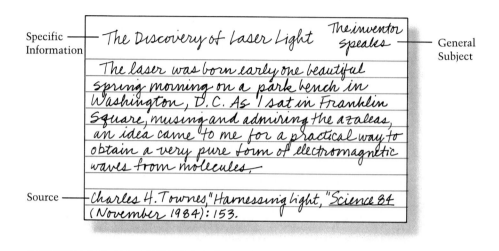

Specific Information

The Discovery of Laser Light   The inventor speaks

General Subject

The laser was born early one beautiful spring morning on a park bench in Washington, D.C. As I sat in Franklin Square, musing and admiring the azaleas, an idea came to me for a practical way to obtain a very pure form of electromagnetic waves from molecules.

Source

Charles H. Townes, "Harnessing Light," *Science 84* (November 1984): 153.

you wish to consider for your speech. An incomplete source citation makes it difficult to find the information again if you need to recheck it; hurried scribbles, too, are hard to decipher later.

Many people find that notecards are easier to use than a notebook because they can be shuffled by topic area or type of support. If you use a notebook, however, try recording each item on half a page. Since most of your information will not fill a page, this will save paper; cutting the sheets in half will make it easier to sort your data or to adopt a classification scheme and relate information to particular themes or subpoints of your speech. When preparing notecards, place the subject headings at the top of the card and the complete source citation at the bottom, as in the sample presented above. This way, the card can be classified by general subject (top right heading) and by specific information presented (top left heading).

You need not, of course, always follow these directions exactly. You will find, however, that you will need a classification system so you can put your hands on specific pieces of information as you construct your speeches.

Using Source Material Ethically:
In Pursuit of Excellence

Plagiarism has been defined as "the unacknowledged inclusion of someone else's words, ideas, or data as one's own."[24] One of the saddest things an instructor has to do is to cite a student for plagiarism. In speech classes, students occasionally quote material from *Reader's Digest, Newsweek, Time, Senior Scholastic,* or other easy-to-obtain sources, not realizing how many speech teachers habitually scan the library periodicals section. Even if the teacher has not read the article, it soon becomes apparent to most of the class that something is wrong—the wording is not similar to the way the person usually talks, the speech does not have a well-formulated introduction or conclusion, and the organizational pattern is not one normally used by speakers. Often, too, the person who plagiarizes an article reads it aloud badly, another sign that something is wrong.

Plagiarism is not, however, simply undocumented verbatim quotation. It also includes (1) undocumented paraphrases of others' ideas and (2) undocumented use of others' main ideas. For example, if you paraphrase a movie review form *Newsweek* without acknowledging that staff critic David Ansen had those insights, or if you use the motivated sequence as a model for analyzing speeches without giving credit to Alan Monroe for developing it, you are guilty of plagiarism.

Suppose you ran across the following excerpt from Kenneth Clark's *Civilisation: A Personal View:*

> It was the age of great country houses. In 1722 the most splendid of all had just been completed for Marlborough, the general who had been victorious over Voltaire's country: not the sort of idea that would have worried Voltaire in the least, as he thought of all war as a ridiculous waste of human life and effort. When Voltaire saw Blenheim Palace he said, "What a great heap of stone, without charm or taste," and I can see what he means. To anyone brought up on Mansart and Perrault, Blenheim must have seemed painfully lacking in order and propriety. . . . Perhaps this is because the architect, Sir John Vanbrugh, although a man of genius, was really an amateur. Moreover, he was a natural romantic, a castle-builder who didn't care a fig for good taste and decorum.[25]

If you were to use the excerpt in writing a speech, you should do so carefully. The following examples illustrate plagiarism and suggest ways to avoid it:

1. *Verbatim quotation of a passage* (read it aloud word for word) To avoid plagiarism: "Kenneth Clark, in his 1969 book *Civilisation: A Personal View,* said the following about the architecture of great country estates in eighteenth-century England: (then quote the paragraph)."
2. *Undocumented use of the main ideas:* "In eighteenth-century England there was a great flurry of building. Country estates were built essentially by amateurs, such as Sir John Vanbrugh, who built the splendid Blenheim Palace for General Marlborough. Voltaire didn't like war and he didn't like Blenheim, which he called a great heap of stone without charm or taste. He preferred the order and variety of houses designed by French architects Mansart and Perrault."
   To avoid plagiarism: "In his book *Civilisation: A Personal View,* Sir Kenneth Clark makes the point that eighteenth-century English country houses were built essentially by amateurs. He uses as an example Sir

John Vanbrugh, who designed Blenheim Palace for the Duke of Marlborough. Clark notes that, when Voltaire saw the house, he said, 'What a
great heap of stone, without charm or taste.' Clark can understand that
reaction from a Frenchman who was raised on the neoclassical designs
of Mansart and Perrault. Clark explains English style arose from what he
calls 'natural romanticism.'"

3. *Undocumented paraphrasing*: "The eighteenth century was the age of
    wonderful country houses. In 1722 the most beautiful one in England
    was built for Marlborough, the general who had won over France. When
    Voltaire saw the Marborough house called Blenheim Palace, he said it
    was a great heap of stones."
    To avoid plagiarism: Use the same kind of language noted under exam-
    ple 2, giving Clark credit for his impressions.

Plagiarism is easy to avoid if you take reasonable care. Moreover, by
citing such authorities as Clark, who are well educated and experienced,
you add their credibility to yours. Avoid plagiarism to keep from being
expelled from the class or even your school, but avoid it for positive reasons
as well: improve your ethos by associating your thinking with that of
experts.

Critical Thinking and the Use of Supporting Materials

It's one thing to consider the range of materials appropriate to your purpose,
then to gather the relevant information; it's quite another to use the information effectively. The effective use of supporting materials is an exercise
in **critical thinking**—assessing the rational requirements for clarifying
thoughts and proving something to someone else. As was suggested earlier,
when you illustrate a central idea or a claim, you have to ask yourself two
important questions: "What information is reasonable as support for my
ideas?" and "What do the listeners need to know in order to accept my
ideas?" Thinking critically about these two questions involves the following subissues:

1. the rational requirements your claims put on you;
2. the range of supporting materials available;
3. the demands a particular audience might make of someone defending
    such a claim;
4. the generally perceived power-to-justify of particular forms of support.

Suppose you want to defend the claim that "All public restaurants should
be smoke-free environments." Thinking about the claim, you might come
to the following conclusions:

1. *Rational requirements of the claim.* This claim demands that you demonstrate the relationship between smoking and health and between passive smoke and health. The first is relatively easy to support, given the Surgeon General's warning and the plethora of studies on the harmful effects of smoking. The second is somewhat more difficult, because one could argue that proper ventilation and separation of smoking and nonsmoking areas will effectively minimize any danger from passive smoke. Complicating the issue is the observation that a smoker's civil rights are being violated by acceptance of your claim. What sort of supporting materials will help you make your case? Providing statistical evidence to support the relationships as well as authoritative or expert opinion on the dangers of passive smoke will be helpful. Using personal narratives that detail the consequences of inadvertently inhaling smoke will make the issue more vivid and compelling. Locating appropriate legal precedents on the constitutionality of smoke-free regulations addresses the civil rights issue head-on.

2. *Range of available materials.* Can you find all the materials you need? Do you have access to medical information and expert testimony on the effects of smoking and smoke inhalation? Do you have access to appropriate legal sources? In other words, it's one thing to contemplate what would make for excellent support but quite another to find it. You may have to settle for thinner evidence than you would like, simply due to your lack of access to certain kinds of material.

3. *Audience demands.* The need to address some issues will depend in large part on who is in the audience. The civil rights issue may be less critical if the audience is the local chapter of the American Cancer Society. Consider the kinds of questions your audience is likely to ask and then attempt to address each one. As a nonsmoker, do I really have to be wary of how close to the smoking section I sit at a restaurant? Am I really in that much danger from inhaling the smoke in a room, when I'm not actually smoking? Do I have the right to a smoke-free environment? What are the appropriate limits to that right and is eating in a smoke-free restaurant within the limits?

4. *Power-to-justify.* You may use any of the forms of support to clarify, to amplify, or to strengthen a central idea or claim. However, some forms tend to accomplish these goals more effectively than others and are more effective with particular audiences. Explanation, comparison, specific instance, and segment statistics are especially helpful in clarifying an idea. These methods allow the speaker to present information that simplifies an idea for the audience. They also are useful when listeners have little background or knowledge about the topic or when the subject matter is complex. Explanations, comparison, illustration, and statistics

on magnitude and trend can help the speaker amplify an idea, expanding on it so the audience can better examine the concept. These forms of support may be especially useful when the audience has only a slight knowledge of the concept. To strengthen or lend credibility to a point, a speaker can use factual illustration, specific instances, statistics, and testimony. These forms strengthen the idea by making it vivid and believable.

Once you have thought through these issues, and selected your materials, ask yourself this question: "When the speech is completed, what reasonable questions will still remain in the audience's mind?" You won't answer all issues and provide support for every contingency in advance, but you can look ahead and anticipate what follows logically from the information you'll be presenting. If your information directly supports the ideas you're advancing, and are relevant to the audience's interests and needs, you'll go a long way toward accomplishing your final goal—obtaining acceptance of your ideas. Following are two outlines that illustrate how supporting material can be used.

Sample Outline for an Informative Speech

In the first outline, note how the speaker has combined verbal and visual material to establish and develop the central idea. In this speech, the supportive material is used to amplify the idea.

How We Breathe

☐ *Central idea*   I.   The human breathing mechanism may be likened to a bellows, which expands to admit air and contracts to expel it.

☐ *Explanation*   A.   When we inhale, two things happen.
                      1.   Muscles attached to the collarbone and shoulder bones pull upward and slightly outward.
                      2.   Muscles in the abdominal wall relax, allowing the diaphragm—a sheet of muscle and tendon lying immediately below the lungs—to fall.
       B.   This permits the spongy, porous lungs to expand.
                      1.   A vacuum is created.
                      2.   Air rushes in.
       C.   When we exhale, two things also happen.
                      1.   Gravity causes the rib cage to move downward.
                      2.   Muscles in the abdominal wall contract, squeezing the diaphragm upward.

Sample Outline for a Persuasive Speech   **187**

VISUAL AIDS: "HOW WE BREATHE"

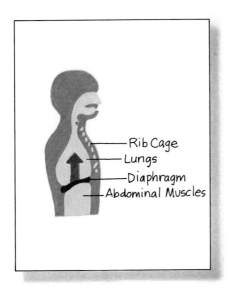

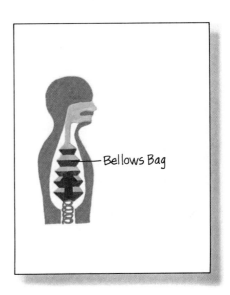

☐ *Comparison*

☐ *Visual aid*
☐ *Restatement
of central
idea*

D. The space available to the lungs is thus reduced.
    1. The lungs are squeezed.
    2. Air is emitted.
E. The similarity between the breathing mechanism
    and a bellows is represented in this diagram:
    (Show "How We Breathe" Diagram)
F. In summary, then, to remember how the human
    breathing mechanism works, think of a bellows.
    1. Just as increasing the size of the bellows bag
        allows air to rush in, so increasing the space
        available to the lungs allows them to admit air.
    2. Just as squeezing the bellows bag forces air out,
        so contracting the space the lungs can occupy
        forces air to be emitted.

Sample Outline for a Persuasive Speech

Study the following outline. Notice that the supporting material is used to strengthen each of the points in the speech. The audience would be unlikely to accept these ideas without further development. Although the proof of a single point may not require the use of supportive materials as numerous or varied as those used in this outline, they show how a number of different forms can be combined.

Cable Television—at Your Service!

☐ *Claim*

I. Cable television soon will revolutionize your everyday life.

☐ *First support-ing statement: hypothetical illustration*

A. Suppose, on a rainy day a few years from now, you decide to run your errands from your living room.
   1. You turn on your two-way communication unit and begin your round of errands:

☐ *Specific instances within the illustration*

      a. On Channel 37, your bank's computer veri-fies the amount of a recent withdrawal.
      b. On Channel 26, you ask the telephone company to review last month's long-distance charges.
      c. On Channel 94, a supermarket lets you scan products, prices, and home-delivery hours.
      d. On Channel 5, you study a list of proposed changes in the city charter.
         1. You can "call in" for further informa-tion.
         2. You can vote from your own home.
      e. Channel 106 gives you access to resource personnel at the public library.

☐ *Restatement of supporting statement*

   2. With "cable television at your service," you have accomplished your day's errands with minimum expenditure of time, gas, and parking-meter money.

☐ *Second sup-porting statement*
☐ *Specific instances*

B. These possibilities, once thought of only as dreams, are becoming actualities across the United States.
   1. Most cities have public-access channels filled with local talent and ethnic programming.
   2. Ann Arbor, Michigan, and Columbus, Ohio, have been leasing channels to private firms and public utility companies.

☐ *Third sup-porting statement*
☐ *Comparison*

C. Cable television soon will be available to virtually every household in the United States at a reason-able cost.
   1. Because the cost is shared by licensee and householder alike, no one bears an excessive burden.
      a. Commercial users find that leasing a chan-nel costs little more than their computer-accounting systems and print/electronic advertising services.

☐ *Statistics*

      b. Studio facilities for the public-access chan-nels are made available at cost in most cable television contracts—normally about $30 per hour.

   c. Current installation charges range from $15 to $50.

   d. Monthly rental fees per household seldom exceed $25 for basic cable service.

2. The technical characteristics of cable television render it inexpensive.

□ *Explanation combined with specific instances*

   a. Some existent telephone lines and equipment can be used.

   b. The conversion box mounts easily on a regular television set.

   c. Studio costs are minimal.

     1. Relatively inexpensive ½″ videotape and broadcasting equipment can be used.

     2. Engineering and production personnel need minimal training for cable systems.

□ *Restatement of claim*

D. Given actual and potential uses, plus the positive cost-benefit ratio, cable television will revolutionize your daily life.

□ *Comparison*

1. Just as the wheel extended our legs and the computer our central nervous system, so will cable television extend our communicative capabilities.

□ *Testimony used as restatement of claim*

2. In the words of Wendy Lee, communication consultant to new cable-television franchises: "We soon will be a nation wired fully for sight and sound. We will rid ourselves of the need for short shopping trips; we will cut the lines in doctors' offices; and we will put the consumer and the constituent into the front offices of his or her corporate suppliers and political servants. The telephone and the motor car will become obsolete."

Chapter Summary

The primary forms of supporting material are *explanations of what, how, and why; analogy or comparison; illustration; specific instance; statistics;* and *testimony*. These materials can be assembled from *printed materials* (newspapers, magazines, yearbooks and encyclopedias, documents and reports, books, and biographies), *radio and television broadcasts, computerized searches,* and *interviews*. Record the information either on notecards or notebook pages, and use it as supporting materials to *clarify, amplify*, and *strengthen* your presentation. Avoid *plagiarism*. Use supporting materials for both informative and persuasive speeches.

References

1. Mary Hoffman, "Mercury: Nothing to Smile About," *Winning Orations 1991*, Reprinted by permission of Larry Schnoor, Executive Secretary, Interstate Oratorical Association, Manketo State University, MN, 56.

2. Wendy Liebmann, "The Changing Consumer," *Vital Speeches*, 58 (April 15, 1992): 410.

3. LaDonna Harris, "Kerner Commission Paper," in Jerry D. Blanche, ed., *Native American Reader: Stories, Speeches and Poems* (Juneau, AK: Denali Press, 1990): 149.

4. Brooke Anderson, "Terrorist Plastic Play Toys," *Winning Orations, 1990*, 18.

5. Harris, 150.

6. Louis Hadley Evans, "Can You Trust God?" Reprinted by permission of the author.

7. John E. Jacob, "The State of Black America," *Vital Speeches*, 58 (June 15, 1992): 536.

8. Harris, p. 149.

9. Janet Martin, "Room at the Top," *Vital Speeches*, 58 (March 15, 1992): 347.

10. John A. Califano, Jr., "Adolescents: Their Needs and Problems," *Vital Speeches*, 44 (August 15, 1978).

11. Liebmann, 411.

12. Todd A. LaSala, "Committed Youth," *Winning Orations, 1991*, 12.

13. Cinda Schmechel, "Cool, Clear Water," *Winning Orations, 1991*, 77.

14. Henri Mann Morton, "Strength Through Cultural Diversity," in *Native American Reader*, 195.

15. Brad Hoeschen, "Charities Telesolicitations: Fundraising or Fraud?" *Winning Orations, 1991*, 53.

16. Eddie Paul Hunter, "Term Limits: A Solution Worse Than the Problem," *Winning Orations, 1991*, 90.

17. Kelly McInerny, "The Pit Bull Problem," *Winning Orations, 1991*, 15.

18. For an entertaining and valuable insight into the fair use of statistics, see Darrell Huff, *How to Lie with Statistics* (New York: W. W. Norton & Company, Inc., 1954).

19. McInerney, 16.

20. Ryan Siskow, "The Double Indignity—Medical Confidentiality," *Winning Orations, 1991*, 33.

21. April Erdmann, "Environmentally Unsafe Farming: An Unsafe Practice," *Winning Orations, 1991*, 39.

22. Sarah Nagel, "[Title Unknown]," *Winning Orations, 1991*, 48.

23. Hoffman, 57.

24. "Academic Honesty and Dishonesty," Louisiana State University, updated from LSU's *Code of Student Conduct* (1981).

25. *Civilisation: A Personal View* (New York: Harper & Row, 1969), 246.

Key Terms

analogy *(p. 162)*

comparison *(p. 162)*

contrast *(p. 164)*

critical thinking *(p. 184)*

explanation *(p. 159)*

factual illustration *(p. 166)*

figurative analogies *(p. 162)*

hypothetical illustration *(p. 165)*

illustration *(p. 165)*

informational interview *(p. 178)*

literal analogies *(p. 163)*

plagiarism *(p. 182)*

specific instance *(p. 167)*

statistics *(p. 168)*

testimony *(p. 171)*

Problems and Probes

1. Read one of the speeches in this text and identify its forms of supporting material. How effectively are they used to meet the purpose of the speech? Discuss your views in small groups within the class—how much agreement is there with respect to the strong or weak points of the speech? If the speaker faced your small group, what should he or she do differently?

2. Arrange to meet classmates in the reference room of your college library. Working in groups of four to six, each group member is to locate two of the items in the left-hand column of the following list. First, determine which of the sources listed in the right-hand column contains the material you need. When you locate your items, show your group the source and indicate where it is shelved.

Weekly summary of current national news	*Book Review Digest*
Brief sketch of the accomplishments of Lee Iacocca	*Congressional Record*
	Encyclopedia Americana
Description of a specific traffic accident	*Facts on File*
Text of Bill Clinton's Inaugural Address	local newspaper
	New York Times
Daily summary of stock prices	*Oxford English Dictionary*
Origin of the word "rhetoric"	*Statistical Abstracts*
Critical commentary on Arthur Schlesinger, Jr.'s *The Disuniting of America*	*Time*
	Vital Speeches of the Day
	Wall Street Journal
Current status of national legislation on education reform	*Who's Who*

Communication Activities

1. Present to the class a five-minute central-idea speech, the purpose of which is either to explain or clarify a term, concept, or process. Use at least three different forms of supporting material in developing your idea. To evaluate the effectiveness of your speech, the instructor and other students will consider the following: (a) adequacy of supporting material; (b) appropriateness of supporting material, both in terms of type and substance; and (c) insight and skill of the development of supporting material.

2. Present to the class a five-minute speech in which you support a specific claim, with the purpose of persuading the audience to accept your ideas. Use at least four different forms of supporting material in developing your justification for the acceptance of your ideas. The class will evaluate your presentation along the lines suggested in activity #1.

3. Listen to or read a speech or other news reports on a controversial subject that is currently in the local, state, or national news. Determine your own position on that issue, and develop your own 5 to 7 minute presentation, gearing it to the audience that's most interested in the issue. Thus, if the issue is of local concern, gear your remarks to the kind of audience that is most likely to be present to hear your ideas. Explain to the class the context and audience in advance of presenting the speech; once the speech is over, the class is to critique in terms of how well they think you responded to the hypothetical audience.

8

ADAPTING THE SPEECH STRUCTURE TO AUDIENCES: THE MOTIVATED SEQUENCE

W hen radical union agitator Joe Hill was about to die by firing squad in 1915, he sent a telegram to his fellow radical unionist Bill Haywood: "I will die like a true-blue rebel. Don't waste any time in mourning—organize."[1] Hill understood that his reasoned arguments and passionate denunciations of capitalist mine owners would produce no change unless there was organization. Now he, of course, was talking about organizing people, but the same can be said about ideas: unless presented in a strategically sound structure, the motivational appeals of Chapter 6 and the supporting materials of chapter seven would fall scattered among the listeners. Organization, structuring, provides direction and force; it's the gun barrel that directs your ideas toward their targets.

There are many ways to organize speech materials. Depending on the topic, your purpose, and audience needs, some approaches will work better than others. Before looking at those differences, however, we first will examine the nature of structure as a general concept and study one general-purpose organizational pattern known as the motivated sequence. In Chapter 9 we'll lay out other patterns for internally organizing speeches.

Organization from the Listener's Perspective

As you know from experience, people don't respond readily to random displays of information, no matter how accurate it is. If you're surrounded by multiple kinds and forms of information, you quickly sort it into categories of things or events. If you were given a box of junk and told to memorize what's in it, it wouldn't take you long to sort into piles: perhaps paper, cloth, plastic, and metal things, perhaps alphabetically, perhaps age or size. As soon as you knew you had to handle the materials mentally, organization would be required.

People actively seek organization in their environment, imposing it if they cannot find it naturally. Watch young children: they learn early that one set of furniture goes in a bedroom, another set, in a kitchen, a third, in a living room. They learn that animate (dogs) and inanimate (toys) objects are treated differently. By elementary school, they can determine what is *foreground* in a picture and what is *background* or supporting detail. Such processes of differentiation lend coherence to their perceptions of their worlds. They also can complete or fill in missing elements in fields. If someone says to you, "One, two, three, four," you almost automatically continue with "five, six, seven, eight." Cartoonists draw a few pen lines of a well-known person, and most readers will identify the individual. Or, if you see an unclosed circle, you'll likely perceive it as a circle because of its resemblance to complete ones you've seen.[2] Generally speaking, the principles of **differentiation** and **closure**—of sorting items into groups and of psychologically completing pictures or experiences—are central to our understanding of verbal organization or order as well.

The key idea underlying verbal organization is this: *people use their language to structure—that is, to make sense out of—their world.* Think of some of the language strategies you use to organize parts of your life:

- *Numerical order.* "In the first place, second, third, finally." Such language use establishes sequence.
- *Physical space.* "To the left, in the middle, to the right"; "west, east, north, south." Establishing spatial relationships allows you to "see" a kind of physical order through language.
- *Topics or types.* "Executive, legislative, judicial branches of government"; "animal, vegetable, and mineral"; "past, present, future." Dividing a subject into manageable and memorable topics helps you understand relationships.
- *Narrative order.* "Once upon a time . . ."; "I heard a story the other day . . ."; "I awoke with a start that morning." Turning a series of events into a story—with a beginning, a middle, and an end, even a "moral" or message—is a way of making disorganized experiences coherent and of giving them a point or application.
- *Logical inference.* "Because of this . . . , therefore . . ."; "As evidence for this assertion"; "I believe that because . . ." Arguments, as we'll see in Chapter 17, hook together causes with effects, instances with general principles, values with ways to act upon them.
- *Hierarchies.* "Higher, lower"; "inside, outside"; "under class, middle

class, upper class"; "important, unimportant"; "main points, secondary points." We often build hierarchies out of social or intellectual judgments to help us understand or argue for what's more or less central to our lives.

These are just some of the language devices we use to organize or order parts of our worlds. In fact, you've spent all of your life using language to bring order to your environment. Our job in this chapter is not to teach you patterns for order, but, rather, to get you to think strategically about organizing your message—why you're using a particular organizational pattern, what you expect an audience to do when you use it.

We also need to discuss a second important proposition about order: *structure is both psychological and logical.* That is, sometimes the order we impose on our environment imitates or focuses on physical characteristics in a kind of scientific way. So, early in this century, American philosopher John Dewey used a *problem-oriented* focus in devising his "psycho-logic" approach to resolving problems. In presenting a pattern for thought, which he called *reflective thinking,* Dewey applied the scientific method to individual and group problem-solving. To Dewey, careful individuals tend to follow a systematic procedure for solving problems. First, people become aware of a specific lack or disorientation in their worlds. Second, they examine this deficiency to determine its scope, causes, and implications. Third, they search for new orientations or operations that would remedy the deficiency, solve the problem. Fourth, they compare and evaluate possible solutions. Finally, they select a solution—the course of action that seems most likely to put their mind at rest and to alleviate the real-world dimensions of the problem.[3]

We also know that individuals can be inner-directed or *motivation-centered.* They care less about how things in the environment relate to each other and more about how they impact on themselves individually. Salespersons and advertisers began recognizing this principle in the 1920s. They realized that people buy cars not simply to get from here to there (i.e., to solve a real-world problem of locomotion), but also to create or reinforce a certain self-image. We buy particular styles of clothing to identify with others who wear that style; we make conscious decisions to get a "Paris" look, a "preppie" look, a "Grateful Dead" look. Our personal motivations, fears, hopes, and desires control our orientations to the outside world.

Alan Monroe (1903–75), the original author of this book, knew Dewey's work well. He also had had personal experience in training sales personnel in the 1920s. As he thought about Dewey's psycho-logic and the various sales techniques he'd taught people to use, Monroe discovered that he could unite both procedures—one based on the scientific method and the other rooted in an understanding of human motivation—to form a highly functional organizational pattern that is especially responsive to human goals.

THE MOTIVATED SEQUENCE

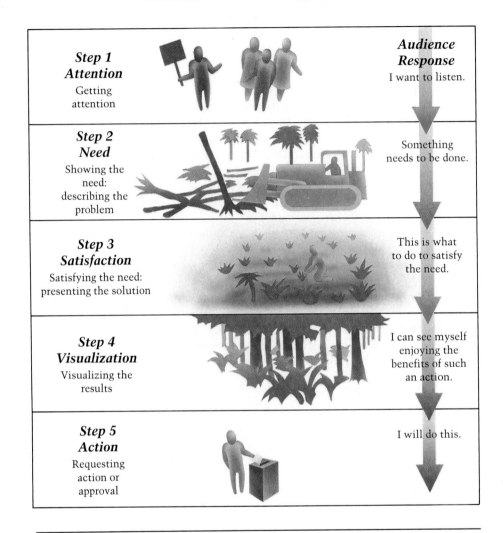

Step 1
Attention
Getting
attention

Audience
Response
I want to listen.

Step 2
Need
Showing the
need:
describing the
problem

Something
needs to be done.

Step 3
Satisfaction
Satisfying the need:
presenting the solution

This is what
to do to satisfy
the need.

Step 4
Visualization
Visualizing the
results

I can see myself
enjoying the
benefits of such
an action.

Step 5
Action
Requesting
action or
approval

I will do this.

Since 1935, when the first edition of this textbook was published, that structure has been called **Monroe's Motivated Sequence.** The rest of this chapter will be devoted to this holistic structure for organizing messages.

Five Basic Steps of the Motivated Sequence

The motivated sequence is functionally similar to Dewey's problem-solving or reflective-thinking procedures. The concept also derives its name from its relationship to human motives; the natural progression of the basic steps respond to a listener's desire for coherence and order. Thus, in terms of the preceding discussion, the motivated sequence is problem oriented and motivation centered.

There are five basic steps in the motivated sequence. As a starting place, you must get people to *attend* to a problem or to feel strongly enough to be willing to hear more about the deficiency you want them to help correct. Then, you can address more specific needs or desires, in relation to an individual's personal sense of *need*. When wants or needs have been aroused, you can attempt to *satisfy* them by showing what can be done to solve the problem or to relieve the impact of the problem on their lives. Simply describing a course of action may be insufficient; hence, you can move to *visualizing* what the environment or situation would be if the action were carried out or, conversely, what it would be like if the action were not taken. With these tasks completed, you can appeal to the audience members to *act*—to put into practice the proposed solution to the problem.

Thus, the motivated sequence is composed of five basic steps in the presentation of verbal materials:

1. **Attention:** the creation of interest and desire
2. **Need:** the development of the problem, through analyzing deficiencies and relating them to individual needs and desires
3. **Satisfaction:** the proposal of a plan of action that will correct the deficiencies and thereby fulfill individual needs and desires
4. **Visualization:** the verbal depiction of the environment as it will look with the deficiency corrected and the plan implemented
5. **Action:** the final call for personal commitment and specific acts

As you think through the order of these steps, recall Maslow's concept of a hierarchy of needs and desires that build naturally upon one another. In a similar fashion, speeches proceed from one step to the next; omitting the attention step, for instance, may result in listeners not hearing the remainder of your ideas. While the sequential patterning of the steps is not a hard and fast rule, adhering to its general order increases the likelihood of success. As a holistic organizational tool, the motivated sequence can be used to structure many different sorts of speeches, on many different topics. As your purpose shifts from informational to persuasive or actuative, the specific form each step takes likewise shifts.

As an overall pattern of development, the most obvious use of the motivated sequence is in persuasive or actuative situations. For example, it can structure the major points of a speech urging classmates to join a blood donors' group being formed on campus: (*attention*) "If you had needed an emergency transfusion for a rare blood type in Washington County on December 23, 1992, you might not have received it." (*need*) "Blood drives seldom collect sufficient quantities of blood to meet emergency needs in an area such as this one." (*satisfaction*) "A blood donors' association guarantees a predictable, steady supply of needed blood to the medical community." (*visualization*) "Without a steady supply of blood, our community

Monroe's Original Rationale

Principles and Types of Speech was first published in 1935; in the more than fifty years that have passed, new concepts have been introduced, while original concepts have been revised and updated. Throughout, listeners and their reaction to messages have remained a central theme. In the editions preceding this one, the motivated sequence has been an integral part of this listener-oriented approach. The following passages are excerpted from Alan H. Monroe's Preface to the first edition. They clearly support the role the motivated sequence continues to play in speech development.

"The names of the conventional divisions (introduction, body, conclusion) have been discarded in favor of a 'motivated sequence' of five steps, each of which is named to correspond with the function of that step in securing a particular reaction from the audience. These steps are named *attention, need, satisfaction, visualization,* and *action.* Thus, the student is made to realize by the very names of the divisions themselves that he [sic] must first gain attention, then create a feeling of need, satisfy that need, make his audience visualize the satisfaction, and finally impel his listeners to act. It is obvious, of course, that not all five of these steps are needed in every speech. . . .

"This approach to the problem of speech construction is not an untried theory. It has been used for nine years in actual classwork. The ease with which

will face needless deaths; with it, emergencies like yours can be met with prompt treatment." (*action*) "You can help by filling out the blood donors' cards I am handing out."

You also can use the motivated sequence to convey information: (*attention*) "Does the prospect of getting AIDS frighten you?" (*need*) "If we are to be less frightened by this insidious disease, we all need to be better informed about the ways we can be infected and about the myths concerning how it can be acquired." (*satisfaction*) "AIDS can be acquired through specific sexual practices by both males and females and through sharing needles used for drug intake; it cannot be acquired from kissing, from toilet seats, or from sitting across from a person with AIDS." (*visualization*) "With this information, I hope to have allayed irrational fears by being very specific

students grasp the idea and the improvement in the functional effectiveness of their speeches has been marked since this method was adopted. Much less often are their speeches mere exhibitions of skill in 'literary' composition, and more often do students adapt their remarks to the actual audience addressed.

"The history of this particular departure from customary practice deserves brief comment. Books on the psychology of business had long used the functional terms, attention, interest, desire, and action, to describe the process of selling merchandise. Professor G. R. Collins applied this sequence to the public sales talk. In 1926, Dr. P.H. Scott and I conceived the idea of applying this method to all speeches which sought to influence belief or action. In 1929, Mr. J. A. McGee, then on our staff, published a book containing a statement of this approach [John A. McGee, *Persuasive Speaking* (Scribner, 1929)—a 300-page textbook that sold for $1.60].

"Mr. McGee, however, limited his discussion to persuasive speeches; his conception of the various steps as sharply defined structural units, all five of which must always be used, prevented him from applying the method to many types of speech where action is not desired. On the other hand, I consider the steps as having a cumulative function, the speaker using only as many of them as the purpose of his speech requires. In this way I have applied the functional approach not only to persuasive speeches but to all types of speeches. Here again the actual use of this approach in my advanced classes on 'Forms of Address' has proved its practical value in demonstrative and informational speeches as well as in those which seek to persuade."

From then until now, the *functional* characteristic of the motivated sequence has stood the test of time. Irrespective of the changes that have been made over the years in particular applications, the dominant principles underlying its use remain as Monroe first used them in the classroom and then articulated them in the first edition of this textbook.

FOR FURTHER READING
Monroe, Alan H. *Principles and Types of Speeches.* Chicago, IL: Scott, Foresman and Company, 1935, vii–viii, x.

about when you are and when you are not at risk." (*action*) "This information can be useful as you consider the meaning of 'safe sex,' as well as when you encounter people with AIDS."

Sample Speech

Following is a speech that was prepared by April Erdmann of Morehead State University (Kentucky) and presented to the 1991 Interstate Oratorical Association contest. As you read over the speech, note that the attention step (paragraph 1) tries to convince an audience to extend what knowledge of environmental problems it already has; the need step (paragraphs 2–4) features information probably unfamiliar to most students; the satisfaction step (paragraph 5) is comparatively short, because of course Ms. Erdmann is not addressing farmers as her primary audience; the visualization step (paragraphs 6–7) has enough detail so that even nonexpert listeners can understand the changes that are possible in agricultural practice; and the action step (paragraphs 8–9) leaves the world of the farmer behind to concentrate specifically on actions a student audience can take.

Environmentally Unsafe Farming: An Unsafe Practice[4]
April Erdmann

Attention Step

It's obvious to anyone who reads magazines and newspapers or watches TV that the 1990's is indeed the decade for the environmentally aware. After all, we now recycle all our paper products, use words such as deforestation and greenhouse effect in everyday conversation, and we've even designated an entire day for cleaning up the earth, but while millions of Americans are busy recycling aluminum cans and boycotting styrofoam, there is still one environmental danger lurking in the shadows and in a sense, creeping across the rural countrysides of America, and that is the problem of environmentally unsafe farming. More specifically, the abuse of agrichemicals, or any chemical that is used for farming. In order to further understand environmentally unsafe farming we will first define the problem and its effects on society, then look at some alternatives to conventional farming, and finally pose some reasonable steps of action that we can take to prevent further damage. /1

Need Step

Environmentally unsafe farming can be defined as any agricultural practice which depletes our natural resources used for farming, or is detrimental to other environmental resources, such as our water supplies. One aspect of this problem is that many of the chemicals that are sprayed on our food have not been tested by the Environmental Protection Agency. An article in the *Journal of the American Medical Association*, June 9, 1989, stated that there was no toxicological data on one-third of all agrichemicals, minimal data on another third and reliable data on only one-tenth. That means that approximately 90% of the pesticides sprayed on the foods we eat and that drain into the water we drink have not been properly tested for poisons. These statistics open special cause for concern when we realize just how many agrichemicals farmers actually use. According to an article in the January 20, 1990, issue of the *Congressional Quarterly*, 450 to 500 million pounds of pesticides are applied to crops each year. That's a lot of untested agrichemicals that are being sprayed on our food. /2

In recent years, a lot of pressure has been put on the government by environmental groups to limit the use of agrichemicals. Because of this pressure the EPA has already withdrawn 27 agrichemicals from the market due to evidence of health hazards. Furthermore the EPA now considers agriculture the largest source of surface water pollution due to the drainage of these chemicals off the soil. Tests by the EPA in states such as Iowa, Florida and Minnesota have detected agrichemicals in groundwater which supplies 50% of all drinking water. An article in the June 4, 1990, issue of *Business Week Magazine* stated that a 1988 EPA survey found traces of pesticides in the groundwater of 26 states and detected nitrates exceeding current safety standards in about 20% of the private wells in Iowa, Kansas and South Dakota. This groundwater contamination is not limited to only the states I have mentioned, though. Any area of our country in which agrichemicals are used is probably experiencing the same problem. /3

Although these statistics are alarming, many farmers argue that these chemicals have no real health effects on the people who consume them. The truth is that many of these chemicals can cause serious health problems. We've all heard that certain chemicals cause cancer, but now there's another health hazard that we need to be aware of when dealing with these pesticides and that is the problem of neurotoxicity or poisons that could affect our nervous systems. According to an article in the December, 1989, issue of *Horticulture Magazine,* the National Academy of Sciences found that nearly two-thirds of all pesticide ingredients were not being tested for neurotoxic effects, and the rest were being tested inadequately. One group of pesticides, called carbamates, which is subject to no type of testing whatsoever, is known to block the action of certain enzymes in the body and overstimulate nerve cells causing cramps, nausea, twitching and mental and behavioral disorders, effects which studies suggest can last for years. In July of 1985, the presence of one of these carbamates in watermelons caused symptoms of short-term nervous system damage in almost a thousand people on the western coasts of the United States and Canada. Although these examples are scary, we need to realize that a lifetime of consumer risk from pesticide residue may equal only half a season for a farmer. Carbondisulfide, a substance present in pesticides that is not subject to testing, has been known to disrupt brain function and has been linked to lethargy, recurring memory loss, insomnia, difficulty concentrating, and pain and weakness of the arms and legs in farmers who use these chemicals. So, these agrichemicals can cause serious health effects when they contaminate our food and drain through the soil into our water, but is there any alternative to this conventional method of farming with agrichemicals? /4

Satisfaction Step

Actually, there are several alternatives. One of the most obvious is organic farming which uses absolutely no chemicals and is done mostly through manual labor. Unfortunately, for the farmer who grows an extensive amount of crops, this is not a viable option. It would be nearly impossible to walk through hundreds of acres of farmlands pulling weeds and checking for insects. So, if organic farming is not the answer to this problem, what is? Well, one solution may be sustainable agriculture, which according to the June, 1990, issue of *Scientific American* can be defined as techniques which produce adequate amounts of high quality food, protect our resources and are environmentally safe and profitable. Instead of depending on purchased materials such as pesticides and fertilizers, a sustainable farm relies as much as possible on beneficial natural resources drawn from the farm itself. /5

Visualization Step

One example of successful sustainable agriculture is Joe Maddox, a farmer in Colorado City, Texas. He once tried to eliminate mesquite, a type of plant, on his 22,000 acre sheep and cattle ranch by dousing it with pesticides. Now he just lets the mesquite grow and covers it with pasture to control its spreading. He also used to spray for cockleburs, a plant that would get into the wool of his sheep, but then he began to realize that these agrichemicals were affecting Lake Spence, a nearby source of drinking water for many people. Now Maddox baits cocklebur stands with salt to attract the cattle and the cattle crush the cockleburs underfoot. /6

Another example of good sustainable agriculture is Fred Kirshenman. According to an article in the May 21, 1990, issue of *Time Magazine,* when this farmer from Medina, North Dakota, discovered that the soil on his 3,100 acre farm was getting harder to till and he was having to apply more expensive pesticides and fertilizers, just to achieve the same yield, he became the first person in his township to stop using agrichemicals, and the results were worth it. By rotating crops and using special plowing techniques he was actually able to improve the quality of his soil and he still maintains an average harvest of thirty-three bushels of wheat per acre, which is as good, if not better than any of his neighbors who use conventional farming. Furthermore, he's been able to make a profit through farm products such as sunflowers and cattle, and he hasn't had to borrow operating funds in nine years. The June, 1990, *Scientific American* article reported that farmers who practice the reduction of agrichemicals generally report that their production costs are lower than those of nearby conventional farms. Sometimes, the yields from sustainable farms are lower, but that is offset by lower production costs, which leads to equal or greater net returns. So, farmers can incorporate sustainable agriculture into their routines to help stop this problem, but what can we do? /7

Action Step   First and foremost, we need to change our attitudes about produce. One problem with organic farming is that although the food is almost always fresher than that which is grown conventionally, many times it just doesn't look as good because it hasn't been sprayed with appearance enhancing chemicals. According to an article in the August, 1990, issue of *OMNI Magazine,* many times vegetables are sprayed with man-made toxins, picked before they are ripe, and then pumped with chemicals to make them appear appropriately fresh and rosy so that when they're shipped 2,000 miles to a grocery store, they look like they've just been picked out of the garden. Unless your produce manager assures you that this food was grown safely though, don't assume that it was. According to an article in the December, 1990, issue of *Food Technology,* when a group of consumers were asked to rate the importance of sixteen product characteristics, 94% said appearance, while only 17% rated organically grown as important. These statistics show that we need to develop a major attitudinal change for own health. This past summer I worked in the produce department of a grocery store and I asked my produce manager if the foods in our supermarket were grown safely. He told me that because chain stores, such as ours, usually had requirements for large volume, most of the food we sold was grown conventionally. The previously mentioned *Food Technology* article suggests that if you want to insure that you are getting the best quality food, that you buy your produce from health food stores, consumer food cooperatives and farmer's markets which are generally unable to meet the large volume requirements of supermarket chains. During the summer you can see small fruit and vegetable stands set up just about anywhere. This is the perfect opportunity to stop and ask the actual person who grew the food or his Cousin Joe what type, if any, chemicals were used, so don't hesitate to stop and support a local farmer or gardener who you can be sure uses environmentally safe techniques. Finally, since most of us are now able to vote or will be able to shortly, be sure to vote yes on farm bills and other legislation that supports environmentally safe farming. This way, you'll be ensuring your own health as well as that of the farmers who grow our food. /8

So, now we've taken a look at environmentally unsafe farming and its effects on society, we've seen some alternatives to this problem and finally we've posed some reasonable steps of action that we can take to prevent further damage, so maybe, since the 1990's is indeed the decade for the environmentally aware, we can stop that one danger of environmentally unsafe farming from lurking in the shadows, and in a sense, bring it into the light, where it belongs. /9

Structure and Development of the Steps in the Motivated Sequence

Now that we've illustrated the motivated sequence in its entirety, we need to examine more closely the individual steps, noting in particular their internal structuring, the methods for developing them, and the kinds of materials that can be used effectively in each.

The Attention Step

As a speaker, your first task is to gain attention. The attributes of attention and the major devices for obtaining it were covered in Chapter 3. As you plan this step in your speech, review these devices and determine which ones might best stimulate audience interest in your topic. If the audience is lethargic or tired, you need to begin with something more innovative than "Today I'd like to. . . ." Thus, the nine factors of attention discussed in Chapter 3 (activity, reality, proximity, familiarity, novelty, suspense, conflict, humor, and the vital) take on special relevance in the opening moments of your presentation.

Your manner of delivery also affects the attentiveness of your audience; the vigor and variety of your gestures and bodily movements and the flexibility and animation of your voice are important determinants of audience enthusiasm and interest in your subject. Your credibility, or *ethos*, as it is judged by your listeners, also assists you in securing their attention. If they already have high regard for you, they're more likely to be attentive as you begin your presentation. The color and impressiveness of your language and style also affect the audience's willingness to attend to your message. A lackadaisical delivery, coupled with a colorless and uninteresting style, is counterproductive. Fundamentally, however, you capture and hold attention through the *types of ideas* you present to your listeners. Your ideas must tap their sense of interest and personal motivation before they will feel compelled to listen.

Although gaining attention is an initial step in bringing your ideas to an audience, remember that *keeping* attention also is vitally important. Keep

In order to capture and hold attention, a speaker must present ideas that tap listeners' interests and personal motivation.

the same attention devices in mind as you develop the remaining steps in the motivated sequence; in particular, they can be used to heighten attention during the need and visualization steps. An enthusiastic delivery and style also improve your chances of success, as does your satisfaction of the audience's initial assessment of you as a responsible, ethical individual through careful, complete presentation of ideas.

The Need Step

Assuming the audience is attending to you and your message, you must lay out reasons for being concerned about the issue you're discussing: Why is the information or viewpoint vital to their interests? Why should they think the problem is urgent? To provide answers to such questions, the need step can be set up effectively like this:

1. *Statement.* Offer a clear statement of the need. State the central idea or claim, and even offer it phrased in more than one way to make the point clearly.

   The Iowa River is being poisoned by agricultural chemical runoff.

2. *Illustration.* Present one or more illustrations of specific instances to give listeners an initial idea of the problem's seriousness and scope—its importance or significance.

> *The Army Corps of Engineers' annual study of fish kills in the Coralville Reservoir indicates they're at three times the national average and increasing with each passing year.*

3. *Ramification.* Using the types of supporting materials discussed in Chapter 7, clarify your statement of need and justify the concern you're expressing. Add more examples, additional statistics, testimony from experts, and other forms of support to drive your analysis forward with force.

> *Water from the Iowa River provides Iowa City with half its drinking water. The Water Works department tests that water every day in the spring. A five-year overview of their figures shows that nitrates in our drinking water have climbed from the above-average to the low-danger level. Last spring Water Works Director Calvin Shrien said that "If agricultural chemical use isn't better controlled in northern Iowa, towns like Iowa City in the southern part of the state will have to import drinking water from outside the area."*

4. *Pointing.* Impress upon your listeners the issue's seriousness, scope, and significance to them. Tie it to their health, happiness, security, or other interests.

> *So, are you ready to start buying most of your drinking water? Are you ready to brush your teeth with Perrier, make cocoa with LaCroix, and fill your dog's water dish with Evian? Iowa may seem like a clean-air, healthy place to raise kids and tomatoes, but its water quality is deteriorating faster than it is in major American cities.*

In the need step, you have two primary goals: to make your subject clear and to relate it to the concerns and interests of your audience. While you may not need to use all four tactics every time you discuss some need, you at least should think about them. When arguing for the development of a nuclear-free Europe, for example, you wouldn't need to do much with illustration and ramifications, though still the statement of the need and pointing—how does the problem affect listeners in the middle of the United States—are important. Adjust the development of the need step to your topic, the audience's knowledge base, and their concerns.

The Satisfaction Step

The purpose of this step is to help your listeners understand the information you're presenting or to obtain their assent to the action you're proposing. The structure of this step varies, depending whether your purpose is primar-

In the satisfaction step of a speech to actuate, a speaker can demonstrate the workability of a proposed action and answer objections that might arise.

ily informative, entertaining, or persuasive. Consider this step for each type of speech:

The Satisfaction Step in a Speech to Inform.   When your primary goal is to give listeners a clear understanding of a topic, this step is met when the need for information has been satisfied. Consider the speech on agricultural chemical runoff, for example. As an informative speech, it doesn't include a well-developed "plan," as would a speech to persuade or actuate, but you certainly would want to inform your listeners about the many interlocking problems that would have to be solved to stop river poisoning.

1. *Initial summary.* Briefly state the main ideas you'll cover.

   Detoxifying something as long and big as a river is no easy task. Cleaning up the nation's rivers, including the Iowa River, will happen only when we return to natural fertilizers, develop more biodegradable chemical fertilizers, divert runoff from agricultural fields to holding ponds, and improve filtration systems in our towns and cities.

2. *Detailed information.* Discuss the facts and explanations pertaining to each of the main ideas. For our speech on agricultural runoff, that would produce a four-part detoxification process: natural fertilizers, biodegrad-

able chemical fertilizers, ways to reroute runoff, and new developments in water filtration.

3. *Final summary.* Restate the main ideas you've presented, together with any important conclusions you want to leave with your listeners.

> *Even in a town as beautiful as Iowa City, we must be concerned about the quality of river water: water that is the life-environment of marine life and the life-elixir of towns on its banks. In this speech, I've discussed both the marine and the human side of the problem, and suggested that the solution to the problem is complex, requiring four different kinds of large-scale efforts.*
>
> *Those of you who came here from Minnesota laugh at this state sometimes, calling it "The Land of 10 Lakes." But, like many of you, I've learned to appreciate the importance and beauty not only of lake life but also river life. By the time the Iowa River flows into Iowa City, it's only about forty-five miles from the end of its journey, in the Mississippi. Here in Iowa City, the Iowa River is broad and slow—great for fishing, canoeing, power-boating, and swimming. This city, this university, this state are enhanced and enriched by the Iowa River and river life. Your experience with it will tell you that, sooner or later, you're going to have to be part of its reclamation. I hope this speech has helped you understand the problems and will guide you as you decide what contributions you can make to keep the river alive.*

The Satisfaction Step in a Speech to Entertain.   When your purpose is to entertain—to present a useful thought or sentiment in a light-hearted, humorous manner—the satisfaction step can constitute the major part of your speech. Your goal is to satisfy the audience that the speech is, in fact, entertaining and that it has conveyed an idea or sentiment worth their time and attention. In developing the satisfaction step in a speech to entertain, follow these guidelines:

1. *Initial statement of theme.* Briefly indicate the sentiment or idea that you will discuss.

2. *Humorous elaboration.* Develop the theme with particular attention to hypothetical and factual illustrations and specific instances that will convey a light-hearted, yet meaningful, message to the audience.

3. *Final summary.* Restate your main theme by connecting your illustrations to the point you wish to make.

The Satisfaction Step in a Speech to Persuade or to Actuate.   In these instances, the satisfaction step is developed as a major subdivision of the speech. The following elements are usually included:

1. *Statement.* Briefly state the attitude, belief, or action you wish the audience to adopt.

2. *Explanation.* Make sure your statement is understood by the audience.

Diagrams or charts may be useful in explaining a complex proposal or plan.

3. *Theoretical demonstration.* Show how this belief or action logically meets the problem illustrated in the need step.

4. *Workability.* If appropriate, present examples showing that this solution has worked effectively in the past or that this belief has been supported by experience. Use fact, figures, and expert testimony to support your claim about the workability of your proposal or idea.

5. *Meeting objections.* Forestall opposition by answering possible objections that might be raised.

These five elements may not be needed in every speech to persuade or to actuate; they also may not appear in this order. For instance, if workability is the key to the success of your proposal, and the audience already is well informed about it, you can shorten the preceding steps and spend most of your time persuading the audience that the idea can work. Conversely, if workability is not the central issue, but an explanation of how the "plan meets the need" is in order, you may spend a great deal more time on this facet. In any case, the elements, in sequence, offer a useful framework for the presentation of a solution to a problem: (a) briefly state what you propose to do, (b) explain it clearly, (c) show how it remedies the problem, (d) demonstrate its workability, and (e) answer objections.

Parallel Development of the Need and Satisfaction Steps. In most persuasive speeches, you will have more than one main point to stress in developing your rationale. Further, each main point may relate to a different facet of the solution you are proposing. To show the relationship between each main point and its relevant solution, you can develop the need and satisfaction steps in *parallel order.* That is, you can present the initial main point under the need step and follow it with the facet of the solution that clearly alleviates the problem identified in that point. This approach can be followed in the presentation of the second, third, and even fourth main points. While the method weakens the cumulative or sequential effect of the motivated sequence, the added clarity often makes up for the loss.

The sequential order and the parallel order for developing the need and satisfaction steps of a speech to actuate are illustrated in the following outlines:

Sequential Order

Attention Step   I. While working for the local hospital's emergency ambulance unit this past summer, I responded to sev-

eral automobile accidents in which the driver was severely injured.
   A. [Vivid description of how the accidents occurred]
   B. [Vivid description of the injuries sustained by the drivers]

Need Step

I. In many of these accidents, the driver either had been drinking or fell asleep at the wheel.
   A. The driver was unable to react properly due to the effect of the alcohol.
   B. The driver awoke too late to take corrective action.

Satisfaction Step

I. In order to combat these two causes of highway accidents, you must do two things above all others.
   A. Do not drive under the influence of alcohol.
   B. Do not drive when you are tired—if you have been driving for a long time, stop and rest.

Visualization Step

I. You will actually enjoy driving more when you have the assurance these actions will bring.

Action Step

I. Resolve right now to do two things when you drive.
   A. Do not drink and drive.
   B. Do not drive when tired.

Parallel Order

Attention Step

I. While working for the local hospital's emergency ambulance unit this past summer, I responded to several accidents in which the driver was severely injured.
   A. [Vivid description of how the accident occurred]
   B. [Vivid description of the injuries sustained by the driver]

Need and Satisfaction Steps (First Phase)

I. *Need:* In some cases the driver had been drinking and was unable to react properly.

II. *Satisfaction:* To assure yourself that you can react properly, do not mix drinking with driving.

Need and Satisfaction Steps (Second Phase)

I. *Need:* In some cases the driver had fallen asleep and awoke too late to take corrective action.

II. *Satisfaction:* To assure yourself that you can take corrective action, do not drive when tired.

Visualization Step

I. You will actually enjoy driving more when you have the assurance that these actions will bring.

Action Step I. Resolve right now to do two things when you drive.
                             A. Do not drink and drive.
                             B. Do not drive when tired.

Whether using sequential order or parallel order, you need to develop support for your statements by supplying an abundance of illustrations, statistics, expert testimony, and comparisons.

The Visualization Step

This step is most commonly included in speeches to persuade and to actuate. The function of this step is to intensify audience desire or willingness to act—to motivate your listeners to believe, to feel, or to act in a certain way. The primary strategy is to project listeners into the future and illustrate vividly the results of accepting or denying the proposed belief or acting or failing to act as the speaker directs. The step may be developed in one of three ways:

- **Positive method.** Describe the favorable conditions that will prevail if the audience accepts your beliefs about the future or your proposals. Use specific examples and illustrations to give audience members a clear sense of what they can look forward to by their agreement.
- **Negative method.** Describe the adverse conditions that will prevail in the future if the audience does *not* adopt the belief you advocate or carry out the solution you propose. Graphically describe the danger or unpleasantness that will result from their denial or inaction. In the case of problems requiring a solution, select the most striking deficiencies you have already illustrated [in the need step], and demonstrate why they will continue or worsen unless the audience adopts your recommendations.
- **Contrast method.** This approach combines both positive and negative perspectives on the future. Forecast the negative possibilities first, then introduce the positive attributes that can be expected if the audience members embrace your ideas or act upon your proposal. By means of such contrast, the bad and good effects—the disadvantages and advantages—are more striking than if they were presented in isolation from one another.

Whichever method you use, realize that the visualization step always must stand the test of reality; the conditions you picture must appear believable and probable. The audience must accept them as real possibilities, not simply as mere chance developments that might accrue from their response to your ideas. In addition, you must make every effort to put your listeners into the picture—to let them see themselves actually living in the future environment you so carefully craft. Use vivid imagery; create mental images that allow the audience members to see, hear, feel, taste, or smell the advantages or disadvantages you describe. The more real you make the

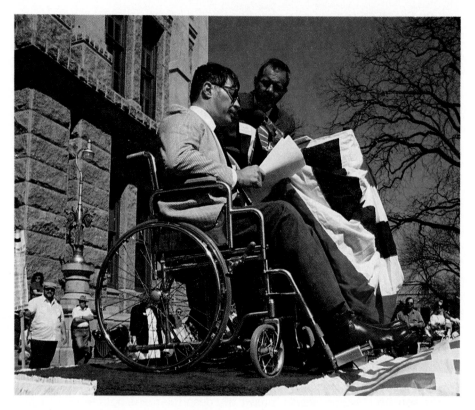

The primary strategy of visualization is to project listeners into the future by vividly illustrating the results of their action or inaction.

projected situation, the greater are your chances of getting a significant, positive response from your audience. The following sample shows how a speaker urging you to plan your college curriculum carefully might develop a visualization step using the contrast method:

> Suppose you enter the university, as nearly 40 percent of our students do, as an "undecided"—either with few interests and even less sense of your educational goals or with many interests that are ill defined or poorly focused. How will you select courses? You might approach the problem in one of two ways: either you "go with the flow," or you seek early advice and plan systematically to ensure graduation after four years.
>
> If you use the first approach, you begin by taking only courses that meet specific requirements (for example, English, speech, math, and science courses). In your second year, you start experimenting with some electives—courses that will not meet specific requirements. You find yourself listening to and accepting your friends' recommendations—"Take Speech 124 because it's easy," "Take Photography 102 because it's cool," or "Take Art 103 because you get to draw what you want." Now comes your junior year. You're nowhere

near a major and you're getting close to the three-quarter mark in your education. Your advisor, your parents, and your friends all nag you. You even get down on yourself. In your senior year, you sample some social work courses, finally discovering something you really like. Only then do you realize it will take three or four more semesters—if you're lucky—to complete a B.S.W. degree.

In contrast, suppose you're one of the other half of the "undecided"—those who seek career and personal advisement early. You enroll for the no-credit "Careers and Vocational Choices" seminar in your first semester. While meeting your liberal arts requirements, you take classes in several different departments to test your interests. During your sophomore year, you work with three or four areas of possible interest; you take more advanced courses in these areas to ascertain your interest and ability. Near the end of your sophomore year, you talk with people in Career Planning and meet frequently with your advisor. By your junior year, you get departmental advisors in two majors, find out you don't like one subject as much as you thought, and consult only the second advisor after midyear. You go on to complete the major, taking a summer course between your junior and senior year to catch up because you are a little behind, and obtain your degree "on time."

Carefully planning, experimenting with possible interests, reasoning thoughtfully about your reaction to different areas of study, and rigorously analyzing your own talents are actions that separate the completers from the complainers four years later, so . . . [*move into the action step at this point*].

The Action Step

As the accompanying table indicates, only the speech to actuate *always* requires an action step. With other speech purposes, such as to inform or to entertain, you may use something resembling an action step: urging further study of the topic dealt with in an informative speech, using humor to engage the audience's interest in further exploration of a subject, or seeking to strengthen a belief or attitude in meeting a persuasive purpose.

The action step should be relatively brief. Two adages apply: "Stand up, speak up, shut up" and "Tell 'em what you're going to tell 'em, tell 'em, and then tell 'em what you told 'em." Insofar as the action step is concerned, clinch your major ideas, finish your speech briskly, and sit down.

Applying the Motivated Sequence

You've now been presented with a description of the steps or stages of the motivated sequence and their roles in the structure and development of speeches. Now, let's examine some brief outlines of speeches representing each of the main types you're likely to give in your life. (Later chapters will go much further into each type—see Part IV.)

APPLYING THE MOTIVATED SEQUENCE TO THE GENERAL PURPOSES OF SPEECH

General Purposes

	TO INFORM *(Understanding, Clarity)*	*TO ENTERTAIN* *(Enjoyment)*
1 Attention Step	Draw attention to the subject.	Draw attention to the theme.
2 Need Step	Show why listeners need a knowledge of the subject, point out what problems this information will help them solve.	Show why the theme is worthy of consideration.
3 Satisfaction Step	Present information to give listeners a satisfactory knowledge of the subject to help them solve these problems; begin and end this presentation with a summary of the main points (normal end of the speech).	Elaborate on the theme through numerous illustrations to elicit a pleasurable reaction from listeners.
4 Visualization Step	Sometimes: briefly suggest pleasure to be gained from this knowledge.	Sometimes: briefly suggest what is to be gained through humorous examination of the theme.
5 Action Step	Sometimes: urge further study of the subject.	Sometimes: implore listeners to consider the lighter side of life.

APPLYING THE MOTIVATED SEQUENCE TO THE GENERAL PURPOSES OF SPEECH

General Purposes

	TO PERSUADE (Belief [Internal])	TO ACTUATE (Specific Action [Observable])
1 Attention Step	Draw attention to the need.	Draw attention to the need.
2 Need Step	Present evidence to prove the existence of a situation that requires a decision upon which listeners must take a position.	Present evidence to prove the existence of a situation that requires action.
3 Satisfaction Step	Get listeners to believe your position is the right one by using evidence and motivational appeals.	Propose the specific action required to meet this situation; get listeners to believe in it by presenting evidence and motivational appeals (as in the speech to persuade).
4 Visualization Step	Briefly stimulate a favorable response by projecting this belief into imaginary operation (normal end of the speech).	Picture the results of such action or of the failure to act; use vivid description (as in the speech to persuade).
5 Action Step	Sometimes: arouse determination to retain this belief (as a guide to future action).	Urge listeners to take the specific action proposed.

Lecture Fees for the Rich and Famous

CNN's Ted Turner:	$35,000	Football commentator John Madden:	$35,000
Feminist writer Gloria Steinem:	$15,000	Former First Lady Rosalyn Carter:	$20,000
Novelist Stephen King:	$20,000	TV interviewer Jane Pauley:	$25,000*
Actress Diana Rigg:	$12,500		
Comic writer Dave Barry:	$10,000		
TV interviewer Barbara Walters:	$25,000		
Comedian Bob Hope:	$100,000		
Conservative Jeane Kirkpatrick:	$20,000		

So, all you need to do is brush your teeth, get a good night's sleep, and practice your speechmaking skills day after day. Who says talk is cheap?

* Matthew Connor, "Lecture Fees of the Rich and Famous," *Forbes FYI* (1992), pp. 74–77.

Using the Motivated Sequence in a Speech to Inform

Generally, informative speeches concentrate on the first three steps of the motivated sequence. You, of course, need to elicit listeners' initial attention and then sustain it throughout the rest of the speech. You also must motivate them to listen, approaching the need step in this way: why should anyone want to know the information you're about to present? Then, to satisfy this need (step 3), you actually supply the material that's the subject matter of your speech. Sometimes, an action step is added in response to the "so what?" question: What should your listeners do with this information? You don't concentrate your attention on the action step in an informative speech, but it can provide a nice conclusion. Four steps of the motivated sequence are applied in the following outline of an informative speech.

Sleep Apnea

Attention Step	I.	Do you snore, or do you know someone who does?
	II.	If you snore, do you find yourself falling asleep at odd times during the day, even though you're not tired?
Need Step	I.	For most of us, snoring is simply a laughing matter.
	II.	For one of ten snorers, it may not be.
		A. These snorers suffer from sleep apnea.
		B. This disease causes the person to stop breathing for short periods of time.
Satisfaction Step	I.	Snoring, when severe enough to cause apnea, produces negative effects on one's health.

A. Apneic snorers suffer from short moments of oxygen deprivation accompanied by higher than normal levels of carbon monoxide, which affect the heart, the brain, and other vital organs.

B. Apneic snorers develop hypertension (chronic high blood pressure) at a much faster rate than nonsnorers.

C. Apneic snorers have a much higher incidence of depression and headaches than nonsnorers.

D. Apneic snorers experience social problems, such as job instability, marital difficulties, inability to concentrate, irritability, and even aggressive behavior at a higher rate than nonsnorers.

II. You can assess the possibility of sleep apnea through a number of methods.

A. Monitor your own snoring with a tape recorder; listen for pauses that last between ten seconds and one or two minutes.

B. Have a sleep partner monitor your snoring pattern; time actual breathing lapses characteristic of snoring behavior.

C. Daytime sleepiness is a major clue to the existence of apnea.

Action Step

I. The next time your rest is interrupted by someone's snoring, remember that, for that person, it may not be a laughing matter.[5]

Using the Motivated Sequence in a Speech to Entertain

As was noted, the speech to entertain may exist for humor in its own right, but more often it uses an occasion for humor to make a serious point. In instances in which you expect the audience only to sit back and enjoy the presentation (for example, at a comic revue), the attention step is the only one required. When you want to both entertain your audience and make a serious point, additional steps are appropriate. In the following outline, all of the steps of the motivated sequence are appropriate to the "moral" that the speaker draws from the discussion of optimism vs. pessimism and the concluding appeal for acting as an optimist.

A Case for Optimism

Attention Step

I. Perhaps you've heard the expression "The optimist sees the doughnut, the pessimist, the hole."

Need Step

I. To the pessimist, the optimist is a fool: the person who looks at an oyster and expects to find pearls is engaging in wishful thinking.

II. To the optimist, the pessimist is sour on life: the person who looks at an oyster and expects to get ptomaine poisoning is missing out on the richer possibilities life can offer.

Satisfaction Step

I. The pessimist responds to every event with an expectation of the worst that could happen.

II. The optimist, on the other hand, looks for the bright side.

    A. The day after a robbery, a friend asked a store owner about the loss. After acknowledging that he had indeed suffered a loss, the store owner quipped, "But I was lucky; I marked everything down 20 percent the day before—had I not done that, I would have lost even more."

    B. The optimist is one who cleans her glasses before she eats grapefruit.

Visualization Step

I. When you look on the bright side, you find things to be happy about.

Action Step

I. Be an optimist: "Keep your eye on the doughnut and not on the hole."[6]

Using the Motivated Sequence in a Speech to Persuade

The following speech outline, urging an end to the colorization of classic films, is not a "complete" speech outline, but its detail shows how supporting material is integrated into the various stages and how the overall speech is developed.

Oppose Colorization

Specific Purpose: To convince listeners that colorization of classic black-and-white movies should not be allowed

Attention Step

    I. If you like classic movies as I do, imagine my surprise in turning on the television to watch *The Maltese Falcon* and discovering that it had been "colorized"—a process that imposes "natural colors" onto films that were originally shot in black and white.

    II. The issue of colorization has divided the Hollywood community and has even generated congressional interest.

Need Step

    I. Ted Turner was behind the original impetus to colorize movies for replay on television.

        A. Turner acquired the MGM film library, which included over 3600 films.

        B. Turner Broadcasting has committed $18 million toward the colorization of 100 classic films, from among those it acquired in the MGM purchase.

    II. There are several objections to the colorization of classic films.

        A. The most common objection concerns the violation of the original integrity of the film.

            1. For example, John Huston, the director of *The Maltese Falcon*, held a press conference to denounce the colorization of his original work.

            2. A contemporary director, Martin Scorsese, has pointed out that colorization of his 1980 movie, *Raging Bull*, would destroy the artistic integrity of the film.

            3. Nicholas Meyer, director of *Star Trek II*, commented, "It is a mind boggling disservice to the artistry of black-and-white films. They [the original producers/directors] photographed these films using the values of black-and-white photography."

        B. Several arts groups have spoken out against the colorization of classic films.

            1. The Director's Guild of America

            2. The Screen Actor's Guild

            3. The Writer's Guild of America

            4. The American Society of Cinematographers

        C. Federal groups and officials also have protested the process.

            1. The National Council on the Arts and the

                      American Film Institute have expressed their opposition to the process.

    2. Representative Richard Gephardt sponsored a Film Integrity Act to provide legal protection for old films.

  D. There is no current law opposing colorization of classic films.

    1. The principle that an artist's work is harmed by colorization has not been supported by law.

    2. In contrast, the principle does have support in both England and France.

Satisfaction Step

I. How should we protect an artist's original work?

  A. I propose that we support legislation similar to that enacted in England and France.

  B. The legislation proposed by Gephardt will accomplish the goal of protection from colorization.

Visualization Step

I. The enactment of legislation will bring a halt to the colorization of black-and-white films.

  A. When you turn on the TV to watch Laurel and Hardy's *Helpmates* or *Miracle on 34th Street,* you can be sure that it is the original version.

  B. Ending colorization will halt a practice that many view as an immoral intrusion on an artist's original work—after all, the new "color" version is a technician's idea of what colors would have looked like, not a producer's or director's.

Action Step

I. What do I want from you?

  A. I hope you agree that colorization harms the artistic integrity of an original work.

  B. I also hope that I have convinced you that colorization is not an idea "whose time has come."[7]

Using the Motivated Sequence in a Speech to Actuate

All five steps of the motivated sequence are used in a speech to actuate; the audience is asked to go beyond a change in belief state or an awareness of new information, to actually behave in certain ways. The following outline illustrates how the previous speech can be altered from one with a persuasive orientation to one with an actuative intent. Because the initial steps would remain the same, only the changes in the action step are shown.

Action Step

I. What do I want from you?

  A. For starters, you can boycott those films already colorized; do not watch Turner's colorized films on television and do not rent colorized versions of classic movies.

    B. Second, you can assist me by talking to your friends and convincing them to join the boycott.

    C. Finally, you can take action by writing your congressional representative or senator and urge legislative action to end colorization.

Chapter Summary

The human need to find or construct structure or order in the world is the basis for the speaker's need for pattern or organization in his or her materials. Listeners need speakers to provide emphasis via distinctions between *foreground* and *background (differentiation)* and via a sense of completeness that provides *closure* to messages. People use language to structure their worlds and generally approach such structuring with either real-world, *problem-centered* methods of investigation or psychologically oriented, *motivation-centered* methods. *Monroe's Motivated Sequence* was introduced early in this century as a means of combining problem- and motivated-centered structures for ideas: it provides an orderly approach to problem solving with a motivational framework. Its five steps—*attention, need, satisfaction, visualization,* and *action*—can be used to structure any type (informative, entertaining, persuasive, actuative) of speech.

References

1. Reprinted from the 19 November 1915 *Salt Lake* [Utah] *Tribune* in *The Oxford Dictionary of Modern Quotations,* ed. Tony Augarde (New York: Oxford University Press, 1991), 102.

2. The principle of closure is one of the Gestalt principles of perception. The term "gestalt" refers to wholeness and has been used to refer to a group of psychologists who've researched these aspects of cognitive processes. For a brief review of basic Gestalt principles, see John R. Anderson, *Cognitive Psychology and Its Implications* (New York: W. H. Freeman & Co., 1980), 53–56; Philip G. Zimbardo, *Psychology and Life,* 13 ed. (New York: HarperCollins Publishers, 1992), 266–8.

3. John Dewey, *How We Think* (Boston: D. C. Heath Co., 1910), 72.

4. April Erdmann, "Environmentally Unsafe Farming: An Unsafe Practice," *Winning Orations 1991.* Reprinted by permission of Larry Schnoor, Executive Secretary, Interstate Oratorical Association, Mankato State University, MN.

5. Information cited in Steve Kaplan, "Snoring," *World and I,* 2 (July 1987): 298–303.

6. Based in part on information from *Friendly Speeches* (Cleveland, OH: National Reference Library).

7. Material based on Debra Wishik, "Colorization: Not a Black and White Issue," *World and I,* 2 (July 1987): 236–41.

Key Terms

action step   (p. 197)

attention step   (p. 197)

closure   (p. 194)

contrast visualization
method   (p. 211)

differentiation   (p. 194)

Monroe's Motivated Sequence
(p. 196)

need step   (p. 197)

negative visualization
method   (p. 211)

positive visualization
method   (p. 211)

satisfaction step   (p. 197)

visualization step   (p. 197)

Problems and Probes

1. Choose a social controversy as a topic for a speech; specify two audiences, one opposing the issue and the other supporting it (for example, a speech on the need for additional day care facilities presented to a liberal audience and a conservative audience). Using the motivated sequence as a pattern, specify how you would develop each step so it is appropriate to each audience. Write a concluding paragraph that explains the differences between the speeches, as they were adapted to the differing positions of the audiences.

2. The motivated sequence has its own internal logic aimed at satisfying audience questions: attention precedes need, need precedes satisfaction, and so on. Working in small groups, discuss the utility of this perspective as a means of responding to audience expectations. On what occasions might you consider eliminating a step or reversing the order of steps? Would any other pattern have equal or greater utility? At the end of the discussion, be prepared to report your conclusions to the rest of the class.

3. Develop brief outlines for an informative and a persuasive speech using the samples in this chapter as guides. What are the major differences between the outlines—which steps are included or left out of the analysis? What do you do differently in each step in orienting your speech toward presenting information or persuading an audience? Following the outlines, write your response to these questions. Hand in your outlines and response for evaluation by the instructor.

Communication Activities

1. Select a topic for an informative, a persuasive, or an entertaining speech. Develop a specific purpose and a brief outline of the speech, following the appropriate steps in the motivated sequence. Assume that the audience will be your classmates. Working in small groups, each member presents his or her abbreviated "speech"; critique each presentation in terms of its appropriate use of the motivated sequence.

2. Select a topic for a speech that could be either persuasive or actuative. Develop a specific purpose and a brief outline, following the appropriate steps in the motivated sequence. When you come to the action step, develop two approaches—one meeting the needs of a persuasive speech, the other an actuative speech. Working in small groups, briefly review the purpose and the elements contained in the persuasive outline, then indicate how you would alter the speech to make it actuative. Does your specific purpose change as you shift from one speech type to another? Critique one another's approaches to this assignment.

THE MOTIVATED SEQUENCE AND PATTERNS OF INTERNAL ORGANIZATION

I n the preceding chapter, we presented an overview of a holistic or basic way of organizing speeches. The motivated sequence is responsive to the thought processes listeners often follow when receiving new information or trying to solve problems. The motivated sequence is general enough to be used in almost any speaking situation, but you may need more guidance. *How much time should you devote to each step?* Some speakers get so carried away with telling stories as attention-getters that they steal valuable time that should have been used on the need and satisfaction steps. And, more urgently, *how are the need and satisfaction steps related logically to each other?* It's true that they're psychologically related, but how can you relate need arguments to satisfaction plans for change?

You'll face such problems when you organize or package materials for audiences. In Chapter 8, after all, we treated simple speeches; in your life you'll probably have to give more complicated messages. How can you organize the insides, the various parts, of your speeches? In other words, are there specific *organizational patterns* useful when you're presenting information and ideas to audiences? We'll first discuss the idea of "organization" or "pattern" generally, expanding some of the notions introduced in the previous chapter, then look at four types of organizational patterns you'll want to consider each time you talk publicly.

Developing Patterns of Internal Organization Within the Steps of the Motivated Sequence

The motivated sequence gives you a solid overall structure, but it doesn't really help you with some of the complicated problems of structure you face inside the speech—especially in the need, satisfaction, and visualization steps.

For example, suppose you're building a speech about problems with the American way of electing presidents. You can think of several needs you could develop: the needs to get better candidates, to speed up the electoral process, to provide more and better information on each candidate's stand on the issues, to reduce the influence of political action committees (PACs) on election outcomes, to control television advertising. As you think about that range of needs, you'll also realize that satisfaction—plans for change—are equally complicated; some of the solutions might involve new campaign laws; some, regulation of advertising; others, revitalization of our political parties and a streamlining of the electoral process; and still others, changes in voter attitudes. So, can you (1) organize all of those needs and plans for change in a reasonable way and (2) construct an organizational pattern that will help your listeners both comprehend and come to accept your arguments?

The same sort of thing could be said about the visualization step. Usually, it's organized chronologically: "If we don't act today, the situation will be worse tomorrow and, sooner or later, become disastrous." Yet, if your need and satisfaction steps are complicated, visualization will become equally difficult. On the issue of reconstituting the American way of electing presidents, you'll probably want to visualize each area of reform: what things will be like with (a) renewed party participation in the process, (b) a national campaign fairness board, (c) spending limits on all aspects of campaigns, and (d) the elimination of the Electoral College. You'd probably want to find a set of topics that covered each aspect of the plan and helped with the visualization process.

Thus, while the attention and action steps usually can be handled pretty easily, the three middle steps often demand a lot of organizational work. Five key criteria for communicating ideas to audiences should be met as you think about speech organization:

1. *The organization of main points must be easy for the audience to grasp and remember.* Listeners will find it easier to track your ideas if they see relationships among the main points. If the structure is clear, they even *anticipate* your next point through the pattern. When that happens, you as speaker know you have them with you.

2. *The pattern must allow full, balanced coverage of the material it orga-nizes.* When making three arguments in support of a claim, you usually want to spend roughly the same amount of time on each, because the first point might be important for some listeners, while the second and third points might appeal to others in your audience. Audiences usually can sense *proportion,* and may well wonder if you spend far more (or less) on one point or another.

3. *The pattern should be appropriate to the occasion.* As we've noted, on some occasions you're expected to observe group traditions. Political fund-raising speeches, for example, are almost always built around a problem-solution format, with a call for action (contributions) finishing them off; audiences on this and other occasions expect certain topics even in certain organizational patterns.[1] Choose a form that meets audience expectations.

4. *The pattern should be adapted to the audience's needs and level of knowledge.* Whereas the motivated sequence is based on listeners' fundamental thought processes, patterns of internal organization depend upon other aspects of audience awareness of an issue or problem. If listeners aren't well informed, say, about problems in the way Americans elect their presidents, you might want to go to a chronological pattern to show them the roots and later evolution of those problems in the need step. If they are knowledgeable, a cause-effect pattern that compacts such an analysis in the need step quickly but then develops a more complicated satisfaction step probably will work better. Speakers always must start at the point where the audience is.

5. *The speech must move forward steadily toward a complete and satisfy-ing end.* As you structure the substantive portions of your talks, give the audience a sense of forward motion—of moving crisply through a series of main points with a clear idea of where you're heading and how. Repeated backtracking to pick up lost points confuses and aggravates your listeners.

These are the primary criteria that should guide you as you assemble the body of your speeches. How can you execute them? We suggest that four types of organizational patterns work well for people delivering oral messages.

Patterns of Internal Organization

The four most useful patterns for structuring the bodies of speeches are chronological, spatial, causal, and topical patterns.

Organizing information into a temporal sequence enables a speaker to describe systematically the evolution of a process or the history of a program.

Chronological Patterns

The defining characteristic of **chronological patterns** is their temporal structuring of happenings or events. They're useful for orienting listeners who know little about a topic or for providing support for ideas via storytelling. Thus, chronological patterns run according to straightforward temporal sequences or to what are called narrative sequences.

Temporal Sequence. To use a **temporal sequence,** you begin at some period or date and move forward (or backward) systematically to provide background information. So, if you wanted to do a speech on why the United States has devoted so much more time and money to manned than unmanned space flights, you'd do well to use a temporal sequence, examining the unmanned rocket flights of the 1950s and 1960s, the Kennedy era commitment to manned flights to the moon, and Nixon era commitments to manned space station and shuttle technology, which continued even after the *Challenger* disaster of 1986. Such a *selection* and *sequencing* of events—and both are strategic moves made by a speaker who uses a temporal sequence—allows you to use the past to *explain* the present.

Narrative Sequence.   If you want to do more than explain or provide background for some problem, however, then you'll want to use a chronological pattern to make a point. *Narratives* are stories that allow you to draw conclusions about a series of events. For example, Aesop's fables are stories (narratives) with morals about human motivations and actions; lawyers, too, tell stories about their clients, the point being to argue for guilt or innocence. In **narrative sequences,** therefore, stories are the source of supporting material for some claim.[2] Suppose you wanted to argue that we need to regulate the way presidential candidates use mass media. A narrative sequence wherein the story comprises the need step and the lessons-to-be-learned as part of the satisfaction step would work well.

The Electrification of Presidential Campaigns[3]

Claim: It is time for Congress to regulate the materials broadcast by presidential campaigns.

Attention Step	[Review of some of the most disgusting presidential ads you've seen.]
Need Step	I. [Review of the worst of the campaign abuses, ending with the question, "How did American politics get to this point?"]
	II. Step by step, we converted our most important kinds of presidential campaign communication to electrical messages. Let me tell you the story of the electrification of presidential campaigns.
	A. Radio came into presidential politics in 1924.
	1. The Republicans held a three-day convention that was broadcast to 5 million people.
	2. But the Democratic convention went on 17 days with bitter floor fights that were high drama for the listeners.
	B. In 1924 the nation also saw its first campaign film.
	1. The Republicans wanted to make Calvin Cool-

idge appear more exciting, so they made a film that showed him off as a tough, active politician.

2. After that, every presidential candidate made either a biographical film about his life or a resume film about his qualifications.

C. While television actually broadcast political materials in 1948, its first widespread use occurred in 1952.

1. CBS with Walter Cronkite broadcast the conventions.

2. Both Eisenhower and Stevenson made TV ads, with Eisenhower's being put together with the help of Walt Disney, Irving Berlin, and an advertising agency.

D. The computer became a force in presidential campaigning in 1960.

1. The 1960 census supplied computerized data on shifts in American population and attitudes quickly enough for use by Kennedy.

2. Direct voter polls also were conducted that year by Kennedy's consultant, Joe Napolitan.

E. Overall, between them, George Bush and Michael Dukakis spent $55 million on media during the general election period of 1988.

Satisfaction Step

I. From the story of the electrification of presidential campaigns, we can draw three important conclusions:

A. When candidates have uncontrolled access to mass media, the costs of campaigning rise astronomically [cite figures from 1960 onward].

B. When candidates start to use primarily electronic media for their campaigns, voter turnout declines [cite figures from 1960 onward].

1. The visualization of attacks on opposing candidates possible with film and TV seem related to voter disillusionment.

2. Voter apathy has been found related to the "distance" created between candidate and voter by television.

C. When attempts are made to control spending (as with the Federal Campaign Spending Acts of the 1970s), the money just enters the campaign in other ways.

1. Single-issue political organizations.

2. The rise of industrial political action committees (PACs).

II. [a plank-by-plank presentation of a plan of action for curbing the cost and impact of electrified image-centered presidential campaigns]

Geographical patterns organize information according to well-defined areas in order to illustrate physical movement and development.

Visualization Step	[depiction of what will happen to the costs and methods of campaigning if we don't regulate it; depiction of what campaigning will look like if we do regulate it.]
Action Step	[Optional: call for first steps and exhortation for listeners to get involved in campaign reform movements.]

Spatial Patterns

Generally, **spatial patterns** arrange ideas or subtopics in terms of their physical proximity or relationship to each other. A specialized form of spatial patterns are **geographical patterns,** which organize materials according to well-known regions or areas; these are especially useful for making comparisons and contrasts between areas or movements across them. So, the evening weather forecast reviews today's high pressure dome over your area, then the low pressure area lying to the west, and the Arctic cool-air mass that seems to be coming in behind that low pressure area from Canada.

ETHICAL MOMENTS

Protected and Unprotected Speech

It is my legal judgment . . . that the testimony of Professor Hill in the morning was flat-out perjury. [Senator Arlen Specter]

If you . . . appear to have a closed mind, doesn't it raise issues of judicial temperament? [Senator Howell Heflin]

Did you ever have a discussion of pornographic films with Professor Hill? [Senator Patrick Leahy]

Why in God's name would you ever speak to a man like that the rest of your life? [Senator Alan Simpson]

I felt I had to tell the truth. I could not keep silent. [Professor Anita Hill]

Law professor Anita Hill was grilled by members of the Senate Judiciary Committee during October of 1991 after she alleged that Supreme Court nominee Clarence Thomas had sexually harassed her—with words. Not only was he alleged to have sought dates with her while her employer, but she said he talked trash, the language of "sexual overtures."

While the American doctrine of freedom of speech allows you to call people names, express your opinions, and declare your politics, it also limits your ability to threaten others with physical, economic, or even psychological force.

The courts have decided that personally aggressive speech, especially in situations of uneven power, is unprotected by the First Amendment's free speech clause.

Clarence Thomas was recommended by the Senate Judiciary Committee to the United States Supreme Court. Yet, that fall Anita Hill's testimony before millions of television viewers brought the issues of sexual harassment and harassing speech to public attention. In the long run, she achieved more than she probably imagined that she could. Anita Hill's name is synonymous with courage.

Material drawn from *Time*, (21 October 1991): 36–40.

The notion of geography, however, need not be applied only to landmasses; you can use it to talk about physical spaces, as when you explain talk about the different services available on the four floors of a university library. In an age when travel is highly popular and comparatively less expensive, you might well find yourself giving a speech using a geographical pattern, as in the following speech on volcanoes:

Eruptions in Your Future![4]

Central Idea: Traveling to the sites of the world's major volcanoes will let you see the creative forces of the earth at work.

Attention Step	[Opening stories about the 7,000-year-ago eruption of Mazama, a 9,900 feet high volcano in southern Oregon, which covered the entire northwestern United States in ash and lava and created what we now call Crater Lake]
Need Step	[Discussion of why listeners should be interested in the sites of recently active volcanoes—what can be learned, aspects of the beauty and power of nature available only at these sites]

Satisfaction Step

I. To give you a taste of what you can see, let me give you a tour of active volcano sites around the world.
   A. We start with the continental United States at Mt. St. Helens in the state of Washington (1991 eruption).
   B. We next journey to the Aleutian Islands off the Alaskan coast, to Mt. Akutan (1990 eruption).
   C. We cross the Pacific to Japan, to Mt. Asama (1991 eruption).
   D. Dropping down to Sumatra, we find Kerinci (1987).
   E. While it's tempting to visit Erebus in Antarctica (1991), we instead cut to Zaire in Africa, Mt. Nyamuragira (1988).
   F. From there, it's up to Etna in Italy (1990), Hekla in Iceland (1991), and home again.

II. Going around the world in this pattern takes us to many of the points where the earth, even as I speak, is regenerating itself.

Visualization Step	[visualization of what it means to see the earth regenerating itself]
Action Step	[Notice that the whole trip is too expensive for most students, but that a visit to one volcano may well be the trip of a lifetime for anyone in your audience.]

You'll find you can use spatial elements, in one form or another, in many of your speeches. Often you'll want to consider *magnitude* or *size*. A discussion of the rail system in the People's Republic of China, for example, would need to consider the great distances involved in traveling through its twenty-six provinces. Or, if you want to compare the services of small-town versus metropolitan banks, you'd probably use a form of spatial pattern but without the physical sense of actual maps. Third, you often will organize single arguments or ideas spatially. A speech on the effects of nuclear fallout could organize damage assessments from "ground zero," or the point of impact, through areas one mile away, to regions ten, fifty, and a hundred miles out.

The great utility of spatial patterns is their visual component. Helping audiences *see* ideas is a virtue for someone using an oral medium of communication.

Causal Patterns

As the name implies, **causal patterns** of organization move either (1) from a description of present conditions to an analysis of the causes that seem to have produced them or (2) from an analysis of present causes to a consideration of future effects. Causal patterns give listeners a sense of physical coherence because ideas are developed in direct relationship with each other; they assume that one series of events results from or causes another. (See page 454 for the tests of causality.) When using a *cause-effect pattern*, you might first point to the increasing number of closed courses (i.e., too few places) in your college each semester and then show the result—it takes students longer to graduate. Or, using an *effect-cause pattern*, you could argue that everyone knows how long it's taking students to graduate, then argue that closed classes are the cause, at least in part. To see the two patterns, compare the following outlines:

Acid Rain (Option 1)

Claim: Acid rain [cause] is a growing problem because it threatens our health and economy [effects].

Attention Step	[Draw attention to the importance of the issue]
Need Step	I. Manufacturing plants across the United States emit harmful acid-forming sulfur dioxide and nitrogen oxides into the air.
	II. The effects of these emissions include damage to important ecological structures.
	A. Lakes and forests are threatened.
	B. The productivity of crop lands is reduced.
	C. Acid particles in the air and drinking water cause 5 to 8 percent of all deaths in some parts of the United States.

PATTERNS OF INTERNAL ORGANIZATION

<table>
<tr>
<td>

Chronological Pattern
Temporal
Narrative

</td>
<td>

Causal Pattern
Cause-Effect
Effect-Cause

</td>
</tr>
<tr>
<td>

Spatial Pattern
Geographical
Magnitude

</td>
<td>

**Topical
Pattern**

</td>
</tr>
</table>

Visualization Step	[Indicate what the long-range consequences will be if we ignore the problem]
Action Step	[Appeal to listeners' self-interest to hold their attention on this issue as something to follow in the future]

Acid Rain (Option 2)

Claim: Acid rain [effect] is primarily the result of modern technologies [cause].

Need Step

I. If we're going to control acid rain, we must learn about and deal with its causes.

II. Human activities cause acid rain.

A. One primary cause is energy production: acids are given off by power plants.

B. A second main cause is motorized transportation, especially trucks and auto emissions.

Both outlines share a common characteristic: each starts with the aspect of the situation *better known* to audience members, and then develops more fully the lesser-known facets of the problem. As a guiding principle, *use a cause-effect sequence when listeners are generally well acquainted with the cause; use an effect-cause sequence when the effect is better known.*

The subject to be discussed may suggest an appropriate organizational pattern. Topical patterns are useful in situations calling for an enumeration of items or parts.

Topical Patterns

Some speeches on familiar topics are best organized in terms of subject-matter divisions that have become standardized. Financial reports are customarily divided into assets and liabilities; discussions of government into legislative, executive, and judicial matters; and comparisons of kinds of telescopes into celestial and terrestrial models. **Topical patterns** are most useful for speeches that enumerate aspects of persons, places, things, or processes. Occasionally a speaker may try a **complete enumeration** of a subject, as in a ten-part sermon on the Ten Commandments. More often, however, a **partial enumeration** of the possible topics or areas is sufficient. So, a speech on volleyball shots for an audience of beginners might include the following:

The Basic Shots in Volleyball

Central Idea: Knowing the basic volleyball shots can increase the playing ability even of beginners.

Attention Step	[Elicit interest through the usual devices]
Need Step	[Point out how the audience can use this information]

Satisfaction Step	I. There are three basic shots in volleyball.
	    A. A "bump" is performed by bringing your shoulders together and clasping your hands under the ball.
	    B. A "set" prepares the ball for another player, so you bring your hands above your head and hit the ball near your forehead with your palms open.
	    C. A "spike" or "kill" is a quick power shot executed with one hand, driving the ball over the net and down toward your opponent's feet.

Visualization Step	[After encouraging them to hit each shot in warmup, visualize the enjoyment they'll have in their weekend backyard or beach games once they can hit each kind of shot]
Action Step	[Review the key points you want listeners to take away from your speech, and encourage them to start working on them next weekend]

Topical patterns are among the most popular and easiest to use in organizing your speech. Given the usual practice of a partial rather than complete enumeration of topics, you may need to justify your limitations and even indicate why you're not talking about other facets. If someone asks "Why didn't you talk about the 'diving save' volleyball shot?" they are telling you that they don't think your limitation of the topic was reasonable; you'd better be ready to answer ("Because in friendly weekend games that shot is dangerous; it should be saved for playing organized or league volleyball, when you play with others who know what they're doing"). All that's required is that the audience understand why some items were included and others weren't. That understanding can come either from your logical development of the topic ("The *Basic* Shots in Volleyball") or from an explicit statement about its scope.

Integrating Patterns into the Motivated Sequence

Having looked at some internal patterns, you can now consider the relationship between the motivated sequence and the chronological, spatial, causal, and topical patterns:

Attention Step—Introduction to Speech
Introductory devices—might use chronological or spatial methods in beginning a hypothetical story; overall, organize the introduction to satisfy the functions discussed in Chapter 10.

Need Step—Body of Speech

Use chronological, spatial, causal, or topical patterns to relate the main points to one another; may even use one pattern for main points and another to organize subpoints (see next section).

Satisfaction Step—Body of Speech

Use any of the patterns to organize this step; may even use one pattern for main points and another for subpoints; whatever pattern is used should be tied in with needs, for the need step/satisfaction step relationship is key to the body of your speech.

Visualization Step—Body or Conclusion of Speech

The positive, negative, and contrastive methods may be put together, topically; a chronological pattern running from past to future or a geographical pattern illustrating effects in different regions is useful.

Action Step—Conclusion of Speech

A specific pattern is not needed; conclusions can either call for specific actions or review the main ideas to give listeners a sense of what they could do with the information, ideas, and proposals you've presented.

This, then, is what we mean when we talk about the "internal patterns of organization." Not only is the speech as a whole organized by the traditional ideas of introduction, body, and conclusion as well as by the motivated sequence, but each section of step itself needs a kind of internal coherence or form. Audiences use formal structures to keep up with you. You've got to not only give them material but also the structures to put it in.

An Arrangement of Main Points and Subpoints

We've suggested that you often use different organizational patterns in different parts of your speech. Look at two examples. First, speeches on travel often combine spatial and chronological patterns, for the spatial allows the speaker to help listeners visualize the subject while the chronological helps the speaker reveal interesting detail:

The Major Cities of India

I. The major cities of western India are Bombay and Ahmadabad.
  A. Bombay
    1. Early history
    2. Development under the British
    3. Condition today

   1, 2, 3—develop as in I.A.

II. The major cities in central India are Delhi and Hyderabad.
  A. Delhi—develop as in I.A.
  B. Hyderabad—develop as in I.A.

Causes and effects are often nicely developed in main point/subpoint sets, where the causes appear in the main points, and the effects, in the subpoints; sub-subpoints then carry illustrations, as follows:

Our Disappearing Salmon

I. Industrial pollution has caused a decline in the U.S. salmon population.
  A. Dam construction has severely affected salmon.
   1. There are fourteen barriers on a major salmon river.
   2. Eleven of the fourteen barriers are hydro-electric facilities.
    a. These facilities produce high water temperatures.
    b. Estimates of fish loss due to excessive temperatures are as high as 16 percent.
  B. Chemical and industrial pollution also have harmed the salmon.
   1. Discharge of chemicals such as PCB has hurt the salmon population.
   2. PCB kills salmon roe (eggs), thus limiting the future population even further.

This lesson is important: *developing your ideas in parallel forms makes them more coherent and clear, and hence more memorable and more powerful.* Controlling the structure of ideas is one of your great weapons for getting an audience to see the world as you see it. If they see the way you see, they're more likely to think and act the way you want them to.

Selecting an Organizational Pattern: Strategies and Determining Factors

Selecting internal organizational patterns isn't something that's wholly arbitrary. As we've been suggesting, there are touchstones that can guide you as you think about selecting one pattern rather than another. Consider the following:

1. *Some subject matters guide you toward particular patterns.* If you're interested in how "proper" relationships between males and females came to be accepted, you can't ignore a chronological pattern. If you're trying to explain some basic principles of professional flower gardening, you'll probably know immediately that spatial (geographical) patterns are the easiest to use. Try to complement the natural divisions in your topic as you put your main points and subpoints in order.

In choosing an organizational pattern, speakers should be sensitive to the demands of the occasion, as well as to listeners' needs, expectations, and knowledge of the subject.

2. *Your specific purpose may suggest which pattern is the most serviceable.* If you're explaining changing definitions of rape and the social effects of these definitions, it would seem logical to use a chronological pattern for the main points, cause-effect units for the subpoints. If your purpose is to argue that an ambulance site should be moved in order to reduce response time, a spatial pattern is demanded. So, as you begin to outline your main points, consider the impact of the topic and your purpose; your organizational pattern should assist you in dramatizing the claim you're advancing.

3. *Finally, consider the needs and expectations of the audience and occasion.* The occasion may call for particular patterns. An audience listening to a speech urging that three creeks be rerouted to make room for a new highway probably expects you to address particular topics: positive impacts of the highway, environmental impact of the rerouting, and costs of the project. Some occasions call for particular topics as well; for example, every presidential inaugural address *must* mention the historicity of the occasion, the binding up of wounds after an ugly campaign, domestic problems, foreign policy problems, and a call for citizens' help. Traditions suggest certain patterns, and you must be sensitive to them as well as to more specific audience expectations.

Edelman on Perceiving Problems

To evoke a problem's origin is to assign blame and praise. Blame for recurring wars and militarism depends upon whether they are seen as originating in the plans of aggressors, the authoritarian character structure of some cultures, the chance occurrence of a sequence of events with which diplomats cannot cope, the logic implicit in industrialized societies, or the will of God. Each origin reduces the issue to a particular perspective and minimizes or eliminates others.*

Political scientist Murray Edelman understands that (1) you have many possible explanations available when you discuss problems, (2) you must select some as your principal points of focus, and then (3) you must tie those explanations carefully to the problem to create a coherent package of problems so that your solutions make sense. Creating a sense of *coherence* is a key—an essential aspect of organizing your speeches. Return to 1991 and the talk by Presidents George Bush and Saddam Hussein to examine their conflicting analyses of war and its causes. Edelman's point will be verified.

* Murray Edelman, *Constructing the Political Spectacle* (Chicago: University of Chicago Press, 1983), p. 17.

While much more could be said about organizational patterns, we'll hold those comments until Chapter 11, on outlining, where we consider more minute aspects of speech form. For now, you ought to be concentrating on *packaging your ideas strategically,* that is, structuring them in ways that make them understandable and palatable to your listeners. Getting others to see problems and solutions in the way you do, after all, is half or more of the battle of getting them act on those problems in constructive ways.

Chapter Summary

Building a conceptually clear structure for your major ideas is crucial. Listeners need to see and comprehend a pattern to your ideas if they're to make sense out of them. As long as the pattern you select is sensitive to your topic, your purpose, and the expectations of the audience and occasion, your message should be received as a logically coherent approach to some idea or problem. Five criteria should guide you toward some pattern: (1) *the organization of the main points should make them easy to grasp and remember;* (2) *the pattern should allow full, balanced coverage;* (3) *the pattern should be appropriate to the occasion;* (4) *the pattern should be adapted to the audience's needs and level of knowledge;* and (5) *the speech must move steadily forward.* Four classes of internal organizational patterns include *chronological (temporal, narrative), spatial* (as well as *geographical), causal (effect-cause, cause-effect),* and *topical (complete* and *partial enumeration) patterns.* Different patterns can be used in multiple ways inside either the traditional (introduction, body, conclusion) or the motivated sequence structure.

References

1. See the case studies of the presidential inaugural address in Herbert W. Simons and Aram A. Aghazarian, eds., *Form, Genre, and the Study of Political Discourse* (Columbia, SC: University of South Carolina Press, 1986), esp. the essays by Karlyn Kohrs Campbell and Kathleen Hall Jamieson, pp. 203–25; Bruce E. Gronbeck, pp. 226–45; Robert P. Hart, pp. 278–300. See also Roderick P. Hart, *The Sound of Leadership* (Chicago: University of Chicago Press, 1987) and Karlyn Kohrs Campbell and Kathleen Hall Jamieson, *Deeds Done in Words: Presidential Rhetoric and the Genres of Governance* (Chicago: University of Chicago Press, 1990).

2. Walter R. Fisher goes so far as to argue that narrative persuasion is the most powerful kind of speaking. See his *Human Communication as Narration: Toward a Philosophy of Reason, Value, and Action* (Charleston, SC: University of South Carolina Press, 1987). See also Kathleen Hall Jamieson, *Eloquence in an Electronic Age: The Transformation of Political Speechmaking* (New York: Oxford University Press, 1988).

3. Information taken from Bruce E. Gronbeck, "Electric Rhetoric: The Changing Forms of American Political Discourse," *Vichiana,* 3rd series, 1st year (Napoli, Italy: Loffredo Editore, 1990), pp. 141–61; and Herbert E. Alexander and Monica Bauer, *Financing the 1988 Election* (Boulder, CO: Westview Press, 1991), chap. 3.

4. The data in this outline taken from *The World Almanac and Book of Facts 1992* (New York: World Almanac, 1991), pp. 529–30.

Key Terms

causal patterns (p. 233)

chronological patterns (p. 227)

complete enumeration (p.235)

geographical patterns (p. 230)

narrative sequence (p. 228)

partial enumeration (p. 235)

spatial patterns (p. 230)

temporal sequence (p. 227)

topical patterns (p. 235)

Problems and Probes

1. Read one of the speeches in this text and examine its organization. Identify the need and satisfaction steps in the development of the speech. What are the major points within each step and how are they arranged? Write a brief paper summarizing the results of your analysis.

2. Read three or four recent presidential inaugural speeches, or speeches related to warfare by Roosevelt (WWII), Truman (Korean Conflict), Nixon or Johnson (Vietnam), or Bush (Persian Gulf). Note the organization of each. How do the addresses differ in terms of their structure? In what ways are they similar? Write a brief paper in which you consider the possible constraints imposed by the situation on the arrangement of points. Specifically, address one of these questions: How does situation affect an inaugural address? How do different wartime situations affect speech-making by presidents? Conclude your analysis by commenting on the clarity and appropriateness of each address as a "good fit" between context and organization.

3. Working in small groups in class, suggest how the main points can be organized in each of the following topics, assume the end product is to be a short in-class speech.

      Why many small businesses fail
      Developments in laser technology
      Digging for sapphires, gold, or opals
      Eat wisely and live long
      Problems of the part-time student
      Racquetball for the beginner
      Appreciating impressionist art
      Computer literacy

Share your results with the rest of the class. How much organizational similarity is there among groups?

Communication Activities

1. Assume that you are preparing a speech on the merits of fraternities and sororities on campus (your position is that they are generally a positive influence on campus life) for each of the following audiences: (1) Student Senate, composed of representatives from dormitories, fraternities, sororities, off-campus students, and nontraditional students; (2) Faculty Senate, composed of representatives from the sciences, social sciences, arts and humanities; (3) Administration, composed of student services staff as well as the president and vice-presidents. Prepare a speech that is organized to meet the needs of each audience. In class, meet in small groups and discuss each approach with your classmates. How are the speeches different? How are they the same?

2. Prepare a five-to-seven-minute speech on a subject of your choice for presentation in class. Before you present the speech, critically appraise the organi-

zation you have used and write a brief paper defending the approach you took in organizing the main points and subpoints. Immediately after presenting the speech, and taking into account comments from the class, write a brief addendum on the experience of presenting the speech: Did it work the way you anticipated? Would you change your approach in any specific area of the speech? Hand in the analysis to your instructor.

10

BEGINNING AND ENDING THE SPEECH

When done well, beginnings serve to orient your listeners to your purpose in speaking; endings provide closure to the ideas advanced. When done poorly, beginnings reflect a lack of attention to purpose and endings reflect your own confusion as to what is important or essential to remember. Planning your beginning, or **introduction,** and ending, or **conclusion,** will help you prepare audiences to listen and direct their attention to what has been said. Just as aerobics instructors begin with warm ups and end with cool downs, so must you lead your audience systematically into the environment of your speech, then take them back to their own worlds at the end. Well-prepared introductions and conclusions allow you and your audience to enter into and separate from a rhetorical relationship, orient your listeners to your central idea or claim and reinforce it at the end, and signal clearly when your speech begins and ends.

Beginnings and endings are easily integrated into the motivated sequence discussed in Chapter 8. Introductions fulfill the attention step; conclusions are tied to either the visualization or the action step. Gaining an audience's attention and bringing closure to your ideas also is affected by strict communication rules within a culture. Adapting to cultural norms to gain attention and to bring a speech to a close, as well as in advancing ideas in the body of the speech, is critical to your success. In this chapter, we'll review the purposes of introductions and conclusions, discuss and examine strategies for beginning and ending your speeches, and consider factors that determine your approach.

Beginning the Speech:
The Functions of Introductions

In making certain that your ideas are as well received as possible, plan your introduction in terms of your analysis of the audience. Several basic questions will guide your opening remarks:

1. Are audience members likely to be *interested* in my topic, or must I work especially hard to gain their attention?
2. Are audience members aware of my *qualifications*, or must I establish my expertise?
3. Are there some special *demands of the occasion* that I should recognize, or am I free to go in any direction I wish? If I do depart from customary expectations, should I justify my departure?
4. Need I work to create *goodwill*, or are audience members likely to be sympathetic to me and my ideas?
5. Will the audience members already understand the *context* for the ideas or proposals, or must I provide historical details to justify speaking on this issue at this time?
6. Will audience members be able to follow this speech easily, or should I *forecast* the major themes early on?

Taking each of these guidelines in turn will further illustrate their relevance for planning appropriate introductions.

First, while you need to consider listener attention throughout the speech, your initial task is to increase your audience's level of interest or take advantage of an already high level. If, for example, your purpose is to convince your peers that they should get involved in off-campus volunteer projects, they may respond negatively ("Not another person asking for my time!"). In a situation like this, you may find it useful to review the factors of attention from Chapter 3 to find ways to relate your topic to their personal interests and needs. You might also consider acknowledging the possible negative response and offer reasons for its reconsideration.

Second, as a student you may have some credibility because you're studying certain subjects or have had certain experiences; however, your peers may not see you as an expert on decisions or actions that involve political or ethical choices. If you're uncertain whether the audience knows or accepts your qualifications, it's usually best to convey your background or personal commitment to the issues at the outset. If the audience is aware, either briefly mention your qualifications to further underscore your personal commitment, or simply move on to more critical issues. The goal is to demonstrate your command of the topic in a way that isn't boastful or overdone.

A third function of an introduction is to speak directly to the audience's expectations about the content and direction of your speech. When leading a discussion of a book for a reading group, you and your audience share a clear sense of what's expected, so you need not deal explicitly with the demands of the occasion. If you're speaking at a commencement or dedication or are presenting or accepting an award, some cultural themes are appropriate to address (see the discussion in Chapter 18. Noting the relevance and importance of these traditional themes is one way of putting your audience at ease, because this strategy clearly suggests your appreciation for the event and its demands.

Fourth, when delivering a short speech in a class, you may not have to create goodwill. However, most audiences appreciate references to how much you value their willingness to listen to you. If your audience isn't sympathetic to your position, recognizing your differences and appealing for a fair hearing is an important strategy. If listeners feel you respect their right to hold different views, they'll be more willing to hear you out. If, in recognizing differences, you appear condescending or otherwise insincere, your attempt at a fair hearing may well fall short of its objective. Aim for warm and cordial personal relations.

Fifth, there will be occasions when the audience is well aware of the issue and its history. Your speech will be considered natural in the context of the issues that are being discussed. On other occasions, however, the audience may be less prepared for the issue or the reasons for its importance. If you're speaking in such a situation, offering some initial background on the topic and its importance will help you orient your audience.

Finally, forecasts are useful in almost all speeches. In forecasting, you provide the audience with a preview of the development of your main ideas at the start; they will find it easier to follow your ideas as you move forward. Forecasting ("In discussing date rape, I will define the term, discuss recent events on campus, and then consider the legal implications") constructs a framework that orients the audience and alerts them to your purpose in speaking.

Introductions need not fulfill *all* of these six guidelines. Sometimes one or more of these will be obvious to your listeners. The utility of the guidelines lies in suggesting what you need to consider in evaluating your audience and occasion, and adapting your introduction accordingly.

Types of Speech Introductions

With the six guidelines in mind, you're ready to select specific introductory strategies. The following are eight ways of beginning a speech:

1. Refer to the subject or problem.
2. Refer to the occasion.
3. Use a personal reference or greeting.
4. Ask a rhetorical question.
5. Make a startling statement of fact or opinion.
6. Use a quotation.

Referring directly to the subject or problem is a very useful introductory strategy when the audience already has a vital interest in hearing the message.

7. Relate a humorous anecdote.
8. Cite a real or hypothetical illustration.

Reference to the Subject or Problem

Referring directly to the issues being discussed is useful when the audience has a vital interest in the topic. When a business conference invites a speaker with a particular topic or theme in mind, it's unnecessary to go into detail justifying the topic's relevance. Instead, the speech can begin with a direct reference to the issue and move on to its development. At other times, it may be useful to "jump in" and allow the initial themes of the speech to build relevance. Howard Rainer combined a *rhetorical question* (discussed below) and a reference to the issues in his message to his university graduation class:[1]

> Is this the right time for a new American Indian revolution to begin? I say, "Yes, it is!" The new revolution or movement in Indian America can start today—at this gathering—if just one of you would catch this same vision I am going to share with you.
>
> Because of the thousands of outstanding Indian people whom I have met and the countless numbers of Indian youth who are anxious and ready for a

movement, I present to you my Master Plan of Action to get this revolution off the ground.

Alicia Croshal, another student speaker, also used this approach in opening her speech on gossip:[2]

> Gossip has a bad reputation. It isn't always bad, and it doesn't always deserve it. Allow me to give you the real scoop. It's so juicy that I'm going to develop four main points instead of three! First, I'll give you a brief overview of the history of gossip. Then, I'll explain how it fulfills psychological needs, how it functions anthropologically, and finally, how gossip is real news.

Although brevity and directness may strike exactly the right note with your audience, it wouldn't be wise to begin all speeches in this manner. To a skeptical audience, a direct announcement may sound immodest, tactless, or even challenging; to an apathetic audience, it may sound dull. Use direct references only when you're certain your audience is in tune with what you have to say and is willing to listen to your ideas.

Reference to the Occasion

Occasions such as commencement addresses, acceptances of awards, holidays, and keynote addresses virtually dictate that you refer to the reason that brings you and your audience together. Setting out the significance of the occasion forges a bond between speaker and listener. Noted historian Arthur M. Schlesinger, Jr., appeared at a National Academy of Science gathering to honor the memory of a brilliant sponsor of the arts:[3]

> It is a high honor to be invited to inaugurate this series of annual lectures in memory of Nancy Hanks and in support of the cause she so nobly served—the sustenance and enrichment of the arts in America. And it is appropriate that this series should be sponsored by the American Council for the Arts, an organization that for 28 years has given the artistic condition of our diverse and combative society searching analysis and vigorous advocacy; all the more appropriate because Nancy Hanks was president of the ACA before she moved on to become the brilliantly effective leader of the National Endowment for the Arts.

If the time, place, or reason for coming together is important, a reference to the occasion belongs in your introduction.

Personal Reference or Greeting

A warm personal expression of goodwill toward the audience or a personal story often serves as an excellent starting point. Personal references are especially useful if your invitation to speak marks a departure from tradition. This was the case in Henri Mann Morton's keynote address to a regional group of National Forest personnel. Without calling attention to the fact that she, a Native American woman, was addressing a group of predominantly white males, Morton acknowledged her appreciation for the opportunity:[4]

> Thank you for honoring me with your gracious invitation to speak at your conference. The Indians and Indian dances you saw last night serve as evidence of the endurance of the Indian spirit.

Personal references also are appropriate if you're well known to the audience. Liz Carpenter, a veteran Washington reporter who served in the government under presidents Johnson, Ford, and Carter, took advantage of her reputation in opening her speech to the National Press Club:[5]

> Dear old friends, colleagues of the press: How great thou art! How great it is to return after ten years and to find you are still here in the town where "try to remember" has become the national anthem. Like Rip Van Winkle, I rub my eyes in wonder at Washington today. Like George Bush, I wonder where I am and where I have been all this time....

If you're unknown to the audience, you need to be wary of coming across too personally. Consider your reaction when someone you don't know greets you as if you were a long-lost friend. It's natural to become rather defensive and skeptical of the person's sincerity. Morton and Carpenter, in separate settings, effectively adapted their use of personal reference to the audience and occasion; doing likewise in your situation will sharpen your image as a sincere speaker.

Rhetorical Question

A rhetorical question is one that is asked without expecting an immediate, direct verbal response. Although you don't want the audience members to answer you aloud, you do want them to think about possible answers. Used sparingly, rhetorical questions can focus audience attention on your subject and involve listeners in your view of it. Using rhetorical questions also depends on the relevance of the subject to the audience. Asking a group of college sophomores "How would you feel if, at age ninety-five, your social security suddenly ran out?" probably isn't geared to their most immediate concerns.

On the other hand, asking "How would you feel if budget cuts meant you couldn't graduate as planned?" would draw the audience into the topic, because their immediate concerns are involved. You may use the rhetorical question as the first step in forecasting the development of the topic: "Why have the cuts been taken?" "What do they mean in terms of your ability to graduate?" "What recourse do you have as a student in protesting the situation?" Shannon Dyer of Southwest Baptist University in Missouri used this approach to open her speech by wondering why whistleblowers didn't prevent the Challenger accident and the Union Carbide plant gas leak at Bhopal, India. She moved on in forecasting her response with additional questions:[6]

> Thus, let's examine the dilemma of whistleblowers. First, who are whistleblowers? Then, what is the high personal price for their warnings? And finally, how can we protect these citizens—the watchdogs of our nation's safety?

Rhetorical questions can unite speaker and audience interest and involvement in the topic. Speakers may also repeat a rhetorical question throughout a speech as the Democrats did with their "Where was George?" refrain in 1988. This strategy often energizes the audience, as they chant the question along with the speaker.

Startling Statement

An inoffensive, appropriate startling statement of opinion or fact is another way to gain attention. Elizabeth Badgley, a student at South Dakota State University, opened her speech with a startling statement that also aroused curiosity:[7]

> Warning! Research has shown this product can cause seizures, memory loss, speech difficulties, insomnia, erratic behavior, and its carcinogenic effects are not known.

She went on to note she was not "speaking of cigarettes or alcohol" but of aspartame, or as it's better known, Nutrasweet. Jeffrey Jamison, a student at Emerson College in Boston, used a one-line opening to arouse interest and focus attention on his topic (he also won first place in the 1991 Interstate Oratorical Association contest):[8]

> One day the Energizer bunny will die.

He went on to note that while the battery energizing the "lovable little pink bunny" will eventually wear out, unsafe disposal of such alkali batteries "will become one of America's most serious environmental threat[s] during the next three to five years."

Overdoing this technique does have its dangers. Few things disgust an audience more than an overplayed, silly startling statement; false drama, melodramatic stories, and bad shock techniques (for example, screaming your first two sentences and then saying, more quietly, "Now that I have your attention. . . .") should be avoided. Do *not* bring a Saturday night special into your classroom as part of your speech on gun control. Scaring the wits out of people is more than ethically dubious; akin to terrorism, it's inhumane. Aim for suspense, as did Badgley, rather than emotional arousal for its own sake.

Pertinent Quotation

You can also convey the theme of your address or create interest in a topic with a *quotation*. To be effective, the quoted material should be simple and direct; the audience shouldn't have to ponder its meaning or its possible relevance to the situation. Tisha R. Oehmen, a student at Lane Community College, Oregon, used the following "expert opinion" as a means of opening her speech on the proposed diversion of Columbia River water to Southern California:[9]

> "Each day the Columbia River dumps in the Pacific Ocean 90 billion gallons of fresh water. That is 3.7 billion gallons an hour, 61 million gallons a minute, and 1 million gallons a second. This is wasteful and sinful."
>
> These are the words of Los Angeles County Supervisor Kenneth Hahn, as quoted in *The Washington Post*, May 20, 1990. This is how Hahn prepared his Board of Supervisors for his proposal to siphon water out of the Columbia River to quench the thirst of his drought-stricken city.

Oehmen then argues against Hahn's analysis, pointing out that "the Columbia's diversion would not only scar the landscape, but the proposed diversion would slow shipping, cripple irrigation, harm the fragile salmon run, and reduce the available electricity." By providing the audience with a strong reason for approving the proposal, she indirectly recognizes how difficult it will be to sway opinion in the other direction, especially among Californians who desperately need additional water resources. The quotation and Oehmen's subsequent remarks function well in setting the stage for the presentation.

Humorous Anecdote

Telling a funny story or relating an amusing personal experience can effectively arouse audience interest. The story, however, should conform to these rules:

1. *Be sure the story is at least amusing, if not absolutely funny.* If it isn't, or if you tell it badly, you'll embarrass yourself and your audience. Be particularly careful with stories that depend on your audience understanding idiomatic expressions or regional phrases (such as "wicked good" in "Downeast" country).

2. *Be sure the anecdote is relevant to your speech.* If its subject matter or punch line isn't directly related to you, your topic, or at least your next couple of sentences, the story will be perceived as a mere gimmick, bringing your sincerity into question. Audiences tire quickly of speakers who begin with an irrelevant "A funny thing happened on my way here. . . ."

3. *Be sure it is in good taste.* In a public gathering, an off-color or doubtful story violates accepted standards of social behavior and can undermine an audience's respect for you. Avoid racial, religious, ageist, and sexist humor. If the audience is composed of diverse ethnic groups, the story may not include what some consider an appropriate topic for humor.

All three of these rules were obeyed by George V. Grune, CEO of The Reader's Digest Association, Inc., as he delivered a commencement address to the Graduate School of Business at Rollins College. Note that he successfully combines several introductory techniques—reference to issue and occasion with a humorous story:[10]

> This morning I'd like to talk about global marketing and the opportunities it offers American business today—and each of you individually. I understand international marketing was a favorite subject for many of you, and I suspect earning a living is uppermost on your minds, considering the occasion we celebrate today.
>
> There is a story about a king who once called three wise men together and posed the same problem to each: "Our island is about to be inundated by a huge tidal wave. How would you advise the people?"
>
> The first man thought long and hard and then said, "Sire, I would lead the people to the highest spot on the island and then set up an all-night prayer vigil."
>
> The second man said, "Master, I would advise the people to eat, drink and be merry for it would be their last opportunity to do so."
>
> The third wise man said, "Your majesty, if I were you, I would immediately advise the people to do their best to *learn how to live under water.*"
>
> As you progress in your business career, you'll face many challenges that will test your ability to in effect "learn how to live under water." Those who adapt and find new solutions to complex issues will be the most successful. And nowhere is that more true than in the global arena.

After relating his anecdote, which helped put the audience at ease, Grune went on to develop his main theme: the challenges facing students of international marketing.

Real or Hypothetical Illustration

A human-interest story, taken from real life, from literature, or from spontaneous invention involves the audience with the issues to be discussed. As
with humor, illustrations need to be relevant and in good taste. Such stories
orient the audience to the topic and demonstrate its importance. Kelly
McInerney, a Regis College student, used this factual illustration to drive
home her point about the dangers of pit bulls:[11]

> Six year old Lindsay Rael was your average fun-loving little girl. Yet in seconds,
> her whole life changed when she was attacked by two pit bulls. Had it not been
> for the heroics of two neighborhood teenagers who pulled the dogs off of the
> child and, in Lindsay's words, "saved my life," she might not be here today.
> With stitches from her nose to her ear and both arms in casts, Lindsay was
> released from a Denver hospital on February 16, 1991. This shy little girl must
> deal with scarification, plastic surgery and face the world as a different person
> at only six years old. But the most terrifying fact of all is that this is not an
> isolated incident.

McInerney's presentation shows that real or hypothetical illustrations can
rivet attention, dramatizing an issue far more than the supporting statistical
information. Kathleen Tracy, a student at St. Joseph's University in Pennsylvania, used a hypothetical illustration based on fact to introduce her
discussion of the lives of Romanian orphans under the government of
Ceausescu:[12]

> Imagine living 23 hours a day, 365 days a year in a 10 by 20 foot darkened room
> with no windows, sharing only three beds with nine other people. At noon you
> are led out of this room for one hour of "recreation." During this hour you are
> placed on a toilet seat for two minutes while you are spoon-fed one small cup
> of soup, three ounces of milk and one small roll. For the remaining 58 minutes
> you are led outside to brave the 20 degree temperatures in nothing more than
> cotton pants and a t-shirt. You are then taken back to your room to await
> tomorrow's hour of freedom. But that's only if you're lucky. If this sounds too
> horrible to imagine, don't worry too much; your average life expectancy is only
> eleven years.

When inventing an illustration, the most important factor is the story's
believability. Tracy responds to the possibility that the story is too farfetched for belief by noting that her description is "the average day in the
life of one of Romania's forgotten children in one of the many state-funded
orphanages set up under the government of Nicolae Ceausescu."

Combining Introductory Techniques

As noted in earlier examples, introductions may be combined. You may find
it appropriate to cite your qualifications, increase goodwill, and forecast the

rest of your speech before moving into the substantive portion of your remarks. Moving the audience toward the first main point of your speech is the rationale for combining techniques. Assume the following speaker is addressing the Faculty Senate on a proposal to eliminate the university's physical education requirement:

- "I am pleased that you are allowing me to speak to you today on the physical education requirement. As far as I know, this is the first time a student has been asked to address the Faculty Senate. Your invitation demonstrates your commitment to shared responsibility for academic requirements." [*reference to occasion*]
- "As a recreation major, I'm especially pleased to be talking with you so that I can explain how it is that someone majoring in a physical education discipline is nonetheless opposed to mandatory physical education at this school." [*personal reference*]
- "When the Romans preached 'A sound mind in a sound body,' they did not seek a gymnasium filled through coercion, but through attractive programs and courses." [*quotation*]
- "Must students go through this school forced into physical activities they do not choose for themselves, or can we find ways to draw them into exercises and sport?" [*rhetorical question*]
- "I am going to demonstrate to you today that we can fill the gym with students through smart programming and a curriculum of classes and nonclass experiences. First I will discuss the results of a student body survey we conducted last semester, then I will present a plan for meeting the student body's exercise and competitive needs, and finally I will tell you why it is an educational improvement over compulsory physical education." [*claim plus forecast*]

Using introductory techniques relevant to the topic, audience, and occasion will enable you to get your speech off to a productive start. Not only are these techniques helpful at the outset; they also may be used throughout the speech. Rhetorical questions, for example, can be used to move from one main point to the next. Quotations, especially from expert sources, serve as testimony in support of your claim. Illustrations that relate to the audience's own experience or provide new information are useful at any point in the speech. Humorous anecdotes can relax an audience, especially if you have been presenting serious or difficult material. A startling statement, even in the middle of the speech, can focus attention on what you're saying and why it's important.

Ending the Speech: The Functions of Conclusions

Once you've developed the introduction that provides a smooth transition to your presentation, it's time to consider how to end your speech. At worst,

BEGINNING AND ENDING A SPEECH

| *Beginning the Speech* | *Body of Speech* | *Ending the Speech* |

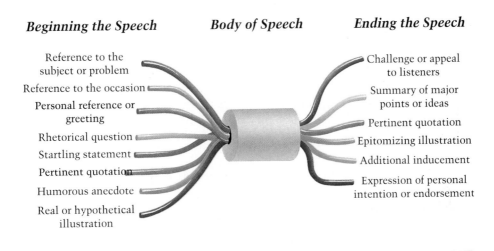

Beginning the Speech:
- Reference to the subject or problem
- Reference to the occasion
- Personal reference or greeting
- Rhetorical question
- Startling statement
- Pertinent quotation
- Humorous anecdote
- Real or hypothetical illustration

Ending the Speech:
- Challenge or appeal to listeners
- Summary of major points or ideas
- Pertinent quotation
- Epitomizing illustration
- Additional inducement
- Expression of personal intention or endorsement

the audience thinks you've ended long before you actually do or that you simply "run out of gas" and quit, leaving them confused as to what has just happened and why. A **conclusion** provides a sense of closure and will leave your audience aware of your central goal. The key question to ask about endings is "What do I want my audience to believe, remember, or do as a result of my presentation?" Consider the following issues:

1. How should I *signal* that the speech is ending?
2. Does the content lead naturally to a *"So what"* question?
3. What *mood* do I want the audience to be in when I conclude?

Many speakers use customary expressions to *signal* that the end is at hand: usually they employ expressions such as "In summary," "In conclusion," "What, then, is the significance of this plan for our local community? In closing, let me reaffirm its central implication . . . ," or "Lord Byron provides an appropriate closing for the values I wish to entrust to your care today. . . ." These statements refocus audience attention on the message of the speech. Adopting any one of these signals provides a transition from the main body of the speech to your conclusion. Once used, however, you need to actually conclude. Continuing to talk much longer only irritates your audience.

The tendency of the audience to ask "So what?" at the close of a presentation can be dealt with in a straightforward manner. There may be a large difference between your enthusiasm for the topic and that of the audience, in which case they'll want to know why they should worry about your subject or be interested in it. In the end, the significance of your ideas must be adapted to your *listeners'* needs, wants, and desires. Otherwise, you'll be wasting valuable time talking past their own interests.

Finally, the audience's mood may be critical to the acceptance of your ideas. Do you want to leave listeners inspired, excited, and willing to work on behalf of your proposals? Do you want them to share your anger and disgust with the proposals or tactics of others? Will it make a difference if they're left stunned by your remarks, indifferent to your enthusiasm, or simply unaffected by your ideas? If so, work to ensure that they're involved in the message and influenced by your enthusiasm and interest. A strong and effective conclusion can pull together the many reasons for belief and action into a tightly constructed appeal that will have the desired effect on the audience.

Types of Speech Conclusions

Speakers frequently use one or more of the following techniques for bringing their talks to an appropriate end:

1. Issue a challenge or an appeal to the listeners.
2. Summarize the main points or ideas.
3. Provide an appropriate quotation.
4. Epitomize the point with an illustration.
5. Offer an additional inducement for accepting or acting upon the proposal advocated.
6. Express your own intention or endorsement.

Challenge or Appeal to Listeners

Using this technique, you appeal directly for support or action or remind listeners of their responsibilities in furthering a cause. Such an appeal must be compelling and contain a suggestion of the principal ideas or arguments presented in the speech. Howard Rainer closed his speech to the Fort Defiance graduating class with a precise challenge:[13]

> Yes, this Indian revolution, this movement, can happen. It can have the power to spread all over Indian America.
>
> If you don't think we have this power, laugh at my words! Then we will have to wait another hundred years. Can we afford the wait? Are you ready and willing to sacrifice for the new Indian revolution? Then stand up and say, "Count me in!"
>
> What are you waiting for?

The challenge effectively recalled the central point of his address—the potential for a new Indian revolution in the values and opportunities

A speaker can conclude by openly appealing for support or by reminding listeners of their responsibilities in furthering a cause they believe in.

afforded Indians—and called for direct participation on the part of those listening.

Ben Wainscott, a student at Northwest Missouri State University, anticipated a "So what?" question and chose to respond to it directly:[14]

By this point in the speech you may be wondering, "My God, what does he want me to do now?" I'm not asking you to boycott any products, sign any petitions or write your congressman. I am asking you to do something that I sincerely hope you practice when you leave this room today, that you do next week, next month and next year. All I'm asking is this: Say cheese. Just smile at people more often. Laugh a little bit more. Make it easier to show your pearly whites. There is no subject more important than that of your own personal health and happiness. It will change your life and the lives of those around you. You owe it to them and you owe it to yourself. And if I have said just one thing today to make you realize that you need to smile and laugh more often, then I have completed 100% of my goal. If not, I've failed miserably. But just remember this, I gave this whole speech today without one reference to the song "Don't Worry, Be Happy," and I think that's more than enough to smile about.

By combining a direct challenge with a clear statement of the central purpose of this message with a touch of humor, Wainscott brought his message to an effective close.

Summary of Major Points or Ideas

Summaries are especially helpful when your speech is complex; they also can be used to recall the *forecasting* used in your introductory comments. Summaries are an effective way to "tell your audience what you told them." A summary in an informative speech allows you to pull together the important strands and to highlight the essential pieces of information. In a persuasive speech, a summary allows you to review the main points of your argument one last time. If something hasn't been clear to the audience, restating it in the summary may clarify the point's relevance or significance in the overall argument.

Ben Smith, an Ohio State University student, recalled the overall structure of his address and returned to the opening illustration in closing his appeal for greater control of pleasure boats:[15]

> We have seen the problem of boating accidents, we have seen the causes; and finally, we have seen the solutions. We have seen the problem of boating accidents is an avoidable tragedy. We began by looking at a crowded parking lot. Well, let's look there again. This time all the cars go at the regulated speed. They follow right-of-way laws, use turn signals and go in the same direction. Add a couple more police officers and you have a safer parking lot. If we can make these changes on the water, perhaps we can make America's water safer as well.

Kathleen Tracy, whose hypothetical illustration of the forgotten children of Romania was cited earlier, closed with a concise summary and an appeal for continued concern and action:[16]

> We have seen that an irrational population policy produced the horrible conditions that exist in these Romanian institutions today, and we have viewed some of the atrocities that continue to be committed. However, most importantly, we have seen that we can remedy the situation through relief missions, donations or even adoptions so that these children have not just one hour of freedom a day, but 24 hours, during which time they're clothed properly, fed well and loved. We can't erase the atrocities already committed at the hands of a brutal dictator, but each of us can, in any small way possible, help remember and provide for these forgotten children.

A reference to the occasion, pertinent quotation, or personal greeting can remind listeners of the significance of an event. This technique can also offer additional inducement to the audience to accept or act on your position.

Pertinent Quotation

At times, the words of others can bring closure to your ideas. If the quotation is relevant and contributes to the mood you wish to establish, you can make a powerful impression in the minds of your listeners. Notice how Denalie Silha, a student at North Dakota State University, closed her speech on rethinking retirement policies with a unique quotation:[17]

> Listen to Warren Buffett, who has built an investment empire. When asked a few years ago about leaving a woman in charge of one of his companies after celebrating her 94th birthday, he replied, "She is clearly gathering speed and may well reach her full potential in another five or ten years. Therefore, I've persuaded the board to scrap our mandatory-retirement-at-100 policy. My God, good managers are so scarce I can't afford the luxury of letting them go just because they've added a year to their age."

Silha's example focuses audience attention on the issues she presented and asks why mandatory retirement policies should continue.

If you use a quotation at the beginning of a speech, referring back to it in your conclusion is an easy way to tie the speech together. Chui Lee Yap began a speech on ethnocentrism by quoting from Aldous Huxley: "Most ignorance is vincible ignorance. We don't know because we don't want to know." After explaining the reasons for American ignorance of other cultures, Yap concluded, "As Huxley implied, cure of our not knowing—is our wanting to know."[18] Christine Keen, Issues Manager for the Society for Human Resource Management, uses a similar approach in her discussion. She begins by noting "the Chinese have a curse: 'May you live in interesting times.' And these certainly are interesting times." After noting the challenges facing human resource managers, she closes by reminding the audience of the opening lines: "For at least the next decade, then, we will all live in interesting times. And it's up to us to determine if that's a curse or a blessing."[19]

Epitomizing Illustration

If you use an illustration in the introduction to orient your listeners to your main ideas, you can also use it again at the close of your speech. A closing illustration should be both *inclusive* and *conclusive*; that is, it should incorporate the main focus of your speech and be forceful in tone and impact. As with quotations, you can use illustrations to *frame* your presentation. Tim Dolin, a student at Marshall University in West Virginia, used this approach in his speech on the dangers of hepatitis-B:[20]

Opening
Joseph Blackwood was recently diagnosed as suffering from terminal cirrhosis of the liver. The diagnosis was unique not only because Mr. Blackwood was only 35 but also because Mr. Blackwood did not drink. His cirrhosis is a side effect of a viral infection he contracted in 1984.

Closing
It is too late for Joseph Blackwood to be vaccinated. It is not too late, however for us to have the foresight Mr. Blackwood lacked to protect ourselves and those we love from Hepatitis B.

In this fashion, Dolin not only ties together the central points but also brings into focus the preventive measures that individuals can take to avoid the tragedy epitomized in his story.

Additional Inducement

You can add to the force of your message by bringing forward an additional reason for being concerned or taking the action you propose. This is the approach used by Brian Swenson, a student at Dakota Wesleyan, South Dakota, to close his discussion of gun safety and children:[21]

Today, we have looked at a few cases of child shootings, some facts and statistics about child shootings and what you should do if you own a gun to prevent this from happening to your children or other children. Now, maybe you still think that you don't need to lock up your gun and that this won't happen to you; but, I have one more statistic for you. One child is killed everyday with a handgun and for every child killed ten others are injured. Now, I have a question for you. Is your child going to be one of the ten that are injured or is it going to be that one that is killed? The choice is yours.

Brian Twitchell began and ended his speech on the causes and effects of depression with the story about the little Dutch boy and the dike. In his conclusion he added this additional reason for sharing his concern:[22]

> Why should you really care? Why is it important? The depressed person may be someone you know—it could be you. If you know what is happening, you can always help. I wish I had known what depression was in March of 1978. You see, when I said David Twitchell could be my father, I was making a statement of fact. David is my father. I am his son. My family wasn't saved; perhaps now yours can be.

Expression of Personal Intention or Endorsement

A statement that indicates you're willing to put yourself on the line and follow your own advice is particularly valuable when your personal reputation with the audience is high. If you can indicate your own intent to take action, you reinforce your sincerity and increase your overall credibility with the audience. In 1812, the Shawnee Indian leader, Tecumseh, was attempting to unite eastern Indians in a war against the encroaching white race. The Choctaw chief Pushmataha, Tecumseh's equal as a leader and an orator, opposed war. In closing his address refuting the call for war, Pushmataha makes his position absolutely clear:[23]

> Listen to the voice of prudence, oh, my countrymen, ere you rashly act. But do as you may, know this truth, enough for you to know, I shall join our friends, the Americans, in this war.

That his appeal was successful is verified by the fact that the Choctaw did not join Tecumseh.

Combining Concluding Techniques

In an introduction, you can address more than one of the functions of a conclusion by ensuring that your audience leaves knowing what you meant for them to remember and why. If you were addressing the Faculty Senate as in the earlier example (p. 254), your conclusion might contain the following:

- "As I have demonstrated in this brief review, the student body survey strongly supports the elimination of the P.E. requirement. Second, if my plan, or one similar to it, is adopted by the campus, we can meet the same needs of physical health and well-being, but on a basis that is not mandatory." [*summary*]
- "In demonstrating that my plan is an improvement, we can recall the advice of the Romans: A 'sound mind in a sound body' can be better achieved through attractive programs engaged in by willing, enthusiastic students." [*quotation*]
- "My challenge to you is to support the elimination proposal, but to go further, by enacting a program that meets goals that are appropriate for today's youth—those of an active and physically sound student body." [*personal challenge*]
- "For my part, rest assured that I will continue to seek support for an active, voluntary program of physical exercise." [*statement of personal intent*]"

You need not limit yourself to only one closing technique. Use those which, taken together, add force to your ideas, and enable you to finish on a strong, positive note.

Selecting Introductions and Conclusions

The preceding sections have concentrated on the functions of introductions and conclusions and the means of fulfilling them. In general, each of the means can be an effective way of satisfying the functions of introductions or conclusions. Obviously, some techniques are more relevant or better suited than others for fulfilling a particular function. For example, a real illustration works better than a hypothetical one in stating your qualifications; a personal reference may be the most direct means of all. Conclusions that contain pertinent quotations or epitomizing illustrations may create an appropriate mood more effectively than a summary of major points.

As you approach each facet of the total speech, think through what you want to accomplish and adopt the approach that has the best chance of meeting your goal. As noted in Chapter 1, creating a speech involves a *rhetorical sensitivity* to the situation in which you find yourself. There are some natural constraints on what you can and should do:

1. *What are your experiences and abilities?* The best source for real illustrations is your own life. Stories of your experiences come across naturally as you tell them. Stories that you've discovered through research, on the other hand, need to be rehearsed so that they sound "natural." Your experiences also may be the best basis for claiming qualifications in an area; otherwise, you need to illustrate, through explicit statements

or the quality of your research materials, that you know what you're talking about. Your abilities as a speaker also may constrain your choices. If you don't tell funny stories in a natural, relaxed manner, attempting a humorous anecdote may not be wise. On the other hand, if you're known as a clown and want to be taken seriously for a change, you need to set forth your qualifications explicitly and, in concluding, create a serious mood for the consideration of your views. Humor may not be your best vehicle under these circumstances.

2. *What is the mood and commitment of the audience?* If you're speaking on a subject already announced and known to be controversial, gaining attention through a startling statement or a humorous anecdote may seem highly inappropriate. If the audience is indifferent or has already heard several presentations on the same subject, a direct reference to the subject may be perceived as dull and unoriginal. A rhetorical question that forces them to think for a moment or a startling statement that creates curiosity may be appropriate. Both induce listeners to participate directly, rather than to listen passively.

3. *What does the audience know about you and your commitment to the subject?* If you're already known as an expert in an area, stating your qualifications would be repetitious and may even convey conceit. If your personal experience and depth of feeling are generally unknown, you'll want to reveal these through personal reference, or, as Michael Twitchell did (see page 261), through an additional inducement at the close of your address. Either approach establishes both your knowledge and your personal involvement in the subject. Allow time to pass before you attempt to bring deeply felt experiences before an audience, however, especially those involving loss of life. If you appear emotionally shaken or teary-eyed, the tension level will increase as the audience shares your personal discomfort. The effectiveness of your personal revelation will be correspondingly decreased. Using a challenge or statement of personal intent also is an effective means of demonstrating your commitment to the subject.

4. *What constraints are imposed by the situation or setting?* A somber occasion, such as a funeral or a dedication of a war memorial, is hardly the place for hilarious stories. On the other hand, some serious occasions, such as commencements, can be enlivened by humor. The student speaker who ended his high-school address by waving a beer bottle and proclaiming "This Bud's for you" quickly discovered that his attempt at humor was received well by only part of his audience. The faculty and parents did not react as pleasantly as did his peers. Not everything goes, even when *you* see nothing wrong with the story or allusion. A reference to the occasion or personal greeting may be an appropriate reminder to the audience that you, as well as they, appreci-

ate the significance of the occasion. Pertinent quotations and epitomizing illustrations, at the beginning or end, also can convey a sense of the event's meaning for everyone present.

This discussion of the use of appropriate introductions and conclusions is not intended to be exhaustive. Rather, it illustrates the general approach to *thinking through* possible audience reactions as you select various means of introducing and concluding your speech. A "thought-through" speech will be perceived as well prepared by your listeners, whether they ultimately agree with you or not.

Sample Outline for an Introduction and a Conclusion

An introduction and a conclusion for a classroom speech on MADD and SADD, anti–drunk driving organizations, might take the following form. Notice that the speaker uses one of the factors of attention—suspense— together with startling statements to lead the audience into the subject then concludes by combining a final illustration with a statement of personal intention.

Introduction
I. Many of you have seen the "Black Gash"—the Vietnam War Memorial in Washington, DC.
   A. It contains the names of more than 40,000 Americans who gave their lives in Southeast Asia between 1961 and 1973.
   B. We averaged over 3000 war dead a year during that anguishing period.
II. Today, another enemy stalks Americans.
   A. The enemy kills, not 3000 per year, but over 20,000 citizens every twelve months.
   B. The enemy is not hiding in jungles but can be found in every community in the country.
   C. The enemy kills, not with bayonets and bullets, but with bottles and bumpers.
III. Today, I want to talk about organizations that are trying to contain and finally destroy the killer.
   A. Every TV station in this town carries a public service ad that says "Friends Don't Let Friends Drive Drunk."
   B. Those ads are trying to rid our streets of that great killer, the drunk driver.
   C. In response to that menace, two national organizations—Mothers Against Drunk Driving and Students Against Drunk Driving—have been formed and are working even in this community to make the streets safe for you and me.
IV. [*Central Idea*] MADD and SADD are achieving their goals with your help.
V. To help you understand what these familiar organizations do, first I'll tell you something about the founders of MADD and SADD; then, I'll describe

their operations; finally, I'll mention some of the ways community members get involved with them.

[Body]

Conclusion

I. Today, I've talked briefly about the Lightners and their goals for MADD and SADD, their organizational techniques, and ways you can get involved.

II. The work of MADD and SADD volunteers—even on our campus, as I'm sure you've seen their posters in the Union—is being carried out to keep you alive.

   A. You may not think you need to be involved, but remember, after midnight one in every five or fewer drivers on the road is probably drunk.

   B. You could be involved whether you want to be or not.

   C. That certainly was the case with Julie Smeiser, a member of our sophomore class, who just last Friday was hit by a drunk driver when going home for the weekend.

III. If people don't take action, we could build a new "Black Gash"—this time for victims of drunks—every two years, and soon fill Washington, DC, with monuments to needless suffering.

   A. Such monuments would be grim reminders of our unwillingness to respond to enemies at home with the same intensity with which we attacked enemies abroad.

   B. Better would be a positive response to such groups as MADD and SADD, which are attacking the enemy on several fronts at once in a war on motorized murder.

IV. If you're interested in learning more about MADD and SADD, stop by Room 324 in the Union tonight at 7:30 to hear the president of the local chapter of SADD talk about this year's activities. I'll be there; please join me.

Chapter Summary

Introductions function *to raise interest, to indicate the speaker's qualifications, to recognize the demands of the occasion, to create goodwill,* and *to forecast the development of the speech.* The types of introductions include *referring to the subject, referring to the occasion, using a personal reference or greeting, asking a rhetorical question, making a startling statement of fact or opinion, using a quotation, telling a humorous anecdote,* and *using an illustration.* In concluding a speech, you should decide how strong a *summary* you need, consider the *"So what?"* question, think about an appropriate final *mood* for your speech, and *signal a sense of finality.* Useful techniques for ending a speech involve *issuing a challenge or appeal, summarizing, using a quotation, using an illustration, supplying an additional inducement to belief or action,* and *stating a personal intention.* Which techniques for beginning and ending a speech you use usually depend upon *your experiences and abilities, the mood and commitment of your audience, the audience's knowledge of you and your commitments,* and *situational constraints.*

References

1. Howard Rainer, "Hear My Words," in Jerry Blanche, ed., *Native American Reader.* (Juneau, AK: Denali Press, 1990), 156.

2. Alicia Croshal, "Gossip: It's Worth Talking About," *Winning Orations, 1991,* 1. Reprinted by permission of Larry Schnoor, Executive Secretary, Interstate Oratorical Association, Mankato State University, Mankato, MN.

3. Arthur M. Schlesinger, Jr., "America, the Arts and the Future," in Owen Peterson, ed., *Representative American Speeches 1987–88.* (New York: H. W. Wilson Co., 1988), 60:127.

4. Henri Mann Morton, "Strength through Cultural Diversity," in *Native American Reader,* 194.

5. Liz Carpenter, "Reflections from the Grassroots," in *Representative American Speeches 1987–88, 60:181–82.*

6. Shannon Dyer, "The Dilemma of Whistleblowers," *Winning Orations 1989.*

7. Elizabeth Badgley, "Nutra + Sweet = ? The Sweet and the Not-so-Sweet," *Winning Orations 1991,* 108.

8. Jeffrey E. Jamison, "Alkali Batteries: Powering Electronics and Polluting the Environment," *Winning Orations 1991,* 43.

9. Tisha R. Oehmen, "Not a Drop to Drink," *Winning Orations 1991,* 96.

10. George V. Grune, "Global Marketing: Global Opportunities," *Vital Speeches of the Day,* 55 (July 15, 1990).

11. Kelly McInerney, "The Pit Bull Problem," *Winning Orations 1991,* 15.

12. Kathleen Tracy, "The Forgotten Child," *Winning Orations 1991,* 99.

13. Rainer, p.158.

14. Brent Wainscott, "Title Unknown," *Winning Orations 1990,* 73.

15. Ben Smith, "Cruisin' for Danger," *Winning Orations 1990,* 89.

16. Kathleen Tracy, 102.

17. Denalie Silha, "Rediscovering a Lost Resource: Rethinking Retirement," *Winning Orations 1991,* 81.

18. Chui Lee Yap, "Ethnocentrism," *Winning Orations 1983.*

19. Christine D. Keen, "May You Live in Interesting Times," *Vital Speeches* 58 (Nov. 15, 1991):83, 86.

20. Tim Dolin, "The Next Polio?" *Winning Orations 1990,* 113, 117.

21. Brian Swenson, "Gun Safety and Children," *Winning Orations 1990,* 103.

22. Brian Twitchell, "The Flood Gates of the Mind," *Winning Orations 1983.*

23. Pushmataha, ". . . He Whose Passions are Inflamed by Military Success, Elevated too high by a Treacherous Confidence, Hears no longer the Dictates of Judgement," in *Native American Reader,* 83. The introduction to the excerpt is based on Blanche's commentary. As Blanche notes, this may not be an exact rendering of the words used; nevertheless, it certainly meets the spirit of the Choctaw's "reverence for the spoken word" (83).

Key Terms

additional inducement (p. 260)

challenge or appeal (p. 257)

conclusion (p. 255)

epitomizing illustration (p. 260)

expression of personal intent (p. 261)

humorous anecdote (p. 251)

introduction (p. 244)

personal greeting (p. 248)

pertinent quotation (p. 251, 259)

real or hypothetical illustration (p. 253)

reference to subject or occasion (p. 247)

rhetorical question (p. 249)

startling statement (p. 250)

summary of major points (p. 258)

Problems and Probes

1. After listening to a speech in at least two different settings [i.e., public lecture, public meeting, student meeting, televised address], compare and contrast the techniques used in introducing and concluding the separate presentations (they need not be on the same issue). Which are most useful or effectively used; which are not as useful, or although useful, are poorly executed by the speaker? In writing your evaluation, provide sufficient context so that a person who isn't present can understand what happened in each setting.
2. Assume you've been asked to speak on a controversial issue. Assume further that the setting for the speech will include three different occasions: a classroom speech, where audience members are mixed in their support or rejection of the issue; a 'pro' audience, sympathetic to your position; and a 'con' audience, hostile to your position. Indicate how your introduction and conclusion would be changed as you move from one setting to another. What would you do differently with respect to the techniques used, and why?

Communication Activities

1. In class groups, devise *two* excellent introductory strategies for the following speakers to use in the situations noted:

Speaker	Situation
Anita Hill	Keynote address, women's convention
Jimmy Carter	Seminar on human rights
Hillary Clinton	Keynote address, Children's Rights conference
Joe Garagiola	Dinner meeting, Division I baseball coaches

2. Devise one-minute introductions and conclusions to your next informative speech; deliver them in class to small groups in round-robin fashion. Have the members of the group evaluate the introductions as to interest and effectiveness (you may need to highlight what the body of the speech will attempt to accomplish before presenting the sample conclusion).

3. If videotape equipment is available, the instructor will present one or more sample introductions and conclusions by contemporary political or other speakers (for example, drawn from C-SPAN). In class discussion, critique the effectiveness of the introductions, and propose alternative means of beginning or ending the speeches. An alternative: in small groups, develop alternative introductions or conclusions, present those to the class, and discuss the respective quality of the original versus the alternative developed in class.

11

OUTLINING
THE SPEECH

"Outlining" is a word likely to bring back terrifying visions of eighth-grade English. You weren't quite sure why you had to do it; you hated it because you couldn't always think of both an A and a B to go under major heading II; and when you were all done, you were convinced it took more work than it was worth. Outlining rules seemed even more arbitrary than grammatical rules about using the words "which" and "that."

Although this is not the chapter of the book you're most looking forward to reading, the fact is that outlining is an important tool for the speaker. Speakers need outlines for two reasons:

1. *Testing.* An outline allows you to see your ideas—both those present and those absent. When you actually outline a speech, you can discover what ideas you've overemphasized to the exclusion of other notions, and what you've left out. A speaker's outline is a testing device.

2. *Guiding.* When you're actually delivering a speech, an outline is the preferred form of notes for many, perhaps even most, speakers. A good speaking outline shows you where you've been, where you are, and where you want to reach before you sit down; it helps you emphasize the right elements; it even can provide you with special speaking directions ("show map here"; "slow down here").

Outlines for speakers come in multiple forms, depending upon the purpose for which they've been constructed. In this chapter, we must begin

By sketching the structure of your speech in advance of delivery, you can determine whether the major sections fit together smoothly.

with a discussion of good outline form, to make sure you haven't completely forgotten what you were supposed to learn in eighth grade. Then, we'll get into the heart of the matter: types of outlines and ways to use them as testing instruments and as speaking guides.

Requirements of Good Outline Form

There are many different "good" outline forms, depending on the way you want to use them. Let us begin with the complete, full outline to review the five great rules of outline structures.

1. *Each item in the outline should contain only one unit of information.* An important purpose of a full outline is to show you how pieces of information are related to each other, so this rule is key.

    Incorrect

    I. Athens, Greece, should be the permanent site for the Olympic Games because they have become more and more politicized in recent years.
        A. The U.S. decision to boycott the 1980 Summer Olympics was political.
        B. The U.S.S.R. decision to boycott the 1984 Summer Olympics was political.
        C. Also, the costs are prohibitive, and returning the Games to their homeland would place renewed emphasis on their original purpose.

Notice that point C introduces two new ideas about costs and the Games' purpose. Those are important ideas and deserve emphasis equal to the matter of politics.

Correct

I. Athens, Greece, should be the permanent site for the Summer Olympic Games.
    A. The Games have become more and more politicized in recent years.
        1. The U.S decision to boycott . . .
        2. The U.S.S.R. decision to boycott . . .
    B. Costs for building new sites in new locations each four years are becoming prohibitive.
    C. Returning the Games to their homeland would place renewed emphasis on their original purpose.

In this version, the three reasons for urging the claim on the listeners are clear and are equally emphasized.

2. *Less important ideas in the outline should be subordinate to more important ideas.* You already know this is true; the trick is to actually carry it out so that listeners will understand the rational structure of your arguments.

Incorrect

I. The cost of medical care has skyrocketed.
    A. Operating room fees can run to tens of thousands of dollars.
        1. Hospital charges are high.
        2. A private room can cost $1,500 a day.
    B. X-rays and laboratory tests are extra.
    C. Complicated operations may cost over $50,000.
        1. Doctors' charges constantly go up.
            a. Office calls usually cost between $30 and $50.
        2. Drugs are expensive.
        3. Most antibiotics cost from $2 to $3 per dose.
    D. The cost of even nonprescription drugs has mounted.

This outline is a mess. A listener would feel bombarded by numbers and general references to hospitals and doctors, but probably couldn't sort it all out. To help the listener grasp the main ideas, notice what happens when the material is sorted by category-of-cost, in a topical outline:

Correct

I. The cost of medical care has skyrocketed.
    A. *Hospital charges* are high.
        1. A private room may cost as much as $1,500 a day.
        2. Operating room fees may be tens of thousands of dollars.
        3. X-rays and laboratory tests are extra.

B.   *Doctors' charges* constantly go up.
1.   Complicated operations may cost over $50,000.
2.   Office calls usually cost between $30 and $50.
C.   *Drugs* are expensive.
1.   Most antibiotics cost from $2 to $3 per dose.
2.   The cost of even nonprescription drugs has mounted.

The second form highlights the three main topics; it also subordinates examples, which are the supporting materials, to the three main arguments. The key word here is *fit:* what example fits within or under what topic? Reasons fit within or under claims: supporting materials fit within or under reasons.

3.   *The logical relation of items in an outline should be shown by proper indentation.* Yes, yes, you probably had nightmares about indentation in eighth grade, but you can handle it now. The rules are simple: the "biggest" or most important ideas start in Roman numerals on the left; the next biggest or most important are usually indented four or five spaces; the next level of thought is indented the same number of spaces; and so on. Second lines of any given sentence are indented the same (or sometimes one space more) than the first line, so that the numbering system stands out. Letting the numbers stand out allows the *form* of the ideas to be clear.

I.   Picking edible wild mushrooms is no job for the uninformed.
A.   Many wild species are highly toxic.
1.   The angel cap contains a toxin for which there is no known antidote.
2.   Hallucinogenic mushrooms produce short-lived highs, followed by convulsions, paralysis, and possibly death.
B.   Myths abound regarding ways to choose "safe" mushrooms.
1.   Mushrooms easily peeled still can be poisonous.
2.   Mushrooms eaten by animals are not necessarily safe.
3.   Mushrooms that don't darken a silver coin in a pan of hot water could be toxic.[1]

4.   *A consistent set of symbols should be used.* Each layer of indentation has its own set of symbols. The most popular set looks like this:

I.   Main idea
A.   Major sub-point or topic
1.   Aspect of the sub-point or topic
a.   Perhaps a statistic or quotation
(1)   Perhaps bolstering support

The important point is not to use only this set, but to be consistent, so that both you and any readers understand the rational structure of your thoughts.

An outline can serve as the basis for oral presentation. As you speak, the outline keeps you on track and reminds you of points you want to cover.

5. The first four requirements apply to all outlines. One last rule is made for complete, formal outlines: *all main points and subordinate points in formal outlines should be written as full sentences.* Full sentences maximize the clear expression of your ideas, because this sentence structure allows for the full articulation of human thought. For the speaker, using complete sentences forces you to reason your way through points that are fuzzy and incomplete. It may be painful to write complete sentences, but it's one of the ways you can guarantee good thinking.

Types of Outlines

Now that you've been back through the traditional rules of outline form, we can discuss how speakers use them *strategically:* to gain some rhetorical advantages from outlines. Consider where you are in the speech preparation process: you've picked purposes and central ideas or claims, developed your big ideas, dug up some supporting materials, and considered how to arrange everything to your advantage into introduction, body, and conclusion. Now you're ready to actually build the speech, and an outline is one of your main tools.

Most speakers go back and forth between their speech materials and their outlines. At first, given your initial research, the outline may start to "write

Memory and Organization

If you lost your outline, would you remember the major items? Even with the outline present, could you give your speech without complete reliance upon it, trusting your memory of the points and their sequence? Further, how many points should a speech attempt to cover? What difficulty would the audience have if you were to offer seventeen reasons for the rejection of nuclear power? These issues are answered in part by research relating organizational processes to human memory. In a classic study, Miller concluded that there is a limit to the number of items a person can easily recall; according to Miller, the "magic number" is seven, plus or minus two. More recent research has suggested that a more manageable number is five, plus or minus two. Using this research as a guideline would suggest that your list of seventeen items on nuclear power should be reduced to no more than five to seven points.

We routinely recall more than seven items, however (otherwise how would you pass a test in biology?). How is this possible, given the assumption that there is a limit on human memory? One of the

itself"—but not for long. Translating your materials into a structured speech can reveal problems in your proposed presentation. For example, you may discover that you have four pieces of testimony supporting one idea but none supporting another equally important one. Or, you might find three illustrations for your second point and a not-very-good-one for the third need. Outlining the visualization step might reveal that you need another set of statistical trends to develop the negative method, or you may discover that the chronology you're working with has a major gap in it.

This is what we meant earlier about using an outline to *test* your ideas. As your mental map moves onto paper, you'll almost inevitably find problems you need to solve. As for being a *guide* to your speaking, you'll want to convert the full, testing outline into something with shorter phrases and even single words—something that reminds you of what you wanted to say. Sure, some people try to speak from the fully developed outline; they're the ones you see shuffling through too many sheets of paper, losing their places, squinting to read individual sentences, and droning on once they finally decide just to read the whole thing to their audience.

ways we manage the additional data is by "chunking," or taking small bits of information and organizing them into discrete groupings. Your seventeen items on the hazards of nuclear power, for example, might be "chunked" into subsets involving internal safety procedures, mechanical failures, supervisor training issues, past violations of safety standards, and design flaws. These chunks, which are easier to recall than the multiple items, can serve as the main points in your presentation. The more specific instances within each subset can serve as your subpoints, fleshing out the case you wish to make.

As this chapter has noted, the effective outlining of ideas involves *coordinating* concepts of equal emphasis or merit and properly *subordinating* specific items to each "coordinate" point. Thus, in an outline, level *I* and level *II*, or level *A* and level *B*, are coordinate when considered as separate sets. Items *A* and *B* are subordinate when placed under *I* or *II*. This *hierarchical* method of organizing ideas matches the human mind's approach to the recall of items. Thus, three to five coordinate points (level *I*, *II*, . . .) could easily contain additional subpoints under each (*A*, *B*, *C*, . . .). Recalling level *I* also brings to mind the relevant subpoints, while recalling level *II* brings into focus the points under that heading.

FOR FURTHER READING

Mandler, G. "Organization and Memory." In Gordon Bower, ed. *Human Memory: Basic Processes.* New York: Academic Press, 1977, 310–54; G. Mandler's articles in C. R. Puff, ed. *Memory Organization and Structure.* New York: Academic Press, 1979, 303–19; Miller, G. A. "The Magic Number Seven, Plus or Minus Two: Some Limits on Our Capacity for Processing Information." *Psychological Review* 63 (1956): 81–97.

Thus, there are two main types of outlines in public speaking because you use them for two different purposes.

The Full-Sentence Outline

The **full-sentence outline** represents the factual content of the whole speech, arranged in outline form. Whether you use the traditional divisions of the speech (introduction, body, conclusion) or the steps in the motivated sequence (attention, need, satisfaction, visualization, action), each division or step is set off in a separate section:

- The principal ideas are stated as main headings, with subordinate or developmental materials fit underneath.
- Each major idea and all subordinate ones are written in complete sentences.
- Sources for supporting materials often are placed in parentheses at the end of sentences, perhaps in abbreviated form, with a bibliography attached at the end.

Such an outline creates a clear, comprehensive picture of your speech, with only specific wording and cues to delivery left out. In this form, it's a rigorous test of your preparation: is everything you need there? Do you have too much or too little material at specific points? Have you made yourself clear, adapted everything you can to the audience, fit the requirements of the occasion? Are you ready to go? (Sometimes, you can help yourself with the testing process by turning it into a *technical plot outline,* that is, one where you record the kinds of materials you've included to see how strong the speech is [pp. 282].) Here is an example of a full-sentence outline:

Steps in Preparing a Good Outline

I. The first step in preparing a good outline is to determine the general purpose of the speech for the subject you have selected.
  A. You will need to limit the subject in two ways.
    1. First, limit the subject to fit the available time.
    2. Second, limit the subject to ensure unity and coherence.
  B. You also will need to phrase the specific purpose in terms of the exact response you seek from your listeners.
II. The second step is to develop a rough outline of your speech.
  A. First, list the main ideas you wish to cover.
  B. Second, arrange these main ideas according to the methods discussed in Chapters 8 and 9.
  C. Third, arrange subordinate ideas under their appropriate main heads.
  D. Fourth, fill in the supporting materials to be used in amplifying or justifying your ideas.
  E. Finally, review your rough draft.
    1. Does it cover your subject adequately?
    2. Does it carry out your specific purpose?
III. The third step is to put the outline into final form.
  A. Begin this process by writing out the main ideas as complete sentences or as key phrases.
    1. State the main ideas concisely, vividly, and—insofar as possible—in parallel terms.
    2. State the major heads so that they address directly the needs and interests of your listeners.
  B. Write out the subordinate ideas in complete sentences or in key phrases.
    1. Are they subordinate to the main idea they are intended to develop?
    2. Are they coordinate with other items at the same level (that is, are all A–B–C series roughly equal in importance; are all 1–2–3 series roughly equal in importance)?
  C. You now are ready to fill in the supporting materials.
    1. Are they pertinent?
    2. Are they adequate?
    3. Is there a variety of types of support?
  D. Finally, recheck the completed outline.
    1. Is it written in proper outline form?

A complex sentence outline can be distracting and confusing when used as a speaking outline, whereas the key words in a phrase outline are easy to see as you stand in front of an audience.

2. Does the speech, as outlined, adequately cover the subject?
3. Does the speech, as outlined, carry out your general and specific purposes?

The Phrase Outline

The phrase outline and the full-sentence outline use the same indentation and symbol structure. The major difference is that each item in a **phrase outline** is referred to in shorthand—key words, even a single word. Speakers use phrase outlines in two ways: informally, in developing a *rough outline* or preliminary sketch of their speeches; and, more formally, as a *speaking outline,* or the text they actually carry with them to the lectern or table. Developed as a phrase outline, the previous full-sentence outline looks like this:

Sample Phrase Outline

I. Determine general purpose
  A. Limit subject
    1. Fit available time
    2. Assure unity and coherence
  B. Phrase in terms of listener response

II. Develop rough draft
   A. List main ideas
   B. Arrange main ideas
      1. Motivated sequence
      2. Traditional pattern
   C. Arrange subordinate ideas
   D. Add supporting materials
   E. Review rough draft
      1. Adequacy?
      2. Meet specific purpose?
III. Final outline form
   A. Complete sentences or key phrases
      1. Concise, vivid, parallel phrasing
      2. Address needs and interests of listeners
   B. Subordinate ideas—complete sentence or key word
      1. Under appropriate main head
      2. Coordinate with subordinate ideas of equal weight
   C. Add supporting materials
      1. Pertinent
      2. Adequate
      3. Variety
   D. Review outline
      1. Good form
      2. Adequate coverage
      3. Meets purpose

Preparing an Outline

You should develop your outline, as well as the speech it represents, gradually, through a series of stages. Your outlines will become increasingly complex as the ideas of your speech evolve and as you move it closer to its final form. There are three stages you will have to move your outline through, each of which has a specific function:

1. Develop a *rough outline* that establishes the topic of your speech, clarifies your purpose, and identifies a reasonable number of subtopics.
2. Prepare a *technical plot outline* of your speech in order to evaluate the strengths and weaknesses of your prospective presentation.
3. Finally, recast your material into a *speaking outline* that compresses your technical plot into key words or phrases that can be used to jog your memory when you deliver your speech.

Developing a Rough Outline

Suppose your instructor has assigned an informative speech on a subject that interests you. You decide to talk about drunk driving because a close friend was recently injured by an intoxicated driver. Your broad topic area is *drunk driving.*

In the six-to-eight minutes you have to speak, you obviously can't cover such a broad topic adequately. After considering your audience (see Chapter 4) and your time limit, you decide to focus your presentation on two organizations—Mothers Against Drunk Driving (MADD) and Students Against Drunk Driving (SADD).

As you think about narrowing your topic further, you jot down some possible ideas. You continue to narrow your list until your final ideas include the following:

1. Founders of MADD and SADD
2. Accomplishments of the two organizations
3. Reasons the organizations were deemed necessary
4. Goals of MADD and SADD
5. Action steps taken by MADD and SADD
6. Ways your listeners can help

You can help your listeners to follow your ideas by clustering similar ideas. Experiment with several possible clusters before you decide on the best way to arrange your ideas.

Your next step is to consider the best pattern of organization for these topics. A chronological pattern would enable you to organize the history of MADD and SADD, but it would not allow you to discuss ways your listeners could help. Either cause-effect or effect-cause would work well if your primary purpose were to persuade. However, this is an informative speech, and you don't want to talk about the organizations as only the causes of the effect of reduced alcohol-related accidents. Of the special patterns, an inquiry order might work. You discard inquiry order, however, when you realize that you don't know enough about audience members' questions to use this organizational pattern effectively. After examining the alternatives, you finally settle on a topical pattern. A topical pattern allows you to present three clusters of information:

1. Background of MADD and SADD—information about the founders, why the organizations were founded
2. Description of MADD and SADD—goals, steps in action plans, results
3. Local work of MADD and SADD—how parents work with their teenagers and with local media to accomplish MADD and SADD goals

As you subdivide your three clusters of information, you develop the following general outline:

I. Background of MADD and SADD
   A. Information about the founders
   B. Reasons the organizations were founded
II. Description of the organizations
   A. Their goals
   B. The action steps they take
   C. Their accomplishments so far

III. Applications of their work on a local level
   A. "Project Graduation"
   B. Parent-student contracts
   C. Local public service announcements

A **rough outline** identifies your topic, provides a reasonable number of subtopics, and shows a method for organizing and developing your speech. Notice that you've arranged both the main points and subpoints topically. A word of warning: *you should make sure that the speech doesn't turn into a "string of beads" that fails to differentiate between one topic and the next.*

The next step in preparing an outline is to phrase your main headings more precisely. Then you can begin to develop each heading by adding subordinate ideas. As you develop your outline, you'll begin to see what kinds of information and supporting materials you need to find.

Developing a Technical Plot Outline

A **technical plot outline** is a diagnostic tool used to determine whether a speech is structurally sound. Use your technical plot outline to discover possible gaps or weaknesses in your speech. After completing your rough outline and learning more about your topic through background reading, you're now ready to assemble a technical plot outline.

Begin by examining your rough outline. Be flexible—if you discover that you must rearrange some topics or drop others to fit your time limits or audience's interests, then do so. Next, write each item of the outline as a complete sentence to convey your meaning clearly and precisely. Remember the requirements of good outline form discussed earlier. You should add to your outline a bibliography of the sources you consulted.

Lay the complete sentence outline beside a blank sheet of paper. On the blank sheet, opposite each outline unit, identify the corresponding supporting materials, types of motivational appeals, factors of attention, and other devices. For example, indicate on the blank sheet of paper wherever you have used statistics; you might also include a brief statement of the function of the statistics.

Then, examine the list of supporting materials, motivational appeals, factors of attention, and so on. Is there adequate supporting material for each point in the speech? Is the supporting material sufficiently varied? Do you use motivational appeals at key points in the speech? Do you attempt to engage your listeners' attention throughout the speech? Answering these questions with your technical plot outline can help you to determine whether your speech is structurally sound, whether there is adequate supporting material, whether you've overused any forms of support, and whether you have effectively adapted your appeals to the audience and content.

Perceptual Grouping: The Organization of Subordinate Points

What basic principles do we use to organize information into meaningful patterns? Gestalt psychologists have studied this question in detail for years. They believe that organization is basic to all mental activity and that it reflects the way the human brain functions. Although the assumptions of Gestalt psychology have less influence in the study of cognition and perception today than they did in the past, they provide us with some clues to patterns of thought.

As suggested in this chapter, psychologists have argued that human knowledge is derived analogically; that is, people learn by adding new bits of information to old constructs. Although the information that we encounter changes, the constructs remain constant. There are several relatively static constructs that people use to group new bits of information:

1. *Proximity*—we group stimuli that are close together.
2. *Continuity*—we tend to simplify and to find similarities among things rather than differences.
3. *Contiguity*—we connect events that occur close together in time and space.
4. *Closure*—we complete figures by filling in the gaps or adding missing connections.
5. *Similarity*—we group items of similar shape, size, and color.

Methods for learning new vocabulary or for remembering people's names are often based on these simple constructs. For example, you use the principle of *proximity* when you remember the word *acerbic* (meaning sharp, bitter, or sour) because it resembles the word *acid*. When you stumble over the word *acerbic* in a sentence, you guess its meaning from its use and context by employing the principle of *closure*. You easily connect "acerbic" with "acerbity" because of the principle of *continuity*. When trying to remember someone's name, you might "flash back" to the first time you met that person, thus applying *contiguity*. Or, that person might remind you of another person with the same name because of their *similarity* in appearance.

You can adapt these constructs to organize the substructure of your speeches. When you do so, you'll be providing your listeners with unfamiliar information in patterns of thinking that are familiar to them. Consider the constructs for organizing subordinate points shown in the table on the facing page.

STRATEGIES FOR ORGANIZING SPEECH INFORMATION

Organization Strategy	Main Construct	Explanation	Example
Parts of a Whole	Proximity	You help your audience perceive how the new information is all part of a whole.	"The grip, shaft, and head are the main parts of a golf club."
Lists of Functions	Continuity	You show your audience the connections between new information.	"The mission of a police department consists of meeting its responsibilities of traffic control, crime detection, and safety education."
Series of Causes or Results	Contiguity	You show your listeners the relationship between items of new information.	"The causes of high orange juice prices may be drought, frost, or blight in citrus-producing states."
Items of Logical Proof	Closure	You connect separate items of information along a coordinated line of reasoning.	"We need a new high school because our present building (a) is too small, (b) lacks modern laboratory and shop facilities, and (c) is inaccessible to handicapped students."
Illustrative Examples	Similarity	You help your audiences accept your main point by grouping specific cases or examples.	Cite the outcome of experiments to prove that adding fluoride to your community's water supply will help prevent tooth decay.

Sample Technical Plot Outline

What follows is the complete content of an outline with its technical plot. For illustrative purposes, all items in the outline are stated as complete sentences. Such completeness of detail may be desirable if the occasion is especially important or if you have difficulty framing thoughts extemporaneously. Frequently, however, you will need to write out only the main ideas as complete sentences and state the subordinate ideas and supporting materials as key phrases. Check with your instructor if you have any doubt about how detailed to make your outline.

Notice how these constructs are based upon the five constructs people use to make sense of new information.

These constructs also function as criteria against which your organizational coherence can be checked. Are your most important ideas *near,* or *proximate,* to each other? Do they advance a chain of thinking in a coherent manner implying *continuity?* Are they linked together or *contiguous?* Are they sufficiently comprehensive to permit accurate *closure?* Are they *similar* enough to suggest they belong together as main points?

As a public speaker, you can take advantage of the innate constructs by which the human brain organizes new information. You can use the constructs of proximity, continuity, contiguity, closure, and similarity to make your message more accessible to your listeners.

FOR FURTHER READING
For elaboration of the constructs previously discussed, see Lyle E. Bourne, Jr., and Bruce R. Ekstrand, *Psychology: Its Principles and Meanings,* 4th ed. (New York: Holt, Rinehart & Winston, 1982), chap 3; Dennis Coon, *Introduction to Psychology,* 3rd ed. (St. Paul: West, 1983), 104–124; Henry Gleitman, *Psychology* (New York: W. W. Norton, 1981),

228–253. For recent reviews of Gestalt psychology, see Rudolph Arnheim, "The Two Faces of Gestalt Psychology," *American Psychologist,* 41 (1986): 820–824; Ronald H. Forgus and Lawrence E. Melamed, *Perception: A Cognitive-Stage Approach,* 2nd ed. (New York: McGraw-Hill, 1976), 177–182; and Michael Kobovy and James R. Pomerantz, eds., *Perceptual Organization* (Hillsdale, N.J.: Lawrence Erlbaum Associates, 1980).

Friends Don't Let Friends Drive Drunk[2]

[The introduction and conclusion of this speech were developed in detail in Chapter 10, Beginning and Ending the Speech, pages 264–265]

First topic: background on founders, helping create emotional identification

I. MADD and SADD were founded under tragic circumstances.
    A. MADD was founded in 1980 by Candy Lightner.
        1. One of her daughters was killed by a drunk driver.
        2. She wanted to protect other families from a similar tragedy.

B.   SADD was founded by Lightner's other daughter.
1.   The loss of her sister hurt her deeply.
2.   She knew the importance of peer pressure in stopping teenage drinking and driving.

Second topic:
description

II.   You can understand MADD and SADD better if you know something about their goals, operations and effectiveness.

First subtopic:
goals

A.   MADD and SADD were organized the way they were because the Lightners have specific goals they wish to achieve.
1.   They want the general public to carry out the agitation necessary to effect changes.

Specific instances

a.   Members of the public can put pressure on government officials.
b.   They can write letters-to-the-editor.
c.   They can campaign for state and local task forces.
d.   They can do all this for a minimal investment of money.
2.   They want to expose the deficiencies in current legislation and drunk driving control systems.

Statistics
(segments)

a.   They want to toughen the laws on operating a motor vehicle when intoxicated [statistics on variations in state laws].

Specific instances

b.   They want to pressure judges to hand down maximum instead of minimum penalties [specific instances of light sentences].

Statistics
(segments)

c.   They want to see more drunk driver arrests from city, county, and state law enforcement agents [statistics on arrest rates].
3.   They want to help the families of other victims.
a.   Most MADD and many SADD members have been victims themselves.

Testimony

b.   Families are taught to put their energy into getting something done [quotations from pamphlets] as well as into mourning.
4.   And finally, MADD and SADD want to educate the general public.
a.   They want to make people conscious of the tragedies of drunk driving.
b.   They want to focus media attention on the problem.

Second subtopic:
action steps

B.   MADD's steps for action demonstrate the thoroughness with which the organization understands the processes of public persuasion.

Throughout, extended hypo- thetical illustration exemplifies the steps

1. First, a local chapter sets its goals.
2. Second, it educates its organizers goal by goal so that everyone knows the reasons behind each step.
3. Third, it sets research priorities.
   a. One group might check on local arrest records.
   b. Another might examine drunk driving conviction rates for various judges.
   c. A third might work with local media to find out how to secure time and space for a public service announcement on drunk driving.
   d. A fourth might talk with local schools and churches about safe prom nights.
4. Fourth, once the research is complete, the local chapter can formulate its plans of action.
5. Fifth, it can "go public" with action teams and task forces.

Testimony

6. This five-step process parallels the campaign model for public persuasion devised by Herbert W. Simons in his book *Understanding Persuasion.*

Third subtopic: results of MADD/ SADD work Statistics (magni- tude)

C. Although still young, organizations such as MADD and SADD already have had significant effects.
1. By 1984, there were 320 MADD chapters across the country.
2. About 600,000 volunteers are now working on MADD projects.
3. State laws already are changing.

Specific instances

   a. In 1982 alone, 25 different states enacted 30 pieces of drunk driving legislation as a result of MADD's lobbying.
   b. After petitions were submitted by the organizations, Congress raised the manda- tory legal drinking age to 21.
   c. In Florida, convicted drunk drivers must have red bumper stickers on their cars reading, "CONVICTED DUI."

Statistics (trends)

4. Fatalities from drunk driving have decreased [quote pre-1980 and post-1980 statistics].
5. MADD also takes credit for increasing the popularity of low-alcohol beer, wines, and wine coolers.

Third topic: local projects

III. You can work with MADD and SADD on local pro- jects.
A. Set up a workshop in local high schools for parent-child contracts.

Explanation

    1. In such a contract (which has no legal status) the teen agrees to never drive drunk, calling on the parent for a ride instead, while the parent agrees to ask no questions and to impose no special penalties for the teen's intoxication.

    2. The contract reinforces the importance of not driving drunk and makes the commitment to safety a mutual commitment.

  B. Set up a SADD "Project Graduation."

Example

    1. With the cooperation of the schools and, sometimes, local youth organizations or churches, a community can sponsor non-alcoholic postprom parties.

    2. They allow prom-goers a chance to stay up late, have fun, and celebrate without alcohol.

  C. Work with local media to use public service announcements to halt teen and adult drunk driving.

Specific instances

    1. MADD chapters can order ads you may have seen on TV.

      a. Some oppose drunk driving.

      b. Some tell you to designate a nondrinking driver from among your group.

      c. Others urge hosts of parties to not let drunk guests drive.

Specific instance

    2. SADD chapters also can order ads and school posters, nonalcoholic party kits, and the like [show sample items].

Developing a Speaking Outline

As you probably realize, a technical plot outline would be very difficult to use when you were actually delivering your speech on MADD and SADD. A technical outline is too detailed to manage from a lectern; you will probably be tempted to read it to your listeners because it includes so many details. If you read your outline, however, you'll lose your conversational tone.

Therefore, you need to compress your technical plot outline into a more useful form. A **speaking outline** is a short, practical form to use while delivering your speech. This form consists primarily of summaries of the complete sentences in your technical outline. The actual method you use to create your speaking outline will depend on your personal preference; some people like to work with small pieces of paper, others with notecards. Whatever your choice, however, your speaking outline should serve several functions while you're addressing your audience: (a) it should provide you with reminders of the direction of your speech—main points, subordinate ideas, and so on; (b) it should record technical or detailed material such as statistics and quotations; and (c) it should be easy to read so that it does not

SAMPLE SPEAKING OUTLINE (ON NOTECARDS)

Notecards for a speech on MADD and SADD

FRIENDS DON'T LET FRIENDS DRIVE DRUNK

I. Background
   A. MADD 1980 Cindy Lightner
   B. SADD her other daughter for hi-school kids

II. Description
   A. Goals
      1. public agitation (gov't. officials, letters to editor, task forces, all for little money)
      2. expose deficiencies in current legis. & control
         a. tougher laws state by state (STATISTICS)
         b. pressure judges (JUDGE NORTON, SANDERS, HANKS)
         c. more arrests (STATISTICS)
      3. public education
         a. more conscious
         b. media attention

   B. MADD's action steps
      1. goals (what community needs most)
      2. educate organizers
      3. set research priorities (arrest records, conviction rates, PSA's, prom nights)
      4. formulate plans of action
      5. go public[1]
         (note on Simon's *Understanding Persuasion*)

   C. Results
      1. 320 MADD chapters by 1984
      2. 600,000 volunteers
      3. state laws changing
         a. 1982 25 states, 30 pieces of legis.
         b. Congress drinking age to 21
         c. Florida, red bumpersticker, CONVICTED DUI
      4. fatalities down (statistics)
      5. popularity of low-alc beers, wines, coolers

   III. Local projects
      A. contracts
      B. prom night (Operation Graduation)
      C. PSA's and publicity
         1. MADD TV ads
            a. after drunk driving
            b. sober group member
            c. host/guest --*Friends don't let friends d.d.*
         2. SADD projects
            a. school posters (SHOW POSTER)**
            b. non-alc party kits
            c. ads

detract from the delivery of your speech. Each notecard or piece of paper should contain only one main idea.

There are four main characteristics of properly prepared speaking outlines:

1. Most points are noted with only a key word or phrase—a word or two should be enough to trigger your memory, especially if you've practiced the speech adequately.
2. Ideas that must be stated precisely are written down fully, for example, "Friends don't let friends drive drunk."
3. Directions for delivery are included, such as "SHOW POSTER."
4. Emphasis is indicated in a number of ways—capital letters, underlining, indentation, dashes, and highlighting with colored markers (find methods of emphasis that will easily catch your eye, show the relationship of ideas, and jog your memory during your speech delivery).

Chapter Summary

Arranging and outlining often are viewed as heinous tasks by students, yet if the different services outlines provide speakers are understood, they're seen as tools in helping you to complete your speech preparation thoroughly and confidently. There are five requirements for good outline form: (1) *each item should contain only one idea;* (2) *less important ideas should be subordinate to more important ones;* (3) *logical relationships should be shown through proper indentation;* (4) *a consistent set of symbols should be used;* and (5) *in complete outlines, all main points and subordinate ideas should be written as full sentences.* Two types of outlines are important to speakers: the *full-sentence outline,* used to show the fully developed speech and to test it, often in a *technical plot outline;* and the *phrase outline,* used as a *rough outline* when you're developing a speech and later as a *speaking outline* when you're at the lectern. Overall, then, outlining helps speakers through the three phases of speech preparation: a rough outline helps you focus your thinking, a technical plot outline helps you assess the rationality and appeal of your ideas, and a speaking outline aids you in developing the speech as planned.

References

1. Information taken from Vincent Marteka, "Words of Praise—and Caution—About Fungus Among Us," *Smithsonian* (May, 1980): 96–104.

2. The material for this speech—including the statistics we haven't directly included—was drawn from the following sources: "MADD From Hell," *Restaurant Hospitality* (April, 1990); "One Less for the Road?" *Time* (May 20, 1985); "Rascal, MADD Party with High Schoolers," *Advertising Age* (November 20, 1989); "War Against Drunk Drivers," *Newsweek* (September 13, 1982); "They're Mad as Hell," *Time* (August 3, 1981); "How to Get Alcohol Off the

Highway," *Time* (July 1, 1981); "Health Report," *Prevention Magazine* (June, 1984); "Water Water Everywhere," *Time* (May 20, 1985); L. B. Taylor, *Driving High* (New York: Watts, 1983); Sandy Golden, *Driving the Drunk Off the Road* (Washington, DC: Acropolis Books, 1983); and U.S. National Highway Traffic Safety Administration, *How to Save Lives and Reduce Injuries—A Citizen Activist Guide to Effectively Fight Drunk Driving* (pamphlet) (Washington, DC: U.S. Government Printing Office, 1982).

Key Terms

full-sentence outline *(p. 275)*

phrase outline *(p. 277)*

rough outline *(p. 282)*

speaking outline *(p. 282)*

technical plot outline *(p. 282)*

Problems and Probes

1. Revise both *a* and *b* below, following the guidelines for correct outline form.
   a. The nuclear freeze concept is a good idea because it allows us to stop nuclear proliferation and it will help make us feel more secure.
   b. I. We should wear seatbelts to protect our lives.
   II. Studies indicate seatbelts protect children from serious injury.
   III. Studies indicate seatbelts reduce risk of head injury.
2. Select a speech from this text or from a speech anthology available in the library. Develop a full-sentence outline for the speech, then an abbreviated phrase outline. Add to these outlines a technical plot in which you indicate the forms of support, attention factors, and motivational appeals used by the speaker. Hand in your written outlines and technical plot. Your instructor may have you meet in small groups to compare your analyses of a single assigned speech.

Communication Activities

1. For a speech assigned by the instructor, draw up a full-sentence outline and a technical plot in accordance with the samples provided in this chapter. Hand in your speech outline in time to obtain feedback before presenting your speech.
2. Working in small groups, select a controversial topic for potential presentation in class. Brainstorm possible arguments that could be offered on the pro and con sides. With these as a basis, develop a phrase outline of the main points to be presented on both sides.
3. For the next round of classroom speeches, your instructor will divide the class into groups and ask each student to outline the presentations of their respective group members. Working in groups, compare and contrast the outlines of what was heard with the speaker's own outline.

PART THREE

CHANNELS

"*It may therefore be fairly concluded, that to neglect all or any part of the labour which constitutes correct delivery; whether it be the due management of the voice, the expression of the countenance, or the appropriate gesture, is so far an injury to the cause in which the speaker is engaged, and so far deprives his composition of its just effect.*"

Gilbert Austin
Chronomia; Or a Treatise on Rhetorical Delivery (1806)

USING
LANGUAGE TO
COMMUNICATE

T he preceding chapters concentrated on preparing, organizing, and adapting messages to their intended audiences. The next three chapters focus on **encoding** these messages—the processes for giving expression and form to ideas, attitudes, feelings, and values. These processes, or channels, include the choice of language (the subject in Chapter 12), the use of visual aids (Chapter 13), and the control of bodily and vocal behaviors (Chapter 14). Each channel is not simply a conduit, an empty pipe, through which "content" flows. In fact, each channel helps shape and complete that content. Words, the impact of graphs and other visual aids, the various shadings to meaning given by tone of voice or body posture interact to shape the meaning the speaker desires. We begin with language—the choices of wording and style for making your meaning clear and compelling.

Speaking in a language that the audience understands is critical to success. Languages and dialects contain idiomatic expressions whose meaning may be quite different from the literal meaning of the words of the expression. Imagine talking to a foreign audience, using contemporary expressions such as the eastern regionalism "wicked good" or teen slang such as "chill out." Even when you don't use such colloquial expressions, you must still be careful to use terms that are within the audience's range of knowledge or experience, or you must define the terms as you use them in your speech.

For instance, if you were discussing recent archeological finds in the ancient lands of the Philistines, references to "Hathor-type sistrum," shekels, *begá*, and *bat* may be lost on an audience unless they're experts in the field. In fact, with a general audience, the reference to *bat* may, without explanation, be confused with the American game of baseball (*bat* refers to a liquid measure equivalent to 32 quarts).[1] Audiences can only **decode** terms for which they have referents or with which they have experience.

Language is both a referential and a relational channel of conveying ideas. In discussing archaeological finds, a **referential language** is used to identify persons, places, things, feelings, or other characteristics of a people and their environments. But referential language has both **denotative** and **connotative** dimensions. In its denotative role (its dictionary definition), references to shekels and *bat* name precise objects. In the connotative role of language, terms such as "chill out" and "wicked good" go beyond their denotative definition to encompass different associations or meanings attached to the word or phrase.

In addition to its referential role, language also is **relational**.[2] There are innumerable phrases in our language that encode our relationships to each other. When you say "May I please have the . . . ," you signal that you're asking for cooperation rather than commanding action, regardless of your formal relationship with the person (as employer, for example). You change the relational sense of the language when you instead say "Give me the. . . ."

You call upon all of these dimensions of language in the act of speaking to others. To put ideas into language is to *style* them, whether to a single listener or to a formal, public audience. A **speaking style** is a set of verbal and nonverbal cues that speakers and listeners both understand. For both, the style represents a particular mode of human interaction. Commonly identified styles include an evangelical style, an academic style, a colloquial style, and even a discombobulated (confused) style.

Your individual speaking style for any occasion sets up a social-psychological relationship with your audience. The relationship is social in that it's wholly or in part influenced by conventions—the normal way in which people in this setting interpret symbols. Rap is a conventional manner of speaking that differs radically from an academic address—the social relationship implied by each style virtually excludes the other. The "psychological" aspect of style indicates that the style is yours; an individualized expression, it's your own personal signature.[3]

Essentials of Effective Word Choices

The creation of clear, compelling language in a style suited to you, the topic, audience, and occasion requires attention to five key factors in word choice: accuracy, simplicity, coherence, intensity, and appropriateness.

Accuracy

Achieving a precise meaningful style requires that you select words that accurately describe what you intend to convey. President Bush was criticized repeatedly for his use of "the [fill in the noun] thing"; his lack of precise language left the audience grasping for his meaning. If you give a presentation on the dangers of nuclear power without bothering to learn the technical terms normally associated with nuclear energy, it will put you at a distinct disadvantage when your opponent employs those terms in a way that conveys their meaning. The distinction between you and your opponent suggests a greater expertise in the situation.

In their referential sense, words represent concepts and objects. In speaking positively about "American democracy," you may assume that your listeners clearly understand your meaning. Your listeners may, however, attach a different meaning than you intended to convey. Democracy doesn't mean the same thing to a citizen of the United States as it does to a citizen of China. In fact, the term "democracy" does not necessarily mean the same thing to a member of the political right as it does to a member of the left.

Students of general semantics continually warn us that "the word is not the thing" it represents and that language is not fixed and timeless.[4] People, words, and meanings continually change, though at different rates. The force of fixed meaning is evident in expressions such as "once a con, always a con." An ex-convict has great difficulty living beyond or outside of the label. A person released from prison can change, but the label "ex-con" traps a person in his or her past. The terms used not only *select* a particular vision or meaning for the person, but also *deflect* or *reject* other possible labels.[5] A person is more than a label.

To avoid imprecision or vagueness, choose words that express the exact shade of meaning you wish to communicate. A thesaurus is an excellent source in selecting words that allow you to refer to a concept or object, but offer slight variations that may be more forceful or clear than the more general word. The common, ordinary verb "point" could be replaced with aim, direct, refer, hint, imply, suggest, denote, indicate, signify. Do you want to say the action "points to," "refers to," "hints at," or "implies"? Similarly, the verb "shine" may be replaced with radiate, scintillate, gleam, glisten, glitter, glow. Which is the most accurate expression of what you mean: saying "his small face positively shone with pleasure," "his small face radiated pleasure," or "his small face gleamed with pleasure"?

Simplicity

Speak so that everyone in the audience, regardless of her or his experience or education, can understand your message. Simplicity does not mean that your language is simplistic or that you come across as condescending in talking down to your audience. You can still "talk with" rather than "talk to" an audience while using words that are within your listeners' common range of experience or that can be defined so they can easily comprehend your presentation. Saying "difficult to understand" rather than "esoteric" or "to establish" rather than "to ascertain " will enable you to communicate ideas to your audience in a manner that neither confuses them nor insults

Abraham Lincoln said, "Speak so that the most lowly can understand you, and the rest will have no difficulty."

their intelligence. When a simpler and more common term is available, choose it over a longer or less familiar term, unless accuracy is damaged as a result. In that event, use the less familiar term and define it using more commonly known and understood words. Billy Sunday, the famous evangelist, gave this example:[6]

> If a man were to take a piece of meat and smell it and look disgusted, and his little boy were to say, "What's the matter with it, Pop?" and he were to say, "It is undergoing a process of decomposition in the formation of new chemical compounds," the boy would be all in. But if the father were to say, "It's rotten," then the boy would understand and hold his nose. "Rotten" is a good Anglo-Saxon word, and you do not have to go to the dictionary to find out what it means.

In choosing words, then, select those that accurately and clearly convey the precise meaning you wish to express.

Coherence

Listening to oral messages requires concentration. As a listener, you don't have the luxury of going back over the text, as you do when you read a textbook, nor do you have punctuation marks that distinguish one idea from another. To be understood, your oral message must be logically constructed or coherent. To achieve coherence, you need to organize your ideas so the audience can see connections between points (see Chapters 8 and 9). In addition, you can use signposts to help audiences see those connections and follow the development of your ideas. As noted in Chapter 10, forecasting the development of your main points ("The four major points to be covered are. . . ."; "The history of this issue can be easily divided into two periods. . . .") provides convenient signposts for your audience. At the end of your presentation, summaries ("The four points I have discussed are. . . ."; "The two periods just covered [restate them] represent. . . .") also function as signposts.

Signposts are words (*first, next, thus, finally*) or phrases (*as a result, in consequence*) that keep the audience on track. Signposts such as "the history of this issue begins with . . ." or "before considering the recent events, we need first to clearly understand. . . ." also provide helpful clues to the overall structure of your message. Signposts function as connectives or transitions between ideas. The following are additional connectives or transitions that are typically used in oral presentations:

In the first place . . . The second point is . . .

In addition to . . . notice that . . .

Now look at [name it] from a different angle . . .

You must keep these three things in mind to fully grasp the significance of the fourth . . .

What was the result? Well, . . .

Turning now to . . .

These signposts are neutral—they tell the audience that another idea is coming but do not suggest more subtle logical relationships that may exist. However, you can improve the clarity and forcefulness of your ideas, and thereby increase coherence, by clearly invoking relationships that imply *parallel/hierarchical, similar/different,* and *coordinate/subordinate* relationships:

- *Parallel*: Not only . . . but also . . .
- *Hierarchical*: More important than these . . .
- *Different*: In contrast . . .
- *Similar*: Similar to this . . .
- *Coordinated*: One must consider X, Y, and Z.
- *Subordinated*: On the next lower level is . . .

LANGUAGE INTENSITY CHART

	Subject	*Verb*	*Object*
Positive	A Doctor of Philosophy at an institution of higher learning	discussed	dialectical perspectives on life and living.
Neutral	The philosophy professor at State U	outlined	Karl Marx economic and social theories.
Negative	An effete intellectual snob at the local haven for druggies	harangued our children with	Communist drivel.

Forecasting and closing summaries clarify the *macrostructure* of your message. If audiences know in advance of the substantive portion what they will hear and at the close of the speech is reminded of that overall structure, they'll have an easier time recalling your central idea or claim. The signposts noted above are elements of a speech's *microstructure*—they give an audience an understanding of what is happening, step by step, through the body of the speech.

Intensity

Your feelings about the subject, occasion, and audience will color your choice of words. Through selecting highly positive, neutral, or negative words, you communicate your attitude. Consider, for example, the following "attitudinally weighted" terms:

Highly Positive	*Relatively Neutral*	*Highly Negative*
savior	G. I.	enemy
patriot	soldier	baby-killer
freedom fighter	combatant	foreign devil

These are organized roughly in order of their intensity of feeling, from the highly positive "savior" to the highly negative "foreign devil." The term you select communicates your position on an issue; hence be sure that your choice accurately reflects your actual attitude or feeling.

How intense should your language be? John Waite Bowers has suggested a useful rule of thumb: let your language be, roughly, one step more intense than the position or attitude of your audience.[7] If the audience is sympathetic to the position you take on an issue, you can afford to be more intense. Conversely, if they're hostile, a more neutral language—one that reflects a willingness to consider opposing points of view—will be more likely to secure a fair hearing. Adapting your language choice to the audience will maximize the chance that your ideas will be heard as you intend them—that your listeners will not be so "put off" by your inappropriate intensity that they discard your ideas without critically appraising their merit.

Appropriateness

Appropriateness helps you meet the expectations imposed by the topic, the audience, and the occasion. Even if an audience is sympathetic, a solemn and formal occasion may not be the most appropriate place for a highly intense expression of feeling. Such occasions call for language that is as dignified, serious, and restrained as the occasion itself. Just as you would not employ slang expressions in a speech dedicating a memorial, you also would refrain from using a shrill style at a banquet in honor of retirees. Suiting your language to the tone of the occasion as well as to the audience will ensure that your style is perceived as appropriate and *fitting* for the moment. An occasion that allows for informal language choices, but with an audience that is older than you are, requires informal colloquialisms that are within the range of experience of your listeners. "Gee whiz," "high camp," "cool," "neat," "far out," and "awesome" represent different generations of language use; in using any of these, you need to define those the audience may not recognize immediately—or may have heard but not clearly understood. When the expression is unique to an earlier era, refrain from any expression that appears to ridicule the phrase; after all, it was as perfectly acceptable in their era as "totally awesome" is in yours.

Selecting an Appropriate Style: Strategic Decisions

The qualities of an effective speaking style discussed above (accuracy, simplicity, coherence, intensity, appropriateness) are essential for clear and understandable communication. There are also other strategies that can be used to further control the impression the audience has of you, your ideas, and even the occasion itself. The combination of these strategies, which give your speech its distinctive character or dominant effect, is generally referred to as **tone**. Do you come across as a free spirit or as a somber, serious student of life? Is your message cast primarily as a logical argument, or are you telling stories that will support your ideas? Are you primarily concerned with how you'll be received, with how the message will be accepted, or both? Each possibility reflects a different tone that is communicated to the audience. It tells them where you're coming from.

While tone is an elusive quality of oral communication, it nevertheless can be identified in terms of its primary dimensions. The five dimensions are written vs. oral style; serious vs. humorous atmosphere; person-centered vs. group-centered and material-centered emphases; gendered vs. gender-neutral nouns and pronouns; and propositional vs. narrative form. The following discussion will assist you in adapting a preferred tone to your message.

Written vs. Oral Style

The fact that oral speech developed long before written language has far-reaching implications. It is presumed that oral speech arose directly from early humanity's contact with a harsh environment and still retains features of its origin. Generally, spoken language is looser and less complicated because it appears in more informal contexts than written language. There will be more personal pronouns and personal references, and greater redundancy in the oral message, with more familiar and easy-to-use words than in a written message.[8] In essence, the ideas presented orally will be "dressed up" when you re-draft them as part of a written proposal or essay. They may convey the same message, but in the written version there will be a greater degree of formality and precision in the use of complete sentences. Consider the following difference between formal and informal messages:

Formal Style	*Informal Style*
Please remit payment immediately.	Pay up!
May I be of assistance to you?	Whatchawant?
The insertion of lye in drainpipes will have a detrimental effect on the structural integrity of the drain.	It eats pipes!

As should be clear, you'd be more likely to use a formal style in written messages and the informal style in an oral message. As speakers, we tend to gravitate toward the formal style when faced with a serious message or an audience that wants a forthright, well-considered treatment of a topic. Carrying the formality too far, however, can result in a style that is stilted and stiff. Consider the following example:

Formal I: I am pleased that you could come this morning. I would like to use this opportunity to discuss with you a subject of inestimable importance to us all: the impact of inflationary spirals on students enrolled in institutions of higher education.

Formal II: Thanks for coming. This morning, I will be addressing a problem of concern to us all—the rising cost of going to college.

Both of these styles are appropriate for a serious discussion of the issues. Nevertheless, version II is far easier to comprehend, and its shorter, more direct approach saves the speaker valuable time getting to the message. After all, hearing the message is why the audience is there or interested in the topic. A well-crafted, complex, prolix message won't incite their attention or interest. Even when you feel it's imperative to write out your message—in order to ensure accuracy in citing specific information or to get complex ideas across as clearly as possible—craft the message along the lines suggested in version II rather than I.

Serious vs. Humorous Atmosphere

Your speaking style contributes greatly to the atmosphere of the speaking occasion. Your word choice, demeanor, tone of voice, physical energy, and the like combine to create either a serious or a humorous atmosphere. At a commencement address, you'll speak in a way designed to create a reflective mood in your audience, appropriate for the occasion. On the other hand, at a reunion of high school classmates, you'll want to create a more convivial, social atmosphere.

This doesn't mean that humor isn't appropriate at a commencement, or that a serious theme cannot be inserted into a reunion. Rather, it suggests that situations bring different emphases to bear on what is expected. Funerals are somber occasions, but stories that evoke fond memories of amusing times in the past don't detract from a tone that is generally reflective and meditative. Victory speeches are times for celebration, humor, joy, and a feeling of unity; above all, such occasions are not times for speaking ill of the vanquished (especially if the game could have gone either way in the final moments). The focus on humor and a joyous mood doesn't mean that such speaking occasions are frivolous or totally fun-oriented; a serious note can be struck with respect to the work that a team has yet to do in improving its game.

As you will see in Chapter 18, entertainment speeches have worthy purposes; they can be persuasive and serious in their goals, and they can have their somber, reflective moments. The social commentator (such as Dave Barry) who throws humorous but barbed comments at pompous, silly, or corrupt officials is very concerned about social reform.

Whether serious or humorous, the **speech atmosphere** comprises the mindset or attitude you wish to instill in your audience. A serious speaker

A speaker may wish to create a sober atmosphere, a time for personal reflection and commitment. Any attempts to create such a mind-set should be undertaken with the speaking situation and the speakers' purposes in mind.

urging future doctors to remember the things that are most important in life might say, "Rank your values and live by them." That same idea expressed by actor Alan Alda came across to the same audience in a humorous vein:[9]

> We live in a time that seems to be split about its values. In fact it seems to be schizophrenic.
>
> For instance, if you pick up a magazine like *Psychology Today*, you're liable to see an article like "White Collar Crime: It's More Widespread Than You Think." then in the back of the magazine they'll print an advertisement that says, "We'll write your doctoral thesis for 25 bucks." You see how values are eroding? I mean a doctoral thesis ought to go for at least a C-note.

The most important considerations in deciding whether to be serious or to strive for a more humorous atmosphere include whether (a) you are by inclination funny or proficient at telling humorous stories, (b) the topic lends itself to humor or is more suited to serious language, (c) the audience is receptive to either a serious or a humorous style, and (d) the occasion allows for humor. Once these considerations are reviewed, the choice between a relatively serious or humorous atmosphere will be easy to make.

Person-Centered vs. Group-Centered or Material-Centered Emphases

There will be times when you want your own ideas, values, and actions to be the center of attention. What is important to the audience is what *you* think or are willing to do. In such a person-centered setting, the more frequent use of "I" instead of "we" is appropriate. On other occasions, you'll want to focus attention on the group, as a whole. In this group-centered setting, you become one with the audience and you'll use the term "we" because both speaker and audience are charged with the responsibilities or desires embodied in the speaker's message. On yet other occasions, the speaker will distance himself or herself from the message; the references will be in the third person toward people, institutions, and the like. In this material-centered setting, the ideas are the critical focus of attention.

Obviously, these three focal points are often mixed in any given address. That is, a speaker will mix references to "I," "we," "they," and "it." One term may dominate a particular section of a speech or an entire message. Consider the following examples of "I" directed, "you/we" directed, and "they/it" directed language taken from a speech given by Allen H. Neuharth, chair of the Freedom Foundation. The occasion was Neuharth's acceptance of the DeWitt Carter Reddick Award for Outstanding Achievement in Communication, on April, 1992, by the College of Communication of the University of Texas at Austin:[10]

> *"I" Directed*: In 1952, just two years out of the University of South Dakota, a classmate and I started a weekly statewide sports tabloid newspaper called *SoDak Sports*. We begged, borrowed and stole all the money we could—about $50,000. Two years later, we had lost it all, our venture went belly-up and we were bloodied and bowed. I ran away from home, went to Miami, found a job as a reporter for $95 a week.
>
> There, when I wasn't working or having fun in the sun, I thought a lot about what went wrong with my plan to become rich and famous in South Dakota. Gradually, I got it. I didn't really have a plan. I only had an idea. I hadn't really considered the risk/reward ratio. I hadn't figured out how to pay the rent. My first venture went broke because of mismanagement. I had mismanaged it. Once you admit you're the one who screwed up, it's much easier to get up off the floor, dust yourself off and try again.
>
> *"You/We" Directed*: . . . we must overcome our reluctance to criticize ourselves or our co-workers or competitors. Most in the media are unbelievably thin-skinned. We spend most of our lifetime criticizing or analyzing everyone else—politicians, business people, academicians. But we seldom turn that spotlight on ourselves. Our egos are enormous.
>
> *"They/It" Directed*: The media, thanks to instant satellite communication, is the glue that is bringing this globe together. Without the satellite—and instant global communication—there would have been no Tiananmen Square sit-in in

Beijing. No breakdown of the Berlin Wall. No marches in Poland, Romania and Czechoslovakia. And the hardliners would not have flunked revolution 101 in the old Soviet Union last August.

Neuharth mixed the three emphases in an appropriate and effective manner. Given his own reputation as a journalist (he was involved with Gannett's creation in 1982 of *USA Today*), he had the authority to comment on his own background, the desire to have all journalists act in a certain way, and on the media's influence on world events. In this setting, to have used only one approach would have been less compelling and potentially less effective. In using the person-centered approach, Neuharth was building a positive relation with his audience; the group-centered approach builds on that relationship, indicating that he's willing to accept the same tasks or challenges as he's handing out to the audience. The material-centered approach distances the audience and speaker from the material, to better assess and judge its merits. The key considerations are the relevance of each approach to the situation you will face, the likelihood that the audience will be receptive to the dominance of one, two, or the mixture of all three.

Gendered vs. Gender-Neutral Nouns and Pronouns

Words reveal attitudes and values you hold toward objects, concepts, and persons. Referring to a segment of a mixed audience (see Chapter 5) in terms of gender ("As you girls know . . .") may well place you in serious trouble with members of your audience. **Gender-linked words** are those that directly or indirectly identify males or females—*policeman, washerwoman, poet, poetess, steward, stewardess*. Pronouns such as *he* and *she* and adjectives such as *his* and *her* are also gender-linked terms. **Gender-neutral words** are those that do not directly or indirectly denote gender—*chairperson, police officer, flight attendant*.

Today's audiences are more conscious than ever before of gender-linked language. The important consideration is that you don't overtly or indirectly alienate your audience by using language that's considered inappropriate or insensitive. Just as many African-Americans took offense at Ross Perot's expression "you people" (which they took as meaning they remained outside his world), choosing gender-linked language can offend both women and men.

As a speaker, there are three troublesome gender issues that will affect your language choices:

1. *Inaccurately excluding members of one sex.* Some terms inaccurately portray social-occupational conditions in the world as if the gender referenced were the only gender involved, or that could be involved, in the future. "A nurse sees *her* patients eight hours a day, while a doctor sees *his* only for a few moments." "A loan officer often has trouble telling *his* clients no; a teller has no difficulty saying no to *her* customers." "An elementary-school principal has *his* duties; a teacher has

Gendered vs. Gender-Neutral Communicator Style

This feature of communication, unlike the discussion of language use, refers to the possibility that men and women differ dramatically in the actual *style* they employ in communicating to others. Thus, where *gender-linked* referred exclusively to specific terms or words used by a speaker, *gendered* refers to an overall approach taken by a speaker. According to recent research, male communicators are expected to be dominant, argumentative and verbally aggressive, assertive, relaxed, and dramatic. Female communicators, on the other hand, are expected to be friendlier, more open, more responsive, and more nonverbally animative, especially in terms of eye contact and facial expression.

These differences, while reported in the literature, don't necessarily translate into generalizations about all men or all women as communicators. A danger in listing these proposed differences is that they become written in stone as generic differences that differentiate communicator styles. Indeed, they do *not* describe traits or attributes that are inherent to one sex or another—the style depicted is influenced by the values of the commu-

hers." Both men and women hold these positions, so giving the impression that only one gender is involved in each role is misleading and demeaning.

There is a second issue. In cases in which there is a predominance of males or females in a profession, one might argue that referring only to males or females simply reflects reality. This argument neglects an important feature of language: *terms not only select, but also deflect and even reject alternate realities.* Thus, by continually referring to one gender, the language itself builds a picture of reality that has the force not only to *exclude* members of the opposite sex from being perceived as participants, but also to validate that exclusion. Speaking of nurses as only women, of principals as only men, or of tellers as only women creates a mind-set that accepts this interpretation as the normal, appropriate condition. Over time such associations acquire a sense of perma-

nity in which one lives. The style also is depicted by the culture; as Klopf reports, Japanese men and women differ on some dimensions while being similar on others. The key point is that members of other cultures don't necessarily adopt the same styles as Americans.

The issue remains as to whether the "expectations" in fact represent actual behaviors. In more precise research, *none* of the above differences actually surfaced in male and female perceptions of their *actual* behaviors. That is, the kind of style differences noted above are *expected* differences, rather than differences that actually exist in the behaviors of men and women. As Staley and Cohen suggest, "Apparently males and females appear to see themselves similarly for the most part; however, they are seen as exhibiting fairly distinct male and female communication styles by others or at least are expected to do so" (200). To conclude, on the basis of the present research, that men and women display distinctly different styles would be inadvisable. The evidence is still somewhat inconclusive but leans in the direction of greater similarities than differences between the

sexes. To the extent that such differences are predicated on social relationships and standards of behavior in society at large, one could expect greater merger of styles where differences may exist, rather than the reverse.

Sources: This research is reviewed in Constance Courtney Staley and Jerry L. Cohen, "Communicator Style and Social Style: Similarities and Differences between the Sexes," *Communication Quarterly*, 36 (1988): 192–202. The terms used to depict differences in style are taken directly from their review of literature, virtually verbatim; also see Donald Klopf, "Japanese Communication Practices: Recent Comparative Research," *Communication Quarterly*, 39 (1991): 130–143.

nence ("this is the way it has always been and shall always be") that makes it very difficult to initiate changes. The sense of *naturalness* created through this naming process lends itself to an opposite expression: "it is *unnatural* for women to fight or fly combat missions." Using gender-neutral language in these kinds of situations is a way of giving credence to the possibility that both men and women can be represented.

2. *Stereotyping male and female psychological or social characteristics.* Real men don't cry or eat quiche. A woman's place is in the home. The Marines are looking for a few good men. Little girls are made of sugar and spice; little boys are made of snails and puppy dog tails. The only form of communication faster than telephone is tell-a-woman. Men are assertive; women are pushy. He's a real character, she's a scatterbrain.

In fact, none of these is true of either gender. Real men do cry and eat quiche. A woman's place is in the Senate. Little girls and little boys aren't made of any of these ingredients, thankfully! Men gossip as much as women do. Women can be assertive; men can be pushy. Women possess character; men may be witless. Stereotypes, if repeated publicly as part of a speech, will alienate you from your audience. The expression "to Jew them down" is as offensive to members of the Jewish community—and non-members, as well—as any gender-linked noun is to many men and women, because it unfairly and inaccurately attaches a specific social characteristic to an ethnic group. Today's audiences are less tolerant of inaccurate and denigrating stereotypes of any kind, whether racial, ethnic, or gender-linked.

3. *Using gendered nouns inappropriately.* Historically many occupations have been held by one gender, and that fact was reflected by their terminology. Mailman, fireman, and policeman were once historically accurate labels. That is no longer true. The "-ess" ending on words to denote female (stewardess) reflects an earlier epoch, when such terms were current and acceptable but is now considered inappropriate. To continue to use such terms may imply that you favor such exclusionary stereotypes and leave you open to charges of social insensitivity. Hearing language that is personally offensive, regardless of the reason, may cause your listeners to refuse to listen further to your address.

These three problems demand serious reflection on your own habits as a language user. A speaker who habitually uses sexist language (language that is gender-linked) is guilty of ignoring important speaking conventions that have taken shape over the last twenty years or so. What can you do to avoid sexist language? There are four steps you can take to permanently recast your own language, so as not to give undue offense in speaking:

1. *Speak in the plural.* Say "Bankers are" or "Principals are" when referring to occupational groups. Then you can use "they" if you don't wish to repeat the noun. Often, use of the plural will assist you in speaking in a gender-neutral manner.

2. *Say "he or she" or "she or he" when referring to a singular subject.* There will be times when the plural is inappropriate or awkward. Our language has not yet coined a neutral singular pronoun, hence you're best advised to incorporate reference to both genders. For example: "A student majoring in communication has to enroll in an internship. *He or she* can. . . ." You also can continue the reference to the student in the third person, "The student major can . . . ," avoiding the use of either "he" or "she."

3. *Remove gender inflections.* Adopting the term *flight attendant* instead of *stewardess* (actually, that has been done across the profession) is a

painless change. Switching from fireman to firefighter, chairman to chairperson or chair, from seamstress to tailor, or from manning the station to staffing the station is equally painless.

4. *Use gender-specific pronouns when they accurately and appropriately identify the person, process, or activity.* It's acceptable to use *she* in reference to a mother, *her* in reference to a specific woman who has been named already in the speech (likewise with *he* or *his*). It's appropriate to discuss former and current presidents in masculine terms; it would not be appropriate to group all candidates for the presidency, past and present, in the same way.

All in all, the use of gender-neutral idioms reflects your respect for the audience—that they're entitled to every consideration due them as equal participants in a search for the best course of action. Gender-neutral language affirms the essential humanity of all beings. Gender differences are important in many facets of everyday living, but when they dominate talk, they become ideologically repressive; gender-linked language limits our horizons by restricting who we are, and who and what we may become. Being gender-neutral in your everyday talk, as well as in your speaking situations, removes a critical barrier to effective communication.

Propositional vs. Narrative Style

Finally, speaking styles can be largely propositional or narrative. Propositional styles emphasize a series of claims, with supporting evidence for each, that culminate in a general proposition. In this style, the claims suggest what action should be taken or what policy should be adopted or rejected. Narrative style, on the other hand, couches claims and evidence in a more informal, often personal, story that epitomizes the general claim being advanced. Thus, both *argue*, in the sense that they're claims on an audience's attention, belief, and action; however, they do so in radically different ways. In the following illustrations of *propositional* and *narrative* approaches, assume that you, as the speaker, want to persuade your classmates to use their academic advisors on a regular basis.

Propositional Style

I.   You ought to see your advisor regularly because he or she can check on your graduation requirements.
  A.   Advisors have been trained to understand this school's requirements.
  B.   They also probably helped write the department requirements for your major, so they know them, too.
II. You ought to see your advisor regularly because that person usually can tell you something about careers in your field.
  A.   Most faculty members at this school regularly attend professional meetings and find out what kinds of schools and companies are hiring in your field.

Speaking styles vary greatly. Some are highly propositional, whereas others are narrative.

      B.   Most faculty members here have been around a long time and, thus, have seen what kinds of academic backgrounds get their advisees good jobs after school.

III. You ought to see your advisor regularly to check out your own hopes and fears with someone.

      A.   Good adivsors help you decide whether you want to continue with a major.

      B.   If you decide to change majors, they often will help you find another advisor in another department who can work with you.

Narrative Style

   I. I thought I could handle my own advising around this school, and that attitude got me into trouble.

      A.   I could read, and I thought I knew what I wanted to take.

      B.   I decided to steer my own course, and here's what happened.

II. At first, I was happy, taking any course I wanted to.
  A. I skipped the regular laboratory sciences (chemistry, biology, physics) and took "Science and Society" instead.
  B. I didn't take statistics to meet my math requirement but instead slipped into remedial algebra.
  C. I piled up the hours in physical education so I could have a nice grade-point average to show my parents.
III. When I was about half done with my program, however, I realized that:
  A. I hadn't met about half of the general education graduation requirements.
  B. I wanted to go into nursing.
IV. Therefore, I had to go back to freshman- and sophomore-level courses even though I was technically a junior.
  A. I was back taking the basic science and math courses.
  B. I was still trying to complete the social science and humanities requirements.
V. In all, I'm now in my fifth year of college, with at least one more to go.
  A. My classmates who used advisors have graduated.
  B. I suggest you follow their examples rather than mine if you want to save time and money.

Either style can be effective, depending on the audience's expectations and the speaker's resourcefulness in generating an effective argument. The propositional form provides a concise, logical series of "should" statements to direct audience action. In the narrative form, your talent as a storyteller is put to the test. While the above examples suggest the use of either style as the structure for the body of an entire speech, speeches may combine both. Neuharth (pp. 302) used a narrative style in discussing his own life experience, then moved on to a propositional form in relaying his views on the kinds of reforms journalists must engage in.

Identifying the best style for your speech (formal/informal; serious/humorous; person/group/material-centered; gendered/gender-neutral; and propositional/narrative) is influenced by your own personality, your purpose in speaking, the demands of the subject, and the expectations of the audience and occasion. While your own style may not fit exactly into any one of the styles suggested, if it meets these conditions, it will be an appropriate response to the rhetorical situation.

Rhetorical Strategies

Rhetorical strategies—the words you use to give meaning and impact to your ideas—help define your speaking style and establish the atmosphere in which your ideas are heard. There are countless strategies available to speakers; this section will concentrate on four of the most common rhetorical choices—definition, restatement, imagery, and metaphor—and ways to use them effectively.

Definition

Your speech topic and the needs of the audience will determine whether it's essential to define your terms. If the topic concerns issues beyond the normal experience and knowledge of the audience, you'll probably need to define new terms or common words used in a technical manner to increase audience understanding. Eight types of definition are useful to speakers.

Defining from Dictionaries.   A dictionary definition is a **reportive definition**, which means that it indicates how people in general use a word. Dictionary definitions categorize an object or concept and specify its characteristics: "a *calla lily* is a tropical plant [category] with a white showy petallike part surrounding a yellow spike [characteristics]" (*Oxford American Dictionary*, 1980). While this definition is accurate and descriptive, it also is fairly general—there may be other plants with features similar to those of the calla lily. Thus, you may need to follow this definition with a picture or drawing or to employ additional material to convey your intended meaning. In defining certain technical phrases, you may need to resort to specialized dictionaries, such as *Black's Law Dictionary* or the *Dictionary of Foreign Terms*.

Defining in Your Own Words.   Occasionally a word has so many meanings that speakers have to indicate which one they wish to use. Then you must use a **stipulative definition**—one that states the sense of the word you wish to convey: "By 'rhetoric' I mean the act of using language in a way that influences the beliefs, values, or actions of others."

Defining in the words of others.   Instead of your own words, you might paraphrase (or cite verbatim) those of an acknowledged authority: "As Kenneth Burke suggests, rhetoric is the process of using *'language as a symbolic means of inducing cooperation in beings that by nature respond to symbols.'* For the remainder of this presentation, I will elaborate on what that definition means to the study of human communication."[11] The use of an **authoritative definition** may be more credible than one you cite on your own authority.

Defining Negatively.   Sometimes you can further clarify a term by telling an audience how you are *not* using a term or concept. In addition to a stipulative or authoritative definition of rhetoric, for example, you might say "By rhetoric, I am not referring to the way the term is used in ordinary parlance or by politicians when they denigrate an opponent as indulging in 'mere rhetoric.' " A **negative definition** helps define the parameters or boundaries of the term you're using—audiences have a clearer idea of your intent in using a particular word or phrase.

Defining from Origins. An idea or term can also be clarified by explaining its origins or etymology:

> Sincere comes from two Latin words—*sine* meaning *without* and *ceres* meaning *wax*. In early Rome, a superior statue was one that had no flaws that had to be filled with wax. A superior statue was thus said to be *sine ceres*—*without wax*. Today, the phrase *a sincere person* carries some of that same meaning.

An **etymological definition** illustrates the original sense of the term or explains how a common usage has been derived from an earlier formulation. A **genetic definition**, on the other hand, explains the history of an idea or a word: "*Nostalgia* or *nostalgic* used to refer to what today we ordinarily call homesickness—the suffering or pain caused by a wish to return to home and family. Today it has lost this original sense. Now it refers to a more wistful longing for years past." Either form of definition gives the audience a sense of the background of a term's use; as in the case of stipulative definitions, etymological and genetic definitions give a term or a phrase added precision.

Defining by Example. If a concept is highly technical or unfamiliar to an audience, using an **exemplar**—an example that epitomizes the meaning you desire to convey—may be helpful. It's important to select an example that's known or familiar to your audience: "The building we are in today, Old Capitol, is a perfect example of what I want to talk about—Georgian architecture."

Defining by Context. You also can refer to the context in which a term or phrase is most commonly used: "The difference between *imply* and *infer* can be understood by looking at a conversation between two people. When Jennifer spoke to Jack, her message *implied* she wanted to study tonight; Jack *inferred* from Jennifer's comments that she wanted to study. When I speak directly, I *imply* a certain meaning; when you interpret my words, you *infer* the meaning you thought I had in mind. Obviously, miscommunication may occur—my implied meaning is fuzzy, your inferred understanding is not at all what I had in mind." A **contextual definition** also can refer to an actual event or situation: "I am using 'revolution' as a way to describe the events that produced the democracy movement in China." Context helps to "place" a term in a specific environment, limiting its possible meanings and clarifying your particular meaning.

Defining by Analogy. Defining by analogy is an appropriate means of conveying technical information; an **analogical definition** compares a process, event, object, or term that your audience finds unfamiliar or unknown to something with which the audience is familiar or knowledgeable. For example, to illustrate the function of cryogenic tanks you might say "Hospitals and labs use cryogenic tanks, which work much like large thermos bottles, to freeze tissue samples, blood, and other organic matter." The value of the analogy lies in its accuracy—is the allusion to thermos bottles an accurate description of the process? Comparing nuclear fission to the action of billiard balls when a rack is struck by a cue ball may be appropriate, but only at a very superficial level.

Defining by Describing Operations.   Some words or concepts are best defined in operational terms. You can explain abstract verbal concepts by discussing them in functional terms. Thus, a social scientist might offer this **operational definition** of *intelligence*: "An intelligence quotient is a person's performance on the Wechsler-Bellevue Intelligence Test compared with the performance of other members of the population." Operational definitions have the advantage of making abstract concepts concrete. The value of such definitions lies in their reliability; do they define what they claim to? Thus, one might challenge an operational definition by claiming that the operation cited is not an accurate indication of the phenomena being tested or evaluated: "The Wechsler test ignores the cultural diversity of the population; hence its scores are not accurate indexes of intelligence."

Restatement

Unlike written messages, oral messages don't have the advantage of second looks. This increases the pressure on the speaker to be clear and precise in conveying a message. One of the best means of making certain there's little doubt about your intent is to restate your ideas through intentional repetition. This can be accomplished in two ways: *rephrasing* is saying the same thing in different words; *reiteration* is using different vantage points to describe or explain your meaning.

Rephrasing.   The most elegant example of skillful rephrasing is found in John F. Kennedy's inaugural address:[12]

> Let the word go forward from this time and place, to friend and foe alike, that the torch has been passed to a new generation of Americans—born in this century, tempered by war, disciplined by a hard and bitter peace, proud of our ancient heritage—and unwilling to witness or permit the slow undoing of those human rights to which this nation has always been committed, and to which we are committed today at home and around the world.

> Let every nation know, whether it wishes us well or ill, that we shall pay any price, bear any burden, meet any hardship, support any friend, oppose any foe to assure the survival and success of liberty.

John F. Kennedy's inaugural address is an example of the effect of skillful rephrasing to clarify a message and to make it more specific.

Consider the impact if Kennedy had only said: "We'll do everything we can to protect human rights and assure the survival of liberty." While the message is essentially the same, the briefer statement does not have the same forcefulness. In Kennedy's skillful use of rephrasing, our will to pursue our ends is unmistakable; the briefer statement doesn't convey the same sense of will.

Reiteration.   A central idea or claim can be illustrated from multiple viewpoints. Reiteration involves using different perspectives on a central theme to drive a point home or to fully illustrate its meaning. Henri Mann Morton used this approach to underscore the society's balance between cultural uniqueness and our common humanity by citing the words of a Cheyenne philosopher, High Chief:[13]

> In this land there are many horses—red, white, black, and yellow. Yet it is all one horse.

> There are also birds of every color, red, white, black, and yellow. Yet, it is all one kind. So it is with all living things.

> In this land where once there were only Indians, there are different races, red, white, black, and yellow. Yet, it is all one people.

It is good and right.

High Chief was a wise man. He knew that cultural uniquenesses have a strength of their own. At the same time, he recognized our common humanity.

While rephrasing and reiteration are extremely useful in clarifying ideas and adding force to their importance, they can be overused. Be careful not to employ these techniques where the ideas are so clear and common that rephrasing is unnecessary. Also be wary of too much rephrasing or reiteration—once the point is sufficiently clear and its importance strengthened, it's time to move the speech forward.

Imagery

Our impressions of the world come to us through the sensations of sight, smell, hearing, taste, and touch. In speaking, you can convey these sensations to other persons through words, since you may not be in a position to actually touch other people, have them experience the taste of an exotic food, or spray an exotic perfume for them to smell. The primary senses through which you will reach your audience are the *visual* and *auditory*. Your audience can see you, your movements, and your facial expressions; can observe the visual aids you present as part of your message; and can hear what you have to say.

There are, however, ways to stimulate listeners' senses more indirectly by using language that has the power to recall images they have previously experienced or to arouse sensations in the imagination. In essence, you can seek to provide a "you are there" experience for your audience, where your words transport them to another time and place. The language of imagery is divided into seven classes or types; each relates to the particular sensation it seeks to evoke in your audience:

1. *Visual* (sight)
2. *Auditory* (hearing)
3. *Gustatory* (taste)
4. *Olfactory* (smell)
5. *Tactual* (touch)
6. *Kinesthetic* (muscle strain)
7. *Organic* (internal sensations)

Visual Imagery.   To achieve a visual image, you want your audience members to form a mental picture. Wendy Liebmann, President of WSL Marketing, provides such a mental picture in her description of the consumer in the next century:[14]

America in the 21st century will be characterized by its differences, not its similarities. American in the 21st century will be a mosaic of different ethnic groups and cultures that no longer view assimilation as their American Dream.

THE TYPES OF IMAGERY

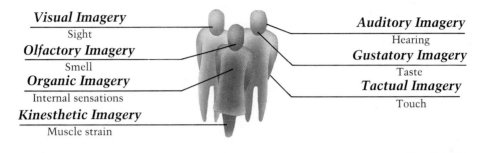

Visual Imagery
Sight

Olfactory Imagery
Smell

Organic Imagery
Internal sensations

Kinesthetic Imagery
Muscle strain

Auditory Imagery
Hearing

Gustatory Imagery
Taste

Tactual Imagery
Touch

By the year 2000, nearly one-third of the U. S. population will be non-white or Hispanic. By the year 2056, the "average" American will be African, Asian, Hispanic, or Arabic. In California, parts of Florida and Texas, Spanish—not English—will be the predominant language.

But America in the 21st century will be characterized not *only* by its ethnic diversity, but also by the aging of its population.

Picture it. Twenty-first century America. An aging nation. No longer a nation of youth.

In building this comprehensive picture of the 21st century American, Liebmann provides specific terms to form the image of the individual: diverse, older, cautious, cynical.

Auditory Imagery.   To communicate a sense of sound to your audience, select words that convey what the audience would hear if it were in a given situation. Kelly McInerney combines a clear visual image with that of an auditory image in her discussion of the potential demise of the African elephant:[15]

> As the sun rises in Kenya, an elephant crosses the savanna to the edge of a water hole, its trunk raised to catch the first scent of danger. Satisfied that the way is clear, it signals and is joined by a companion. In greeting, the two twist their trunks together, flap their ears and hit tusk against tusk, sending a sharp cracking sound across the hills. That same crack of ivory against ivory can be heard 10,000 miles away in Hong Kong and Tokyo, where ivory traders stack tusk upon tusk—more than 800 tons laundered free of illegality. You see, the beauty of the elephant's ivory tusks is also its curse, and in man's quest for "white gold" he has been anything but indifferent.

In this example, note how the auditory imagery forms the transition between a perfectly natural greeting between animals, and the sounds that dominate the visual scene of tusks being stored for later sale.

Gustatory Imagery. Creating an image that simulates the actual *taste* of something can be accomplished through mention of its saltiness, sourness, or spiciness. Remember that foods have texture as well as taste. Creating an image of popcorn at the movies, for example, can be achieved in part through mention of the tangy flavor of salt, the crunchiness of unpopped kernels, and the sweetness of its buttery flavor. Your goal is to prompt your listeners to use their imaginations in recreating the experience.

Olfactory Imagery. If you're using, say, the popcorn image, you can transfer the sense of *smell* to your audience by describing the experience of entering the movie lobby and encountering the powerful, enticing aroma. If your audience already has had the experience, you may only need to "transport" them to that place and let their imagination take over. The same would be true of the variety of pleasant and intriguing smells as one strolls past Indonesian, Pakistani, Thai, or Mexican restaurants.

Tactile Imagery. Tactile imagery conveys a sense of physical contact with an object, in terms of its texture and shape, pressure, and its temperature. Through your language, create images that allow the audience to "feel" how soft, smooth, sharp, or slimy a thing is, to sense the physical pressure one feels carrying a heavy object, walking into a blustery wind, or wearing shoes one size too small. Sensations of hot and cold also can be described through descriptive imagery.

Kinesthetic Imagery. This imagery describes the sensations associated with muscle strain and neuromuscular movement. You can take your listeners on a short trip with a marathon runner as she or he enters the twenty-sixth mile of a twenty–six mile race with language that relays a sense of the tired muscles, sore feet, constricted chest—all to be replaced by a sudden rush of adrenaline as the finish line draws near.

Organic Imagery. You communicate sensations such as hunger, dizziness, or nausea through organic imagery. The sensation of dizziness as you struggle through rarified mountain air to reach a summit, conveying how the bottom dropped out of your stomach when the airplane hit an air pocket, and describing the lightheadedness you felt when you ascended too rapidly while scuba diving—these are the kinds of feelings you can communicate to audiences through an appropriate choice of words. Used with discretion, you can make vivid the experiences you and others have had without becoming gruesome, grotesque, or disgusting.

Combinations of Imagery.   The seven types of imagery may be referred to as "doorways to the mind."[16] As devices that open new levels of awareness, they will affect people in different ways, so you should incorporate more than one form of imagery to convey your ideas. In the following example, note how the speaker combines various sensory appeals to arouse listener interest and reaction:[17]

> The strangler struck in Donora, Pennsylvania, in October of 1948. A thick fog billowed through the streets enveloping everything in thick sheets of dirty moisture and a greasy black coating. As Tuesday faded into Saturday, the fumes from the big steel mills shrouded the outlines of the landscape. One could barely see across the narrow streets. Traffic stopped. Men lost their way returning from the mills. Walking through the streets, even for a few moments, caused eyes to water and burn. The thick fumes grabbed at the throat and created a choking sensation. The air acquired a sickening bittersweet smell, *nearly* a taste. Death was in the air.

In this example, college student Charles Schaillol used vivid, descriptive phrases to affect the senses of his listeners: *visual*—"thick sheets of dirty moisture"; *organic*— "eyes to water and burn"; *gustatory/olfactory*— "sickening bittersweet smell, nearly a taste." The value of Schaillol's illustrations lies in their plausibility: does the word picture ring true for the audience? The value also lies in their appropriate arousal of feeling, by tapping the imagination to create the image desired. If the speaker had simply said "Death was in the air in Donora," he would not have conveyed anywhere near the same sense of what was happening in that town.

Metaphor

The images created by appealing to the various senses are often the result of using a **metaphor**—a comparison of two dissimilar things. Schaillol's "fog . . . thick sheets" metaphor illuminates the image he wishes to present. To be successful, as rhetorical critic Michael Osborn notes, a metaphor should "result in an intuitive flash of recognition that surprises or fascinates the hearer."[18] By connecting dissimilar things, metaphors extend our knowledge and increase our awareness of a problem, object, or person. A reference to a table's "legs" may illuminate the object, but it lacks fascination. When they're fresh and vivid, metaphors can be powerful aids in evoking feelings ("balanced on four slender toothpicks, the antique table swayed under the heavy load").

One of the most effective metaphors in recent years, however, was one Jesse Jackson used at both the 1984 and 1988 Democratic National Conventions. The power of an everyday object—in this case a quilt—to organize ideas and appeals is demonstrated in the following quotation from his 1988 address:[19]

America's not a blanket woven from one thread, one color, one cloth. When I was a child growing up in Greenville, S.C., and grandmother could not afford a blanket, she didn't complain and we did not freeze. Instead, she took pieces of old cloth—patches, wool, silk, gabardine . . . —barely good enough to wipe off your shoes with.

But they didn't stay that way very long. With sturdy hands and a strong cord, she sewed them together into a quilt, a thing of beauty and power and culture.

Now, Democrats, we must build such a quilt. Farmers, you seek fair prices and you are right, but you cannot stand alone. Your patch is not big enough. Workers, you fight for fair wages. You are right. But your patch, labor, is not big enough. Women, you seek comparable worth and pay equity. You are right. But your patch is not big enough. Women, mothers, who seek Head Start and day care and pre-natal care on the front side of life, rather than jail care and welfare on the back side of life, you're right, but your patch is not big enough.

Students, you seek scholarships. You are right. But your patch is not big enough. Blacks and Hispanics, when we fight for civil rights, we are right, but our patch is not big enough. Gays and lesbians, when you fight against discrimination and [for] a cure for AIDS, you are right, but your patch is not big enough. Conservatives and progressives, when you fight for what you believe, right-wing, left-wing, hawk, dove—you are right, from your point of view, but your point of view is not enough.

But don't despair. Be as wise as my grandmama. Pool the patches and the pieces together, bound by a common thread. When we form a great quilt of unity and common ground we'll have the power to bring about health care and housing and jobs and education and hope to our nation.

We the people can win.

Metaphors of unity always are present in times of division and crisis, but few have been more powerful than this homely image from one of America's premier orators.

As suggested earlier in this chapter, words are not neutral conduits for thought. Words not only reflect the "real" world outside your mind, but also, as critic Kenneth Burke suggests, help shape our perceptions of people, events, and social contexts. Language has a potent effect on people's willingness to believe, to feel, and to act.

Sample Speech

Henri Mann Morton presented the following keynote address at the Northwest's Colville and Okanogan National Forest conference on cultural diversity on March 23, 1989. As a Native American woman, she was in an excellent position to comment on the issues related to the theme of the conference. While she affirms the goal of workforce parity, she also reminds her audience of the cultural heritage against which parity must be measured.

As you read the speech, pay particular attention to the language. While simple, precise, and clear, it also contains appeals made more powerful by the use of metaphoric language in weaving both propositional and narrative style in a well crafted presentation. She also utilizes both personal and group-centered styles in conveying ideas.

Strength Through Cultural Diversity
Henri Mann Morton

Thank you for honoring me with your gracious invitation to speak at your conference. The Indians and Indian dances you saw last night serve as evidence of the endurance of the Indian spirit. /1

American Indian cultures survived Anglo-European contact and the spirit endures in Indian people. The most valuable and cherished of our resources are our young people. They represent:

>   the power of the mind
>   the power of our history as a people
>   the power of continuity; and the all important
>   Power of the Indian spirit. /2

There is power in words, as well. Look at your 1995 goal of parity in the workforce, represented by the words: "Strength Through Cultural Diversity." They are words—good words; good words, which make for a positive change and a positive commitment to minority people, and to women. They are powerful words. /3

The Northwest is the homeland of many native American tribes: Spokane, Colville, Yakima, Coeur d'Alene. We must never forget that American Indians were the first people to live in this beautiful country. They were the sole inhabitants for a long period of time and during that time evolved their own distinctive cultures. Following Indian-white contact they remained the majority population for a time, and today are the minority in their homeland that they were first to love. /4

The power of this land is rooted in the premise of cultural pluralism based upon the fact that Indian tribal groups historically co-existed in this area for centuries prior to Indian-white contact. They have provided us with a powerful model of cultural diversity. Today, about 500 distinct tribal groups are located in 26 states, and they each possess unique world views. Native Americans/ American Indians believe in the dualities of life, such as: sky-earth; sun-moon; love-hate; wisdom-ignorance, etc. Of them all, however, the most powerful is: man and woman. Together they make the perfect whole, and are a part of the great sacred circle of life. /5

Many tribes view life as a road or a path around this earth (circle), which some of them call the "Road of Life." American Indians have walked this road, on this good earth for a long time. We must remember that—

America's first cultures were Native American.
America's first workforce was Native American.
America's first men were Native American.
And America's first women were Native American. /6

The Native American woman comes from a tribally diverse and culturally unique way of life. Her past on this continent extends back in time for thousands upon thousands of years. /7

Indian origin accounts provide the basis for their beliefs that their worlds were created here; consequently, Native Americans believe they have been here for all time. For example, Cheyenne genesis—our oral historical account states we were created here, and further sets out the concept of earth as grandmother and sacred life giver. /8

Other tribal views:
1. Hopi: Spider Grandmother created four races of people from different colored clay: red, white, black, and yellow; spread over them the white substance, cape of wisdom; sang over them the Creation songs—words of the song indicative of the power of words; agreed to live a life of poverty and to be responsible stewards of the land.
2. Iroquois: Clan Mother.
3. Cherokee: Beloved Woman.
4. Piegan: Manly-Hearted Woman.
5. Cheyenne: Sun Dance Woman.

Each establishes a strong attitude of respect toward Indian women. /9

I am an American Indian woman. My grandmothers have been here for all time. The land you strive to protect is my grandmother—my mother. She is oldest woman—first woman. She is sacred; she is our beloved earth woman. We must revere her. /10

I am the direct descendant of these who were first to love this beautiful country and still do. /11

I am the granddaughter of those who welcomed many of our grandmothers and grandfathers—your grandparents—to this country. It is now our country. /12

We were multi-tribal; heterogeneous as the indigenous people of America, and following Anglo contact exchanged the term "multi-tribal" for "multi-cultural," so we could embrace those who came to live with us. /13

Prior to non-Indian contact, we as American Indians were culturally diverse. We were familiar with the concept of "cultural diversity," and recognized that those cultural differences made us strong. Cultural diversity made for strength—there was/is strength in cultural diversity. Cultural diversity makes our country strong. It has made us a great nation and we all have an opportunity to achieve the American dream. /14

American Indians are the minority of minorities. They number 1.5 million; less than one percent of our population. Though small in numbers we are the fastest growing ethnic group, with a young population. Unfortunately, they are American society's "miners' canaries." /15

The treatment of American Indians indicates the political-economic-social-humanistic climate of this country. It signals a shift from a healthy environment to one that is dangerous, if not lethal. /16

Education history is an example of this assimilationist goal. A 1969 report to the White House concluded that policymakers are uninformed and lack basic knowledge about American Indians. Based upon experience, this lack of knowledge could be expanded to include all minorities. /17

Unfortunately, I would characterize American society as a "multiculturally disrespectful" one. /18

We all need to develop skills and knowledge in becoming culturally respectful. /19

"Code of Ethics": (from *The Sacred Tree.* Four Worlds Development Press: The University of Lethbridge, Lethbridge, Canada, 1984). /20

Respect means "to feel or show honor or esteem for someone or something". . . . Showing respect is a basic law of life.

—Treat every person from the tiniest child to the oldest elder with respect at all times.

—Special respect should be given to elders, parents, teachers, and community leaders.

—Touch nothing that belongs to someone else (especially sacred objects) without permission, or an understanding between you.

—Speak in a soft voice, especially when you are in the presence of elders, strangers, or others to whom special respect is due.

—Treat the earth and all of her aspects as your mother. Show deep respect for the mineral world, the plant world, and the animal world. Do nothing to pollute the air or the soil. If others would destroy our mother, rise up with wisdom to defend her.

—Show deep respect for the beliefs and religion of others.

—Listen with courtesy to what others say, even if you feel that what they are saying is worthless. Listen with your heart. /21

I have oftentimes asked the question, "What is an American?" I could come up with a definition; so could you. I do know, however, that there is no one model American. /22

We need only review our history as a country to know that it has been oriented toward monoculturalism. The "melting pot" philosophy has prevailed, characterized by statements such as "be American." Further, we are all too aware of issues such as chauvinism; Manifest Destiny; Christianity; and a social distortion of reality. I agree with the individual in "Tracks" who said, "The melting pot theory is a fallacy." I would add that its tragic results are cultural genocide. /23

An American Indian philosopher once said, "It is not necessary for eagles to be crows." This statement clearly articulates the foolishness of forcing the culturally different into mainstream America, to become white American clones. As a country, we appear to be obsessed with "cloning" entire cultures, the cloning to be accomplished by the American "melting pot." /24

Judging from the current makeup of the U.S. Forest Service workforce, employment practices have resulted in homogeneity that is not representative of a culturally diverse society, nor one that is equally representative of males and females. By and large, recruitment and hiring patterns established over time, have resulted in a predominantly white male agency. /25

I am a Cheyenne Indian woman, about as far removed from this view of the world that an individual can be. Shaped by a different culture, my worldview is different, in which both the beauty and harshness of life must be maintained in a delicate balance, and which also recognizes the interdependence of all things in the universe. This interdependent view of life is maintained and ordered by the four basic human values of respect, acceptance, understanding, and love. /26

As American Indians, historically we have had three powerful agencies of oppression. They are:

1. The church: "Christianize these pagans."
2. The government: "Assimilate these who were here first"—daring them to remain outside the melting pot.
3. Education systems: "Civilize these 'savages'"—fails in providing multicultural education background. /27

All three are guilty of committing cultural genocide and institutional racism, either deliberately or inadvertently, by commission or omission. /28

Schools have been extremely guilty of perpetuating a socially distorted view of the world in its homogenizing process, and its attempts to "whitewash" the culturally different child. We have to face the fact that a lack of knowledge or understanding of cultural differences provides the perfect breeding ground for exploitation of minorities. /29

Textbooks, and the teachers that teach from them, not only denigrate American Indian cultures, but they are intellectually dishonest, as well, when they teach that Christopher Columbus discovered America. /30

In his 1969 White House Study, quoted in the 1969 *Kennedy Report*, Alvin Josephy, Jr. (a non-Indian), would have policy makers acknowledge "five basic truths about American Indians":

1. Indians have been here for thousands of years.
2. This is their homeland.
3. Their own distinct cultures have evolved. (We have our own visions of the American dream.)
4. We were not forced into abandoning our cultures.
5. Assimilation and acculturation occur on individual terms. /31

Acculturation is a two-way street. It can be positive. /32

American Indian contributions are not only numerous but significant, as well:

1. Some 200 drugs known to and used by Indians are today listed in the official pharmacopoeia of the United States.
2. Significant contributions in the area of agriculture:
    a. potato
    b. corn, or maize
3. Twenty-five state names and many other place names are of Indian origin.
4. "Peace as law" is an Iroquoian model for the U.S. government. /33

"To the Iroquois, peace was the law. They used the same word for both. They found it not in some imagined retreat from the world, but in human institutions, especially in a good government. Their own Confederacy, which they named the Great Peace, was sacred. The chiefs who administered the League were their priests. /34

"In their thought, peace was so inseparable from the life of man that they had no separate term by which to denominate it. It was thought of and spoken of in terms of its component elements: as Health (soundness of body and sanity of mind), Law (justice codified to meet particular cases), and Authority (which gives confidence that justice will prevail). /35

"Peace was a way of life, characterized by wisdom and graciousness. /36

"Their symbol for this Peace was a Tree, and the Tree had roots in the earth. . . . /37

"Like the spires of our churches, the Great White Pine which 'pierces the sky' and 'reaches the sun', lifted the thoughts of the Iroquois to the meanings of peace—the Good News which they believed the Great Spirit . . . had sent Deganawidah [the promulgator of the League] to impart to them. /38

"In general, the Tree signified the Law, that is, the constitution, which expressed the terms of their union. But there were other important elements in the symbol. /39

"The Branches signified shelter, the protection and security that people found in union under the shadow of the Law. /40

"The Roots, which stretched to the four quarters of the earth, signified the extensions of the Law, the Peace, to embrace all mankind. Other nations, not yet members of the League, would see these roots as they grew outward, and, if they were people of goodwill would desire to follow them to their source and take shelter with others under the Tree. /41

"The Eagle That Sees Afar, which Deganawidah placed on the very summit of the Tree, signified watchfulness. 'And the meaning of placing the Eagle on the top of the Tree', said Deganawidah, 'is to watch the Roots which extend to the North and to the South and to the East and to the West, and the Eagle will discover if any evil is approaching your Confederacy, and will scream and give the alarm and come to the front.' /42

" 'The Eagle,' said Deganawidah, 'shall have your power.' It was a reminder to his people that the best political contrivance that the wit of man can devise is, it is impossible to keep the peace unless a watchful people stands always on guard to defend it. /43

"Then Deganawidah uprooted the Tree and under it disclosed a Cavern through which ran a stream of water, passing out of sight into unknown regions under the earth. Into this current he cast the weapons of war, the hatchets and war-clubs, saying, 'We here rid the earth of these things of an Evil Mind.' /44

"Then, replacing the Tree, 'Thus,' he said, 'shall the Great Peace be established, and hostilities shall no longer be known between the Five Nations, but peace to the United People'." /45

We live in a rapidly changing world. Our environment is undergoing an equally rapid change. Times have changed very quickly. Change has come about so quickly that the Forest Service work environment has failed to maintain pace. /46

Speaking of rapidly changing times, our Cheyenne medicine people, who are the keepers of the Cheyenne culture and people, move very slowly and are cautious in the way they do things, thereby slowing time. /47

The Taos Pueblo, too, have their time concept, as articulated by one of their elders:

"Some things must change. Some things must never change." /48

This requires a balance between change and cultural continuity, so as to maintain a healthy and whole ecosystem and life. /49

Change is natural. Yet it seems to be our nature as human beings to fear change. /50

I can understand that the very thought of a culturally diverse work force can cause apprehension, misunderstandings, fear, and resultant backlash. We as Cheyennes initially feared the white man. Teachings of our powerful Cheyenne prophet told us what to expect. He emphasized destruction of the earth. Teachings of my great-grandmother: "Understand that sometimes the white man is but a child, new to this land." /51

Indians encourage thinking with the heart. Thus, thinking with both the heart and the mind about cultural diversity, and the strength to be gained therefrom, can be cause for celebration. With clarity of vision we can celebrate the natural diversity of the universe and of our world. /52

Our forests would be so monotonous if there were only one kind and one color of tree; one kind of plant; one kind of animal; and soil of one kind of consistency and color. /53

As humans you are all unique and possess individual beauty. You have your values as individuals, and ours as Americans. /54

American Indians have strong value systems; namely:
1. Patience
2. Honesty
3. Acceptance
4. Respect /55

They are essentials for maintaining good interpersonal relationships and are requisite for excellent intercultural relations. /56

Lakota elders were asked what their children and grandchildren should learn. They all agreed that basics were important. They further agree that above all, children should learn to get along with each other. Further, that they must continue to work for the good of Indian communities. /57

American Indians know how to work. Misconception: all are good with their hands. The truth is that we are good with our minds as well. /58

Today here in the Pacific Northwest, fishing is sport. For those who have to do it for a living, it is hard work. /59

Among Plains Indians, for the men, killing a buffalo involved knowledge and skill; for women, tanning a hide was hard work. /60

For all time we have had to provide for ourselves. We know what it is to work. Men and women were equal partners in maintaining their homes and communities. We had a tribally representative workforce. /61

If the Forest Service is going to reach parity in its workforce policies, attitudes, and practices, of necessity, it must be culturally congruent and responsive to gender. /62

Programs and services must be designed or modified to meet the special and unique needs of culturally different employees. /63

This does not mean lowering standards, either! /64

This is nothing more than respectful recognition of the importance of culture and the dynamics that result from cultural uniquenesses. /65

I am concerned about preparing our students to work in the real world. /66

Can I assure them that it is culturally respectful? /67

What kind of attitudes and perceptions will they have to confront about women and minorities? /68

What about upward mobility and promotions? Is it systematic and just? Is it fair? How effective are your mentorship programs? /69

What about backlash students can anticipate to counteract misconceptions that women and minorities are getting all the jobs? /70

You are to be applauded for your commitment to cultural diversity in the U.S. Forest Service workforce. I mean this in all sincerity since we are witnessing the unfortunate intensification of white supremacist attitudes and movements even here in the Northwest, specifically the Aryan Nations in Idaho, and on some college and university campuses across the nation. /71

I share your 1995 vision of a racially, culturally, gender-based, and humanistically representative workforce in which attitudes of respect, acceptance, and understanding are all pervasive. /72

The vision I see is dedicated to a love of life, to a love of people, and love of the environment, particularly of the land—the earth, she who is our grandmother, who must be revered and protected; she upon whom we walk and live; she who supports our feet and gives us life; she who nurtures us, her children. We all share this bond and as culturally diverse people we can draw strength from our rich cultural diversity. /73

I would like to share with you this Cheyenne philosophical belief: "A nation is not conquered until the hearts of its women are on the ground. Then it is done, no matter how brave its warriors nor how strong its weapons." /74

This shows the acceptance of, and respect for, the power of women. As equal partners of men, who too, have their own power, we then can see why the most powerful of all pairs in the universe are men and women working together. /75

This is my tribute to you as human beings. /76

Thank you for letting me walk my journey of life with you. /77

I have faith in you as intelligent and sacred beings. Keep up the good work you have begun. /78

Finally, I would like to leave you with the words of one of our Cheyenne philosophers, High Chief, who said:

> In this land there are many horses—red, white, black, and yellow. Yet, it is all one horse.
> There are also birds of every color, red, white, black, and yellow. Yet, it is all one bird. So it is with all living things.
> In this land where once there were only Indians, there are different races, red, white, black, and yellow. Yet, it is all one people.
> It is good and right. /79

High Chief was a wise man. He knew that cultural uniquenesses have a strength of their own. At the same time he recognized our common humanity. /80

You, too, know this, indicated by your powerful theme of "Strength Through Cultural Diversity." /81

I want to be around in 1995 when you reach your goal. /82

Chapter Summary

Successful speeches generally are characterized by *accurate, simple, coherent, properly intense*, and *appropriate* language choices. In selecting a speaking style appropriate to you, the occasion, your subject matter, and the audience, you must make decisions about *written vs. oral language*, a *serious vs. humorous atmosphere*, a *person-centered vs. group-centered or material-centered emphasis, gendered vs. gender-neutral nouns and pronouns*, and *propositional vs. narrative forms of presentation*. As far as your rhetorical strategies are concerned, consider: (1) *definition* (in your own words, negatively, from original sources, by examples, by context, by analogy, by describing operations), (2) *restatement* (both rephrasing and reiteration), (3) *imagery* (visual, auditory, gustatory, olfactory, tactual, kinesthetic, and organic), and (4) *metaphor*. Language choices, and the resulting speaking styles, form speakers' most crucial channels of substantive communication.

References

1. See Seymour Gitin, "Last Days of the PHILISTINES, "*Archaeology*, 45 (May/June, 1992): 31.

2. These dimensions are also called the *content* and *relationship* dimensions of language by Simons and by Watzlawick, Beavin, and Jackson. See Herbert W. Simons, *Persuasion: Understanding, Practice and Analysis*, 2nd. ed. (New York: Random House 1986), 78, working from P. Watzlawick, H. J. Beavin, and D. D. Jackson, *Pragmatics of Human Communication: A Study of Interaction Patterns, Pathologies and Paradoxes* (New York: W. W. Norton, 1967).

3. For a discussion of the concept *signature*, see Anthony Hillbruner, "Archetype and Signature: Nixon and the 1973 Inaugural," *Central States Speech Journal* 25 (Fall, 1984): 169–81.

4. For fuller discussion of these ideas, see Mary Morain, ed., *Bridging Worlds Through General Semantics* (San Francisco: International Society for General Semantics, 1984); Ross Evans Paulson, *Language, Science, and Action: Korzybski's General Semantics: A Study in Comparative Intellectual History* (Westport, CT: Greenwood Press, 1983).

5. Kenneth Burke, *Language as Symbolic Action* (Berkeley, CA: University of California Press, 1966), 45.

6. Quoted in John R. Pelsma, *Essentials of Speech* (New York: Crowell, Collier, and Macmillan, 1934), 193.

7. John Waite Bowers, "Language and Argument," in G. R. Miller and T. R. Nilsen, eds., *Perspectives on Argumentation* (Glenview, IL: Scott, Foresman, 1966), esp. pp. 168–72.

8. See Lois Einhorn, "Oral Style and Written Style: An Examination of Differences," *Southern Speech Communication Journal* 43 (1978): 302–11. For further analysis of the differences between oral and written styles, see John F. Wilson and Carroll C. Arnold, *Public Speaking as a Liberal Art*, 5th ed. (Boston: Allyn and Bacon, 1983), 227–29. For an incisive analysis of the role of orality and literacy in rhetoric's beginning in ancient Greece, see Tony Lentz, *Orality and Literacy in Hellenic Greece* (Carbondale, IL: Southern Illinois University Press, 1989).

9. Alan Alda, "A Reel Doctor's Advice to Some Real Doctors," in Stephen E. Lucas, *The Art of Public Speaking* (New York: Random House, 1983), 364.

10. Allen H. Neurath, "Acceptance Address," Dewitt Carter Reddick *Award: Address by the 1992 Recipient.* [pamphlet] College of Communication, University of Texas at Austin, 1992. Not paginated.

11. Kenneth Burke, *A Rhetoric of Motives* (Berkeley, CA: University of California Press, 1969), 43.

12. From *Public Papers of the Presidents of the United States: John F. Kennedy* (Washington, D.C.: U. S. Government Printing Office, 1961).

13. Henri Mann Morton, "Strength Through Cultural Diversity," in J. Blanche, ed., *Native American Reader* (Juneau, Alaska: Denali Press, 1990), 205.

14. Wendy Liebmann, "The Changing Consumer," *Vital Speeches*, 58 (April 15, 1992): 410.

15. Kelly McInerney, "Title Unknown," *Winning Orations, 1990*, 14. Reprinted by permission of Larry Schnoor, Executive Secretary, Interstate Oratorical Association, Manketo State University, Mankato, MN.

16. Victor Alvin Ketcham, "The Seven Doorways to the Mind," in William P. Sandford and W. Hayes Yaeger, eds., *Business Speeches by Business Men* (New York: McGraw-Hill Book Co., 1930).

17. Charles Schaillol, *Winning Orations.*

18. Michael Osborn, *Orientations to Rhetorical Style* (Chicago: Science Research Associates, 1976), 10.

19. Jesse Jackson, "Common Ground and Common Sense," *Vital Speeches*, 54 (August 15, 1988).

Key Terms

analogical definition (p. 311) *genetic definition* (p.311)

auditory imagery (p. 315) *gustatory imagery* (p. 316)

authoritative definition (p. 310) *kinesthetic imagery* (p. 316)

connotative language (p. 293) *metaphor* (p. 317)

contextual definition (p. 311) *negative definition* (p. 310)

decoding (p. 293) *olfactory imagery* (p. 316)

denotative language (p. 293) *operational definition* (p. 312)

encoding (p. 292) *organic imagery* (p. 316)

etymological definition (p. 311) *referential language* (p. 293)

exemplar definition (p. 311) *relational language* (p. 293)

gender-linked words (p. 303) *reportive definition* (p. 310)

gender-neutral words (p. 303) *rhetorical strategies* (p. 309) sign posts *(p. 296)*

speaking style *(p. 293)*

speech atmosphere *(p. 300)*

stipulative definition *(p. 310)*

tactual imagery *(p. 316)*

tone *(p. 299)*

visual imagery *(p. 314)*

Problems and Probes

1. Working in small groups, discuss the use of gender-linked versus gender-neutral words; in your view, which situations require greater attention to gender-neutral language?

2. Working in small groups, create a list of ten relatively neutral words or expressions. For each word or phrase listed, list 2-to-3 attitudinally weighted terms that are positively "loaded" and 2-to-3 that are negatively "loaded" (Example: Neutral: "old"; Positive: "mellow"; Negative: "senile").

3. Using varied and vivid imagery, prepare a written description of one of the following:

Sailboats on a lake at sunset

Windsurfing on a windy day at the lake

Having fun with friends

Roller-blading through downtown

Communication Activities

1. Prepare a speech concerning an issue that you can get excited about. Use language in a way that conveys the sense of excitement that you feel and that you wish your audience would feel as well. Pay particular attention to words that convey images.

2. Prepare a speech that focuses on defining a concept or an object that is not known by most, if not all, in the audience. Concentrate on language that conveys the "unknown" or relatively unknown to an audience.

3. Develop a four-to-five minute *manuscript* speech on a topic that is of vital concern to you—one that you feel indignant about and want your audience to share your feelings. Incorporate the advice offered in this chapter regarding varied definitional strategies, imagery, and metaphor.

CHAPTER 13

USING VISUAL
AIDS IN
SPEECHES

This has been called the **ocularcentric century**.[1] That is, ours has become a time when sight threatens to be the dominant sense. Television, film, transparencies, VCRs and videotape, videodiscs, CD ROM and related digital technologies, overhead and opaque projectors, billboards, poster art, banners trailing from airplanes, sidewalk tables with samples from a store's "today only" sale—our world is filled with visual communications. No time or place before yours has been so visually oriented. Entire companies—from such famous ones as major media studios down to small-town graphics production shops in people's basements—exist because of Americans' willingness to pay for good pieces of visual rhetoric.

The public speaker, of course, always has been in the visual communication business. Your physical presence in front of an audience is a powerful visual statement; your body, your facial expression, and your intense eyes and indicative gestures all combine to make the visual channel of public speaking a carrier of significant messages. Your use of *visual aids* makes the world of sight an essential part of oral communication transactions. From objects a second grader brings to school for "Show and Tell" to the flipcharts that sales trainers use, speakers multiply and deepen their communication messages when they use visual channels well.

Research on visual media, learning, and attitude change has revealed helpful information about the impact of visual aids on audiences.[2] Much advice, however, still flows directly from veteran speakers to those new at public presentations. In this chapter, we'll mix advice from social-scientific research with wisdom from old pros. First, we'll deal with the general functions of visual aids; then we'll examine various types and look at some advice on how to use them to greatest effect.

The Functions of Visual Aids

Visual materials provide punch for any presentation in two ways: (1) they help listeners comprehend and remember your material, and (2) they improve the persuasive impact of your messages.

Comprehension and Memory

While the old saying that "A picture is worth a thousand words" may be something of an exaggeration, its truths are reflected in research. Visual research has demonstrated that bar graphs, especially, make statistical information more accessible; simple drawings enhance recall; and charts and such human interest visuals as photographs help listeners process and retain data.[3] Pictures have significant effects on children's recall and comprehension during storytelling.[4] Your own experience probably bears this out. Recall the high school teachers who worked with models, maps, slides (transparencies) or overheads, and video; most likely you'll remember their presentations better than those in other classes where visual materials were rare or non-existent.

Persuasiveness

In addition to improving comprehension and memory, visuals can heighten the persuasive power of your ideas because they engage listeners actively. Lawyers, for example, aware of the dramatic effects of good visuals, often include visual evidence of injuries or crimes in their cases in order to capture the jury. Some lawyers even have experimented with video technology to create powerful portrayals, with recreations of dangerous conditions at an intersection in an involuntary manslaughter case or anatomical figures showing fatal wounds in a homicide case.

Undeniably, your credibility and persuasiveness are enhanced by good visuals.[5] Visual materials satisfy the "show-me" attitude prevalent in a vision-oriented age; they provide a crucial means of meeting listener expectations.[6]

Types of Visual Aids

To give you the broadest possible look at visual aids, we'll divide them into two broad classes: *actual objects* and *symbolic representations of actual objects.* Then we'll examine more particular types and give you some tips on how to use them in your talks.

Actual Objects

The objects that you bring to a presentation, including your own body, can be categorized under two headings: (a) *animate* (living) objects and (b) *inanimate* (nonliving) objects.

Animate Objects.   Live animals or plants can, under some circumstances, be used to enhance your speeches. If your speech explores the care and feeding of laboratory mice, you can reinforce your ideas by bringing to the speech one or two mice in a properly equipped cage. Describing the differences between two varieties of plants may be easier if you demonstrate the differences with real plants. Discretion and common sense about what's possible and in good taste will help make visuals work for you rather than against you. You might be stretching your luck, for example, by bringing a real horse into the classroom to show how one is saddled or by bringing in an untrained puppy to show how one is paper trained.

You want to use the actual object to focus audience attention on your speech, not to distract the audience with the object. A registered Persian cat may seem to be a perfect visual aid for a speech about what judges look for in cat shows until the cat gets loose in the classroom or causes allergic reactions; then your message may be lost in the process.

Speakers who demonstrate the yoga positions, warm-up exercises, ballet steps, or tennis strokes they discuss in their speeches add concreteness and vitality to their presentations. For example, a senior nursing major might add credibility by wearing a uniform when demonstrating CPR.

Remember to control the experience. Make sure that members in the back rows can see you. Demonstrate a yoga position from a sturdy table top rather than from the floor. Slow the tempo of a tennis stroke so that the audience can see any intricate action and subtle movements. One advantage of properly controlled visual action is that with it you can control the audience's attention to your demonstration.

Inanimate Objects.   Demonstrations are often enhanced by showing the actual object under discussion. A speech about stringing a tennis racket is enhanced by a demonstration of the process with an actual racket. A speech about the best way to repair rust holes in an automobile fender is clarified by samples of the work in stages. Cooking or house remodeling demonstrations are enlivened with samples prepared before the presentation, since the presenter usually doesn't have time to complete the actual work during the presentation.

Most importantly, you want to keep audience attention focused on the message of your speech. To do this, place the object between you and the audience as much as possible. If you stand in front of the object or to the side, you risk blocking the audience's view, disrupting their focused attention and frustrating them.

Symbolic Representations

When you can't use actual objects or your own physical movement to clarify your message, you can resort to using **symbolic representations**, or objects, tokens, or images, that represent the content of your speech. These representations may be relatively *concrete*—such as photographs, slides, films, or videotapes—or *abstract* drawings—such as graphs, charts, and models.

Concrete Representations.   **Concrete representations** closely resemble the content of the speech. *Photographs* can give the audience a visual sense of your topic. With photographs you can illustrate flood damage to ravaged homes or depict the beauty of a wooded area threatened by a new shopping mall. One problem with photographs, however, is that audiences may not be able to see details from a distance. You can compensate for this shortcoming by enlarging photos so that people can see them more easily. Avoid passing small photos through the audience because such activity is noisy and disruptive. The purpose of a visual aid is to draw the attention of all members of the audience simultaneously.

Slides (35 mm transparencies) allow you to depict color, shape, texture, and relationships. If you're presenting a travelogue, you need slides to show your audience the buildings and landscape of the region. If you're giving a speech on the history of the steam engine, slides can help you to show various steam engines in operation. If you're speaking against the construction of a dam, you can enhance your persuasiveness by showing slides of the white water that will be disrupted by the dam. If you're discussing stylistic differences among famous artists, slides of art works from the Baroque and Neoclassical periods can illustrate the distinctions you need to make.

Using slides requires familiarity with projection equipment. It also requires some forethought about the setup of the presentation. Attention to small, seemingly inconsequential details will make a major difference in how smoothly the presentation goes. Do you know how to change the projection lamp? Did you bring along a spare bulb just in case? Will you need an extension cord? Do you know to remove a jammed slide? If you operate on the assumption that whatever can go wrong will, you'll be prepared for most problematic circumstances.

Videotapes and *films* can also be useful in illustrating your points. Videotaped segments from several current situation comedies can dramatically reinforce your claim that minorities are underrepresented in television. Two or three videotaped political ads can help you illustrate methods for packaging a candidate. Again, familiarity with the operation of a videocassette recorder or film projector ensures a smooth presentation. Too often, speakers assume that the equipment will be provided and a skilled technician will be available, only to find that no one knows how to run the

Symbolic representations convey information in various ways. For instance, a photograph of a sailboat (top) gives an audience a realistic but complicated view of the object, whereas an abstract representation, such as a diagram (bottom), strips away unnecessary details to illustrate the object more clearly. Also abstract, yet highly visible, a model (center) provides a three-dimensional image of the object, allowing a speaker to point out its parts and discuss their functions.

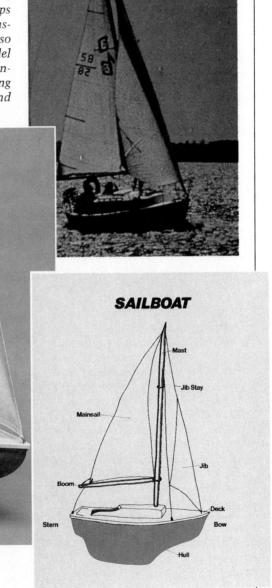

SAILBOAT

Mast

Jib Stay

Mainsail

Jib

Boom

Deck

Stern

Bow

Hull

Can Pictures Lie?

an pictures lie? Aren't they each worth a thousand words because seeing is believing, showing is better than telling? Not really, especially in the ocular centric age. Consider:

- Hopes for finding American soldiers missing in action (MIAs) in Vietnam often depended upon photos that seemed to show American soldiers standing with signs with current dates on them. Those pictures were faked.
- Thanks to electronic scanners, you now can easily add to or subtract from pictures, printing the altered photos so cleanly that the forgery is almost impossible to detect.
- During the 1992 campaign, political action committees (PACs) ran ads that showed Bill Clinton holding hands in victory on the Democratic Convention stage with Ted Kennedy. What the PAC had done was put a picture of Kennedy's head on Vice President Al Gore's body.
- During the 1988 campaign, another PAC ran an ad whose text included straightforward, descriptive statements: "As governor Michael Dukakis vetoed mandatory sentences for drug dealers. He vetoed the death penalty. His revolving-door prison policy gave weekend furloughs to first-degree murderers not eligible for parole. While out many committed other crimes like kidnapping and rape. And many are still at large. Now Michael Dukakis says he wants to do for America what he's done for Massachusetts." Those statements were spoken, however, against pictures that (1) showed the sun setting over a prison with guards in the watchtowers; (2) a revolving gate where prisoners, many representing minorities, presumably were being let out as quickly as they were being put in; and (3) another shot of the guards, guarding, we now knew from the pictures, prisonerless prisons at night—when crime increases.

Pictures can be altered to "say" something that isn't true. Or, they can add imaginings to words in order to intensify them, even focus them on a particular idea that someone wouldn't dare say aloud ("African-American men are being let out of prison so they can kidnap and rape white women").

The visual channel can be very helpful to both speaker and audience when it is used in morally defensible ways. It can be destructive of the truth when it's not.

machine properly. Such delays increase your nervousness and detract from your presentation.

Models can dramatize your explanations. **Models** are reduced or enlarged scale replicas of real objects. Architects construct models of new projects to show clients. Developers of shopping malls, condominiums, and business offices use models when persuading zoning boards to grant needed rights-of-way or variances. You can use models of genes to accompany your explanation of gene splicing. As with other visual aids, models need to be manageable and visible to the audience. If you are using a model that comes apart so that different pieces can be examined, practice removing and replacing the parts beforehand.

Abstract Representations.   If you need to illustrate the growth of inflation or show how social security revenues will be spent in the next six months, you'll find yourself resorting to more abstract representations than those previously discussed. **Abstract representations** show ideas symbolically, often in numbers. The form of the representation—drawings, charts, graphs—will depend on the formality of the situation. If you're brainstorming building renovation ideas with a prospective client, quick sketches may suffice. However, if you're meeting with the client's board of directors, the same rough drawings will be inadequate. The board will expect a polished presentation, complete with a professionally prepared prospectus. Similarly, chalkboard drawings may be sufficient to explain cell division to a group of classmates, but when presenting the same information as part of a Science Fair project, you need refined visual support materials. The care with which you prepare these visuals will convey either an attitude of indifference or concern to your audience.

Chalkboard drawings are especially valuable when you want to present an idea step by step. By drawing each stage as you discuss it, you can control the audience's attention to your major points. Coaches often use this approach when showing players how to execute a particular play. Time lines and size comparison diagrams can also be sketched on a chalkboard. To visually represent the history of the civil rights movement in the United States, you can create a time line that illustrates key events, such as the arrival of the first slaves in Jamestown, the Emancipation Proclamation, and the 1965 Voting Rights Act. Take care, however, that you don't rely on the board so much that you spend the majority of your speech with your back to your audience.

Speakers can use *overhead projectors* just as they would use chalkboards—illustrating their points as they talk. However, overhead projectors offer some advantages over chalkboards. One advantage of an overhead projector is that you can turn it off when you've made your point, thus removing any distraction from your message. Another advantage is that you can uncover one part of a transparency at a time, keeping the remainder covered so as to control the flow of information. Finally, you can prepare transparencies before the speech, giving them a more professional appear-

BAR GRAPHS

Bar graphs visually illustrate relationships. Changing spacing and size of bars can affect the visual message.

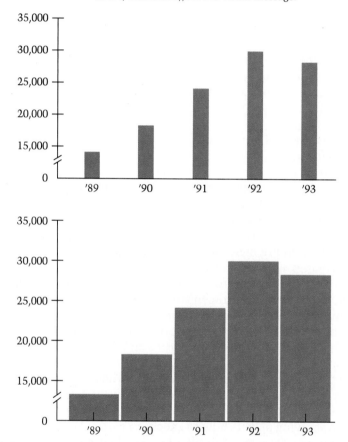

ance than chalkboard drawings. During the speech you can point to the transparency or add to it to emphasize your claims.

When you're using either a chalkboard or an overhead projector, be aware of your technique. First, make your drawings large enough so that the audience can see them. Second, if you continue to talk to the audience as you draw, be brief; your audience's attention will wander if you talk to the board or to the light source for more than a minute or two. Third, consider the visual field while you draw—where should you stand to avoid blocking the audience's view of your visuals? Fourth, when you're through talking about the illustration, erase it or turn off the projector.

Graphs show relationships among various parts of a whole or between variables across time. There are several types of graphs:

LINE GRAPHS

Line graphs can reveal relationships, but they also can deceive the unwary. These two graphs show the same data, but the use of different spacing makes the U.S. economy seem much more volatile in the second version than the first. Always look at the scales and their units when trying to interpret line graphs.

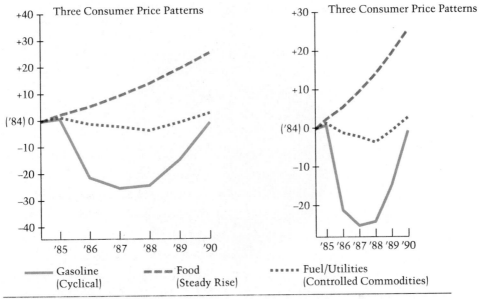

Three Consumer Price Patterns

——— Gasoline (Cyclical)   ▬ ▬ ▬ Food (Steady Rise)   •••••• Fuel/Utilities (Controlled Commodities)

Source: Bureau of Labor Statistics.

1. **Bar graphs** show the relationships between two or more sets of figures. If you were illustrating the difference between lawyers' and doctors' incomes or between male lawyers' and female lawyers' incomes, you would probably use a bar graph.

2. **Line graphs** show relationships between two or more variables, usually over time. If you were trying to explain a complex economic correlation between supply and demand, you would use a line graph.

3. **Pie graphs** show percentages by dividing a circle into the proportions being represented. A charitable organization could use a pie graph to show how much of its income was spent on administration, research, and fund-raising campaigns. Town governments use pie graphs to show citizens what proportion of their tax dollars go to municipal services, administration, education, recreation, and law enforcement.

4. **Pictographs** represent size and number with symbols. A representation of U.S. and Russian exports of grain might use a miniature drawing of a wheat shock or ear of corn to represent 100,000 bushels; this representa-

PIE GRAPH

A pie graph shows percentages of a whole; this graph reveals the percentages of survey respondents who rated U.S. airline service.

Ratings of Overall Quality of Service by U.S. Airlines

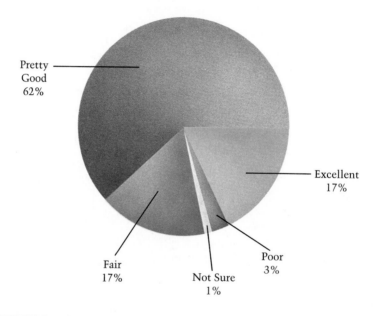

Pretty Good 62%

Excellent 17%

Poor 3%

Fair 17%

Not Sure 1%

Source: Business Week/Harris Poll conducted December 12–16, 1988.

tion would allow a viewer to see at a glance the disparity between the exports of two countries.

Your choice of bar, line, pie, or pictorial graphs will depend on the subject and the nature of the relationship you wish to convey. A pie graph, for example, can't easily illustrate discrepancies between two groups; nor can it show effects of change over time.

Regardless of the type of graph you choose, when you are preparing a graph, you must be very careful not to distort your information. A bar graph can create a misleading impression of the difference between two items if one bar is short and wide while the other is long and narrow. Line graphs can portray very different effects of change if the units of measurement are not the same for each time period. You can avoid misrepresenting information by using consistent measurements in your graphs and by using a computer to generate your graphs (see page 347).

PICTOGRAPHS

The speaker uses artistic skill to depict the number of houses (represented by television sets) being accessed by cable systems. The artistry draws attention to the information.

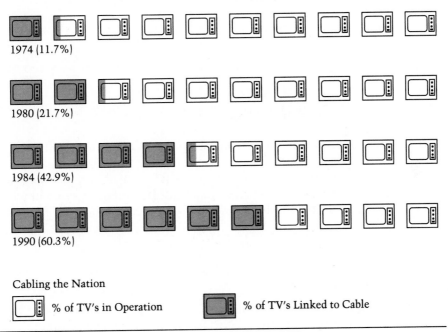

1974 (11.7%)

1980 (21.7%)

1984 (42.9%)

1990 (60.3%)

Cabling the Nation

% of TV's in Operation   % of TV's Linked to Cable

Source: USA Today, January 28, 1985; The World Almanac 1992.

Charts and **tables** condense large blocks of information into a single representation. If you want to discuss what products are imported and exported by Japan, you can break down imports and exports on a table. If you want to show the channels of communication or the lines of authority in a large company, your presentation will be much easier to follow if your listeners have an organizational chart for reference.

There are two special types of charts: **flipcharts** unveil ideas one at a time on separate sheets; **flowcharts** show the chronological stages of a process on a single sheet. Both flipcharts and flowcharts may include drawings or photos. If you present successive ideas with a flipchart you'll focus audience attention on specific parts of your speech. If you present successive ideas with a complete chart, however, the audience may stray from your order of explanation to read the entire chart. You can use a flowchart to indicate what actions might be taken across time—for example, a flowchart will allow audiences to visualize the stages of a fundraising campaign.

As long as the information is not too complex or lengthy, tables and charts may be used to indicate changes over time and to rank or list items and their costs, frequency of use, or relative importance. Tables and charts should be designed so that they can be seen and so that they convey data simply and clearly. Too much information will force the audience to concentrate more on the visual support than on your oral explanation. For example, a dense chart showing all the major and minor offices of a company may simply overwhelm listeners as they try to follow your explanation. If the organization is too complex, you may want to develop a series of charts, each one focusing on a smaller unit of information.

Strategies for Selecting and Using Visual Aids

To decide which visual aids will work best for you take into account four considerations: (a) characteristics of the audience and occasion; (b) the communicative potential of various visuals; (c) your ability to integrate verbal and visual materials effectively; and (d) the potential of computer-generated visual materials to help you with your communication tasks.

Consider the Audience and Occasion

Before you select specific visual aids, common sense will tell you to think about your listeners:

- Do you need to bring a map of the United States to an audience of college students when discussing the westward movement of population of this country?
- If you're going to discuss a football team's offensive and defensive formations, should you diagram them for your audience?
- Can you expect an audience to understand the administrative structure of the federal bureaucracy without providing an organizational chart?

How readily an audience can comprehend *aurally* (by ear) what you have to say is another more difficult question to answer. It may be quite difficult, for example, to decide what your classmates know about the organization of such groups as the National Red Cross or what Rotary Club members know about the administrative structure of your college. Probably the best thing you can do is to speak with several of your listeners ahead of time. This and other forms of audience research can help you decide on how to use the visual channel.

As part of your preparation process, take into account the speaking occasion. Certain occasions demand specific types of visual support materials. The corporate executive who presents a report on projected future profits to a board of directors without a printed handout or diagram will probably put his or her credibility in jeopardy. The military adviser who calls for governmental expenditures for new weapons without pictures or drawings of the proposed weapons and printed technical data on their performance is not likely to be a convincing advocate. An athletic coach without a chalkboard at halftime likely will only confuse some of the players. In short, if you speak in situations where speakers traditionally have used certain visual aids, meet those expectations in your own work. If an occasion doesn't appear to require certain visual supports, analyze the occasion and your topic further for different visual possibilities. Use your imagination. Be innovative. Don't overlook opportunities to make your speech more meaningful, more exciting, and more interesting for your listeners.

Consider the Communicative Potential of Various Visual Aids

Keep in mind that each type of visual aid is best at communicating a particular kind of information. Each type also must blend with your spoken presentation as well as with your audience. In general, pictorial or photographic visuals can make an audience *feel* the way you do. For example, you can use slides, movies, sketches, or photographs of your travels in Sri Lanka to accompany a speech on social conditions in equatorial Asia. Direct representations can be filled with feeling and show an audience what you experienced in another place or situation.

Visuals containing descriptive or written materials, on the other hand, are especially useful in helping an audience to *think* the way you do. Models, diagrams, charts, and graphs about the population and economy of Sri Lanka could help you persuade your listeners to conclude that the United States should increase its aid to that country.

Integrate Verbal and Visual Materials Effectively

To be maximally effective, visual aids must work in harmony with your spoken messages. Visuals should save time, increase the impact of your speech, clarify complex relations, or generally enliven your presentation. Consider the following suggestions for making your visuals work for you:

1. *Design abstract symbolic representations with care.* Use contrasting colors (red on white, black on yellow) to highlight different kinds of information in an organizational chart or to differentiate segments of a pie graph or bars in a bar graph. As a rule, color commands more attention than black and white.

2. *Keep charts and other graphic aids clear and simple.* Research has demonstrated that plain bar graphs are the most effective way to display statistical comparisons.[7] The reason may be that bar graphs represent abstract numbers in concrete visual form. Make sure that your bar graphs work for you: do they make the essential information stand out clearly from the background? Let simplicity guide your presentation.

Artist Paul Klee on the Visible

Kunst gibt nicht das Sichtbare wieder, sondern macht sichtbar. [Art does not reproduce the visible: rather, it makes visible.]*

Paul Klee's statement is also true of visual aids. They aren't simply things or objects in themselves that are given to an audience. Rather, when you incorporate visual aids—videos, board drawings, actual objects—into your speech, they become communication systems in their own right. The visual becomes every bit as much a communication channel as the verbal is. Klee (1879–1940) understood this principle. His paintings exaggerated features of human beings in order to help us see what we hadn't seen before. Your visual aids do the same thing.

* From the entry on Paul Klee, *The Oxford Dictionary of Modern Quotations*, ed. Tony Augarde (New York: Oxford University Press, 1991), p. 128.

3. *Make your visual large enough to be seen clearly and easily.* Listeners get frustrated when they must lean forward and squint in order to see detail in a visual aid. Make your figures and lettering large enough to be seen from the back of the room. Follow the example of John Hancock who, when signing the Declaration of Independence in 1776, wrote his name large enough to "be seen by the King of England without his glasses."

4. *Make your visuals neat.* Draw neatly, spell correctly, make lines proportional, and make letters symmetrical. Too often, beginning speakers throw together visuals at the last moment. They forget that visual aids contribute to audience assessment of their credibility. Misspelled words and sloppy graphs will lower listeners' estimation of your competence.

5. *Decide how to handle difficult visual aids in advance.* Decide on a visual aid and practice with it well in advance, especially for demonstration speeches. Suppose you want to demonstrate tombstone dabbing or making paper casts of old tombstone faces. Tombstones are heavy. Do you bring one to class? Tombstone dabbing takes time and is very messy. How much of the process do you show? You could discuss in

detail the chemicals used for cleaning stone surfaces, the different kinds of paper, various dabbing techniques, and locations of interesting tombstones. How detailed should you get? Unless you think through such questions in advance, you'll undoubtedly find yourself making some poor decisions in mid-speech.

6. *Be prepared to compensate orally for any distraction your visual aid may create.* Remember that you must compete with your visual aid for your listeners' attention. Listeners may find the visual aid so intriguing that they miss part of your message. You can partially compensate for any potential distraction by building reiteration into your speech. By repeating your main ideas you can be reasonably certain that your listeners will follow your thoughts. As added insurance, you might also keep your visual aid out of sight until you need to use it.

7. *Be prepared to coordinate slides, films, overhead projections, or videotapes with your verbal message.* Mechanical or electronic messages can easily distract your listeners. If your audience concentrates harder on the moving images than on your words, however, you defeat your own purpose. You need to talk louder and move more vigorously when using a machine to communicate, or you need to refuse to compete with the machine at all; that is, show the film or slides either *before* or *after* you comment on their content. Whatever strategy you choose, make sure your visual materials are well integrated into your oral presentation.

8. *Hand your listeners a copy of the materials you wish them to reflect on after your speech.* If you're making recommendations to a student council, you should provide copies of your proposal for the council's subsequent action. Or, if you're reporting the results of a survey, your listeners will better digest the most pertinent statistics if you give each listener a copy of them. Few people can recall the seven warning signs of cancer, but they might keep a wallet-sized list handy if you provided them with it. Of course, you would not duplicate your entire speech for everyone—select only those items with lasting value. Time the distribution so it doesn't interfere with your speech.

   These suggestions should enable you to take advantage of the communicative potential of visual media. Good visual aids don't detract from your message. Instead, they fit your ideas and leave the audience with a feeling of completeness.

Evaluate Computer-Generated Visual Materials

When considering visual aids, you can tap into the expanding world of computer graphics. While you may not be able to produce results similar to those on the latest televised football game, you can still use readily available computer-generated visual materials. Here are some suggestions for ways to use such materials:

1. *Use computer graphics to create an atmosphere.* It's easy to make

Well thought out computer-generated visual aids can give your presentation a level of professionalism and class and enhance your credibility.

computer banners with block lettering and pictures. Hang a banner in the front of the room to set a mood or establish a theme. For example, a student urging her classmates to get involved in a United Way fundraising drive created a banner with the campaign slogan, "Thanks to you, it works, for all of us." Initially, the banner captured attention; during the speech the banner reinforced the theme.

COMPUTER-GENERATED VISUAL AIDS

A computer with a decent graphs program can generate visual materials. You will probably have to enlarge them at a graphics store; that cost often is worth the quality of the aid. The sample below is from a speech on energy-saving electronic magnetic preheating systems. This is the fourth picture from a series of ten, listed along the right-hand side of the picture. They were assembled into a flip chart for a sales presentation.

Source: International Institute for Energy Conservation.

2. *Enlarge small computer-generated diagrams.* Most computer diagrams are too small to be seen easily by an audience. You can use a photo duplicating machine that enlarges images sometimes 140 to 200 percent of the original size to make a more visible diagram.

3. *Consider enhancing the computer-generated image in other ways.* Use markers to color in pie graphs or to darken the lines of a line graph. Use press-on letters to make headings for your graphs. Convert computer-generated images into slide transparencies for projection during your speech. Mixing media in such ways can give your presentations a professional look. If you have access to the right technology, you can create three-dimensional images of buildings, machines, or the human body.

4. *Know the limitations of computer technology.* Remember that you're the lead actor and your visuals are props. Choose the visuals that fit your purpose, physical setting, and audience needs. Computers are most effective when processing numerical data and converting them into bar, line, and pie graphs.

Chapter Summary

In the ocularcentric twentieth century, visual aids comprise an important channel of communication even in oral settings. They can *aid listener comprehension* and *add persuasive impact* to a speech. There are two main types of visual aids: *actual objects* and *symbolic representations.* Actual objects include both *animate objects* (living plants, animals, and even the speaker) and *inanimate objects* (nonliving things). Symbolic representations include *concrete representations* (chalkboard drawing, graphs, charts and tables, and computer-generated materials) as well as *abstract representations.* In selecting which visual aids to use in particular speeches, consider *the audience and occasion, the communicative potential of various visual aids, ways to integrate verbal and visual materials effectively,* and *the best use of computer-generated materials.* Coordinating the verbal and visual channels can add enormous impact to your oral presentations.

References

1. Jacques Ellul, *The Humiliation of the Word,* trans. Joyce Main Hanks (Grand Rapids, MI: William B. Eerdmans, 1985). See also Martin Jay, "The Rise of Hermeneutics and the Crisis of Ocularcentrism," in *The Rhetoric of Interpretation and the Interpretation of Rhetoric,* ed. Paul Hernadi (Durham, NC: Duke University Press, 1989), 55–74.

2. The general theories of Gestalt psychology (which undergird much of visual theory) are reviewed understandably in Ernest R. Hilgard, *Theories of Learning* (New York: Appleton-Century-Crofts, 1956). Their applications can be found, among other places, in Rudolph Arnheim, *Visual Thinking* (Berkeley: University of California Press, 1969); John M. Kennedy, *A Psychology of Picture Perception* (San Francisco: Jossey-Bass, 1976); and John Morgan and Peter Welton, *See What I Mean: An Introduction to Visual Communication* (London: Edward Arnold, 1986). For discussions of research on media and learning, see E. Heidt, *Instructional Media and the Individual Learner* (New York: Nichols, 1976) and Gavriel Salomon, *Interaction of Media, Cognition, and Learning* (San Francisco: Jossey-Bass, 1979).

3. William J. Seiler, "The Effects of Visual Materials on Attitudes, Credibility, and Retention," *Communication Monographs* 38 (1971): 331–34.

4. For more specific conclusions regarding the effects of various kinds of visual materials, see F. M. Dwyer, "Exploratory Studies in the Effectiveness of Visual Illustrations," *AV Communication Review* 18 (1970): 135–50; G. D. Feliciano, R. D. Powers, and B. E. Kearle, "The Presentation of Statistical Information," *AV Communication Review* 11 (1963): 32–39; Seiler; M. D. Vernon, "Presenting Information in Diagrams," *AV Communication Review* 1 (1953): 147–58; L. V. Peterson and Wilbur Schramm, "How Accurately Are Different Kinds of Graphs Read?" *AV Communication Review* 2 (1955): 178–89; and Virginia Johnson, "Picture-Perfect Presentations," *Training & Development Journal* 43 (1989): 45.

5. Joel R. Levin and Alan M. Lesgold, "On Pictures in Prose," *Educational Communication and Technology Journal* 26 (1978): 233–44. See also Marilyn J. Haring and Maurine A. Fry, "Effect of Pictures on Children's Comprehension of Written Text," *Educational Communication and Technology Journal* 27 (1979): 185–90.

6. To read a thoughtful exploration of the relationships between ideas and visuals, see Edgar B. Wycoff, "Why Visuals?" *AV Communications* 11 (1977): 39, 59.

7. See Feliciano, et al., "The Presentation of Statistical Information"; Vernon, "Presenting Information in Diagrams"; and Peterson and Schramm, "How Accurately Are Different Kinds of Graphs Read?"

Key Terms

abstract representations (p. 337)

bar graphs   (p. 339)

charts   (p. 341)

computer-generated visual materials   (p. 345)

concrete representations (p. 334)

flipcharts   (p. 341)

flowcharts   (p. 341)

graphs   (p. 338)

line graphs   (p. 339)

models   (p. 337)

ocularcentric century   (p. 331)

pictographs   (p. 339)

pie graphs   (p. 339)

symbolic representations (p. 334)

tables   (p. 341)

Problems and Probes

1. Think of several courses you have taken in high school and/or college. How did the instructors use visual aids in presenting the subject matter of these courses? Were such materials effectively used? Was there a relationship between the subject matter and the type of visual aid used? Give special consideration to proper and improper uses of the chalkboard by the instructors. What communicative functions are best served by the chalkboard? least served? Are there special problems with the use of visuals when audience members are taking notes while listening? Prepare a brief written analysis of these questions, including several illustrations from the classes. How might your instructors have expanded or improved the visual presentation of information?

2. Visual aids capture appropriate moods, clarify potentially complex subjects, and sometimes even carry the thrust of a persuasive message. Examine magazine advertisements and "how-to" articles in periodicals, look at store windows and special displays in museums and libraries, and observe slide-projection lectures in some of your other classes. Then (a) using the types considered in this chapter, classify the visual materials you have encountered; (b) assess the purposes these materials serve—clarification, persuasion, attention focusing, mood setting, and others; (c) evaluate the effectiveness of each of

the materials you have examined; and, finally, (d) prepare a report, a paper, or a journal entry on the results of your experiences and observations.

Communication Activities

1. Present a short oral report in which you describe a speech you will give and the ways you will incorporate visual materials and coordinate them with the verbal materials. Specify the characteristics you might try to build into each visual aid to maximize clarity. If you can, bring in some rough-draft examples of the visuals for the purpose of illustrating your intentions.

2. Prepare a short speech explaining or demonstrating a complex process. Use two different types of visual aids. Ask the class to evaluate which aid was more effective. Try this same speech without the use of any visual materials. What new pressures do you feel as a speaker? How can you deal with them? Can you still give an effective presentation?

3. Repeat activity #2 with a classmate. Working together, develop two different visual aids to enhance your joint presentation. Plan a performance in which the two of you share the delivery responsibilities. When one speaker talks, the other may be in charge of displaying visual aids. How effective are these duet performances? How does having a thoroughly initiated partner increase the speaking options?

14

Using Your Voice and Body to Communicate

" T he *last* thing I want to do this semester is give a speech in front of an audience. I suppose I'll have to, since there's nothing else open, but the thought of it really unnerves me." If these thoughts crossed your mind sometime prior to signing up for a course in public communication, consider yourself in good company. History tells us that many famous speakers had to overcome severe problems of delivery before others would listen to their ideas. Abraham Lincoln suffered from extreme speech fright; Eleanor Roosevelt appeared awkward and clumsy; John F. Kennedy had a strong regional dialect and repetitive gestures. Each of these famous speakers, and many others, realized that the effectiveness of a speech depends not only on careful research and organization, but also on how ideas are presented.

The manner in which a speech is presented affects its reception. If you've heard a recording or seen a video of Martin Luther King's "I Have a Dream" speech, you're aware of the difference that hearing him makes, compared to simply reading a copy of the speech. The same is true of Jesse Jackson—his use of repetition doesn't read nearly as well as it sounds when heard. It is important to be aware that the actual presentation of the speech adds to the impact of the ideas.

In presenting a speech, you'll need to consider how your delivery will affect how your audience perceives you. Will they see you as deeply committed to the claim you advance, as sincerely interested in the information you impart? Or will they see you as indifferent to whether they agree with you or your information? How the audience perceives you and the message is, in part, a product of the way in which you present yourself and your ideas. Your voice and bodily movements—the *aural* and *visual channels of communication*—help transmit your feelings and attitudes toward yourself, your audience, and your topic.

You may have seen speakers who reluctantly approach the platform with downcast eyes and grimacing faces, literally dragging their feet and fussing with their notes on the way to the front of the room. Their sense of self-confidence and their attitude toward the audience and the occasion betray them before they even begin. Even if the ideas are important and the speech is well crafted, the audience will have difficulty listening because they expect the worst. Conversely, if a speaker moves with apparent confidence, takes a moment at the platform to organize notes and glances at the audience as if to say "I'm ready, are you?" the audience will be more favorably disposed to listen critically.

A well presented speech communicates self-confidence and personal competence. To assist you, we'll discuss ways to effectively use your voice and body to communicate.

Using Your Voice to Communicate

Your voice is an instrument that helps convey the meaning of language. As we have noted, it does affect your listeners' perception and interpretation of your message.[1]

You communicate your level of enthusiasm for your central idea or claim through your voice. Knowing about the characteristics of **vocal quality** will help you communicate your interest in your ideas and, in turn, make them more interesting for your listeners. Recall a play-by-play account of a sports event by your favorite announcer such as the basketball announcer Dick Vitale or baseball announcer Joe Garagiola. The vividness they create depends, in large part, on their vocal intensity.

Our culture prizes one essential vocal quality above all others—a sense of **conversationality**.[2] The most successful speakers of our time make their listeners feel they're being addressed personally. Even speakers who address millions through the mass media on evening newscasts or nightly talk shows speak as though they're engaging each listener in a personal conversation. Such conversational quality comes primarily from the realization that they're talking "with" not "at" an audience. You should adapt your voice to the public speaking situation without losing the interpersonal qualities expected in everyday conversation.

We'll begin this chapter by reviewing some of the general characteristics of an effective speaking voice and by considering the ways to adapt it to particular speaking situations.

The most successful speakers of our time have possessed the vocal quality of conversationality, the ability to make listeners feel they are being directly, personally addressed.

The Effective Speaking Voice

Successful speakers use several vocal attributes to emotionally color ideas. The attributes include intelligibility, variety, understandable stress patterns, and control of emotional quality.

Intelligibility

As a listener, your ability to comprehend a speech's message is dependent in part on the speaker's *loudness, rate, enunciation,* and *pronunciation.* During personal conversation, you may not give much thought to any of these attributes. A soft speaking voice may be easily heard by a person seated next to you; a faster than normal speaking rate may even garble some words ("whatchawan?") without sacrificing intelligibility. You may even mispronounce words, only to have your friend correct you immediately or simply ignore the slip because it isn't critical to their impression of your competence or interest in the issue. When speaking in public, however, these four attributes assume a far greater significance.

LOUDNESS LEVELS

As you can see, noise varies considerably. How could you adjust your volume if you were speaking to a "quiet" audience? What if you were competing with a lawnmower outside the building?

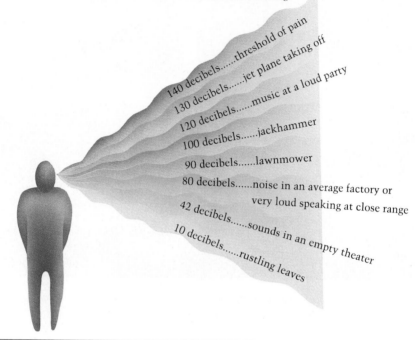

140 decibels......threshold of pain

130 decibels......jet plane taking off

120 decibels......music at a loud party

100 decibels......jackhammer

90 decibels......lawnmower

80 decibels......noise in an average factory or very loud speaking at close range

42 decibels......sounds in an empty theater

10 decibels......rustling leaves

Adjust Your Volume. Probably the most important single factor in intelligibility is how well the audience can hear you. Your speaking volume is related to the distance that exists between you and the audience and the amount of external noise. The farther away your listeners are (if you don't have a microphone), the louder you must talk. Keep in mind that your voice always sounds louder to you than your listeners, so even if they're relatively close, you still need to project your voice to ensure they can hear what you're saying.

In addition to distance, the external noise that you must compete with affects how loudly you'll have to speak. An air conditioner or fan may be heard more easily than your voice in the back of a room if you don't project over the sound it makes. Even an empty theater generates noise (at 25 decibels); when it holds an audience, the noise level rises to 42 decibels. If you were speaking to plant workers in an average factory, the noise level you would compete with is about 80 decibels—the same as very loud speaking at close range.

If you're uncertain how loud you should be, you can either ask your audience if they can hear you in the back of the room or watch their expressions as you begin to speak. If they look as if they're straining to hear or even using nonverbal signals to indicate you should increase the volume, you'll need to speak more loudly. In a classroom situation, you also can ask your instructor if you're speaking loudly enough.

Control Your Rate.   In animated conversation, you may well speak at the rapid verbal **rate** of 200-250 words per minute. As words tumble out in ordinary conversation, you may give little thought to how fast you're speaking. Listen to speakers from a different country—even if you understand a little of their language (Spanish, Italian, or French, for example), you may find it incredibly hard to "keep up" because they speak so much faster than you can discern their individual words. The experience is no different in traveling to different regions of the United States and finding that people talk at rates you're not used to. A fast rate is especially characteristic of people raised in the North, Midwest, Southwest, or West.

During informal conversation, the difficulty is lessened in part by the fact that the sounds carry only a short distance. In large auditoriums, echoes may further distort sounds, making it more difficult to follow rapid delivery; if the speech is presented outdoors, words often seem to drift and vanish into the open air—more quickly than they can be "caught" if the rate is too rapid.

When addressing large groups, slow your ordinary conversational rate down by about ⅓, to around 120-to-150 words per minute. While you don't often time your own rate of delivery, again you can ask the audience or pay close attention to their nonverbal signals as you speak. If your speaking rate is too fast for the occasion, rest assured that someone will inform you; that message may be far more pleasant if you appear to be genuinely concerned about how well your listeners follow your rate of delivery.

Adjusting your rate does not mean that you will or should speak at the same rate throughout your presentation. Just as the sports announcer varies his or her rate as the game's excitement rises or falls, so too will you need to vary your rate to reflect the intensity of your commitment, the importance of key ideas, or the emotionality of your appeal. Consider, for example, how Michael Dukakis was criticized for not varying his voice when asked if he would favor the death penalty for a person convicted of assaulting or raping his wife. His dead-pan delivery made it appear he was unemotional and lacked intense convictions. Listeners expected a more rapid rate, delivered in a more strident, louder voice.

Enunciate Clearly.   **Enunciation** refers to the crispness and precision used in forming your words. Most of us are "lip lazy" in that we tend to slur sounds, drop syllables, insert new sounds, and skip over beginnings or endings of words (as in "quitcherbellyachin"). While this may be highly normal and accepted during informal conversation with friends, it's inappropriate in more formal settings, such as a public presentation. When speaking in public, you will need to concentrate upon the clear and distinct enunciation of syllables and words. You will need to remind yourself to say "going" instead of "go-in," "just" instead of "jist," "wash" instead of "warsh," "roof" instead of "ruf," and "orange" instead of "ornch." This means thinking about how the word sounds when you use it informally, how it should sound in more formal settings, and then adjusting your delivery to suit the situation. Slowing your informal rate of delivery will help, as it will allow you more time to form consonants, use all of the syllables of a word, and vocalize beginnings and endings of words.

Meet Standards of Pronunciation.   Whereas enunciation refers to precise vocalization, **pronunciation** refers to the regional or national pattern of how various words should be vocalized. Is the small stream a "crick" or "creek," do we trace our "r-o-o-ts" or "ruts" when we construct a family tree? Your enunciation of a word may be clear, as in "Ayuh" or "Bangor," but the audience may laugh as your pronunciation reveals you as an outsider. In Maine, for example, Calais is not "Callay" but "Callus"; in Illinois, "Des Plaines" is not "De Plain" but "Dez Plains"; in Montana, "Havre" is not "Hauve" but "Have-er." These examples call attention to various **dialects** found in the United States.

Since dialects have different rules for vocabulary, grammar, and pronunciation, a clash of dialects can result in confusion and frustration for both speaker and listener. Occasionally an audience may make negative judgments about the speaker's credibility—that is, the speaker's education, reliability, responsibility, and capability for leadership—based solely on dialect.[3] Such judgments of credibility occur because dialects and even professional jargon contribute heavily to what paralinguists call *vocal stereotypes*.[4] News anchors, for example, have reacted to the potential for negative judgments by adopting a "midwestern American" dialect—a manner of speech that is broadly accepted across the country. This dialect avoids calling attention to itself, as would a Downeast or a pronounced Southern accent. Many speakers alter their dialect to suit the situation: formal or "midwestern" when dealing with a general audience, and informal when talking to local folk. When you speak, analyze the situation to determine whether your regional dialect is appropriate, or whether you should use the grammar, vocabulary, and vocal patterns of middle America.

Variety.   As you move from intimate conversation to more public encounters, you may lose the spontaneity and animation that generally accompanies informal communication. Varying characteristics of your voice, such as rate, pitch, force, and using pauses effectively will help you compensate for the more formal nature of public speaking situations. In essence, varying your voice will make the presentation more *pleasant* to listen to.

We've already considered varying the rate of speech. Three aspects of **pitch** (the musical "notes" in your speaking voice) are relevant to effective vocal communication. First, your normal **pitch level**—whether soprano, alto, tenor, baritone, or bass—is adequate for most everyday conversation.

However, adapting your normal level by altering the **pitch range** can effectively provide emphasis or call attention to your ideas. It also prevents you from becoming monotonous—a speaking voice that incorporates very little change in rate or pitch level. Given the distances that sounds must travel between speaker and audience and the length of time speakers talk, you should exaggerate your range of sounds. Raise your pitch higher than your normal level, and drop it lower. Usually, the more emotionally charged your ideas, the more intense your commitment, or the more critical the message, the more you should vary your pitch.

The key to successful control of pitch ultimately depends on understanding the importance of **pitch variation**. Use the full pitch range you're capable of in giving ideas and thoughts their appropriate measure of emphasis. As a general rule, use higher pitches to communicate excitement and lower pitches to create a sense of control or solemnity. Be wary of "faking it," using a highly emotive pitch level when the subject does not merit such an emphasis. Just as an audience expects a certain level when the subject calls for intensity and strong feeling, as expressed through the voice, they also dislike artificially induced emphasis.

As a second rule, let the sense of the sentence control your pitch variations. For example, abruptly moving your voice up at the end of a question is called a "step." A more gradual or continuous pitch inflection is termed a "slide." Minnie Pearl's opening lines to her act and Ed McMahon's introduction of Johnny Carson stand out as classic examples of exaggerated use of both types of vocal change. Minnie Pearl stretches the first word out while raising the pitch level, then drops it slightly to place a different emphasis on the next phrase. Ed McMahon successively raised his voice until he reached a high pitch level on the beginning of "Johnny," then stepped down the scale on the end of the word. While you may not wish to incorporate such exaggerated usage in your own presentation, the basic principle is applicable to most public occasions. By mastering the use of steps and slides, you can call attention to your word choices and make your meaning clearer and more precise.

Stress Patterns. A third significant aspect of vocal behavior is **stress patterns**—the ways in which sounds, syllables, and words are accented. Without vocal stress, everything in a speech would sound the same, and the message would appear emotionless and possibly incomprehensible. A computer communicates without vocal stress; matching its style of speech wouldn't be advisable in either informal or formal settings. Vocal stress is achieved through vocal emphasis and through the judicious use of pauses.

Vocal Emphasis. **Emphasis** is achieved through adroit changes in vocal energy (volume/loudness), intonation (pitch), and speed (rate). By "punching" words, you make them stand out in the context of other phrases or words being used. Emphasizing different words, even in individual sentences, can have the impact of changing the meaning. Consider the sentence "Jane's taking Tom out for pizza tonight":

1.   JANE'S taking Tom out for pizza tonight. (not Sue or Mary)
2.   Jane's taking TOM out for pizza tonight. (not Jim or John)
3.   Jane's taking Tom OUT for pizza tonight. (rather than staying home)
4.   Jane's taking Tom out for PIZZA tonight. (not seafood or hamburgers)
5.   Jane's taking Tom out for pizza TONIGHT. (not this weekend)

Without careful control of vocal force, a speaker is liable to give expression to messages subject to many possible meanings. A lack of vocal stress not only creates the impression that the speaker is bored, but also can cause needless misunderstandings.

Emphasis is also fostered through changes in pitch and rate. You can use relatively simple changes in pitch, for example, to tell an audience where you are in the speech:

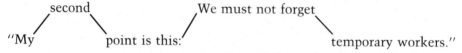

In this sentence, the audience can hear that the speaker has completed the first main point and has moved to the second, and is also alerted not only to the subject "temporary workers" but also to the thrust of what will be said about them.

Variations in rate can indicate the relationship between ideas:

> [*moderate rate*] We are a country faced with . . . [*fast rate*] balance of payments deficits, rising health care costs, high unemployment, a weakened economy...[*slow rate*] and-a-stif-ling-na-tion-al-debt.

In this illustration, the speaker builds a vocal freight train: starting moderately, picking up speed in the middle, and slowing at the end. The audience will not miss the fact that the national debt is most important in this list of economic woes. Variations such as this will help you communicate what is important in your message.

Use Helpful Pauses.   **Pauses** are intervals of *silence* between or within words, phrases, or sentences. When placed immediately before a key idea or the climax of a story, they punctuate thought to create suspense; when placed immediately after a major point or central idea, they add emphasis, and give an audience time to digest the material just presented. Introduced judiciously into the speech, pauses can express feeling more forcefully than words. Clearly, silence can be a highly effective communicative tool if used intelligently and sparingly, and if not embarrassingly prolonged.

Sometimes, speakers fill silence in their discourse with sounds— "umm," "ah," "uh," "er," "well-ah," "you-know," "like," and other meaningless fillers. What's your response to the speaker who opens a speech with

A listener's judgment of a speaker's personality and emotional commitment often centers on that speaker's vocal quality—the fullness of the tones and whether the voice is harsh, husky, mellow, nasal, breathy, or resonant.

"Today, ah, I would, like, you know, to speak to you about a, uh, well-uh, pressing, uh, like, a pressing problem facing this, um, campus." These kinds of vocal intrusions convey hesitancy and lack of confidence; they don't inspire listeners to examine the merit of the ideas critically.

While fillers are annoyances and you should keep them to a minimum, their prevalence suggests a misunderstanding of the function of silence.[5] Silence is not a negative factor in speaking. Pausing between ideas, or at the end of an important point can be helpful, provided the silence is not too prolonged. Pauses communicate a point's importance, and the audience has the chance to consider its implications. Silence also can be used before expressing an idea or conclusion, in building anticipation or suspense. So, don't be quick to simply fill in the empty space between thoughts. Use pauses to advantage in speaking.

Controlling Emotional Quality.   Your voice can be heard as relatively full or thin, as harsh, husky, mellow, nasal, breathy, or resonant. Depending on the vocal quality, an audience may judge you as angry, happy, confident, fearful, sincere, or sad. **Emotional characterizers**, including cues such as laughing, crying, whispering, inhaling, or exhaling, help an audience understand how you're feeling about what is being said.[6] Consider a few of the ways you could say the following sentence: "I can't believe I ate the whole thing." You could express the idea as if you were reporting a fact, as though it were an impossible achievement, or as an expression of wonder about what just happened. In communicating these different shades of meaning, you will find yourself varying loudness, rate, pitch, and vocal stress.

Practicing Vocal Control.   Utilizing the full range of your voice to convey meaning is a prime factor in the impression you make on an audience. While the ultimate impression is not one you can completely control, it's essential to do what you can to narrow the range of possible interpretations the audience can place on you, your sincerity, or the merit of your ideas. Practice is the most important tool in gaining mastery over your own voice and in managing impressions. Before any vocal skill can be natural and effective with listeners, it must become so automatic that the speaker can incorporate it with little conscious effort. In gaining confidence in delivery, you will be able to achieve the sense of conversationality so highly valued in our society.

Using Your Body to Communicate

Where the voice gives meaning through the aural channel, your body conveys meaning through the visual channel. Audiences pay attention to the visual messages you send in their assessment of you and your ideas. You can use your physical presence before the audience to help create clarity and to convey your commitment to the ideas. Actions, just as words, convey meaning.

Dimensions of Nonverbal Communication

In recent years, research has re-emphasized the significance of nonverbal behaviors in communicative encounters.[7] Basically, these roles can be reduced to three generalizations:

1. *Speakers reveal and reflect their emotional states by their nonverbal behaviors in front of audiences.* Feelings and emotions are read through facial expressions, physical action such as walking, moving your head, arms, shoulders, and hands. Misinterpretation of cues also is a potential problem as different cultures will signal these feelings in a variety of ways. For example, embarrassment may be shown by an Arab by lowering his head and slightly sticking his tongue out, while a Missouri farm boy may lower his head or blush.[8]

Knowing how different cultures express feelings through nonverbal messages is an important part of managing your own meaning. In fact, in some cultures, the preponderance of communication comes through nonverbal sources. Japanese, Korean, and Taiwanese cultures, for example, rely more on their surroundings and environment than on verbal messages for information. Cultures may have specialized terms for particular nonverbal signals; the Korean term *nunchi* means "to communicate through your eyes."[9]

2. *Speaker's nonverbal cues enrich or elaborate the message that comes through words.* A solemn face can reinforce the dignity of a funeral eulogy. The words "either you can do this, or you can do that" can be illustrated with appropriate arm and hand gestures. Taking a few steps to the left or right tells an audience that you're moving from one idea or argument to another.

3. *Nonverbal messages create a reciprocal interaction sent from speaker to listener and from listener back to speaker.* Listeners frown, smile, shift nervously in their seats, and engage in many types of nonverbal behavior.

   This chapter concentrates on the speaker's control of "body language." There are four areas of nonverbal communication that concern every speaker: (1) proxemics, (2) movement/stance, (3) facial expressions, and (4) gestures.

Proxemics.　An important dimension of nonverbal communication, **proxemics** refers to the use of space by human beings. Two components of proxemics are especially relevant to public speakers:

1. *Physical Arrangements.* The layout of a room in which you're speaking, including the presence or absence of a podium, the seating plan, the location of chalkboards and similar aids, and any physical barriers between you and your audience.

2. *Distance.* The extent of separation between you and your audience.[10]

In most public speaking situations, both components will have a direct bearing on your message. In facing a seated audience, the lectern, table, or speaker platform will set the audience apart from you as speaker. The literal distance created by physical barriers also has psychological ramifications, because the audience may feel removed from you and your message. In churches, for example, the physical setting is not accidental—the minister is normally raised above the audience by a platform, and stands behind a lectern that, by its size alone, conveys an image of power and commands respectful obedience. Reducing the physical barriers is one way to create a more informal, relaxed, or even intimate setting for your message. For example, you can stand beside the lectern instead of always behind it. You

CLASSIFICATION OF
INTERHUMAN DISTANCE

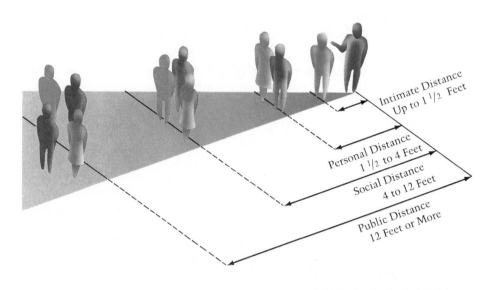

Intimate Distance
Up to 1 1/2 Feet

Personal Distance
1 1/2 to 4 Feet

Social Distance
4 to 12 Feet

Public Distance
12 Feet or More

can move in front of it or come down off the platform to the audience's level. If there is a table between you and the audience, you can establish a more informal atmosphere by sitting on it during your presentation.

Speakers in most public speaking situations talk across what Edward T. Hall refers to as "public distance"—twelve feet or more away from their listeners.[11]

While you can reduce the distance by moving to the front of a lectern, some members of the audience will still be farther from you than you'd like. To communicate with people at that distance, you obviously cannot rely on your normal speaking voice or small changes in posture or muscle tone. Instead, to compensate for the distance, you can use larger gestures, broader shifts of your body from place to place, and increased vocal energy. This will make it easier for a listener seated at the back of a large room to catch the meaning implied by your movement. Raising your eyebrows to express wonderment may be effective for those in the front rows, but if not seen by those in the back, you'll lose the impact.

While there is no single rule for using space wisely, there are some guidelines that can be followed to maximize use:

1. *The formality of the occasion affects your impact—the more solemn or formal the occasion, the more distance and barriers.* Lectures, prepared

PHYSICAL ARRANGEMENTS
FOR PUBLIC SPEAKING

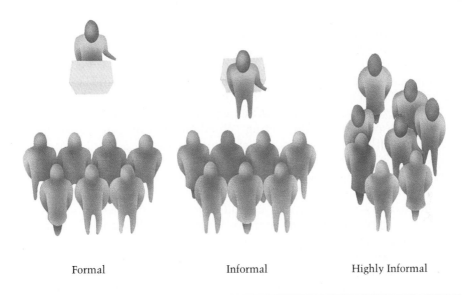

Formal   Informal   Highly Informal

reports, and the like are better suited to presentations from behind the lectern. A "folksy" relaxed style would not be well received at a formal occasion.

2. *The nature of your material may require the use of a lectern, such as when you have extensive quoted material or statistical evidence.* Put simply, you need someplace handy to place notes or other materials that you want to use in presenting your message. Visual aids also may require special equipment, such as an easel, table, or overhead projector. As natural aids to your message, these should be positioned so the audience has a clear view of the visual material.

3. *Your personal preference can be considered.* You may feel more at ease with a lectern that you can work from, even as you move to one side or the other during the presentation.

4. *Cultural constraints should be considered.* Each culture has its own preferences for how meetings are conducted. While factors such as physical arrangement and distance aren't the only variables that distinguish what's acceptable in a particular culture, it would be wise to consider whether actions that you find acceptable might offend your audience.[12]

These guidelines will help you refine and become comfortable with ways to reduce barriers and use distance while meeting the expectations of the audience.

Movement and Stance.   **Movement**—shifts you make from one spot to another during delivery—and **stance (posture)**—standing in a relaxed or rigid manner with head and shoulders erect or slumping—provide another set of nonverbal cues for your audience. They tell audiences whether you're comfortable and confident, tired and disinterested, and energetic or lethargic. Each possibility conveys a different meaning; your audience will incorporate the meaning attached to movement and stance into its general assessment of what you're saying. Whether done on purpose or not, by standing stiffly erect a speaker may, without saying a word, you suggest either "This is a formal occasion," or "I am tense, even afraid, of this audience." Leaning forward, physically reaching out to the audience, says silently but eloquently, "I am interested in you. I want you to understand and accept my ideas." Sitting casually on the front edge of a table and assuming a relaxed posture communicates informality and a readiness to engage in a dialogue with your audience.

In addition to communicating your state of mind, movement also can signal transitions from one idea to another. You can lead your audience through the speech by moving from one side of the lectern to another or by moving toward the audience and then moving back behind the lectern. Changes in posture can also communicate tone shifts: leaning forward may indicate intensity and importance, while moving back to a more relaxed stance will signal an emotional transition in the subject. In this manner, you can more effectively regulate the audience's reception of your message.

However, movement and stance can work against you as well as for you. Aimless pacing back and forth is distracting to an audience. A nervous bouncing or swaying makes the audience tense and uneasy. Standing too stiff and erect may also cause you to lose rapport with the audience. Your movement, in other words, should relate to the subject and to the atmosphere you wish to create. Purposeful movement helps your speech and produces the sense of self-assurance and control you want to exhibit.[13]

Facial Expressions.   When you speak, your face communicates as well as your words. Your facial expressions tell audiences about your self and your feelings. What Paul Ekman and Wallace V. Friesen call **affect displays** are given to an audience through the face; audience members scan your face to see how you feel about yourself and how you feel about them.[14] In addition, facial details cue listeners into specific interpretations of the *content* of your message: are you being ironic or satirical? How sure are you of your conclusions? Is this a harsh or pleasant message? Are you having fun with these ideas, or do they bore you silly? From your own expressing, you know that the face is an important component in expressing an emotional state to listeners.

In communicating emotion and other attributes, you can use facial expression to establish a visual bond with an audience. The speaker who looks down at the floor, who reads excessively from notes or a manuscript, or who delivers a speech to the back wall has severed **visual bonding.** Our culture, as well as others, values and expects eye-to-eye contact as a sign that a speaker is earnest, sincere, forthright, self-assured, and professional. In essence, regular eye contact is an essential means of establishing credibility with an audience.[15]

While you cannot control your facial reactions or expressions completely, you can make sure that your facial messages don't belie your verbal ones. In practical terms, this means that when you're expressing anger, your face should be communicating anger; when you're expressing delight, your face should convey pleasure; and when you're pleading with an audience, your face should convey determination. Otherwise, you'll confuse your audience and they'll doubt your sincerity.

Gestures.   **Gestures** are purposeful movements of the head, shoulders, arms, hands, or other areas of the body. They support and illustrate the ideas you're expressing. Fidgeting with your clothes, a pencil you brought to the lectern, or clutching the sides of the lectern are examples of non-purposeful movement that distracts from any gestures you might use, to say nothing of other physical movements. The effective public speaker commonly uses three kinds of gestures.

1. *Conventional Gestures.* Physical movements that follow the dictates of conventional or customary behavior have specific symbolic meanings for your audience. These gestures condense ideas because they're shorthand movements for what would take many more words to convey. The raised-hand "stop" gesture of the police officer directing traffic, the sign language of deaf persons, and the arm signals of football referees are examples of conventional gestures.

2. *Descriptive Gestures.* Physical movements that depict the size, shape, or location of an object help the audience comprehend what's being discussed or explained. Such gestures draw pictures for audiences. A speaker might use thumb and fingers to describe an "O" ring of the Challenger space shuttle or raise one arm to indicate the height of a stranger.

3. *Indicators.* Throwing up arms to indicate disgust, pounding the lectern to communicate anger, shrugging shoulders to indicate puzzlement, or pointing a finger in issuing a warning are all examples of gestures as indicators. Such gestures encourage listeners' feelings through arousal as they convey a state of mind and simultaneously urge similar responses from them. Your facial expression and other body cues usually reinforce such gestures.[16]

Nonverbal behaviors play an important role in effective oral communication. Facial expressions and gestures, for instance, convey cues to help listeners interpret the contents of a message.

Characteristics of Effective Gestures.   Many of the above gestures are ones you already know, are well practiced at using, and you know when and where they're expected. You will, however, need to consider which gestures will clarify and add interest to your presentation. Four characteristics that will help you evaluate the role of gestures are (1) relaxation, (2) vigor and definitiveness, (3) proper timing, and (4) appropriateness.

Relaxation.   If your muscles are tense, your movements will be correspondingly tight and stiff, and any gesturing you do will seem awkward and probably ill-timed as well. You should make a conscious effort to relax your muscles before you start to speak. You might "warm up" by taking a few unobtrusive steps, by rearranging your notes, or even by breathing deeply.

Vigor and Definitiveness. Good gestures are lively, vigorous, and definite. They communicate dynamism, matching your vocal energy. By putting enough force into your gestures to illustrate your conviction and enthusiasm, you can help support an assessment that you are a credible, sincere speaker. Furthermore, by matching the gestures to the importance of the ideas, and using them purposefully, you can avoid seeming ill-prepared. Exaggerated or overused repetitive gestures do little to help distinguish ideas.

Timing. The proper time to employ a gesture is when the idea is spoken. The stroke of a gesture—the shake of a fist, movement of a finger or of the hand—should fall exactly on, or slightly precede, the point the gesture is designed to emphasize. Improper timing looks ludicrous; consider how a speaker looks when the gesture comes after the word or phrase it was intended to reinforce.

Appropriateness. Consider your audience in thinking about whether the use of a gesture is "fitting" for a particular occasion. A Portuguese audience, for example, is rather reserved; hence an overly physical speaker would not be received as well as one who matched gestures and physical movement to the audience's natural reserve. A Spanish audience would tend toward the opposite extreme; greater dynamism shown through gestures would be fine. If you know that your audience will be culturally diverse, don't automatically assume that your normal approach would be fitting; check intercultural communication resources to determine what may be appropriate or taboo for different members of the audience.[17]

Nonverbal Channels: Strategic Choices

While complete control of your vocal and bodily behavior is difficult to achieve, and well-nigh impossible to attain at all times, you can learn to orchestrate your voice and movements. While we have treated language, visual aids, voice, and body as discrete channels of communication, in practice they interact together to convey a message. The following suggestions provide an overview of the choices you can make in integrating language and visual aids with body and voice to present a coherent, consistent message to an audience.

1. *Start with yourself.* What kind of person are you? With which kinds of styles and actions are you normally most comfortable? Ask yourself questions about whether you're basically quiet and reserved or excitable and extroverted, whether you enjoy vigorous physical exercise or avoid exertion, whether you talk easily on your feet or prefer to sit while

Facial Expression

A person's facial expression can reveal or conceal attitudes and feelings. This principle was recognized over a century ago by Charles Darwin, whose *The Expression of the Emotions in Man and Animals* (1872) continues to stimulate research. For example, working from Darwin's principles, Paul V. Ekman and his colleagues have developed an entire research program around the analysis of facial movements and their potential communicative value. Their goal was to determine whether facial expressions are universal; that is, whether persons of diverse cultures all identify specific expressions as revealing the same particular emotion.

Three experimental approaches were utilized to test this hypothesis. In one approach, photos displaying six different emotions were shown to subjects. The subjects, from various literate cultures, were asked to identify the emotional state represented in each photo by choosing a term from a list provided by Ekman and his colleagues. In a second

approach, designed to test whether cultures with limited or no contact with Westerners would also identify the same emotional expressions, three photos were given to New Guinea natives. Each subject was told a hypothetical story (e. g., this person has just learned his son has died) and was asked which of the three photos would correspond to the feelings of the person in the story.

The third approach was designed to test whether Westerners could recognize the expression of emotions by non-Westerners. In this case, New Guinean subjects were asked to display specific emotions while being videotaped. In both pre-literate (New Guinea) and literate cultures, Ekman found that *"observers label certain facial expressions of emotion in the same way regardless of culture."* New Guineans, without exposure to Western cultural habits, agreed with their Western counterparts on the identity of several emotions (e.g., happiness, sadness). Similarly, college students without prior knowledge of New Guinean culture

---

talking, whether you're comfortable with broad movements or feel silly shouting at an audience. The point is, you should *not* try to copy a speaker or other person you admire. Even if your personality is similar (and especially if it isn't) you will find that adopting another's behavior or style appears "affected."

You should *not* reach for delivery techniques that are unnatural to your self-image. In our culture, there is a rather broad range of acceptable modes of public speaking, from the energetic, rhythmic delivery patterns of Jesse Jackson to the soothing contemplative delivery patterns

were able to identify certain emotional states represented in the videotapes.

Ekman and his colleagues developed the Facial Action Scoring Technique (FAST) to discriminate between and among various facial expressions. The technique is based on photos representing different expressions in three areas of the face: brows/forehead, eyes/eyelids, and lower face (mouth, chin). To obtain a score, coders view tapes of facial expressions (isolated by facial area), and code them according to their "fit" with a set of criterion photos demonstrating various poses.

FAST and other coding techniques have led to more specific studies of facial expression. For example, studies have isolated which areas of the face reveal which emotional states. Fear and sadness are shown, and recognized, from an analysis of the eyes and eyelids; surprise, on the other hand, is best determined by an analysis of the mouth region of the face. Studies also have linked the detection of deception to changes in facial expression. Deception may be the result of masking one's true feelings in a situation where revealing them is inappropriate ("put on a happy face") or may be the result of deliberate attempts to lie. You may have noticed that even though a person says "I'm not angry," the eyes may tell another story, revealing a state of anger that the words deny.

This research is applicable to your own speaking situation, because knowing the relationship between "face" and "emotion" helps you interpret the facial expressions of audience members. The ability to detect such emotional responses as happiness, surprise, fear, sadness, anger, disgust, and interest provides you with a more accurate assessment of your audience's reception of the message.

FOR FURTHER READING

Cody, Michael J. and H. Dan O'Hair. "Nonverbal Communication and Deception: Differences in Deception Cues Due to Gender and Communicator Dominance," *Communication Monographs*, 50 (1983): 175–92. Ekman, Paul, ed. *Emotion in the Human Face*, 2nd. ed. (Cambridge: Cambridge University Press, 1982). Ekman, Paul. *Telling Lies* (New York: W. W. Norton Company, 1985). Ekman, Paul, et al. "Universals and Cultural Differences in the Judgments of Facial Expression of Emotion," *Journal of Personal and Social Psychology*, 53 (1987): 712–17. McDermott, Jeanne, "Face to Face, It's the Expression that Bears the Message," *Smithsonian*, 16 (1986): 112–23. Matsumoto, David, "Cultural Influences on Facial Expressions of Emotion," *The Southern Communication Journal*, 56 (1991): 128–37.

of Barbara Walters. Do not model yourself on someone else; learn instead to work publicly with the qualities of the person you really are.

2. *Within the constraints of the audience and the occasion, plan a proxemic relationship with your audience that reflects your own needs and attitudes toward your subject and listeners.* If you feel more at home behind the lectern, plan to have it placed accordingly. If you want your whole body visible to the audience yet feel the need to have notes at eye level, stand beside the lectern and arrange your cards on it. If you want

to relax your body, and are sure you can compensate for the loss of action through increased vocal energy, sit behind a table or desk. If you feel physically free and want to be wholly "open" to your audience, stand in front of a table or desk. As far as possible, make the physical arrangements and distance to the audience work for you.

3. *The farther from your listeners, the more important it is for them to have a clear view of you.* The speaker who crouches behind a lectern in an auditorium of 600 people soon loses contact with them. The farther away your audience is, especially in situations where you can do little to decrease the distance, the harder you must work to project your voice and body outward: a louder than normal voice and broader, more expansive gestures and other physical movements will make it easier for audience members to see how your physical actions supplement your speech. Think about large lecture classes you have attended or political rallies you have observed. Recall delivery patterns of speakers that worked well in such situations; select and adapt those that will work comfortably for you.

4. *Insofar as practical, adapt the physical setting to the visual aids you plan to use.* If you're going to use such visual aids as a chalkboard, flipchart, working model, or process diagram, remove any objects, such as the tables and chairs, that would obstruct the listeners' view insofar as possible. If it isn't easy to remove obstacles, you might ask the audience members who can't see your aids to move to another part of the room. In many cases, it's better to acknowledge such logistical difficulties and give audience members a chance to move than to plunge ahead as though the obstacles were unimportant.

5. *Adapt the size of your gestures, the amount of your movement, and the volume of your voice to the size of the audience.* Keep in mind what Edward Hall said about distance. You should realize that subtle changes in facial expressions, small movements of your fingers, and small changes in vocal characteristics cannot be detected when you're standing twenty-five feet or more away from your audience.

6. *Continuously scan your audience from side to side and from front to back, looking specific individuals in the eye.* Continuous doesn't mean constant motion, giving the impression of a "swivelhead." Rather, it means that you must be aware, and let listeners know you're aware, of the entire group that is in front of you. Take them all into your field of vision periodically, especially those that sit on the outer edges closer to you, outside your normal field of vision. At times, physical arrangements may make this awkward; a group may ask you to speak and provide less than ideal conditions for maintaining contact, such as speaking with some persons actually behind you. In such situations, the best you can do is to either turn away from some to "check in" with those behind you, or suggest that those behind you might physically

move chairs to a more visually comfortable position. Recognizing audience members by looking directly at them helps you establish a visual bond and helps keep their attention from wandering. Direct contact also enhances your credibility.

7. *Use your body to communicate your feelings about what you are saying.* When you're angry, don't be afraid to gesture vigorously (provided that the audience will not be unduly offended by your anger or your animated action). When you express tenderness, let your face show how you feel; a tightly contorted face would not fit the mood, but a relaxed, smiling one would. By using the same emotional indicators you would on a one-to-one basis with the same group of listeners, you'll find it easier to create a conversational atmosphere.

8. *Use your body to regulate the pace of your presentation and to control transactions.* Shift your weight, or move from one side of the lectern to another to convey transitions between ideas. Move more when speaking at a faster rate; move less when the occasion requires a serious, reflective mood. By orchestrating voice and movement together with the content, you'll convey more accurately and more forcefully the precise meaning you want to get across to the audience.

9. *Adjust both vocal characteristics and head movements when you must use a microphone.* When you find yourself in a situation where you'll use a microphone, there are several things to consider. The mike tends to "explode" certain sounds if you're too close, and won't pick up others when you're too far away. Given the variety and sophistication of microphones and sound systems, check to see if you can experiment prior to the speaking occasion—a sound system check, with someone in the back of the room, will help you adapt during the actual speaking encounter. If that isn't possible, testing the microphone for a moment before you begin is an acceptable alternative. Ask the audience if they can hear and understand you before getting into your opening remarks. There are additional guidelines for using a mike:

   - Practice with mikes on your own to become more comfortable holding them and gauging the possible distance at which you can speak effortlessly yet clearly.
   - Use a slower rate when using a public address system. You'll get used to the echo effect as your first two words will have reverberated before you say the next two.
   - Remember to decrease your volume and to minimize variations in volume. Think of speaking into a microphone as speaking at an intimate distance—five or six inches from someone's face. At that distance, you talk more softly than in normal conversation, and you usually don't vary your volume as much. By using this approach you'll avoid suddenly "blasting" the audience with a voice that's louder than usual.

- Likewise, pay attention to enunciation and pronunciation. If you're normally "lip lazy," form words more carefully into a mike. If you normally "pop your plosives"—hit your *p's* and *b's* harder than others—hold back. If you forget, the mike's popping sounds will quickly remind you to smooth out your delivery.

10. *Finally, use your full repertoire of descriptive and regulative gestures while talking publicly.* Strive to recreate the same approach you use in talking normally. If you're naturally animated when talking to friends, carry that same behavior over into the speaking situation, adapting as needed to fit the occasion and subject. Let your hands rest comfortably at your sides, relaxed but ready to use. Occasionally, rest them on the lectern. If you put them in your pockets, behind your back, or cross them in front of you, you'll make it difficult to use them promptly and efficiently. Use descriptive gestures to indicate size, shape, or relationship; use conventional gestures to give visual dimension to your ideas. There is no "right number" of gestures to use; rather, their relationship to the ideas and regulative flow of your speech should be natural and easy to comprehend.

Selecting the appropriate method of presentation and using your voice and body productively enhances your chances of gaining support for your ideas. Practice is a key element. Through practice you can evaluate vocal changes and bodily movements and decide which work best for you in complementing your ideas. The more confident you become in getting ready to speak, the more naturally and comfortably your ideas will flow, once you get started. The nonverbal channel supplements the verbal in clarifying and supporting your ideas.

Chapter Summary

Every speaker should effectively use the *aural* and *visual channels* of communication. The voice, when used well, enables a speaker to convey a clear and compelling message. A flexible speaking voice has *intelligibility, variety*, and understandable *stress patterns*. *Loudness, rate, enunciation*, and *pronunciation* create regional speech differences known as *dialects*. Changing *rate, pitch, stress*, and *pauses* influence an audience's involvement with the presentation and help eliminate monotonous delivery. *Emotional characterizers* communicate shades of emotional meaning to listeners.

Physical movements complement vocal quality to add clarity to the message. Speakers can use space, or *proxemics*, to create physical and psychological intimacy or distance. *Movement* and *stance* regulate communication. *Facial expressions* communicate feelings and provide important clues to meaning. *Eye contact* establishes visual bonding with listeners, making them feel a part of the communication situation. *Gestures* enhance listener responses to messages, if those gestures are relaxed, definite, and properly timed.

Vocal and physical behaviors need to be adapted to the personality of the speaker, the occasion, and the audience. In particular, speakers need to consider the expectations of the audience, including how cultural diversity affects the reception of particular behaviors. Your credibility as a speaker, as well as the credibility of your message, depends in part on how well you integrate appropriate vocal and physical behaviors and the content of your message.

References

1. R. Geiselman and John Crawley, "Incidental Processing of Speaker Characteristics: Voice as Connotative Information," *Journal of Verbal Learning and Verbal Behavior*, 22 (1983): 15–23.

2. W. Barnett Pearce and Bernard J. Brommel, "Vocalic Communication in Persuasion," *Quarterly Journal of Speech*, 58 (1972): 298–306. Thomas Frentz, "Rhetorical Conversation, Time, and Moral Action," *Quarterly Journal of Speech*, 71 (1985): 1–18.

3. Mark L. Knapp, *Essentials of Nonverbal Communication* (New York: Holt, 1980).

4. Klaus R. Scherer, H. London, and Garret Wolf, "The Voice of Competence: Paralinguistic Cues and Audience Evaluation," *Journal of Research in Personality*, 7 (1973): 31–44; Jitendra Thakerer and Howard Giles, "They Are—So They Spoke: Noncontent Speech Stereotypes," *Language and Communication*, 1 (1981): 255–61.

5. For an excellent analysis of the function of silence, see Peter Ehrenhaus, "Silence and Symbolic Expression," *Communication Monographs*, 55 (1988): 41–57.

6. Bruce L. Brown, William J. Strong, and Alvin C. Rencher, "Perceptions of Personality from Speech: Effects of Manipulations of Acoustical Parameters," *Journal of the Acoustical Society of America*, 54 (1973): 29–35.

7. For recent research on nonverbal communication, see J. DeVito and M. Hecht, *The Nonverbal Communication Reader* (Prospect Heights, IL: Waveland Press, 1990); M. L. Hickson and D. W. Stacks, *Nonverbal Communication: Studies and Applications*, 2nd ed. (Dubuque, IA: Wm. C. Brown, 1989); J. Burgoon and T. Saine, *Nonverbal Communication: The Unspoken Dialogue* (New York: HarperCollins Publishers, 1990).

8. Larry M. Barna, "Stumbling Blocks in Intercultural Communication," in Larry A. Samovar and Richard E. Porter, eds., *Intercultural Communications: A Reader*, 6th ed. (Belmont, CA: Wadsworth, 1991), 345–52.

9. Richard E. Porter and Larry A. Samovar, "Basic Principles of Intercultural Communications," in *Intercultural Communication: A Reader*, 20.

10. For a fuller discussion of each of these components, see Burgoon and Saine.

11. See Edward T. Hall, *The Hidden Dimension* (New York: Doubleday, 1969), Chapter 10. For a concise critique of Hall's theory, see Carol Zinner Dolphin, "Variables in the Use of Personal Space in Intercultural Transactions," in *Intercultural Communication: A Reader*, 320–31.

12. For a discussion geared to communication in organizational contexts, see William V. Ruch, *International Handbook of Corporate Communication* (Jefferson, NC: McFarland, 1989). Also see Dolphin.

13. Albert E. Scheflen, "The Significance of Posture in Communication Systems," *Psychiatry*, 27 (1964): 321.

14. Paul Ekman, *Emotion in the Human Face*, 2nd ed. (Cambridge: Cambridge University Press, 1982).

15. For a difficult but rewarding analysis of the management of demeanor, see Erving Goffman, *Interaction Ritual: Essays on Face-to-Face Behavior* (New York: Doubleday, 1967), 5–46. For the importance of eye contact in intercultural communication, see William V. Ruch, *International Handbook of Corporate Communication.*

16. For a more complete system of classifying gestures, see Paul Ekman and Wallace V. Friesen, "Hand Movements," *Journal of Communication*, 22 (1972): 360.

17. For an excellent introduction to what may be appropriate or offensive, see William V. Ruch, *International Handbook of Corporate Communications.*

Key Terms

affect displays (p. 364)

conventional gestures (p. 365)

conversationality (p. 352)

descriptive gestures (p. 365)

dialects (p. 356)

emotional characterizers (p. 360)

emphasis (p. 357)

enunciation (p. 355)

gestures (p. 365)

indicators (p. 365)

movement (p. 364)

pauses (p. 358)

pitch (p. 356)

pitch level (p. 356)

pitch range (p. 357)

pitch variation (p. 357)

pronunciation (p. 356)

proxemics (p. 361)

rate (p. 355)

stance (posture) (p. 364)

stress (p. 357)

visual bonding (p. 365)

vocal quality (p. 352)

Problems and Probes

1. The instructor will divide the class into small groups. Given the physical constraints of your classroom (size, furniture, etc.), each group will design a speaker-audience configuration that differs from the traditional arrangement of chairs and lectern or table. A representative from each group will explain his or

her group's alternative room arrangement. The class then will discuss the pros and cons of the different suggestions in terms of the effective use of space.

2. The instructor will divide the class into small groups. Each group will be given an excerpt from a speech, a play, or a short piece of fiction (selected by the instructor). In working on an oral presentation of the material, each group will be assigned to implement a different facet of vocal presentation (rate, pitch, stress; different dialects; expanded gestures and physical movement). After a representative of each group presents his or her group's "rendition" of the material to the class, the class as a whole will discuss the influence of shifts in vocal presentation on the impact or meaning of the material.

Communication Activities

1. Present a two-to-three minute speech in which you need to work with the chalkboard or use your hands and body to illustrate an action or technique (clear any visual aids or materials with your instructor in advance).

2. Prepare and present a speech that's designed to get an audience to share in your excitement about an event, experience, or challenging task. Integrate vocal energy and variations with appropriate physical movement to convey your sense of excitement. Your goal is to make the audience "see" and "feel" the subject of your speech as intensely as you do.

3. Using a Dr. Suess book, assign different members of a small group various roles or sections; present an excerpt from the book. Emphasize variations in vocal stress, pitch, rate, etc.

PART FOUR

TYPES

"*All the ends of speaking are reducible to four; every speech being intended to enlighten the understanding, to please the imagination, to move the passion, or to influence the will. Any one discourse admits only one of these ends as the principle.*"

George Campbell
The Philosophy of Rhetoric (1776)

15

SPEECHES TO INFORM

In the electronic age, a staggering amount of information is literally at our fingertips. Keying appropriate terms into any one of several electronic databases such as Compuserve or Prodigy accesses encyclopedias, current events, sports, and numerous networks devoted to special interests. Pure information rarely, if ever, signifies its own importance or meaning; it requires human beings to shape, explain, interpret, and act on it. In other words, *mere information is useless until someone puts it together in ways to make it clear and relevant to the lives of others.* One means of conveying information in understandable terms is through public communication; speakers sift through the available information, interpret its likely meaning and significance, and assemble it into a readily comprehensible package for public consumption.

This chapter will focus on the essential features of all informative speeches, then discuss the various types of informative speeches and the standard ways each can be organized.

Essential Features of Informative Speeches

To achieve their goals, informative speeches must contain these essential characteristics: clarity, association of new ideas with old ones, coherence, and motivational appeal.

Clarity

Maximum **clarity** is achieved when the message is easy to follow and the language is easy to comprehend. These two qualities can be achieved by paying close attention to guidelines concerning organization and style:

Organization. There are three basic rules for organizing an informative speech:

1. *Don't try to cover too many points.* Confine the speech to three or four principal ideas, with facts and ideas grouped under each of these main heads. Even if you know a great deal more, you will find it necessary to select that which is most relevant and essential in order to limit your remarks to the time allotted.

2. *Clarify the relationship between your main points by observing the principles of coordination.* Carefully worded transitions help your audience follow your message: "*Second,* you must prepare a concise statement of your educational goals as part of your application." "The verdict of the first trial about the Rodney King beating was *followed by* widespread rioting in Los Angeles." "*Even more critical* than the Stamp Act Crisis just mentioned were the Townshend Duties." "*Before concluding,* I want to briefly mention one last issue for your consideration." Such transitional statements allow listeners to follow you from point to point and to discern relationships between points.

3. *Keep your speech moving forward according to a well-developed plan.* Do not jump back and forth between ideas, charging ahead and then backtracking.

Style. The guidelines for general style follow those discussed in earlier chapters:

1. *Use a precise, accurate vocabulary without getting too technical.* Consider two means of conveying information about finishing off a room after the walls were panelled:

   a. "You take these here long sticks and cut them off at angles in this box with a saw attached. Just make sure the corners match."

   b. "This piece is ceiling molding; it goes around the room between the wall and the ceiling to cover the open seams between the paneling and the ceiling tiles. You can easily make the corners of the molding match by using a mitre box, which has grooves that allow you to cut 45-degree angles. Assuming the length is, let's say 120", I can show you how easy it is to do it yourself."

Televised Information

Public-speaking textbooks discuss the importance of shaping and interpreting information so that listeners are given not only the facts but also ways to understand them. In public speaking, the shaping and interpreting processes occur in words, in things you say about facts or ideas. In the case of television news, however, meaning is also communicated in other ways, a fact that bothers critic and communications scholar Neil Postman of New York University. His 1985 book *Amusing Ourselves to Death* expresses his concerns about televisual discourse and the meanings it makes for us.

Postman calls the eighteenth century the Age of Exposition. That century witnessed the peak of printing's power. The printed word, in the forms of books, newspapers, pamphlets, and political broadsides, surrounded the citizens of the western world. Print taught people to read ideas one at a time, to link them together with the kinds of verbal transitions discussed in Chapter 12, and even to criticize each other in logical and relevant ways.

Postman terms the twentieth century, however, the Age of Show Business. With the advent and dominance of television in our lives, according to Postman, information and ideas come to us chopped into little pieces, into the sound bites and video clips of televised news. The average length of a network television shot is 3.5

In this illustration, **a** is a decidedly inferior explanation; **b**, on the other hand, contains some technical terms, but the speaker uses them in a context that makes them clear to the listener. Most audiences want to know the correct terminology for handling tasks; they don't wish to have a speaker convey information that's imprecise or incomplete since, if they follow the information, they may find themselves embarrassed by their lack of knowledge.

2. *Simplify when possible, including only as much technical vocabulary as you need.* In the above illustration, it may not be necessary to go into a longer explanation of the different types of molding and their names. If you're a computer expert, talking to an audience of generalists in the language of experts may not be helpful. Balance the technical terms with clear definitions and explanations so that the audience has a chance to understand without being overwhelmed.

seconds; the average length of network news stories is 45 seconds. When continuing stories, such as a presidential campaign, are involved, as Professor Kathleen Jamieson of the University of Texas-Austin noted at the 1988 Speech Communication Association convention, coverage of a particular candidate's activities is closer to 18 seconds a night.

Postman argues that all of this leads to a "peek-a-boo world," in which information pours down upon us in extremely small units, in which discontinuity rather than coherence and continuity is a fact of life (with television's main transition being "And now . . . this"), and in which the credibility of the information giver is more important than reason or logic. Reminding us that people often pointed out contradictions between what then-President Ronald Reagan said from one day to the next, Postman notes that Reagan's illogic did not really bother the American people very much because they have become conditioned to absorb information in unconnected bits. They really didn't notice.

In one sense, then, Postman's research suggests that we may be swimming upstream in our battle to demand of public speakers logical coherence—carefully described and explicitly interpreted ideas. Should we then give up the fight to improve public communication? That view is too cynical. Better is Postman's own effort: to return in face-in-face speaking situations to older practices, where people spoke to each other via well-chosen words with clear and adequate information appropriately interpreted for five, ten, or twenty minutes at a time. While the speed and razzmatazz of MTV is entertaining, it should not be mistaken for informative communication.

FOR FURTHER READING

Postman, Neil. *Amusing Ourselves to Death: Public Discourse in the Age of Show Business.* New York: Penguin Books, 1985.

3. *Use reiteration when it clarifies complex ideas, but avoid simply repeating the same words.* Rephrasing helps solidify ideas for those who may be hearing them for the first time: "Unlike a terrestrial telescope, a celestial telescope is used for looking at the moon, planets, and stars; that is, its mirrors and lens are ground and arranged in such a way that it focuses on objects thousands of miles, not hundreds of feet, away from the observer."

Adherence to these guidelines, in addition to following the suggestions presented in Chapters 8, 9, 11, and 12, will help you present ideas in a clear, comprehensible, coherent manner.

Association of New Ideas with Familiar Ones

Audiences grasp new facts and ideas more readily when they can associate them with what they already know. Therefore, in a speech to inform, try to

ASSOCIATION OF NEW IDEAS
WITH FAMILIAR ONES

Snail Shell
(Single Unit)

House
(Single Unit)

Honeycomb
(Multi-Unit)

Condominium
(Multi-Unit)

connect the new with the old. Determining the kinds of connections that will work depends on a close analysis of the audience. Their prior experiences and knowledge will help you determine what images, experiences, analogies, and metaphors to use in your speech. You also may have to discuss the background and experiences of the audience with someone who knows more about their characteristics.

At times, the connections will be obvious. A college dean talking to an audience of manufacturers on the problems on higher education might present her ideas under the headings of raw materials, casting, machining, polishing, and assembling. She thus translates her central ideas into an analogy that these particular listeners are sure to grasp and appreciate. On occasion, however, you may need to rely on more common experiences to relate new ideas. For example, you might explain the operation of the human eye pupil by comparing it to the operation of a camera lens aperture.

Coherence

Coherence depends in part on clear and effective organization—using a pattern that fits your ideas together into a meaningful whole. Sometimes it's relatively easy to convey the sense of coherence, as when giving a speech on the nature of the different colleges within a university or when giving one on the structure of the federal government—there are only a certain number of items to cover.

At other times, you'll have to illustrate comprehensiveness and relationships between parts in other ways. Some of these may suggest themselves as you engage in further research; for example, you could discover differences in terms of size, rank order of importance, or location that will begin to order the main points. Other ways will depend on your inventiveness. For example, if you were to explain the Nielsen television program rating system, you might discuss only three aspects of the system: what it is, how it works, and how it is used to determine which programs continue or are canceled. To give the speech an extra measure of coherence, you could use a question-answer organizational approach within the body of the speech:

> People who worry about the effect of the Nielsen ratings on what they watch usually ask three questions: "What *is* a Nielsen rating?" "How is the rating done?" and "Why do the networks rely on it for making their decisions on shows?" To answer these common questions in explaining the "what," "how," and "why" of TV ratings, I will. . . .

Notice that the speaker used a common trio of words—what-how-why—in forecasting what would be covered.

Coherence depends in part on the perception of completeness—that a subject has been discussed in a holistic fashion. Unfortunately, it's difficult to do justice to many subjects in the time you have to speak. You can still achieve coherence in these instances by acknowledging that the speech is not an exhaustive account, but that within its boundaries, you will cover the issues most critical or those of greatest interest to the audience. Justifying your approach will help the audience place your perspective into a broader context.

Motivational Appeals

Motivating your audience to listen is normally thought of in terms of persuasive speeches. Nevertheless, there is a positive role for **motivational appeals** in informative settings. Blithely assuming that because you're interested in an event, group, project or task does *not* necessarily mean everyone else is, or that they want to hear about it. To you, having a pet boa constrictor may be the most natural kind of pet to own; after all, they don't bark, ruin the couch, and only eat once a month. However, until your listeners are convinced that an informative speech on owning a snake is vital to their own lives, they may be unwilling to even entertain the topic, much less the actual purchase. Likewise, a speech on Lichtenstein may be of vital interest to you, but it may be a "yawner" to your audience.

Types of Informative Speeches

The format of an informative presentation will depend, in large part, on four things: the nature of the situation, the level of knowledge and the expectations of the audience, and your expertise in assembling and interpreting the relevant information. While the format will vary considerably as a result of these considerations, there are four general types into which most informational presentations will fit: definitional speeches, explanatory speeches, instructional speeches, and oral briefings. These four represent common ways in which people package or integrate information to meet the needs of others. As each is discussed, guidelines for organizing and sample outlines will be presented.

Definitional Speeches

Curiosity and a "need to know" drive the concern for messages that define, clarify, and otherwise make useful information that we don't understand or haven't had the opportunity to check out for ourselves. The curious person may simply want to know "What is a CD-ROM?" or "What is meant by the expression, 'e-mail?'" That same person will be driven by a more specific need if he or she will use the information to evaluate products on the market for an employer.

In both cases, a limited dictionary definition probably will not suffice—while it may clarify and explain, it does little more. In contrast, the **definitional speech** *defines concepts or processes in ways that make them relevant to the situation or problem the audience faces.* A speech on CD-ROMs would go beyond a specific definition into its potential applications, cost factors, and future prospects. In the same way, a speech on e-mail wouldn't stop with a definition of electronic mail.

In the process of explaining, the definitional speech will have two characteristics. First, it will present a *vocabulary* ("CD-ROM," "electronic mail") for dealing with the objects, people, and processes under consideration. Second, it will provide an *orientation* or way of thinking about the information. The orientation (or in contemporary political language, "spin,") will depend in large part on how the speaker has selected and shaped the information to be presented. Assuming an objective and fair stance on CD-ROMs or e-mail, you would be provided with the information you need to understand the term and to react toward it in the future, based on your own needs and interests. Your aim as a speaker is to package information into a coherent whole; your aim as a listener is to gain an understanding and a way of thinking about the information that assists you in making decisions.

Structuring the Definitional Speech. Speeches of definition aren't difficult to organize; however, because of their narrow focus they pose greater challenges in engaging audiences psychologically.

Introduction. Because speeches of definition treat either unfamiliar or familiar concepts in a new light, their introductions must create curiosity and need in listeners. Creating curiosity is a special challenge in speeches on unfamiliar concepts, for we all are tempted to say, "Well, if I've made it this far without knowing what black holes are, why dark matter is important, or why studying astronomy is beneficial, why start now?" The answer, to a large extent, depends on your ability to make people wonder about the unknown. Creating a sense of wonder may be a way to engage the audience, to get them asking not "Why should I listen?" but saying "Ok, tell me more."

Speeches on both unfamiliar and familiar concepts must be attentive to listeners' needs and wants. Include specific motivational appeals in your informative speech: "Watching a collegiate basketball game is a lot more fun if you know what's going on. Knowing the difference between man-to-man defense and a zone defense and how they're used increases your enjoyment of the game. You also gain a greater appreciation of the skill it takes to play the game at the collegiate level." This offers a specific rationale for an audience member to be drawn into the subject, at least long enough to hear what else you have to say.

Body. Most speeches of definition use a topical pattern (see Chapter 9) because such speeches usually describe various aspects of a thing or an idea. It seems natural, for example, to use a topical pattern when giving a speech on computer programming as a career option: duties, skills, and training required are three topics that are appropriate to cover in this kind of speech.

Other patterns may also serve your specific purpose well. For example, you might use an effect-cause pattern, and incorporate an analogy to discuss the principle of diminishing marginal returns: the audience may be familiar with the diminishing effect of higher grades on their academic average as they move through the college experience. Even though they work harder, later grades have less impact on their actual average. Once they understand the effect, you can go on to relate that to the principle and illustrate how and why it occurs.

Review the following outline for a speech on cancer, paying particular attention to how the introduction and body are organized.[1]

What Does Cancer Mean?

I. "You have cancer" is a phrase that can strike fear into the hardiest among us. Fear of the unknown is the most difficult to accept. Thus, if we are to understand cancer, we must know more about what the term means.
   A. My intent is to acquaint you with several terms that, together, will give us a better understanding of cancer.
   B. I will review a common process whereby cancer cells form tumors in your body.
II. There are several terms used in the scientific discussion of cancer. Not all are clearly understood.
   A. "Carcinogen": Chemicals, viruses, and physical events (such as exposure to ultraviolet rays) may lead to cancer.

    B. "Activation": The carcinogen must be chemically changed in order to start the malignant process.

    C. "Detoxification enzymes": These are naturally occurring chemicals in the body that detoxify—take the poison out of substances ingested into the body.

        1. Most carcinogens entering the body are detoxified and can cause no harm.

        2. In some cases, the detoxification process goes wrong, and the carcinogen is rendered capable of entering a cell's nucleus and attaching itself to DNA.

    D. "DNA attachment": The DNA is the central code that determines the function of the cell, the central operating system of the human computer.

        1. The second line of defense occurs when scavenger molecules attack the activated carcinogen and render it harmless.

        2. DNA has a third line of defense, as invading activated carcinogens can be isolated by DNA repair molecules.

        3. Unfortunately, these lines of defense can also fail.

    E. "Cell mutation and division": Remember your junior-high biology? Cells divide and create exact replicas.

        1. If the defenses have failed, an active carcinogen is attached to DNA inside a cell.

        2. Cell division will produce two new cells with the carcinogen-affected DNA.

    F. "Promoter chemicals": These are chemicals near the mutated cell that foster its multiplication, to the detriment of other nonmutants nearby.

        1. The mutant cell may also be attacked by a second carcinogen.

        2. If all of the defenses fail again, a second mutation occurs.

        3. After several cycles of mutation and promotion, a group of cells may begin to form a tumor.

III. I hope this review of the major terms and their meanings gives you a better understanding of the process produced "cancer."

Conclusion. Conclusions for speeches of definition frequently include a concise summary and a sense of how your listeners can apply the ideas. For example, a speech on the use of a stairmaster could conclude with a review of the vocabulary used in describing it and how you want them to think about this as a form of exercise. The key element is to signal the end and to give the audience an appreciation of the important items covered instead of simply stopping.

Instructional Speeches

The sign "THIS IS NOT YOUR REAL LIFE; IF IT WERE YOU WOULD HAVE BEEN GIVEN BETTER INSTRUCTIONS" testifies to the impact of instructions in our daily affairs. Almost daily, you're the recipient of instructions—in the classroom, at a job, purchasing a new product—that are designed to make your life easier. In addition to giving instructions to someone about how a product works, what tasks to complete in a specific order in a chemistry class, or how to connect into a new computerized database at work, people also show or demonstrate processes or tasks involved. An **instructional speech** offers a verbal explanation of a complex process; a **demonstration speech** goes further by providing a visual dimension, illustrating the actual product or process for the audience. To clarify the process, both use visual aids—pictures, graphs, charts, or overheads.

Speeches utilizing instruction alone or coupled with demonstration have two essential features. First, they involve the *serial presentation of information*, usually in clearly defined steps or phases. Such speeches normally are organized, therefore, in chronological or spatial patterns. Second, they demand *absolute clarity*, simply because listeners are expected to repeat or reproduce the steps through which you take them. Whether you need to add a *demonstrative* component will depend on the seriousness of the task, its complexity, and the amount of time you've been allotted. Offering training tips to an audience at a dog obedience class, for example, would be far easier with a dog that responds to the verbal or visual commands you're discussing. Just talking it through may not be as interesting or as informative. While pictures of "before" and "after" help explain how effective a particular process is, actually performing some of the tasks during the speech to show how the results are obtained may be far clearer to the audience.

Structuring Instructional Speeches.   While the organizational facet of instructional speeches is fairly easy, the main challenge lies in integrating your speech within the physical demands of the setting.

Introduction.   Unlike with definitional speeches, you generally won't have to deal with engaging your audience's willingness to listen. The reason why audiences need to listen is usually clear in the context of the situation. For example, if you're giving a workshop on how to fill out a 1040 tax form or how to build an ice boat, listeners already have the prerequisite interest in the issue. Otherwise, they wouldn't have come to hear you. In some cases, such as giving instructions to mid-level managers on how to make the most use of their new electronic mail capabilities or in situations where the audience isn't there voluntarily (such as a speech classroom), you may have to pay closer attention to motivational issues. In the first case, listeners may be reluctant to learn the newest applications; in the latter case, the atmosphere is more artificial than in other contexts. Normally, however, you'll need to concentrate on previewing the speech and on encouraging attention throughout:

1. *Preview your speech before getting down to specifics.* If you are going to take an audience through the 10 steps involved in e-mail log-in and file transfers, give them an overall picture of the process before getting into step one.

2. *Encourage them to follow along, even through some of the more difficult steps.* The steps involved in e-mail may seem simple enough at the

Informative speeches take many forms. A speech of definition seeks to define concepts and processes in ways that make them relevant to a situation or problem. Instructions are verbal communications that explain complex processes, whereas demonstrations are verbal and nonverbal messages explaining and illustrating such processes. In an oral report, a speaker assembles, arranges, and interprets information in response to a request by a group. Finally, an explanatory speech is one in which the speaker either clarifies a concept, process, object, or proposal or offers a supporting rationale for a contestable claim.

outset, but it may be hard to follow the correct command sequence especially for an audience not used to working with computers. By using a handout that lists all of the commands in their proper sequence, and by demonstrating the process at each stage, you can encourage an audience to stay with you through the full sequence of steps.

Body.   As suggested earlier, organize instructional and demonstrative speeches in a chronological and/or spatial pattern. If the process is serial, it makes sense to go through each step in the order it's encountered. Once the organizational pattern is set, it's easier to deal with the more typical prob-

lems associated with this kind of speech: matters relating to rate, scale, and integrating the verbal with the visual:

1. *The problem of rate.* How do you properly demonstrate techniques when the natural sequence takes far more time than the speech allows—glue needs to dry between step one and step two, for example. Two approaches are useful. First, if the time needed is relatively short, you can fill in the period with other material that is of interest to the audience and is pertinent to the process you're explaining. Second, bring samples of the product or process at different stages. Cooking shows, for

example, don't leave you waiting the half hour or hour it takes to cook a crawfish étouffée. Instead, they have precooked a sample at each critical stage of the process, so that you can both see how the dish is developed and what it looks like at the end. To illustrate how to fill holes in an old rusted fender for example, you can bring small samples of the project at critical stages.

2. *The problem of scale.* How do you show audiences how to repair a fender, when the object is both large and heavy? Conversely, how do you show an audience the intricacy of cross-stitch when only those in the front row will be able to see the technique? With large objects, cut them down to a size that is easier to bring to the class or workshop; with small objects, increase the scale in order to make it easier to see the process. With the fender, use a scrap piece that has a rusted hole to be filled in. In demonstrating a particular stitch in cross-stitch, use a larger piece of fabric stretched over a frame, yarn and an oversized needle, and stitches that are in inches instead of millimeters. Using approaches like these will allow you to make a process visible or manageable to all in the audience.

3. *The problem of coordinating the verbal and the visual.* Both instructions and demonstrations involve telling and showing virtually simultaneously. To keep yourself from becoming unglued or confused, practice the speech in advance so you're accustomed to the order of ideas and objects. Decide where to stand when showing a slide so you don't block the audience. If you're using a pointer to indicate certain features on a slide, move in from the side and then move away. If you need to draw on the board, stop talking for a few seconds while you sketch a diagram. If the diagram will take a long time, move back and forth between portions of the diagram and explanations (talking to the blackboard may make it more difficult for the audience to hear you). If you're using physical objects, be sure you are familiar with their use prior to attempting an explanation.

By thinking through technical and procedural issues, you'll be better prepared to deal with structuring and presenting your instructional speech. The following example illustrates how the introduction and body of the speech might be organized in a speech on how to plant tomatoes.

How to Plant Tomatoes

Coordinate verbal and visual materials

I. First, you must select a variety of tomato seed that's suited to various geographical, climatological, agricultural, and personal factors. [*Display chart, showing varieties in columns along with their characteristics.*]

   A. Some tomatoes grow better in hard soils; some in loose soils.

   B. Some varieties handle shade well; some direct sunlight.

   C. Some are well suited to short growing seasons; others to long seasons.

   D. Each variety tends to resist certain diseases, such as blight, better than others.

II. Once you have selected a variety (or maybe even two, so that they mature at different times) you must start the seeds.

Coordinate verbal and visual materials

   A. Prepare a mixture of black dirt, peat moss, and vermiculite as I am doing. [*Do it, indicating proportions.*]

   B. Fill germination trays, pots, or cut-off milk cartons with the germination soil, and insert seeds. [*Do it.*]

Reduce time delay (rate)

   C. With water, sunlight, and patience, your plants will grow. I can't show you that growth here today, but I can use these seedlings to illustrate their care along the way. [*Bring out half-grown and fully grown seedlings.*]

Coordinate verbal and behavioral actions

     1. When the seedlings are about an inch or two tall, thin them. [*Demonstrate.*]

     2. At about six inches [*show them*], you can transplant them safely.

     3. But, you'll know more about which plants are strong if you wait until they are ten to twelve inches tall. [*Show them plants of different strengths.*]

   D. Now you are ready to transplant the seedlings to your garden.

     1. Carefully unpot the seedlings, being sure not to damage the root network [*Demonstrate.*]

Coordinate visual and verbal materials; enlarge materials

     2. Put each seedling in a hole already prepared in your plot; this diagram shows you how to do that. [*Show an enlarged drawing that illustrates hole size and depth, a mixture of peat moss and vermiculite in the bottom, and spacing of plants.*]

     3. Pack the garden soil firmly but not so hard as to crush the roots.

     4. Water it almost every day for the first week.

Coordinate verbal and visual materials; reduce size of materials

     5. Put some sort of mulching material—grass clippings, hay, black sheets of plastic—between the rows if weeds are a problem. [*Another drawing or picture.*]

E.   Once you know your plants are growing, cage or stake each plant. [*Show sketches of various styles of cages or stakes and discuss the advantages of each.*]

Conclusions.   Conclusions for demonstration speeches usually have three parts. First, the instructions are *summarized* in order to enable audiences to pull the individual parts together and think about those things they still don't understand. Second, some *bolstering* needs to take place. People trying their hand at new processes or procedures usually get into trouble the first few times and need to be reassured that, through practice, they'll become proficient. Finally, *future help* should be offered. What sounds simple in a well-ordered and clearly demonstrated presentation may be much more difficult in actual execution by someone not as familiar or as expert in the processes. If possible, note when and under what circumstances you'd be available to offer additional assistance.

Oral Briefings

An **oral briefing** is a speech that assembles, arranges, and interprets information gathered in response to a request from a particular group. Briefings may be designed to bring audience members up-to-date on the status of a project or new product, to preview or propose new initiatives to an audience, and to orient audiences toward the values or customs of others (for example, new employees of a company or a sales team that is traveling to another country).

Depending on the nature of the request and the audience's level of knowledge, the briefing may be *general* or highly *technical.* In the first case, you can rely on personal experience and historical background and description to convey an understanding of the issue being considered. In a situation requiring more technical information, you'll have to consider the level of expertise in the audience and adapt your presentation accordingly. With a relatively unsophisticated audience, your presentation may rely on analogies to events, processes, or products with which they are familiar. In this way, you can move them to an understanding of a new event or product by noting its similarity to others they have experienced. If you're speaking as an engineer to other engineers, your audience expects more technical information. In this case, you'll need to be concerned with precise, specific technical data and with its implications—what does the data mean?[2] In any case, briefings require attention to the concrete and specific—you cannot get by with generalities.

In addition to being general or technical, briefings may be *factual* or *advisory.* The factual briefing concentrates on assembling, arranging, and interpreting raw information; the advisory briefing goes beyond that to make recommendations relative to the information—what should be done as a result of the information.

Briefing audiences requires that you consider your role as an *expert*—as the source of predigested information for a group of people who, in turn, will act on what you have to say. That role carries with it the obligation to prepare with special care and the necessity to present ideas with clarity and balance. The success of a business, the government's legislative program, or a group's future may depend on your ability. Just as important, your job may depend on your ability to meet these demands. The following guidelines will be helpful in ensuring your concentration on the tasks at hand.

1. *The information you present must be researched with great care.* Although you may be asked to present statistical generalizations in only a five-minute report, your research must be extensive and solid. The audience will expect you to have at hand the concrete data on which the generalizations are based, especially if those generalizations are controversial or seem extraordinary. A quarterly report for a business that relies on material gathered from only one of several territories not only is incomplete; the conclusions drawn may be heavily skewed, especially if the territory isn't representative of the company as a whole. Furthermore, the information needs to be balanced and as free of bias as possible. In a business setting, you need to ensure your audience has all of the facts about how sales are going. While concreteness and completeness may suffer in a short presentation, having the appropriate information to back up the speech, and noting your willingness to share it in a question-answer session, is essential.

2. *When making recommendations rather than merely reporting information, be sure to include a complete rationale for the advice you present.* Suppose, for example, that as a wheelchair-bound person, you have been called on to brief your student government on the status of access for the disabled on your campus and to make recommendations on how the assembly can help make the campus more accessible.

   First, you can use your own experience in listing the problems. Second, you will need to gather additional information about the current status of access. How well has the campus met the requirements specified in the recent American Disabilities Act? What plans does the campus have for remedying deficiencies? Beyond physical access, what is being done to ensure transportation? Are there enough volunteers to help students who may need assistance? How aware is the campus of the needs—would it help to have a seminar or awareness day sponsored by student government? How can students help students, either as individuals or through the collective resources of an organization such as student government?

   Beyond gathering information and ideas relevant to a review of the situation and possible recommendations, you should consider a rationale for what is being advised. Why is it necessary to involve student government? What difference can student government make with respect to access for the disabled? If student government were to act as recommended, what other benefits might accrue besides making life on campus better? Would there be more action from other campus officials if the students got involved? In building the rationale, you also need to consider which recommendations are the most feasible, the least costly, the most essential. In ranking the recommendations from short-term–easy-to-enact to long-term–more-difficult-to-enact, you have applied distinct criteria: the time involved (now; later) and the ease with which change can be effected (easy; difficult).

Organizing the recommendations in this way alleviates potential concerns by illustrating, in advance, what can be done and in what order it can be considered. As a wheelchair-bound individual you may have strong credibility, but the audience will also be concerned about your fairness. Thus, it will be important to illustrate, through your information and your recommendations, that you have considered all of the issues in a balanced manner and have arrived at the most judicious recommendations.

3. *Make full use of visual aids when briefing audiences.* Because your speech often is short and to the point, yet contains information that may be complex and new to the audience, it will be to your advantage to use visual aids. Overhead transparencies, large posters with graphs or charts, pictures easily seen by the audience, and other materials will allow you to convey information in fewer words, and hence cover more ground in the presentation. The advice in Chapter 13 on using visual aids is pertinent.

4. *Stay within the boundaries of the charge you are given.* Whether your briefing assignment is general or technical, you're the primary source of information at that moment. Thus, being sensitive to the audience's expectations and needs is essential. What's expected of you in this situation? Were you asked to gather information only, or were you charged with the responsibility of offering recommendations? Does the audience assume that you'll emphasize information from the past, current trends, or future prospects? Are cost implications expected in assessing a proposal?

In most cases, you'll be given a specific task with either explicit or implicit parameters. If you depart too far from that task—if you make recommendations when you're only expected to present data, or the reverse, you're likely to create ill will among your listeners. The audience will concentrate on its disappointment rather than on what has been provided. If you are uncertain about what's expected of your presentation, clarify the boundaries within which you're to operate. In that way, you'll meet the audience's expectations.

Structuring Oral Briefings.   These speeches require more attention to structural considerations than do the other informational speeches.

Introduction. For the most part, you won't have to motivate your audience. In most cases, they already know why you're speaking and are already interested in the *content of the report.* You can begin an oral briefing, however, by briefly *reminding* an audience of the reasons or recapping the charge you were given. You also may wish to *describe the procedures* you used to gather information—where you went for information, how you obtained specific pieces, problems encountered in meeting your charge. Third, it's essential to *forecast* the ideas or issues to be covered in the presentation, because it prepares the audience to listen. Finally, *pointing ahead to any action* they are to take as a result of the information will help audience members place your remarks in the context of their potential future behavior. Thus, the key to a good briefing introduction is *orientation*—reviewing the past (their expectations and your preparation), the present (your goal in this presentation), and the future (their responsibilities following the presentation).

Body. The principles underlying a choice of pattern are easy to state: *use a pattern that is best suited to topic and audience expectations.* Have you been asked to provide a history of a group or of a problem? Have you been asked to review the current status of plans for a new building or new product? Then a chronological pattern will respond to topic needs and audience expectations. Does the audience want to know why they face a present situation? A cause-effect format might be more useful than a strict chronology, as the former points more directly to actions or events that influenced the current circumstances. Have you been asked to brief the audience on the new organizational structure being proposed for your group? If so, a topical approach might be best.

Report from the Final Examination Committee

I. My committee was asked to compare and contrast various ways of structuring a final examination in this speech class and to recommend a procedure to you. [*The reporter's "charge."*]
    A. First, we interviewed each one of you.
    B. Then, we discussed the pedagogical virtues of various exam procedures with our instructor.
    C. Next, we deliberated as a group, coming to the following conclusions. [*Orientation completed.*]
II. At first we agreed with many students that we should recommend a take-home essay examination as the "easiest" way out.
    A. But, we decided our wonderful textbook is filled with so much detailed and scattered advice that it would be almost impossible for any of us to answer essay-type questions without many, many hours of worry, work, and sweat.
    B. We also wondered why a course that stresses oral performance should test our abilities to write essays.

III. So, we reviewed the option of a standard, short-answer, in-class final.
   A. Although such a test would allow us to concentrate on the main ideas and central vocabulary—which has been developed in lectures, readings, and discussion—it would require a fair amount of memorization.
   B. And, we came back to the notion that merely understanding communication concepts will not be enough when we start giving speeches outside this classroom.
IV. Thus, we recommend that you urge our instructor to give us an oral examination this term.
   A. Each of us could be given an impromptu speech topic, some resource material, and ten minutes to prepare a speech.
   B. We could be graded, in this way, on both substantive and communicative decisions we make in preparing and delivering the speech.
   C. Most important, such a test would be consistent with this course's primary goal and could be completed quickly and almost painlessly.

Conclusion.   Most often, oral briefings end with a conclusion that mirrors the introduction. The purpose or reason for the presentation is recalled, the main points are reviewed, and those who participated in data collection (if the effort was not yours alone) or made it possible for you to collect data are thanked publicly. Finally, a motion to accept the report may be offered, if appropriate in the setting, or the audience may be instructed as to their next actions based on the briefing. Questions from the audience also may be invited. Conclusions to briefings are best if they are quick, firm, efficient, and pointed.

Explanatory Speeches

An **explanatory speech** has much in common with the speech of definition, because they share the function of clarifying a concept, process, or event. Normally, though, an explanatory speech is less concerned with the word or vocabulary involved than with connecting one concept with a series of others. For example, a speech of definition on political corruption would concentrate on the term, telling what sorts of acts committed by politicians are included by the term. An explanatory speech on corruption would go further into the subject, perhaps indicating the social-political conditions likely to produce corruption or the methods for eliminating it. The clarification involved in an explanatory speech is considerably broader and more complex than that of a speech of definition.

The key to most explanatory speeches, however, lies in the speaker's point of view or rationale. Suppose, for example, you wanted to tell an audience how the American Revolution came to be. You could offer a great number of explanations, depending on your point of view. One explanation might be economic, so you would stress that the Revolution was the result of disagreements between Americans and Britons over trade and tax policies. Another might be political, so you would note that the Americans felt a strong need for self-government. A third might be social or cultural, so you would argue that the Revolution could not occur until the colonists had a strong sense of their own social identity as separate from the mother country. In a speech on AIDS, on the other hand, you might concentrate on biochemical processes of contagion, the physiological processes of debilitation, the psychological trauma encountered, the environmental means by which diseases spread, or even the sociological relationships between subgroups of people.

All of these approaches are equally "correct," in that they offer precise information on the topic. There are probably as many different explanations of phenomena as there are vantage points. By now you have heard multiple explanations of why the homeless need assistance, of urban decay, and how health care costs might be handled. Sociological, economic, or political perspectives may have dominated these discussions, depending on the speaker's preference or the needs of the audience or occasion.

Explanatory speeches are required whenever audiences are confused about a situation or lack the requisite information on their own. An explanation is called for when key concepts are fuzzy, when the available information is less complete than what you can provide, when effects cannot easily be attributed to their causes, or when competing claims are at loggerheads. Questions of "what," "how," and "why" dominate the reasons for providing explanatory answers.[3] The answer you provide may not be the most complete available, given the time allotted. Nevertheless, you can offer clear, defensible rationales for understanding concepts, relationships, processes, or events.

Structuring Explanatory Speeches. Unlike definitions, explanatory speeches are more complex and difficult to organize.

Introductions. Introductions to explanatory speeches can use many of the techniques discussed thus far. You may have to raise curiosity in some instances: how many of your classmates are really concerned about the status of child care services on campus or the current status of social security benefits? You usually have to generate a desire to listen if your topic seems distant or remotely connected to their actual day-to-day lives. If the explanation covers complex material, previewing the main points will help audiences follow what will be discussed. Encouraging people to follow along, especially with difficult material, also may be appropriate; you can indicate that you'll go into greater detail as you hit complex issues or that you'll be happy to elaborate on points after the speech.

Body. The body of most explanations fits into either causal or topical patterns of development. If you are trying to explain how or why something exists or operates as it does, either cause-effect or its reverse works well. If you're trying to explain how a problem can be solved, addressing the problem and then the solution may be the most practical structure. These two organizational patterns are well suited to explanations because explanations emphasize the interconnection of events, phenomena, or ideas.

Conclusion. Typically, the conclusion of an explanatory speech develops additional implications or calls for particular actions. If, for example, you've explained how contagious diseases spread through geographical areas, you probably should conclude by discussing some actions listeners can take to halt the process of contagion. If you have explained the concept of children's rights by using the example of a young child who divorced his mother in order to be adopted by his foster family, you can close by asking your listeners to consider what these rights mean to them—how does it change their behavior or actions toward young children?

Suppose your major is archaeology, and you decide to discuss recent controversial claims regarding how the first "humans" acted in their environment. Consider the following outline to see how some of this advice can be put to work:

Did Early Humans "Ape the Apes"?[4]

General Purpose: TO INFORM
Specific Purposes: To increase audience understanding of recent controversial issues regarding how the first humanoids acted in their environment, and to illustrate how difficult it is to know for certain how humans behaved.

Introduction:

Curiosity: Raise their curiosity by asking "when did we first become more 'human' than 'animal-like' in our behavior?"

Desire: Indicate that increasing their knowledge will give them a clearer conception of the difficulty in knowing exactly how the early humans lived and acted.

Body:

Organizational pattern: Using both spatial and chronological patterns, develop an understanding of the issues involved in archaeological research on the first humans. For example:

I. The research of Louis and Mary Leakey, and more recently their son Richard, in Tanzania, Kenya, and Ethiopia resulted in an interpretation of "man as hunter" and "woman as gatherer."
   A. The major archaeological "finds" at Olduvai Gorge in Kenya, Koobi Fora in Kenya, and Hadar in Ethiopia are marked on the wall map to my left.
   B. The initial find was at Olduvai; Louis Leakey discovered what he termed "encampments" of men and women, with scattered bones and stone implements.
      1. He named these early humans "*Homo habilis*" or "handy man." They also are termed "hominids" to separate them from later humans.
      2. Leakey argued that the males were the hunters and women the gatherers.
   C. Louis and Mary's son, Richard, discovered even earlier remains in northern Kenya, at Koobi Fora. He followed the same interpretation in arguing the remains were sites of male hunters and female gatherers.

(*Transition*) The interpretation of the Leakeys was initially applauded, but more recently has been challenged by others.

II.   The challenge to this interpretation asks, in effect, "How did the Leakeys know what hominids were doing millions of years ago—the evidence from the sites is insufficient to support their interpretation."

    A.   Using precise geological measures, Richard Potts of the Smithsonian Institution assessed the Olduvai sites and concluded that they were not encampments where men hunted and women gathered.

        1.   The sites give evidence of activity by both carnivores and hominids.

        2.   The sites were "caches" where implements were stored, rather than actual living sites.

    B.   There are several arguments which support Potts' conclusions.

        1.   The sites were concentrated in selected areas and represent deposits over time.

        2.   Bones that show evidence of being transported from an original place are marked by stone cuts.

        3.   Bones also show evidence of carnivore marks superimposed on those made by stone cuts.

        4.   Uncut and unformed stones were found with cut stones, indicating a "cache" where hominids might return.

(*Transition*) A second conclusion, based on this finding, is that men and women were not definitely split in their duties, and in fact these early humans or hominids may have been more like their ape ancestors than like later hunters.

III.   In challenging Richard Leakey's interpretation, there are experts who believe that the *Homo habilis* were scavengers, not hunters.

    A.   The evidence suggests that the hominids chased carnivores, such as lions, away from a kill with stones, then proceeded to take what they wanted from the carcass.

    B.   The evidence also suggests that the "caches" were sites to which they returned with their meat to rest and eat; when night fell, they resorted to sleeping in trees rather than on the open ground.

Conclusion:

These new interpretations suggest early hominids were more like apes than later humans. They did not have spears or fire, hence stalking and killing game was not as likely as scavenging. With this in mind, we can better appreciate the difference that fire and more advanced weapons made in their lifestyle. Finally, the newer interpretations suggest how difficult it is to be certain about the lifestyle of our ancestors. As you read or hear new conclusions about our ancestors, keep an open mind. Newer findings may reveal even these conclusions to be premature.

Sample Speech

In the following informative presentation, David Archambault, President of the American Indian College Fund, seeks to overcome the misinformation and lack of information about the American Indians. In the process, he offers a response to questions that people would either ask or "most *like* to ask," reviews the reasons American Indians do not feel Columbus discovered America ("we knew we were here"), their fate at the hands of settlers and soldiers, and their role in deciding their own future, especially as it relates to colleges created to serve Indian needs. The speech follows a general chronology from the time of Columbus to the present day, offering a clear account of the American Indian view on its own history, and on its role in "building a better America" for the future of not only American Indian children, but all children in the United States.

Columbus Plus 500 Years
Whither the American Indian?[5]
David Archambault

Thank you and good afternoon. Hau Kola. That is how we Lakota say "Greeting, Friends." I am happy to be here today to represent Native American people. I am a Ikoeya Wicaska—an ordinary man. We think of an ordinary man as not superior to anyone else or for that matter to anything else. We—all people and all things—are related to each other. /1

We begin our spiritual ceremonies with the phrase "Oni takuya Oyasi," which means all my relations. We believe that all people are ultimately part of one nation—the nation of mankind, but that this nation is only one of many nations that inhabit the Mother Earth. To us all living things are nations—the deer, the horses, things that crawl, things that fly, things that grow in and on the ground. All of these nations were created by the same Power, and none is superior to another. All are necessary for life. We are expected to live and work in harmony. /2

In my travels I have learned that many Americans in mainstream society are uninformed or ill-informed about American Indians. /3

So let me begin by responding to questions people most often ask about us—or questions people might most *like* to ask. /4

No, we don't consider that Columbus discovered America. Estimates of the number of people who lived in the so-called New World at the time Columbus arrived run from 40 to 100 million or more. Hey, we knew we were here. It was Columbus who was lost. Maybe that poem ought to say,

> "When Columbus sailed the ocean blue, it was he—not America—who got discovered in 14-hundred, ninety-two." /5

Yes, American Indians are American citizens. After World War I, a nation grateful for the contributions of Indians to the war effort made all American Indians full citizens. /6

No, we are not "prisoners" on the reservations. We can leave any time. Many have. But the rest of us don't want to. We don't want to be assimilated into the dominant culture. We want to preserve our own culture and traditions. I'll tell you later how we hope to do that. /7

Yes, we have a unique status in the United States. We are both citizens and sovereign people. That comes from our history as nations—or tribes—defeated by Europeans, who, after giving up on trying to Christianize and civilize us, recognized our right to self-determination. I'll come back to this, too. /8

No, not all Indians are alike. There is diversity among *tribal* nations just as there is among *European* nations. American Indians in 500 or so tribes speak more than 200 languages and dialects. /9

Yes, many American Indians have an especially tough time of it today with alcohol and other health problems, with poverty and inadequate education- and job-opportunities, and with just trying to figure out their own identity. Only we Indians can provide the leadership needed to solve these problems. /10

Finally, no, we don't care—at least most of us don't—whether you call us "Indians," "Native Americans," "Indigenous People," or "Amerinds." An Indian comedian tells it this way:

> "I know why white people call us Indians," he says. "When Columbus got here, he thought he had arrived in the Indies, so naturally he called the inhabitants 'Indians.' I'm just thankful he didn't think he had arrived in Turkey." /11

Today I want to share with you some of our history and culture and our hopes for the future. It is important to American Indians—and I think to you as well—that *all* Americans know more about the first people to come to this land, about where we are and what we are doing and where we are headed. If we are to respect our differences and value what we have in common, we must begin with understanding. /12

During this quincentenary of Columbus's voyage, attention is once again focused on what the white man brought to this land and on Columbus himself. This man who made such a remarkable journey has become the stuff of legend as well as history. He is admired and detested, exalted and condemned. Columbus Day will surely never be a favorite holiday among Indians, but we should consider Columbus for what he was—not for what we may wish he had been. /13

Columbus was a skilled and courageous mariner who led his ships across unchartered waters. He found land and people unknown to Europeans. He discovered a sea route between Europe and America. Never mind that Norse explorers and perhaps others had made the trip earlier. It was Columbus who recorded ways for others to make it across the waters—and back again. /14

Columbus came here, however, not to trade, but to conquer; he came to enrich himself and enslave his captives. His mission, in the words of his royal charter, was to "discover and acquire" all new lands as well as "pearls, precious stones, gold, silver," and other valuables. He would write back to Spain,

> "From here, in the name of the Blessed Trinity, we can send all the slaves that can be sold." /15

Columbus was a man of his time. He felt inspired by his God, empowered by his monarch, and reassured by the rightness of his cause. He was sailing, as the saying had it, for "God, glory, and gold." If he had objected to enslaving others and taking their lands, someone else may have gotten that royal charter. To me, Columbus is neither hero nor villain, but rather a symbol of a world forevermore transformed. His culture and mine have never fully made peace. /16

Tens of millions of native people would die during and after the years of Columbus's four voyages to our shores—die of gunfire from soldiers who wanted their lands and precious metals; die of maltreatment while forced to work as slaves; die of white man's diseases, such as smallpox and typhoid, for which they had no immunity. /17

These native people had been hunters and fishermen and gatherers and farmers and weavers and traders. They had created stable, even advanced, societies. They had highly developed agricultural and trading systems. If was they who had grown the first potatoes and the first corn and the first tomatoes. They understood mathematics and architecture and calendar systems. They were rich in art and culture as well as in gold and silver. The Incas, the Mayans, the Aztecs, and many others—civilizations all destroyed, their people subjugated. /18

In North America, too, Indians lost their lands, their economy, and their freedom to Europeans. At times, the new settlers were not quite sure what to do about these native people. The Indians had welcomed them, fed them, traded with them. They were people who respected their environment. They had developed intricate political and social systems. The Iroquois, for example, had the world's only true democracy—a Supreme Chief, a legislative council,

and a judicial branch as well as universal suffrage and direct representation. It was a system the Founding Fathers of the new nation would study and learn from. /19

But the Indians were in the way—in the way of new settlements and new riches. So for a long time, the objective was to get rid of the Indian. "The only good Indian is a dead Indian," the saying went. Whites even slaughtered the buffalo so the Indian could not hunt. The Indians fought back—often ferociously. But they lacked the manpower and the arms to resist. /20

Sometimes they pleaded. In a remarkable speech in 1879, Chief Joseph of the Nez Perces addressed his conquerors with these words:

"All men were made by the same Great Spirit Chief," he said. "They are all brothers and all should have equal rights. . . . Let me be a free man, free to talk and think and act for myself—and I will obey all of your laws." /21

Often they made treaties: 800 of them, in fact—nearly half of which were ratified by the U.S. Senate in full accord with the federal Constitution. Each of these treaties—every one—was violated by a nation that prides itself on keeping its word. /22

The Indians could not resist, but they could not be exterminated either. And so the government moved them to reservations—a movement with a long and sordid history. One of the most notorious chapters in that history was recorded in the 1830s when tens of thousands of Cherokees, Choctaws, and Creeks were forcibly moved from the Southeastern United States to what is now the state of Oklahoma. The Cherokees called it the "trail of tears." Along the way, nearly one-quarter of them died of starvation and disease. /23

The reservations were run by those who believed the way to "civilize" us was to take away our language and culture and religion. Our children were called savages and taken from us. They were put in boarding schools where they were educated—dare we say "brainwashed?"—with the white man's ways. Their teachers vowed to "kill the Indian and save the child." The idea was that if the white man couldn't get rid of the Indian, perhaps he could at least get rid of the Indian's culture. /24

Not until the 1930s was an effort made to give Indians limited sovereignty, allowing them to carry on their traditions and pass along their culture to their children. /25

But by the 1950s, the new watchword was assimilation. Break up the tribes, move Indians into mainstream society. In other words, make them "real Americans." Once again, the emphasis was on destroying Indian culture. /26

Only during the past several decades has there been a growing realization that we American Indians must determine our own destiny. We must be free to cherish our traditions and our culture, but also learn to live and work with the society around us. We must learn to walk in both worlds. /27

Can we do it? Yes, we can. It will require education for economic development and self-sufficiency. It demands that we create opportunity and hope for future generations. /28

This idea is not original with me. It was taught to us by a great leader of the Lakota people—my people—the great Chief Sitting Bull. He taught us that Indian children could succeed in modern society and yet retain the values of their culture, values such as respect for the earth, for wildlife, for rivers and streams, for plants and trees; and values such as caring for each other and for family and community. /29

He taught us that we must leave behind more hope than we found.

"Let us put our minds together," he said, "and see what life we can make for the children." /30

That is why there is an American Indian College Fund. It is to carry out the dream of Sitting Bull: to bring together the best minds in the Indian and non-Indian world to build a better future for our children. Our mission is twofold: to raise badly needed funds, of course, but also to help the general public understand the heritage of American Indians. /31

There are 26 colleges located on or near reservations in the United States. They were created by and for Indians. Three are four-year colleges; the others, two-year schools. Most are fully accredited and the rest are earning accreditation. /32

In the schools, our children are prepared for both worlds. The schools maintain a rigorous academic discipline while preserving Indian heritage and culture. Our students study math and science and business management, as well as American Indian philosophy, traditions, and language. They learn what it means to be Indian—and gain greater understanding of the world around them. /33

And it's working. Young American Indians who attend our colleges go on to further education and employment. They become productive, active citizens with confidence and pride in their tribal heritage. Many return to the reservation to work. Above all, they learn to value learning and to value the wisdom of those who came before us. /34

The colleges do something more. They serve their communities. They offer job training and day care, health clinics and counseling services, public-affairs and literacy programs. They provide leadership and support for economic development of the reservations. In short, they are committed to service and renewal. /35

Not long ago researchers from the Carnegie Foundation for the Advancement of Teaching spent two years studying our colleges. The schools, the Foundation concluded,

"are crucial to the future of Native Americans and to the future of our nation."

The Foundation called accomplishments of the schools "enormously impressive" and said they

"give hope to students and new life to their communities." /36

But the report also pointed to the need for expanded science labs and libraries and other facilities and urged the federal government to keep promises it has made. Congress had authorized payment of nearly six-thousand dollars for each full-time equivalent student at tribal colleges. But the amount actually appropriated is only about half that. /37

I feel a special commitment to the work of these colleges—not only because I temporarily head the effort to raise private funds and public awareness for them but, more important, because of what they mean to my life and the lives of my people. /38

More than 100 years ago, our great chief Sitting Bull was murdered. His people—frightened that they too would be killed—set out on foot across South Dakota along with Chief Big Foot. Carrying their children, they fled across the frozen prairie through the bitter subzero cold 200 miles to seek refuge on the Pine Ridge reservation in southwestern South Dakota. /39

On December 29, 1890, near a creek now known to all the world as Wounded Knee, Chief Big Foot and his followers were massacred. No one knows who fired first, but when the shooting was over, nearly 300 Indians—men, women, and children—lay dead and dying across the valley. Their bodies were dumped into a mass grave. The survivors were unable to hold a burial ceremony, a ceremony we call the wiping away of tears. It meant the living could never be free. /40

On the 100th anniversary of the massacre at Wounded Knee, several hundred of us on horseback retraced the journey of Big Foot and his band during those final days. We arrived at dawn at the site of the mass grave at Wounded Knee and completed the wiping of tears ceremony. The Si Tanka Wokiksuye, the Chief [Big] Foot Memorial Ride, was a mourning ritual that released the spirits of our ancestors and closed a tragic chapter in our history. /41

We have the opportunity now to help rebuild our nation. And I do not mean just the Indian nations. On this 500th anniversary of Columbus's voyages, we together can build a better America, a nation enriched by the diversity of its people and strengthened by the values that bring us together as a community. /42

Let us make this anniversary a time of healing and a time of renewal, a time to wipe away the tears. Let us—both Indian and non-Indian—put our minds together and see what life we can make for our children. Let us leave behind more hope than we found. I think Sitting Bull would be proud of us all. /43

Thank you. Tosha Akin Wanchin. /44

Chapter Summary

Overall, informative speeches are greater challenges than most people realize. Information isn't useful to listeners until it's been carefully selected, structured, and cast into motivational appeals that draw them in. As noted at the outset, "facts" are seldom enough for human beings; as an informative speaker, it's your task to interpret those facts in a manner that brings their meaning and significance across to listeners. The four types of informative speeches—*definitional, instructional, briefings,* and *explanatory*—are the most common formats you will encounter in developing information for an audience. Irrespective of the format, your informative speech will need to strive for *clarity, ways to associate old ideas with new ones, coherence,* and *ways to motivate people to listen.* Evaluate the various organizational strategies available to you in structuring your presentation so that it meets the needs of the situation and audience.

References

1. Material for this outline drawn from Boyce Rensberger, "Cancer—the New Synthesis: Cause," *Science 84,* 5 (September 1984): 28–33, and from Wendy Gronbeck, an oncology nurse.

2. For a discussion of oral briefings, see James Benjamin and Raymie E. McKerrow, *Business and Professional Communication: Concepts and Practices* (New York: Harper/Collins, 1994), Ch. 10.

3. For an interesting discussion of the what/how/why aspects of explanation, see W. V. Quine and J. S. Ullian, *The Web of Belief* (New York: Random House, 1970), Chapter 7, "Explanation."

4. Outline adapted from Brian Fagan's article, "Aping the Apes," *Archaeology,* 45 (May/June, 1992): 16–19, 67. Also see Richard Potts, *Early Hominid Activities at Olduvai Gorge* (New York: Aldine de Gruyter, 1988).

5. David Archambault, "Columbus Plus 500 Years," *Vital Speeches,* 58 (June 1, 1992), 491–93.

Key Terms

association of new ideas with old (p. 381)

clarity (p. 379)

coherence (p. 382)

definitional speeches (p. 384)

demonstration speeches (p. 387)

explanatory speeches (p. 396)

instructional speeches (p. 387)

motivational appeals (p. 383)

oral briefing (p. 392)

Problems and Probes

1. Attend an event in which an informative speech will be presented, such as an oral briefing or guest lecture, or listen to an informative presentation on television or radio. Write a short paper summarizing the content of the speech

and analyzing the strategies the speaker used to convey ideas. Consider the following questions: How interested did the audience appear—did the speaker need to motivate them to listen? If so, how well do you think it worked? Did the speaker appropriately limit main ideas to three or four? If not, was this a problem in terms of comprehension or retaining interest? Did the speaker utilize visual aids or demonstration materials in a manner that made it easy to follow the presentation? Was the organization of the speech appropriate for the topic and setting?

2. Working in groups, discuss the kinds of speech topics that you and others would like to hear about within each of the speech types discussed in this chapter. Indicate, where appropriate, the kinds of visual materials that might be used to enhance interest and better convey the information you think would be essential to cover in your topic. Also, pay particular attention to the restrictions placed on your setting—can you bring relevant or needed materials to this setting or would the class have to move to another location to hear the presentation? List at least three topics and, as appropriate, the kind of visual material that would be useful. Be prepared to share your conclusions with the class.

Communication Activities

1. Describe a unique place you have visited—for example, a church in a foreign city, a historical site, a local museum or other site of interest to the audience. Deliver a four- or five-minute speech to the class in which you describe this place as accurately and vividly as possible. Then ask the class to take a moment to envision this place. If possible, show them a picture of what you have described. How accurately were they able to picture this place? How might you have ensured a more accurate description? What restrictions did you feel without the use of visual aids?

2. Plan a two- to four-minute speech in which you will give instructions. For instance, you might explain how to calculate your life-insurance needs, how to canvass for a political candidate, or how to make a group flight reservation. This exercise is basically descriptive, so limit yourself to using a single visual aid.

3. Prepare a speech to inform for delivery in class. Using one of the following topics or a similar one approved by your instructor, select and narrow the subject to be covered, develop appropriate visual aids, and settle on the order or pattern you will follow in setting forth the information. Take special pains to make clear why the audience needs to know the material you are presenting. Suggested topics:

Contemporary American writers (artists, musicians)
How to become a better listener
A first lesson in aircraft-recognition
Changing perspectives in American foreign policy
How to read lips
The romance of archaeology
Exercising to control weight
How television programs are rated

CHAPTER 16

SPEECHES TO PERSUADE AND ACTUATE

S o, you finally fight through the crowds to Tiger Stadium in Detroit, having picked up a bag of boiled peanuts a man was vending in the parking lot. As you enter the stadium, someone's selling programs, and someone else, souvenir caps and pennants. Next to the restroom is the concessions stand with Stroh's beer and Ballpark hotdogs. The outfield billboards are covered with the names of Detroit Federal, Ford, Little Caesar's Pizza, and Dayton-Hudson's department store. In the program, some of your favorite players are endorsing soft drinks and sports equipment. And oh yes, there actually are baseball players on the field. . .

It has been said that professional sports competitions are simply excuses for mass advertising. These same people will tell you that the television networks are not in the business of delivering programs to you. Rather, their primary job is to deliver you to the advertisers—to attract enough of you to watch an ad so that the advertisers will get a good return on their investment in *Evening Shade* or *60 Minutes*. You cannot escape persuasion in this country. It is the 20th century's primary capitalistic tool and, by now, the heart even of its politics and many of its social arrangements.

The general purpose of persuasion is to change or reinforce attitudes or behaviors. The speaker or writer who persuades makes a very different demand on an audience from the one who informs. Informative communicators are satisfied when listeners understand what's been said. Persuaders, however, attempt to influence listeners' thoughts or actions. Persuaders request or demand that the audience agree with or act upon messages. Occasionally, persuaders seek to reinforce ideas or action, urging listeners to defend the present system and reject proposed changes. Whatever the spe-

Persuasive speaking is the process of producing oral messages that increase personal commitment; modify beliefs, attitudes, or values; or induce action.

cific purpose, the general purpose of all persuaders is to convince audiences of something.

Broadly, persuasion encompasses a wide range of communication activities, including advertising, marketing, sales, political campaigns, and interpersonal relations. Given this book's focus on speechmaking, we'll narrow our thinking in this chapter to three types of speeches. *Persuasive speaking is the process of producing oral messages that (1) increase personal commitment, (2) modify beliefs, attitudes, or values, or (3) induce action.* Before we can talk about these three types of speech—which we will call speeches of *reinforcement, modification,* and *actuation*—we need to consider some general problems that all persuaders face: (a) the need for you to adapt your work to listeners' psychological states; (b) the requirement that you recognize the diverse populations in your audience and provide each listener with reasons for accepting your claims; (c) and the absolute need to enhance your credibility when selling ideas to audiences. Such problems will take us back to Chapters 5 and 6 briefly, but, from a practical or applied perspective. These three topics take us into the psychological springs to action. From there, we'll go to the three types of persuasive talk.

Three Problems Faced by Persuaders

Persuading others is a challenging task. No matter what advertisers seem to assume, people don't change their long-standing beliefs, values, or behaviors on a whim; they need convincing rationales. Speakers must provide "good reasons"[1] for listeners to alter their thoughts or actions. Good reasons are not simply rational or logically reasonable; rather, they are always determined by (1) listeners' psychological states, (2) sources of ideas (reference groups) acceptable to listeners, and (3) their assessment of the speaker's personal credibility.

Adapting Messages to Listeners' Psychological States

The phrase **psychological state** refers generally to the complex of beliefs, attitudes, and values that listeners bring to a speech occasion. While there are hundreds of ways to talk about psychological states, in this chapter we'll limit ourselves to four so that you can sample different ways to think about listeners' states of mind.

Psychological Orientation (VALS).   A popular book of a decade ago was Arnold Mitchell's *The Nine American Lifestyles*.[2] He and some teammates set up the Stanford Research Institute's **Values and Lifestyles Program**, or **VALS**, in an attempt to understand motives, lifestyles, and governing values of groups of people. They set up the program because they understood that (1) people are governed by entire constellations of attitudes, beliefs, opinions, hopes, fears, needs, desires, and aspirations that are too complex to chart neatly on sheets of paper, but (2) they nonetheless have relatively consistent ways of acting at any given time of their lives. There are patterns to people's development and actions; **lifestyles** are relatively systematized ways of believing and acting in the world—fairly consistent orientations people bring to their decision making.

The VALS program is an effort to capture those lifestyles in an analytically useful way. After considerable surveying and interviewing of Americans, Mitchell's team divided citizens up into four comprehensive groups that in turn are subdivided into nine lifestyles (see Table 16.1).

These categories and the percentages of U.S. adults in each of them came from 1980 research, so the numbers may have changed by now, but the system itself is solid. VALS defines groups of people who habitually respond to problems and their solutions in comparatively predictable ways.

- *Survivors* are the poverty-driven people—ill, depressed, withdrawn, under-educated, lacking self-confidence.
- *Sustainers* are closely related to survivors, although sustainers are more angry, distrustful, and anxious, and have the motive to advance economically, if possible.
- *Belongers* are the stereotypical middle-class Americans—traditional, conforming, family-oriented, "moral," mostly white, often female.

Table 16.1   MITCHELL'S VALS TYPOLOGY

***Need-Driven Groups* (11% of U.S. adults)**

Survivor lifestyle (4%)

Sustainer lifestyle (7%)

***Other-Directed Groups* (67% of U.S. adults)**

Belonger lifestyle (35%)

Emulator lifestyle (10%)

Achiever lifestyle (22%)

***Inner-Directed Groups* (20% of U.S. adults)**

I-Am-Me lifestyle (5%)

Experiential lifestyle (7%)

Socially Conscious lifestyle (8%)

***Combined Outer- and Inner-Directed Groups* (2% of U.S. adults)**

Integrated lifestyle (2%)

- *Emulators* are the great strivers, working hard to become richer and more successful than they are; members of this group are often young, competitive, and ambitious.
- *Achievers* are the more successful models of emulators, and are often professionals, comfortable, affable, wealthy.
- *"I-Am-Mes"* lead off the inner-directed group; they're highly emotional and flighty, both aggressive and retiring, conforming and innovative—always searching for their selves.
- The *Socially Conscious* are driven by their concern for others, societal issues, trends, and events.
- *Integrated* people balance the strengths of the outer- and inner-directed people.[3]

These brief descriptions don't really capture the detail Mitchell offers in VALS on each group. He and his associates have been able to sculpt very specific profiles for members in each lifestyle, including attitudes toward others, consumption patterns, level of environmental concern, and so on. Were you a marketing analyst or political consultant, you'd want to explore each lifestyle's sets of beliefs, attitudes, values, and usual behavioral patterns carefully. As a speaker with few survey research resources, however, you'd use VALS in a different way. You know you're not likely to have many representatives of the need-driven groups (survivors and sustainers) in your classrooms, although you could well meet them on the street if you're conducting a voter registration drive in an inner-city neighborhood. You also know from experience that you'll find many outer-directed people (emulators and achievers comprise the core of many college or university student bodies), with inner-directed folks (especially from the societally conscious lifestyle) also well represented. Considering such psychological orientations as you prepare speeches is a good idea.

Let's look at an example. Suppose you were attempting to help a neighborhood association clean up some vacant lots in order to set up a park. Were you talking to your classmates, many of whom probably fall into the outer-directed (especially emulators and achievers) groups, you would want to feature appeals aimed at that particular psychological orientation:

Example 1: Outer-Directed Audience

I. We should help the neighborhood association clean the lots and build the park because:
   A. You would be demonstrating that even busy college students have the *ambition* to take on serious community projects.
   B. You would show the community that you have the *leadership skills* and *technical abilities* to carry it out.
   C. You would have done something of which you could be *proud* and which you could put on your *resume* under "community service."

Giving the same speech to a neighborhood group, which is likely to contain survivors and sustainers, would require a different set of ideas:

Example 2: Need-Driven Audience

I. You ought to be involved in the neighborhood cleanup and park construction because:
   A. The lots are now breeding grounds for *rats* and other *vermin* that make your life miserable.
   B. *Drug dealers* might be driven out of the neighborhood if those lots are cleaned up.
   C. The presence of a park would increase your *property value* and even help you renters pressure your landlords to fix up your apartments.
   D. A park would give you a *free place* to visit and enjoy on spring days and summer nights.

These two sets of appeals, of course, have been designed for radically different audiences; need-driven and outer-directed groups are as different as groups can be. Seldom, however, are your audiences drawn purely from one group or another. This means that, normally, you must *segment* the listeners, then *target* appeals to each segment in the ways that we discussed in Chapter 5.

Example 3: Mixed-Group Audience

I. You ought to get involved with the neighborhood park project because:
   A. You can increase the value of your property and improve your living conditions (*sustainers*).
   B. You'll demonstrate you're a part of this community, even in your student days (*belongers*).
   C. You'll be living out your values in a tangible way (*experiential people*).
   D. [etc.]

Even a general analysis of psychological orientation, therefore, helps you choose among the different ways you can urge change and even phrase the specific appeals you use.

Predisposition Toward the Topic. As noted in Chapter 5, an audience can have five possible attitudes toward your topic and purpose: (1) favorable but not aroused to act; (2) apathetic toward the situation; (3) interested but undecided about what to do; (4) interested in the situation but hostile to the proposed attitude, belief, value, or action; or (5) hostile to any change from the present state of affairs. Furthermore, such predispositions can be either relatively fixed or tentative and may vary from subgroup to subgroup within the audience. Given this sort of variability, consider the following suggestions as you design your speech:

1. *If you sense much audience hostility toward your message, present both sides of the issue you're discussing.* A **one-sided speech** offers only arguments in favor of your claim, while a **two-sided speech** cites opposing arguments but then refutes them. If you expect resistance, you simply must acknowledge and then try to neutralize it through refutation.[4]

2. *If listeners' beliefs seem relatively fixed, they're likely to be part of **belief networks** that you need to address.* The more central or highly significant that beliefs, attitudes, and values are, the greater the likelihood they are part of a network of interconnected beliefs. A study by

Prescott demonstrated clearly, for example, that people who are against abortion are likely to be in favor of physical punishment for children and capital punishment for criminals and be against prostitution, nudity, premarital sex, and drugs.[5] As a persuader, therefore, you must assess the degree to which your position runs counter to a full network. When you think it does, you must either (a) try to deal with the whole network (very, very difficult) or (b) seek to isolate one issue from the others. By stressing the unique problems encountered by physically abused children, for example, you might be able to get listeners to separate this question from related ones (the importance of discipline, parental rights, or punishment as training).

3. *You also must deal not only with the strength of attitudes but also their saliency.* **Saliency** refers to the relevance and interest level of a belief, attitude, or value for an individual. For example, topics currently on the front page often are highly salient, as are topics of regular conversation. The saliency of an issue ought to affect your persuasive strategies in significant ways:

   - *When topics are highly salient, listeners are more likely to be familiar with the central issues.*[6] You need to spend less time in providing a background for salient topics; on the other hand, audiences may well have certain expectations on salient topics. Be up to date.
   - *On salient topics, listeners are more likely to resist changes in their beliefs and attitudes.*[7] Treat this situation as you would a hostile one, by acknowledging the audience's resistance in the need step and then demonstrating clearly in the satisfaction step how the solution is consonant with many related beliefs and attitudes.
   - *When saliency is high, increase the number of strong arguments you offer; when saliency is low you'll be more effective if you increase the number of both strong and weak arguments.*[8] Those "in the know" won't put up with weak or frivolous arguments, although such arguments sometimes work on nonsalient issues.
   - *The more central and salient the listeners' values are, the more likely the listeners are to be hostile.*[9] Issues such as the decriminalization of drugs or the rights of persons with alternative lifestyles are not only salient but, for some, challenge their most basic values about protection of the body or of family values. Your best bet in such situations is to go for small changes now—changes in the law to allow marijuana use in cancer treatment programs or to legalize gay and lesbian marriages—in hopes of pushing for more basic changes later.
   - *Quote salient authorities.* It makes a difference whether you cite Lyndon LaRouche or Jesse Jackson on an issue concerning social

welfare. Especially if listeners aren't ready to take the time to work on issues and consider information about them seriously, the saliency of authorities becomes crucial.[10]

Cognitive Complexity.   **Cognitive complexity** is a matter of an individual's sophistication—not simply the number of things a person knows, but rather his or her ability to deal with a wide range of causes, implications, and associated notions when thinking about an idea or event. Cognitive complexity is made up of partly intelligence, partly maturity, and partly experience. While research is only just starting on this topic, some findings are well established:

1. Cognitively complex audiences (e.g., college or university audiences) demand and can follow *sophisticated argument.*
2. They respond better to *two-sided* than *one-sided* arguments.
3. They require much more *evidence* before they'll change their beliefs and attitudes.
4. Cognitively complex speakers usually generate more *strategically sound tactics* and hence are more competent communicators.
5. If cognitively complex listeners work hard to test your ideas and then accept them, those people are likely to stay persuaded longer than less complex listeners.[11]

Given that most of your audiences are cognitively complex (until you become an elementary school teacher or a social worker in the back counties of some rural states), you cannot get by with a few easy arguments when persuading. You must be ready both to defend your claim and answer objections from the other side with such people.

Degrees of Change.   Finally, so far as psychological states are concerned, you must recognize that people will change only so much as a result of your speeches. It's extremely difficult, except in rare circumstances such as radical religious experiences, to make wholesale changes in people's beliefs, attitudes, and values. Generally, you ought to strive for **incremental change**—step by step movement toward a goal. The distance you can move a listener is determined by (1) *initial attitude* and (2) the *latitude of change* the person can tolerate.

Suppose that the possible attitudes toward a topic like abortion are set up on a scale running from "extremely favorable" to "extremely unfavorable," like this:

1 extremely favorable toward legalized abortion
2 moderately favorable
3 mildly favorable
4 neutral

INCREMENTAL APPROACH TO ATTITUDE CHANGE

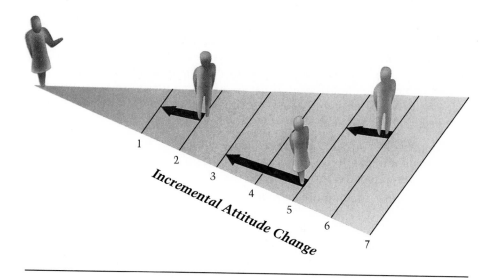

5   mildly unfavorable
6   moderately unfavorable
7   strongly unfavorable toward legalized abortion

Trying to convince someone who is strongly unfavorable (7) that abortion should remain legal (1) would probably fail, even if you presented both sides of the argument. Most radical "anti's" could only be moved a short way because of a single speech—to moderately or mildly unfavorable if you were a skilled arguer—if at all. Trying to change listeners too much can produce a **boomerang effect**; often, persuasive attempts backfire and create more rather than less resistance to ideas. In the face of a strong "1" speech, most "7s" become even more committed to their position.[12]

The precise degree of change people tolerate varies from individual to individual and topic to topic. *Authoritarian* individuals, for example, are governed by strong, clear moral codes, and hence tend to support conservative causes, defer to authority figures, and express strong aversion to what they see as "social deviants"—those who violate the normal social and moral orders of the community.[13] Such people have a narrow **latitude of acceptance**; on a numerical scale, you must assume their views are firmly anchored in one or two positions—on the abortion scale, a 1–2, 6–7, or something similar.

As targets of persuasion, authoritarian individuals present interesting problems. On the one hand, their seeming rigidity makes them difficult audiences; *usually, you must seek incremental change—small changes— when you are dealing with authoritarian listeners*. Yet on the other hand, if you have a firm base in expertise and trustworthiness, and if you are advocating attitude changes and actions that can be tied to traditional social–moral values, you're likely to do well with such people. *Highly credible persuaders advocating traditional value-centered changes often can move authoritarian listeners to action*. These apparently contradictory generalizations, of course, are easily reconcilable when one considers their latitudes of acceptance: such people may indeed have narrow latitudes of acceptance, but once someone gets inside of that range with ideas, its very narrowness and intensity become the grounds for belief, attitude, and behavioral change.

Obviously, you cannot interview all audience members, assessing their lifestyles, predispositions toward the topic, degree of cognitive complexity, and the width of their latitudes of acceptance or rejection. Few speakers (political candidates are certainly exceptions here) scientifically assess the psychological states of their listeners. But, good audience analysis allows you to guess shrewdly, then adjust your appeals and plans of action accordingly. Talk with people; check with such civic attitude-testers as Chambers of Commerce; read local newspapers and other sources of information on community problems, attitudes, and responses to those problems. All such sources of information on psychological states will help you maximize your chances for successful persuasion.

Drawing Upon Diverse External Reference Groups

Reference groups are collections of people and organizations that affect individuals' beliefs, attitudes, and values. They are collectivities "from which an individual derives attitudes and standards of acceptable and appropriate behavior and to which the individual refers for information, direction, and support for a given lifestyle."[14] You may or may not hold actual membership in such groups; you might belong to the Young Republican Club and not to the Sierra Club (an environmental lobby), and be influenced strongly by both. You voluntarily join some reference groups; you might believe in the legal rights of everyone and so join the American Civil Liberties Union. Others you are a part of involuntarily—for example, you are born male or female and a member of an ethnic group. You share values with some of your reference groups; hence they have a positive effect on your attitudes and behavior, while those with values dissimilar from yours produce negative reactions in you. As a result, the National Right to Life Committee probably affects your thinking about abortion in either positive or negative ways; because it probably affects you, it is a reference group, even if you don't join or support it. Reference groups can be classified as *membership and nonmembership groups, voluntary and involuntary groups*, and *positive and negative groups*.

Beliefs, attitudes, and values are based, in part, on the traditions and customs of reference groups, although people differ in their degree of direct reliance.

With this background, consider some of the ways you can use reference groups in your persuasive and actuative speeches:

1. *First, make reference groups you want to use* salient *to your listeners.* You need to bring some group to a conscious level and make sure the group seems relevant to the topic at hand. For example, during the 1992 presidential election the Roman Catholic church in Iowa took a stand against the proposed Equal Rights Amendment for the state. The church thus was brought to mind among many voters, but to some its opinion was thought irrelevant to the ERA. As a speaker on ERA, therefore, you would have had to assess the saliency of the church's position in your speech.

2. *Cite the opinions of voluntary, positively viewed groups whose values* coincide *with positions you're taking.* This is a kind of testimony— useful, as we saw in Chapter 7, as orienting and probative supporting materials. So, many ERA supporters in Iowa cited testimony from the National Organization for Women (NOW) during the debates over the amendment.

3. *Cite voluntary, negative, nonmembership groups when they* oppose *the position you're advocating.* Such groups are "devil-groups," groups peo-

ple vilify and actively act against. Such references play into an "us versus them" orientation and, whether you like it or not, some listeners are as willing to act against something as for something else. They possess what are called *negative attribution styles.*[15] Thus, the Roman Catholic church's opposition to the ERA was seen as a "devilish" intrusion of the church into matters of citizenship and state by supporters of the ERA.

4. *The more significant a person's* roles *in any group, the more the group's norms and beliefs influence that person's thoughts and behavior.* So, it was easier to whip the Democratic Party County Central Committee into a frenzy at campaign time than ordinary Democratic party members, and, conversely, it was more difficult to produce radical business attitude changes in executives than in frontline workers.[16] In the ERA campaign, group leaders spoke out much more fervently for and against the amendment than rank-and-file members of groups.

5. *Talk about reference groups to create a sense of security, of belongingness.* Aligning your views specifically with those of positive membership groups important to listeners not only helps you create acceptance, but create long-lasting acceptance.[17] The importance of *women* as a group supporting the ERA was stressed in the 1992 Iowa campaign, playing on a sense of belongingness, and, as a matter of fact, over 60 percent of the female voters cast their ballots in favor of it. (Nonetheless, the amendment lost in 1992.)

Finally, as we've noted throughout this book, you're usually facing diverse audiences, which means that you must work many reference groups into most speeches in order to reach various segments of your audience. *You must aim for broad-based support of your position.* Thus, supporters of Iowa's Equal Rights Amendment in 1992 argued it ought to be passed because it was endorsed by many different kinds of organizations— economic, political, social, religious, professional. Its ads mentioned such groups as the Des Moines Chamber of Commerce; the Iowa Higher Education Association; the American Federation of State, County, and Municipal Employees; the League of Women Voters; the Iowa Council of Churches; and the Iowa Democratic Party, in order to make many different reference groups salient to the voting decision.

Enhancing Personal Credibility

The issue of authority brings us to the third essential dimension affecting the persuasive process. A good deal of your potential effectiveness depends upon your perceived credibility, or ethos. In Chapter 1, we outlined several factors that can determine listeners' perceptions of your credibility—their sense of your expertise, trustworthiness, competency, sincerity or honesty, friendliness and concern for others, and personal dynamism. While you should work to maximize the potential impact of all of these factors whenever speaking, regardless of purpose, they are especially important when you seek to change someone's mind or behavior. The following guidelines can assist you in making decisions about the use of credibility as an effective tool in persuasion.

First, when speaking to people who are relatively unmotivated and who don't have enough background information to critically assess what they hear, the higher *your credibility the better your chances of being a successful persuader.* Conversely, if your credibility is low, even strong arguments will not overcome your initial handicap.[18] This fact should give you a clear sense of why your own credibility is an important component in your chances for success.

Second, *you can increase the likelihood of being judged credible when seeking to persuade an audience by taking steps to enhance your image of competence and sincerity.* People who don't take the time to weigh your reasons and evidence are unlikely to change their beliefs and values if they think you've done a poor job of researching the issues or are insincere. There are several things you can do to increase the audience's perception of your *competence*: (1) carefully set forth all of the competing positions, ideas, and proposals relevant to a topic *before* you come to your own judgment; (2) review various criteria for judgment to show that your recommendations or positions flow from accepted and generally held criteria; and (3) show that the recommendations you offer actually will solve the problems you identified in the need step of your speech. You can increase the audience's sense of your *sincerity* by: (1) showing yourself to be open to correction and criticism should any listener wish to question you (a calmly delivered, relevant response does more to defuse hecklers than responding in kind);[19] (2) exuding personal warmth in your relations with the audience; (3) maintaining direct eye contact with listeners; and (4) recognizing anyone who has helped you understand and work on the issue or problem.

Third, *heighten audience members' sense of your expertise, friendliness, and dynamism, especially when seeking to move them to action.* People are unlikely to change their routines on your recommendation unless they feel that you know what you're talking about, that you have their best interests in mind, and that you're excited about your own proposal. *Expertise* can be demonstrated by (1) documenting your sources of information; (2) using a variety of sources as cross-checks on each other; (3) presenting your information and need analyses in well-organized ways; (4) using clear, simple visual aids when they are appropriate or necessary; (5) providing adequate background information on controversial issues; (6) competently separating causes from effects, short-term from long-term effects, hard facts from wishes or dreams, and one proposal from others; and (7) delivering your speeches in a calm and forthright manner.

A sense of *friendliness* and *concern* for others can be created by (1) treating yourself and others as human beings, regardless of how controversial the topic is and how intensely you disagree with others, and (2) depersonalizing issues, talking in terms of the "real-world" problems rather than in terms of personalities and ideologies. Finally, an audience's sense of your *dynamism* can be enhanced by (1) speaking vividly, drawing clear images of the events you describe; using sharp, fresh metaphors and active rather than passive verbs; and expressing your ideas with a short, hard-hitting oral style rather than a long, cumbersome written style and (2) using varied conversational vocal patterns, an animated body, direct eye contact rather than reliance upon your notes, and a firm upright stance.[20]

A public speaker's principal communicative virtue is the presence of a living, active human being behind the lectern—a person who *embodies* a message, whose own values are expressed in and through the message. People command more attention and interest than written words, and people, unlike films and videotapes, can feel, can react to audience members, and can create a sense of urgency and directness. Hence, personal credibility is an extremely valuable asset for the persuader and actuator.

Types of Persuasive and Actuative Speeches

Although there are many ways to classify persuasive and actuative speeches, we'll examine them in terms of their psychological and behavioral force. That is, in classifying these speech types, we're concerned with the *demands* each type makes upon an audience's mental state and level of activity. We will examine speeches of reinforcement, modification, and actuation.

Speeches of Reinforcement

Americans are joiners. To get our political, economic, social, and personal work done, we constantly organize ourselves into groups and associations. Action-oriented groups gather and package the latest information, keep on top of issues that are important to the members of the group, and propose solutions to specific problems. Service groups organize charities, perform volunteer work, and provide support for other activities in communities.

An inevitable fact of group life is that, as time goes by, members' interest in activities declines, membership drops, and the cause for which the group was formed gets lost in the myriad of causes competing for the attention and support of the people in the community. Periodically, people need to be reminded of why they joined the group, what its services are, and how the group helps them meet their personal goals.

In public speaking, **reinforcement** is a process of calling up the original beliefs and values that caused people to join a group in the first place and of reinvigorating audience members so they once more contribute their time, energy, and finances to the tasks needing to be done. In a practical sense,

Using Fear Appeals

Among the most potent appeals to audiences are fear appeals. Research suggests that fear appeals are so powerful that they actually can interfere with a listener's ability to process information critically. However, research indicates that fear appeals retain their effectiveness over extended periods of time.

Sometimes fear appeals are used for laudable goals such as the Juvenile Awareness program at New Jersey's Rahway State Prison (the basis of the 1977 television special "Scared Straight"). In this program, delinquent youths are introduced to convicts who describe the horrors of prison life. Results suggest that the program helps deter youths from further delinquent activity.

However, fear appeals are always accompanied by the potential for misuse. The possibility of misuse raises a number of ethical considerations. Think about the following applications to your classroom speaking. Evaluate the ethics of each situation. What would you do if you were the speaker? Why?

1. You're planning a persuasive speech to convince your audience that war is morally wrong. You are totally committed to peace and believe that anything you can do to maintain peace in this world is your moral

reinforcement speeches are *epideictic*—they seek to increase adherence to, or rejection of, a particular set of values. As Perelman and Olbrechts-Tyteca observe, "epideictic discourse sets out to increase the intensity of adherence to certain values, which might not be contested when considered on their own but may nevertheless not prevail against other values that might come into conflict with them. . . . In epideictic oratory, *the speaker turns educator*" (emphasis added).[21]

Reinforcement speeches are called for when listeners are mentally apathetic and physically lethargic. People behave as though they are unconcerned about the problem. This is often the case with fund-raising drives for charitable causes: every fall the United Way asks you to contribute; public lobbies, such as Common Cause or the Nature Conservancy, periodically send out appeals for financial assistance. In cases in which apathy is less extreme, the committed still need an extra nudge to dip into their pockets and give assistance. Televangelists crusade for dollars on behalf of their continuing ministries. Whether the state of apathy and lethargy is extreme or moderate, the message is oriented toward reaffirming basic verities,

obligation, so you exaggerate some of the facts about recent world conflicts to frighten your audience about the results of war.

2. You give a speech on the increase of date rape on college campuses. In order to convince your audience that date rape is wrong and extremely common, you create scenarios that appeal to the fears of your listeners. Your scenarios are so vivid that several of your listeners, who are rape survivors, are visibly overcome with emotion. One of the listeners is so upset that she must leave the classroom during your speech. Everyone in the audience sees her leave.

3. Knowing that the arousal of fear impedes the ability to think critically, you decide to arouse fears in your listeners so that they fail to perceive that your argument is unsound. You feel that it is your listeners' responsibility to listen critically and if they are willing to accept unsound arguments, they're fools.

4. You feel very strongly that the college president is wrong to continue investing college money in countries where torture and imprisonment without trial are legal. You present a very persuasive speech about your feelings. In your speech, you appeal to your audience's fears by suggesting that the college president is actually propagating torture and corrupting the values of U.S. citizens to the point that someday torture and imprisonment without trial might be legal in the United States. Your listeners become so incensed, as a result of your speech, that they march to the president's house and set his car on fire.

5. You're preparing to give a speech on hate crimes in the United States. You want to make sure that you have your audience's attention before you begin, so you decide to present the details of a series of grisly murders committed in your town by a psychopath—even though these murders were not motivated by hate but by mental illness, and so they aren't examples of hate crimes.

reeducating audience members about the values that attracted them to the group in the first place.

The key to reinforcement speaking is *motivation*. While people may say, "Sure, I support the Republican party," or "Yeah, I agree with SADD's efforts to control drug and alcohol use in the schools," they may not be motivated to act upon the basis of their convictions. They need to have their original commitment resurrected. Jesse Jackson's speech to the delegates at the 1988 Democratic National Convention is one example of a speech designed to serve an educative function and gain active support for the Democratic party.

Speeches of Modification

Unlike speeches of reinforcement, speeches of **modification** seek specific psychological changes in one's belief state, attitudes toward an object, or basic values. Speeches of this type have been the central feature in the art of rhetoric since the time of the early Greeks. Whether your present or future role is that of a student, businessperson, lawyer, minister, sales clerk, doctor, or parent, the task of changing the views of others is a constant demand of your daily life. Using the categories of beliefs, attitudes, and values described in chapter five, we can examine three subtypes of speeches aiming at modifying the views of listeners.

Changing Beliefs. The psychological basis for most speeches aimed at changing someone's beliefs about the world is *differentiation*. That is, one can get you to change your beliefs about anything from eating seaweed to the balance of power between Isreal and its Arab neighbors by persuading you to perceive those matters in different ways. Persuaders who want you to differentiate between your old way of looking at something and a newer way of seeing it may use one or more of three basic strategies:

1. *Selective description.* A persuader may accentuate the positive and ignore the negative. Someone might persuade you to consider tofu an acceptable food by assuring you that its vitamin and mineral content is superior to that of foods in your normal diet, while ignoring your questions about its taste or processing costs. As we have seen, because it's a one-sided strategy, selective description wouldn't be an advisable tactic in situations where the audience is informed or strongly hostile toward the message.

2. *Narrative.* A persuader may use narrative forms, as we discussed them earlier, by telling a story about the United States preparedness level going into the Korean Conflict, ending with the moral that the country can never let its guard down. Two features of storytelling are essential if the narrative is to have persuasive force. First, listeners must perceive the story to be probable; it must make coherent sense to them. Second, the story must possess what Fisher terms "narrative fidelity"—it must appear consistent with other stories listeners have heard.[22] When both features are present, a story can function as a powerful image to move an audience.

3. *Appeals to uniqueness.* Someone attempting to get you to change your beliefs about a politician may convince you that the candidate is "not like all the others," pointing to unique aspects of her background, experience, public service, honesty, and commitment to action.

These three strategies are effective to the extent that listeners perceive the message to be important, novel, and plausible. The message must be one that isn't already well internalized by the audience members (they aren't already convinced), and the rationale for change must appear credible to them. Finally, the change itself must be seen as feasible or practical.[23]

Changing Attitudes. Attitude change is probably the most heavily researched psychological change of this century.[24] Given the previous discussion of attitude as predisposition, you're aware that this form of change involves modifying one's evaluation of an object from "good" to "bad," or at least to "neutral." Because attitudes are attached to beliefs ("Opportunities for women are increasing in this country [belief] and that is good [attitude]"), sometimes persuaders attempt to change an attitude by attacking a belief. If a speaker can show that opportunities for women are *not* increasing, or even demonstrate that the rate of increase is minimal or insignificant, he or she then can link that assertion to a negative attitude ("The slow rate of increase is harmful to women"). Because attitudes are organized into clusters around a value, they can sometimes be changed by getting people to think in different valuative terms.

Attitudes can be changed not only by attacking underlying beliefs or over-arching values, but also by direct assault. Parents attempt to instill any number of attitudes in their young children by repeatedly offering short "lectures" (for instance, "Spinach is good for you" and "Don't give in to peer pressure—be an individual"). Repetition often has the desired effect, as children accept the attitude as their own and live by its creed. Recall Michael Dukakis at the 1988 Democratic National Convention repeating his parents' refrain "Much has been given you; you have much to give" as an attitude that became his personal rationale for seeking public office. Such direct assaults can be termed *brainwashing* when "they" (enemies or malicious people) use this technique and *education* when "we" (friends or "right-thinking people") use it. From our perspective, the cult members who armed and barricaded themselves in the Davidian compound outside Waco, Texas, in 1993 were victims of brainwashing. From their perspective, they may have felt in the presence of a divine individual who had taught them well; hence, they went willingly to their deaths.

Changing Values.   Perhaps the most difficult challenge for any persuader is to change people's value orientations. As noted in earlier chapters, values are fundamental anchors, basic ways of organizing our view of the world and our actions in it. They are difficult but not impossible to change. Three techniques often are used:

1. *Valuative shifts.* Like differentiation, this technique asks an audience member to look at an issue or a proposal from a different valuative vantage point. The person asking you to buy insurance, for example, tells you to look at it not simply as financial protection (a pragmatic value) but as family protection and a source of peace of mind (sociological and psychological values). Such appeals can persuade people to shift their valuative orientation and see an issue or proposal in a new way. While the issue remains unchanged, its relationship to the audience member is transformed from a negative one ("I don't need financial protection") to a positive one ("You're right, the *family* will need protection if something happens to me").

The transcendence technique for altering values approaches the issue from the perspective of "higher" values. Oliver North used such appeals in his defense during the 1988 Iran-Contra hearings.

2. *Appeals to consistency.* When you hear such appeals as "The American Legion favors . . . " you as a member of that organization are being asked to approve a certain measure in order to remain consistent with others in your reference group. Those for whom peripheral cues are important are likely to respond to this type of appeal. When someone projects a value orientation from the present to the future ("If you like horror films, you'll positively love the Friday the Thirteenth series"), he or she is appealing to cognitive consistency.

3. *Transcendence.* This sophisticated method for getting you to change your values approaches the issue from the perspective of a "higher" value. Oliver North used such appeals in defense of his actions during the Iran-Contra hearings. By appealing to "patriotic duty," he defended what appeared to many to be direct violations of the law. In this way, he sought to redefine his actions as consistent with higher national values, and, therefore, as excusable. Senator George Mitchell responded to North during one phase of the hearings by presenting a different hierarchy of values: patriotic duty does not stand above adherence to the

law, regardless of the situation. From Mitchell's perspective, the actions were inexcusable.

Thus, speeches of modification may seek a change in beliefs, attitudes, or values. Speeches designed to bring about these kinds of changes in listeners demand a higher level of communicative competence than most other types of speeches. As you know from experience, however, these competencies can be acquired by speakers willing to think through situations calling for such kinds of persuasion and willing to spend time on thorough speech preparation.

Speeches of Actuation

Moving uncommitted or apathetic people to action is a chore many prefer to avoid. For example, you may have heard such expressions from friends and acquaintances as "I don't like to ask people to contribute money to a cause, even if it's worthy," "Don't ask me to solicit signatures for that petition—I feel like I'm intruding on others' privacy," or "I'm just not persuasive enough to get people to volunteer to work at the Kiwanis Auction—ask Mary." If all of us felt this way, little would be accomplished. In some cases, simply making a living requires that we move others to action. Even if you take one of these positions, some day you will have to engage in the task of creating a speech of **actuation**.

Consistent with our earlier definition of persuasion, *an actuative speech seeks, as its final outcome, a set of specifiable actions from its audience.* These actions may be as diverse as giving personal time to an activity (visiting a local nursing home), contributing money to a cause or product (donating to the Wildlife Fund), or changing a habit (stopping smoking). There are two types of audiences for whom actuative speeches are generally appropriate: (1) those who believe in the idea or action but are lethargic about doing anything and (2) those who doubt the value of the action and are uninformed or uninvolved. The second situation is our concern here.

Actuative speeches addressed to the uninvolved listeners among us demand significant behavioral change. The goal might be as short range as making a profit the next quarter of the fiscal year or as long range as sociopolitical transformation of society. Whatever the extent or loftiness of the goal, all actuative speeches depend upon making a set of needs salient for an audience, then demonstrating that a certain course of action will satisfy those needs.

As in the case of speeches of reinforcement and modification, the key to effective actuation is motivation. No matter how wonderful the new products, how exciting the political candidate, or how worthy the cause, unless a listener is personally convinced that the product, candidate, or cause will make a significant change in his or her life, your speech will fail to have its intended effect.

Resistance to Counterpersuasion

In this chapter we've concentrated on the issue of persuading—increasing or otherwise changing people's acceptance of certain beliefs, attitudes, and values. We haven't, however, focused on the ways in which you can increase your listeners' resistance to ideas that run counter to your own. Besides persuading them to accept your beliefs or attitudes, you also may need to protect them against *counterpersuasion*, attempts by others to influence your audience away from your position. By protecting your listeners from counterpersuasion, you can strengthen their adherence to your claim.

McGuire and his associates conducted a research program on resistance to ideas. They argue that "cultural truisms"—audience-held attitudes that appear so basic and correct as to seem invulnerable to attack—are, in fact, very vulnerable to counterpersuasion. Because people haven't had to defend these attitudes, they haven't developed the appropriate defensive skills; because they believe these cultural truisms to be invulnerable, they lack the motivation to develop strong defenses against counterpersuasive attempts.

Consider, for example, the statement "Democracy is the best form of government." How well prepared are you, for

Structuring Persuasive and Actuative Speeches

The overall structure of a persuasive or an actuative speech incorporates the features of the motivated sequence—attention, need, satisfaction, visualization, and action—relevant to the specific type of speech. Within each step, as appropriate to the topic and occasion, other patterns of organization can be used to bring a sense of coherence and cohesiveness to each step. (See Chapters 8 and 9 for more details on organizing speeches.)

The Motivated Sequence and Reinforcement Speeches

The visualization and action steps are the crucial elements in most reinforcement speeches. This is because the listeners are already convinced of

instance, to present specific arguments in defense of this claim? If you're ill prepared, you're far less resistant to counterpersuasion than you might think. The antidote for your lack of preparation might involve an *inoculation* strategy: hearing refutations of the arguments that might be advanced in attacking your attitude. Inoculation provides you with a basis for responding to an attack, thereby increasing your resistance to counterpersuasion.

In addition to creating an inoculation strategy, you can increase resistance to counterpersuasive attempts either by forewarning audience members or by simply encouraging them to think seriously about their own behaviors and attitudes. *Forewarning* means letting audience members know in advance that they'll be exposed to a counterpersuasive attempt—that someone will try to change their beliefs or values in ways that you, and they, may not desire. Time is a crucial variable; the more time between forewarning listeners and an attack on their attitudes, the stronger will be their resistance to the counterpersuasive message. Time allows them to formulate reasons to support their own attitudes and to reject possible arguments against them. Thinking about their beliefs and attitudes focuses attention on the actions that they are comfortable with retaining, and, like forewarning, gives them time to develop reasons to resist change.

A third strategy that increases resistance involves the amount of knowledge that people bring to a situation. For example, Hirt and Sherman found that individuals with greater knowledge are more resistant to refutational arguments. Thus, you can increase potential resistance to messages that are contrary to your own by adding to the audience's knowledge about the issues involved.

FOR FURTHER READING
Hirt, E. R. and S. J. Sherman. "The Role of Prior Knowledge in Explaining Hypothetical Events." *Journal of Experimental Social Psychology* 21 (1985): 591–43; Petty, Richard E., and John T. Cacioppo. *Communication and Persuasion: Central and Peripheral Routes to Attitude Change.* New York: Springer-Verlag, 1986.

the importance of the problem and are predisposed to accept particular solutions. The most important goal in a reinforcement speech is to get listeners to renew their previous commitments and to charge once more into the public arena to accomplish a common objective. Thus, a typical reinforcement speech following the motivated sequence usually has a short attention step, a need step that documents recent gains and losses (especially losses, since they illustrate the desirability of reengagement), little or no satisfaction step, a more fully developed visualization step (which lets listeners "see" themselves as reengaged with the issues), and an action step that focuses on particular actions to take now or in the near future (as audiences for these speeches are usually ready to respond quickly to appeals for renewed efforts).

In the following brief outline, the speaker is urging her players to rededicate themselves as they initiate a week of practice prior to playing for the league championship. There's little reason for a lengthy attention or need step, as the players are committed to the game and its role in their lives; the major emphasis is on reminding them of what they've done to get to this point and what remains to be done.

You're Already Winners

Specific Purpose: To reinforce the listeners' previous commitment to the team and to their own involvement in the sport

Attention Step
  I. "Winning isn't everything; it's the only thing." For us, this will not mean "win at all costs."
 II. Integrity and commitment yield winners.

Need Step
  I. The way we use our time during our last practices is critical.
     A. "You play as you practice."
     B. Work ethic determines results.
 II. Academically, you're already winners.
     A. You are proven student athletes with the highest academic average of any team on this campus.
     B. The seniors will graduate.
III. Athletically, you're already winners.
     A. We can win the league championship.
     B. Integrity has earned positive recognition.

Satisfaction/Visualization Step (combined, as the solution [win the game] is accepted)
  I. Why not quit now while you're ahead?
     A. It insults your commitment to excellence.
     B. It lets your fans down.
     C. It lets me down.
 II. Renew commitment to hard work, fun, and a winning attitude.
     A. These are the ingredients that led to our past success.
     B. They will be sufficient to carry us through this week, into the game, and beyond.
III. What does winning this final game mean?
     A. It means being satisfied with your own participation as a player and team member.
     B. It means recognition for you and the university.

Action Step
  I. Now is the time to do what has to be done.
     A. Practice hard.
     B. Play the championship game with all your heart.
 II. Win or lose, be satisfied with your individual effort.
     A. Individual and team integrity and discipline count.
     B. "Winning is everything" if done for the right reasons.

The Motivated Sequence and Speeches of Modification

Regardless of the nature or scope of the psychological modification you ask of your listeners, you can use the motivated sequence. When asking people to accept your judgments about a person, a practice, an institution, or a theory, you can seek to do these things:

1. Capture the *attention* and interest of the audience.
2. Clarify that a judgment concerning the worth of the person, practice, or institution is *needed* by showing (a) why such a judgment is important to your listeners personally and (b) why it is important to their community, state, nation, or world.
3. *Satisfy* the need by (a) setting the criteria upon which an intelligent judgment may be based and (b) advancing the judgment you believe to be correct and showing how it meets the criteria.
4. Picture the advantages that will accrue from agreeing with the judgment you advance or the evils that will result from failing to endorse it (*visualization* step).
5. If appropriate, appeal for acceptance of the proposed judgment (*action* step).

The use of the motivated sequence to present a claim of value is illustrated in the following outline for a speech presenting the reasons for continuing the struggle against sex discrimination.

The Invisible Woman

Specific Purpose: To persuade the class to judge a person on the basis of ability rather than gender

Attention Step
I. Incredible. Inexcusable. Inequitable. This is the present status of women in the work world.
   A. The 1910 *Farmers' Home & Advocate Journal* describes women as "invisible."
   B. The invisible woman exists today.
II. Inequity exists for me, exists nationally, and exists on this campus.

Need Step
I. Inequity in the workplace must end.
II. My first-hand experience is proof of inequity.
   A. Thirty years ago, I earned $1 to $4 less than male co-workers doing the same work.
   B. Women who work alongside their husbands do not qualify for Social Security death benefits.
III. Inequity exists at the national level.
   A. A 1982 study concluded that income inequity existed in over 100 occupations.

    B. In the early 1980s, male school administrators earned more per year than female counterparts.

    C. Male elementary-school teachers earned more per year than female counterparts (females = 80% of work force).

    D. Male computer systems analysts also outearned women.

IV. Inequities in the work force also exist on this campus.

    A. The last seven years have seen little change in the percentage of women faculty.

        1. Tenure-track women faculty = 14% of the total faculty (nationwide availability is 23%).

        2. Percentage of female faculty hired in 1981–83 dropped 25% since 1977.

    B. The university has been slow to address the problem.

Satisfaction/Visualization Steps

  I. Equality between the sexes is recognized in tuition charges, graduation requirements, and exams.

 II. It is right, fair, and long past due that women be paid the same as men for equal work.

Action Step

  I. I am not asking that women be "one of the boys."

 II. What I want: an America that judges qualifications rather than gender.[25]

The Motivated Sequence and Actuative Speeches

Demands for action can be issued and defended very efficiently by using the motivated sequence. In fact, the desire to structure speeches that move people to action (to buy a product or to engage in another specified behavior) was the impetus behind Alan Monroe's development of this organizational scheme. Rather than examine an outline of a speech to actuate, we will look at a sample student speech.

Sample Speech

Following is a speech prepared by Denalie Silha of North Dakota State University for an Interstate Oratorical Association contest in 1991. Ms. Silha had to dispel some myths about the elderly before she could convince her young audience that retirees ought to be considered a "lost resource" rather than a throwaway population. Her opening story captured a sense of the expertise that can come with age (Paragraph 1), Paragraph 2 generalized the matter and forecast the organization of the speech, and Paragraphs 3–9 developed a series of needs: size of over-65 population, increased improvement in health and vitality of this group, special areas such as daycare that could use retirees as valued employees, and the needs that retrained retirees could solve for the society at large. Paragraphs 10 and 11 then provide the formal satisfaction step, 12 and 13 refer to earlier portions of the speech (especially Paragraphs 7 and 8) that served as the visualization of the good results retraining could provide, and the speech finishes with a call to action in the form of testimony from a large investment brokerage that had a company led by a 94-year-old woman—a definite challenge to the audience to break away from its stereotypes about old people. The speech is very well put together and well-adapted to the rhetorical task of modifying existing beliefs.

Rediscovering a Lost Resource: Rethinking Retirement[26]
Denalie Silha

Meet Bill Ames—beefy, amiable, and a 66-year-old bargain extraordinaire. Bill retired three years ago. But his former employer, Varian Associates, wanted him to come back to work—desperately. You see, Ames is one of the few people around who knows how to properly test a Klystron tube, an expensive piece of equipment essential to satellite communications. As it turned out, all Varian had to do was ask. Ames readily agreed to work part-time, happy to escape the boredom he'd discovered in retirement. /1

Bill Ames is not an isolated case. As is documented in the January 30, 1989, issue of *Fortune* magazine, the median age of the U.S. population is increasing dramatically. There is a devastating problem facing American society today. That problem is the growing number of Americans over the age of 65 who are retired and out of the workforce. Today, we'll explore this problem in detail. To do so, we'll look at why the growing number of older Americans—those over age 65—who are forced into retirement—is a problem. Subsequently, we'll discover workable solutions to this dilemma. Once the problem and several practical solutions have been revealed, I'll present several feasible steps which we should take to implement them. /2

So, why has mandatory retirement at age 65, a standard readily accepted by Americans in the past, suddenly become a problem? During most of human history, only 1 in 10 people has lived to the age of 65. In today's America, 8 in 10 zoom past their 65th birthday, according to the April 16th *U.S. News and World Report*. They have become the fastest-growing population in the country—their numbers outpacing teenagers for the first time ever. As the baby boom generation matures and life expectancies increase, the nation will have a much larger older population. This, coupled with a decline in the birthrate, will mean a workforce dramatically different from today's. Twelve percent of the American population is now over age 65, according to the May, 1990, *Science* magazine, and this figure will rise to 20% by the year 2020. What this means is that within the next 30 years, the percentage of our population who are over the age of 65 will double! Given these projections, there will be one retiree for every two workers. This is in contrast to the current figure of approximately four workers supporting each retiree. If these projections are correct, that the income of every two workers rather than four workers will be supporting each retiree, we can deduce that a much more significant portion of your paycheck and mine will be deducted for Social Security. Obviously, at least economically speaking, the significance of this problem spans well beyond older Americans to include those of us just entering the workforce. /3

What is important about this new generation of older people is its difference not just in size but in vitality and outlook. Many of these older Americans are willing and able to work. According to Alvar Svanborg, of the University of Göteborg in Sweden, "today's 70 year olds are healthier, more vital, and intellectually. . . more capable than 70 year olds a decade ago." /4

A society whose citizens are living longer should enable them to work longer. They are older, but they are not the frail incompetents we tend to depict them as. At this point you may be thinking, "Personally, I can't wait to retire." But according to surveys by Lou Harris and the American Association of Retired Persons, "40% of retired people would actually prefer to be back in the workforce, holding a job and holding their heads a tad higher." Perhaps retirement at age 65 should be an option rather than a mandate. /5

Certainly, these seniors should be allowed to remain in the workforce longer if they are willing and able to do so. But as the U.S. enters the 1990's, we must address the needs and concerns of our older citizens in ways which benefit them, as well as society. We can and should be retraining seniors to work in fields where shortages exist. Some employers have discovered that to hold onto these valuable employees longer they must keep them motivated. Thus, these innovators have started retraining seniors. /6

One prime example of retraining seniors to work where shortages exist is in the day-care field. In some communities, toddlers are being paired with seniors in day-care centers. Such links fulfill important social as well as economic needs. Vast numbers of children in our mobile society are growing up deprived of the important contact with older people. Even their grandparents may live far away and see them only once or twice a year. Further, the media portray older adults as passive and unproductive. "By forging a link between the generations, older people are feeling appreciated, children are broadening their horizons, and both groups are making new friends." Seniors express feelings of "being young again" and say the experience "gives me something special to wake up for" as is reported by *Educational Leadership*, May of 1989. /7

Further, by retraining seniors to work in such fields as day-care centers an economic need for society is fulfilled as well. Currently, turnover in day-care centers is high because the centers cannot afford to pay competitive wages. The wages such centers can afford to offer do not provide young men and women an income level necessary to raise a family. Rather than continuing to face employee shortages in such facilities, the retraining of seniors would meet these needs while providing a welcome supplement to social security. Thus, the children benefit, the centers benefit, the seniors benefit, and society benefits. /8

In addition to retraining for day-care, similar retraining programs include organizing phone links between older people and latchkey kids, who return to empty homes after school. Still another possibility is to utilize seniors as management consultants. According to Matilda Riley, Director of the National Institute on Aging, "Throughout the health care system, there is a pressing demand for assistance from older people in a range of positions from nursing home aides to management consultants." Innovative retraining programs such as these can certainly benefit older Americans as well as society. /9

Now that we've determined that forced retirement at age 65 is an unnecessary problem which hurts older Americans as well as society in general, let's take a closer look at how we can effectively solve this problem. First and foremost, retirement at age 65 must be made an option rather than a requirement. According to the April 9, 1990, issued of *Fortune* magazine, "unless the trend toward earlier retirement is reversed, many folks will spend more years as retirees than as workers. This cannot and should not be the case. Certainly, older Americans should be given the option to retire, however, they should not be forced to do so." /10

Second, National or State funded retraining programs need to be established for the nation's seniors. By funding such programs through government agencies initially, the impetus would be set for businesses to follow suit. Some innovative corporations have "seen the light" with regard to retraining experienced employees. According to the April 1, 1990, *U.S. News and World Report*, one-third of the reservations staff at Days Inn is older workers and running short on teenage help, McDonalds actively recruits older employees. It's not enough, however, for a handful of corporations to stand as models. Public leaders must set the agenda by making this an issue and cause these trends to spread to thousands of other employers, large and small. /11

But what can we—here in this room—do to foster this necessary trend to employ willing and able older workers? First, we need to adjust our attitudes. Each one of us must begin to look for older Americans who want to volunteer to help us. Older Americans can be a vital resource to aid us in school and in the workplace. It is up to us to seek out their help. For too long, we have held the inaccurate notion that older Americans are elderly Americans. It is up to each of us to change this attitude individually, as well as collectively. And, furthermore, it is up to each one of us to do the asking. /12

Today, we've taken a closer look at this significant problem of the growing number of Americans over age 65 who are forced into retirement. We've examined the dramatic costs to society if the contributions of these able-bodied Americans continue to be ignored. And finally we've posed several workable solutions which must be implemented to correct this injustice. /13

Listen to Warren Buffett, who has built an investment empire. When asked a few years ago about leaving a woman in charge of one of his companies after celebrating her 94th birthday, he replied, "She is clearly gathering speed and may well reach her full potential in another five or ten years. Therefore, I've persuaded the board to scrap our mandatory-retirement-at-100 policy. My God, good managers are so scarce I can't afford the luxury of letting them go just because they've added a year to their age." /14

Chapter Summary

The rhetorical arts of persuasion and actuation are fundamental to any democratic society. Not only are they the heart and soul of capitalism, American mass media, and politics, but they're necessary to the operation of your everyday life. Effective persuasive speaking is a function of *adapting to an audience's psychological states* (psychological orientations, predispositions toward the topic, cognitive complexity, and latitudes of acceptance), *drawing upon diverse external reference groups*, and *enhancing personal credibility*. The strategies discussed under each of these topics are not exhaustive, but they suggest mental habits of audience analysis that speakers must employ each time they attempt persuasion. To increase your effectiveness, use them whenever you seek to *reinforce* an audience's commitment to shared values, to *modify* listeners' *beliefs*, *attitudes*, and *values*, or to move them to *action*. The motivated sequence is of great help as you plan all three kinds of persuasive speeches.

References

1. For a discussion of the full range of rhetorical and narrative materials that count as "good reasons," see Walter R. Fisher, *Human Communication as Narration* (Columbia, SC: University of South Carolina Press, 1987), chs. 2 and 3.

2. Arnold Mitchell, *The Nine American Lifestyles: Who We Are and Where We're Going* (New York: Macmillan, 1983).

3. Drawn from Mitchell, chs. 1 and 2, using many of his words for describing each category.

4. For background on the one- vs. two-sided speeches, see Herbert W. Simons, *Persuasion: Understanding, Practice, and Analysis*, 2nd ed. (New York: Random House, 1986), 28–30.

5. J. W. Prescott, "Bodily Pleasure and Origins of Violence," *The Futurist* (1975): 64–74. The main source of research on central and peripheral beliefs, attitudes, and values is Milton Rokeach, *Beliefs, Attitudes, and Values* (San Francisco: Jossey-Bass, 1968); much of this is summarized in Erwin P. Bettinghaus and Michael J. Cody, *Persuasive Communication*, 4th ed. (New York: Holt, Rinehart & Winston, 1987), 18–22.

6. Richard E. Petty and John T. Cacioppo, *Communication and Persuasion: Central and Peripheral Routes to Attitude Change* (New York: Springer-Verlag, 1986), 83.

7. Petty and Cacioppo, 129.

8. Petty and Cacioppo, 153.

9. Petty and Cacioppo, 87.

10. Petty and Cacioppo, 143.

11. Petty and Cacioppo, 20-21.

12. The idea that attitudes in part are cognitions existing on a continuum is central to many psychological theories; the classic source for this idea is R. P. Abelson, et al., *Theories of Cognitive Consistency: A Sourcebook* (Chicago, IL: Rand McNally, 1968). See the summary in Kay Deaux and Lawrence S. Wrightsman, *Social Psychology*, 5th ed. (Pacific Grove, CA: Brooks/Cole, 1988), 182–209.

13. Deaux and Wrightsman, 391–95. For a review of the basic research on authoritarian personality, obedience to authority in the famous Milgram experiments wherein subjects were supposedly administering electric shocks to others, and social explanations of authoritarianism, see Philip Zimbardo, *Psychology and Life*, 13th ed. (New York: HarperCollins, 1992), 585–92.

14. Zimbardo, 580–81.

15. Zimbardo, 640.

16. Such notions are developed in classic reference group theory as described in H. H. Kelley, "Two Functions of Reference Groups," in H. Prohansky and B. Seidenberg, eds., *Basic Studies in Social Psychology* (New York: Holt, Rinehart & Winston, 1965), 210–14. See also Bettinghaus and Cody, ch. 4.

17. Diane M. Mackie, "Systematic and Nonsystematic Processing of Majority and Minority Persuasive Communications," *Journal of Personality and Social Psychology*, 53 (1987): 41–52.

18. Petty and Cacioppo, 205.

19. R. E. Petty and T. C. Brock, "Effects of Responding or Not Responding to Hecklers on Audience Agreement with a Speaker," *Journal of Applied Social Psychology*, 6 (1976): 1–17.

20. A complete summary of research on credibility, which supports these conclusions, is found in Stephen Littlejohn, "A Bibliography of Studies Related to Variables of Source Credibility," in Ned. A. Shearer, ed., *Bibliographical Annual in Speech Communication: 1971* (New York: Speech Communication Association, 1972), 1–40. Research which shows that credibility tends to vary from situation to situation and topic to topic is represented by such studies as Jo Liska, "Situational and Topical Variations in Credibility Criteria," *Communication Monographs*, 45 (1978): 85–92. For a contemporary account of the relationship between source credibility and attitude change, see Petty and Cacioppo.

21. Chaim Perelman and L. Olbrechts-Tyteca, *The New Rhetoric: A Treatise on Argumentation*, trans. John Wilkinson and Purcell Weaver (Notre Dame, IN: University of Notre Dame Press, 1969), 51.

22. Fisher ch. 5.

23. Donald Dean Morley and Kim B. Walker, "The Role of Importance, Novelty, and Plausibility in Producing Belief Change," *Communication Monographs*, 54 (1987): 436–42. The theory is presented in Donald Dean Morley, "Subjective Message Constructs: A Theory of Persuasion," *Communication Monographs*, 54 (1987): 183–203.

24. Deaux and Wrightsman, 160-209; Gerald R. Miller, Michael Burgoon, and Judee K. Burgoon, "The Functions of Human Communication in Changing Attitudes and Gaining Compliance," in Carroll C. Arnold and John Waite Bowers, eds., *Handbook of Rhetorical and Communication Theory* (Boston: Allyn and Bacon, 1984), 400–74.

25. Adapted from a speech by Fran Biersman, in R. R. Allen, and R. E. McKerrow, *The Pragmatics of Public Communication*, 3rd ed. (Dubuque, IA: Kendall/Hunt Publishing Co., 1985), 351–53.

26. Denalie Silha, "Rediscovering a Lost Resource: Rethinking Retirement," *Winning Orations 1991*, ed. Larry G. Schnoor, Executive Secretary (Mankato, MN: Interstate Oratorical Association, 1991), 78–81.

Key Terms

actuation (p. 427)	*one-sided speech* (p. 413)
belief networks (p. 413)	*psychological state* (p. 410)
boomerang effect (p. 416)	*reference groups* (p. 417)
cognitive complexity (p. 415)	*reinforcement* (p. 421)
incremental change (p. 415)	*saliency* (p. 414)
latitude of acceptance (p. 416)	*two-sided speech* (p. 413)
lifestyles (p. 410)	*Values and Lifestyles Program*
modification (p. 423)	*(VALS)* (p. 410)

Problems and Probes

1. Analyze the differences between an appeal to persuade and an appeal to actuate in relation to the essential features of persuasion discussed in this chapter (adaptation to psychological state, change by degrees, saliency, credibility) for each of the following situations: (a) you want your parents to stop smoking; (b) you try to convince your best friend not to drop out of school; (c) you want a stranger to donate money to the local Hospice program. In what ways do your appeals differ? What variables account for the differences? Which factors are the most difficult to analyze in each of these situations and why?

2. Comment on this statement: "Most people act out of desire rather than reason; they only use reason to justify to themselves and others what they want to do anyway." If this statement has merit, how would it affect the development of a speech to actuate? Develop at least three specific principles that a speaker might consider if the statement is true.

Communication Activities

1. Develop and present to the class a five-to-seven-minute speech. Follow the steps in the motivated sequence appropriate to the type of speech chosen: reinforcement, modification, or actuation. As you construct your speech, keep in mind the strategies discussed in this chapter, both in terms of the essential features of all persuasive speeches and those specific to your speech. Adapt to the audience members as you deem appropriate from your analysis of their beliefs, attitudes, and values.

2. Present a five-to-eight-minute speech with the specific goal of persuading audience members to take an action you recommend. Show that a problem or situation needing remedy exists and that they should be personally concerned about potential solutions. In presenting the solution, indicate why you believe that action on their part will be a concrete, influential move toward a remedy

(do not simply say, "Write your . . ."; indicate why it would help). On a future "checkup" day, see how many listeners have taken the recommended action. This task can be an assignment for the entire class with a questionnaire used on "checkup" day to see which recommended actions were taken. As possible speeches, you might urge an audience to sign a petition asking for a specific change on your campus (for example, establishing a day-care center), or you might ask class members to write letters to the editor of the local newspaper urging that a particular community action be taken or avoided (be sure to provide the address). You also might ask them to attend an informational meeting of a newly organized campus group or a meeting of the student government to protest its position on an issue important to you.

CHAPTER 17

ARGUMENT AND CRITICAL THINKING

W e live in an information age that constantly bombards us with requests, appeals, and pleas to change our beliefs or to adopt new behaviors or actions. Sorting through these multiple and at times contradictory claims requires a critical spirit—a willingness to apply personal reasoning skills to others' ideas as well as to our own. Thinking critically is central to your participation in the social world.[1]

Employing a critical spirit isn't a matter of putting others or yourself down; it's a process of careful assessment, evaluation, and judgment of the reasons offered in support of a claim. As you engage in critical evaluation, you become an arguer, a person who argues with others or even with yourself as you assess the reasons for and against adopting a proposed belief or action. The critical spirit has two essential applications in public speaking:

1. Through **arguing,** a speaker presents reasons giving support and force to claims.
2. Through **critical thinking,** a listener evaluates the reasons offered prior to accepting or rejecting the claims.

Argument and critical thinking are bound together in public communication. Exchanging views in the social world automatically includes the critical assessment of those ideas. As a result, this chapter begins with an examination of the social process involved in arguing with others. Then, the chapter will consider the critical evaluation of claims and conclude with some tips to improve your effectiveness as an arguer.

Argument as a Social Process

Engaging in **argument** commits you to following the social conventions governing public deliberation. These conventions may be explicit (parliamentary procedure) or implicit (respect for others' ideas). Through **argumentation,** people arrive at reasoned conclusions about facts, values, and policies. The reliance on reason constitutes the major difference between argumentation and mere fighting. As such, argumentation is a form of persuasion in that it seeks to change the beliefs, attitudes, values, and behaviors of others. At the same time, it's a form of mutual truth-testing, helping participants arrive at the best possible conclusions, given the information available at the time. Thus, the process is more thoroughly *rule-governed* than other forms of public presentation. In addition, four major social conventions apply to arguing with others: (a) bilaterality, (b) self-risk, (c) fairness, and (d) rationality.

Bilaterality

Arguing is inherently **bilateral**—that is, it requires at least two people or two competing messages. Even when arguing with yourself, you assume two incompatible positions. Controversy is inherent in the process: we don't argue with others or ourselves about what's self-evident. Argumentation occurs when others have different points of view than we do. When candidates for public office present their campaign ideas, they expect counterargument from opposing candidates. They may even engage in face-to-face debates in which they express their opposing views in response to questions from a moderator or panel. In your own immediate environment, arguments may occur in a variety of settings—where you live, study, attend class, or eat. While these situations aren't as formal as debates, they nonetheless share many of the same features: reasons are given and refuted; claims are advanced and withdrawn.

Self-Risk

Arguing with others entails risk. There's always the chance that your ideas won't be accepted. If you wish to argue, however, that's a risk you must accept. For example, if you argue that all hospital personnel and patients should be subject to mandatory AIDS testing, opponents will likely claim that such action is impractical and unnecessary. If your opponents succeed in convincing an audience that their objections have merit, you'll either have to acquiesce or find stronger arguments to overturn the objections. In arguing, there's a moral obligation to yield to a stronger argument.[2]

Fairness

Fairness in argumentation depends on the commonly accepted standards of a social group; it entails allowing others to have their say. Thus, you

Argumentation is inherently bilateral: it requires at least two competing messages. Reasons are given and refuted; claims are advanced and withdrawn.

commit yourself to a version of what the Federal Communications Commission calls a *fairness doctrine*—every viewpoint must be given equal access to the airwaves. In argumentation, arguers must have the ability to say, "I have the right to be heard. You may reject my claims and reasons, but first you must hear me out." For this reason, most legislative bodies are reluctant to cut off debate. They are committed to upholding the First Amendment right of expression through the fairness doctrine. While we may not agree with a point of view, we have an obligation to uphold the other's right to self-expression.

Rationality

Rationality is the central element in the assessment of reasons (critical thinking) and their presentation (arguing). The reasons you offer for your claim must be seen as good reasons for accepting the argument—they must be relevant to the issues, supported with clear reasoning and solid evidence. You'll be held accountable for the claims you advance. In particular, rational argumentation adheres to standards of **validity** and the **soundness** of arguments. An argument is considered *valid* if its pattern of reasoning follows the applicable rules for its development; an argument is *sound* if its content offers good reasons for the adoption of the claim. Applying the tests of reasoning and detecting fallacies in your own arguments (see pp. 455–58), as well as in those advanced by opponents, will make you both a competent arguer and an astute critical thinker.

In some cases, argumentation follows formal rules that govern who may speak when and for how long, as well as how decisions will be reached. A presidential debate, for example, is conducted in accordance with a unique set of rules agreed to by the participants. A legislative body argues in accordance with agreed-upon **parliamentary procedures** (such as those set forth in *Robert's Rules of Order*).[3] Since such technical rules are an important feature of argumentation in small-group or deliberative settings, parliamentary procedure is included in one section of the *Speaker's Resource Book* at the end of this textbook.

In argument, all four of these social conventions—bilaterality, self-risk, fairness, and rationality—must be observed. In arguing, for example, that *Roe* v. *Wade* should be overturned, you have an obligation to demonstrate that an unborn fetus's rights supercede those of the mother (commitment to rationality). As you speak, you also must recognize that others have the right to voice their disagreement with your proposal (commitment to fairness) and that they may refute your argument (commitment to self-risk). An opponent may assert that the alleged right isn't universal, hence should be the decision of the mother (commitment of bilaterality). No matter what the claim, each arguer has the right to ask "Why do you believe this?" and "Why should I believe this?" (commitment to rationality). Arguing with others and engaging in critical thinking means being willing to analyze claims in accordance with these conventions.

The discussion of social convention has employed the concept "argument" in several senses. For our purposes the following distinctions are useful:[4]

1. **Argument**—the actual "product" that results from the combination of a *claim* plus supporting *reasons* and *evidence*
2. **Arguing**—the individual act in expressing a claim plus supportive reasons
3. **Argumentation**—the process of engaging others in controversy; the give and take of argument-counterargument (The term also can apply to the *study* of argument as both product and process.)

In formal encounters, the above terms can be sorted into three distinct *levels:* I. The Unit of Argument; II. The Argumentative Speech; and III. The Argumentative Process. Speeches given by the proponents of change are

THE LEVELS OF ARGUMENTATION

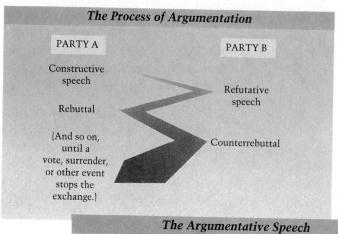

The Process of Argumentation

PARTY A

Constructive speech

Rebuttal

(And so on, until a vote, surrender, or other event stops the exchange.)

PARTY B

Refutative speech

Counterrebuttal

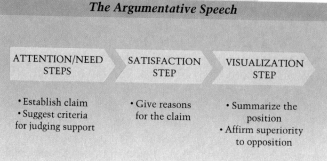

The Argumentative Speech

ATTENTION/NEED STEPS

SATISFACTION STEP

VISUALIZATION STEP

• Establish claim
• Suggest criteria for judging support

• Give reasons for the claim

• Summarize the position
• Affirm superiority to opposition

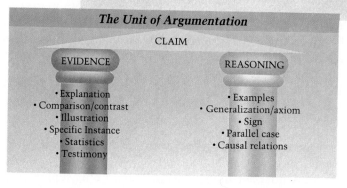

The Unit of Argumentation

CLAIM

EVIDENCE

REASONING

• Explanation
• Comparison/contrast
• Illustration
• Specific Instance
• Statistics
• Testimony

• Examples
• Generalization/axiom
• Sign
• Parallel case
• Causal relations

often called **constructive speeches,** while those of opponents are termed **refutative speeches.** Each person or side may then continue the argument through a series of **rebuttal speeches** designed to respond to the most recent charges of the opponent. In each case, the speech includes (a) an introduction that sets out the claim and suggests criteria for assessing it; (b) a body organized around a series of reasons and evidence that supports the claim;

and (c) a conclusion that summarizes the position and indicates why your position is superior to your opponent's. Ultimately, the process ends when resolution is reached, the formal time frame for the debate comes to an end, or the parties agree to suspend interaction until a future time.

Elements of Argument

The analysis of argument begins with the **claim** being advanced, then examines the nature of **evidence** used in support of the claim and the major **reasoning patterns** (sometimes referred to as the **warrants** or **inferences**) used to connect evidence to claims.

Types of Claims

The majority of argumentative speeches assert that (a) something is or is not the case; (b) something is desirable or undesirable; or (c) something should or should not be done. The first step in constructing a successful argument is to determine clearly the nature of the claim you wish to establish.

Claims of Fact.   If you were trying to convince your listeners that incentive-based recycling is more cost-efficient than mandatory recycling, you would be presenting a claim of fact—asserting that an audience is justified in believing that this state of affairs exists or will exist. When confronted with a **factual claim,** two questions are likely to arise in the mind of a critical listener:

1. *By what criteria or standards of judgment should the truth or accuracy of this claim be measured?* Some standards are rather obvious. If you were asked to judge a person's height, using a yardstick or other instrument would provide the answer. Listeners look for similar kinds of yardsticks when asked to evaluate more complex claims. What, for example, is meant by "cost-efficient" in the recycling claim? Against what standard, precisely, is the accuracy of the claim to be judged?

2. *Do the facts of the situation fit the criteria as set forth?* Do lower taxes or subsidies for garbage disposal satisfy the "cost efficient" standard? In demonstrating that the facts are adequate, set forth your criteria in clear terms, then relate the facts in a way that illustrates the connection between them and the criteria.

If your audience disagrees with your claim, they may choose to attack the criteria or the facts themselves. At the very least, when there is direct opposition to your claim, you know what you need to cover in your rebuttal.

Claims of Value.   A claim also may incorporate value judgments in asserting that your idea is worthy or that the idea of an opponent is undesirable or

Argumentativeness and Verbal Aggression

Is being an arguer a positive or negative trait? How about the individual who argues by attacking the person rather than the substance of the argument? Isn't he or she violating the conventions of argumentation outlined in this chapter? Don't some people really like to engage in argumentation, while others seem to acquiesce in order to avoid an argument?

Infante and his colleagues conducted a series of studies on *argumentativeness* and *verbal aggression*. They conceptualized *argumentativeness* in positive terms, as a socially desirable trait that predisposes an individual to assess reasons and to present arguments in accordance with appropriate social conventions. Students strongly oriented toward arguing with others were found to have experienced greater training in argumen-

tation. They also reported a higher overall grade point, were born earlier in the family birth order (which is consistent with other research on the assertiveness of first-borns), preferred smaller classes (presumably because it is easier to engage in argumentation), and tended to be more liberal.

More importantly, Infante et al. found that "high argumentatives" are *not* less likely than "low argumentatives" to value the importance of maintaining general social relations or getting along with peers. Enjoying a good argument does not mean a person cannot respect others. In actual argumentation, those who scored high on an "Argumentativeness Scale" displayed less flexibility in the positions they advocated, appeared more interested in arguing and willing to argue, were perceived as more skillful

unjustified. In these cases, you are articulating a **value claim** that, as with a factual claim, is supported by (a) standards or criteria and (b) by the illustration of how your value term meets those criteria. In the preceding example, you might also claim that incentive-based recycling is *superior* to mandatory recycling. Providing consumers with incentives to recycle may yield cost-efficiency with respect to collection and disposal, less bureaucracy involved in managing, and more positive feelings about the effort. These advantages are offered as evidence in support of the judgment of superiority; they may also be balanced by a discussion of disadvantages associated with mandatory programs. In essence, the relative weight of advantages versus disadvantages determines the adequacy of the value term.

arguers, and were more enthusiastic in their conduct of the argument.

While argumentativeness is linked to assertive behavior, *verbal aggressiveness* is related to hostility and reflects a willingness to verbally abuse a person in the act of arguing. While argumentatively oriented people may resort to verbal aggression under some circumstances, the two "traits" are distinct psychological responses. People higher in argumentativeness are no more likely than others in engage in aggressive behavior. Two sources of verbal aggression are frustration with the way another person is arguing or with a recognition of one's own skill deficiencies and prior experience or social conditioning to respond aggressively. A person scoring high on the "Verbal Aggressiveness" scale is more likely to attack an opponent's competence, tease an opponent, use facial expressions and other nonverbal cues to attack the opponent's self-concept, and use profanity.

As this research suggests, argumentation can be a constructive, positive activity when it adheres to the social conventions. Arguing well with others can be personally enjoyable regardless of the outcome, but using verbal aggression is destructive to other people and diminishes the quality of any decisions that might be reached.

FOR FURTHER READING

Infante, Dominic A. "The Argumentative Student in the Speech Communication Classroom: An Investigation and Implications." *Communication Education* 31 (1982): 141–48; Infante, Dominic A. "Trait Argumentativeness as a Predictor of Communicative Behavior in Situations Requiring Argument." *Central States Speech Journal* 32 (1981): 265–72; Infante, Dominic A., and Andrew Rancer. "A Conceptualization and Measure of Argumentativeness." *Journal of Personality Assessment* 46 (1982): 72–80; Infante, Dominic A., and Charles J. Wigley III. "Verbal Aggressiveness: An Interpersonal Model and Measure." *Communication Monographs* 53 (1986): 61–69; Infante, Dominic A., J. David Trebing, Patricia E. Shepherd, and Dale E. Seeds. "The Relationship of Argumentativeness to Verbal Aggression." *Southern Speech Communication Journal* 50 (1984): 67–77. Infante, Dominic, Bruce L. Riddle, Cary L. Horvath, S. A. Tumlin. "Verbal Aggressiveness: Messages and Reasons." *Communication Quarterly* 40 (Spring, 1992): 116–26.

Claims of Policy.   A **policy claim** recommends a course of action you want the audience to approve. The above example might be phrased as "The federal government *should* establish incentive-based recycling programs." The policy claim incorporates fact and value claims as its primary "proofs":

> *Policy:* The Federal Government should establish incentive-based recycling programs . . . because . . .
>> *Value:* Incentive programs are superior to mandatory programs . . . because . . .
>>> *Fact:* Incentive programs are more cost-efficient.
>>> *Fact:* Incentive programs will produce a more receptive attitude toward recycling.

ETHICAL MOMENTS

The Use of Evidence

The use of evidence generates several potential ethical dilemmas. Consider the following issues:

1. Should you suppress evidence that contradicts a point you are making? If your opponent isn't aware of the information, should you mention it?

2. What about the use of qualifiers? Should you leave in all of the "maybe's" and "possibly's" when you read or paraphrase a quotation? If you have to submit a written text or outline, you can use ellipses (the three dots that indicate something is missing from the original) where the qualifiers once were.

3. Does it make any difference if you overqualify a source? If you've discovered an article by a staff researcher at the National Endow-

ment for the Arts on the issue of funding controversial art, will it hurt to pretend the information is from an Associate Director of the agency? It would increase the credibility of the information, and who's to know? Should you care?

4. What difference does it make if the poll is conducted by the National Right-to-Life Committee or Planned Parenthood's Pro-Choice Committee? What if each organization asks polling questions in such a way as to encourage a response favorable to their position? Can you just say that "a recent national poll found that 75% of our citizens favor abortion rights?" You haven't really lied in suppressing the polling agency or the actual questions asked, have you? Is this acceptable?

The key term in the policy claim is *should*—it identifies a proposed policy or defends a policy or action that's presently the case. For our purposes, those policy claims examined will *challenge* the present system, procedure, or way of doing things. In these instances, these subsidiary questions are most relevant:

1. *Is there a need for such a policy or course of action?* If your listeners don't believe a change is called for, they aren't likely to approve your proposal. This doesn't mean you should avoid new ideas; rather, it suggests that the importance of establishing a *need for change* depends upon the audience's level of comfort with the status quo.

448

2. *Is the proposal practical or workable?* Can we afford the expenses it would entail? Will it meet the need as identified? Does such a policy stand a reasonable chance of being adopted? Arguing that in any future conflict only persons aged 65 or over should be drafted into the Armed Forces may be interesting, but is it even remotely possible that audiences would agree? Why would we want to adopt this idea?

3. *Will the benefits of your proposal be greater than its disadvantages?* People are reluctant to approve a proposal that promises to create conditions worse than the ones it's designed to correct. Burning a building to the ground to get rid of rats may be efficient, but hardly desirable. Drafting 65-year-old men and women may save the lives of those between 18 and 24, but aren't there some other reasons not to support this idea? The benefits and disadvantages must be carefully weighed in concluding that a proposal is indeed comparatively better than the present course.

4. *Is the offered proposal superior to any other plan or policy?* Listeners are hesitant to approve a plan if they have reason to believe that an alternative course is more practical and more beneficial. During the 1992 presidential race, for example, Bush, Clinton, and Perot argued for their respective solutions to the poor economy and negated their opponents' plans. With the alternatives in front of them, the American people could choose the plan they felt would be more practical and beneficial.

From what you've learned about the three types of claims, you should be able to see the importance of knowing in advance what expectations the claim itself entails. If you are arguing a policy claim, will you need to answer all four of the above issues, or does the audience already accept one or more of them? If your central claim is one of fact or value, what criteria should be used as bases for judgment, and how well does your evidence meet them? Finally, unless there are reasons for delay, you should announce the claim you are supporting or opposing early in the presentation. If your listeners don't see the precise point you're making, your strongest arguments and appeals will likely prove useless.

Evidence

As you discovered in Chapter 7, supporting materials clarify, amplify, and strengthen the ideas in your speech. They provide evidence for the acceptance of your claim and its supporting points. Evidence is a crucial part of developing a clear, compelling argument and can be presented in any of the forms already discussed: explanation, comparison and contrast, illustration, specific instance, statistics, and testimony.

The primary goal in selecting evidence is to obtain material that's *relevant* to the argumentative claim being advanced. There is no single rule for choosing relevant material. Examples or testimony relevant to one claim won't necessarily be relevant to a related claim, or they may be relevant but not particularly strong. In considering the relevance of your supporting materials, consider their *rational* and *motivational* characteristics.

Rationally Relevant Evidence.   The type of evidence you select should reflect the type of claim you advocate. For example, if you argue that shark fishing should be more heavily regulated, you'll probably choose examples of poor fishing practices or statistical evidence that relates to overfishing and potential loss to the ecosystem. If you are arguing that your college's athletic program isn't meeting Title IX requirements, you'll need to show the percentage of men and women participants and the current levels of funding for men's and women's sports programs. You'll also want to provide testimony that indicates the guidelines used by universities to gauge their compliance. In many cases, the claim advanced suggests the kind of evidence that will be most relevant. Always ask yourself, "Given this claim, what evidence is naturally suggested by the subject matter?"

Motivationally Relevant Evidence.   Listeners often require more than logically relevant support. Your evidence also must create a compelling desire on their part to be involved, to endorse the belief, or to undertake a course of action. That is, to motivate your listeners you must answer the "So What?" question. The selection of motivational materials can be guided by two questions:

1. *What type of evidence will the audience demand?* To orient your thinking, turn this around and ask, "As a member of the audience, what would I expect as support for this claim in order to accept it?" What motivated you may well motivate the audience. And, as noted above, some evidence seems naturally connected to certain subjects. A claim regarding relative costs of competing plans suggests things like statistical graphs or charts. A claim regarding the attitudes of consumers suggests testimony from experts who have studied consumer behavior and poll data reflecting direct questions addressed to consumers. If the audience is able to say "Yes . . . but . . ." after hearing your evidence, you haven't covered the ground as comprehensively as they require.

    A claim that says "The President has done a poor job managing the economy" may be supported with relevant testimony from experts. That alone, however, may not be sufficient to allay audience suspicions that the experts are wrong, or that the President's hands were tied by Congress. Thus, the context in which you are arguing also plays a role in determining what will motivate audiences to accept your message. Careful audience analysis and consideration of the occasion will help determine what will motivate your listeners.

2. *Which specific pieces of evidence will your listeners be most responsive to?* You should pose this question once you've determined the type of evidence required in your argument. For example, if you've decided to use expert testimony to support your argument, whom should you quote? If you're using an illustration, should you use a factual example from the local group or develop one of your own? Will your listeners be more moved by a personal story than a general illustration?

Reasoning (Inference)

Once you have a claim and evidence, you must illustrate its connection— why or how does this evidence support this claim? Using different forms of reasoning or inference provides the connective. Patterns of reasoning are habitual ways a culture or society uses inferences to connect the material supporting a claim with the claim itself. Basically, there are five reasoning patterns: reasoning from examples, generalization, sign, parallel case, and causal relations.

Reasoning from Examples. Often called **inductive reasoning, reasoning from examples** is a matter of examining a series of known occurrences and drawing a general conclusion, or it is using a single instance to reason to a future instance of the same kind. The conclusion is probable rather than certain: "In every election in our community over the past few years, when a candidate leads the polls by 10 or more points with a month to go, he or she has won. Thus, my candidate will surely win next month." Maybe so— but maybe not. The inference in this case can be stated as "What is true of the particular cases is true of the whole class, or, more precisely, future instances of the same class."

As another example, consider the kinds of evidence collected by the National Cancer Institute about the relationship between diet and cancer. Making an inductive leap based on case histories that showed people with high fiber diets had fewer instances of digestive tract cancer, the NCI issued this advisory: "High fiber diets help prevent certain types of cancer." This statement doesn't mean that using a high fiber diet precludes a form of cancer, only that such a diet does lessen the chances.

Note, however, that a single instance can be a powerful illustration on which to base a conclusion. One can argue that one death at an intersection supports the need for a traffic light, or that the death of one child from a three-wheel vehicle (recently banned after multiple injuries and deaths) is sufficient evidence to support the ban of all such vehicles. In sum, reasoning from examples doesn't ensure support for your claim but may suggest a high degree of probability.

Reasoning from Generalization or Axiom.   Applying a generally accepted truth to a specific situation is a form of **deductive reasoning.** Where inductive reasoning is typified by an inferential leap on the basis of the evidence, deductive reasoning produces a conclusion that is true if the premises are true. For example, you may have learned in a consumer course that buying goods in large quantities saves money (the generalization or evidence). On the basis of that statement, you might shop discount stores on the theory that because they purchase goods in quantity, they will pass the reduced cost on to the consumer, thereby saving you money (claim deduced from the evidence). To the extent that the **generalization** holds true, your experience has to hold true as well.

As a further illustration, consider a nonsensical argument:

All elephants have green trunks. (generalization)

Dumbo is an elephant. (secondary premise)

Dumbo has a green trunk. (claim)

If the generalization is true and the secondary premise is true, the conclusion *has* to be true. If the secondary premise suggested "Dumbo has a green trunk," you could not conclude "Dumbo is an elephant," as there may be other animals with green trunks. Thus, deductive reasoning has to follow accepted rules of reasoning from the generalization to the conclusion. The inference you draw between the generalization, secondary premise, and claim focuses attention on the strength of the evidence and on the reasoning involved in reaching a claim.

Reasoning from Sign.   This pattern uses an observable mark, or symptom, as proof of the existence of a certain state of affairs. **Sign reasoning** occurs when you note the appearance of a rash or spots on your skin (evidence) and conclude you have the measles (claim). Signs aren't causes; a rash doesn't cause measles, an ambulance siren doesn't cause the accident or crisis it responds to. Reasoning from sign is central to detective work, whether in your own investigation of a situation, a doctor's assessment of an illness, or a police detective's study of motives for a crime.

However, isolating the signs and reasoning to a probable conclusion based on what they suggest may yield an erroneous conclusion; thus sign reasoning doesn't produce certain evidence in all cases. Some evidence is certain—as in the claim that the temperature has to be below 32 degrees F, since there's ice on the pond. Other evidence is less than certain—motive, weapon, and opportunity don't prove a person committed a crime. In these and other cases, there may be several interpretations of the same evidence. Even though sign reasoning can be problematic, we nonetheless use signs as indicators; otherwise we wouldn't predict economic trends will continue or change, the weather will be cold or warm, or a political candidate will surely win or lose an election.

Reasoning from Parallel Case.   Another common reasoning pattern involves comparing similar events or things and drawing conclusions based on the comparison or **parallel case.** The claim that your state should adopt a motorcycle helmet law might be supported by noting that a neighboring state, with similar characteristics, has one and the result has been lower death and head injury rates. In essence, you are claiming "What happened there can happen here." The political candidate's claim that what he or she has done for a community or state can be repeated in a larger arena, while not precisely parallel, draws strength from this type of argument. As the variables separating the cases grow in size and significance, this reasoning pattern will become less forceful.

Reasoning from Causal Relations.   **Causal reasoning** assumes that one event influences or controls other events. You can reason from a specific cause to an effect or set of effects, or vice versa. For instance, assume that alcohol abuse on a campus appears to be increasing. Is the increase the result of lax enforcement of existing rules? Do loopholes allow for greater abusive situations to develop, in spite of best intentions? Are today's students more prone to abuse than in previous years? Pointing to one or more of these as the cause sets the stage for an analysis of potential solutions. The principle underlying this pattern is one of constancy: every effect has a cause.

Evaluating Arguments

Central to thinking critically is testing the reasoning pattern for weaknesses, both as a user and as a consumer. An assessment of the adequacy of your reasoning can take one of two forms: an analysis of specific patterns of reasoning, or an analysis of possible fallacies in reasoning.

Tests for Reasoning

Each pattern has its own unique set of criteria for establishing a valid, sound argument. Within the context of each pattern, apply the following questions to your own arguments and to those of others.

Reasoning from Examples:

1. *Have you looked at enough instances to warrant generalizing?* You don't assume it's now spring because of a one warm day in late February.
2. *Are the instances fairly chosen or representative?* Deciding never to shop in a store because a clerk was rude isn't exactly working on the basis of a representative sample, let alone sufficient. You'll want to judge the store in a variety of situations—if you find that rudeness is the norm rather than the exception, your claim may be justified.

3. *Are there important exceptions to the generalization that must be accounted for?* While it is generally true, from presidential election studies, that "As Maine goes, so goes the nation," there have been enough exceptions to that rule to keep candidates who lose in a Maine primary campaigning until the election.

Reasoning from Generalization or Axiom:

1. *Is the generalization true?* Even well accepted beliefs (such as the belief that the world is flat) may well be wrong. If the generalization isn't true, the conclusion or claim will necessarily be weakened—it may yet be justified, but not on the basis of this argument.
2. *Does the generalization apply to this particular case?* Usually, discount stores offer better deals, but on occasion one can find better prices at sales at local neighborhood stores. While "birds of a feather flock together" applies to birds, it may not apply to a group of humans.

Reasoning from Sign:

1. *Is the sign fallible?* Many signs constitute circumstantial evidence rather than infallible proof. The signs may all point to a thunderstorm, but as they alone don't cause the storm, it may or may not arrive.

Reasoning from Parallel Case:

1. *Are there more similarities than differences between the two cases?* Two items may have many features in common but there also may be significant differences that would weaken your argument. As suggested, too many differences seriously negate the effectiveness of the parallel argument.
2. *Are the similarities you've pointed out the relevant and important ones?* There are two students down the hall who dress in similar clothes, have the same major, and get similar grades; does this mean that if one is nice, so is the other one? Probably not, because the similarities you've noticed are relatively unconnected to niceness.

Reasoning from Causal Relations:

1. *Can you separate causes and effects?* We often have trouble with "Which came first?" kinds of issues. Do higher wages cause higher prices, or the reverse? Does a strained homelife cause a child to misbehave, or is it the other way around?
2. *Are the causes sufficient to produce the effect?* Causes must not only be *necessary* to produce an effect, they also must be *sufficient*. While air is necessary for fire to exist, it isn't all that's required or we would be in a state of constant fire.
3. *Did intervening events or persons prevent a cause from having its normal effect?* Causes do not always produce their expected effects; they may be interrupted by other factors. An empty gun does not shoot; droughts drive up food prices only if there is insufficient food on hand, the ground was already dry, or cheap alternatives are unavailable.

4. *Could any other cause have produced the effect?* Some effects may be produced by different causes; thus, you need to search for the most likely cause in a given situation. Although crime often increases when communities deteriorate, increased crime rates can also be caused by many other changes. A sagging economy could also be a possible reason for higher crime. Perhaps crime only appears to have risen; in actuality people are keeping better records.

5. *Is the cause really a correlation?* Correlations aren't necessarily causally related. Two phenomena may vary together without being related in any way. For example, since Abraham Lincoln's assassination, presidents elected in a year divisible by 20 (until President Reagan) died in office. However, the year was inconsequential in causing the death.

Detecting Fallacies in Reasoning

In addition to applying the foregoing tests, critical thinking requires the analysis of potential **fallacies** or flaws in the reasoning or inferential leap being made. (In essence, you are asking "Can you get here from there?") A convenient scheme divides the most frequent abuses of reasoning into three categories: (a) **fallacies in evidence;** (b) **fallacies in reasoning;** and (c) **fallacies in language.**

Fallacies in Evidence. As the label suggests, these fallacies occur in the way we use supporting material in reaching claims. Three stand out as potential abuses: **hasty generalization; false division;** and the **genetic fallacy.**

Hasty Generalization (faulty inductive leap): This fallacy occurs when the conclusion is based on far too little evidence. If the answer to the question "Have enough instances been examined?" is no, a flaw in reasoning has occurred. Urging a ban on 747's because one was involved in an accident or on aerosol sprays because one blew up in a fire is insufficient support for the claim being urged.

False Division: The assertion that there's only one way to divide a process or idea is often fallacious. There may be numerous ways to "divide the pie," depending on one's purpose. "Only" claims—"the only way to deal with AIDS victims is to isolate them" or "the only way to prevent crime is to institute a death penalty"—are weak assertions on our attention and belief. In fact there are other ways to deal with these issues besides the way advanced by a speaker.

Genetic Fallacy: This argument rests on origins, historical tradition, or sacred practice: "We've always done it this way; therefore this is the best way." The fact that an idea or institution or practice has been around a long time may have little bearing on whether it still should be. Many people who defended slavery referred to the Biblical practice of slavery. Times change, and new values replace old ones, suggesting that new practices may be more in tune with present values. Genetic definitions or arguments can provide

Converse. An 80-year winning streak.

Advertisers frequently ask consumers to purchase products because celebrities endorse them. In detecting fallacies in reasoning, consumers need to ask, "Is the celebrity an expert on the topic?"

appropriate historical significance, but they are, by themselves, hardly proof of the justice or adequacy of a practice or tradition.

Fallacies in Reasoning.   Among the fallacies that may occur in moving from evidence to claim are the following: **appeal to ignorance, appeal to popular opinion, sequential fallacy, begging the question,** and **appeal to authority.**

Appeal to ignorance (argumentum ad ignorantum): The expression "You *can't* prove it *won't* work" illicitly uses double negatives. Incomplete knowledge also doesn't mean a claim is or isn't true: "We can't use radio beams to signal extraterrestrials because we don't know what languages they speak"; "We've never been able to prove he did the deed; therefore he must not have." These are illogical claims because they depend on a state of ignorance. In countering such claims, utilize arguments from parallel cases and from examples since they both transcend the "unknown" in providing support for a claim.

Appeal to popular opinion (argumentum ad populum): "Jump on the bandwagon" and "Everyone is going" are appeals to group support. If others support the position, then you're pressured into supporting it as well: "But, Dad, everyone is going to the party!" Even if most people think something is the case, it still may or may not be true. There's ample evidence of false notions or theories that were once accepted by a populace to give one pause when hearing this kind of argument. While popular support indicates the worth assigned to a cause or event, it doesn't support factual claims.

Sequential fallacy (post hoc, ergo propter hoc): This phrase literally translates from the Latin as "After this; therefore because of this." A primitive kind of causal argument because it reasons solely from order in time, this fallacy is often heard: "I slept near a draft last night and woke up with a nasty head cold"; "The milk turned sour after she went through the barn; thus she is a witch" (from the Salem Witch trials). In some cases, the influence may in fact be the cause, but you need more evidence to support the connection: "I called him last night and today he recanted his story, as I advised him to."

Begging the question (petitio principii): Rephrasing an idea, then offering it as its own reason, begs the question. It is tautology, or circular thought: "Abortion is murder because it is taking the life of the unborn" rephrases the claim (it is murder) to form the reason (it is taking life). In other cases, begging the question occurs in the form of a *complex question:* "Have you stopped cheating on tests yet?" assumes you have cheated in the past, when that may not be proven. Saying "yes" admits past cheating; saying "no" admits to both past and present cheating. You can't win either way you go. Claims of value are especially prone to *petitio principii* arguments.

Appeal to authority (ipse dixit): "Because s/he says it" fallacies occur when someone who is popular but not an expert is used in support of a claim. Television advertisers commit this fallacy in using celebrities to endorse a product when they may have no natural or legitimate claim to expertise about that product. Ask, "Is the source an expert on this topic?" to test whether this fallacy has occurred.

Fallacies in Language.   Some fallacies are inadvertently or unconsciously formed simply by the way we use words. There are five linguistic fallacies that are common in public debate: **ambiguity, non-qualification, is-faults, persuasive definition,** and **name-calling.**

Ambiguity: A word may have more than one meaning; using a term without clarifying its specific meaning can result in confusion and in inaccurate claims: "Some dogs have droopy ears. My dog has droopy ears. My dog is *some* dog!" The confusion rests with the word "some"—its first use suggests "not all" dogs, while the second word suggests "outstanding/ exceptional." Such shifts in meaning can result in flawed claims.

Nonqualification: Qualifying terms such as "might," "maybe," or "possibly" may fall by the wayside in an argument; as they do, the likelihood of the claim being true diminishes dramatically. It may be true that "Our brand results in fewer cavities," but it may be far more accurate to say "Our brand *may* result in fewer cavities *if* you follow a program of regular hygiene and professional dental care." When the qualifications are underplayed, the argument is distorted.

Is-Faults: "Is" can refer either to *classification* ("Mary is a female") or to *attributes* ("Mary is a radical"). While "is" connects the person to an "object" in both cases, they are of quite different character; gender is an inherent biological condition, while a political position is subject to change. Using the connective "is" with attributes suggests permanence, when that isn't the case. Condemnatory speeches and advertisements often contain such fallacies.

Persuasive Definition: Value terms and other abstract concepts are open to special or skewed definitions that are unique to the person or group offering them: "Liberty means the right to own military weapons"; "Real men don't wear cologne"; "A true patriot doesn't protest against this country while on foreign soil." Each of these definitions sets up a particular point of view that is capricious and arbitrary. You could say that persuasive definitions are self-serving, as they promote an argument at the expense of more inclusive definitions of the same terms. If you accept the definition, the argument is essentially over.[5] Substituting a definition from a respected, widely accepted source is a way of challenging this fallacy.

Name-calling: There are several forms of this fallacy; all involve attacking the person rather than the argument. *Argumentum ad hominem* is an attack on the special interests of the person: "Of course you're defending her; she's your cousin." *Argumentum ad personam* attacks a personal characteristic of the individual: "No wonder you're arguing that way; dweebs always think that way." In these two cases, being related is not proof of defense, and dweebs may have ideas as good as anyone else's. *Ideological appeals* link ideas or people with emotional labels: "A national health care program is a socialist, un-American plot to destroy the very fiber of this democracy." This appeal links the program to something the speaker, and hopefully the listener, considers sinister. If both are in agreement, the argument passes without serious critical examination of its merits. Claims ought to be judged on their own terms, not on the people or ideas with which they may or may not be connected.

These are some of the fallacies that find their way into causal and formal argumentation. A good basic logic book can point out additional fallacies.[6] If you know about fallacies, you'll be better able to construct sound arguments and to assess the weaknesses in your opponent's arguments. Also, thinking critically can protect you from being taken in by unscrupulous politicians, sales personnel, and advertisers.

Strategies for Developing Arguments

As you begin to develop an argumentative speech, you should consider the following practical suggestions:

1. *Organize your arguments, using the strongest first or last.*[7] The **primacy-recency effect** suggests that people develop a mental set on

hearing arguments, then critique later arguments in light of the initial ones presented. A high degree of controversy may lessen these effects, since people are engaged in the arguments throughout; a weakly motivated audience, on the other hand, may be more positively affected by the initial arguments. If your purpose is to ensure that the listeners hear and retain the most powerful argument, you may wish to build toward it, carrying your audience with you as you provide stronger and stronger reasons for adopting the claim. The "clincher" may well be the one they retain the longest, since it comes at the end of the presentation.

2. *Use a variety of evidence.* You can't bank on any one piece of material to move an audience toward your position; hence a broad variety of evidence appealing to relevance and motivation will strengthen your effectiveness. For example, if you wish to argue for restrictions on shark fishing, you can cite statistical evidence of overfishing that is depleting the population. You also can offer graphic video evidence showing definned sharks being dumped back into the ocean to die (shark fin soup is an expensive delicacy in some countries). The latter is a more moving illustration of the reason for restrictions on fishing.

3. *Avoid personal attacks on your opponent.* Keep your remarks focused on the issues, not on the person. This indirectly enhances your credibility, especially when members of the audience sympathize with an opponent's position. If you can argue without becoming vicious and personal, you'll earn the listeners' respect, if not their agreement.

4. *Know the potential arguments of your opponent.* The best defense is a good offense, but it stands to reason that prior knowledge of the opponent's reasons will go a long way toward strengthening your own claims. Investigating your opponent's position as thoroughly as possible gives you a competitive advantage; you'll be less likely to be surprised or caught off guard by an argument.

5. *Finally, practice constructing logical arguments and detecting fallacious ones.* Ultimately, arguing well depends on your understanding of logical reasoning. The common denominator of all arguments, despite their different content, is the patterns of reasoning people use. If you have a clear grasp of the basic building blocks, including the material presented in this chapter, your skill development will proceed at a much faster pace.

Sample Speech

Policies are supported by particular factual assertions, as well as values. The advisability of an action is based on (1) the credibility of the facts offered in its support, and (2) on the audience's willingness to accept the value judg-

Often the best advocates know their opponent's arguments better than their opponent does. Such knowledge enables them to prepare a response and boosts their confidence in their ability to argue well. Anticipating an opponent's arguments also helps a speaker concentrate on ideas and, therefore, avoid several logical fallacies.

ments being made. In many cases, a speaker must reorient an audience's thinking, especially if they find a present practice unobjectionable. Mary Hoffman of Winona State University faced this problem in her analysis of the dangers posed by a product used by dentists to fill cavities.

In developing her position that the use of mercury-based fillers (silver amalgam) should be discontinued, Ms. Hoffman began by reviewing the history of the practice. In paragraphs 7–12 she presented a summary of the known dangers of mercury, a prime ingredient in silver amalgam, and offered additional support in the form of research studies that indicated that mercury is released into the body through the normal act of chewing. She then goes on, in paragraphs 13–16, to indicate that the Federal Drug Agency and the American Dental Association both continue to discount the dangers of the product and recommend its usage. She concludes with her claim that, in spite of their refusal, the FDA and ADA must seek to discontinue use until further studies to clarify the danger are conducted. In the interim, she observes that all we can do is become informed about the dangers and seek alternatives until the safety of the product is assured.

Mercury: Nothing to Smile About
Mary Hoffman[8]

Perhaps there is nothing we fear more than a trip to the dentist. While none of us enjoy the poking and scraping that accompany the visit, we all recognize the need for this semi-annual ritual. After leaving the office, we would like nothing better than to be able to say, "look ma, no cavities," like the kid on the Crest commercial. But I'm willing to bet that didn't happen to any of us very often. Instead, we probably returned a few weeks later and left with numb lips and new fillings. While these fillings may slow the advance of the cavity creeps, they may be causing serious health problems. Silver Amalgam, which has been used in dental work for over one hundred and fifty years, was always assumed to be harmless, but new research suggests it may be very dangerous. Despite recent Food and Drug Administration attention to the problem, far too many questions remained unanswered. /1

In order to better understand and deal with this dangerous situation, let's first examine the history of silver amalgam fillings; second, investigate the problem and its effects; and finally, examine steps that must be taken to ensure dental safety. /2

Silver-amalgam fillings, the dull silverish fillings that many of us have in our mouths have been in use for more than one hundred and fifty years, according to the October 15, 1990, issue of *Newsweek*. Silver amalgam is really only 35% silver and is 50% mercury. The compound also contains zinc, copper and tin. This combination of metals is used because it is both strong and durable. Fillings must withstand the stress of constant chewing and silver amalgam is well suited to handle that pressure. The average silver-amalgam filling lasts five to ten years, with some lasting as long as forty. /3

Other filling materials do exist, but none are as effective. Plastic composites are simply not strong enough for use in back teeth and gold fillings are complicated and expensive to install. /4

Over the past one hundred and fifty years, according to the March, 1986, issue of *Consumer Reports*, more than one hundred million Americans have had silver-amalgam fillings installed. /5

These little pieces of metal are designed to protect the rest of our teeth, and they do a pretty good job. But while silver-amalgam fillings are keeping our smiles healthy, they may be making the rest of us sick. /6

It has always been known that mercury in large doses is deadly—it can cause tremors and mental deterioration. In smaller doses, it is responsible for insomnia, anxiety and minor tremors. But the amount of mercury in a filling, or even a mouthful of fillings isn't enough to cause a problem, right? Wrong. In 1979, researchers at the University of Iowa discovered that not only do the fillings release mercury while they are hardening, vigorous chewing, such as the type used to chew gum, releases maximum amounts of mercury vapor into the mouth. According to the August 27, 1990, issue of *Newsweek*, each silver-amalgam filling contains mercury equaling the weight of an eighth of a tea-spoon of sugar, so if you have eight fillings, you are chewing on a teaspoon of mercury. The October, 1990, issue of *Newsweek* reports that fillings can be the largest single source of exposure to inorganic mercury. Unfortunately, the mercury doesn't simply leave the body through exhalation, it makes its way into body tissue. In 1987, researchers at the Karolinske Institute in Sweden discovered that a group of people with silver-amalgam fillings had three times as much mercury in their brains, and nine times as much in their kidneys as people who did not have the fillings. /7

Even though scientists have known that the fillings release mercury for twelve years, the American Dental Association has always claimed that the amount of mercury released is not significant. Researchers at the University of Calgary disagree. They filled teeth in six sheep with silver amalgam and in only two months discovered that the test animals experienced a loss of kidney function from 16–80% while the control animals suffered no loss. /8

A study done on primates, about as close to humans as subjects get, showed monkeys with amalgam fillings had mercury in their kidneys, gastrointestinal tracts and jaws. And, the February 2, 1990, issue of the *Economist* reports that primates with the fillings have a high level of a new antibiotic-resistant bacteria in their tissues. It is feared that this bacteria will be passed along to those who don't even have the fillings. /9

Some medical professionals maintain that the mercury released from the fillings is causing serious health problems. Hal Huggins, a Colorado dentist, believes mercury poisoning caused by fillings can create symptoms like those of diseases from Leukemia to depression. "Sixty Minutes" reported a case in which a wheelchair-bound patient believed to have multiple sclerosis had her silver-amalgam fillings removed and was walking within two weeks. /10

While cases of truly serious illnesses being caused by the fillings are few, any release of a substance as toxic as mercury must be cause for concern. According to the October 20, 1990, issue of *Science News*, continual exposure to low levels of mercury can cause insomnia, tremors and memory loss. Atlanta dentist Ron Dressler states, "I have over three hundred scientific references on mercury toxicity and I can no longer in good conscience put those things in people's mouths." /11

Not only are the fillings potentially dangerous while we are alive, they even pose problems for others after we die. The August 27, 1990, issue of *Newsweek* reports that when bodies are cremated, the mercury vaporizes and escapes into the air. British geologist Allan Mills says the average crematorium releases 24 pounds of mercury each year. If conditions are calm in the area, the mercury will stay concentrated in dangerous levels. /12

The FDA accepted silver amalgam as safe in 1976 simply by employing a grandfather clause used for common medical products. While the Iowa study exposing the dangers of silver amalgam was completed in 1979, the FDA didn't actually study the substance until this year, twelve years after potential dangers were discovered. According to the April, 1991, issue of *Dentistry Today,* an FDA panel convened to hear testimony on March 16. After less than a month of study, the organization refused to ban silver amalgam but urged more studies to ease public fear, explaining that there are still concerns about safety. The FDA is notorious for inefficiency. It is not surprising that after waiting twelve years to study a substance used by millions, the organization decides in less than a month not to ban the substance despite continuing health concerns. /13

Despite the evidence that amalgam fillings pose a health threat, the ADA continues to deny that any danger exists. The December, 1990, edition of "Sixty Minutes" says the ADA maintains that any mercury released into the mouth is in safe and minuscule amounts. The organization forbids members to remove fillings for the sake of removing mercury and threatens to revoke the license of any dentist who does. /14

When telling members, dentists and technicians, how to handle the substance, however, the ADA is much more cautious. Persons creating the fillings are told never to let the material touch their skin, by wearing a mask and gloves at all times. The amalgam is also to be kept under lock and key. /15

Not only does the ADA claim existing fillings are safe, it continues to encourage the use of amalgam in new fillings, claiming that no proof exists that the material is harmful. /16

Silver-amalgam fillings are certainly a cause for concern, but I'm not suggesting you have all your fillings removed. In fact, according to *Consumer Reports,* not only does removal take a large bite out of your pocketbook, it releases even higher amounts mercury into the mouth, even if only temporarily. Removing fillings is not going to solve the problem because the true concern is not so much the fillings themselves as it is the FDA and ADA stand on the issue. By continuing to advocate the use of silver amalgam, the associations put millions of people at risk. /17

Rather than becoming part of the solution, the FDA has made itself a larger part of the problem. By refusing to ban the substance, the FDA makes it possible for the ADA to continue its stubborn stance. The FDA must undertake further research and seriously consider either banning or reclassifying the substance. According to *Dentistry Today,* reclassifying silver amalgam as a Class III substance would require manufacturers to submit results of safety and effectiveness tests. /18

In order to ensure the safety of dental patients, the ADA, despite the FDA's ruling, must discontinue the use of silver amalgam while researching both its safety and alternative materials. The organization must lift the ban against member dentists removing the fillings so that people who want to have their fillings removed have a safe place to have the work done. Just as doctors and pharmacists are required to inform patients of potential side effects of drugs, dentists must be required to inform patients of potential effects of silver amalgam. Dentists need to inform patients of all their filling options, rather than simply assuming they want silver amalgam because it is the least expensive. /19

OK, the FDA and the ADA can help solve the problem, but what about us, the people who constantly fight the cavity creeps? Our best alternative is to be informed. We need to ask our dentists what he or she has used or is using to fill our teeth and if the answer is silver amalgam, we need to ask about alternatives. If you or someone you know suffers from symptoms of mercury poisoning, ask your doctor or dentist. If you don't feel you are getting a straight answer from the first professional you talk to, get a second opinion. As members of the ADA feel pressure from their customers, the ADA will feel pressure from its members to recognize and deal with questions concerning the safety of silver amalgam. /20

Over 100 million people chew on mercury and more are added to the list each day. Despite evidence that shows silver-amalgam fillings are potentially dangerous, the American Dental Association continues to insist that no danger exists. Until dental patients force the ADA and FDA to attend to the problem, the cavity creeps may be the least frightening things in our teeth and our trips to the dentist may be more frightening than we ever imagined. /21

Chapter Summary

Argumentation is a persuasive activity in which a speaker offers reasons and support for claims in opposition to the claims advanced by others. Arguing with others engages people in tasks central to *critical thinking*: assessing the reasons offered in support of claims. The process of arguing is governed by *social conventions*, including *bilaterality, self-risk, reasonableness,* and *rationality.*

Public argumentation, at its most general level, consists of *constructive* and *refutative* speeches, often structured in accordance with specific rules of procedure. Within single argumentative speeches, particular *arguments* consist of (1) the *claim* to be defended, (2) the *evidence* relevant to the claim, and (3) the *reasoning pattern*, or inference, used to connect the evidence to the claim. Claims of *fact* assert that something is or is not the case, claims of *value* propose that something is or is not desirable, and claims of *policy* attempt to establish that something should or should not be done. Evidence is chosen to support these claims because it is *rationally* or *motivationally relevant.* There are five basic reasoning patterns: *reasoning from example, reasoning from generalization or axiom, reasoning from sign, reasoning by parallel case,* and *reasoning from causal relation.* Each of the inferential, or reasoning, patterns can be tested by applying specific questions to evaluate the strength or soundness of the argument. Critical thinkers also should be on the alert for *fallacies* committed during an argumentative speech. Fallacies are flaws in the reasoning process and include, as general groups, *fallacies in evidence, fallacies in reasoning,* and *fallacies in language.*

Speakers seeking to develop argumentative speeches, either to initiate support for a position or to offer a refutation of an opponent's position, should consider the general strategies presented in this chapter. As you become more adept at constructing your own presentations, you also will increase your skill in critically appraising the arguments of your opponents.

References

1. Harvey Siegel, *Educating Reason: Rationality, Critical Thinking, and Education* (New York: Routledge, 1988), 1–47. The importance of critical thinking has been underscored in two recent national reports on higher education: The National Institute on Education's *Involvement in Learning: Realizing the Potential of American Higher Education* (1984); and the American Association of Colleges' report, *Integrity in the College Curriculum: A Report to the Academic Community* (1985). For a summary of research on critical thinking in the college setting, see James H. McMillan, "Enhancing College Students' Critical Thinking: A Review of Studies," *Research in Higher Education,* 26 (1987): 3–29.

2. Douglas Ehninger, "Validity as Moral Obligation," *Southern Speech Communication Journal,* 33 (1968): 215–22.

3. Henry M. Robert, *Robert's Rules of Order Newly Revised,* ed. Sara Corbin Robert, Henry M. Robert III, William J. Evans, and James W. Cleary (Glenview, IL: Scott, Foresman, 1981).

4. For a summary of the senses in which the term can be employed, see Joseph Wenzel, "Three Perspectives on Argument: Rhetoric, Dialectic, Logic," in *Perspectives on Argument,* ed. J. Schuetz and R. Trapp (Prospect Heights, Il: Waveland Press, 1990).

5. Charles L. Stevenson, *Ethics and Language* (New Haven, CT: Yale University Press, 1944), Chapter 9.

6. For further study of informal logic, see Irving M. Copi and Keith Burgess-Jackson, *Informal Logic,* 2nd. ed. (New York: Macmillan, 1992).

7. Sarah Trenholm, *Persuasion and Social Influence* (Englewood Cliffs, NJ: Prentice-Hall, 1989), 242–43.

8. Mary Hoffman, "Mercury: Nothing to Smile About," *Winning Orations, 1991,* 55–58.

Key Terms

arguing (p. 440)

argument (p. 441)

argumentation (p. 441)

bilateral (p. 441)

causal reasoning (p. 453)

claim (p. 445)

Problems and Probes

1. How influential are political debates in campaign years? Locate studies of presidential debates, and present your critical summary in written form or as part of a general class or small group discussion.

2. Assess editorials and letters to the editor in the campus or local paper—locate and identify fallacious reasoning or reasoning that fails to meet the tests discussed in this chapter. Be prepared to offer oral examples of the kinds of reasoning detected, and indicate why you feel that reasoning is invalid or unsound.

3. Assume you're going to give a speech favoring mandatory military service to an audience of students hostile to your proposal. Outline your arguments using the Toulmin model of argument as discussed in the Speaker's Resource Book. What factors do you consider as you construct and frame your argument? Assume several counterarguments are offered by your fellow students—what new factors must you consider in rebuilding your case for service?

Communication Activities

1. Prepare a ten-minute argumentative exchange on a topic involving you and one other member of the class. Dividing the available time equally, one of you

will advocate a claim; the other will oppose it. Adopt any format you both feel comfortable with. You may choose: (a) a Lincoln/Douglas format—the first person speaks four minutes; the second, five; and then the first person returns for a one-minute rejoinder; (b) an issue format—you both agree on, say, two key issues, and then each speaks for two and a half minutes on each issue; (c) a debate format—each speaker talks twice alternatively, three minutes in a constructive speech, two minutes in rebuttal; and (d) a heckling format—each of you has five minutes, but during the middle of each speech the audience or opponent may ask questions.

2. Turn the class into a deliberative assembly, decide on a motion or resolution to be argued, and then schedule a day or two for a full debate. This format should use particular argumentative roles: advocate, witness, direct examiner, cross-examiner, summarizer. It allows each speaker to be part of a team; what you do affects not only yourself but also other speakers on your side of the argument. (For guidance in the use of this format, see John D. May, ed., *American Problems: What Should Be Done? Debates from "The Advocates"* [Palo Alto, CA: National Press Books, 1973]).

18

SPEECHES ON SPECIAL OCCASIONS

W hen asked the question "Who are you?" most people respond in terms of social categories: "I'm a college student" (educational institution), "I'm a Baptist" (religious assembly), "I'm an Italian American" (ethnic collectivity), "I'm a computer programmer" (work group), "I'm one of the Gonzalez kids from Ponderosa Street" (familial and geographical identification), "I'm a Puerto Rican" (societal roots). All of this is not to say, of course, that there is no real "you" behind those labels; it's to say that you often think of yourself, not as some free-floating, autonomous individual, but in terms of the social groups that are so thoroughly a part of your life. Even when mentioning yourself, you often bring in social roles: "I'm Jake, Thad Garner's son," or "I'm Sarrina, Nancy Pei's friend."

Groups and our consciousness of roles not only form part of our identities but they also have authority over us. They can regulate our behavior because, after all, they often predate us. We are thrust into preexisting families, with their own rules or customs, and into social and political institutions that make claims upon our loyalty and actions from the day we're born. Social groups and institutions provide us with services, control our behaviors, and, yes, mark us for who we are. It is little wonder that people maintain very special relationships with the groups and institutions to which they belong.

In this chapter, we'll look at several kinds of speeches you may give in the presence of or as the representative of some of those groups and institutions. Before we discuss those speech types, however, we'll have to deal boldly with one of the major problems of our time—the fragmentation of society,

People to tend to think of and identify themselves in terms of social groups and roles.

the challenge of communicating in an age of diversity. Special-occasion speeches are absolutely crucial types of public talk. Unless we're willing to think about what holds us together—what makes us into a *community*—informative, argumentative, and persuasive speaking will produce no results.

Ceremony and Ritual in a Diverse Community

The word "community" comes from the Latin *communis*, meaning "common," or, more literally (with the *-ity* ending), "commonality." A community is not simply the physical presence of people—say, those who live in the same town (a local community) or who worship together (a religious community). A **community** is a group of people who think of themselves as bonded together, whether by blood, locale, class, nationality, race, occupation, gender, or other shared experience or attribute.

The phrase "who think of themselves" is key here. Really, of course, you share blood type with members of your family, but why is that important to your concept of family? Why not eye color or hair shade or shoe size instead? Of course there really are biological differences between males and females, but why is one's gender important in determining who gets paid more, who draws combat duty in time of war, or who's generally expected to raise the kids? Both college professors and preachers go to school about the same amount of time, yet we pay experienced professors about twice as much as experienced preachers—how come? Yes, skin comes in many different colors, but why have we made so much of that fact?

The point here is simple but absolutely important: *While physiological, psychological, and social differences between people are real, the importance attached to those differences is socially constructed in arbitrary ways.*

Social Definitions of Diversity

A **social construction** is a mechanism used by group members to understand, interpret, and evaluate the world around them. There is no such thing, as Nelson Goodman notes, as "perception without conception."[1] Human beings cannot "see" their world without framing it, usually in language. Words store our experience of the world; just uttering "pit bull" brings to mind for most people frightening stories of their own or other people's experiences. Words encode our common attitudes; as we noted in Chapter 12, we have multiple words for the same object ("officer of the law," "cop") because our feelings about such people vary. Words express our evaluations; the difference between a "student-athlete" and a "jock" is a difference in how we value what the person does while at school. Saying that "we socially construct our world" isn't to say that we create it in some brute way; the physicality of the world is real, solid, and you'll literally hurt your toe when it bumps into a desk. Rather, it is to say that *human beings orient themselves to the world via language.* We see, interpret, and evaluate the *Dasein* (the "out-there") via language.

It follows, then, that, at one level or another, communication always is the attempt to get others to see, interpret, and evaluate the world as you do. The language you share with your culture mates helps you to get others to see as you do, but meanings are not stable. They vary from time to time, context to context, and even person to person. "Democracy" means one thing in the United States, another in the Russian republics, because of differing traditions, governmental institutions, and personal experiences. When a U.S. and Russian citizen talk to each other about democratic institutions, they must be careful to indicate very concretely how each is seeing, interpreting, and evaluating the world when using that term.

So, this is the point of this chapter: Periodically, communities must stop to define themselves, their beliefs, attitudes, and values, their place in the world. We do this on **special occasions**—and hence this chapter. But, as we have seen throughout this book, arriving at definitions shared by everyone is very, very, difficult: *In an age of diversity, there is a tendency to fragment society rather than to share beliefs, attitudes, and values as a community.* The great challenge of special-occasion speaking, therefore, is to get a society to live the motto stamped on American money: *E pluribus unum,* "Out of many, one."

Public Address as Community Building

Let's get more specific. We talked about reference groups in Chapter 16. You're both passively and actively related to groups; you both draw self-definition from groups and seek new information or reinforcement from them. Hence, many people are born into a religious community whose doctrines and rites make indelible marks on them; when faced in later life with such crises as unwanted children, the death of loved ones, or decisions about marriage, those people often turn to that community for solutions. As a community, the **reference group** can be both definer and extender of the individual. Thus, reference groups make claims on individuals when they are seen as salient to a problem or event.

Just as your group memberships change over time, so does the power of particular groups to affect your thought and actions.[2] Yet, traces of groups from your youth follow you through life. The question we face in this chapter goes beyond that social-psychological truth: *your sense of group identity, of community, is created largely through public talk.* The language of reference groups is inscribed in your memory. You may have memorized and learned to recite in a group the Boy Scout law and oath, each recitation reinforcing the Scouts' beliefs and values ("On my honor I will do my best, to do my duty to God and country, and to obey the Scout law. . . "). Many churches have ceremonies of group confession of sins and profession of faith, and most depend upon speechmaking—preaching—to instill and reinforce doctrine and morals. Your civic education begins with pledging allegiance to the flag; it broadens when you participate in Memorial Day, Fourth of July, and Labor Day ceremonies (which include public addresses); and that education is reviewed every time the president appears on television or hopefuls campaign for local, state, and national office. The rituals and public addresses are social constructions that emphasize and give expression or life to particular views of the world. Your sense of community undoubtedly is built out of bits and pieces of social constructions reinforced in you since your childhood.

As Michael Walzer puts it, "The state is invisible; it must be personified before it can be seen, symbolized before it can be loved, imagined before it can be conceived."[3] The same is true with most reference groups in your life. You cannot see group standards, only individuals' behavior; you cannot feel the influence of groups outside of the words and other symbols they use to define their claim upon you. Those memories of group norms, often tied to particular pieces of languages, are buried inside you, ready to be resurrected on later occasions.

Finally, groups remind you of their claims upon you on special occasions, in special rituals. David Kertzer has described **ritual** as follows:

> Ritual action has a formal quality to it. It follows highly structured, standardized sequences and is often enacted at certain places and times that are themselves endowed with special symbolic meaning. Ritual action is repetitive and, therefore, often redundant, but these very factors serve as important

means of channeling emotion, guiding cognition, and organizing social groups. I have defined ritual as action wrapped in a web of symbolism.[4]

Confirmation or bar mitzvah services, the act of "hooding" a new Doctor of Philosophy during graduation, reciting the Pledge of Allegiance in school—these are kinds of ritual actions that Kertzer is talking about. All rituals are structured, standardized, and repetitive, with times and places set aside for ritual observances. Ritual is imbued with symbols and with public address to provide the means of channeling, guiding, and organizing that Kertzer mentions.

Speeches on special occasions are themselves, then, ritualized and often structured, standardized, and so on. If introductions of speakers often seem trite, that's because introducing someone into your community is a ritualized activity. If many nomination speeches sound alike from campaign to campaign, that's because few of us really want surprises in our campaign processes. Surprise could lead to change, and change in turn could upset our political system. In speeches for special occasions (except, as we shall see, speeches to entertain), the emphasis is upon ritualized tradition rather than revolutionary change. In one form or another, the goal of special-occasion speeches is always to socially construct the world in ways consonant with group traditions—to get you to see, interpret, and evaluate the world through the eyes of the group in which the public address is occurring.

Now, then, we come to the great challenge of special-occasion speechmaking. *In an age of diversity, when each of us has been socialized into any number of specific ethnic, social, political, and religious groups, each of which makes demands upon our beliefs, attitudes, and values, how can we create a sense of shared community?* Is it possible to share "community" when people are divided into two genders, innumerable religions, younger and elderly peoples, multiple ethnic groups, a growing number of political parties, and Mac versus IBM users? How can public speakers reach across differences to create a sense of mutual identity among listeners? Or, if people do feel a sense of community, what can we do ritualistically and rhetorically to make them sensitive to the demands of community upon them?

Let's now look at some types of special-occasion talk: speeches to introduce, pay tribute, create goodwill, and entertain. How do we live out *E pluribus unum?*

Speeches of Introduction

Speeches of introduction usually are given by a member of the group that's to hear the speech and are designed to prepare that group to accept the featured speaker and the speaker's message into the group's community and standards. In a sense, a speech of introduction asks for *permission* for an outsider to speak; that permission, presumably, is based upon what the nonmember can contribute to the group. The group must want to hear the outsider before the featured speaker can be successful. If the speaker is a member of the group, the introduction should serve as a reminder of his or her role and accomplishments within the community.

Purpose and Manner of Speaking for Speeches of Introduction

The purpose of a speech of introduction is, of course, to create in the audience a desire to hear the speaker you're introducing. Everything else must be subordinated to this aim. You aren't being called upon to make a speech yourself or to air your own views on the subject. You're only the speaker's advance agent; your job is to sell him or her to the audience. This task carries a twofold responsibility. First, you must arouse the listeners' curiosity about the speaker and/or subject, thus making it easier for the speaker to get the attention of the audience. Second, you must do all that you reasonably can to generate audience respect for the speaker, thereby increasing the likelihood that listeners will respond favorably to the message that's presented.

When giving a speech of introduction, your manner of speaking should be suited to the nature of the occasion, to your familiarity with the speaker, and to the speaker's prestige. If you were introducing a justice of the United States Supreme Court, for instance, it would hardly be appropriate to tell a derogatory joke about him or her. Nor would this approach be tactful if the speaker were a stranger to you, or the occasion serious and dignified. On the other hand, if you are presenting an old friend to a group of associates on an informal occasion, a solemn and dignified manner would be equally out of place.

Formulating the Content of Speeches of Introduction

The better known and more respected a speaker is, the shorter your introduction can be. The less well known he or she is, the more you will need to arouse interest in the subject or build up the speaker's prestige. In general, however, observe these principles:

1. *Talk about the speaker.* Who is he? What's her position in business, education, sports, or government? What experiences qualify him to speak on the announced subject? Build up the speaker's identity, tell what he knows or what she has done, but don't praise his or her ability as a speaker. Let speakers demonstrate their skills.

2. *Emphasize the importance of the speaker's subject.* For example, in introducing a speaker who's to talk about the oil industry, you might say, "All of us drive automobiles that run on petroleum products. A knowledge of the way these products are manufactured and marketed is,

Rituals and Power

We've discussed speeches for special occasions as community building. They're also important for community maintaining, and therein lies one of their great powers. We seldom think about our routine activities as "powerful," yet a whole line of research in cultural studies is working to substantiate that claim. Of recent vintage is Kertzer's *Ritual, Politics, and Power*. A professor of anthropology at Bowdoin College, Kertzer investigates the influence of ritual in politics.

He defines "ritual" as "action wrapped in a web of symbolism," as "highly structured, standardized sequences . . . often enacted at certain places and times that are themselves endowed with special symbolic meaning" (p. 9).

Symbolization is the key here. Some highly standardized sequences of behavior, such as brushing your teeth or getting dressed, have little or no symbolic significance; they are simply habits or routines. Rituals are structured actions to which we attach particular collective significance, often about how the past is related to the present and how the present should affect the future. A political ritual, Kertzer notes, "helps us cope with two human problems: building confidence in our sense of self by providing us with a sense of continuity—I am the

therefore, certain to be valuable to our understanding and perhaps to our pocketbooks."

3. *Stress the appropriateness of the subject or of the speaker.* If your town is considering a program of renewal and revitalization, a speech by a city planner is likely to be timely and well received. If an organization is marking an anniversary, one of the speakers may be its founder. Reference to the positions these persons hold is obviously in order and relates the speaker more closely to the audience.

Organizing Speeches of Introduction

The necessity for a carefully planned introduction depends upon the amount of time available and the need to elaborate on the topic's importance or the speaker's qualifications. A simple introductory statement, "Ladies and Gentlemen, the President of the United States," obviously

same person today as I was twenty years ago and as I will be ten years from now— and giving us confidence that the world in which we live today is the same world we lived in before and the same world we will have to cope with in the future" (p. 10). As a group, thus, we celebrate our pasts and construct our futures in the present; ritual is the mechanism of that celebration.

The notion of power comes into the picture when we consider politics as the processes whereby vested interests in a society struggle for domination. Republicans fight Democrats for legislative or executive control; a section of town unrepresented on the city council fights to get a seat; a lobbyist for the American Association of Retired Persons pushes for increased state appropriations to elderly services budgets; the Hispanic voters of Texas ask presidential candidates to take stands against the "English-language only" movement. Political struggle can be harsh, even fatal, in some societies. Citizens attempt to ritualize political fighting: they invent rules of "parliamentary procedure" to ritualize partisan debate; press traditions dictate the kinds of questions that are asked of presidents in their news conferences; the transfer of power from one executive to another is ritualized in inaugural ceremonies, and coronation ceremonies for kings and queens are often lavish beyond description.

The power in such rituals, according to Kertzer, lies in their abilities (1) to control the actual struggles for power and (2) to help convince the witnesses (the populace) that authority is being wielded benevolently, in their name. The rhetoric of special occasions, thus, is a two-edged discourse of power and community maintenance.

FOR FURTHER READING
Kertzer, David I. *Ritual, Politics, and Power.* New Haven, CT: Yale University Press, 1988.

requires little in the way of organization. For longer, more involved introductions, consider how much attention should be devoted to the background and expertise of the speaker and to the interest, importance, or urgency of the topic. A good way to start is to make an observation designed to capture the attention of the audience and then to proceed to develop topics that relate the speaker and message to group interests, desires, or needs. Remember that your introduction should not be longer than the speech it introduces; aim for brevity.

Sample Speech

The virtues of an excellent introduction, displaying tact, brevity, sincerity, and enthusiasm, are evident in the following introduction prepared by Benita Raskowski.

Introducing a Classmate
Benita Raskowski

We've all come to know Sandy Kawahiro in this class. When we introduced ourselves during the first week of the semester, you learned that Sandy was raised in Hawaii, later moving to the West Coast to live with an uncle. Sandy's first speech dealt with his experiences in California's Sonoma Valley as a minority person for the first time in his life and of the pressures those experiences put upon his values and behavior. In his second speech, Sandy offered an explanatory speech on his post-collegiate career, industrial relations.

Today, Sandy's going to combine his personal and professional life. If you followed the state legislature's recent public hearings on discrimination on the job, or saw CBS' special report on work environments in Japan two nights ago, you know how important human relations training can be to a successful business operation. This morning, Sandy will continue some of those ideas in a speech arguing for further development of human relations programs in executive training packages. The speech is entitled "Human Relations Training on the Job: Creating Color Blindness."

Speeches of Tribute

As a speaker you may be called upon to pay tribute to another person's qualities or achievements. Such occasions range from the awarding of a trophy after a successful softball season to delivering a eulogy at a memorial service. Sometimes tributes are paid to an entire group of people—teachers, soldiers, mothers—rather than to an individual. In all these circumstances, the focus is upon relationships between the community and the individual or group being paid tribute. Honorees are being held up for praise because of the ways in which they have contributed to or represented the community as a whole.

Farewells

In general, **speeches of farewell** fall into one of three subcategories. When people retire or leave one organization to join another or when persons who are admired leave the community where they've lived, the enterprise in which they've worked, or the office they've held, public appreciation of their fellowship and accomplishments may be expressed by associates or colleagues in speeches befitting the circumstances. Individuals who are departing may use the occasion to present farewell addresses in which they voice their gratitude for the opportunities, consideration, and warmth given them by co-workers and, perhaps, call upon those who remain to carry on the traditions and long-range goals that characterize the office or enterprise.

At a dedication, the speaker says something appropriate about the purpose to be served by whatever is being dedicated or commemorated.

In both situations, verbal tributes are being paid. What distinguishes them is whether the departing person is *speaking* or is being *spoken about*. More rarely, when individuals—because of disagreements, policy differences, or organizational stresses, for example—resign or sever important or long-standing associations with a business or governmental unit, they may elect to use their farewell messages to present publicly the basis of the disagreement and the factors prompting the resignation and departure from the community.

Dedications

Buildings, monuments, and parks may be constructed or set aside to honor a worthy cause or to commemorate a person, group, significant movement, historic event, or the like. At such **dedications,** the speaker says something appropriate about the purpose to be served by whatever is being set aside and about the person(s), event, or occasion thus commemorated.

Memorial Services

Services to pay public honor to the dead usually include a speech of tribute, or **eulogy.** Ceremonies of this kind may honor a famous person (or persons), perhaps on anniversaries of their deaths. For example, many speeches have paid tribute to John F. Kennedy and Martin Luther King, Jr. More often, however, a eulogy honors someone personally known to the audience and recently deceased.

At other times, a memorial honors certain qualities that person stood for. In such a situation, the speaker uses the memorial to renew and reinforce the audience's adherence to ideals possessed by the deceased and worthy of emulation by the community.

Purpose and Manner of Speaking for Speeches of Tribute

The purpose of a **speech of tribute** is to create in those who hear it a sense of appreciation for the traits or accomplishments of a particular person or group. If you enable your audience to realize the essential worth or importance of that person or group, you've succeeded, but you have to go farther than this. By honoring the person, you may also arouse deeper devotion to the cause or values he or she represents. Did the person give distinguished service to the community? Then others should serve as well. Was the person a friend and helper to young people in trouble? Then others should do youth work as well. Create a desire in your listeners to emulate the person or persons honored—that is community building.

When delivering a speech of tribute, suit the manner of speaking to the circumstances. A farewell banquet usually blends an atmosphere of merriment with a spirit of sincere regret. Dignity and formality are, on the whole, characteristic of memorial services, the unveiling of monuments, and similar dedicatory ceremonies. Regardless of the general tone of the occasion, however, in a speech of tribute avoid high-sounding phrases, bombastic oratory, and obvious "oiliness." A simple, honest expression of admiration presented in clear and unadorned language is best.

Formulating the Content of Speeches of Tribute

Frequently, in a speech of tribute a speaker attempts to itemize all the accomplishments of the honored person or group. This weakens the impact because, in trying to cover everything, it emphasizes nothing. Plan, instead, to focus your remarks, as follows:

1. *Stress dominant traits.* If you are paying tribute to a person, select a few aspects of his or her personality that are especially likeable or praiseworthy, and relate incidents from the person's life or work to illustrate these distinguishing qualities.

2. *Mention only outstanding achievements.* Pick out only a few of the person's or group's most notable accomplishments. Tell about them in detail to show how important they were. Let your speech say, "Here is what this person (or group) has done; see how such actions have contributed to the well-being of our business or community."

3. *Give special emphasis to the influence of the person or group.* Show the effect that the behavior of the person or group has had on others. Many times, the importance of people's lives can be demonstrated not so much by their particular material accomplishments as by the influence they exerted on associates.

Organizing Speeches of Tribute

Ordinarily you'll have little difficulty in getting people to listen to a speech of tribute. The audience probably already knows and admires the person or group about whom you are to speak, and listeners are curious to learn what you are going to say about the honoree(s). Consider the following steps in preparing your speech:

1. *Direct the attention of the audience toward those characteristics or accomplishments that you consider most important.* There are two commonly used ways to do this: (a) make a straightforward, sincere statement of these commendable traits or achievements or of the influence they have had upon others, and (b) relate one or more instances that vividly illustrate your point.

2. Were there obstacles or difficulties that the person or group being honored had to overcome? *If so, dramatize the impact of the accomplishment by noting these problems and their successful resolution.* Thus, you might describe the extent of the air pollution problem in a large city before paying tribute to the individuals who developed and enforced an effective pollution-control plan.

3. *Develop the substance of the tribute itself—relate a few incidents to show how the personal or public problems you have outlined were met and surmounted.* In doing this, be sure to demonstrate at least one of the following: (a) how certain admirable traits—vision, courage, and tenacity, for example—made it possible to deal successfully with these prob-

lems, (b) how remarkable the achievements were in the face of the obstacles encountered, (c) how great the influence of the achievement was on others.

4. *Synthesize the attributes of the person or group into a vivid composite picture of the accomplishment and its significance.* (a) Introduce an apt quotation. Try to find a bit of poetry or a literary passage that fits the person or group to whom you're paying tribute and introduce it here. (b) Draw a word picture of a world (community, business, or profession) inhabited by such persons. Suggest how much better things would be if more people had similar qualities. (c) Suggest the loss the absence of the individual or group will bring. Show vividly how much he, she, or they will be missed. Be specific: "It's going to seem mighty strange to walk into Barbara's office and not find her there ready to listen, ready to advise, ready to help." In closing, connect the theme of the speech with the occasion on which it is presented. Thus, in a *eulogy,* suggest that the best tribute the audience can pay the person being honored is to live as that person did or to carry on what he or she has begun. In a *dedication* speech, suggest the appropriateness of dedicating this monument, building, or plaque to such a person or group and express hope that it will inspire others to emulate its accomplishments. At the close of a *farewell* speech, extend to the departing person or persons the best wishes of those you represent and express a determination to carry on what they have begun. If *you* are saying farewell, call upon those who remain to carry on what you and your associates have started.

In summary, by isolating character traits that others can emulate, dramatizing accomplishments so that others will be inspired, illustrating the honoree's vision and courage, and synthesizing the person's significance in terms of group standards, you aren't only honoring an individual's accomplishment but also pulling the listeners together in a community. Even a highly diversified audience can be galvanized into a collective if your topics and language help individual listeners to see the world of the honoree in a particular way.

Sample Speech

Harold Haydon offered the following remarks at the unveiling of *Nuclear Energy,* a bronze sculpture created by Henry Moore and placed on the campus of the University of Chicago to commemorate the achievement of Enrico Fermi and his associates in releasing the first self-sustaining nuclear chain reaction at Stagg Field on 2 December 1942. The unveiling took place during the commemoration of the twenty-fifth anniversary of that event. Haydon was Associate Professor of Art at the university.

Notice in particular how Haydon verbally controls the way the audience is to see—to understand, interpret, and evaluate—*Nuclear Energy*. The first three paragraphs ask the listeners to contemplate commemorative sculpture—its historical foundations and present-day functions.

Paragraphs 4 and 5 suggest that there's a spiritual side of scientific discovery that must always be honored. The sixth paragraph deals with the controversy involved with nuclear energy, but deflects that social-political debate by talking, instead, of the importance of artistic recognition. This allows Haydon in paragraphs 7, 8, and 9 to celebrate the union of science and art, the spirit of both people of science and people of art. Haydon thus asks the audience to see the heroic aspects of both science and art (while not looking at the possibly evil effects of science). He controls our vision masterfully.

The Testimony of Sculpture
Harold Haydon[5]

Since very ancient times men have set up a marker, or designated some stone or tree, to hold the memory of a deed or happening far longer than any man's lifetime. Some of these memorial objects have lived longer than man's collective memory, so that we now ponder the meaning of a monument, or wonder whether some great stone is a record of human action, or whether instead it is only a natural object. /1

There is something that makes us want a solid presence, a substantial form, to be the tangible touchstone of the mind, designed and made to endure as witness or record, as if we mistrusted that seemingly frail yet amazingly tough skein of words and symbols that serves memory and which, despite being mere ink blots and punch-holes, nonetheless succeeds in preserving the long human tradition, firmer than any stone, tougher than any metal. /2

We still choose stone or metal to be our tangible reminders, and for these solid, enduring forms we turn to the men who are carvers of stone and moulders of metal, for it is they who have given lasting form to our myths through the centuries. /3

One of these men is here today, a great one, and he has given his skill and the sure touch of his mind and eye to create for this nation, this city, and this university a marker that may stand here for centuries, even for a millennium, as a mute yet eloquent testament to a turning point in time when man took charge of a new material world hitherto beyond his capability. /4

As this bronze monument remembers an event and commemorates an achievement, it has something unique to say about the spiritual meaning of the achievement, for it is the special power of art to convey feeling and stir profound emotion, to touch us in ways that are beyond the reach of reason. /5

Nuclear energy, for which the sculpture is named, is a magnet for conflicting emotions, some of which inevitably will attach to the bronze form; it will harbor or repel emotion according to the states of mind of those who view the sculpture. In its brooding presence some will feel the joy and sorrow of recollection, some may dread the uncertain future, and yet others will thrill to the thought of magnificent achievements that lie ahead. The test of the sculpture's greatness as a human document, the test of any work of art, will be its capacity to evoke a response and the quality of that response. /6

One thing most certain is that this sculpture by Henry Moore is not an inert object. It is a live thing, and somewhat strange like every excellent beauty, to be known to us only in time and never completely. Its whole meaning can be known only to the ever-receding future, as each succeeding generation reinterprets according to its own vision and experience. /7

By being here in a public place the sculpture *Nuclear Energy* becomes a part of Chicago, and the sculptor an honored citizen, known not just to artists and collectors of art, but to everyone who pauses here in the presence of the monument, because the artist is inextricably part of what he has created, immortal through his art. /8

With this happy conjunction today of art and science, of great artist and great occasion, we may hope to reach across the generations, across the centuries, speaking through enduring sculpture of our time, our hopes, and fears, perhaps more eloquently than we know. Some works of art have meaning for all mankind and so defy time, persisting through all hazards; the monument to the atomic age should be one of these. /9

Speeches of Nomination

The **speech to nominate** contains elements found in both speeches of introduction and speeches of tribute. Here, too, your main purpose is to review the accomplishments of a person you admire. This review, however, instead of standing as an end in itself (tribute) or of creating a desire to hear the person (introduction), is made to contribute to an actuative goal—obtaining the listeners' endorsement of the person as a nominee for an elective office.

  In a speech of nomination, the manner of speaking generally is less formal and dignified than when you're giving a speech of tribute. It should, however, be businesslike and energetic. In general, the content of the speech follows the pattern of a speech of tribute, but the illustrations and supporting materials should be chosen with the intent of showing the nominee's qualifications for the office in question. Although the speech to nominate has certain special requirements, fundamentally it's a speech to actuate; therefore, begin with a statement of your intent—to rise to place a name in nomination. Second, describe the qualifications required by the job, the problems to be dealt with, and the personal qualities needed in the individual to be selected. Next, name your candidate and state this person's qualifications for the position—describe the individual's training, experience, success in similar positions, and personal qualities. Your objective is to show why you believe your nominee is an excellent choice for the position. Finally, urge audience endorsement as you formally place the person's name into nomination.

An alternative to this pattern is to begin with the name of the nominee. This is an acceptable practice if the audience is already favorably disposed toward the nominee. If your choice is likely to stir opposition, however, it may be wiser to establish first the qualities needed for the position and then, in naming your candidate, indicate how this nominee's qualifications will satisfy the requirements.

Not all nominations, of course, need to be supported by a long speech. Frequently, especially in small groups and clubs, the person nominated is well known to the audience, and his or her qualifications are already appreciated. Under such circumstances, all that is required is the simple statement: "Mr. Chairman, given her obvious and well-known services to our club in the past, I nominate Marilyn Cannell for the office of treasurer."

Speeches to Create Goodwill

The fourth type of special-occasion speech we will discuss is the **speech to create goodwill.** While ostensibly the purpose of this special type of speech is to inform an audience about a product, service, operation, or procedure, the actual purpose is to enhance the listeners' appreciation of a particular institution, practice, or profession—to make the audience more favorably disposed toward it. Thus, the goodwill speech is also a mixed, or hybrid, type. Basically, it is informative but with a strong underlying persuasive purpose.

Typical Situations Requiring Speeches for Goodwill

There are numerous situations in which goodwill speeches are appropriate; three are typical:

Luncheon Meetings of Civic and Service Clubs. Gatherings of this kind—semisocial in nature with an atmosphere of congeniality—offer excellent opportunities for presenting speeches of goodwill. Members of such groups are interested in civic affairs and in the workings of other people's businesses or professions.

Educational Programs. School authorities, as well as leaders of clubs and religious organizations, often arrange educational programs for their patrons and members. Speakers are asked to talk about the occupations in which they are engaged and to explain the opportunities offered and the training required in their respective fields. By using illustrations and tactful references, a speaker may—while providing the desired information—also create goodwill for his or her company or profession.

An educational program provides the public with desired information, while creating goodwill for speaker's company or profession.

Special Demonstration Programs. Special programs are frequently presented by government agencies, university extension departments, and business organizations. For example, a wholesale food company may send a representative to a nutritionists' meeting to explain the food values present in various kinds of canned meat or fish products and to demonstrate new ways of preparing or serving them. Although such a speech would be primarily informative, the speaker could win goodwill indirectly by showing that his or her company desires to increase customer satisfaction with its products and services.

Manner of Speaking in Speeches for Goodwill

Three qualities—modesty, tolerance, and good humor—characterize the manner of speaking appropriate to goodwill speeches. Even in plant tours, there could be people who question the values espoused by the company and the way or the places where it markets its products. Speakers must be able not only to act as information sources on the company but also as persuaders who work to change uninformed beliefs and hostile attitudes. You must know and present the facts clearly and show a tolerant, patient attitude toward others. Representatives of airline companies shouldn't attack trucking companies or bus lines, as that probably will gain little but ill will.

And exercise good humor; be enthusiastic and create good feelings through your humor.

The challenge of diversity, therefore, is present even when you are running a campus tour for visitors or a rescue-relief drive being supported by your employer. Diversified audiences will likely have stereotypical views—that all chemical plants are evil, that universities are filled with ivory-tower big spenders, that churches sponsoring relief drives are just trying to convert everyone to their religious viewpoint. Your challenge is to array information and valuable appeals in such a way as to attack those stereotypes. You must talk like a modest, tolerant, good-humored individual, not a company public relations trainee.

Formulating the Content of Speeches for Goodwill

In selecting materials for a goodwill speech, keep three suggestions in mind. First, present novel and interesting facts about your subject. Make your listeners feel that you're giving them an inside look into your company or organization. Avoid talking about what they already know; concentrate on new developments and on facts and services that aren't generally known. Second, show a relationship between your subject and the lives of your listeners. Make them see the importance of your organization or profession to their personal safety, success, or happiness. Third, offer a definite service. This offer may take the form of an invitation to the audience members to visit your office or shop, to help them with their problems, or to answer questions or send brochures.

Organizing Speeches for Goodwill

Because of its close relationship to speeches to inform and to persuade, the organization of materials we have just described can be discussed in terms of the motivated sequence.

Attention Step. The purposes of the beginning of your speech are to establish a friendly feeling and to arouse the audience's curiosity about your profession or the institution you represent. You can gain the first of these objectives by a tactful compliment to the group or by a reference to the occasion that has brought you together. Follow this with one or two unusual facts or illustrations concerning the enterprise you represent. For instance: "Before we began manufacturing television parts, the Lash Electric Company confined its business to the making of clock radios that would never wear out. We succeeded so well that we almost went bankrupt! That was only fifteen years ago. Today our export trade alone is over 100 times larger than our total annual domestic business was in those earlier days. It may interest you to know how this change took place." In brief, you must find a way to arouse your listeners' curiosity about your organization.

Need Step. Point out certain problems facing your audience—problems with which your institution, profession, or agency is vitally concerned. For example, if you represent a radio or television station, show the relationship of good communications to the social and economic health of the community. By so doing, you'll establish common ground with your audience. Ordinarily the need step is brief and consists largely of suggestions developed with only an occasional illustration; however, if you intend to propose that your listeners join in acting to meet a common problem, the need step will require fuller development.

Satisfaction Step. The meat of a goodwill speech is in the satisfaction step. Here is the place to tell your audience about your institution, profession, or business and to explain what it is or what it does. You can do this in at least three ways. You can relate interesting events in its history. Pick events that demonstrate its humanity, reliability, and importance to the community, to the country, or to the world of nations. You also can explain how your organization or profession operates. Pick out those things that are unusual or that may contain beneficial suggestions for your audience. This method often helps impress upon your listeners the size and efficiency of your operation or enterprise. You also might want to describe the services your organization renders. Explain its products; point out how widely they are used; discuss the policies by which management is guided—especially those you think your audience will agree with or admire. Tell what your firm or profession has done for the community: people employed; purchases made locally; assistance with community projects; or improvements in health, education, or public safety. Do not boast, but make sure that your listeners realize the value of your work *to them*.

Visualization Step. Your object here is to crystallize the goodwill that your presentation of information in the satisfaction step initially has created. Do this by looking to the future. Rapidly survey the points you have covered or combine them into a single story or illustration. To approach this step from the opposite direction, picture for your listeners the loss that would result if the organization or profession you represent should leave the community or cease to exist. Be careful, however, not to leave the impression that there is any real danger that this will occur.

Action Step. In this step, you make your offer of service to the audience. For example, invite the group to visit your office or point out the willingness of your organization to assist in a common enterprise. As is true of every type of speech, the content and organization of the speech for goodwill must be adapted to meet the demands of the subject or occasion. You should, however, never lose sight of the central purpose for which you speak: to show your audience that the work you do or the service you perform is of value to them, that it somehow makes their lives happier, more productive, interesting, or secure.

Although its purpose is primarily to entertain, an after-dinner speech normally offers important information relevant to the group at hand.

Speeches to Entertain

To entertain an audience presents special challenges to speakers. As you may recall, we identified "to entertain" as an independent type of speech in Chapter 4 because of the peculiar force of humor in speechmaking. Discounting slapstick (of the slipping-on-a-banana-peel genre), most humor depends primarily upon a listener's sensitivities to the routines and mores of one's society; this is obvious if you have ever listened to someone from a foreign country tell jokes. Much humor cannot be translated, in part because of language differences (puns, for example, do not translate well) and in even larger measure because of cultural differences.

Purpose and Manner of Speeches to Entertain

Like most humor in general, **speeches to entertain** usually work within the cultural frameworks of a particular group or society. Such speeches may be "merely funny," of course, as in comic monologues, but most are serious in their force or demand on audiences. After-dinner speeches, for example, usually are more than dessert; their topics normally are relevant to the group at hand, and the anecdotes they contain usually are offered to make a point. That point may be as simple as deflecting an audience's antipathy toward the speaker, as group centered as making the people in the audience feel more like a group, or as serious as offering a critique of society.

Waving the Bloody Shirt and the Burning Flag

The phrase "waving the bloody shirt" dates from the year 1868, when tax collector and school superintendent A. P. Huggins was roused from his bed, ordered to leave the state, and given 75 lashes by members of the Ku Klux Klan. Huggins reported the incident to the military authorities, and an officer took his bloodied shirt to Washington and gave it to Radical Republican Congressman Benjamin Butler of Massachusetts. Later, when giving a speech in support of a bill permitting the president to enforce Reconstruction laws with military force, Butler waved Huggins's shirt. From then on, Republican orators regularly "waved the bloody shirt," blaming the South for starting the Civil War and accusing it of disloyalty to the Union and to its flag.

Similarly, in the late 1980s and early 1990s people have burned the U.S. flag to protest nationalism and to call attention to threats to freedom of speech and the Bill of Rights. In reaction, many people have "waved the burning flag,"

Speakers seeking to deflect an audience's antipathy often use humor to ingratiate themselves. For example, Henry W. Grady, editor of the *Atlanta Constitution*, expected a good deal of distrust and hostility when, after the Civil War, he journeyed to New York City in 1886 to tell the New England Society about "The New South." He opened the speech not only by thanking the Society for the invitation but also telling stories about farmers, husbands and wives, and preachers. He praised Abraham Lincoln, a Northerner, as "the first typical American" of the new age; told another humorous story about shopkeepers and their advertising; poked fun at the great Union General Sherman—"who is considered an able man in our hearts, though some people think he is a kind of careless man about fire"; and assured his audience that a New South, one very much like the old North, was arising from those ashes.[6] Through the use of humor, Henry Grady had his audience cheering every point he made about the New South that evening.

Group cohesiveness also can be created through humor. Politicians, especially when campaigning, spend much time telling humorous stories about their opponents, hitting them with stinging remarks. In part, of course, biting political humor degrades the opposition candidates and party; how-

denouncing flag burning as unpatriotic and as a symbol of anti-American sentiment. "Waving the bloody shirt" and "waving the burning flag" represent particular persuasive strategies in special occasion speaking. In special occasion speeches, you're likely to hear patriotic recitals of the lives of martyrs who died that we might enjoy freedom, of traditional values and their symbols, and of the United States as the democratic bulwark, impervious to the assaults of all other political systems around the world.

Buried in this kind of public speaking are difficult ethical moments. Certainly as Americans we should know our history and who our martyrs were; we should be able to openly discuss values and the topics of patriotism and allegiance; and the United States, for better or worse, is expected to play a significant role in the international scene.

1. But what if our definition of patriotism begins to preclude discussion of alternative viewpoints?

2. What if references to traditional American values halt the examination of values of other people's cultures?

3. When does the defense of democracy become cultural imperialism—an attack on all other cultures, economies, and political systems?

Special occasion speaking *is* a time for reflecting upon one's own culture and belief systems, but such situations can easily be used to batter someone else's culture and thoughts. What the Greeks called *epideictic* oratory, the oratory of praise and blame, is talk filled with ethical minefields. At what point does waving the bloody shirt or the burning flag stop, rather than encourage, dialogue?

ever, such humor also can make one's own party feel more cohesive. For example, Democrats collected Richard Nixon's 1972 bumper stickers, which said "Nixon Now," cut off the *w*, and put them on their own autos. Democrats did endless turns on the names Bush and Quayle in 1988. Likewise, Republicans poked fun at Michael Dukakis, laughing at a picture of him seated in a tank and savaging his foreign policy statements. Such zingers allow political party members to laugh at their opponents and to celebrate their membership in a "better" party.

Finally, speeches to entertain can be used not merely to poke fun at outsiders, but even to critique one's society. Humor can be used to urge general changes and reform of social practices.

Formulating the Content of Speeches to Entertain

When arranging materials for speeches to entertain, develop a series of illustrations, short quotations or quips, and stories, each following another in fairly rapid succession. Most important, make sure that each touches upon a central theme or point. An entertaining speech must be more than a comic monologue; it must be cohesive and pointed. The following sequence works well for speeches to entertain:

1. Relate a story or anecdote, present an illustration, or quote an appropriate passage.
2. State the essential idea or point of view implied by your opening remarks.
3. Follow with a series of additional stories, anecdotes, quips, or illustrations that amplify or illuminate your central idea. Arrange those supporting materials so they are thematically or tonally coherent.
4. Close with a restatement of the central point you've developed. As in step 1, you can use another quotation or one final story that clinches and epitomizes your speech as a whole.

Sample Speech

The following speech by cartoonist Garry Trudeau of *Doonesbury* fame illustrates the principles for arranging speeches to entertain and demonstrates pointedly that such speeches can have very serious purposes—in this case, a critique of American attitudes toward impertinence. Notice that he began the speech with humorous observations, but then let his point about impertinence emerge sharply, with sarcasm his primary use of humor through the latter portions of the speech. In all, this commencement speech delivered at Vassar College in 1986 suited his occasion, the times, and his audience.

The Value of Impertinent Questions
Garry Trudeau[7]

Ladies and gentlemen of Vassar:

My wife, who works in television, told me recently that a typical interview on her show used to run 10 minutes. It now runs only five minutes, which is still triple the length of the average television news story. The average pop recording these days lasts around three minutes, or, about the time it takes to read a story in *People* magazine. The stories in *USA Today* take so little time to read that they're known in the business as "News McNuggets." /1

Now, the average comic strip only takes about 10 seconds to digest, but if you read every strip published in the *Washington Post*, as the President of the United States claims to, it takes roughly eight minutes a day, which means, a quick computation reveals, that the Leader of the Free World has spent a total of 11 days, 3 hours and 40 minutes of his presidency reading the comics. This fact, along with nuclear meltdown, are easily two of the most frightening thoughts of our times. /2

There's one exception to this relentless compression of time in modern life. That's right—the graduation speech. When it comes to graduation speeches, it is generally conceded that time—a generous dollop of time—is of the essence. This is because the chief function of the graduation speaker has always been to prevent graduating seniors from being released into the real world before they've been properly sedated. Like all anesthetics, graduation speeches take time to kick in, so I'm going to ask you to bear with me for about a quarter of an hour. It will go faster if you think of it as the equivalent of four videos. /3

I want to speak to you today about questions. About pertinent questions and impertinent questions. And where you might expect them to lead you. /4

I first learned about pertinent questions from my father, a retired physician who sued [sic] to practice medicine in the Adirondacks. Like all parents racing against the clock to civilize their children, my father sought to instruct me in the ways of separating wheat from chaff, of asking sensible questions designed to yield useful answers. That is the way a diagnostician thinks. Fortunately for me, his own practical experience frequently contradicted his worthiest intentions. /5

Here's a case in point: A man once turned up in my father's office complaining of an ulcer. My father asked the pertinent question. Was there some undue stress, he inquired, that might be causing the man to digest his stomach? The patient, who was married, thought about it for a moment and then allowed that he had a girlfriend in Syracuse, and that twice a week he'd been driving an old pick-up down to see her. Since the pick-up frequently broke down, he was often late in getting home, and he had to devise fabulous stories to tell his wife. My father, compassionately but sternly, told the man he had to make a hard decision about his personal priorities if he was ever to get well. /6

The patient nodded and went away, and six months later came back completely cured, a new man. My father congratulated him and then delicately inquired if he'd made some change in his life. /7

The man replied, "Yup. Got me a new pick-up." /8

So the pertinent question sometimes yields the impertinent answer. In spite of himself, my father ended up teaching me that an unexpected or inconvenient truth is often the price of honest inquiry. Of course, you presumably wouldn't be here if you didn't already know that. I'm confident that your education has been fairly studded with pertinent questions yielding impertinent answers. /9

But how many of you have learned to turn that around—to ask the impertinent question to get at that which is pertinent? /10

I first came across the impertinent question in the writings of that master inquisitor, Studs Terkel. He himself claims to have adopted it from the physicist Jacob Bronowski, who once told him, "Until you ask an impertinent question of nature, you do not get a pertinent answer. Great answers in nature are always hidden in the questions. When Einstein in 1905 questioned the assumption held for three hundred years that time is a given, he asked one of the great impertinent questions: "Why? How do I know that my time is the same as yours?' " /11

The impertinent question is the glory and the engine of human inquiry. Copernicus asked it and shook the foundations of Renaissance Europe. Darwin asked it and is repudiated to this day. Thomas Jefferson asked it and was so invigorated by it that he declared it an inalienable right. /12

Daniel Defoe asked it and invented the novel. James Joyce asked it and reinvented the novel, which was promptly banned. /13

Nietzsche asked it and inspired Picasso, who restated it and inspired a revolution of aesthetics. /14

The Wright brothers asked it and their achievement was ignored for five years. Steven Jobs asked it and was ignored for five minutes, which was still long enough for him to make $200 million. /15

Whether revered or reviled in their lifetimes, history's movers framed their questions in ways that were entirely disrespectful of conventional wisdom. Civilization has always advanced in the shimmering wake of its discontents. As the writer Tristan Vox put it, "Doubt is precisely what makes a culture grow. How many of what we call our classics were conceived as the breaking of laws, exercises in subversion, as the expression of doubts about the self and society that could no longer be contained?" /16

The value of the impertinent question should be self-evident to Americans, for at no time in human history has it been asked more persistently and to greater effect than during the course of the American experiment. It is at the very core of our political and cultural character as a people, and we owe our vitality to its constant renewal. /17

Today, the need for that spirit of renewal has never seemed more pressing. There is a persistent feeling in this country that many of our institutions have not measured up, that with all our resources and technology and good intentions, we as a nation are still a long way from fulfilling our own expectations. The social programs that have failed to eliminate poverty, an educational system which has seen its effectiveness seriously eroded, the chemical breakthroughs that now threaten man's environment, the exploding booster rockets, malfunctioning nuclear power plants—these are but some of the images that have shaken our confidence. According to a recent poll, the only American institution that still enjoys the trust of a majority of college students today is medicine; only 44% of those polled trust educational institutions, 29% trust the White House, 23% trust the press and only 21% say they trust religion. /18

It's difficult to think of an institution in this country that has not had to reexamine its agenda, to ask impertinent questions about the purpose and the means of its mission. Society's leaders, whose number you join today, face a wall of public cynicism. As professionals, they have to speak more clearly about what they *can* do. As citizens, they have to speak clearly about what they *should* do. /19

Nowhere is the need for accountability more urgent than in what is shaping up to be the largest coordinated national undertaking of your generation—the Strategic Defense Initiative. It may well become the most fiercely contended issue of your times. Already 6,500 college scientists, including a majority of professors in 109 university physics and engineering departments, have declared their opposition to SDI and have signed a "pledge on non-participation" in a project they have called "ill-conceived and dangerous." The group, including 15 Nobel Prize winners, maintains that the weapons system is inherently destabilizing and the further pursuit of its development is likely to initiate a massive new arms competition. /20

The actions of these scientists constitute an extraordinary repudiation of the amorality of indiscriminate weapons research. Science, since it leads to knowledge, has all too frequently led its practitioners to believe that it is inherently self-justifying, that there is nothing dangerous about splitting atoms in a moral vacuum. These attitudes are held in abundance by some of the brightest people of your generation, who are already hard at work on what nearly *all* of them concede is a dangerous fantasy. /21

Listen to these comments from the young Star Warriors still in their 20s working on particle beams and brain bombs at Lawrence Livermore National Laboratory: /22

This from the inventor of the atomic powered x-ray laser, "Until 1980 or so, I didn't want to have anything to do with nuclear anything. Back in those days I thought there was something fundamentally evil about weapons. Now I see it as an interesting physics problem." /23

His co-worker, another brilliant young physicist, says he has doubts about the wisdom of SDI but concurs that "the science is *very* interesting." /24

A third member of the team had this to say: "I think that the great majority of the lab's technical people view the President's (Star Wars) speech as somewhat off the wall and the programs being proposed as being, in the end, intrinsically rather foolish. But obviously, the lab is benefiting right now and will continue to benefit, and everybody's happy with the marvelous new work." /25

Marvelous new work, indeed. As a TRW recruiting brochure put it recently, "We're standing on the first rung of a defense development that will dominate the industry for the next 20 years." Why? Because weapons manufacturers think Star Wars will work? On the contrary, at a recent trade show, McDonnell Douglas boasted on one wall its Star Wars hardware while on a facing wall, it displayed proposed Star Wars countermeasures, including a "maneuvering re-entry vehicle" and a "defense suppression vehicle." GA Technologies is already marketing the latest in "survivable materials" to protect American missiles from a *Soviet* defensive system. /26

No one in the defense industry seriously believes in a "peace shield"; in fact they're betting against it. If an American SDI is big business, then the hardware needed to overcome the anticipated Soviet response is even bigger business. The industry is further encouraged by the mindless momentum of the program, as evidenced by the recent admission of Reagan's undersecretary of defense that he pulled the $26 billion price tag out of the air. /27

Said the official, "I tried to figure out what the hell we're talking about. [Congress] wanted a number and kept on insisting on having a number. OK. First year was $2.4 billion, and I figure, OK, best we could handle is maybe a 20%–25% growth." /28

Little wonder that during the program's first year, the money could not be spent fast enough to use up the yearly appropriation. Undeterred, the following year the administration asked for $2.5 billion, greater than its request for all the basic research financed by the National Science Foundation and Department of Energy combined. /29

It should not surprise us that so many in the scientific establishment find this obscene. Said computer scientist David Parnas, who recently quit an SDI advisory panel, "Most of the money spent will be wasted; we wouldn't trust the system even if we did build it. It is our duty . . . to reply that we have no technological magic (that will make nuclear weapons obsolete). The President and the public should know that." /30

To question the rationale of the SDI enterprise should be, as Mr. Parnas suggests, a question of simple duty. It shouldn't have to be an impertinent question, but that's exactly what it's becoming. The Star Wars juggernaut may already be unstoppable. $69 billion dollars will be spent by 1994. A representative of Hughes Aircraft recently predicted, "By 1988, it may be institutionalized." Lobbies are already being mobilized, interests are becoming entrenched, foreign governments are already being involved, on the sound theory that Star Wars will be harder to stop if it becomes part of Allied diplomacy. And all around the country, some of the most talented men and women of your generation are being recruited to solve "an interesting physics problem." /31

The impertinent question. We need it now more than ever. /32

And yet, sadly, healthy skepticism is at odds with the prevailing sentiment of our times. As Tristan Vox sees it, "arguments abound to the effect that a nation does not grow great by doubting itself, indeed the self-criticism was the trap that American democracy had laid for American greatness." /33

We've been here before. It was called the '50s. This supposedly conservative doctrine holds that the very qualities from which this country has traditionally drawn its strength—idealism, openness, freedom of expression—are naive and dangerous in a cold war struggle. It maintains that America's raucous squabbles, our noisy dissent—in short, its very heritage—have weakened us as a nation and caused it to lose its unchallenged supremacy. /34

As the *New Republic*'s Mike Kinsley put it, "Talk about blaming America first." /35

In such an atmosphere, the impertinent question comes with risks. Ask the two engineers at Morton Thiokol who protested the launch of the doomed Challenger space shuttle. Ask any Pentagon procurement whistle-blower. Ask David Stockman. The mere fact of this president's widespread popularity casts suspicions on the motives of even the loyalest of oppositions. There is, of course, no question that this president seems to have fulfilled a deep yearning in many Americans to feel positively about their country. And yet, the Reagan presidency often reminds me of a remark made by a woman to sportscaster Heywood Broun following the victories of the great racehorse Secretariat in the Triple Crown. After the trauma of Vietnam and Watergate, she told Broun, Secretariat had "restored her faith in mankind." /36

I would submit to you that Ronald Reagan is the Secretariat of the '80s. He has restored our faith in ourselves, and for that, we are all in his debt. It does not, however, exempt his administration from criticism from concerned citizens who love their nation as much as he does. One of the things that has always distinguished this country from most others is that we've always challenged ourselves to do better. As a satirist, I can't foresee any administration, Republican or Democratic, under which the basic message wouldn't be the same—that it's possible to do better. /37

This is the true glory of America. This hope is what stirs me as a patriot—not a winning medal count at the Olympics, not the ability to drop 9,000 servicemen on a Caribbean golf course, not jingoistic commercials that tell me that the pride is back, America, when for many of us the pride never left, and certainly not by the fantasy of 1,000 laser rays criss-crossing the heavens in software-orchestrated precision, obliterating a swarm of supersonic projectiles. /38

Skeptical? You bet. You're looking at a man who has attended 16 graduations, at four of which, including one technical college, the microphone failed. /39

The impertinent question. The means by which we reaffirm our noblest impulses as a people. But what about the impertinent question as it pertains to us as individuals? Bronowski had an addendum to his comments on the subject. "Ask the same kind of question," he charged Studs Terkel, "not about the outside, but the inside world; not about facts but about the self." /40

This is impertinence of the gravest sort. The inner life finds very little currency in this, the age of hustle. David Stockman has written of a leadership circle which is intellectually inert, obsessed by television, bored by introspection and ideas of substance. Meanwhile, all across town, the sad stories of sleaze abound, 110 to date, all pointing the new prevailing ethic of corner-cutting and self-advancement, whose only caveat is the admonition not to get caught. /41

It can seem a pretty grim picture. Indeed, as you look around you, you see very little to distract you from this narrow path. And yet that is exactly what your liberal education—with its emphasis on ideas, on inquiry, on humanist values—sought to do. As the president of my alma mater once observed, "The whole point of your education has been to urge you to see and feel about the connectedness among things and how that connectedness must be fostered so that civilization is sustained." /42

Our understanding of the interdependencies of the human experience is the only force which keeps a society from fragmenting. The extent to which you seek that understanding is the extent to which you will be strong enough to repudiate the callousness you see around you. /43

This won't please you, but let me share a little of what one of the more astute voices of your generation, 24-year-old David Leavitt, has written about his peers: "Mine is a generation perfectly willing to admit its contemptible qualities. But our contempt is self-congratulatory. The buzz in the background, every minute of our lives, is that detached ironic voice telling us: At least you're not faking it, as they did, at least you're not pretending as they did. It's okay to be selfish as long as you're up-front about it." /44

This is a pretty bleak portrait of the values of a generation, and my guess is I'm staring at hundreds of exceptions. My further guess is that the yearning for moral commitment is as intense as it always was, but that the generation with no rules, the generation that grew up in the rubble of smashed idealism, fallen heroes and broken marriages is deeply suspicious. /45

Columnist Ellen Goodman has speculated that this is why apartheid and the soup kitchen have emerged as the causes of choice; they offer that stark unambiguous clarity that World War II offered their grandparents, that sense that there is no good news about the other side of the argument. But Goodman, being incorrigibly of her era, also believes that micro evolves into macro; that to be involved inevitably leads to decisions between imperfect options; that many of you will take risks, make mistakes, and become citizens in spite of yourselves. /46

I'm afraid there's simply no other way. If ours becomes a society intolerant of failure and uncompassionate in the face of suffering, then surely we are lost. With the uncertainties of the future hedging in on you, you need to assess your commonalities. You need to say how you would treat other people, and how you would have them treat you back. /47

The best your college education can do for you now is to remind you that it's one thing to be self-absorbed and quite another to be self-aware. It comes down to a matter of being open, of seeing. It comes down to a matter of remaining intrigued enough by life to welcome its constant renewal. In short, it comes down to the impertinent question. /48

From those of us floundering out here in the real world, to those of you preparing to enter it, may I just say, welcome. We need you. /49

Thank you and good luck. /50

Chapter Summary

Speeches on special occasions are grounded in communities' ceremonies or rituals for defining and reinforcing those communities' fundamental tenets. Speakers on such occasions face the special challenge of getting diversified audiences to see, interpret, and evaluate the world through the beliefs, attitudes, values, and rituals of the group observing the occasion. We define ourselves and live up to standards of behavior within *reference groups*, and yet, when those groups clash, *social constructions* of the world must be built through language. Types of speeches on special occasions include *speeches of introduction, speeches of tribute* (farewells, dedications, memorial services), *speeches of nomination, speeches to create goodwill*, and *speeches to entertain*. Most of these forms are built so as to construct and reinforce community standards, although speeches to entertain often are used to critique group beliefs and practices in order to contribute to a better community.

References

1. Nelson Goodman, *Ways of Worldmaking* (Indianapolis, IN: Hackett, 1978), 6.

2. For a discussion of the kinds of group activity that reinforce the power of groups over your life, see James E. Combs, *Dimensions of Political Drama* (Santa Monica, CA: Goodyear, 1980), "The Functions of Ritual," 20–22. Cf. Philip G. Zimbardo, *Psychology and Life*, 13th ed. (New York: HarperCollins, 1992), "Constructing Social Reality," 595–607.

3. Michael Walzer, "On the Role of Symbolism in Political Thought," *Political Science Quarterly* 82 (1967): 194.

4. David I. Kertzer, *Ritual, Politics, and Power* (New Haven, CT: Yale University Press, 1988), 9.

5. Harold Haydon, "The Testimony of Sculpture," *The University of Chicago Magazine* (1968).

6. Henry W. Grady, "The New South," *American Public Addresses: 1740–1952*, ed. A. Craig Baird (New York: McGraw-Hill Book Co., 1956), 181–85.

7. Garry Trudeau, "The Value of Impertinent Questions," *Representative American Speeches* 1986–1987, ed. Owen Peterson (New York: H. W. Wilson, 1987), 133–42.

Key Terms

community (p. 469)	*ritual* (p. 471)
dedications (p. 478)	*social construction* (p. 470)
eulogies (p. 478)	*special occasion* (p. 470)
reference group (p. 471)	*speeches of farewell* (p. 476)

Problems and Probes

1. This chapter has argued that goodwill speeches usually are informative speeches with underlying persuasive purposes. Describe various circumstances under which you think the informative elements should predominate in this type of speech, and then describe other circumstances in which the persuasive elements should be emphasized. In the second case, at what point would you say that the speech becomes openly persuasive in purpose? If you prefer to work with advertisements, scan magazines to find public service ads that emphasize what a company is doing to help society with its problems or to promote social-cultural-aesthetic values. Then ask yourself similar questions about these advertisements.

2. In this chapter we have discussed speeches of introduction and tribute, but we have ignored speakers' *responses* to them. After you have been introduced, given an award, or received a tribute, what should you say? Knowing what you do about speeches of introduction and tribute, what kinds of materials might you include as attention, satisfaction, and visualization steps?

Communication Activities

1. Assume that you are to act as chairperson on one of the following occasions (or on a similar occasion):
    a. A student government awards banquet
    b. A special program for a meeting of an organization to which you belong
    c. A kickoff banquet for a schoolwide charity fund-raising program
    d. A student-faculty mass meeting called to protest a regulation issued by the dean's office

In your role as chairperson, (a) plan a suitable program of speeches or entertainment, (b) allocate the amount of time to be devoted to each item on the program, (c) outline a suitable speech of introduction for the featured speaker or speakers, (d) prepare publicity releases for the local media, (e) arrange for press coverage. Work out a complete plan—one that you might show to a steering committee or faculty advisor.

2. Your instructor will give you a list of impromptu special-occasion speech topics, such as:
    a. Student X is a visitor from a neighboring school; introduce him/her to the class.
    b. You are Student X; respond to this introduction.
    c. Dedicate your speech-critique forms to the state historical archives.

    d.   You have just been named Outstanding Classroom Speaker for this term; accept the award.

    e.   You are a representative for a Speechwriters-for-Hire firm; sell your services to other members of the class.

You will have between five and ten minutes in which to prepare and then will present a speech on a topic assigned or drawn from the list. Be ready also to discuss the techniques you used in putting the speech together.

3. Giving speeches to entertain is quite difficult because humor is a delicate art that only few can master; however, many audiences, as well as speakers, have come to expect the inclusion of jokes and funny stories in even the most serious presentations. Collect jokes, anecdotes, and cartoons that fit a certain genre, such as ethnic, religious, or sex-role-related. Analyze your collection with audience adaptation in mind. How might these jokes be offensive to some groups? How might they be modified so they are no longer offensive? How useful is material that is offensive even though it seems funny to you? Also collect jokes, anecdotes, and cartoons that are not offensive to anyone and suggest how they might be useful in speaking situations. Be prepared to share your observations with your classmates.

SPEAKER'S RESOURCE BOOK

The *Speaker's Resource Book* contains brief discussions of concepts and practices that extend the content of the preceding chapters. All are relevant to a broader understanding of the communicative concepts, situations, and practices that speakers may engage in.

I. COMMUNICATION CONCEPTS

COMMUNICATION MODELS

A model is a picture or representation of a thing or a process that identifies the key parts or elements and indicates how each element affects the operations of all of the other elements. A communication system can be reduced to such a model—in fact, to many models, depending upon what aspects of communication are of primary interest.

Before examining some communication models, however, you might legitimately ask, "Who cares?" "Of what importance or use are models?" While it's undoubtedly true that some speakers create and deliver extraordinarily powerful speeches without having seen—much less drawn up—a communication model, the fact is that most of us need help in conceptualizing the oral communication process; its primary features are not always clear. Furthermore, armed with models that direct our attention to particular aspects or features of oral communication, we're more likely to create strategically sound and situa-

tionally sensitive speeches than if we're unaware of the importance of particular elements or aspects of communication.[1] Models can control our perception of the communication process; in turn, the way we perceive communication can govern our practice.

For example, one of the earliest definitions of communication came from the Greek philosopher-teacher Aristotle (384–322 B.C.).[2] He defined communication, then called "rhetoric," as "the faculty of observing in any given case the available means of persuasion" (*Rhetoric* 1335b). With his stress upon "observing in any given case the available means" and with his long lists of things a speaker might want to say when talking in the Greek law courts and assemblies, his was a *speaker-centered* model of communication. Translating some of his Greek concepts into more contemporary language, his model looked essentially like the figure below.

As time passed, rhetoricians, or communi-

ARISTOTLE'S MODEL

A SPEAKER **discovers** logical, emotional, and ethical proofs,

arranges those materials strategically,

clothes the ideas in clear and compelling words, and

delivers the resulting speech appropriately.

BERLO'S MODEL

A **Source** encodes a **Message** for a **Receiver,** who decodes it (the S-M-R model).

cation theorists, became less concerned with the speaker or writer and more concerned with types and contents of actual messages. For example, in the late eighteenth and nineteenth centuries, the "belletristic" approach to communication education developed in the schools. After learning as much as they could about language—its origins, main elements, and eloquent use—students were put through a series of exercises. These began with the construction of relatively simple descriptive passages; moved on to more complicated historical narratives; and culminated in the writing of argumentative, persuasive, and literary works.

All of this emphasis upon preparing various kinds of messages led to *message-centered* theories of communication, which could be used to describe both oral and written discourse. The simplest and most influential message-centered model of our time came from David Berlo[3] (see the figure shown above). This model was useful for the post–World War II world of communication study for several reasons. (1) The idea of "source" was flexible enough to include mechanical, electronic, or other nonhuman generators of messages. (2) "Message" was made the central element, stressing the transmission of *ideas.* (3) The model recognized that receivers were important to communication, for they were the targets. (4) The notions of "encoding" and "decoding" emphasized the problems we all have (psycholinguistically) in translating our thoughts into words or other symbols and in

deciphering the words or symbols of others into terms we can understand.

The model was popular. It does, however, tend to stress the manipulation of the message—the encoding and decoding processes; it implies that human communication is like machine communication, like signal sending in telephone, television, computer, and radar systems. It even seems to stress that most problems in human communication can be solved by technical accuracy—by choosing the "right" symbols, preventing interference, and sending efficient messages.

The problems of human communication, however, are not as simple as that. Even when we know what words mean and choose the right ones, we still can misunderstand because we all have different experiences and interests in life. Even when a message is completely clear and understandable, we often don't like it. Problems in "meaning" or "meaningfulness" often aren't a matter of comprehension but of reaction; of agreement; of shared concepts, beliefs, attitudes, values. To put the *com-* back into communication, we need a *meaning-centered* theory. While there are many such theories, perhaps one of the simplest was that offered by theorist Wilber Schramm in 1954[4] (see the figure on page 503).

This model is elegant, picturing the meaning-sharing process simply and graphically, It essentially argues that, in any given signal (message), you and I will comprehend and understand each other to the degree that our "fields of experience" (interests, feelings,

SHRAMM'S MODEL

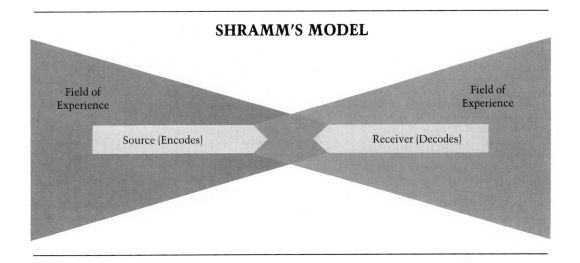

values, goals, purposes, information, ideas) overlap. That is, we can communicate in any given situation only to the degree that our *prior* experiences are similar.

Before we assume we've frozen interhuman communication in a simple process, we must take into account three other aspects of people-talk: feedback, context, and culture. (See Chapter 1.)

Our model now includes all the elements of a communication system that we need. To understand how systems operate, though, you also must keep in mind some of the characteristics of the elements we've alluded to:

1. *Sources* and *receivers* hold differing bundles of beliefs, attitudes, values, expectations, skills.
2. *Messages* are encoded into a variety of symbol systems (words, gestures, tones of voice, pictures, bodily postures).
3. *Contexts* provide almost innumerable cues that help receivers interpret what's being said or done.
4. *Cultures* provide even more complex rules for offering and interpreting messages.

If you look at the model on page 504 carefully, then examine the one offered in Chapter 1, you'll note some important similarities. That is because this *general* model of human communication formed the basis for the *specific* model of public speaking—one kind of human communication—we've been operating from in this textbook. As a matter of fact, were you to go through the entire book with this model in hand, you'd discover that the language, general advice, and even lists of specific "do's" and "don'ts" throughout the preceding chapters are grounded in this model. The stress upon making rhetorical choices based on your assessments of situation, audience, and purpose; the references to communication rules and roles; the expressed hope that you'll develop a broad range of oral communication skills are all rooted in this model.

Communication models are merely pictures; they are even distorting pictures, because they stop or freeze an essentially dynamic interactive or transactive process into a static picture. Nevertheless, a well-drawn model—and certainly you're able, if you think about it, to draw a model that reflects your own view of communication practices—can direct your attention to key aspects of human communication and, hence,

A CONTEXTUAL-CULTURAL MODEL

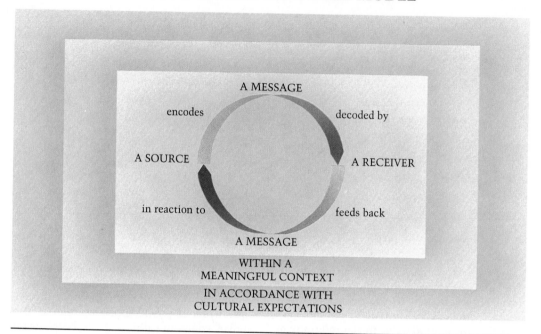

A MESSAGE

encodes   decoded by

A SOURCE   A RECEIVER

in reaction to   feeds back

A MESSAGE

WITHIN A
MEANINGFUL CONTEXT

IN ACCORDANCE WITH
CULTURAL EXPECTATIONS

affect your oral communication performance. A picture may well be worth a thousand words—especially if it helps you shape those words into a coherent, powerful speech.

References

[1] For a helpful and more sophisticated introduction to communication models, see C. David Mortensen, *Communication: The Study of Human Communication* (New York: McGraw-Hill, 1972), Chapter 2, "Communication Models."

[2] Aristotle's speaker-centered model received perhaps its fullest development in the hands of Roman educator Quintilian (ca. A.D. 35–95), whose *Institutio Oratoria* was filled with advice on the full training of a "good" speaker-statesman.

[3] Simplified from David K. Berlo, *The Process of Communication* (New York: Holt, Rinehart, and Winston, 1960).

[4] From Wilbur Schramm, "How Communication Works," in *The Process ad Effects of Communication*, ed. Wilbur Schramm (Urbana: University of Illinois Press, 1954), 3–26.

ETHICS AND PUBLIC SPEAKING

Four types of ethical demands are made upon the responsible speaker: the demands you make upon yourself, the demands imposed upon you by the situation, the particular audience's sense of what will be ethically proper, and constraints imposed by societal standards of conduct.

1. *Self*. You are the best judge of your personal standards of conduct. Not all people are willing to sell a car they know is a lemon without mentioning the possibility of problems. While there may be a sucker born every minute, every speaker isn't inclined to exploit that possibility in selling his or her ideas to an audience. Each of us has limits beyond which we are uncomfortable in advancing ideas or selling products. First and foremost, then, you need to be consistent with your own standards for the ideas you advocate, the information you dispense, and the techniques you use.

2. *Situation*. Some people will attempt to take advantage of a situation in order to sell an idea or a product. News stories about elderly persons who've been swindled are all too common. For this reason, there are laws that restrict conduct in particular situations. "Truth in advertising" legislation, disclosure of information by used car dealers, provisions for ensuring that estimates are given and agreed to before work is performed on your car or home, and "truth in lending" statutes all work to limit the range of unethical practices that people might otherwise be prone to commit. Adhering to legal statutes or to situational standards dictated by custom also will help prevent irresponsible speech.

3. *Audience*. Some audiences are more gullible than others. One audience's level of knowledge, interest, or even comprehension may make it possible to capture that audience without its realizing that you've been less than candid or honest. Another audience, in contrast, will appraise your ideas critically. What does this mean for you as a public speaker? Should you take advantage of the less critical listeners and hope to slide your ideas past them without their noticing that the reasoning and support are weak? Your own standards and those implicit in the situation should prevent you from taking this route.

4. *Society*. If your standards and those of the specific situation are not sufficient to pre-

vent unethical practices, the standards of the society often prove potent enough to prevent abuses. Where there are no formal laws or rules to follow, communities have established general standards that a speaker violates at his or her peril.

None of these standards operates in isolation. Taken together, they form a whole and act as a check on ethical abuse.

Guides to Practice

Thinking about being ethical in your presentation and actually being ethical are quite different. Knowing what should be done is no guarantee against mistakes. The following guidelines will help you translate the previously mentioned cautions into actual practice.

Advocate Ethically Based Proposals. Audiences can challenge your techniques of presentation as unethical, or they can challenge the ideas themselves. Your position on topics that evoke heightened emotional feelings (for example, abortion) may be rejected on ethical grounds. If the audience feels your proposal is questionable, how far will you get with it, regardless of the techniques you use? You have an obligation to be sensitive to community standards regarding the ideas and proposals you submit for approval and action. You may be convinced that the proposal is ethical, but you may still need to persuade your audience that it doesn't violate community standards.

Protect the Rights of Others. The language you use and the claims you advance should not be so abusive as to libel or slander others. You need to defend claims about the wrongdoing of others and state your case in clear, precise terms without resorting to loaded language or name calling. When in doubt, be very careful in your accusations regarding the behavior of other people.

Subordinate Techniques to Ideas. You want the audience to focus upon your message, not upon the artistry of your approach, style, or delivery. Whatever techniques you use should be in the service of the message, rather than so transparent that they assume a significance of their own. Techniques perceived as "too smooth" may cause the audience to question the sincerity of your motives in persuading them. Going beyond what an audience feels is reasonable for the topic under discussion or the situation will bring attention to your techniques and damage your effectiveness.

Responsible speech, in essence, requires sensitivity to the total communicative situation. Speaking with knowledge and skill, drawing upon your knowledge of your self, the situation, the audience, and the broader community standards and limiting the potential for abuse by following the above guidelines will help you practice ethically responsible communication.

ANALYZING AND CRITICIZING THE SPEECHES OF OTHERS

The bulk of this book has been concerned with making you a more skillful producer of oral messages. Except for some comments on listening in Chapter 2 we haven't discussed explicitly the matter of analyzing and evaluating the messages of others. Because during your lifetime you'll spend more hours listening than talking, however, you certainly should know something about speech analysis and criticism. In a short space, we can only introduce the subject; you might learn enough here to want to study and practice speech analysis and criticism later.

What Is Speech Analysis and Criticism?

For most people, the word *criticism* calls up images of parents lecturing their kids, of politicians shouting at each other in a "Did not! Did too!" sort of way, or of teachers telling you about your shortcomings. Those kinds of negative or corrective judgments are part of what criticism *can* be about, but they are only that—negative judgments. There is much more to a complete act of criticism.

Suppose you come out of a classroom lecture and say to a friend, "That was the worst lecture I've heard all term." Your friend replies, "How so?" You answer, "The professor was disorganized, he turned his back on us most of the time and talked to the chalkboard, and the point he made about audience analysis

as the single most important part of public speaking was just plain dumb." Your friend responds, "Oh, I don't know about that. He did outline the lecture pretty well, I thought, and of course he turned his back—he had a lot to write down. And what do you mean, audience analysis is 'just plain dumb'?" "Well," you counter, "he didn't really follow the outline—remember when . . . ?" On it goes, until you both agree or get tired of discussing the topic.

In dialogues like this one, you're engaging in analysis and criticism. *Criticism is an argumentative process of analytical description and reasoned evaluation aimed at producing interpretations and judgments.* It's argumentative in that it's based on a disputable claim ("That was the worst . . ."). It's a process in that it's aimed at another party, either someone who responds or someone who simply reads what you've written. Analytical description provides the "evidence" one uses to support the claim. The evaluative aspects of criticism aren't simply self-reports of likes and dislikes, but are based on accepted criteria for judgment (in the example, on the positive values of good organization, eye contact with audiences, and audience analysis).

The goals of criticism—what someone else should get from your efforts to criticize well—are twofold:

1. *Interpretation.* Critics are in the business of getting others to view something in a

particular way, from a particular vantage point. In our example, you tried to get your friend to examine the professor's effort from three perspectives—organizational skills, delivery skills, and assertions about audience analysis. All three of these points of view fit under a general category one could call "technical speaker competencies"; technical speaker competencies are a kind of vantage point for evaluating that teacher's lecturing on that day. (Other vantage points, each with its own vocabulary, could have been used.)

2. *Judgment.* Also, criticism as a kind of argumentative discourse usually ends in judgment. A critic normally ends up asserting that someone or something is beautiful/ugly, useful/useless, ethical/unethical, good/bad. In a fully rounded piece of criticism, those judgments are reasoned, are argued for in the ways we talked about argumentation earlier in this book.

All criticism, therefore, includes three elements: (1) an interpretive-judgmental assertion, (2) evidence in support of that assertion, and (3) a perspective or way of looking at something that makes the assertion in some way important or worthy of consideration. More specifically, then, rhetorical criticism or speech criticism focuses on informative and persuasive messages: often, but not only, speeches, for persuasion also can be sought via newspapers, magazines, radio and television programs, propagandistic art, and so on. The rhetorical critic or analyst seeks to interpret and judge those rhetorical messages in particular ways and from certain perspectives.

Speech Criticism versus Speech Evaluation

As you'll recall from Chapter 2, you evaluate classroom speeches and others you hear from your personal perspective and from the speaker's as well. From your personal perspective you ask, "What's in this speech for me? What can I learn? What should I be wary of? What does this person think of me?" From the speaker's perspective—as when you are giving

someone feedback about his or her oral performance—you ask, "How did this person come across? Was the claim or central idea clearly stated? Was the speech well organized and easy to follow? Were the supporting materials adequate? Was the language clear and appropriate?" *Speech evaluation,* then, is aimed at oneself and at the speaker—for the listener's and the speaker's personal benefit.

Speech criticism usually is quite different. It is an *independent* message aimed at a *public.* Speech analyses and criticisms are messages about other messages. A speech seeks to accomplish an informative, persuasive, or entertaining purpose, while criticism of that speech interprets and judges that performance or transaction *with another, usually larger, purpose in mind.* That larger purpose is determined in part by what you, the analyst-critic, want other people to understand about the performance or transaction, and in part by what your readers (your public) want to learn.

Types of Speech Analysis and Criticism

That last statement leads us to consider the range of purposes critics and readers can have, which in turn produces a list of types of rhetorical criticism. Actually, there are almost as many purposes and types of criticism as there are individual critics, especially when you think about specific purposes as we discussed them in Chapter 3; however, most of the specific purposes can be placed under one of the three following categories.

To Account for the Effects of Communication.
Perhaps the most common end of rhetorical analysis is to account for the effects of a message or speaker upon an audience. Almost anyone, with sense and a bit of energy, can describe many of these effects. In assessing the effects of a presidential speech, for example, you can:

- Note the amount of applause and its timing
- Read newspaper accounts and commentary on it the next day
- Check public opinion polls, especially

those assessing the president's performance thus far and those dealing with the particular subject of the speech

- Notice how much it is quoted and referred to weeks, months, or even years after it was delivered
- Examine votes in Congress and election results potentially affected by the speech
- Read memoirs, diaries, and books treating the event, the speaker, and the speech
- Read the president's own accounts of the speech[1]

Mere description of effects, however, isn't criticism; after all, you can do that without even reading the speech. The important phrase in this purpose, therefore, is "accounting for." Rhetorical analysts discussing the effects of a speech take that extra step, delving into the speaking process to see if they can discover what in the message, the situation, the speaker, and other elements of the speech produced those results. That's no easy task, yet it's central to improving our knowledge of speechmaking and its effects on society. Following are examples of where you might look in the communication process to find elements that can account for a message's reception by an audience:

1. *The situation.* Did the situation make certain demands the speaker had to meet? A series of events, the traditions of discourse surrounding the occasion (that is, the expectations we have about inaugurals, sermons, and the like), or even the date of the speech (it is one thing for a presidential aspirant to make promises in October, but quite another for the elected person to make them in January)—all these can provide critics with clues to situational demands.

2. *The speaker.* Did the speaker have the authority or credibility to affect the audience, almost regardless of what he or she said? Some speakers have such a reputation or carry so much charisma that they can influence an audience with the sheer power and dynamism of their words and

presence. The rhetorical critic is interested in such phenomena and seeks to find specific word patterns and speech behaviors that account for listeners' reactions to these factors.

3. *The arguments.* Did the speaker's message strike responsive chords in the audience? Were the motivational appeals those to which this audience was susceptible? Why? Were the beliefs, attitudes, values, and ideological orientations advanced by the speaker likely to have made impressions on this audience? Why? Were the supporting materials—and specific combinations of the various types—useful in helping an audience comprehend and accept the overall message? Why? (These "whys" usually have to be answered by assessing the temperament of the times, the dominant ideologies in the culture, and the facts of the situation, as well as the internal and external characteristics of audiences discussed in Chapter 5.)

4. *Uses of modes of communication.* Were the linguistic, paralinguistic, bodily, and visual modes of communication used effectively? In other words, as a critic you must look at more than the words on a printed page. Oral communication always needs to be explained as completely as possible, either from videotapes, films, or—if necessary—newspaper descriptions of the speaker and occasion.

A solid analysis of communication effects, therefore, demands a careful integration of "who did what to whom, when, and to what effect." It demands thoughtful assessment— the hard work of deciding which among all of the elements of the speaking process were responsible for particular aspects of audience reaction. Ultimately, your quest for "why" will lead you to look at more than the speech itself. For example, determining why the audience was particularly receptive to President Johnson's call for a "blank check" during the 1964 Gulf of Tonkin crisis will require a historical examination of public attitudes at the time. To determine the effect of President Carter's debates on his 1976 victory and 1980 defeat will require more than an analysis of his arguments or his use of the media in both campaigns.

At times, it may be necessary to combine scientific research with historical explanation. An example will illustrate this point. Two teams of rhetorical analysts—Andrew A. King and Floyd D. Anderson, and Richard D. Raum and James S. Measell—were interested in techniques presumably used by Richard Nixon, Spiro Agnew, and George Wallace to polarize public opinion and divide voting groups in order to win elections in the '60s. King and Anderson examined with considerable care the speeches of Nixon and Agnew between 1968 and 1970, while Raum and Measell looked at Wallace's speeches between 1964 and 1972. Neither team felt that a mere listing of argumentative and linguistic techniques was enough, for the listing did not provide them with answers to the question "Why did these techniques work?" Both teams, therefore, read the social-psychological literature on the concept of *polarization*. King and Anderson then used this research to shed light on ways words can be used to affirm a group's identity (in this case, that of the silent majority), and on methods for isolating or negating the voting power of an opponent. The concept of polarization seemed to explain why those tactics supposedly created two different political power blocs, or "societies," in the late 1960s.

Raum and Measell, however, went further. They not only examined the tactics and psychological dimensions of polarization, but also looked at the concept as they deemed it to occur in specific situations. George Wallace's effectiveness, they concluded, lay in the kinds of people he appealed to, in his vocabulary—which charged his audiences emotionally—and in the ways in which Wallace made himself a social redeemer who could save the country from the "enemy."[2] You may not find it necessary to resort to such sophisticated strategies to explicate a message's effects.

Nevertheless, your analysis of a contemporary speech may be based on information you possess about how people behave in crowds, what their attitudes are, or what a particular psychological theory would predict given certain speech strategies. This information becomes a central part of your critical evaluation.

To Explore the Critical Dimensions of Communication.   So far, we've been discussing a focus on criticism that examines the effects of speeches—changes in attitudes or behavior, voting shifts, and acknowledgment of a speaker's rhetorical expertise are potential items in this process of arriving at a critical judgment. This is not, however, the only way of looking at a speech. A speech, after all, is many things on many different levels; hence, it's possible to talk about a number of different critical perspectives. A *critical perspective* is, in language we already have used, a human design or purpose. It is the reason-for-being of a piece of criticism, the particular viewpoint a critic is interested in bringing to bear on a discourse. Just as you can be looked at in a number of different ways—as a student, as a son or daughter, as an employee, as a lover—so, too, can a speech be examined from different vantages, depending upon the observer's purposes or designs. For example, speeches have been viewed critically in the following ways:

1. *Pedagogically.* You can use the speech as a model, as a way of examining public communicators who have made judicious rhetorical choices. You can learn how to speak well, in part, by looking at and listening to other speakers.

2. *Culturally.* You can examine a discourse to acquire a better understanding of the times. For example, you may look at speeches from the Revolutionary War period or from the nineteenth century to better understand *how* our ancestors thought, *how* the great American values were spread through the society, and *how* we as a nation came to be what we are.

3. *Linguistically.* Because human beings are symbol-using animals—because we're distinguished from other animals by the complexity of our symbol systems—it makes sense to be particularly interested in the language used in public discourses. Some critics look at oral language to better comprehend the communicative *force* of words—how some words plead, others persuade, still others threaten, and so on. Some critics are concerned with *condensation symbols*—the process by which certain words (for example, *communist* in the '50s, *hippie* in the '60s, *polluter* in the '70s, *yuppie* in the '80s) acquire a broad range of ideologically positive or negative connotations. Other critics are especially interested in *metaphors*—in ways we describe experiences vicariously with words ("He's an absolute *pig*") or, in the case of *archetypal metaphors*, ways by which we can capture the essence of humanity by appealing figuratively to the great common human experiences (light and dark metaphors, birth and death metaphors, sexual metaphors, and so on). Whatever approach linguistic critics take, however, they ultimately seek to illuminate what it means to communicate as a symbol-using human being.

4. *Generically.* A great number of critics have addressed the problem of classifying speeches into types, or genres. For example, in this book, we've generally classified speeches into four basic types—speeches to inform, to entertain, to persuade, and to actuate—because the groupings help you accomplish certain *purposes*. Other critics classify speeches by *situation* or *location*—for instance, the rhetoric of international conflict, the rhetoric of the used-car lot, the political-convention keynote address—in order to uncover the ways in which the location or expectations created by the occasion determine what must be said. Others argue that speeches are best categorized by *topic*

because certain recurrent themes congregate around recurrent human problems. Hence, they write about the rhetoric of war and peace, the rhetoric of women's issues, of reform or revolution. Whatever approach critics use in the process of classification, however, they all generally have a single goal: to categorize speeches in order to find *families of discourses* that have enough in common to help us understand dominant modes of thought or modes of expression typical of an age, problem, or set of speakers.

Pedagogical, cultural, linguistic, and generic critics, therefore, all examine specific aspects of discourses, features they think deserve special attention. They make this examination in order to learn what these aspects tell us about communication practice (*pedagogy*), the condition of humanity (*culture*), the potentials of language codes (*linguistics*), or the dominant species of discourse (*genres*).

To Evaluate the Ethics of Communication.

In an age of governmental credibility gaps, charges of corporate irresponsibility, situational ethics, and the rise of minorities who challenge the prevailing social and ethical systems of the United States, a host of ethical questions have come to concern speech analysts: Can we still speak of the democratic ideal as *the* ethical standard for speakers in this country? What are the communicative responsibilities that attend the exercise of corporate, governmental, and personal power?

For example, President Nixon's speech on November 3, 1969, in which he talked about the "silent majority," his quest for peace, and three alternatives for ending the war in Vietnam—escalation, withdrawal, or gradual de-escalation—naturally aroused considerable controversy. One critic, Forbes Hill, found no special ethical problems in the speech because the president's appeals to the majority of Americans were consistent with the country's values at that time. Another, Robert P. Newman, assuming the "democratic ideal" as his standard, decried the speech because he claimed that it violated the individual's right to know fully all that a government plans and does. A third critic, Karlyn K. Campbell, argued that the standards initially set for evaluating the alternatives were violated later in the speech, and Philip Wander and Steven Jenkins accused the president of lying.[3] Thus, each critic assumed a particular ethical posture, and from that posture proceeded to evaluate the speech in accordance with his or her own views and biases.

Essential Critical Activities

Rhetorical analysis, no matter what its specific purpose, always demands certain activities of the critic. No matter what goal you're attempting to accomplish, as a critic you need a way of talking about the speech event, a plan for observing or reconstructing it, and a method for writing up your critical thoughts.

A Coherent Vocabulary for Rhetorical Evaluation. Perhaps the most difficult task a beginning critic faces is that of settling on a rhetorical vocabulary, a way of talking. The "who? what? when? where? why? how?" questions of the journalist may provide a starting point for analysis, but they won't get a critic very far in examining a speech. Unlike the journalist, the critic is engaged in a systematic, coherent pursuit of specialized knowledge *about* communication. The description of the event itself is only a part of that process; therefore, the actual analysis demands a language that "talks about" talk. There are many such critical vocabularies. Consider one example.

Lloyd Bitzer argues that the *rhetorical situation* almost literally dictates what kinds of things ought to be said, to whom they ought to be said, and in what forms the messages should be presented.[4] More specifically, he maintains that situations are marked by *exigencies* (events, peoples, or happenings that call forth discourse from someone because they are important, serious, demanding, and so

on), by *audience expectations* (thoughts of who should say what to whom, when, and where), and by *constraints* (the limits of choices speakers can make—for instance, the rules governing congressional debate, the boundaries of social propriety, the availability or not of certain audiences). If a speaker in a rhetorical situation satisfies the reasons calling forth talk, meets the audience's expectations, and abides by the constraints, the speech will be considered a *fitting response* to the situation.[5] Thus, in Bitzer's model, the main emphases are upon *the primacy of situation and the importance of speech competencies*.

Bitzer's approach to rhetorical analysis and his vocabulary are especially useful when, as a critic, you're studying the speeches of representatives of particular groups. The behaviors of heads of state, congressional politicians, leaders of churches, labor unions, and the like in part are dictated by the groups they represent. They aren't speaking for themselves as individuals, but rather for groups or institutions. Hence, no matter what they believe personally, their public utterances always must be consistent with the organization's goals, reinforce its viewpoints, and voice its concerns. They may even be pressured by the forces inherent in certain occasions—by what custom dictates *must* be said in inaugurals, in Labor Day speeches, in Easter sermons, and the like. In short, when speakers are constrained by situationally imposed roles, Bitzer's approach and vocabulary help us examine how these constraints affect the way people talk publicly and upon what bases we judge them competent speakers.

Careful Observation. The second task you must grapple with as a critic is that of deciding *what* to look at and *how*. In part, of course, this problem is solved by your selection of a vocabulary. If, for example, you use a textbook vocabulary, you know you'll have to isolate motivational appeals, look for an arrangement pattern, and see if you can find out how the speaker delivered the message. Yet, the vocabulary doesn't, as a rule, exhaust your task of looking. You may need to expand it to include searches for information both inside and outside the speech text itself.

Outside Observation. Often you have to look for relevant information about the speech, the speaker, the audience, and the situation *outside* the actual text of what was said. As we've already suggested, if you're interested in the effects of a presidential speech, you'll probably want to check public opinion polls, memoirs, diaries, the results of subsequent voting on the issue or issues, and newspaper and magazine reactions. If you're working from the textbook vocabulary, you'll probably need to see what the audience knew about the speaker beforehand (prior reputation), what kind of people made up the audience present, and what ratings were given to radio or television broadcasts of the speech. If you are doing a cultural analysis of the speech, you'll have to read whatever you can find on the cultural values and mores of the era in which the speech was delivered.

You cannot, for example, do a study of Daniel Webster as a typical ceremonial orator of the 1830s or 1840s without having a solid grasp of what Americans were doing and thinking about during that early national period. Webster's political generalizations, metaphors, and sweeping vision of the Republic make little sense unless you're acquainted with political-economic expansion, the settling of the Midwest and West, the growing fight between states' righters and nationalists, the problem of slavery, and other key cultural battles that characterized the period. Many kinds of critical studies of speeches, therefore, require you to spend time in the library with newspapers, magazines, history books, and biographies.

Inside Observation. As a critic, you also will have to live with the speech for a while. Often, an initial reading of it produces either a "So what?" or a "What can I say?" reaction. You should read it time and again, each time subjectively projecting yourself into the situation, into the frame of mind of the speaker and the audience. You probably should even read the speech aloud (if you don't have a recording or videotape of it), trying to capture emphases, rhythms, and sounds. Part of inside observation, then, is a process of "getting the feel" of the speech.

The other part is discovering the key points on which it turns. Certain statements or phrases in great speeches became memorable because they were pivotal. They summarized an important idea, attitude, or sentiment. As you read over, say, Cicero's "First Oration Against Cataline," you're impressed by the initial series of eight rhetorical questions, which immediately put the Roman audience into an abusive frame of mind. You may be similarly impressed by the way Queen Elizabeth I used *I* and *we* in her speeches in order to make her dominance over Parliament eminently clear, or by British Prime Minister David Lloyd George's preoccupation with light-dark archetypal metaphors, which elevate his discourse. Contemporary speeches, too—those published in *Vital Speeches of the Day,* for example—have certain elements in common: a heavy reliance upon particular forms of support, especially statistics, quotations from authorities, and explanations.

In other words, looking inside speeches intently forces your critical apparatus to operate. Your mind begins to catch points of dominance and memorability—aspects of discourse you find noteworthy and even fascinating. When those insights are coupled with research you've done on the outside—in newspapers, magazines, books, and the like—you'll soon find that you have something critical to say about a particular speech or group of speeches.

Composing Your Critical Evaluation. Acts of criticism are arguments. Your critical evaluation functions as a *claim* that must be supported with specific reasons justifying its soundness. Your process of observation and the vocabulary you use come together into a cogent explanation of why the speech was effective, how certain identification strategies functioned, or why cultural symbols in a speech were ignored by the audience. The following outline of a plan for writing your critical evaluation isn't the only way in which your argument may be organized. Nevertheless, it may be helpful as a general guide to the organization of your critical response. The plan also may be useful for term papers or research papers you'll be asked to write.

A Plan for Writing Speech Criticism

I. Introduction
   A. As a starter for your paper, introduce a quotation, a description of events, a statement of communication principles, or whatever will indicate your approach to the speech or your point of view about it.
   B. Make *a statement of questions or claims*—the point or points you wish to develop or establish in the paper.
   C. Make *a statement of procedures*—how you propose to go about answering the questions or proving the claims.
II. Body
   A. After you've thus described the basic speech material or the situation with which you are dealing, take the steps of your critical analysis one point at a time, looking, for example, at *exigencies/audience expectations/constraints/fittingness* if you're using Bitzer's critical techniques, making sure in this approach that you've carefully described the situation around which you're building your analysis.
   B. As you offer the subpoints or claims, liberally illustrate them with quotations from the speech or speeches you're analyzing, quotations that serve as evidence for your point of view or argument. Also quote from other critical observers to further support your position if you wish.
III. Conclusions
   A. In your *summary*, pull the argument of your paper together by indicating how

the subpoints combine to present a valid picture of public communication.
   B. Draw *implications*, commenting briefly upon what can be learned from your analysis and this speech (or set of speeches) about communication generally. That is, you say in effect that this is a case study of something having larger implications.

With a coherent vocabulary for thinking about public communication, with patient and thoughtful observation, and with a plan for reporting your reactions, you should be able to produce useful and stimulating evaluations and analyses of speeches, Ultimately, your practice in communication criticism will help you better understand the ways by which public discourse affects the beliefs, attitudes, values, and behaviors of yourself and your society.

In this short, appendix, we have been able to describe only *briefly* a few critical frameworks or approaches and to allude to a limited number of actual speeches and speaking events. A good general introduction to rhetorical criticism suitable for undergraduate students is Malcolm O. Sillars's *Messages, Meanings, and Culture: Approaches to Communication Criticism* (New York: Harper-Collins, 1991).

Reference Notes

[1] For an example of how skilled critics search out the effects of a controversial speech of this kind, see Paul Arntson and Craig R. Smith, "The Seventh of March Address [Daniel Webster]: A Mediating Influence," *Southern Speech Communications Journal* 40 (Spring, 1975): 288–301.

[2] Andrew A. King and Floyd D. Anderson, "Nixon, Agnew, and the 'Silent Majority': A Case Study in the Rhetoric of Polarization," *Western Speech* 35 (Fall, 1971): 243–55; Richard D. Raum and James S. Measell, "Wallace and His Ways: A Study of the Rhetorical Genre of Polarization," *Central States Speech Journal* 25 (Spring, 1974): 28–35.

[3] Forbes I. Hill, "Conventional Wisdom—Traditional Form: The President's Message of November 3, 1969," *Quarterly Journal of Speech* 58

(December, 1972): 373–86; Robert P. Newman, "Under the Veneer: Nixon's Vietnam Speech of November 3, 1969," *Quarterly Journal of Speech* 56 (December, 1970): 432–34; Karlyn Kohrs Campbell, "Richard M. Nixon," *Critiques of Contemporary Rhetoric* (Belmont, CA: Wadsworth, 1972): 50–57; and Philip Wander and Steven Jenkins, "Rhetoric, Society, and the Critical Response," *Quarterly Journal of Speech* 58 (December, 1972): 373–86.

[4] Lloyd F. Bitzer, "The Rhetorical Situation," *Philosophy & Rhetoric* 1 (Winter, 1968): 1–14.

[5] For a study clearly illustrating Bitzer's method of analysis, see Allen M. Rubin and Rebecca R. Rubin, "An Examination of the Constituent Elements in Presenting an Occurring Rhetorical Situation," *Central States Speech Journal* 26 (Summer, 1975): 133–41.

A MODEL FOR ORGANIZING AND EVALUATING ARGUMENTS

Writing in 1958, the British philosopher Stephen Toulmin proposed that arguments be diagrammed in a visually clear pattern that would help ensure that all elements–implicit and explicit–were recognized. The following elements, and the visual model that illustrates the relationships between and among them, will aid you in analyzing and critiquing your and others' arguments.

1. *Claim.* Put simply, what are you proposing for audience consideration? This can be, as we suggested in Chapter 17, a claim of fact, value, or policy.
2. *Data.* What materials, in the form of illustrative parallels, expert opinion, statistical information, research studies, and the like, can you advance to support the claim?
3. *Warrant.* What is the relationship between the parallel case, statistical data, or expert opinion and the claim? Upon what kind of assumption or inferential pattern does its acceptance as support for the claim depend? Materials don't function as evidence or support for no reason; *facts do not speak for themselves.* What makes an audience believe in the strength of the reasons as support lies in the following kinds of assumptions that warrant acceptance of the link between data and claim:
   a. An expert knows what he or she is talking about.
   b. Past economic, social, or political practices are reliable predictors of future occurrences.
   c. Inferential patterns (for example, cause, sign) suggest the linkage is rational.

We know, for instance, that an expert's credibility is a major determinant in gaining acceptance of the opinions being offered. In the development of the argument, this factor operates as an implicit *warrant* connecting the opinion to the claim. In matters involving economics, we know that the regularity of certain marketplace functions, such as supply and demand, exert a powerful influence on events. Hence, when we claim that the prices of finished products will rise as a result of the increases in the cost of raw materials, we are tacitly assuming the normal operation of the marketplace. Likewise, the value of using parallel cases as support for your position rests on the regularity of an inferential pattern: when two cases are parallel, similar results can be expected.

4. *Backing.* Does the audience accept the relationship between the data and the claim as given? If not, what further data would help supporting the warrant? When the warrant linking a reason and claim is accepted by the audience, explicit development of this facet of the argument is unnecessary. If an audience already under-

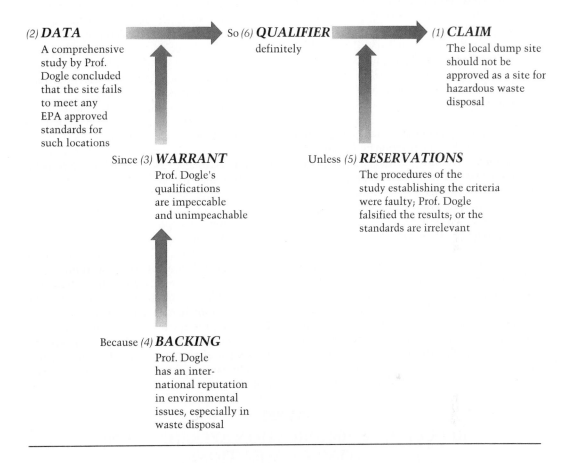

(2) DATA
A comprehensive study by Prof. Dogle concluded that the site fails to meet any EPA approved standards for such locations

So **(6) QUALIFIER**
definitely

(1) CLAIM
The local dump site should not be approved as a site for hazardous waste disposal

Since **(3) WARRANT**
Prof. Dogle's qualifications are impeccable and unimpeachable

Unless **(5) RESERVATIONS**
The procedures of the study establishing the criteria were faulty; Prof. Dogle falsified the results; or the standards are irrelevant

Because **(4) BACKING**
Prof. Dogle has an international reputation in environmental issues, especially in waste disposal

---

stands the logical pattern of an analogy and believes that the substance of the argument being presented is analogous, spending time to support the analogous nature of the relationship would be pointless.

When a relationship between the reason and the claim isn't automatically accepted, you'll have to provide additional support focused on the warrant rather than the original claim. Thus, in supporting an argument against continued economic aid to the "Contras" with testimony from a politician, you might need to establish her

expertise to increase the likelihood of audience acceptance.

5. *Reservations.* Can significant counterarguments be raised? In most cases, arguments on the opposite side aren't only readily available, but may even be as strong as your own reasons. Anticipating reservations in advance will help you strengthen your own argument. In general, these can be thought of as "unless" clauses in your argument.

6. *Qualifiers.* How certain is the claim? Note that we do not ask how certain *you* are; you may be absolutely sure of something

for which you cannot offer verifiable support. How much can one bank on the claim that you are putting forward as an acceptable basis for belief or action? Are you *sure* that economic aid will be used for military purposes? Such qualifiers as *probably, presumably, virtually,* and *may* should be incorporated into the claim to reflect the strength of the argument.

These six elements operate as a general framework for the construction and analysis of an argument. The interrelationships between and among the elements can best be displayed through a visual diagram. The numbers in the diagram correspond to the elements discussed. (See the figure on page 515.)

The model has three principal uses in organizing your arguments. First, by setting forth the arguments' components in the manner indicated, you'll be able to capture visually the relationships among the components. How, for example, are the data you present linked to the claim? What sort of warrants (assumptions, precedents, rules of inference) are you using to ensure that the audience sees the connection between the data and the claim?

Second, once you've written a brief description of the data and have identified the warrant on which its relationship to the claim rests, you can more clearly determine whether you wish to offer the claim as definite, or as only probable, likely, or possible. You'll also be reminded to reflect on the audience's grasp of the warrant. Is it a generally accepted relationship—will it be in this case?

Finally, by thinking through the possible reservations that others will have to your argument you'll be in a better position to shore up weaknesses in advance and, where necessary, to build a stronger base from which to respond to issues that might undermine rather than directly refute your case.

The elements also help sharpen your ability to question an argument. The data may be misleading or in error, the relationship between the data and claim may be highly questionable (lacking a strong warrant); there may be so many reservations that the claim must be highly qualified; advocates may be pushing claims harder than the data will warrant. Using the model as a means of thinking about arguments can help you determine whether a claim goes beyond what can reasonably be supported by the evidence and available warrants.

REDUCING COMMUNICATION APPREHENSION: SYSTEMATIC SOLUTIONS

Researchers have estimated that as much as 20 percent of the college population may experience *communication apprehension,* defined as "an individual's level of fear or anxiety associated with either real or anticipated communication with another person or persons."[1] The consequences of a high level of communication apprehension include lowered self-esteem, lowered academic achievement, and, in general, negative effects on a person's relationships with other people.[2] This personality trait affects all areas of a person's communica-

tive efforts, from calling on the telephone to presenting a public speech.

Communication apprehension is distinguished from the experience of *stage fright,* which involves specific situations in which a person is orally presenting material in a public setting (for instance, a play, speech, or panel presentation). Stage fright is a normal experience; it may or may not be accompanied by high communication apprehension. Thus, a person who has no major problems interacting with others in most situations can feel nervous when called upon to present ideas in public.

In this section, we will focus on three major treatment approaches and suggest ways in which they might be adapted to the reduction of your own stage fright.[3] As such, the advice will supplement that offered in chapters 1 and 3.

Systematic Desensitization

Systematic desensitization is a treatment program that assumes that you *do* have the ability to accomplish a specific task. Your fear is so great, however, that it impedes your successful behavior. For example, assume that you're afraid of height, and, as an actor, must walk the catwalks of the theater. Walking, as a behavior, isn't the problem. The fear of height causes you to become nauseated when on the catwalk and, thus, is potentially harmful. Persons trained in systematic desensitization would establish an ascending series of events that would provoke increasing amounts of your fear. They would ask you to imagine each aversive situation while in a relaxed state. Once you're able to accept a low-level fear-producing situation, you'd be asked to imagine a slightly higher-level situation. This would continue until you were able to imagine yourself on the catwalk and remain relaxed.

Cognitive Restructuring

As in the case of systematic desensitization, a treatment approach via cognitive restructuring assumes that you have the necessary behaviors but are unable to enact them due to your anxiety. This approach further assumes that your fear is a result of a misperception of the event and that you lack sufficient reinforcement to overcome your misperception. In the program, a trained counselor would seek to correct your perception of the event. In particular, the consultant would seek to change your mostly negative "self-talk" regarding the situation. You probably are your own worst critic; your presentation isn't as bad as you tell yourself it is. In cognitive restructuring, you'd be counseled to see the event in more realistic, and less personally negating, terms.

Skills Training

Unlike the other programs, this approach assumes your anxiety is due primarily to a lack of skilled behavior. Thus, if you'd been taught specific skills, you'd be able to react more competently and comfortably in a situation. A trained instructor would use a variety of teaching strategies (coaching, modeling, rehearsal, goal setting, actual performance) to help you acquire specific behaviors. Special programs have been created as part of college interpersonal and public communication courses (separate sections, workshops, or labs) to help students reduce their apprehension. Typically, these programs have focused on those experiencing a high level of apprehension.[4]

Reducing Stage Fright

Systematic desensitization is a program that requires expert assistance. Thus, the advice offered here won't include this approach as one you could undertake on your own or with the assistance of an untrained person. We might assume that both cognitive restructuring and skills training would be beneficial aids. That is, you can work on your perception of the event—is it as terrible as you think? Are you really as poor a speaker as you think? By talking with a public speaking instructor, or simply by asking friends who observe your performance, you may get a clearer picture of your strengths and weaknesses. Being willing to let go of your own perceptions and to accept the critique of others is essential to the restructuring of your perspective on the situation.

Second, we might assume that your skills can be refined and improved. By taking this route, your self-confidence may grow, and you'll find it easier to control your anxiety. There are several things you can consider, either on your own or with an instructor's assistance.

1. *Audio- or videotape.* If the necessary equipment is available, you can practice your presentation and play it back on an audio or video recorder. A careful critique of your performance with or without assistance (if your own attitude is generally negative, self-appraisal may simply reinforce a negative image) will suggest areas for improvement.
2. *Role playing.* You or an instructor can create role-playing situations that simulate the behaviors that you need to refine. If these are realistic, they'll help you feel more comfortable when you face an actual public-speaking situation.
3. *Rehearsal.* Practice your presentation before the live event, and ask friends or an instructor to critique your performance.
4. *Goal setting.* This can be a formal procedure worked out with an instructor, or your own informal assessment of what you want to work on.[5] Define a goal and then a set of specific behaviors that you want to accomplish in meeting that goal. For example, you might express this goal: "I want to be more articulate in the next presentation." A specific behavior would be: "I want to reduce the use of such words as *like* and *you know* to no more than two in the entire performance."

Reference Notes

[1] James C. McCroskey, "Oral Communication Apprehension: A Summary of Recent Theory and Research," *Human Communication Research* 4 (1977): 78.

[2] McCroskey, 78–96; Susan R. Glaser, "Oral Communication Apprehension and Avoidance: The Current Status of Treatment Research," *Communication Education* 30 (1981): 321–41.

[3] Glaser's essay is used as the basis for this review.

[4] For additional information on treatment programs, see Jan Hoffman and Jo Sprague, "A Survey of Reticence and Communication Apprehension Treatment Programs at U.S. Colleges and Universities," *Communication Education* 31 (1982): 185–93; Karen A. Foss, "Communication Apprehension: Resources for the Instructor," *Communication Education* 31 (1982): 195–203.

[5] Gerald M. Phillips, "Rhetoritherapy vs. the Medical Model: Dealing with Reticence," *Communication Education* 26 (1977): 34–43.

GENDER AND COMMUNICATION

In Chapter 12, we discussed specific strategies for using gender-neutral language. While our earlier discussion alluded to the ideological and social reasons for making these changes, they deserve further attention. As will become clear, the reasons go beyond using nouns and pronouns that are inclusive or neutral.

That women are at a disadvantage in most public-speaking contexts is supported by cultural history and affirmed by contemporary research. From a cultural perspective, there's a long history of women being relegated to secondary roles. Historically, women's voices have been silenced in a male-dominant public culture. Within this country, as late as the nineteenth century, women weren't supposed to speak in public. Women abolition speakers, such as the Grimke sisters, broke cultural barriers as they raised their voices in protest over slavery. Even though women won the right to vote, and more women are now giving voice to their concerns and are participating in public-policy controversies, recent empirical research still perceives male speakers as more accurate in their presentation of ideas and more credible generally. Conversely, women are perceived as lacking power, as being passive. In their study of sex-linked language differences in a public setting, Mulac, Lundell, and Bradac

(1986) concluded that "generally the female speakers . . . were comparatively complex, literate, tentative, and attentive to emotional concerns. Their discourse suggested a relatively powerless condition. By contrast, the males were egocentric, nonstandard, active, controlling, and intense. Their discourse focused on the here-and-now" (p. 124).

Stereotypes that lend tacit support to these perceptions are summarized as follows by Borisoff and Merrill (1985):

> The stereotypically feminine speaker is soft spoken, self-effacing, and compliant. More emotional than logical, she is prone to be disorganized and subjective (p. 11). The masculine model is that of a speaker who is direct, confrontative, forceful and logical, whose few, well-chosen words are focused on making a particular point (p. 13).

The use of gender-neutral language assists in removing the negative impact of these stereotypes. While their power and influence in directing people's public talk are gradually lessening, they still are reference points against which change is measured.

Speaking your mind in a public setting requires an ability to assert yourself. As the above stereotypes suggest, women are generally perceived as less assertive than men. The relative absence of assertiveness (though by no means entirely absent in women's public speech) is seen in the style of language and speaking that women engage in.

In general, women tend to project a quality of hesitancy or uncertainty in their choice of language, and in the way in which they phrase their questions and requests. For example, women tend to use standard pronunciation to a greater extent than do men. They also phrase requests in more polite language than men (men tend to make requests sound more like commands, while women phrase them in terms that allow the recipient a choice of declining). As might be expected from this difference, men's language choices tend to be more hostile than those of women.

Women also engage in more "corrective" talk, choosing to remind others of an inappropriate use of standard pronunciation, or inappropriate word choice. Tag questions ("I am on time, aren't I?") may be effective in some contexts, but are often used to reflect uncertainty. When used by women, who tend to use them more frequently than men, tag questions intensify the negative or limiting effects of the stereotype.

Women also use qualifiers, such as *likely*, *maybe*, or *possibly*, more often than men. This use is in contrast to the "directness" of male talk and furthers the negative image. Disclaimers, such as "I haven't thought this through . . ." have the same impact. In public settings, women are generally polite and "wait their turn" to speak, while men far more often interrupt in an attempt to be heard. Not only do men talk more, they also don't acknowledge comments from women in the same manner as similar comments from men.

The communication variables that differentiate male and female talk are much more complicated than can be discussed here. The solution to the problems implied by the stereotypes for both men and women are not simple—it isn't the case that women should simply talk like men, or vice versa. A gender-neutral language is one way to lessen the impact of both stereotypes in the public speaking setting. Using language that's inclusive—that references both genders—equalizes individuals in terms of their gender. Given research that clearly indicates that references to "men" or "mankind" are *not* seen as inclusive of both sexes, the switch to a more inclusive, nonspecific language is an appropriate means of valuing all members of a mixed-sex audience. Adopting such language behaviors also moves a speaker closer toward what some term an "androgynous" style—a set of behaviors that isn't gender-specific, but rather is open to both male and female speakers. Using language and emotion appropriate to the situation, whether a speaker is male or female, is to place the demands of the rhetorical occasion first, and the "traditions" of gender second. Hesitancy and tentativeness may have their natural place in a public setting, and language should reflect these tendencies whenever appropriate, but neither gender should be locked into a feminine or masculine stereotype simply by acknowledging what the situation calls for.[1]

For Further Reading

Mulac, A., T. L. Lundell, and J. J. Bradac. "Male/ Female Language Differences and Attributional Consequences in a Public Speaking Situation:

Toward an Explanation of the Gender-Linked Language Effect." *Communication Monographs* 53 (June, 1986):115–29.

Reference Notes

[1] This discussion is indebted to Deborah Borisoff and Lisa Merrill's *The Power to Communicate: Gender Differences as Barriers* (Prospect Heights, IL: Waveland Press, 1985) and to Judy C. Pearson, *Gender and Communication* (Dubuque, IA: Wm. C. Brown Publishers, 1985).

II. COMMUNICATIVE SITUATIONS

CONSTRUCTING INTERVIEW QUESTIONS

While everyone knows that answers to questions often determine one's success in achieving major goals in interviews, too often most of us forget how equally important questions are. We all must learn how to phrase different types of interview questions and how to organize them in order to elicit the information we seek.

Types of Interview Questions

A skill you must possess as both interviewer and interviewee is facility in asking questions. Six types of questions are often asked, and you must possess the ability to ask each type in appropriate situations. *Primary questions* introduce a topic or area of inquiry, while *follow-up questions* probe more deeply or ask for elaboration or clarification. Thus, if you're interviewing a local newspaper editor for a speech, you might begin with "What background did you have before becoming editor?" and follow up with "Would you elaborate on your experience as a copy editor—what did you do in that position?"

You also will develop *direct questions* ("How long have you been the editor?") and *indirect questions* ("What is your goal for the

paper five years from now?"). Direct questions allow you to gather information quickly, while indirect probes let you see interviewees "thinking on their feet," structuring materials and responses and exploring their own minds. Interviewers also use both *open* and *closed* questions. A closed question specifies the direction of the response—"Do your editorials create public concern about local issues?" An open question allows the interviewee to control the categories of response—"How do you perceive your role in the community?" Closed questions require little effort from the interviewee and are easy to "code" or record; open questions allow interviewers to observe the interviewee's habits, to let them feel in control of the interaction. Of course, these various types of questions overlap: you can use a direct or indirect question as your primary question; a closed question can be either direct ("Do you function most as editor, reporter, or layout specialist?") or indirect ("Of the various jobs you perform—editor, reporter, layout specialist—which do you enjoy the most?").

As you plan interviews, you must learn to blend questions of all six types. This blend is called an *interview schedule*.

Interview Schedules

An interview schedule is your effort to organize specific questions to systematically elicit the materials and opinions you are looking for. Like any other organizational pattern, an interview schedule should have a rationale, one that (1) permits you to acquire systematic information or opinion and (2) seems reasonable to the interviewee, avoiding confusing repetitions and detours. Interview schedules normally are built in one of two forms—the *traditional* and the *branching schedule.*

Traditional Schedule of Questions

I. "What was your background before becoming an editor?" (primary, indirect, open question)
   A. "How many journalism courses did you take in college?" (follow-up, direct, open question)
   B. "What kinds of practical experience did you obtain in your newswriting course?" (follow-up, direct, open question)
II. "How do you perceive your role in the community?" (primary, indirect, open question)
   A. "Several letters to the editor have complained about your bias in favor of the largest employer in the town. How do you respond to these criticisms?" (follow-up, indirect, open question)
      1. "Do you ignore the largest employer when writing editorials, or do you consider its position and then write what you believe in?" (follow-up, direct, closed question)
      2. "Do you find it difficult to take positions counter to those of the largest employer?" (follow-up, direct, open question)

Branching Schedule of Questions

1. "Did you take courses in journalism prior to becoming a journalist?"

If yes:	If no:
2. "Did you take courses in newswriting?"	2. "What type of practical experience did you have?"

If yes:	If no:
3. "Did you obtain practical experience in the newswriting course?"	3. "Did you do primarily features or general news items?"

If yes:	If no:
4. "What specific assignments did you have?"	4. [Note: Go to next area of inquiry.]

Notice that the traditional schedule of questions uses an organizational pattern that first extracts information and then follows with more probing questions. This pattern allows the interviewee to think through his or her experiences concretely before you ask for self-reflection or evaluation. Were that reversed, the interviewee might be asked to evaluate an experience before having recalled it clearly, most likely producing a less-than-complete evaluation. Notice, too, the mixing of types of questions in the traditional schedule to keep the interaction progressing.

A branching schedule is used in situations in which the interviewer knows rather specifically what he or she is looking for. Survey or polling interviewers often use this schedule. In our example, a student is using a branching schedule to explore the background of a local newspaper editor. In a complete branching schedule, the *If no* questions would likewise have "branches" beneath them; nonetheless, our illustration indicates the essential logic of the pattern.

No matter what types of questions you use and what specific organizational pattern for questions you devise, remember these important points:

1. *Plan you questions* before going into an interview so that you know your goals and proceed toward them.
2. *Organize your questions* in a manner that seems rational and prepares interviewees adequately before asking them to make abstract, complex evaluations.

THE EMPLOYMENT INTERVIEW

The employment interview can be a crucial communicative experience. The outcome may enhance your career aspirations or simply ensure that the rent will be paid on time. Either way, you often have a lot at stake in an interview situation. Seldom will you enter an interview with no real concern over whether the interviewer responds positively to you, or whether you actually get the job. The suggestions offered regarding building self-confidence (see Chapter 3) apply to the interview situation as well. By being prepared in advance, you'll be able to respond appropriately to the questions you're asked. The following guidelines may be helpful in preparing for and participating in an interview.

Preparing for an Interview

As you prepare for an interview, consider the following questions:

1. *Why do you want this job?* Aside from the fact that jobs means money, what's your reason for seeking this particular job?
2. *What knowledge or skills does the job require?* What skills, talents, abilities can you contribute? List the major skills that you possess; which ones are most relevant to this particular job? What courses or work experiences would be especially meaningful in this position? What should you stress in explaining your qualifications?
3. *What information can you gather about the company before the interview?* What homework should you do to indicate that you're seriously interested in this company and what it offers? Check with a campus placement office or with a local employment agency; they may have useful information available. If the company is a large national firm, check business publications for relevant information. Call the company's public relations office and request an annual report or other informative materials.
4. *What working conditions (location, extent of travel, benefits, salary) are you willing to accept?* How much of this information is available in the job description? If not mentioned there or by the interviewer, what issues are important enough for you to raise during the interview? Make a short list of your key concerns; refer to the list as the interview progresses to see what important concerns still need to be raised.
5. *What is the most appropriate apparel for the interview?* How will the interviewer expect you to dress? How do you want to present yourself?

By thinking through these and similar questions, you can go into an interview with a clear idea of what you want to accomplish.

Participating in an Interview

An interviewer seldom gets down to business in the initial moments of the interview. There is a brief time for exchanging social talk about the day, last night's game, and so on. This time allows you to relax and to establish a communicative relationship with the interviewer. Does the interviewer seem to be friendly, outgoing, and relatively informal in conducting the interview? Or is the interviewer likely to be all business once the obligatory social niceties are out of the way? You'll need to adapt to the social atmosphere that the interviewer seeks to establish. During this brief time, both of you are gaining first impressions of the other.

Follow the interviewer's lead. When he or she is ready to move to more formal questions, you should be able to shift gears and begin answering and asking questions regarding the position for which you are applying. The interviewer generally will begin with background information about the position and will ask general questions about your academic and work experience. As you respond to general questions, be wary of "overtalking" a question —going on and on without end. Give precise answers, developed in sufficient detail to respond fully to the question.

You'll be expected to ask questions as well as respond to them. Appropriate questions may include asking the interviewer what he or she likes about the company, what the opportunities for advancement are, how much travel would be involved, and what kind of equipment you'll be working with. Asking questions about salary and benefits can be a delicate matter. If you probe too much or spend an inordinate amount of time on details, the interviewer may get the impression that you're only interested in making a buck. If the interviewer doesn't offer the information, you can ask what the expected salary range will be and what benefits, in general terms, the company has for its employees. You want to appear interested in how supportive the company is; at the same time, you want to demonstrate your willingness to earn a salary.

Be sensitive to the interviewer's cues that the session is coming to an end. This might be an appropriate time to review your notes and ask if you could get some information on one or two brief points that were not covered. Asking a dozen specific questions of no clear importance, however, won't create a positive impression. As the interview closes, you can pull together your earlier statements regarding your qualifications and briefly restate them for the interviewer. This gives you a chance to express your perception of what you can contribute to, and why you are interested in working for, the interviewer's company.

Sending a follow-up note thanking the interviewer for his or her time and reiterating your interest in the position is a helpful touch. Besides being a social nicety, it gives you a chance to clarify any points made, to add information you felt was not adequately covered in the interview, or simply to say "thanks" for an enjoyable experience.[1]

Reference Notes

[1] For further information on employment interviewing, consult Lois Einhorn, Patricia Hayes Bradley, and John E. Baird, Jr.; *Effective Employment Interviewing* (Glenview, IL: Scott, Foresman, 1982).

GROUP DISCUSSION: PARTICIPATION

Although most of this book deals with public speaking, it's important also to look at group communication as another important kind of multiperson public communicative activity. A group discussion is a shared, purposeful communication transaction in which a small group of people exchanges and evaluates ideas and information in order to understand a subject or solve a problem.

As this definition suggests, there are two major kinds of discussion. In a *learning, or study, discussion*, participants seek to educate each other, to come to a fuller understanding of a subject or problem. People interested in art, computer programming, or religious study, for example, may gather monthly to share thoughts and expertise. In an *action, or decision-making, group*, participants attempt to reach an agreement on what the group as a whole should believe or do, or they seek ways to implement a decision already made. A city council will decide what to do with its federal revenue-sharing funds; a subcommittee in a business may be asked to recommend useful ways to expand markets.

You'll probably spend much personal and

work-related time in group discussions. Your communicative tasks in those groups will be complicated by the fact that, as a participant, you're focusing in three directions at once: on yourself, on others in the group, and on the group's task.

Focus on Self

Because you are you and not someone else, you must focus on your own needs, desires, attitudes, knowledge, opinions, hopes, and fears. You participate in group discussions because, reasonably, you expect some sort of gain. That gain can be emotional, as you become accepted by others. It can be reinforcing, as you use others to add authority to ideas or positions you want to defend publicly.

Focus on Others

In a group, however, you cannot be completely self-absorbed. Other members also have their biases, priorities, and experiences. As a participant, you're partially responsible for *group maintenance*—for building a supportive social-emotional atmosphere in which everyone feels comfortable even in times of conflict, in which mutual respect is a norm or expectation, and in which there is interdependence and honest openness to others.

Focus on the Task

In addition to everyone's feelings, the group's purpose must be kept in mind. You have joined a group to accomplish something—to learn something, to solve a problem, to launch a plan or campaign. If you don't keep that task in mind, you're liable to run down blind alleys and around irrelevant issues, to spend more time talking about next week's fishing trip than the job to be done.

Participating in a group can be tricky business, therefore, because you're looking in these three directions at once. If you lose sight of yourself, you're a mere pawn. If you forget about "them," you are a tyrant. If you ignore the task, you're probably going to have to attend yet another meeting. In essence, as a discussant, you must engage in a mental jug-gling act, keeping track of your self, of others, and of the group's progress toward its goal.

Knowing and Revealing Yourself in Discussions

Let us begin with you. You have both rights and responsibilities as you consider your own head and heart. The following suggestions include both head and heart.

Preparing.   Obviously, you must enter a discussion prepared to participate. Getting intellectually ready for a discussion guarantees two things. First, it ensures that you're able to offer positive contributions and, hence, uphold your end of the bargain that constitutes "groupness." Second, it protects you from glib but shallow sales pitches, silly proposals, ignorant allies, and overpowering opponents.

Getting Background on Others.   You ought to have information not only on the topic but also on the other participants. This may not be a problem in a group that has a history, but it certainly can be in newly formed work teams and committees. The more you know about others, the better able you'll be to anticipate the sources and strengths of your opposition, to know how to object without hurting someone's feelings, to guess at how tenacious various individuals will be.

Introducing Ideas.   As a discussion proceeds, you must calculate how and when to introduce your ideas, opinions, and feelings. This is the only way you can be true to your self. Several tasks for introducing ideas have proven successful.

Hitchhiking.   In this tactic, you link your idea to one that someone else has stated. It seems perfectly natural to say, "Carl said that we needed to consider the impact of this proposal on our clerical staff, and I agree. As a matter of fact, I've done some thinking about this problem, and . . . ." In this way, you build on someone else's notions and probably gain an ally.

Summary. "So far, we've isolated three causes for declining school enrollments and I think they're accurate, but I wonder if there isn't a fourth reason . . . ." In this tactic, you give everyone who has contributed to the discussion a psychological stroke and then seek to move the discussion into new territory—yours.

Shift in viewpoint. Consider: "We've looked at the problem of child abuse from the perspectives of the child and of the abusing parent. What about those teachers, doctors, social workers, and other professionals who suspect they've seen a case. What's their role in all this?" This sort of introductory statement, once more, recognizes the ideas and feelings of others while it allows you—with the group's blessing—to intrude your own position.

Disagreement. You might say, "Jean, I certainly can understand why you think no more parking ramps should be built downtown, but I think you've examined only two of the factors involved. Before we reach a decision on the issue, I think we must look at two additional factors . . . ." In this way, you express your disagreement softly. You leave Jean with the feeling you are accepting her analysis and integrity, yet you give yourself an entering wedge. In these tactics, take care that your remarks actually fit with what has been going on.

Listening to and Evaluating Others.
To protect yourself in a discussion, you must be a rapt and careful listener. You must be able to see through the swarm of words from an eloquent advocate. You must be sure you don't have mistaken impressions, for the consequences of misunderstanding can be great, both interpersonally and intellectually. To understand the full implications of what others say, consider the following listening techniques.

Questioning. Don't be afraid to ask polite questions of others: "I didn't follow that; could

you repeat it?" "Can you translate that for me?" "I'm curious—where did you read that?" If you phrase the question in terms of your own needs, you won't seem to be suggesting that the other person is unclear or incorrect. Questioning in this way is relatively nonthreatening.

Rephrasing. To check on your own listening abilities, and to make sure you know what position you are disagreeing with, try rephrasing another person's ideas: "Let's see if I followed you. First you said that . . . and then you noted that . . . , right?" Putting someone else's ideas into your own words protects you and can save the group time, especially if others also need the translation.

Recording. Take notes. If, say, you're in a decision-making group and the discussion becomes protracted, by the time you arrive at a solution stage, people may have forgotten all the problems to be solved. Keeping track throughout the discussion will save embarrassment and make your own contributions useful later.

Reacting to Disagreement and Criticism.
Not only must you carefully evaluate the ideas of others, but you should be mentally ready to react to their analyses of you. Be a debater, and focus on the disagreement rather than on the personalized attack. This goal can be accomplished in several ways.

Interpreting. "Let's see if I can figure out what part of my analysis you're having trouble with." By focusing on the substance of the disagreement, you're telling the group that you want to ignore personal innuendoes and keep the group as a whole on track.

Turning the other cheek. In all humility, you could say, "I'm sorry what I said bothered you so much, Fred. Let's see if we can resolve this issue." Poor Fred looks pretty bad after this response, and you can come out more highly credible.

Confronting the attacker. Especially if another person seems to be disrupting and attacking everyone, you (and the rest) may have to confront that person directly: "Janet, you don't seem to be happy with the way we're handling this. What can we do to make you more comfortable and to get on with the task at hand?" In thus confronting a particularly nasty person, you're extending the group's good wishes and sympathy, attempting to return the common focus to the job to be accomplished. With all three techniques, you are protecting your self, which is essential to your own well-being.

Taking Care of Others in Discussions

Another focal point is the other members of the group. Without that focus, you aren't doing your part to keep them happy and productive. A supportive social-emotional atmosphere, even in times of disagreement, is a must. There are many ways to build a supportive atmosphere.

Stroking.   It never hurts to give psychological strokes to other group members. It costs you little (unless your pride and ego get in the way), and it keeps everyone working and playing together. "That's a great idea!" "Thanks for the suggestion. It makes me see this question in a different light." "That's beautiful, Ralph." Such personal reactions to others show mutual trust and support.

Criticizing Constructively.   It doesn't hurt, either, to do a little stroking even while you are disagreeing with someone. There are ways to fight ("That's the dumbest thing I've ever heard!"), and there are ways to criticize constructively. These can involve (1) bringing in additional authorities to erode the other person's position, (2) politely cataloguing facts that have been ignored, (3) introducing alternative statements of value ("You look at this as a political question, but I wonder if it's not more a matter of human rights"), and (4) calling for a discussion of the implications of an idea ("I think your plan sounds decent, but do you think it will alleviate the first problem we mentioned?"). The important point, as you communicate your criticisms, is to go as far as you can in depersonalizing the disagreement.

If possible, keep the focus on *authorities* (who do the attacking instead of you), on the *facts* (which we would love to think speak for themselves), on *value* positions, and on the hardheaded *implications*.

Accepting Correction.   Not only must you be able to disagree positively with someone else's misrepresentation or misunderstanding of you, but you'll do the group a favor if you can gracefully accept others' positions and ideas as correctives to your own. It's tempting to be the gamester and to fight back inch by inch, but if you see the basic logic of someone's analysis or if you note that group opinion is running counter to your own, you'll have to surrender–or leave. You can get into a huff or a blue funk, or you can retreat with the aplomb of Robert E. Lee of Appomattox. Your ego cries out, "You fools! One day you'll see my wisdom!" but your sense of commitment to others demands, "OK, I'm still having a little problem with all this, but if the rest of you think we should try, then I'll certainly go along" or "I didn't realize some of those implications of my proposal, Joan. Thanks for pointing them out. Are there other proposals that won't have those bad effects?" Eating a little crow certainly leads to occasional indigestion, but sometimes it is better to cave in a bit than to be beaten to death. In this way, you'll live to argue another day.

Being Patient.   Patience is perhaps the essential quality in your focus on other group members. You're often forced to be an extraordinarily saintly, patient person while discussing. Just as you think you've carved out a piece of truth and wisdom, so does everyone else. Work hard at allowing them—even forcing them—to show you the error of your ways. Ask them to repeat, to go further, to extend. Keep them talking in the hope that their contributions will be given full consideration. What they say may even be good! Especially with somewhat hesitant or reticent people, you often must gently prod them along, even if you know your own ideas will triumph.

Patience is a small price for ultimate victory; it might actually produce a good suggestion or two, and it certainly will promote a positive social-emotional climate. It can be inefficient at times, but that's something you occasionally have to tolerate in groups.

Achieving the Group's Goals in Discussions

Finally, you must focus on the goal or task of the group. We often think, perhaps wistfully, that it's the leader's job to keep a discussion moving forward. It is, but leaders often need help, occasionally miss important points here and there, sometimes get flustered, and perhaps let the group get bogged down in an overextended discussion of an issue. While there is usually a person designated "leader," leadership must be shared by all participants from time to time. Even if you don't have the word *boss* emblazoned on your forehead, you still have some responsibilities for moving the group ahead. A few of these responsibilities have already been suggested. Others are strictly procedural matters to which you should attend.

Knowing the Agenda. An *agenda* is an agreed-upon list of tasks to be accomplished or questions to be answered in a particular session. Know when it's appropriate to bring up a matter you are interested in. Knowing the agenda allows you (and the rest) to keep the discussion orderly and progressive and tells you something about timing your remarks.

Asking Procedural Questions. Never be afraid to ask questions about what's happening in a discussion: "Are we still on point three, or have we moved to point four?" Is there some way we can resolve this question and move ahead?" "Can we consider the feasibility of Art's proposal before we move on to Brenda's?" Such questions can seem inordinately naive, and, if asked with a sneer in your voice, could reflect badly on the leader, yet sometimes naive questions are absolutely necessary.

Summarizing. Seldom can a single leader carry out all of the summarizing that most groups need. A good summary allows you to check bases, to see what has been agreed to and what remains to be done. Summaries can be simple: "Now, as I heard you two, Jack said this and this, and Bob said that and that, right?" or they can be elaborate attempts to trace through the whole of a discussion so that members have it clearly in mind before you adjourn.

Arbitrating. Another important leadership function that shouldn't fall solely on the leader's shoulders is that of arbitrating disputes. Being the peacemaker is sometimes risky business, for both parties may go for your throat, yet if a discussion is going to be mutually supportive and satisfying, and if it's going to get its job done, then each person occasionally will have to help it get over intellectual and emotional rough spots. Sometimes you can arbitrate by offering a *compromise:* "OK, is it possible for us to accept a part of Proposal A and a part of Proposal B and forge those parts into a new Proposal C? It might go this way. . . ."

At other times, you're going to have to call for *clarification:* "Bill, you think Ron's idea is defective because of this, and you, Ron, seem to be saying that Bill has missed the point about the riverfront land, right?" By pointing out the idea in conflict rather than the personalities in conflict, you perhaps can deflate it.

You may occasionally have to offer a *gentle reprimand:* "Whoa! If you two don't quit beating each other to death, we'll never get done in an hour! Let's see if we can get to the nub of the matter here." By thus holding out the standards of efficiency and expediency, you may succeed in getting two people to clarify, to remember the rest of the group, and to charge ahead.

Participating in a discussion can be a tremendously rewarding and efficient way of making your own ideas and feelings public, of learning new information and perspectives, of making key decisions at work or at home, and of implementing plans or proposals. You'll achieve maximum satisfaction and gain, however, only if you constantly keep in focus yourself, others, and the task. Monitor all three focal points steadily. You must have some degree of trust (or even suspicion); you must

do your part in bringing out the best in others; you must remember that discussion is an interdependent activity with both social-emotional and intellectual components; you must abide by faith in a quasi-democratic outlook on life.

GROUP DISCUSSION: LEADERSHIP

Our culture has a particularly ironic way of cooling down zealots and go-getters. If you're the person in your organization, business, or classroom with ideas, enthusiasm, and commitments, you're immediately made the group's leader. Suddenly, where you once were a strong advocate and a hard worker in the trenches, you now are expected to be impartial, organized, wise, knowledgeable about procedures, politically shrewd, and able to turn out the ever-present report in forty-eight hours.

Groups sometimes make shameful demands of their leaders; yet if they didn't most groups wouldn't get anything done. Someone ultimately has to be in charge, to execute the group's *leadership functions*—handling procedural aspects of group operation, seeing that ideas are explored fully and fairly, and taking care that the feelings and contributions of everyone in the group are brought out. In this short review of leading meetings and of leadership functions, we'll discuss three phases of a leader's job: premeeting preparation, running the meeting, and postmeeting evaluation. By examining the responsibilities in these three phases, perhaps we can demystify the leader's jobs and necessary skills.

Phase I: Premeeting Preparation

As a leader, your principal job throughout all three phases is to operate as a *facilitator*.

While leadership in general is diffused among all members of a group (because all are responsible for helping produce a quality end-result), "the" leader has special duties. This is especially true in Phase I, premeeting preparation. Group members are counting on you to do what you can to make the actual discussion, committee, team, session, or meeting function smoothly. Although your tasks will vary with the precise goal and the degree of formality of the group, they may include some of the following.

Announcing the Time and Place. You'll probably be responsible for getting information about the meeting to interested parties. This may include contacting the group members (one hopes you got telephone numbers on a sign-up sheet earlier), making sure the room or facility is open and available, letting the press know of the meeting if it is open to the public. It's a small task, but overlooking it can produce disastrous results.

Assembling Background Material. You may also have to get some general materials ready for the meeting. The business team leader digs through old files to find out how the firm last approached this question and to unearth pertinent cost-benefit statistics, sales histories, or whatever. If these sorts of backgrounding activities are carried out carefully, you'll save the group a lot of frustration and wheel-spinning during the actual discussion.

Constructing an Agenda. Even if the topics for the upcoming meeting were announced in the previous meeting, a group usually needs more guidance. That guidance often takes the form of an *agenda,* a structured list of topics, questions, resolutions, and the like. Agendas vary, obviously, in detail and length; their completeness depends upon the specialization of the group and the expertise of its members.

Final Check of Arrangements. Just before the meeting is to begin, you may have to check on the facilities one last time. Are the seating arrangements conducive to discussion? If there are microphones, are they working? Are the refreshments prepared? Make sure your meeting is not problematic because you have overlooked the "little" details people expect leaders to care for.

Phase II: Running the Meeting

With careful preplanning, you should have little trouble actually running the meeting. Your primary jobs are to keep the discussion progressing toward its goal and to serve the participants in whatever ways you can. To carry out these two jobs, you'll probably use some of the following communication techniques in each stage of the meeting.

Beginning the Meeting. Of course, you will have to start the meeting. This may involve nothing more complicated than a "Can I have your attention, please? It's time we begin." In other settings, you may have responsibilities for opening remarks, a short speech orienting the group to the meeting's purpose, the procedures you'll follow, and the like. Prepare opening remarks carefully, so that you won't embarrass yourself, not forget anything, and *not* drone endlessly. You're a facilitator, not an orator. If this is a formal meeting of an organization, you may have to begin it in the usual parliamentary fashion:

1. Call to order
2. Review of the minutes of the previous meeting

3. Reports from committees or officers
4. Review of old business (considerations carrying over from the previous meeting)
5. New business (new resolutions and considerations)

Whatever the situation, begin the meeting crisply and clearly. Your group will thank you for your sense of organization and your concern that they have time to talk.

Leading the Discussion. Once the discussion is launched, you should stay out of the substance of it as much as possible. Think of yourself as an interested troubleshooter. You're watching for confusion, omissions, conflict, procedural tangles, and the like. When you see any of these sorts of problems, only then do you move in. In most groups, you have several major responsibilities during the discussion.

Bringing out reticent individuals. Except in the most formal parliamentary groups, you ought to be on the lookout for nonparticipants, people who hang back because they are hesitant or because talkative souls are dominating the group. "What do you think, Harry?" is a simple but effective way to bring someone out. If that doesn't work, you may need to add a bit of encouragement: "Harry, you're the person here closest to our problems in Missouri. We really could use your thoughts." If you still get no response, move on, looking back at Harry periodically to see if he's ready to talk yet.

Summarizing at key points. Another essential job is that of objectively summarizing particular ideas, conflicts, analyses, and agenda items. A summary from a leader does several things for a group: (1) it shows them you're a fair leader, summarizing both sides of a dispute cleanly; (2) it gently reminds them to finish off a particular point and move on; (3) it catches up members whose minds have drifted off to other matters; and (4) if well done, it can push a group to a decision. Don't be afraid to take notes to make summaries accurate and well structured.

Tying down the key facts, generalizations, and cause-effect relationships.   Even though you try to stay out of the discussion as much as possible, often you're needed to fill out the factual picture, to go after a particularly obvious causal relationship no one has mentioned, to intrude a valuative perspective needing consideration, and so forth. Because you don't want others to think you're running the meeting with a heavy hand, try to draw out the missing information, relationship, or value from the participants, if possible. Tact is all-important; if you're going to make a statement, you might even want to ask the group's permission. A leader can always make a direct reference to a document members supposedly are familiar with: "So far, we've not said anything about Appendix B in the Jackson Report. Should its recommendations be considered now?" Try to leave the matter up to the group; you thus preserve your objectivity and impartiality.

Handling conflict.   All methods for handling conflict are applicable here: depersonalizing the conflict, using outside authorities to undercut positions, trying to get the participants in the melee to settle it themselves, and referring to the need for dispatch. A leader is in a tricky position when it comes to conflict. On the one hand, a leader realizes that conflict can be creative and can lead to group-generated agreements. Conflict is absolutely necessary for testing ideas and exploring positions, feelings, and proposals. On the other hand, if it becomes dominant and personalized, conflict can destroy a group.

The skillful leader watches to see if it's getting too bloody; watches noncombatants to see if they are getting bored, scared, or frustrated; and watches the clock. Then the leader moves in gingerly, with something like: "OK, you two certainly have demonstrated how complex and touchy this issue is. We really, however, must keep progressing, so how about the rest of you? Does anyone else have an opinion on it?" If you can succeed in getting the rest of the group to pick up on the controversy—and, hopefully, resolve it—your job is done. Go to harsher measures only if the combatants won't quit. Try to slow down the dominating individuals and more equitably spread the communicative load. Reprimand if necessary, but only in the name of the group itself.

Terminating the discussion.   It's the leader's job to terminate the discussion. You must find a way of ending it positively. Your greatest ally in this, of course, is the clock: "Excuse me, but even though I'm finding this discussion fascinating and enlightening, we've got to quit in five minutes. Any last word or two before we break?" Beyond actually stopping the proceedings, the articulate leader moves to a summary of what has been discussed and decided, what remains open, and what is left to be treated in another session. A round of thanks (naming names, even) never hurts. A clear wrap-up sets important notions in members' minds, getting them ready for further consideration or discussion at another time.

Phase III: Post-Meeting Responsibilities

Too many leaders forget their post-meeting responsibilities. Some of these duties are courtesies (thank-you notes to those who brought refreshments, for example); others are economic (paying bills if hall rental and catering were involved). Other important details have to do with the ongoing life of the organization (minutes of the meeting, plans for the next meeting, refiling of materials used, reports to others in the organization, or evaluations to be passed on to your successor).

Because, as leader, you're in so many ways responsible for the social-emotional and substantive life of the organization, be sure you carry out such duties promptly. If people don't receive minutes of the meeting for a month or more, they'll think less of you and will have forgotten some of the salient features of the discussion you can only hint at in the minutes. Thank-you notes leave a good impression and probably prod the recipients to render good service the next time the group meets. If the news release detailing the results of the meeting doesn't get to the press the next day, your group's decisions, recommendations, or actions will be old news and hardly fit to print. Even though you're tired, finish off your post-meeting duties quickly. It will pay off in what you accomplish and in how people think of you.

Being a leader, as you can see, isn't an easy job. Leadership demands forethought, anticipation, organization, impartiality, sensitivity, and good sense. By spacing your tasks, however, you can serve your club, organization, or group as an effective leader.

GROUP PRESENTATIONS: PANELS AND SYMPOSIA

When a group is too large to engage in effective roundtable discussion, when its members aren't well enough informed to make such discussion profitable, or when subgroups in the larger collectivity represent distinct viewpoints on important issues, a *panel* of individuals—from three to five, usually—may be selected to discuss the topic for the benefit of others, who then become an audience. Members of a panel are chosen either because they're particularly well informed on the subject or because they represent divergent views on the issue.

Another type of audience-oriented discussion is the *symposium*. In this format, several persons—again, usually from three to five—present short speeches, each focusing on a different facet of the subject or offering a different solution to the problem under consideration. Usually, the short presentations are followed by periods of discussion among the symposiasts and question-and-answer sessions with the onlooking audience. The symposium is especially valuable when recognized experts with well-defined points of view or areas of competence are available as speakers and, thus, is the discussion procedure commonly used at large conferences and conventions.

The following techniques are useful in preparing for and participating in group and conference presentations.

Preparation for Panels and Symposia

Because in panels and conferences you're one of a team of communicators, it's important that you take others into account as you prepare your remarks. This taking-into-account involves considerations you don't have to face in other speaking situations. First, *you have to fit your comments into a general theme.* If, say, the theme of your panel is "The State of the U.S. Constitution at the Beginning of Its Third Century," not only will you be expected to mention "U.S. Constitution," "two hundred years," and the like, but probably you'll also be expected to say something about how the Constitution has been interpreted over those two hundred years, what's happening today, and how you see the interpretation evolving. The theme, in other words, affects how you'll treat your subject, and perhaps even forces you to approach it in a particular way.

Also, *remember that you may be responsible for covering only a portion of a topic or theme.* In most symposia and panels, the speakers divide the topic into parts to avoid duplication and to provide an audience with a variety of viewpoints. For example, if the theme is the state of American culture, you might be asked to discuss education, while others will examine social relations, the state of science and technology, and leisure time, thus dividing the theme *topically*. Alternatively, you might be asked to discuss *problems* (depersonalization, the "plastic" world, the limits of the work force) while other participants examine *solutions* (individual, corporate, ethical, political). Part of your preparation, therefore, involves coordinating your communicative efforts with those of others.

The more you know about the subject under discussion, the better. To be ready for any eventuality, you must have a flexibility born of broad knowledge. For each aspect of the subject or implication of the problem you think may possibly be discussed, make the following analysis:

1. *Review the facts you already know.* Go over the information you've acquired through previous reading or personal experience and organize it in your mind. Prepare as if you were going to present a speech on every phase of the matter. You'll then be better qualified to discuss any part of it.

2. *Bring your knowledge up-to-date.* Find out if recent changes have affected the situation. Fit the newly acquired information into what you already know.

3. *Determine a tentative point of view on each of the important issues.* Make up your mind what your attitude will be. What three or four steps might be taken to attract new members into your club? On what medical or health-related grounds should cigarette smoking be declared illegal? Be ready to state and substantiate your opinion at whatever point in the discussion seems most appropriate, but also be willing to change your mind if information or points of view provided by others show you to be wrong.

4. *To the best of your ability, anticipate the effect of your ideas or proposals on the other members of the group or the organization of which the group is a part.* For instance, what you propose may possibly cause someone to lose money or to retract a promise that's been made. Forethought

about such eventualities will enable you to understand opposition to your view if it arises and to make a valid and intelligent adjustment.

Participating in Panels and Symposia

Your style and vocal tone will, of course, vary according to the nature and purpose of the discussion as a whole, the degree of formality that's being observed, and your frame of mind as you approach the task. In general, however, *speak in a direct, friendly, conversational style.* As the interaction proceeds, differences of opinion are likely to arise, tensions may increase, and some conflict may surface. You'll need, therefore, to be sensitive to these changes and to make necessary adjustments in the way you voice your ideas and reactions.

Present Your Point of View Clearly, Succinctly, and Fairly. Participation in a panel or symposium should always be guided by one underlying aim: to help the group think objectively and creatively in analyzing the subject or solving the problem at hand. To this end, you should organize your contributions not in the way best calculated to win other people to your point of view, but rather in the fashion that will best stimulate them to think for themselves. Therefore, instead of stating your conclusion first and then supplying the arguments in favor of it, let your contribution recount how and why you came to think as you do. In this way, you give other members of the group a chance to check the accuracy and completeness of your thinking on the matter and to point out any deficiencies or fallacies that may not have occurred to you.

Maintain Attitudes of Sincerity, Open-Mindedness, and Objectivity. Above all, remember that a serious discussion isn't a showplace for prima donnas or an arena for verbal combatants. When you have something to say, say it modestly and sincerely, and always maintain an open, objective attitude. Accept criticism with dignity and treat disagreement with an open mind. Your primary purpose is not to get your own view accepted, but to work out with the other members of the group the best possible choice or decision that all of you together can devise and, as a team, to present a variety of viewpoints to the audience.

PARLIAMENTARY PROCEDURE AND SPEECHMAKING

In groups, parliamentary procedure often is used to regulate discussion and decision making. The primary intent of procedural rules is to ensure that discussion is orderly and that minority voices have the opportunity to be heard. Although it can be used to frustrate members' wishes (as is sometimes the case in legislative assemblies), on the whole, parliamentary procedure is a useful aid to a group's decision-making processes. We cannot cover all of these procedural rules, but we'll introduce the major devices and offer some practical advice regarding their use.

Major Procedural Rules

The table on pages 536–37 outlines the most often used procedural rules and indicates whether they require a second, whether they permit discussion, and what support they require for approval. First, however, we'll define the major categories of motions.

The *main motion* is the proposal brought before the group. It may be introduced very simply: "I move that. . . ." The content of the main motion depends upon what you want the group to act upon (for example, "I move that we hold the fund-raising event on October 5"; "I move that we authorize the president and the treasurer to review existing needs and purchase equipment as needed to get us ready for the new year"; "I move that this group go on record as opposing the Equal Rights Amendment"). The motion may simply express the sentiment of the group and require very little discussion prior to a formal vote, or the motion may be highly controversial and engage group members in impassioned debate over the proposal's merits. When motions are controversial, the use of *subsidiary, incidental,* and *privileged motions* becomes important.

Subsidiary motions have a direct bearing on the main motion. They seek to alter the content of the motion, to change the time of discussion, or to place the motion before a subgroup for further study. The motion to postpone indefinitely has the effect of killing future discussion of the proposal. Perhaps the most confusing of the subsidiary motions is that which seeks "to amend." If an amendment is offered and seconded, the discussion must focus on the merits of the proposed change in the main motion. Once discussion has concluded, the *amendment* is passed or negated. In either case, the discussion now must revert to the main motion, either as originally presented (the amendment failed) or as altered (the amendment passed). Once discussion is concluded (assuming no new amendments are offered), the vote is taken on the main motion as presented or altered.

As long as you work backward from any amendment to the main motion, voting at each step, you'll avoid controversy and confusion. When discussion seems to lag or becomes highly repetitive, the *previous-question motion* ends discussion. Voting on the previous question also causes confusion, as some may think they're voting on the main motion. All the previous-question motion does is seek agreement to stop discussion. In some groups, moving the previous question can be handled informally. Once it has been moved, the chair can ask if there are any objections to ceasing discussion. Hearing none, the chair can move immediately to a vote on the main motion. This saves time by avoiding a separate vote to close debate when the result is clearly favorable. Amendment, previous-question, and the remainder of the subsidiary motions can be raised at any time—they take precedence over the main motion and over each other. The following sequence could occur:

1. The main motion is presented and seconded; discussion ensues.
2. The main motion is amended, seconded, and discussion continues.
3. A member seeks to limit discussion to ten minutes; this is seconded but isn't open to discussion.
4. Another member moves to amend the limit-discussion motion by striking ten minutes and inserting twenty minutes. This is seconded and discussion begins until someone reminds the group that the amendment isn't debatable because the motion to which it's applied in this case isn't open to discussion.
5. The chair reminds everyone that the motion before the group is the amendment to limit discussion to twenty minutes instead of ten. The group votes on the amendment; it fails.
6. The chair announces that the motion to limit discussion to ten minutes is now before the group and isn't open to discussion. The chair calls for a vote; the motion passes.
7. Eight minutes of discussion ensue, during which the previous question is called. The chair asks if there is any objection; hearing none, she bypasses a formal vote on the previous question and reminds everyone that the vote is on the *amendment* to the main motion. The amendment passes.

8. The chair reminds everyone that discussion is now open on the main motion as amended. A member moves to refer the motion as amended to a committee. This is seconded and discussion ensues on the move to a committee. The chair reminds the group that the discussion limit has passed and asks if everyone is ready to vote on the referral-to-committee motion. Hearing no objection, the chair calls for a vote; the motion fails.
9. The chair restates the motion as amended and once again asks if the group is ready to vote. Hearing no comment, the chair asks if all are ready to vote. The chair restates the main motion as amended, and the vote is taken. The motion passes.

Although ordinary discussion may not be so contorted, this sequence does suggest the confusion that group members can create for themselves if they don't have a clear sense of the rules of procedure (and a chair that seeks to make each step clear).

Incidental motions also affect the progress of a main motion. They're important in reserving rights for individuals who are attempting to influence the flow of events. The motion to *suspend the rules* allows a person to introduce a proposal out of its normal order; the *point of order* motion can come at any time during a discussion and allows a member to remind a group that it isn't following accepted rules of procedure (for example, in point 4 of the previous illustration, the discussion of an amendment to the limit-discussion motion could be questioned by rising to a point of order). If the chair did not know the rules and said, "It's OK, let's continue discussion," a member would have the right to appeal the decision of the chair. Check the accompanying table and note the problem that's been created. Is the appeal debatable? When in doubt, discuss. After all, the purpose is not to alienate members but to regulate the discussion. The motion to *divide a question* is useful when the main motion contains more than one main idea. It also can be used when you sense that one part of a motion may pass and a second portion may fail. By moving to divide, you may save part of the proposal.

Privileged motions also help regulate the process. There is little to be gained by a *call for the orders of the day* if everyone but you is satisfied with the events of the meeting. If, on the other hand, the group appears restless and is wandering around several topics, it may be good to issue this form of reminder. The *question of privilege* protects an individual's right to hear what is going on or to understand what action is being voted on. The motions to *recess* and to *adjourn* aren't intended to frustrate a group's desire to resolve whatever problem is before it. If there's a great deal of tension, it may be wise to request a recess in order to allow tempers to cool; likewise, if tensions persist, it might be useful to suggest an adjournment to a specific time. The *unclassified motions* provide a means to bring a topic that has been tabled at a previous meeting before the group, or to alter action that has been taken (*to reconsider, to rescind*). Take special note of the restrictions on the use of these latter motions (see the table, notes 13 and 14).

Speaking in Parliamentary Groups

If you're in a meeting governed by parliamentary rules, there are several things you can do to increase your effectiveness:

1. *Know the appropriate rules yourself.* Don't depend upon a good chair to keep you informed regarding the process. The more knowledgeable you are, the less confused you'll become as the process of using parliamentary rules unfolds. Also, you'll be able to counteract efforts to use the rules to create an unfair advantage for one or more persons.

2. *Listen carefully.* Stay on top of what's going on. If the chair doesn't keep the group on track by constantly reminding members what's pending, you may need to take on that responsibility. Hopefully, you and others will be kept informed regarding what is on the floor by a conscientious leader.

3. *Ask questions.* If you aren't sure about the procedures or become lost in the parliamentary thicket, don't hesitate to raise a question of personal privilege. Be specific in asking the chair or the parliamentarian (if one is appointed) what's on the floor or what motions are appropriate under the circumstances.

4. *Speak to the motion.* Limit your remarks to the specific motion on the floor. Don't discuss the entire main motion if an amendment is pending; instead, comment directly on the merits of the amendment.

5. *Avoid unnecessary parliamentary gymnastics.* If group members yield to the temptation to play with the rules, parliamentary procedure becomes counterproductive. The rational process of decision making is undermined by such game playing. Refrain from piling one motion on top of another, cluttering the floor (and the minds of members) with amendments to amendments. Also guard against raising petty points of order. Parliamentary procedure is instituted to ensure equal, fair, controlled participation by all members. It provides a systematic means of the introduction and disposal of complex ideas. Unnecessary "gymnastics" will impede rather than foster group decision making.

A comprehensive guide to parliamentary procedure, adopted by many groups in their by-laws, is *Robert's Rules of Order*. Consult this or other guides to answer questions that go beyond the material presented in this review.

PARLIAMENTARY PROCEDURE FOR HANDLING MOTIONS

Classification of Motions	Types of Motions and Their Purposes	Order of Handling	Must Be Seconded	Can Be Discussed	Can Be Amended	Vote Required [1]	Can Be Reconsidered
Main motion	To present a proposal to the assembly	Cannot be made while any other motion is pending	Yes	Yes	Yes	Majority	Yes
Subsidiary motions (2)	To postpone indefinitely (to kill a motion)	Has precedence over above motion	Yes	Yes	No	Majority	Affirmative vote only
	To amend (to modify a motion)	Has precedence over above motions	Yes	When motion is debatable	Yes	Majority	Yes
	To refer (a motion) to committee	Has precedence over above motions	Yes	Yes	Yes	Majority	Until committee takes up subject
	To postpone (discussion of a motion) to a certain time	Has precedence over above motions	Yes	Yes	Yes	Majority	Yes
	To limit discussion (of a motion)	Has precedence over above motions	Yes	No	Yes	Two-thirds	Yes
	Previous question (to take a vote on the pending motion)	Has precedence over above motions	Yes	No	No	Two-thirds	No
	To table (to lay a motion aside until later)	Has precedence over above motions	Yes	No	No	Majority	No
Incidental motions (3)	To suspend the rules (to change the order of business temporarily)	Has precedence over a pending motion when its purpose relates to the motion	Yes	No	No	Two-thirds	No
	To close nominations [4]	[4]	Yes	No	Yes	Two-thirds	No
	To request leave to withdraw or modify a motion [5]	Has precedence over motion to which it pertains and other motions applied to it	No	No	No	Majority [5]	Negative vote only
	To rise to a point of order (to enforce the rules) [6]	Has precedence over pending motion out of which it arises	No	No	No	Chair decides [7]	No
	To appeal from the decision of the chair (to reverse chair's ruling) [6]	Is in order only when made immediately after chair announces ruling	Yes	When ruling was on debatable motion	No	Majority [1]	Yes
	To divide the question (to consider a motion by parts)	Has precedence over motion to which it pertains and motion to postpone indefinitely	[8]	No	Yes	Majority [8]	No
	To object to consideration of a question	In order only when a main motion is first introduced	No	No	No	Two-thirds	Negative vote only
	To divide the assembly (to take a standing vote)	Has precedence after question has been put	No	No	No	Chair decides	No

Privileged motions	To call for the orders of the day (to keep meeting to order of business) [6, 9]	Has precedence over above motions	No	No	No	No vote required	No
	To raise a question of privilege (to point out noise, etc.) [6]	Has precedence over above motions	No	No	No	Chair decides [7]	No
	To recess [10]	Has precedence over above motions	Yes	No [10]	Yes	Majority	No
	To adjourn [11]	Has precedence over above motions	Yes	No [11]	No [11]	Majority	No
	To fix the time to which to adjourn (to set next meeting time) [12]	Has precedence over above motions	Yes	No [12]	Yes	Majority	Yes
Unclassified motions	To take from the table (to bring up tabled motion for consideration)	Cannot be made while another motion is pending	Yes	No	No	Majority	No
	To reconsider (to reverse vote on previously decided motion) [13]	Can be made while another motion is pending [13]	Yes	When motion to be reconsidered is debatable	No	Majority	No
	To rescind (to repeal decision on a motion) [14]	Cannot be made while another motion is pending	Yes	Yes	Yes	Majority or two-thirds [14]	Negative vote only

1. A tied vote is always lost except on an appeal from the decision of the chair. The vote is taken on the ruling, not the appeal, and a tie sustains the ruling.
2. Subsidiary motions are applied to a motion before the assembly for the purpose of disposing of it properly.
3. Incidental motions are incidental to the conduct of business. Most of them arise out of a pending motion and must be decided before the pending motion is decided.
4. The chair opens nominations with "Nominations are now in order." A member may vote to close nominations, or the chair may declare nominations closed if there is no response to his/her inquiry, "Are there any further nominations?"
5. When the motion is before the assembly, the mover requests permission to withdraw or modify it, and if there is no objection from anyone, the chair announces that the motion is withdrawn or modified. If anyone objects, the chair puts the request to a vote.
6. A member may interrupt a speaker to rise to a point of order or of appeal, to call for orders of the day, or to raise a question of privilege.
7. Chair's ruling stands unless appealed and reversed.
8. If propositions or resolutions relate to independent subjects, they must be divided on the request of a single member. The request to divide the question may be made when another member has the floor. If they relate to the same subject but each part can stand alone, they may be divided only on a regular motion and vote.

9. The regular order of the business may be changed by a motion to suspend the rules.
10. The motion to recess is not privileged if made at a time when no other motion is pending. When not privileged, it can be discussed. When privileged, it cannot be discussed, but can be amended as to length of recess.
11. The motion to adjourn is not privileged if qualified or if adoption would dissolve the assembly. When not privileged, it can be discussed and amended.
12. The motion to fix the time to which to adjourn is not privileged if no other motion is pending or if the assembly has scheduled another meeting on the same or following day. When not privileged, it can be discussed.
13. A motion to reconsider may be made only by one who voted on the prevailing side. It must be made during the meeting at which the vote to be reconsidered was taken, or on the succeeding day of the same session. If reconsideration is moved while another motion is pending, discussion on it is delayed until discussion is completed on the pending motion; then it has precedence over all new motions of equal rank.
14. It is impossible to rescind any action that has been taken as a result of a motion, but the unexecuted part may be rescinded. Adoption of the motion to rescind requires only a majority vote when notice is given at a previous meeting; it requires a two-thirds vote when no notice is given and the motion to rescind is voted on immediately.

III. COMMUNICATION PRACTICES

HUMOR IN PUBLIC SPEAKING

In Chapter 18, while discussing the speech to entertain, we briefly discussed humor and its general uses in society. We suggested that humor could be used to (1) deflect an audience's antipathy toward a speaker, (2) make people in the audience feel more like a group than they did before hearing the speech, and (3) offer a critique of one's society in palatable or biting form. We noted that a speech to entertain generally had one of those uses of humor as its specific purpose.

More can and should be said, however, about particular uses of humor in other types of speeches. That is, in almost every speaking situation you may need to use humor in one or more parts of a speech. Following are some of the ways humor can be used in different portions of speeches.

Using Humor in Speech Introductions

Speakers ought to consider using humor in introductions to their speeches if (1) they themselves are tense and can tell relevant stories well enough to relax or (2) the audience is stiff, bored, or hostile, and, hence, in need of a jolt from the lectern. That is, a good story or joke is therapeutic, and, because beginning communication transactions often are traumatic for both speaker and listeners, such therapy often will significantly improve the rest of the communicative exchange. Make sure that the story or joke is *relevant, in good taste,* and *well-told.* That is, don't just tell a story for the sake of telling a story; an audience sees through that technique right away. Don't tell a dirty joke, because even if you offend only one listener, others in the audience are likely to recognize the offense, feel embarrassed, and take their embarrassment out on you. Finally, don't tell jokes if your timing is bad, if you tend to forget the punch line, if you cannot

handle the dialect, and so on. A badly told joke is worse than no joke at all.

Consider the following speech introduction: "I came home the other night to find my eight-year-old ready with a joke. 'Daddy,' he said, 'what's green and red and goes a hundred miles an hour?' 'I don't know,' I said wearily. 'What?' 'A frog in a processor!' he shouted triumphantly. That time of the evening, the story merely turned me green. Upon reflection, however, it has caused me to think about the ways in which modern technology—right down to the food processor on the kitchen counter—has invaded our thinking, our values, yes, even our humor. And today, I want to . . . ."

In this introduction, you won't find a rib-rattlingly funny story; as a matter of fact, most audience members probably would simply smile rather than laugh. That's all right, because the story can still do its job; it still can relax the speaker and the audience. As a matter of fact, if you expect audience members to react with full hilarity to a joke and then they don't, you're liable to be more tense than you were before you started the story. Remember that you're a public speaker *using humor for your purposes*, not a comic.

Using Humor in Midspeech

You also may want to use humor in the middle segments of speeches to (1) lighten a comparatively dense or heavy section, (2) serve as a memorable illustration of an important point, or (3) improve certain aspects of your credibility. More specifically, humor gives:

- *Contrast.* After an audience is hit with a lot of statistics or a pile of philosophical abstractions, a little humor not only provides some important psychological contrast, thereby improving listeners' abilities to attend to your speech (see Chapter 2); it also lifts their spirits and rallies their minds, making them more willing to stay with you for the rest of the speech.

- *Illustration.* Most people can remember a joke more easily than an abstract discussion of something. Even concrete details are more memorable, for many people, if they're offered humorously.
- *Credibility.* One important dimension of credibility is dynamism—the audience's perception of the speaker as an alive, vital human being. A speaker's dynamism ratings—and, hence, overall credibility—improve when humor is used.

Once again, you don't need to work long, involved comic monologues, or even full-blown funny stories into the middle of a speech. Simply the way you *phrase ideas* can add the contrast, make the illustration memorable, and give a little push to your credibility.

Using Humor in Speech Conclusions

Good speakers may also end a speech on a humorous note. Humor can be used in speech conclusions to (1) make the separation of speaker and audience a pleasant event, (2) drive home the main point one last time, or (3) leave the audience with a sense of finality as the speech concludes.

1. *Separation.* When you're listening to good speakers, you often want their speeches to continue; when listening to people you greatly admire, you want to stay in their presence. Even good speakers and admirable lecturers, however, must quit talking sooner or later. To make their separation

from the audience as painless as possible, such speakers often use light humor to make the audience smile or laugh as they leave the rostrum.

2. *Emphasis.* A good story likewise can emphasize the main point of the whole speech; nearly every cleric who has been trained to preach has been taught this type of concluding strategy.

3. *Finality.* The speaker who says, "And so, everything I've been saying can be summed up in the story about the ten-year-old who. . . ." is overtly signalling an audience that the speech is about to end, that the audience should prepare to ask questions, applaud, or leave. Why should you offer such signals to listeners? All of us can think of occasions when we were not sure when a speech was to end, when there was an awkward moment when the speaker thought, "Can I go now?" and listeners thought, "Well, is it over or is she just thinking of the next words?" Signalling the end can reduce some of the awkwardness that otherwise might accompany the end of a good talk.

Overall, therefore, while humor certainly is very important to speeches to entertain, it likewise can be a part of any speech on almost any occasion. Make sure, however, that you use humor appropriately, that you use it to make a point rather than merely to get a cheap laugh, and that you train yourself to tell stories well—naturally, completely, and pointedly. Humor can bond speaker and listener together in a positive relationship and, hence, is a tool important to any speaker's collection of skills.

STRUCTURING ARGUMENTATIVE SPEECHES

Arguing with others usually involves more than a single presentation of your ideas. If you're going to be faced with an opponent's

presentation, there's more pressure to orchestrate the materials that will be used to defend your position. When you have the opportunity to respond formally to an opponent—either in the same setting or at a later time—you need to think in terms of *multiple messages*. More specifically, you need to plan your argumentative approach with respect to (1) constructing your case, (2) anticipating counterarguments, and (3) rebuilding your case.

Constructing Your Case

Your first concern is finding suitable materials for the development of your argument. Assume, for example, that your community is considering the use of its present landfill dump as a site for the disposal of hazardous wastes. In presenting an argument against this proposal at a city council hearing about the merits of the plan, you know that in attacking this policy claim you must (1) gain attention, (2) develop the specific criteria for allowing hazardous waste disposal at the dump, (3) demonstrate the failure of the dump to meet the established criteria, (4) note the advantages to be gained by the acceptance of your analysis, and (5) appeal for a "no" vote on the proposal. As you think about this skeletal outline in terms of your argument, notice that you have several major problems to overcome as you construct your case:

1. You must demonstrate that the *criteria* for allowing hazardous waste disposal provide a relevant, comprehensive, and significant set of standards for judging any proposed dump site. If you can't do this, your opponents can argue that the criteria you propose are irrelevant or insignificant, and if your set of criteria is incomplete, your opponent can counter by arguing that you have unfairly "stacked the deck" by your selection of "convenient" standards.
2. Even if your criteria are acceptable, you must address the *relationship* between the criteria and the dump site in question. Does the site meet the standards considered acceptable? However, doing so doesn't mean your opponents will quit the fight; they can still object to the relationship you seek to establish.

3. *The advantages* that would flow from acceptance of your position may appear obvious and important to you, but they often must be weighed against other advantages to be gained by your opponent's position. You may be faced with issues that have a direct impact on the case you're building: for example, a chemical company employing 2000 workers has threatened to close its plant if it cannot use the existing site; the town stands to profit from dump fees charged for disposal and claims a reduction in property tax as a side benefit.

Thus, your carefully constructed case may meet the problems cited in 1 and 2, but will be challenged by counterarguments that shift the focus to the relative merits of safety versus economic health in the community: What level of risk is acceptable in order to sustain the economic life of the community? In so doing, your opponents won't directly refute your allegations but instead will seek to minimize their significance in relation to the economic benefits to be realized. This developmental outline is, of course, only one of several that might be applied; even a cursory inspection of the topic and of the demands of this type of speech will indicate those points you must argue especially well. Returning to problems associated with this hypothetical case—establishing *criteria*, developing a *relationship* between criteria and dump site, and noting *advantages*—think about how you might proceed to solve them.

- *Where can you find supporting materials to establish criteria for determining a dump site's safety?* Are there any governmental studies or agency standards that would be of value? Are there technical reports from scientists? Have respected persons within the community commented on the issue of criteria? What criteria have other communities used when faced with similar questions?
- *How can you demonstrate the reliability of your conclusion that the dump site fails to*

meet the standards? Have other dumps with similar features been used for disposal, and have they been judged successful? Have studies been done to determine the characteristics of the landfill (for example, proximity to underground water sources)? Have scientists or others already commented on the suitability of the site? Once you have specific information on the characteristics of the dump site, the relationship to criteria can be accomplished in a fairly straightforward manner, by citing the relevant features of the dump and drawing conclusions that the site will not meet the necessary conditions adequately. You also could develop, in more dramatic style, a *hypothetical illustration* of what would happen in a "worst-case" scenario if the dump site were utilized.

- *How do you deal with issues that challenge the advantages you cite?* To begin with, the advantages you might stress would center on the health of citizens in the area surrounding the dump site or those affected by its use. Although this general advantage may seem obvious, it may be useful to underline its significance with testimony from medical experts or from respected town leaders on the problems that dumping hazardous waste products would cause. Without anticipating, at this stage of the analysis, other issues that may be brought forward (for example, unemployment, increased revenue), the best approach is to build the strongest case you can for the health issue. When and if the argument shifts to a comparison of advantages, you'll have made it more difficult for the opposition to undermine the significance of your advantage. Leaving it as "obvious" may only serve to quicken its dismissal by the opponents.

With the preceding analysis as a guide, it appears possible to construct a reasonable case for your position. Of course, you still have to assemble the actual materials—the technical data, expert opinion, relevant parallel cases—

that will allow you to present your case. As you put this together, the next element of the process will assist you in carrying your argument forward.

Anticipating Counterarguments

As you construct your case and outline your argument, you will be sensitized to potential attacks. For instance, if you oppose the use of the local community dump as a hazardous waste disposal site, your opponents may counter your arguments by maintaining that your parallel instances are insufficient or irrelevant as evidence of the unsuitability of the present site. Other opponents will no doubt bring up the threatened closure of the town's major employer if the site application isn't approved, or will concentrate their responses upon the projected revenue loss to the city. Thus, even before you actually present what might be called your "constructive case," you need to be aware of some potential objections and vulnerabilities.

Do not, however, build defensive reactions into your initial argument. If you are a speaker who attempts to anticipate and answer all possible objections before they are lodged, you are in double danger. (1) You may appear paranoid, causing listeners to say, "Boy, if she is this unsure, then maybe the proposal isn't any good." (2) Worse, you may actually suggest negative aspects of your proposal others hadn't thought of. You may, in other words, actually fuel discontent by proposing counterarguments. As a rule, therefore, you should set forth your initial case directly and simply, and then sit back and await the counterarguments presented by others.

In sum, reacting critically to attacks on your arguments involves (1) a careful recording of counterarguments so as to be fair and (2) a decision on how to answer germane objections. You have to be cool and dispassionate enough to do both.

Rebuilding Your Case

Having isolated and considered possible counterarguments, your next task is to answer those arguments to rebuild your initial case. This rebuilding requires *rebuttal* and *reestablishment*.

Rebuttal.   Your first rebuilding task is to rebut counterarguments. In our example this would mean answering to the satisfaction of your audience objections based upon revenue loss to the city or potential unemployment if the plant closes because the application fails. To refute the revenue loss argument, you might indicate that the loss is projected rather than actual; you also may be able to demonstrate insignificance if the amount of revenue lost would not appreciably affect local tax rates. The objection regarding projected unemployment is much harder to meet, as there will be members in the audience who depend upon the plant for their own jobs. You might be able to argue that closure is likely on other grounds, hence negative action on the dump site is a moot point. This is, however, a weak counter, as your opponents may quickly point out that approving the application is precisely the gesture the company needs to be convinced that it should remain. You also may be able to rebut the argument by examining the potential impact of such unemployment and by noting the probability of new industry absorbing much of the loss without the same risk to the health and safety of the community. Finally, you may have no other choice but to rebut by facing the possibility straight on and arguing that the risk to health and safety outweighs any possible economic considerations. In this extended illustration, we see most of the principal communicative techniques used by successful respondents.

Answer objections in an orderly fashion.   If two or three objections are raised, sort them out carefully and answer them one at a time. Such a procedure helps guarantee that you respond to each objection and aids listeners in sorting out the issues being raised.

Attack each objection systematically.   A speech that rebuts the counterarguments of another ought to be shaped into a series of steps, to maximize its clarity and accep-

tability. A unit of rebuttal proceeds in four steps:

1. State the opponent's claim that you seek to rebut. ("Joe has said that a management-by-objectives system won't work because supervisors don't want input from their underlings.")
2. State your objection to it. ("I'm not sure what evidence Joe has for that statement, but I do know of three studies done at businesses much like ours, and these studies indicate that . . . ")
3. Offer evidence for your objection. ("The first study was done at the XYZ Insurance Company in 1986; the researchers discovered that. . . . The second. . . . And the third. . . .")
4. Indicate the significance of your rebuttal. ("If our company is pretty much like the three I've mentioned—and I think it is—then I believe our supervisors will likewise appreciate specific commitments from their subordinates, quarter by quarter. Until Joe can provide us with more hard data to support his objection, I think we will have to agree . . . ")

Keep the exchange on an impersonal (intellectual) level.   All too often counterarguments and rebuttals degenerate into name-calling exchanges. When you become overly sensitive to attacks upon your pet notions and other people feel similarly threatened, a communicative free-for-all can ensue. Little is settled in such verbal fights. Reasoned decision making can occur only when the integrity of ideas is paramount, and the calm voice of reason is more likely to be listened to than is emotionally charged ranting.

Reestablishment.   In most instances you cannot be content merely to answer opponents' objections. You also should take the extra step of reestablishing your case as a whole. That is, you should first point out what portions of your argument have *not* been attacked and indicate their importance. Then you should introduce more evidence in support of your reconstructed case—further testimony, additional parallel cases—to bolster your argument as a whole. To return to our earlier example, you might indicate that no one has questioned your evidence on the site's unsuitability or the parallel cases you have presented.

In conclusion, argumentative speaking demands many talents. To argue well, you must be able to determine rationally the evidence and inferences needed to support your claim, to distinguish between solid and fallacious reasoning, and to build both constructive and refutative speeches to meet the demands of give-and-take in public decision making.

RESPONDING TO QUESTIONS

In most meetings (and at other times as well), listeners are given a chance to ask questions of speakers. Panelists frequently direct questions to each other; professors ask students to clarify points made in classroom reports; clubs' treasurers often are asked to justify particular expenditures; political candidates normally must field objections to positions they have taken.

Sometimes, questions require only a short response—some factual material, a yes or no, a reference to an authoritative source. These sorts of questions need not concern us, but at other times, questions from listeners can require a good deal more. Specifically, some questions call for *elaboration* and *explanation*. For example, after an oral report, you might be asked to elaborate upon statistical information you presented or called upon to explain how a financial situation arose. Other questions call for *justification and defense*. In open hearings, school boards seeking to cut expenditures justify their selection of school buildings to be closed. At city council meetings, the city manager often has to defend ways council policies are being implemented. In these situations, a "speech" is called for in response to questions and objections.

Techniques for Responding to Questions

Questions calling for elaboration and explanation are, in many ways, equivalent to requests for an informative speech. Think about them as you would any situation wherein you're offering listeners ideas and information in response to their needs and interests.

Give a "Whole" Speech. Your response should include an introduction, body, and conclusion. Even though you may be offering an impromptu speech (see Chapter 3), you nonetheless are expected to structure ideas and information clearly and rationally. A typical pattern for an elaborative remark might look like this:

1. *Introduction*—a rephrasing of the question to clarify it for the other audience members, an indication of why the question is a good one, a forecast of the steps you'll take in answering it.
2. *Body*—first point, often a brief historical review; second point, the information or explanation called for.
3. *Conclusion*—a very brief summary (unless the answer was extraordinarily long); a direct reference to the person asking the question, to see if further elaboration or explanation is needed.

Directly Address the Question as It Has Been Asked. Nothing is more frustrating to a questioner than an answer that misses the point or drifts off into irrelevant territory. Suppose, after you've advocated a "pass-fail" grading system for all colleges, you're questioned about how graduate schools can evaluate potential candidates for advanced degrees. The questioner is calling for information and an explanation. If, in response, you launch a tirade against the unfairness of letter grades or the cowardice of professors who refuse to give failing grades, you probably won't satisfy the questioner. Better would be an explanation of all the other factors—letters of recommendation, standardized tests, number of advanced courses taken—in addition to grade point averages that graduate schools can use when evaluating candidates. If you're unsure what the point of the question is, don't hesitate to ask before you attempt an answer.

Be Succinct.   While you certainly don't want to give a terse yes or no in response to a question calling for detail, neither should you talk for eight minutes when two minutes will suffice. If you really think a long, complex answer is called for, you can say, "To understand why we should institute a summer orientation program at this school, you should know more about recruitment, student fears, problems

with placement testing, and so on. I can go into these topics if you'd like, but for now, in response to the particular question I was asked, "I'd say that . . ." In this way, you are able to offer a short answer yet are leaving the door open for additional questions from listeners wishing more information.

Be Courteous.   During question periods, you may be amazed that one person asks a question you know you answered in your oral report, and another person asks for information so basic you realize your whole presentation probably went over his or her head. In such situations, it's easy to become flippant or overly patronizing. Avoid these temptations. Don't embarrass a questioner by pointing out you've already answered that query, and don't treat listeners like children. If you really think it would be a waste of the audience's time for you to review fundamental details, simply say that the group doesn't have time to discuss them but that you're willing to talk with individuals after the meeting to go over that ground.

SPEAKING ON RADIO AND TELEVISION: A FEW TIPS

In Chapter 14 you received some advice about talking over a public address system in a large room (page 372). When you not only use a microphone but your remarks are being broadcast via radio and television, you have to make more adjustments in your voice and movement. First, we'll consider three general principles, then move to some tips for speaking on radio and television.

Principle #1. Remember that radio and television are intimate media of communication. To a listener, a radio speaker usually sounds best when talking conversationally; the sound characteristics of radio make it an intimate medium. Think of the FM radio announcer, the public radio interviewer, the

morning drive-time DJ: they all seem to be talking directly to you, only a few feet away. To be sure, "oratorical speech" sometimes is heard during the news or the broadcast of a political event, but that sort of talk isn't nearly as effective on the radio as conversational comments. The same is true of television. Marshall McLuhan called television "cool" because it draws us in, invites us to participate in its programs in the homey setting of our living rooms or dens. With TV, too, conversationality works best.

Principle #2. Articulation is especially important in broadcast speech. The standard studio microphone is very sensitive to a range of pitches and sounds. That means it picks up and broadcasts to the listening audience every little slurp, lisp, glottal stop (vocal click), breathy inhalation, snort, and vocalized "ah" that comes out of your mouth. An auditorium mike sends sounds into a large space, where many of your vocal mannerisms can be absorbed by the walls; the studio mike is sending sound into a small space—a loudspeaker—where all of its characteristics, good and bad, are there for everyone to hear. Careful articulation is very important to broadcast speech.

Principle #3. Changes in vocal characteristics should be accompanied by changes in language. A speech before a large audience in a large auditorium usually demands comparatively formal language structures—the kinds that characterize most addresses to political conventions, congresses, and congregations. Given the sort of intimacy that's often achieved in broadcast talk, however, you usually must use more informal language structures when being interviewed for broadcast. Abraham Lincoln's "Four score and seven years ago" probably would have become "Eighty-seven years ago our ancestors founded this country on the principles of liberty and equality," or a similar construction that could more easily have been fit into broadcast conversational modalities.

These principles suggest that you must alter the way you think about "speech" when it's broadcast. You ought to be thinking of the "speech" as a "talk" or even a "conversation." The following tips may help you achieve that effect:

1. Despite those who tell you how and where to stand, move, and look in the studio, make sure you're comfortable before you talk. You probably will be told not to move, to keep aimed toward the mike, and so on, but don't get twisted into a position in which you aren't comfortable. If you have to strain or if you get tense because your posture is unnatural, it will show up when it comes time to talk.

2. When on television, know where you're going to look. Are you going to look only

at your host? at the camera? at a studio audience? Different kinds of shows are governed by different sorts of "look-space" conventions. Arrange your look-space ahead of time. Nothing makes you look quite so bad as moving your gaze from a person to the camera to an audience member and back again.

3. Don't jerk around when on camera; do what you can to hold your position. Remember that your face is being magnified to 24-to-27 inches in someone's living room. If you twitch, it will be hard for the camera operator to keep you in the frame, and your viewers will get dizzy. Keep your *vocal energy* high, but hold back your *physical movement*.

4. Don't get nervous when you sit closer to someone than you are used to. If you're seated next to a host or an interviewer, the director probably will set you much closer to that person than you are used to sitting; only in that way will the director be able to get a good, sharp picture (a so-called two-shot) of you and the host. Your natural tendency will be to pull back from what Edward Hall called intimate distance. Fight it.

5. Remember that you need not directly look your interviewer in the eye when talking. For some people, staring directly into someone's face for a long time at close range is distracting and embarrassing. When on television, it's easy to look just to the side of someone's face. For people who are used to looking into space when thinking, looking past someone is an acceptable technique.

6. Use your host's name regularly when on the radio. You may have noticed that radio hosts and guests use each other's name regularly; that's because people are always tuning out and tuning in to programs, and names serve as important reference points. Do your part to help keep an audience informed about what's going on.

7. For both radio and television, break your

messages into short pieces. A four- or five-minute speech seems like an eternity on today's broadcasting media; listeners are conditioned to shorter bursts of ideas and information. So, tell your interviewer that you can break up your message into thirty-second or one-minute segments, and ask him or her to help you with the transitions from one part to the next.

8. Avoid white clothing when you're going to appear on television. White shirts and dresses "flair" when photographed under the intense lights of a television studio. Wear medium blues instead of whites, colors instead of black. Don't be afraid, either, of using a little makeup to avoid being bleached out or, in the case of dark-skinned people, shaded out.

9. Do what you can to have a good time. Tenseness, boredom, fright—all seem to be magnified by the radio mike and the television camera. Loosen yourself up in whatever ways you can—by yourself, in informal conversation with the interviewer, and so on. Smile, laugh, and engage the subject with gusto and your media appearance will be a success.

10. Know your cues for summing up and quitting. For both radio and television appearances, you are likely to face time limits. Know for sure what nonverbal or verbal cues will be used to signal that you have a minute or thirty seconds left to go. If you can, prepare a final sentence ahead of time, so you can quite with a sense of finality.

Radio and television appearances allow you and your message to reach a great number of people with minimal effort. Seek out these opportunities, and make the most of them. These few tips will get you started; you'll soon discover additional rules that apply to your own modes of talk in front of the mike and camera.

IV. WORKING BIBLIOGRAPHY: ADDITIONAL READINGS

The bibliography that follows is not meant to be comprehensive, but rather suggestive. Additional books and articles can be found in the reference notes that follow most chapters and the units in this *Speaker's Resource Book*.

Andrews, James R. *The Practice of Rhetorical Criticism.* 2nd ed. New York: Longman, 1990.

Andrews, James R., and David Zarefsky, eds. *American Voices: Significant Speeches in American History 1640–1945.* New York: Longman, 1989.

Arnold, Carroll C., and John Waite Bowers, eds. *Handbook of Rhetorical and Communication Theory.* Boston: Allyn and Bacon, 1984.

Bem, Daryl. *Beliefs, Attitudes, and Human Affairs.* Belmont, CA: Brooks/Cole, 1980.

Bitzer, Lloyd. "The Rhetorical Situation." *Philosophy & Rhetoric* 1 (January, 1968): 1–14.

Bizzell, Patricia, and Bruce Herzberg. *The Rhetorical Tradition: Readings from Classical Times to the Present.* New York: St. Martin's Press, 1990.

Bettinghaus, Erwin, and Michael Cody. *Persuasive Communication.* 4th ed. New York: Holt, Rinehart & Winston, 1987.

Burgoon, Judee K., David B. Buller, and W. Gill Woodall. *Nonverbal Communication: The Unspoken Dialogue.* New York: HarperCollins, 1989.

Campbell, Karlyn Kohrs, comp. *Man Cannot Speak for Her: A Critical Study of Early Feminist Rhetoric and Key Texts of the Early Feminists.* 2 vols. New York: Praeger, 1989.

Combs, James E., and Dan Nimmo. *The New Propaganda: The Dictatorship of Palaver in Contemporary Politics.* New York: Longman, 1993.

Coupland, Nikolas, Howard Giles, and John M. Wiemann, eds. *"Miscommunication" and Problematic Talk.* Newbury Park, CA: Sage, 1991.

Crystal, David. *The Cambridge Encyclopedia of Language.* Cambridge, Eng.: Cambridge University Press, 1987.

Daly, John A., Gustav W. Friedrich, and Anita L. Vangelisti, eds. *Teaching Communication: Theory, Research, and Methods.* Hillsdale, NJ: Lawrence Erlbaum Associates, 1990.

Denton, Robert E., Jr., ed. *Ethical Dimensions of Political Communication.* New York: Praeger, 1991.

Ellis, Donald G. *From Language to Communication.* Hillsdale, NJ: Lawrence Erlbaum Associates, 1992.

Foss, Karen, and Sonja K. Foss. *Women Speak: The Eloquence of Women's Lives.* Prospect Heights, IL: Waveland Press, 1991.

Foss, Sonja K. *Rhetorical Criticism: Exploration and Practice.* Prospect Heights, IL: Waveland Press, 1989.

Foss, Sonja K., Karen A. Foss, and Robert Trapp. *Contemporary Perspectives on Rhetoric.* 2nd ed. Prospect Heights, IL: Waveland Press, 1991.

Golden, James L., Goodwin F. Berquist, and William E. Coleman. *The Rhetoric of Western Thought.* 4th ed. Dubuque, IA: Kendall/Hunt, 1989.

Gudykunst, William B. *Bridging Differences: Effective Intergroup Communication.* Newbury Park, CA: Sage, 1991.

Gusfield, Joseph R., ed. and intro. *Kenneth Burke on Symbols and Society.* Chicago: University of Chicago Press, 1989.

Hart, Roderick P. *Modern Rhetorical Criticism.* Rhetoric and Society Series. New York: HarperCollins, 1990.

Jamieson, Kathleen Hall. *Eloquence in an Electronic Age: The Transformation of Political Speechmaking.* New York: Oxford University Press, 1988.

Jamieson, Kathleen Hall, and David S. Birdsell. *Presidential Debates: The Challenge of Creating an Informed Electorate.* New York: Oxford University Press, 1988.

Jowett, Garth S., and Victoria O'Donnell. *Propaganda and Persuasion.* 2nd ed. Newbury Park, CA: Sage, 1992.

Knapp, Mark, and Judy Hall. *Nonverbal Communication in Human Interaction.* Fort Worth, TX: Harcourt Brace Jovanovich, 1992.

Larson, Charles U. *Persuasion: Reception and Responsibility.* 6th ed. Belmont, CA: Wadsworth, 1992.

Linkugel, Wil A., R. R. Allen, and Richard L. Johannesen, eds. *Contemporary American Speeches: A Sourcebook of Speech Forms and Principles.* 5th ed. Dubuque, IA: Kendall/Hunt, 1982.

Littlejohn, Stephen W. *Theories of Human Communication.* 3rd ed. Belmont, CA: Wadsworth, 1989.

Littlejohn, Stephen W., and David M. Jabusch. *Persuasive Transactions.* New York: HarperCollins, 1987.

McCloskey, Donald N. *The Rhetoric of Economics.* Madison: University of Wisconsin Press, 1986.

Ong, Waler J. *Orality and Literacy: The Technologizing of the Word.* New York: Methuen, 1982.

Osborn, Michael. *Orientations to Rhetorical Style.* New York: Macmillan, 1976.

Pearce, W. Barnett. *Communication and the Human Condition.* Carbondale, IL: Southern Illinois University Press, 1989.

Pearson, Judy Cornelia, Lynn H. Turner, and William Todd-Mancillas. *Gender and Communication.* 2nd ed. Dubuque, IA: William C. Brown, 1991.

Pfau, Michael, David A. Thomas, and Walter Ulrich. *Debate and Argument: A Systems Approach to Advocacy.* New York: HarperCollins, 1987.

Rieke, Richard D., and Malcolm O. Sillars. *Argumentation and Critical Decision Making.* 3rd ed. Rhetoric and Society Series. New York: HarperCollins, 1993.

Ryan, Halford Ross, ed. *Contemporary American Public Discourse: A Collection of Speeches and Critical Essays.* 3rd ed. Prospect Heights, IL: Waveland Press, 1992.

Rybacki, Karyn, and Donald Rybacki. *Communication Criticism: Approaches and Genres.* Belmont, CA: Wadsworth, 1991.

Salomon, Gavriel. *Interaction of Media, Cognition, and Learning.* San Francisco: Jossey-Bass, 1979.

Satterthwaite, Les. *Graphics: Skills, Media and Materials.* 4th ed. Dubuque, IA: Kendall/Hunt, 1980.

Shimanoff, Susan B. *Communication Rules: Theory and Research.* Newbury Park, CA: Sage, 1980.

Sillars, Malcolm O. *Messages, Meanings, and Culture: Approaches to Communication Criticism.* Rhetoric and Society Series. New York: HarperCollins, 1991.

Simons, Herbert W. *Persuasion: Understanding, Practice and Analysis.* 2nd ed. New York: Random House, 1986.

Steil, Lyman K., Larry L. Barker, and Kittie W. Watson. *Effective Listening.* New York: Random House, 1983.

Stewart, Charles S., and William B. Cash, Jr. *Interviewing: Principles and Practices.* 5th ed. Dubuque: William C. Brown, 1988.

Tedford, Thomas L. *Freedom of Speech in the United States.* 2nd ed. New York: McGraw-Hill, 1993.

Weitzel, Al R. *Careers for Speech Communication Graduates.* Salem, WI: Sheffield Publishing, 1987.

Wilcox, Roger P. "Characteristics and Organization of a Technical Report," *Communicating Through Behavior*, eds., William E. Arnold and Robert O. Hirsch. St. Paul: West Publishing, 1977, 201–06.

Wolvin, Andrew D., and Carolyn G. Coakley. *Listening*. 3rd ed. Dubuque, IA: William C. Brown, 1988.

Woodward, Gary C. *Persuasive Encounters: Case Studies in Constructive Confrontation*. New York: Praeger, 1990.

Woodward, Gary C., and Robert E. Denton, Jr. *Persuasion and Influence in American Life*. 2nd ed. Prospect Heights, IL: Waveland Press, 1992.

INDEX

LITERARY CREDITS

Note: Boldfaced numbers refer to entire speech

pages 2,   "Strength Through Cultural Diversity" by Henri Mann Morton from *Native American*
249,   *Reader: Stories, Speeches and Poems,* edited and commentary by Jerry D. Blanche, Ph.D.,
313   pages 194–205. Reprinted by permission of The Denali Press.

page 62   From "I've Been to the Mountaintop" (April 3, 1968) by Martin Luther King, Jr. Copyright
           © 1968 By The Estate of Martin Luther King, Jr. Reprinted by arrangement with The Heirs
           to the Estate of Martin Luther King, Jr., c/o Joan Daves Agency as agent for the proprietor.

page 64   From "Women in Leadership Can Make a Difference" by Geraldine Ferraro, *Representa-*
           tive American Speeches, 1982–1983. Reprinted by permission of Geraldine Ferraro.

page **69**   "Gossip: It's Worth Talking About" by Alicia Croshal from *Winning Orations 1991,*
           pages 1–3. Copyright © 1991 by the Interstate Oratorical Association. Reprinted by
           permission.

pages 159,   Excerpts from "The Changing Consumer: Predicting the Marketplace of the Future" by
165,   Wendy Liebmann from *Vital Speeches of the Day,* April 15, 1992. Reprinted by permis-
314   sion of City News Publishing Company and the author.

pages 159,   "Mercury: Nothing to Smile About" by Mary Hoffman from *Winning Orations 1991,*
461   pages 55–58. Copyright © 1991 by the Interstate Oratorical Association. Reprinted by
           permission.

pages 161,   From "Kerner Commission Paper" by LaDonna Harris from *Native American Reader:*
164   *Stories, Speeches and Poems,* edited and commentary by Jerry D. Blanche, Ph.D., page
           149. Reprinted by permission of The Denali Press.

page 162   From "Terrorist Plastic Play Toys" by Brooke Anderson from *Winning Orations 1990,*
           page 18. Copyright © 1990 by the Interstate Oratorical Association. Reprinted by permis-
           sion.

page 163   Excerpts from "The State of Black America: Excellence, Perseverance, and Preparation"
           by John E. Jacob from *Vital Speeches of the Day,* June 15, 1992, page 536. Reprinted by
           permission.

page 164   Excerpt from "Room at the Top" by Janet Martin from *Vital Speeches of the Day,* March
           15, 1992. Reprinted by permission.

page 165   From "Title Unknown" by Joseph A. Califano, Jr., from *Vital Speeches of the Day,* 44,
           August 15, 1978. Reprinted by permission of City News Publishing Company and the
           author.

page 166   From "Committed Youth" by Todd A. LaSala from *Winning Orations 1991,* page 12.
           Copyright © 1991 by the Interstate Oratorical Association. Reprinted by permission.

page 168   "Charities Telesolicitations: Fundraising or Fraud?" by Brad Hoeschen from *Winning*
           Orations 1991, page 53. Copyright © 1991 by the Interstate Oratorical Association.
           Reprinted by permission.

page 169   "Term Limits: A Solution Worse than the Problem" by Eddie Paul Hunter from *Winning*
           Orations 1991, page 90. Copyright © 1991 by the Interstate Oratorical Association.
           Reprinted by permission.

page 171   From "The Double Indignity—Medical Confidentiality" by Ryan Siskow from *Winning*
           Orations 1991, page 33. Copyright © 1991 by the Interstate Oratorical Association.
           Reprinted by permission.

page **200**   "Environmentally Unsafe Farming: An Unsafe Practice" by April Erdmann from *Winning*
           Orations 1991, pages 37–40. Copyright © 1991 by the Interstate Oratorical Association.
           Reprinted by permission.

page 200   Excerpt from "Can You Trust God?" by Dr. Louis Hadley Evans. Reprinted by permission
           of the author.

PHOTO ACKNOWLEDGMENTS

Unless otherwise acknowledged, all photographs are the property of ScottForesman and Company. Page abbreviations are as follows: (T) top, (C) center, (B) bottom, (L) left, (R) right.

Page 6T AP/Wide World   **Page 6C** J. Sohm/The Image Works   **Page 6B** Novosti/Sygma
Page 10 Bob Daemmrich/Stock Boston   **Page 34** UPI/Bettmann   **Page 40** Diego Goldberg/
Sygma   **Page 43** Mary Kay Denny/Photo Edit   **Page 83** B. Mahoney/The Image Works
Page 90 Bob Daemmrich/Tony Stone Images   **Page 94** Gary Gladstone/The Image Bank
Page 109 Jay Wolf/Picture Group   **Page 112** Don Smetzer/Tony Stone Images   **Page 117** Don
Klumpp/The Image Bank   **Page 136T** Reebok International Ltd.   **Page 136B** Levi Strauss &
Company   **Page 137T** Foote, Cone & Belding   **Page 137B** U. S. Army Photo   **Page 149ALL** Printed
with permission of General Mills   **Page 169** Tim Brown/Tony Stone Images   **Page 180** Bob
Daemmrich/Tony Stone Images   **Page 205** Mark Reinstein/Tony Stone Images   **Page 207** Robert
Clay   **Page 212** Bob Daemmrich   **Page 227** The Stock Market   **Page 230** Robert Frerck/The Stock
Market   **Page 235** David R. Frazier Photolibrary   **Page 239** David R. Frazier Photolibrary
Page 247 Greg Smith/Stock Boston   **Page 256** Paul Merideth/Tony Stone Images   **Page 259** Joel
Gordon Photography   **Page 270** Steve Dunwell/The Image Bank   **Page 273** Bob Daemmrich
Page 277 Michael Newman/Photo Edit   **Page 295** Chicago Historical Society   **Page 301** Brent
Jones   **Page 308** Bob Daemmrich/The Image Works   **Page 313** UPI/Bettmann   **Page 346** Photo
Edit   **Page 354** Comstock Inc.   **Page 361** Bob Daemmrich/The Image Works   **Page 367** J. L. Atlan/
Sygma   **Page 388T** Bob Daemmrich/The Image Works   **Page 388B** Herb Snitzer/Stock
Boston   **Page 389TL** Eastcott/Momatiuk/The Image Works   **Page 389TR** Bob Daemmrich/The
Image Works   **Page 389B** The Image Works   **Page 409** Bob Daemmrich/The Image Works
Page 418 Lawrence Migdale/Stock Boston   **Page 426** Arnie Sachs/Sygma   **Page 442** AP/Wide
World   **Page 456** © 1988/Courtesy Converse, Inc.   **Page 460** John Neubauer/Photo Edit
Page 469 Bob Rashid/Tony Stone Images   **Page 477** Robert Clay   **Page 484** Ellis Herwig/Stock
Boston   **Page 487** John Coletti/Tony Stone Images

What Can I Speak About?
Aids in Finding a Suitable Topic

The beginning speaker often has difficulty selecting a suitable topic for a speech. If you find yourself in this situation, study the following list of possible subjects. Most of the items listed are general areas from which a more precise, narrower subject can be derived. As you scan the list, think in terms of both your and your audience's knowledge and interests and the nature of the occasion (for example, what is expected, how long do you have to speak).

Personal Experience
1. Unique skills
2. Summer jobs
3. Schools attended
4. Academic interests
5. Hobbies
6. Leisure activities
7. Places you have been

The Arts
1. Painting, music, sculpture
2. Theater, cinema, dance
3. Funding for the arts
4. Folk art
5. Literary, artistic awards
6. Rating movies, music
7. Art history
8. Architectural styles—postmodernism
9. Careers in the arts

Science
1. Advances in an area or subject
2. Controversial theories
3. Funding for research
4. History of science
5. Careers in science
6. Major contributions by scientists
7. Medical controversies

Domestic Affairs
1. Social problems
   Crime, gun control, violence
   Homelessness
   Gay rights
   Abortion
   Drug use and abuse, alcoholism
   AIDS
   Health care
   Rural problems
   Sex education in the schools
   Racial, ethnic problems
   Cults
   Child abuse
2. Economic problems
   The federal debt
   Economically deprived citizens
   Legalized gambling
   Welfare
   Trade agreements
   Balance of payments
   Funding education
   Agriculture subsidies
   Foreign ownership in the United States
3. Political problems
   Term limits at state, federal level
   Campaign ethics, costs, funding
   Third party politics
   United We Stand
   Party principles/platforms (Republican, Democrat)
   Presidential campaigning
   Congressional perks
   Scandals